BARRON'S

Stockbroker Examination:

Series 7

3RD EDITION

Michael T. Curley
Member of the Board of Arbitrators
   National Association of Securities Dealers
Member of the Executive Committee
   Credit Division
   Securities Industry Association
Member of the New York Stock Exchange
   Committee
   Series 7 Questions

Joseph A. Walker
Former Member of the New York Stock
   Exchange Examination Qualification
   Committee
Former Chairman of Wall Street Training
   and Consulting, Inc.

BARRON'S

This book is dedicated to my contributing author Joseph A. Walker,
a talented attorney, a gifted teacher,
an accomplished author, a true and loyal friend.

Mike Curley

Acknowledgments

The authors wish to acknowledge Patrick J. Flynn for his professionalism
and expertise in the preparation of this book. Also my wife,
Rosalie Curley, for her invaluable assistance and endless patience.

© Copyright 2007, 2000, 1996 by Barron's Educational Series, Inc.

All inquiries should be addressed to:
Barron's Educational Series, Inc.
250 Wireless Boulevard
Hauppauge, New York 11788
www.barronseduc.com

ISBN-13: 978-0-7641-2380-1
ISBN-10: 0-7641-2380-7

Library of Congress Catalog Card No. 2005044296

Library of Congress Cataloging-in-Publication Data
Curley, Michael T.
    Stockbroker exam : series 7 / Michael T. Curley, Joseph A.
Walker. — 3rd ed.
        p.   cm.
    Rev. ed. of: How to prepare for the stockbroker exam. 2nd ed. 2000.
    Includes index.
    ISBN-13: 978-0-7641-2380-1
    ISBN-10: 0-7641-2380-7
    1. Stocks—United States—Examinations—Study guides. 2. Stockbrokers—
United States—Examinations, questions, etc. I. Title: How to prepare for
the stockbroker exam. II. Title: Stockbroker exam. III. Walker, Joseph A.
IV. Curley, Michael T. How to prepare for the stockbroker exam. V. Title.

HG4910.C846   2005
332.63'22'076—dc22   2005044296

PRINTED IN THE UNITED STATES OF AMERICA

9 8 7 6 5 4 3 2

CONTENTS

INTRODUCTION

— CHAPTER 1 —
CORPORATE SECURITIES

— CHAPTER 2 —
U.S. GOVERNMENT AND AGENCY SECURITIES

— CHAPTER 3 —
MUNICIPAL SECURITIES

Introduction

A MESSAGE FROM THE AUTHOR

To say that the securities industry has changed during the 1980s and 1990s and during this new century would be a gross understatement. It has changed dramatically. During the 1990s we experienced the greatest bull market in history. The year 2000 saw the erosion of huge profits, particularly in the so-called high-tech industry, causing bankruptcies, the depletion of pension funds, and irregularities in accounting procedures. In addition, there have been numerous changes by regulatory authorities such as the Securities Exchange Commission, self-regulatory bodies such as the New York Stock Exchange and the NASD (National Association of Securities Dealers), as well as by individual states. Volume, averages, and indices have risen to amounts unthinkable ten years ago. While the basic products—stocks, bonds, and options—are still the foundation of the industry, offshoots or so-called diversities have increased substantially, attracting many new investors as well as brokers to assist and guide them through their financial future.

The General Securities Registered Representative Series #7 Exam is very comprehensive and difficult. However, this self-study guide along with the chapter questions and answers and the practice final exam and your studious efforts to master this text will prepare you to successfully take the Series 7 Examination.

The text was especially designed as a one-book course as opposed to a kit with a study guide, practice exams, and critiques. The text covers a vast amount of subject matter. The chapters have been arranged in as logical a sequence as possible. I strongly urge you to study the material in the order presented.

As far as the actual Series 7 Exam, it is a six-hour exam consisting of 250 four-part multiple-choice questions. The first 125 questions are covered during three hours in the morning with the remaining 125 questions covered in a three-hour session in the afternoon. In addition, there will be an additional ten questions that will be used by the test committee to ensure that new questions meet acceptable standards. These questions have no effect on the candidate's final score. Consequently, you will answer 260 questions, but only 250 will be scored. A passing score of 70% of the 250 questions is required.

Passing the Series 7 will require a special effort on time and patience. However, the rewards will be great in a most fascinating industry.

Good luck,
Michael T. Curley, Author

REGISTERING FOR THE EXAM

The NASD (National Association of Securities Dealers) requires applicants for the Series 7 Exam to complete a so-called U-4 Form. The organization sponsoring you must send the U-4 Form with your fingerprints to the NASD. The NASD will send a confirmation back to the sponsoring organization.

The Exam

The actual name of the exam is The General Securities Registered Representative Examination Series #7. Within the industry, it is referred to simply as the Series 7 Exam. Your sponsoring organization should make an appointment for you to take the examination. The exam is taken on a computerized testing system. In the event you have any questions, you can contact the NASD Registration Center at 1-800-578-6273.

Do not get intimidated by the computer. The test system was designed so those individuals taking the exam would need no prior experience in operating a computer terminal. In fact, prior to the exam, there is a practice lesson so that you will be familiar with the procedures to answer the questions. A unique feature of this testing system is the ability to recall a question to review and/or change your answer. Your final score will be displayed on the terminal. In addition to your final score, a score profile indicating your performance in specific areas of the examination will be sent to your sponsoring firm.

The NASD Registration Center has a website PROMETRIC.COM. Here you can schedule, reschedule, confirm, or cancel your test appointment. You may also find testing centers closest to you, as well as driving instructions.

As of this writing, the current fee is $200 for the Series 7 Exam.

HELPFUL HINTS

As previously mentioned, the Series 7 Exam consists of 250 four-part multiple-choice questions. Approximately 70 questions are on bonds. Of these 70 questions, approximately 50 are on municipal securities. The next areas of concentration are options, with 30–35 questions, and investment companies, with 15–20 questions. The remaining questions are pretty much equally spread out among the other categories.

At the end of each chapter, there is a 50-question examination along with a removable answer sheet. I strongly urge you to use this answer sheet when taking the exam. After you have corrected your exam, it is a good idea to return to the exam and circle the correct answers. This will serve as an excellent review before taking the final exam. What you will be doing is reading the questions and the correct answer. Keep in mind there are only so many questions that can be asked on this exam and only so many ways a question can be presented. Therefore, repetition is essential.

As far as the questions are concerned, the so-called "Roman Numeral" questions give the candidate the most problems. In the following question, the task is to determine the correct sequence from high to low or low to high.

Classify the debt securities listed below, in ascending order according to the stability of their principal value:

I. A Federal National Mortgage Association Bond
II. An AAA rated corporate bond
III. A Series EE Savings Bond
IV. A U.S Treasury Bond

    (a) I, II, III, IV
    (b) II, I, IV, III
    (c) IV, III, II, I
    (d) III, IV, I, II

(b) The key here is "ascending," which means from lowest stability to highest stability.

The following question is another way in which the Roman Numeral question is used when more than one of the options may be a correct response.

Which issues represent direct obligations of the United States?

I. Export-Import Bank Bonds
II. Series EE Savings Bonds
III. Treasury Bonds
IV. Federal National Mortgage Association Bonds

    (a) II only
    (b) II and III only
    (c) III and IV only
    (d) I, II and III only

(b) Series EE Savings Bonds and Treasury Bonds are direct obligations of the U.S. Government. The others are not.

Other formats of questions are as follows:

Closed Stem

The closed stem is a complete sentence and ends with a question mark (?).

On which of the following is depreciation not permitted?

    (a) rental property whose value is falling
    (b) residential property not used for business
    (c) property whose maintenance exceeds the investment credit
    (d) equipment subject to recapture

(b) Depreciation is permitted only on income-producing property, such as two- or three-family houses.

Open Stem

The open stem is an incomplete statement, and the options represent conclusions to the sentence.

A tax shelter specifically designed for self-employed individuals is:

(a) an Individual Retirement Account
(b) a subsidized deferred account
(c) an SEP–IRA
(d) a Shelter Island plan

(c) SEP–IRAs are for self-employed individuals. IRAs are for employed persons. Choices (b) and (d) do not exist.

Most/Best/Least

In this type of question, the choice requires selecting which answer is better or worse than the others.

Common stocks of which of the following industry issuers would be most likely to decline in value if interest rates in the economy were to rise?

(a) automobile companies
(b) airline companies
(c) machine tool companies
(d) public utility companies

(d) Public utility companies normally have the highest degree of leverage. Therefore, the general rise in interest rates would generally cause net income to decline, thereby reducing earning per share available for common stock and thus its price.

Except or Not

In the except questions, the answer is the exception to the principle so stated.

Although a corporation may have no earnings in a particular year, it is obligated to pay interest on all its outstanding debt instruments except:

(a) convertible subordinated debentures
(b) collateral trust bonds
(c) adjustment (income) bonds
(d) equipment trust certificates

(c) Adjustment (income) bonds pay interest only if earned.

As you can see, it is very important to read the question carefully, and ask yourself what are they asking for? Believe me when I say that people fail the exam not because they don't know the material, but because they misread or misinterpret the question. So take your time, read the question carefully, and ask yourself what are they looking for?

Therefore, read, reread, take the exams, retake the exams, and review the questions with the correct answers. The best of luck to you.

Michael T. Curley, Author

Corporate Securities

BASIC CORPORATE STRUCTURE

A corporation is created by a group of individuals engaged in a business enterprise. Assume that four persons have formed a partnership to engage in the business of manufacturing women's clothing. They would, as a partnership, be subject to certain disadvantages. The business would continue only to the extent of the life of the partners, and the partners would be personally liable for financial losses. This liability would extend beyond their investment in the partnership and could conceivably endanger their personal assets. In addition, the ability to raise capital for expansion would be limited to the abilities of the partners to contribute.

For these and other reasons, the partners might wish to form a corporation, Acme Fashions, Inc.

Corporations are chartered by a state, with the charter being issued by the secretary of state.

In many states the procedure would begin with the filing of a certificate of incorporation. Among the items of information required in the charter would be:

Name and Address of Corporation
Acme Fashions, Inc.
One Main Street
Troy, New York 12345

Purpose of Incorporation
In addition to the obvious activities of the organization, manufacture of clothing, we would include other possible future activities (for example, the purchase and sale of securities, commodities and real estate). As corporations cannot engage in functions not included in their charter, these additions would prevent the need to amend the charter at some later date.

Names and Addresses of Incorporators
Here would be listed the names and addresses of the four incorporators of Acme Fashions, Inc. The four would probably also be named as the officers and as members of the board of directors of the corporation.

Capital Stock Authorized and Issued
As our corporation consists of only four originators, we would authorize a small amount of stock, perhaps 1,000 shares. Of this amount, we would issue 400 shares, 100 to each of our

shareholders. We would also assign a par value to these shares. Par value is used for accounting purposes and does not necessarily relate to the true value of the shares.

Upon receipt of our charter from the state, our capital structure would be:

ACME FASHIONS, INC.
Common Stock

Authorized Stock	–	1,000 shares ($10 par)
Issued and Outstanding	–	400 shares
Unissued Stock	–	600 shares
Treasury Stock	–	0 shares

Treasury stock is stock that has been issued by a corporation but that is later reacquired through purchase or donation. For example, if one of the corporation's stockholders should wish to sever his connection, he might sell his stock back to the corporation. (Some small corporations have agreements with shareholders to repurchase the stock at book value on demand.) Should this stock (100 shares) be repurchased, it becomes known as treasury stock. This stock does not have voting rights or receive dividends while remaining in the treasury. It also would not be used in computing the earnings per share, which would have the effect of inflating earnings. Following such a transaction our capital structure would be:

ACME FASHIONS, INC.
Common Stock

Authorized Stock	–	1,000 shares ($10 par)
Issued and Outstanding	–	300 shares
Treasury Stock	–	100 shares
Unissued Stock	–	600 shares

Generally, a new corporation would issue only one class of stock, usually called common stock. As the company grows and requires additional financing, other securities, such as preferred stocks and bonds, will be added to the capital structure.

COMMON STOCK

Common stock ownership represents an equity interest in a corporation. The holder can in many ways be compared to a general partner in a partnership. The ownership of preferred stock also represents an equity position, but the holder is more similar to a limited partner.

Ownership of common stock carries with it certain privileges.

Privilege I - Voting Rights

Common stock has the inherent right to vote in company affairs. This right is offered in two forms—statutory voting and cumulative voting—and they differ markedly.

Statutory Voting

In this voting procedure, which is the more common of the two, each holder is given one vote per share. In the election of directors, each share is multiplied by the number of seats to be

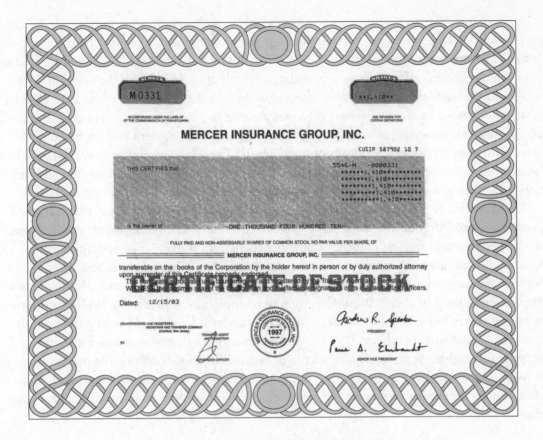

filled on the board of directors. Thus, if three vacancies were to be filled, the holder of 100 shares would be given 300 votes (100 × 3). However, the votes must be cast in equal amounts for each seat. In this case, the 300 votes would be allocated with no more than 100 given to any single candidate. Under this voting method, a majority of the shareholders would elect all of the directors. Minority holders would have no effective say in the election process. This is, perhaps, the reason that statutory voting is used by the majority of corporations.

Cumulative Voting

As in statutory voting, the shareholder in a corporation using the cumulative voting method is given one vote per share multiplied by the number of vacancies to be filled on the board of directors. However, in this procedure the votes could all be cast for one candidate. As in the example above, the holder of 100 shares would have 300 votes (100 × 3). He could choose to cast all of these for one candidate. The possible result could be that a minority of the shareowners would obtain representation on the board. They might ignore the three management choices and instead make their own nomination. By concentrating all of their voting strength in this candidate, they might outvote one of the other three. Although this possibility exists, it does not often occur since minority groups seldom band together to accomplish this purpose.

A common stockholder, though entitled to vote, may surrender this privilege in a number of ways. He might choose not to vote just as an American citizen might opt to stay home on Election Day. More commonly, shareholders surrender their right to vote through a proxy or a voting trust.

A proxy is a short-term surrender of voting rights usually for just one meeting. Under the law, publicly held corporations must supply their shareholders with a proxy, which is comparable to an absentee ballot in a political election. Well before the meeting, the holders are sent the proxy, which contains all matters to be voted upon, including elections to the board of directors. The owner makes his choices and votes for or against the issues. The proxy is returned and the votes cast as directed. Because the votes are cast by someone other than the shareholder this constitutes a surrender of direct voting rights, although the owner's voice is heard in the determination of the issue. Proxies prevent a potential abuse by corporations, which could hold a shareholders' meeting on short notice in some remote location. As few holders would likely attend, the management group would control all corporate decisions without opposition.

A voting trust is a long-term surrender of voting rights, perhaps for many years. It often arises when a corporation is experiencing financial difficulty. The management might contact the shareholders and request that they surrender their right to vote. If agreed, these votes would be placed in a trust to be voted by the named trustees. This would enable the corporation to make more rapid decisions and, perhaps, improve the corporate future. Voting trusts have also been used by corporations that wish to retain family control. The family would own the voting shares but other shareholders, often the majority, would hold voting trust certificates. The voting trust certificate ("VTC") has all privileges of common stock ownership except voting rights. As voting is rarely a major factor in corporate affairs, the market value of the VTC seldom varies greatly from the common shares. In some unusual event, such as a proxy contest for control of a company, however, the value of the voting trust may be a key factor in the market price of the share.

Privilege II - Right to Transfer Shares

With few exceptions, a common shareholder has the right to transfer his shares to someone else without permission of the corporation. Thus, he can sell, assign, or make gifts of his holdings without restriction.

There are occasions when a shareholder might voluntarily agree not to transfer shares for a short period. This often occurs when the shares are received as an employment benefit or as a reward for achievement.

Privilege III - Access to Corporate Books and Records

A shareholder has the right to examine the books and records of the corporation. Since the shareholder is a part owner of the enterprise, this is quite logical. Publicly held companies are required to make reports to shareholders on a regular basis. In addition, the Securities and Exchange Commission requires more detailed information be filed with them by these corporations. As this information is available to the public, there is seldom a need for a shareholder to enforce his access to corporate books. In nonpublic corporations, however, where no such filing requirements exist, a common stockholder may have to employ legal procedures to claim his right to this information. Obviously, a corporation would not be required to disclose information that is confidential and might work to the disadvantage of its business.

Privilege IV - Dividends When Declared

The payment of dividends by a corporation is in effect a reward to the owners. There is no requirement to pay dividends. However, if a dividend is declared it must be paid to all shareowners proportionate to their ownership interest. The company cannot prejudice a group of owners by withholding payment while limiting payment to a chosen few.

Note that on a corporate balance sheet, dividends, unlike bond interest, are not carried as a current liability. They become such only from the time they are declared until the date of payment.

Privilege V - Preemptive Rights

Preemptive rights grant to common stockholders the first right to subscribe to additional stock. This privilege is not inherent as are voting rights and is, in fact, rather unusual in today's investment climate. Some companies, primarily public utilities, grant them as a means of raising additional capital from current shareholders. The use of preemptive rights has declined sharply in recent years, but they do exist as an investment product.

The purpose of "rights" has been to prevent a common stockholder from having his percentage of ownership in a corporation diluted without his acquiescence. If a shareholder in a corporation owns 10% of the outstanding stock, no additional shares could be issued unless he was offered the first privilege to purchase 10% of the new shares. In publicly traded issues, these rights generally give the holder the opportunity to purchase the new shares at a price below the current market value. Thus, the rights would have an intrinsic value of their own.

EXAMPLE

> The XYZ Corporation, which currently has 4,000,000 shares outstanding, wishes to offer an additional 1,000,000 shares through a rights offering to its current holders. Therefore, each stockholder would be allowed to purchase one additional share for each four shares presently held. Assume that Mary Smith owns 400 shares of XYZ Corporation common stock. She would receive 400 rights to subscribe and would be entitled to subscribe to 100 additional shares. If the current market price of XYZ is $40 per share and the subscription price is $32.50, the rights would have a determinable value.
>
> At the time of the original announcement the market price of the stock ($40) would include a right to buy additional shares. Should one purchase a share at $40, he would receive that share plus one preemptive right.

Ms. Smith might wish to know the theoretical value of her rights in order to determine her course of action. If the rights have a sufficient value she may elect to sell them and apply the proceeds to some other purpose. The theoretical value of a right when the stock is trading with rights included (cum rights) can be determined by the following formula:

$$\frac{P}{R+1}$$

"P" (premium) indicates the dollar amount at which the market price of the stock is trading above the subscription price. In our example the premium is $7.50: $40.00 (market price) – $32.50 (subscription price).

"R" (ratio) indicates the number of rights required for subscription to each additional share. As four rights are required for each new share, R is 4. To the ratio we add 1, reflecting the fact that each share purchased would also grant the buyer one right toward purchase of an additional share. This addition negates the value of the right as a part of the market value of the stock. Our calculation would be as follows:

$$\frac{P\ (Premium)}{R\ (Ratio)+1} \qquad \frac{\$7.50}{5\ (4+1)} = \$1.50$$

Thus, each right has a theoretical value of $1.50. Ms. Smith has 400 rights, which upon sale could bring her approximately $600. Her decision to subscribe or sell can now be made on a more factual basis.

At a later date XYZ stock will begin to trade x rights ("XR"). This means that the market price of the stock will no longer include a preemptive right, and it changes our method of computing the value of the right. As there is no longer a right to negate, it would no longer be necessary to add 1 to the ratio. Thus, our formula would be:

$$\frac{P\ (Premium)}{R\ (Ratio)}$$

Using the values from our previous example, the value of the right if XYZ was trading XR (without rights) would be approximately $1.88:

$$\frac{\$7.50}{4} = \$1.875$$

Traders who engage in a market procedure known as arbitrage may find an opportunity to profit by the use of rights. The aim of the arbitrageur is to find a difference in markets that would provide him with a gain. Upon locating this difference, he simultaneously buys one security in one market and sells the same security or an exchangeable one in the same or a different market. For example, if AT&T Corporation stock were trading at $18.74 per share on the New York Stock Exchange and at the same moment was selling at $19 per share on the Boston Stock Exchange, the arbitrageur would simultaneously buy in New York and sell in Boston, achieving a $0.26 per share profit (excluding expenses).

With rights, to use our example, the arbitrageur would first determine the true value of the rights ($1.88). Should the rights be selling below that level, say $1.50, the arbitrage would proceed as follows:

Purchase four rights and sell one share of the stock short. The result would be a profit of $1.50. The four rights would cost $6.00. The subscription would be made at $32.50. Total cost of one share is $38.50. The short sale of the share would have been made at $40, yielding the gross profit of $1.50 per share.

In later chapters we will discuss arbitrage using other investment vehicles such as American Depositary Receipts ("ADRs"), convertible preferred stocks, and convertible bonds. The potential examples of this market technique are virtually unlimited. True arbitrage implies a net profit at the time the trades are simultaneously completed. Obviously, opportunities to reap a profit so easily are difficult to discover. Most arbitrage contains a risk and is generally referred to as risk arbitrage. This topic will be discussed later.

Warrants

Warrants grant to the holder the privilege to subscribe to the common stock of a corporation. Unlike preemptive rights, a warrant is exercisable for a long period of time, often for ten or more years from date of issue and some are perpetual. This time factor makes the warrant an attractive vehicle for potential capital gains.

Generally, a warrant is issued in conjunction with some other security in a package called a "unit." For example, on March 19, 2002, Chiquita Brands International, Inc., issued $250,000,000 of notes maturing March 15, 2009, bearing interest from March 19, 2002, at 10.56% per annum. Warrants were attached as a so-called sweetener to attract the note buyers. The warrant entitled the holder to purchase one share of common stock at a price of $19.23 per share through March 19, 2009. At the time of this writing, Chiquita Brands International, Inc., common stock was selling at $19.93 and the warrant was at $6.00.

The value of the warrant is determined by two factors: intrinsic value and time value. Thus the warrant entitles the holder to purchase one share of common stock at $19.23, and the common stock is selling at $19.63, so the intrinsic value would be $0.40. The difference $3.42 is the time value. The buyer would be paying in the expectation that the common stock will rise during the remaining lifetime of the warrant. In general, this is similar to the premium value of securities options (discussed in a later chapter). However, warrants have a much longer life than options and would command a higher premium.

American Depositary Receipts

American Depositary Receipts ("ADRs") were developed many years ago when American investors became interested in securities of foreign (particularly European) corporations. With the economic recovery that began at the end of World War II, this interest in foreign investment increased markedly, and in the 1970s and early 1980s, it expanded to include Japanese corporations.

ADRs solve a problem that had existed in foreign investment by Americans. For example, if one wished to purchase shares in Royal Dutch Petroleum, the need to have the shares sent to Holland for transfer would be most inconvenient. The time delays would certainly inhibit trading and interest would wane.

By using ADRs, this problem is avoided. The foreign shares are deposited in an American bank in the nation of issue. That bank then issues ADRs in the United States that are tradable and transferable without traveling overseas.

Each ADR often represents one foreign share, but there is no requirement that that be the ratio. Often the ADR equals more or less than one foreign share, and the applicable conditions should be understood by the investor. For instance, Japanese share prices are usually low by design (stock splits, etc.). Therefore, ADRs of Japanese companies often represent ten shares of the underlying foreign security.

In recent years trading has begun in European Depositary Receipts ("EDRs"). These are receipts for American securities that are issued and traded in Europe, giving European investors more convenience in managing their portfolios of securities of American corporations.

ADR holders generally receive all privileges of common stock ownership such as dividends and voting rights, but in some cases they are not granted preemptive rights to subscribe to additional securities. When the company issues rights the bank holding the underlying foreign securities sells the rights and credits each ADR holder with a proportionate amount of the proceeds.

PREFERRED STOCK

Preferred stock is comparable to common stock in that both represent equity ownership in a corporation, but there ends the similarity. The differences between the two classes of equity are threefold:

1. voting rights
2. dividend priority
3. rights in liquidation

Voting Rights

Generally, preferred stock does not vote. All voting power is held by the common stockholders. In this way preferred stock is comparable to the limited partner in a partnership. Although the limited partners make a capital contribution to the organization, only the general partners vote. Voting preferreds do exist, but they are the exception rather than the rule.

Dividend Priority

The dividend on preferred stock must be paid before the dividend can be paid on common stock. This in no way assures that the preferred dividend will be paid but does provide priority over the common. This feature generally makes preferred a more conservative investment and is favored by certain investors. Also, since bonds are debt instruments, they take priority over all stock and provide even more safety than do preferreds. One might question why an investor would purchase preferred stock when bonds of corporations would outwardly seem more attractive. It is possible that the return on the preferred stock is greater than on a bond and thus provides a better investment opportunity. Additionally, under the Internal Revenue Code, corporations may exclude from their tax calculations a large portion of their dividends (currently 70% if a corporation owns less than 29% of issue; if more than 20%, 80% is retained). This exclusion is not available to interest from corporate bonds, thus granting to the preferred stock investor a much higher after-tax yield.

Dividends on preferreds, unlike dividends on common stocks, are usually fixed. Often the dividend is a percentage of the par value. For instance, a Consolidated Edison ($25 par) 12% preferred stock would have a $3 annual dividend (12% of $25), paid in quarterly amounts of $0.75. Even if the fortunes of the company improve sharply, this dividend would remain the same. On the other hand, the variable dividend on common stock could increase in good times, perhaps leading to a higher market price for the shares. Conversely, in poor earnings periods the preferred dividend must be paid before the common dividend, which could be decreased or even eliminated.

Dividends on preferred stock are usually cumulative. That is, dividends not paid in one period accumulate and must be paid before anything is paid on common stock. For example, should our 12% ($25 par) preferred, mentioned earlier, not receive dividends for three consecutive years there would be an arrears of $9 per share. This amount, plus any additional dividends due, would have to be paid in full before anything could be paid to the common stockholder. This in no way guarantees payment of the preferred dividend, but does give it an additional priority over the common stockholders.

Careful investors over the years have profited greatly by purchasing shares of preferred stocks that had large amounts of dividends in arrears. By correctly forecasting a turn for the better in the business of the company they were able to benefit when the arrears were later paid. Additionally, the market value of the preferred stock would increase as the arrears vanished, reflecting the improved financial stability of the corporation.

Some preferred dividends are noncumulative, denying the holder the aforementioned advantages. Careful scrutiny of the terms is a most important function of the investor and his representative.

Participating Preferred

A small number of preferred stocks are also "participating" preferreds. These give the holder the possibility of receiving dividends greater than the stated amount. They are generally used to make a preferred stock more attractive to potential investors. If, for example, our 12% ($100 par) preferred is not particularly interesting to investors at the time the issuing corporation wishes to make an offering, it might sweeten it up by adding a dividend participation to the security. This sweetener might be based on dividend increases to the holder of the common stock. In this case, the 12% ($100 par) preferred would state that if dividends on the common stock exceed $4 per year, the participating preferred holders would share in that excess. Thus, if in some future year the common stockholders received $6 in dividends the participating preferred holder would receive $14 ($12 plus the $2 excess). This characteristic would make the preferred a more desirable holding for many investors.

Participating preferred stocks are rare but have been used successfully to make new offerings more attractive. Their use is not unlike the addition of warrants to an offering of some other security, as mentioned earlier. In either case, the warrant or the participation clause gives added investment value and increases the issuer's ability to raise necessary capital.

Right in Liquidation

Should a corporation liquidate, preferred holders would have rights to payment prior to common stockholders. It must be noted that this particular privilege seldom is of great value. Corporations do not generally liquidate their business if things are going well. Liquidations are more likely to be caused by business problems. In the liquidation process, all creditors, including bondholders, must be paid before any stockholder; there is seldom anything left for these equity owners. However, after creditors have been paid, should assets remain for distribution to stockholders, the preferred comes first. The preferred stockholder must receive the par value of the stock ($100 in our previous example) before the common shareholder receives any payment. While not to be overlooked, this privilege of preferred stock ownership is in most cases of limited importance.

Convertible Preferred

A convertible preferred stock is one that is exchangeable for another security—in most cases, for common stock of the same issuing company. In rare instances the exchange may be for some other security such as a different type of preferred stock or for shares of some subsidiary company.

This conversion privilege makes these shares a breed apart. The holder owns preferred shares with the aforementioned priorities but can, under stated terms and conditions, exchange them for common stock. Thus, should the value of the common shares increase at some future time the convertible preferred holder will share in that gain. From the issuing company's standpoint, convertible preferred shares represent a savings in required dividend payments. At some point the market might demand the issue of nonconvertible preferred stock with a dividend payment of 15% of par value, while a convertible preferred might be issued paying perhaps only 10% of par. The investor accepts this lower return as the shares purchased give the possibility of appreciation based on the performance of the common stock.

When first issued, convertible preferreds are convertible into common at a price higher than the current market price. The conversion benefit will be demonstrated at some future time should the price of the common increase.

EXAMPLE

Acme Button Corporation issues a 10% ($100 par) convertible preferred that allows the holder to make an exchange for common stock at $50 per share. This means that the holder can exchange one share of preferred for two shares of common.

We determine this by dividing the par value—$100—by the conversion price:

$$\frac{\text{Par Value}}{\text{Conversion Price}} \qquad \frac{\$100}{\$50} = 2 \text{ shares}$$

At the time of issue, the common stock of the Acme Button Corporation may be $40 per share, giving no immediate intrinsic value. However, in the future the value may increase dramatically.

Should Acme Button Corporation common trade at $54.50 per share, what would be the equivalent value of the preferred?

Answer: $54.50 × 2=$109.00.

If each convertible share is equivalent to two common shares, then intrinsically the preferred stock is worth twice the common price ($54.50 × 2). This calculation gives us what is known as "parity." Parity is that price at which neither a profit nor a loss would result from conversion. In our example, if the preferred was trading at $109 per share and the holder converted it for two shares of common trading at $54.50, the value would be the same $109 (2×$54.50).

EXAMPLE

If the convertible preferred was trading in the market at $142.50 per share, what would be parity for the common stock?

Answer: $71.25.

We simply divide the price of the preferred ($142.50) by 2, as each preferred is exchangeable for two common.

$$\frac{\text{Preferred Price}}{\text{Conversion Ratio}} \qquad \frac{\$142.50}{2} = \$71.25$$

Quite logically, convertible securities trade at a price that is above parity. Investors pay the additional amount to receive the conversion privilege that may later pay a great reward. They also receive a security (preferred stock) that has priorities over the common stock, as previously discussed.

EXAMPLE

Acme Button Corporation convertible preferred is trading at $90 per share. The common stock is trading at a price that is 10% below parity. What is the market price of the common stock?
Answer: $40.50 per share.

To answer questions such as this most simply, we must first determine parity for the common.

$$\frac{\text{Preferred Price}}{\text{Conversion Ratio}} \quad \frac{\$90}{2} = \$45$$

If trading at parity the common price would be $45 per share. We are told, however, that the common trades 10% below parity. We are left with an easy calculation.

$$\$45 \times 10\% \quad\quad = \$\ 4.50$$
$$\$45.00 - \$4.50 \quad = \$40.50$$

We take 10% of the parity price of $45.00 ($4.50) and subtract from that price ($45.00 – $4.50) to give us the current price of $40.50.
Now we will try a question from the other direction.
Acme common stock is trading at $57.50 per share. The convertible preferred is trading 20% above parity. What is the price of the preferred?

Answer: $138 per share.

Again, we must first compute parity. The preferred is exchangeable for two shares of common stock; therefore, with the common trading at $57.50, parity would be $115.

$$\$57.50 \text{ (Common Price)} \times 2 \text{ (Conversion Ratio)} =$$
$$\$115.00 \text{ (Parity for Preferred)}$$

We are told the preferred actually trades 20% above parity; thus our answer is derived as follows:

$$\$115 \times 20\% = \$\ 23$$
$$\$115 + \$23 = \$138$$

This $23, which the preferred trades above parity, is called the "conversion premium."

A market technique that is the opposite of an arbitrage is called a "reverse hedge." Here the trader who feels that the spread between the common and the convertible preferred is too great will buy the nonconvertible common and sell short the convertible preferred.

> ABC Corporation 8% ($100 par) convertible preferred is exchangeable for common stock at $25 per share. Each share of the preferred is, therefore, exchangeable for four shares of common ($100 divided by $25). The preferred stock is trading at $120, which means that parity for the common is $30 ($120 divided by 4). The nonconvertible common will generally trade below parity. A trader in this situation might conclude that the common should be about 10% below parity, or $27 per share ($30 less 10%). Assume the common stock is trading at $21 per share. If the trader is correct, the common should rise in price to $27 or the convertible preferred should decline to bring the spread into line. He, therefore, does the reverse of a true arbitrage. He "shorts" the preferred and buys the common. The trader will profit on his short position if the preferred declines or will profit on his long position if the common goes up.

A reverse hedge is very dangerous as there is no limit to the possible loss in the short position should the trader's calculations prove to be wrong. We will look at related matters in our later discussion of arbitrage.

Callable Preferred

Many preferred stocks, particularly convertible preferreds, contain a call feature. This entitles the issuer to repurchase the stock at a fixed price in the future. Should the corporation exercise its right to call, the holder must surrender the shares as the agreement was part of the original issuance of the stock.

Perhaps Acme Button Corporation 10% ($100 par) convertible preferred has a call feature that allows the issuing corporation to repurchase the stock under the following terms:

From time of issuance:

Years 1–5	Noncallable
Year 6	108
Year 7	106
Year 8	104
Year 9	102
Year 10 and on	100

Thus, in the sixth year after issue the corporation could call the shares at $108 per share. This would save the dividend payments and could provide a valuable use for internally generated funds.

In convertible preferreds this feature may also lead to what is known as a "forced conversion." Assume the preferred was convertible at $50 per share

$$(2 \text{ shares} = \frac{100}{50} \frac{\text{par}}{\text{conversion price}})$$

Should common stock at one point be trading in the market at $61 per share, parity for the preferred would be $122 per share ($61 × 2). If the preferred were callable at $108 per share and the corporation exercised its privilege, the holder would, of necessity, convert to common. Failure to do this would mean surrendering the shares at the call price of $108 when they could be exchanged for common shares currently valued at $122. Forced conversion will be discussed again in our study of convertible bonds, but the principal is consistent. An investor would convert in these cases to avoid the loss of value that would result if he permitted his securities to be called away from him.

CORPORATE BONDS

A bond is an instrument of debt, representing a loan made to the corporation. Bonds issued by corporations fall into many categories but the basic difference among them is the security behind the borrowing. When an investor buys a bond, she is in effect lending money to that corporation. She will be paid interest at the agreed rate until maturity. Her concern would be the corporation's ability to pay the interest and to pay the principal amount at maturity. Interest, unlike dividends on stock, is an obligation of a corporation, and failure to make payments on schedule leads to a default. The bondholders would then be entitled to the security pledged by the corporation to obtain satisfaction of the debt. Thus, the security is what distinguishes one type of corporate bond from another. In later sections we will discuss debt instruments issued by the U.S. government and government agencies as well as municipalities, but at this point we direct our attention to corporate bonds.

Corporate bonds are often categorized as "money market instruments" and "capital market instruments." Capital markets generally describe debt instruments maturing more than one year from time of issuance, whereas money markets include short-term debt maturing one year or less from date of issue.

Capital Markets

Long-term corporate bonds can be subdivided into any number of types. We use six categories but recognize that many further divisions could be made. We will, however, discuss in detail all current forms of issue.

Mortgage Bond

A mortgage bond is an instrument of debt secured by real property owned by the issuing corporation. Just as an individual may purchase a home and borrow money from a bank pledging the home as security, so may corporations borrow from investors using the real property of the corporation to secure the debt. Should the corporation fail to pay as agreed, the pledged property could be used to satisfy all or part of the debt. For example, Consolidated Edison may borrow $100,000,000 for capital improvements; it would specify certain utility obligations in the borrowing to allow for a foreclosure and payment to the lenders.

Mortgage bonds are issued in many varieties. Principal among these are the open-end and the closed-end mortgage.

In an open-end mortgage, property used to secure a loan can be used to secure a later loan of equal ranking. If our $100,000,000 Con Edison bond was an open-end mortgage, then that corporation could later borrow additional monies pledging the same property as collateral. Further, the investors purchasing the second issue would rank equally with those purchasing the first in the event of a default. Obviously, the buyer must take care to see that the property pledged is more than sufficient to cover all possibilities. Open-end mortgage bonds can normally be issued only by corporations with a high credit standing.

A closed-end mortgage, on the other hand, prohibits that borrower from pledging the security a second time at equal rank. Thus, the lender knows that the pledged real property will be used solely to satisfy his claim in the event of a default. This would not preclude the borrower from pledging this property on a subordinated basis, in which case the buyer of the second issue would have claim only against those assets that remained after the initial lenders had been satisfied.

Other mortgage bonds are issued as consolidated or general mortgage. In this case the issuing corporation does not specify which items of property will serve as collateral but pledges all real property owned to secure its mortgage debt. These are, in effect, a form of open-end mortgage.

Collateral Trust Certificate

A collateral trust certificate is an instrument of debt pledging as security stocks and/or bonds of other corporations. The comparison to one's personal financial dealings is quite direct. For instance, if you need some financing for a project of your own, you would take your General Motors stock to a bank to secure the debt. Should you default, the bank sells the pledged stock to obtain satisfaction. Similarly, Corporation A may issue bonds by placing in trust securities of Corporation B. The trustee, generally a bank, holds the collateral until repayment. Should a default occur, the trustee sells the security to protect the bondholders. These bonds usually contain provisions for increasing collateral should market values decrease. The bondholder is, therefore, reasonably secure against loss.

Collateral trust certificates are not a common form of borrowing, although many such issues do exist (e.g., Shell Oil). In past years they were a common vehicle for the railroad industry. Often a large railroad (New York Central) would own a subsidiary railroad (Michigan Central). The parent would borrow money using the securities of the subsidiary to secure the loan. With the vast changes that have occurred in railroad financing, we see less use of this interesting form of debt security.

Debenture

A debenture is an instrument of debt secured by a promise to pay by the issuing corporation. No specific security is pledged, as is true in other types of corporate debt. A corporation with a high credit rating would have no trouble issuing debentures as investors would have confidence in the issuer's ability to pay. Should a default occur, debenture holders become general creditors and have claim to any assets not pledged to secure other corporate debt.

Debentures are often subordinated to other claims. A subordinated debenture holder would be the last creditor to be paid in the event of a corporate dissolution. Thus, the credit standing of the issuer is of prime importance.

Virtually all convertible bonds are issued as debentures. The issuing corporation gives this bondholder the right to exchange his bond into common stock. This valuable privilege makes it unnecessary to supply any fixed collateral for the loan.

Guaranteed Bond

Though not a specific type of debt, guaranteed bonds have a unique feature. They are issued by one corporation but guaranteed in whole or in part by some other corporation.

Suppose, for example, a small company, ABC Electric Wire Corporation, supplies some item that is needed by some larger company, let's say, General Electric, which may limit its responsibility solely to the payment of interest or solely to payment of principal at maturity. In many cases, the guarantee is as to both principal and interest, giving the investor the same security she would have received had she purchased bonds of the corporation making the guarantee.

Guaranteed bonds are rare but have provided access to credit markets to many corporations that would, if acting independently, find the doors closed to them.

Equipment Trust Certificate

An equipment trust certificate is an instrument of debt pledging as security the actual equipment used by the corporation in the operation of its business. This form of financing is most often used by railroads, which pledge the actual cars operated over the rail system. Other industries, notably airlines and trucking corporations, may also issue this type of bond. When the loan is arranged, a trustee holds title until repayment and makes the interest distribution to the bondholders during the term of the loan. Upon repayment at maturity, the trustee transfers title to the equipment back to the railroad or other issuer. Because the agreement contains provisions for maintenance, insurance, and replacement of the collateral, these securities are considered to be of high investment quality.

Equipment trust certificates have one feature that is unique among corporate bonds. They are usually issued in serial form—that is, portions of the issue mature on different dates. Generally, corporate bonds are issued in term form in which the entire issue matures on the same date. Thus, if the Chesapeake and Ohio borrows $30,000,000 by offering equipment trust certificates, the issue might be structured so that $2,000,000 of the debt would be paid in each of the next 15 years. The amounts paid each year need not be equal, and often the issuers use a balloon form of repayment in which small amounts are repaid in the early years and the largest amount is repaid in the later years.

This form of issuance gives investors the latitude to select from the various maturities offered which best suit their financial planning needs.

Income Bond (Adjustment Bond)

Income bonds, sometimes referred to as adjustment bonds, are not issued as a method of obtaining original financing. Rather, they are issued in exchange for outstanding debt by a corporation experiencing financial problems. Suppose that the XYZ Corporation had outstanding an issue of 6% debentures. Should that corporation default on payment of interest, the bondholders could force a bankruptcy. However, if the corporate assets were minimal, the bondholders would receive little satisfaction. In some cases the corporation sees a possible recovery if it can remain in business and be relieved of the requirement to pay the semiannual interest on its debt. It may, in this instance, offer to exchange an issue of XYZ 8% income bonds for the XYZ 6% debentures. Should the debenture holders agree to the exchange, they would now own a bond with a higher rate of interest should conditions later allow the corporation to resume interest payment.

The key feature of an income bond is that interest must be paid only if sufficient money is earned by the issuer. Should the earnings fall short, there is no obligation to pay and the bond-holder has no recourse but to wait and hope for better days. Should the company be unable to pay for a period of years, the bondholder receives no return on the investment. However, if a banner year occurs in the future, the corporation may distribute the equivalent of a number of previous years' payments. The interest on an income bond is payable only if earned and to the extent earned. Therefore, years may pass with no payments to bondholders followed by a year with a large distribution. Since the holder has exchanged for a bond with a higher interest rate, eventual total payment will increase the return. However, these corporate issuers are financially troubled and happy endings are less than usual.

In some cases the bondholder exchanging his debt for an income bond may not only receive a higher stated interest rate (8% versus 6%) but may also receive a greater principal amount. Thus, to encourage exchange the bondholder may be offered an $1,100 face amount income bond for the $1,000 debenture.

Bonds generally trade "plus accrued interest." This indicates that the buyer of a bond pays to the seller the amount of interest to which the seller is entitled. Bonds generally pay interest twice a year. Should one purchase a bond in September that pays interest on January 1 and July 1 (stated J & J1), the buyer pays an agreed price of perhaps 98 plus the accrued interest from the previous July 1. That interest is refunded with the next interest payment on January 1.

Bond prices are expressed as a percentage of face value. Because the face value of a bond is $1,000, a price of 98 indicates $980 (98% of $1,000). In addition, the buyer in the paragraph above pays interest to the seller for the month of July and August as well as the appropriate portion of September. The following January the buyer receives a full six months' interest from the corporation. This repays him the amount he advanced at time of purchase and gives him the interest due for his period as the bondholder. Interest on corporate bonds and municipal bonds is computed using a 30-day month and a 360-day year. Examples of interest computation will be found in the municipal bond section of this text.

Income bonds are, however, an exception to this general rule. These bonds are traded "flat," which means that there is no accrued interest added to the price paid by the buyer. Should the bond make an interest payment, the holder on that date receives the entire amount distributed. The only other bonds that trade "flat" are those in default of interest payments. A buyer would be foolish to pay interest to the seller when no payment by the issuer is anticipated.

Although interest is not normally a factor in a bond transaction, it could be an important consideration in bonds trading "flat." Should an 8% income bond make a semiannual payment, the holder would receive $40 per $1,000 bond. As a "point" in a bond equals $10 (1% of $1,000), this payment could cause the bond to rise as the payment date nears and fall when the interest has been distributed. Flat bonds trade "ex-interest," just as stocks that pay dividends trade "ex-dividend" on the first day on which the purchaser would not be entitled to the coming payment. Note the difference between a point and a basis point. A point in a bond is $10.00. A basis point is $0.10, which is .010% of $1,000.

Trust Indenture Act of 1939

The indenture is the contract between the issuing corporation (borrower) and the investor purchasing the bonds (lender). It spells out all details covering the loan and includes such items as the interest rate, maturity date, call features, refunding provisions, terms of conversion (if any), and all other conditions of the borrowing. The indenture is printed on the face of the bond certificate.

Under the Trust Indenture Act an independent trustee, usually a bank, is appointed to protect the purchasers of the debt. The trustee oversees the agreement (indenture) to ensure the rights of the bondholders.

Retirement of Debt

Once an issuer has offered debt securities there are a number of ways in which this debt can be retired. Should the bond be issued July 1, 2004, and carry a 20-year maturity, then on July 1, 2024, the company would be required to pay back the bondholders. This redemption at maturity occurs after the bond has reached the agreed date for repayment.

There are, however, four ways by which an issuer may retire debt securities prior to maturity.

Callable Bonds

A call feature entitles an issuer to repurchase bonds prior to maturity under terms that were set at the time of issue. For example, if in June 2004 Florida Power & Light Corporation offered an issue of $100,000,000 first mortgage bonds 5% due June 1, 2034, the bond might allow for a call by the corporation prior to maturity. Generally, there is a period of five or ten years during which the bonds may not be called. This protects the purchaser from losing his investment should interest rates decline. Perhaps Florida Power & Light might carry a schedule like the following:

Years 1–5	Noncallable
Year 6	114
Year 7	113
Year 8	112
⋮	

The call price would decline each year and eventually reach 100 (par), which means 100% of the face value. Bonds cannot be called below par as it would be improper to require the holder of a $1,000 bond to involuntarily accept less than the face value. (Note: Should market factors cause the bonds to trade below 100, the corporation could consider buying them back in the open market rather than exercising the call.)

In the seventh year after issue, a call could be made for the bonds at 113 ($1,130 per $1,000), and the holders would be required to deliver according to the agreement. Florida Power & Light might decide not to call the entire $100,000,000 but just a portion of the issue. In this case, the bonds to be called would be determined by random selection and the holders notified.

Refunding

A refunding is the sale of a new issue of bonds with the proceeds used to retire an outstanding issue. A corporation may have an issue of 8% debentures that were issued some years ago. Should current interest rates allow the company to issue bonds with a 6% coupon, they may elect to refund the older issue. By replacing the 8% bonds with those requiring only a payment of 6%, the company saves 2% each year. On an issue whose face amount is $100,000,000 this represents a $2,000,000 annual savings. Corporations may also use a form of refunding to pay off bonds at maturity. Perhaps the company does not have sufficient capital to meet the payment of a maturing issue. They might sell a new issue of the same face value and use the proceeds to redeem the maturing bonds. In a refunding, the corporation does not receive any cash. The proceeds of the sale are used to retire the outstanding debt.

In order for a corporation to refund an issue, the terms of the refunding must have been included in the indenture. Refunding terms are usually the same as those permitting the bonds to be called. Perhaps the indenture stated in part:

Years 1–5	Noncallable
Year 6	114
Year 7	113
Year 8	112

Thus, should the corporation elect to refund the outstanding debt in the eighth year after issue, it would have to pay the bondholders $1,120 (112% of $1,000) for each $1,000 face amount bond that was refunded. The interest saved might make the payment of this 12% premium advantageous to the corporation.

Sinking Fund

The term "sinking fund" is rather self-descriptive. The corporation agrees to set up a fund to sink the bond issue. A $100,000,000 issue maturing in 20 years might carry a $1,000,000 annual sinking fund. This would mean that each year the corporation would deposit $1,000,000 into the fund, which would be used to repurchase the bonds in the open market. Sinking funds tend to increase the attractiveness of the remaining bonds. Using our example, each year there would be $1,000,000 less of the debt outstanding. This would decrease the amount of interest cost to the corporation and reduce by $1,000,000 each year the amount to be paid off by the corporation at maturity. Sinking fund terms vary and should be carefully studied by the investor. Some even have a "100% sinker," which means that all the bonds will be retired by the sinking fund prior to maturity.

In some cases, bonds may be called by the sinking fund. This takes away from the bondholder the right of choice. If the bonds are called, as described earlier, the holder must surrender them. When the sinking fund operates in the open market the bondholder could elect to retain the bonds should such action be more advantageous.

Conversion

A corporation that issues convertible bonds will frequently see the bonds retired prior to maturity. Convertible bonds give the holder the right to exchange (convert) the bonds to some other security, usually common stock of the same corporation. Suppose a corporation issues a 6% convertible debenture that allows the holder to exchange the bonds for common stock at

$25 per share. This means that the holder has the option to exchange the bond for 40 shares of common stock ($1,000 face value of bond divided by the conversion price of $25 per share). If, at some point in time, the common stock is paying a dividend of $4 per share annually, the bondholder might convert the bond into the 40 shares of stock and receive $160 per year in dividends ($4 per share×40 shares). This is far greater than the $60 in interest (6% of $1,000) that he had been receiving on the bond. Once converted, the bond is retired, thus relieving the corporation of interest payments and the obligation to pay the face amount at maturity.

This feature is one reason why corporations issue convertible bonds. They carry the possibility of being retired prior to maturity and also require a lower interest payment. An issuer might have to pay 8% to issue a nonconvertible bond; a convertible bond might necessitate payment of 6% annually.

Although some convertible bonds are converted at the option of the holder to increase income, more often the exchange is caused by a forced conversion.

EXAMPLE

> The bonds mentioned above are convertible into common stock at $25 per share. Suppose the common stock is trading in the market at $36 per share. "Parity" for the bond would be $144 ($1,440). This is determined by multiplying the price of the stock ($36) by the number of shares into which the bond is convertible (40). If the stock is trading at $36 per share, each $1,000 bond is exchangeable for stock valued at $1,440 ($36×40 shares). Suppose, however, the bond was also "callable" at 106 ($1,060). Should the issuer call the bonds at this price the bondholder would be forced to convert lest he surrender bonds worth $1,440 for the call price of $1,060.

Parity is that price at which neither a profit nor a loss would result from conversion. Using the same bond as in the previous example, we can determine parity when given either the current price of the stock or the current price of the bond.

If given the stock price we simply multiply that price by the number of shares into which the bonds are convertible.

Stock Price	Parity for the Bond
$18 (x 40 shares)	$ 720 (72)
$21 (x 40 shares)	$ 840 (84)
$38 (x 40 shares)	$1,520 (152)
$42 (x 40 shares)	$1,680 (168)
$54 (x 40 shares)	$2,160 (216)

Note: The number of shares into which a bond is convertible is determined by dividing the face value of the bond ($1,000) by the stated conversion price. Thus, if we are told that a bond is convertible into stock at $50 per share, we would divide $1,000 by that $50 price and find that the bond was convertible into 20 shares of stock ($1,000 divided by $50 conversion price).

If we are given the market price of the bond we would determine parity for the stock by dividing that price by the number of shares into which it is convertible. Using our original example of a $1,000 bond convertible at $25 per share, we know that that bond can be exchanged for 40 shares of common stock ($1,000 divided by $25). After making this determination we can easily determine the parity price of the stock when given the market price of the bond. We simply divide the bond price by the number of shares into which it is convertible.

Bond Price	Parity for Common Stock
$ 800 (÷ by 40 shares)	$20 per share (80)
$1,000 (÷ by 40 shares)	$25 per share (100)
$1,200 (÷ by 40 shares)	$30 per share (120)
$1,280 (÷ by 40 shares)	$32 per share (128)
$1,360 (÷ by 40 shares)	$34 per share (136)

Bonds can be retired prior to maturity through (1) call, (2) refunding, (3) sinking fund, and (4) conversion. It is also possible, of course, that a corporation might repurchase its bonds in the open market. It might feel that the market price of its bonds is low. If so, it could use excess corporate funds to repurchase the debt, although it is not required to do so. The result would be, of course, the retirement of the debt.

ANSWER SHEET FOR CHAPTER 1 EXAMINATION

1. Ⓐ Ⓑ Ⓒ Ⓓ   11. Ⓐ Ⓑ Ⓒ Ⓓ   21. Ⓐ Ⓑ Ⓒ Ⓓ

2. Ⓐ Ⓑ Ⓒ Ⓓ   12. Ⓐ Ⓑ Ⓒ Ⓓ   22. Ⓐ Ⓑ Ⓒ Ⓓ

3. Ⓐ Ⓑ Ⓒ Ⓓ   13. Ⓐ Ⓑ Ⓒ Ⓓ   23. Ⓐ Ⓑ Ⓒ Ⓓ

4. Ⓐ Ⓑ Ⓒ Ⓓ   14. Ⓐ Ⓑ Ⓒ Ⓓ   24. Ⓐ Ⓑ Ⓒ Ⓓ

5. Ⓐ Ⓑ Ⓒ Ⓓ   15. Ⓐ Ⓑ Ⓒ Ⓓ   25. Ⓐ Ⓑ Ⓒ Ⓓ

6. Ⓐ Ⓑ Ⓒ Ⓓ   16. Ⓐ Ⓑ Ⓒ Ⓓ   26. Ⓐ Ⓑ Ⓒ Ⓓ

7. Ⓐ Ⓑ Ⓒ Ⓓ   17. Ⓐ Ⓑ Ⓒ Ⓓ   27. Ⓐ Ⓑ Ⓒ Ⓓ

8. Ⓐ Ⓑ Ⓒ Ⓓ   18. Ⓐ Ⓑ Ⓒ Ⓓ   28. Ⓐ Ⓑ Ⓒ Ⓓ

9. Ⓐ Ⓑ Ⓒ Ⓓ   19. Ⓐ Ⓑ Ⓒ Ⓓ   29. Ⓐ Ⓑ Ⓒ Ⓓ

10. Ⓐ Ⓑ Ⓒ Ⓓ   20. Ⓐ Ⓑ Ⓒ Ⓓ   30. Ⓐ Ⓑ Ⓒ Ⓓ

31. Ⓐ Ⓑ Ⓒ Ⓓ   41. Ⓐ Ⓑ Ⓒ Ⓓ

32. Ⓐ Ⓑ Ⓒ Ⓓ   42. Ⓐ Ⓑ Ⓒ Ⓓ

33. Ⓐ Ⓑ Ⓒ Ⓓ   43. Ⓐ Ⓑ Ⓒ Ⓓ

34. Ⓐ Ⓑ Ⓒ Ⓓ   44. Ⓐ Ⓑ Ⓒ Ⓓ

35. Ⓐ Ⓑ Ⓒ Ⓓ   45. Ⓐ Ⓑ Ⓒ Ⓓ

36. Ⓐ Ⓑ Ⓒ Ⓓ   46. Ⓐ Ⓑ Ⓒ Ⓓ

37. Ⓐ Ⓑ Ⓒ Ⓓ   47. Ⓐ Ⓑ Ⓒ Ⓓ

38. Ⓐ Ⓑ Ⓒ Ⓓ   48. Ⓐ Ⓑ Ⓒ Ⓓ

39. Ⓐ Ⓑ Ⓒ Ⓓ   49. Ⓐ Ⓑ Ⓒ Ⓓ

40. Ⓐ Ⓑ Ⓒ Ⓓ   50. Ⓐ Ⓑ Ⓒ Ⓓ

CHAPTER 1 EXAMINATION

1. Bonds that are secured by a portfolio of stocks and/or bonds held by a trustee are called:

   (A) income bonds
   (B) collateral trust bonds
   (C) debenture bonds
   (D) guaranteed bonds

2. To determine a common stock's yield, you need to know its:

   I.   retained earnings
   II. current assets
   III. market price
   IV. annual dividend

       (A) I and IV only
       (B) II and III only
       (C) I and II only
       (D) III and IV only

3. A conservatively capitalized company raises most of its capital through issuance of:

   (A) common stock
   (B) preferred stock
   (C) warrants
   (D) bonds

4. The dividend for participating preferred stock is:

   (A) fixed as to the maximum but not the minimum
   (B) fixed as to the minimum but not the maximum
   (C) payable semiannually to holders of record
   (D) cumulative if it is not paid by the corporation

5. Which of the following preferred issues is likely to fluctuate most in value?

   (A) participating preferred
   (B) cumulative preferred
   (C) callable preferred
   (D) convertible preferred

6. Generally, a holder of an ADR has the same rights as a common stockholder EXCEPT:

   (A) the right to the issuer's financial statements
   (B) preemptive rights
   (C) the right to transfer ownership
   (D) the right to vote

Questions 7–9 are based on the following information:

A corporation decides to make a rights offering to raise $10,000,000 in new capital through issuance of 1,000,000 shares of common stock. Assume it already had 6,000,000 shares outstanding at the time of the announcement.

7. How many rights will the corporation distribute to its stockholders?

   (A) one million
   (B) six million
   (C) seven million
   (D) ten million

8. What is the subscription price per share?

   (A) $4
   (B) $6
   (C) $7
   (D) $10

9. What subscription ratio has been established by the corporation's board of directors?

   (A) six rights are needed for each new share
   (B) ten rights are needed for each new share
   (C) six rights are needed for ten new shares
   (D) there is insufficient information to make this determination

10. Under cumulative voting procedures, if there were five vacancies to be filled on the board of directors and you owned 100 shares of stock you could cast:

   (A) a total of 100 votes
   (B) a total of 100 votes per director
   (C) a total of 500 votes
   (D) a total of 500 votes per director

11. Debentures are:

   (A) secured by real estate holdings
   (B) collateralized by securities owned by the issuer
   (C) backed by the general credit but no specific collateral of the issuing corporation
   (D) protected by the revenues of bridges, tunnels, and toll roads

12. Convertible bonds have all of the following characteristics EXCEPT:

   (A) an ability to protect a short position in a stock they are convertible into
   (B) permissibility to be used as collateral for a loan
   (C) a usually higher yield than nonconvertible bonds issued by the same company
   (D) fluctuations influenced by changes in the market price of the underlying common stock

13. Convertible preferred stocks have all of the following characteristics EXCEPT:

   (A) They have a lower dividend rate than nonconvertible preferreds.
   (B) If converted into common stock, the result will be a dilution of earnings per share.
   (C) If they are called, the holders must always accept the call price.
   (D) Dividends must be paid to preferred stockholders before any dividends may be paid to common stockholders.

14. Although a corporation may have no earnings in a particular year, it is obligated to pay interest on all its outstanding debt instruments EXCEPT:

   (A) convertible subordinated debentures
   (B) collateral trust bonds
   (C) adjustment (income) bonds
   (D) equipment trust certificates

15. Interest rates have risen from 5.10% to 5.30%. From the viewpoint of a prospective purchaser of five $1,000 bonds, what is the increase in interest payments that result from that rise?

   (A) $1
   (B) $2
   (C) $10
   (D) $20

16. Common stocks of which of the following industry issuers would be most likely to decline in value if interest rates in the economy were to rise?

   (A) automobile companies
   (B) airline companies
   (C) machine tool companies
   (D) public utility companies

17. Which one of these instruments is issued to finance foreign trade activities?

    (A) a CD
    (B) an ADR
    (C) a banker's acceptance
    (D) commercial paper

18. When interest rates on good quality bonds move up through 9%, which two of the following occur with outstanding bonds?

    I.   dollar prices rise
    II. dollar prices decline
    III. yield levels rise
    IV. yield levels decline

    (A) I and III only
    (B) II and IV only
    (C) I and IV only
    (D) II and III only

19. What is the dollar price of a 5% bond due to mature in 15 years if it trades on a 5.10 basis?

    (A) 89.29
    (B) 98.96
    (C) 102.12
    (D) 111.20

20. Bonds are most often quoted as a percentage of:

    (A) face value
    (B) book value
    (C) market value
    (D) liquidating value

21. Who are the owners of publicly held corporations?

    I.   the holders of subordinated debentures
    II. the holders of preferred stock
    III. the holders of mortgage bonds
    IV. the holders of common stock

    (A) I and IV only
    (B) II and IV only
    (C) II and III only
    (D) I and III only

22. Although they are privileges of common stock ownership in the United States, one of these items is not a mandated right of stockholders. Which one is not such a right?

    (A) the right to dividend payments
    (B) a residual claim to assets upon dissolution of the company
    (C) the right to a stock certificate
    (D) the right to vote in the important affairs of the company

23. Which of the following comments about treasury stock is true?

    I.   It has voting rights and receives dividends when declared.
    II. It has no voting rights and does not receive dividends.
    III. It is stock that has been reacquired.
    IV. It is authorized but unissued stock.

    (A) I only
    (B) I and III only
    (C) II and III only
    (D) II and IV only

24. Which two of the following statements are true about callable preferred stocks?

    I. If interest rates are lower than the stated (nominal) rate on a callable preferred stock, it is in the best interests of the issuer and the preferred stockholder for the corporation to call the stock.
    II. The callable provision of a preferred stock is a feature designed to be of the best advantage to preferred stockholders.
    III. In a period of falling interest rates, the call price has the effect of limiting the market price at which the preferred stock will sell.
    IV. Long-term individual and institutional investors tend to avoid buying callable preferred stocks.

    (A) I and II only
    (B) I and IV only
    (C) II and III only
    (D) III and IV only

25. In which of these industries would you be least likely to find companies obtaining financing by issuing equipment trust certificates?

    (A) airline
    (B) tractor-trailer
    (C) farm equipment
    (D) oil and gas drilling rigs

26. Which of the following statements is always true of equity securities?

    (A) They are readily marketable.
    (B) They are unsecured.
    (C) They have a fixed rate of return.
    (D) They have a maturity date.

27. Corporations often repurchase their own stock in the open market to:

    I. finance future acquisitions
    II. increase future earnings per share announcements
    III. have stock available for stock option plans for key employees

    (A) I only
    (B) II only
    (C) I and II only
    (D) I, II, and III

28. An investor purchasing which of the following securities acquires the longest-term option privilege?

    (A) calls
    (B) puts
    (C) rights
    (D) warrants

29. The board of directors of a corporation declares a dividend payable one month hence. This dividend can be in the form of:

    I. cash
    II. treasury stock
    III. stock in a subsidiary company
    IV. authorized but unissued stock

    (A) II only
    (B) I and III only
    (C) I, II, and III only
    (D) I, II, III, and IV

30. Choose the only statement below that is true:

    (A) If its earnings are sufficient, a corporation is required to pay a cash dividend to its common stockholders.
    (B) A growth company would be more likely to pay a cash dividend than a stock dividend.
    (C) A stock split and a stock dividend are reflected in exactly the same manner on a corporation's balance sheet.
    (D) The amount of dividends paid by a corporation can have a significant influence on the market price of its stock.

31. In the event of a company's liquidation under terms of a bankruptcy decree, holders of its subordinated debentures would be repaid:

    (A) before existing secured debt instruments
    (B) after bank loans and accounts payable, but before preferred shareholders
    (C) before other existing unsecured debt instruments
    (D) after accounts payable, but before outstanding bank loans

32. In the event of a corporation's dissolution which of the following creditors will be paid first?

    (A) the tax collector
    (B) an account payable
    (C) a senior lienholder
    (D) the subordinated debentures

33. American Telephone & Telegraph Co. $4 convertible preferred ($50 par) is exchangeable for common stock at 47.50. If the preferred stock is trading at 52, where must the common stock sell to be at parity?

    (A) 47.50
    (B) slightly less than 49.38
    (C) slightly more than 54.50
    (D) 52

34. If the common stock is actually trading at 51 the preferred stock is therefore:

    (A) overvalued and will quickly decline
    (B) selling at a 4% premium over conversion value
    (C) underpriced and should quickly rise
    (D) callable at 52, fixing a ceiling on its upward price movement

35. An analyst would most likely classify as a defensive issue:

    (A) a blue chip stock
    (B) a corporate bond
    (C) a utility corporation's common stock
    (D) an aerospace company's security

36. Holders of which of these securities do not receive dividends?

    (A) ADRs
    (B) warrants
    (C) common stock
    (D) preferred stock

37. A corporation issues a bond at par with a 5% coupon that is convertible into common stock at $40. The conversion ratio is therefore:

    (A) 40
    (B) 30
    (C) 25
    (D) 15

38. If the bond increases in value by 20 points, what is the conversion parity of the stock?

(A) $25
(B) $40
(C) $48
(D) $50

39. During a reorganization of a company, voting trust certificates are sometimes issued. An owner of a voting trust certificate:

(A) maintains the right to receive dividends, but gives up the right to vote
(B) gives up all rights of ownership
(C) maintains the right to vote, but gives up the right to receive dividends
(D) gives up the right to both dividends and to vote

40. "Arbitrage" is a term used to describe:

(A) a procedure by which price discrepancy between buying and selling brokers are corrected
(B) the purchase of a security in one market and the sale of the same security in another market at a different price
(C) the method for determining the price of a bond
(D) a method for valuation of corporate assets

41. The most common type of a bond that a strong, well-established company would issue would be a:

(A) debenture
(B) closed-end mortgage
(C) open-end mortgage
(D) convertible

42. The quotation of a corporate bond in a newspaper shows a net change of plus one point. The bond has increased in value by:

(A) $1,000
(B) $100
(C) $10
(D) $1

43. A basis point is equal to:

(A) .100%
(B) .010%
(C) 1.000%
(D) .001%

44. Leverage is typified when:

(A) a trader sells common stock short, buys warrants for the equivalent number of shares, subscribes for the stock, and covers the short sale with it
(B) a company borrows at 6% and puts the funds to work to earn 10%
(C) in a rising market, an investor buys a dually listed stock on the NYSE and sells it later the same day on the CBOE
(D) a corporation redeems its convertible bonds before the maturation date

45. A holder of 200 shares of common stock in a utility corporation receives rights to subscribe to 100 additional shares at $20 when that company attempts to raise $40,000,000 in new capital. How many rights does the stockholder actually receive?

(A) 20
(B) 50
(C) 100
(D) 200

46. Based upon this information, how many common shares were outstanding prior to the offering?

    (A) 2,000,000
    (B) 4,000,000
    (C) 1,000,000
    (D) 40,000,000

47. If the old stock in question 45 was trading at 24.50 cum rights, the theoretical value of each right received by this holder is equal to:

    (A) $4.50
    (B) $1.13
    (C) $1.50
    (D) $2.25

48. A customer owns a perpetual warrant to buy 1 share of XYZ common stock at $30. Today XYZ common is trading at 41.50 and is ex-dividend $.75. What is the market value of the warrant?

    (A) 5.75
    (B) 5.62
    (C) 5.38
    (D) cannot be determined from this information

49. Select the one situation best illustrating a definition of bona fide arbitrage:

    (A) the purchase of a convertible security and its subsequent sale the next day
    (B) the near simultaneous profitable purchase and sale of equal securities in different markets
    (C) the purchase of stock and sale of a security convertible into that stock at approximately the same time
    (D) the purchase of an April 15 call option at 3 and an immediate short sale of the underlying stock at 17

50. XYZ preferred $100 par is convertible into four shares of common and is trading at 104.50. It is also callable at 101. If the market price of the underlying common is now 27.89, which of the following transactions would result in a successful arbitrage?

    (A) purchase 400 shares of the common stock and sell 100 shares of preferred stock "short exempt" (i.e. sale was exempt from the uptick rule)
    (B) purchase the preferred stock and sell an appropriate amount of the common stock "short exempt"
    (C) purchase both the common and the preferred stocks as a guaranteed hedge against further market risk
    (D) purchase the preferred stock and await a call by the corporation, which will inevitably occur at these market price levels

CHAPTER 1 EXAMINATION ANSWERS

1. **B** By definition.
2. **D** To determine the yield on a common stock you divide the annual dividend by the current market price.
3. **A** A capitalization containing only common stock is considered to be a conservative capitalization.
4. **B** By definition. Please note that participating preferred stocks are fairly rare.
5. **D** Because of the conversion feature, convertibles normally follow the fortunes of the common stock. Also, because the dividend rate (stated rate on the preferred) is lower than what it would be otherwise, they are also subject to movement in sympathy with interest rate fluctuations.
6. **B** Although holders of ADRs receive most privileges of common stock ownership, they frequently do not receive preemptive rights.
7. **B** One right for each outstanding share.
8. **D** By dividing $10,000,000 by 1,000,000 shares.
9. **A** Since each share will receive a right, there will be 6,000,000 rights to buy 1,000,000 shares; hence, six rights needed for each share.
10. **C** Under cumulative voting, you multiply the number of directors to be elected by the number of shares you own. In this case, you could cast 500 votes. You could cast it in one lump, or divide it up any way you saw fit.
11. **C** By definition.
12. **C** One of the possible advantages to the issuer of convertible bonds is that they may normally be sold at a yield that is less than the amount they would have to pay if the issue were not convertible.
13. **C** Convertible preferred shareholders have the opportunity of converting. They are not forced to take the call price.
14. **C** Adjustment (income) bonds pay interest only if earned.
15. **C** A basis point equals 10 cents. A rise of 20 basis points in yield equals $2 per bond, or $10 on five bonds.
16. **D** Public utility companies normally have the highest degree of leverage. Therefore, the general rise in interest rates would generally cause net income to decline, thereby reducing earnings per share available for common stock and thus its price.
17. **C** A banker's acceptance is issued to finance foreign trade activities.
18. **D** Rates up equal prices down. Prices down equal yields up.
19. **B** Obviously, the bond is trading at a small discount.
20. **A** Although this is generally true, treasury bills and municipal bonds are quoted on a yield-to-maturity basis.
21. **B** Preferred stock and common stock are ownership interests. Subordinated debentures and mortgage bonds are debt instruments.
22. **A** Choices (B), (C), and (D) properly describe the rights of common stock ownership. Common stock is entitled to dividends only if they are declared by the board of directors.
23. **C** Basically, by definition. Treasury stock does not receive any voting right nor does it receive dividends. It is stock that has been authorized and *issued* but is no longer considered to be outstanding.
24. **D** Choices I and II are incorrect. Call

feature is basically an advantage to the issuer; hence, noncallable preferreds are preferable to callable preferreds. If interest rates were to fall, the corporation might consider calling in the issue and reissuing a new preferred issue with a lower rate. The call provision would tend to limit the upside movement in a period of falling interest rates.

25. **C** In an equipment trust certificate issued by a corporation, operating equipment is pledged as collateral for the loan. An equipment trust can be used in just about any kind of application that you might imagine. However, most farms are run by individuals rather than corporations, and it would be unlikely to find farm equipment financed in this manner.

26. **B** Equity means ownership and hence is unsecured.

27. **D** All of these items describe valid reasons for the acquisition of treasury stock.

28. **D** All of the others have a definite life span. Warrants do, sometimes, but it is normally a long period of time.

29. **D** A dividend may be payable in any of these fashions. Also, but very rarely, a dividend can be in the form of property.

30. **D** Earnings are usually the dominant force in influencing market prices. However, the amount of the dividend can have a tremendous influence on the market price as well.

31. **B** Holders of subordinated debentures are behind all other creditors, but they are before any equity holder.

32. **A** Taxes due are the first claim.

33. **B** The preferred stock has a $50 par value. The formula would be
50 ÷ $47.50 = 1.053
52 ÷ 1.053 = 49.38

34. **C** The parity price of the common is somewhat less than 49.38 and if it actually sold at 51, the preferred is indeed underpriced.

35. **C** Basically, the term "defensive issue" refers to common stock in a company that defends itself from the business cycle. The corporate bond would normally be "defensive," but in normal terminology it is not referred to as a defensive issue.

36. **B** Warrants, and for that matter, options, do not receive dividends. However, if warrants or call options are exercised prior to an ex-dividend date, then the *holder* who exercised would be entitled to receive a dividend.

37. **C** $1,000 face value divided by $40 equals 25 shares.

38. **C** $1,200 divided by 25 shares equals $48.

39. **A** Voting trust certificates are the same as common stock except that the holders do not have voting rights.

40. **B** In arbitrage the investor hopes to profit from a price difference in varying markets.

41. **A** Because debentures, unlike other debt instruments, have no specific security protecting the bondholders, the company's general financial condition is most important.

42. **C** One point (1%) in a bond is equivalent to $10 (1% of $1,000).

43. **B** By definition a basis point equals 10 cents, which is .010% of $1,000.

44. **B** Leverage is simply using money. It is possible to the extent that the earnings generated by the new capital exceed the cost of borrowing the money; that is, the interest charge.

45. **D** The basis for the issuance of rights is always one right per outstanding share.

46. **B** The basis for the offer is one new share for each two shares held. They

are attempting to sell 2,000,000. Thus, they must have 4,000,000 outstanding. Please note that the total number of shares after the offering will be 6,000,000 outstanding.

47. **C** The formula is market price minus subscription price divided by the number of rights needed to buy a new share plus 1.

48. **D** It would appear that the value is something in excess of ten. How-ever, since the warrant is perpetual, there is no way of determining its market value from this information.

49. **B** By definition. An arbitrage is the simultaneous (as far as is possible) purchase and sale of the same or equivalent security in different markets or the same market, in the case of an equivalent security.

50. **B** This defines an arbitrage operation.

U.S. Government and Agency Securities

U.S. GOVERNMENT OBLIGATIONS

The Department of the Treasury is responsible for providing the financing to operate the government. It performs this obligation by issuing marketable and nonmarketable debt securities. Interest from U.S. government securities is exempt from state and local tax but subject to taxation as ordinary income by the federal government.

Treasury Bills (T-Bills)

U.S. treasury bills (T-bills) are short-term obligations issued either at weekly auctions with three- or six-month maturities or at a monthly auction with a maturity of one year. Treasury bills are issued in book entry form only and in denominations ranging from $10,000 to $1,000,000. The minimum purchase must be for an initial amount of $10,000 and in $1,000 multiples thereafter. Unlike all other U.S. government securities, which are issued at a stated interest rate, T-bills are traded at a discount from their face value. The difference between the purchase price of the bills and the par value or the sale value (if sold prior to maturity) is considered interest (ordinary) income, which is subject to federal income tax, but, as noted before, not state taxes.

The discount on a treasury bill is the equivalent of the yield that the investor earns on the bill. Unlike other government securities, it is calculated on the basis of a 360-day year.

Tax Anticipation Bills (TABs)

Tax anticipation bills are occasionally issued by the federal government and are primarily aimed at corporate tax-paying investors. Generally, they mature from one to seven days after normal quarterly corporate income tax payment dates (April 15, June 15, etc.). Although they do not mature until after the tax payment date, they are accepted by the IRS at face value in payment of taxes, giving the investor a higher return than if they were held to maturity. Like treasury bills, tax anticipation bills are issued on a discount basis and are redeemable at face value.

In recent years, the Treasury has been issuing cash management bills (CMBs) in lieu of tax anticipation bills (TABs). CMBs like TABs are issued at a discount and mature at the face value.

Treasury Notes and Bonds (T-Notes and T-Bonds)

As discussed above, treasury bills and tax anticipation bills are securities issued on a discount basis with maturities of one year or less. There are two other types of marketable treasury securities, both of which have coupons and are issued at stated rates of interest. These are notes and bonds. Treasury notes can be issued with maturities anywhere from two to ten years, and treasury bonds are issued with maturities in excess of ten years. Please note that the original maturity date is the only difference between a treasury note and a treasury bond. As a matter of information, in October 2001 the Treasury stopped issuing 30-year treasury bonds, often referred to as the long bond. It was a benchmark for determining long-term interest rates. However, just recently, this bond was reintroduced, and we have it again.

Notes and bonds can be issued either in bearer or registered form. They are issued, quoted, and traded as a percentage of their face value, in fractions stated as 32nds or multiples thereof. A note or bond that is quoted at "98.4–98.16" would indicate that the bid is 98 and $\frac{4}{32}$ and the offer is 98 and $\frac{16}{32}$, equaling a dollar value of $981.25 on the bid side and $985.00 on the offered side.

Maximum liquidity exists for those issues that currently mature within the maturity range of bills. Those maturing between one and two years have near maximum liquidity, and the liquidity for others varies with maturity, technical factors, and investors' long-term goals. Some notes and bonds are callable by the government, generally five years prior to maturity. These obligations are referred to as "term bonds." When calculating yield to maturity on a term bond trading at a premium, you use the call date rather than the maturity date.

U.S. Treasury Strips

In the late 1970s, brokers began cutting off the coupons of treasury notes and bonds prior to their payment dates in effect creating two new securities. A T-note or T-bond bearing no interest, hence the name, zero coupon notes or bonds and stripped securities, which pay interest semi-annually. Zero coupon notes and bonds are sold at a discount. You receive the fair value at maturity, which is your interest payment.

Treasury Inflation-Indexed Securities (TIPS)

A treasury inflation-indexed security (TIPs) is a relatively new security issued by the Treasury Department. The face value of these securities is adjusted based on the Consumer Price Index. However, the interest rate is fixed for the life of the bond. Currently a 3% inflation-indexed treasury security maturing July 2012 has a face value of $1,010. Consequently you would receive 3% interest based on the adjusted face value of $1,010.

Nonmarketable Savings Bonds

Savings bonds are considered nonmarketable because they are offered publicly by the Treasury Department (via an agent) and redeemed directly to the Treasury Department (again via an agent). Hence they do not trade in the open market.

Series EE Savings Bonds

Series EE savings bonds are offered in registered form only at various denominations, with the minimum of $50. They are issued at a discount from face value and redeemed at face value by an agent of the Treasury Department upon maturity. The difference between subscription and redemption prices represents accrued interest for the owner. Commercial banks are not allowed to purchase Series EE bonds. No more than $30,000 of these bonds may be purchased by any individual in one year. Any federal income tax payable by the bondholder may be declared and paid annually or at maturity in one lump sum, depending on the investor's choice. Unlike other bonds, interest on Series EE bonds does not accrue in equal increments over the lifetime of the bond. Instead, interest accrual is small in the early years of the bond and grows much larger in the later years.

Currently, the interest rate on EE bonds is established by the Treasury every six months. It is set at 85% of the average yield for five-year treasury securities for the most recent six-month period.

Series HH Bonds

Series HH bonds are registered securities offered in various denominations beginning at $500. They are issued at face value and redeemed at face value upon maturity. Interest is actually paid by the Treasury Department by a check every six months during the lifetime of the bond. The maximum amount of Series HH bonds that can be acquired by any person is $15,000. (Note: As Series EE and HH bonds are not negotiable, they are generally not acceptable as collateral for a loan.)

Interest Calculation

Interest on U.S. government bonds and notes is computed differently than on corporate and municipal bonds. As the trading volume in governments is quite large, the calculation is more precise. While corporates and municipals use a 30-day month and a 360-day year to calculate interest (a full explanation will be found in the municipal bonds section), U.S. government bond interest is calculated using the actual number of days in each month and a 365-day year. Interest is computed up to but not including the settlement date of the trade.

EXAMPLE _____

Assume that one of your clients made a "regular way," or next business date purchase, of one ($1,000) U.S. government 7½ bond on Wednesday, May 14, 1995. The bond pays interest J & J 1 (January and July 1). How much interest will be added to the cost of his purchase?

Interest Calculation

We must first determine the number of days of interest for May. As this was a regular way trade on Wednesday, May 14, settlement will be on Thursday, May 15. (Regular way trades on governments, unlike those on corporate and municipal securities, are the first business day after the trade.) Up to but not including May 15 gives us 14 interest days in May. We must now calculate the number of days in January, February, March, and April, because your client must pay the seller the accrued interest since the most recent payment (January 1).

January	–	31 days
February	–	28 days
March	–	31 days
April	–	30 days
		120 days

To this we add the 14 interest days for May, giving us a total of 134 days of interest. We now use the formula for interest computation, which is:

$$\text{PRINCIPAL} \times \text{RATE} \times \text{TIME} = \text{INTEREST}$$

Before we proceed to the formula and calculation, we must first determine exactly how many days there are in the six-month period in which the trade took place:

January	–	31 days
February	–	28 days
March	–	31 days
April	–	30 days
May	–	31 days
June	–	30 days
		181 days

*In the event of a leap year, February will have 29 days making the total 182 days.

$$\text{PRINCIPAL} \times \text{RATE} \times \text{TIME} = \text{INTEREST}$$

$$\$1,000 \times .0375 \times \frac{134}{181} = \$27.76$$

We are using an interest rate of .0375%, which is half the annual rate of 7.5%. The result, $27.76, is the interest to be added to the purchase cost of the bond.

Sometimes it is helpful in approaching interest calculation questions to determine beforehand what the approximate answer will be. In our example you know the bond pays $75.00 (7½% of $1,000) per year. This is $37.50 for six months or $6.25 per month. As we have four full months plus about half of May, we know our answer will be somewhat below $30. This approach will prevent calculation errors. If you know the answer will be something under $30 and yet arrive at a figure far from that, you will realize that you have made an error and must recheck your work.

U.S. GOVERNMENT AGENCY SECURITIES

In addition to direct obligations of the U.S. government, there are securities that enjoy federal sponsorship or guarantees to some extent, that is, some are guaranteed by the federal government. These securities can be issued as non-interest-bearing, at a discount from face value, which is payable to the holder at maturity, or they can be issued on an interest-bearing basis with interest calculated on a 30-day month, 360-day year. Interest may be payable either at maturity or semiannually, and the securities are traded on a dollar price basis (fractions in 32nds or multiples thereof).

Government agency securities can be obligations of any one of the following types of agencies:

Government-Sponsored Agencies

Capital stock was originally owned by the U.S. Treasury, but it is presently in the hands of the general public and/or the member organizations served by the particular agency. They are not guaranteed by the U.S. government as to either face value or interest. Some examples are Federal Intermediate Credit Banks (FICB), Federal Home Loan Banks (FHLB), Federal Home Loan Mortgage Corporation (FHLMC—"Freddie Mac"), Federal Land Banks (FLB), Federal National Mortgage Association (FNMA—"Fanny Mae"), and Central Bank for Cooperatives (COOPS).

Federal Agencies

U.S. government corporations and agencies, any corporations or agencies of U.S. government departments, special government agencies—owned by member organizations and federally assisted regional public bodies. The securities of these agencies may or may not be guaranteed by the federal government as to interest and principal. Some examples are District of Columbia Armory Board, Export-Import Bank (EXIM), Federal Financing Bank (FFB), Federal Housing Administration (FHA), Farmers Home Administration (FHDA), Government National Mortgage Association (GNMA—"Ginnie Mae"), Tennessee Valley Authority (TVA), Student Loan Marketing Association (SLMA—"Sallie Mae").

International Institutions

These organizations are sponsored and capitalized by the U.S. government and are composed of most of the free nations of the world. Their securities are not guaranteed by the federal government as to principal or interest. Examples are Asian Development Bank, Inter-American Development Bank, and the International Bank for Reconstruction and Development (IBRD), often referred to as the World Bank.

Interest from federal agency securities is subject to federal tax but not state and local taxes. An exception to this are "Fannie Mae" securities, which are subject to both federal and state taxes.

DESCRIPTION OF GOVERNMENT AGENCIES

Federal Farm Credit Banks

Ownership Banks for Cooperative (COOPS), Federal Land Banks (FLB), and Federal Intermediate Credit Banks (FICB). All issue their own debt obligations. Currently, the Federal Farm Credit Banks issue short-term discount notes and interest-bearing bonds with varying maturities to provide funds for these three organizations. The interest is subject to federal tax; however, it is exempt from state and local taxes.

Purpose To make long-term first mortgage loans on farm properties within their respective district. These loans may not exceed 65 percent of the appraised value of the land mortgage as security.

FHLB - Federal Home Loan Bank

Ownership The system is composed of 12 regional banks, each of which is owned by some of the thrift institutions located in the bank's district, such as S&Ls, building and loan and homestead associations, savings and cooperative banks, and insurance companies. All federal S&Ls are required to become members of the system. Each member is required to purchase capital stock in its regional bank equal to at least 1% of its unamortized mortgage portfolio.

Purpose The banks make loans to member institutions to accommodate unusual credit demands placed upon them because of seasonal and cyclical factors, such as heavy withdrawal of deposits due to "disintermediation."

FHLMC - Federal Home Loan Mortgage Corporation ("Freddie Mac")

Ownership The FHLMC is a subsidiary of FHLB.

Purpose The FHLMC strengthens the existing secondary market in residential mortgages insured by the FHA (Federal Housing Administration) and the VA (Veterans Administration).

FNMA - Federal National Mortgage Association ("Fannie Mae")

Ownership The FNMA is owned by organizations that sell mortgages to it or borrow from it. Most of the sellers are required to purchase capital stock equal to at least 2% of the unamortized mortgages they sell to FNMA.

Purpose The FNMA provides some degree of liquidity to mortgage investments by purchasing when and where such funds are available primarily for residential properties insured by FHA (Federal Housing Administration) or FHDA (Farmers Home Administration) or guaranteed by VA (Veterans Administration).

GNMA - Government National Mortgage Association ("Ginnie Mae")

Ownership The GNMA is a U.S. government corporation within the Department of Housing and Urban Development.

Purpose The GNMA provides special assistance for two types of financing: (1) selected types of residential mortgages originated under special housing programs designed to provide housing of acceptable standards at full economic costs for segments of the national population unable to obtain adequate housing under established home financing programs; and (2) residential mortgages, generally as a means to halt a decline in mortgage lending or home-building activities that might threaten materially the stability of a high-level national economy.

SLMA - Student Loan Marketing Association ("Sallie Mae")

Ownership The SLMA is owned by participants in guaranteed student loan programs, such as commercial banks, S&L associations, colleges, universities, post-secondary vocational schools, and other similar institutions.

Purpose It expands funds available for student loans by purchasing, warehousing, selling, and dealing in them, when insured under the guaranteed student loan program.

TVA - Tennessee Valley Authority

Ownership The TVA is a U.S. government corporation.

Purpose The TVA develops and utilizes the resources of the Tennessee River and adjacent areas through two separate programs: resources development, which is primarily responsible for flood control and navigational improvement; and power, as the sole supplier of electric power for seven states. Electric power generated by this program is wholesaled to several large industrial plants and local public utility companies.

International Bank for Reconstruction and Development (IBRD)

Ownership Even though IBRD is not a government agency, it is financed 90% by the United States.

Purpose This organization was originally founded to finance the reconstruction of Europe after World War II. It now finances and assists so-called developing nations. Interest is completely taxable. This organization is more commonly known as the World Bank.

U.S. GOVERNMENT AGENCY SECURITIES AND MONEY MARKET INSTRUMENTS

The term "money market" is used to define short-term debt instruments that mature one year or less from the date of original issue. Longer-term securities are generally classified as "capital market" instruments. The past years' high interest rates have brought about a growth of money market funds. These investment companies purchase short-term debt securities and pay shareholders at current rates. Since the short-term nature of the securities reduces the risk factor, investors have found these investments most attractive. They can obtain generous returns from these funds without committing investment dollars to long-term debt securities during uncertain market periods. There are many money market securities. The most commonly traded are described below.

B/A - Banker's Acceptances

Definition These are non-interest-bearing drafts or bills of exchange used generally in foreign trade. They are created and traded at a discount from their face value, which is payable at maturity. Discount is calculated on the actual number of days on a 360-day year basis (sometimes quoted on bond equivalent basis). They are created when drafts or bills are drawn by one party against another party's bank, which stamps them "accepted." This means that the bank has accepted the obligation to pay their face value at maturity, hence the term "banker's acceptance."

Credit An acceptance is the primary obligation of the accepting bank and its customer who arranged for the "letter of credit."

Liquidity Many securities dealers and large commercial banks maintain an active secondary market in banker's acceptances.

Initial Maturities Up to 180 days.

Payment Federal funds.

Denominations Various (same amounts as bills of lading or warehouse receipts substantiating letters of credit, giving effect to issuance of B/A).

Form Bearer.

C/P - Commercial Paper

Definition Non-interest-bearing securities issued and traded at a discount from their face value, which is payable to the holder at maturity. Discount is calculated on an actual number of days on a 360-day year basis (sometimes quoted on bond equivalent yield basis).

Credit Direct short-term unsecured promissory notes issued by bank holding companies, finance companies, and industrial corporations.

Markets Direct: Issuers place paper with investors (or their agents, commercial banks, and securities dealers and brokers) at issuers' rates each day until daily borrowing requirements are filled, usually between noon and 2:00 P.M.

Dealers Dealers discount and inventory issuers' paper and rediscount at lower rates (higher prices).

Liquidity Liquidity is limited. C/P should be purchased with the intent of holding it until maturity.

Initial maturities Any number of days up to 270 days can be selected.

Payment Federal funds.

Denominations $25,000 and $100,000, or others if paper is issued on fully invested or interest-bearing basis. $250,000 is considered a round lot.

Form Bearer.

Fully Invested C/P Paper issued at discount (including fully invested). Difference between purchase price and either face value or sale price (if sold prior to maturity) or "buy-back" price is considered as interest (ordinary) income, which is subject to federal, state, and local income taxes.

If $100,000 C/P due in 180 days is discounted at 10%, then investor puts up $95,000.

$$\$100,000 - (\$100,000 \times .10 \times \tfrac{180}{360}) = \$95,000$$

If same investor has $100,000 to put up, how can he become fully invested? Divide available investment funds by net dollar price per $100 for normally discounted C/P to determine face amount of C/P, whose net dollar cost is $100,000. Using above rate and term for our example we have:

$$\$100,000 \div \frac{\$95,000}{\$100,000} = \$105,263.15$$

Proof: $105,263.15 − ($105,263.15 × .10 × 180/360) = $100,000

Interest-Bearing C/P Using the above discounted C/P as an example, we can determine its "bond equivalent yield."

$$\$100,000 - \$95,000 = \$5,000 \text{ (discount earned)}$$

$$\frac{\$5,000}{\$95,000} \times \frac{360}{180} \times 100 = 10.5263\%$$

Thus, C/P may be issued at any face value provided that it bears an interest rate equal to the bond equivalent yield of a discounted C/P.

Fed Funds - Federal Funds

Definition A simultaneous commitment made by one bank to purchase another bank's excess reserves at the local Federal Reserve Bank or its excess demand deposits immediately available at the purchasing bank or elsewhere and to return such funds to the selling bank at a later date, especially when the purchasing bank is short of such funds to meet current loan demands or investment commitments. Transactions may be executed either as discount or interest-bearing paper. Selling bank's situation is a mirror image of purchasing bank's situation.

Credit Secured borrowing: collateral furnished by borrowing bank is similar to that used for repurchase agreements (R/Ps). Unsecured borrowing: selling bank monitors purchasing bank's line of credit with them.

Liquidity High.

Maturities Usually "overnight"; occasionally automatic "rollover" at fixed or current daily rates.

Payment Federal funds.

Tax Features Interest or discount income (expense) treated the same as Fed R/P or reverse R/P.

Fed R/P - Fed "Repo"; Federal Reserve Bank Repurchase Agreement - Fed Reverse R/P; Fed Reverse "Repo" - Fed Reserve Bank Reverse Repurchase Agreement

Definition A simultaneous commitment initiated by local Federal Reserve Banks, as one of their open market operation options, to purchase securities or money market instruments from member banks and sell those back to them at a later date. The purpose is to "free up" members' reserve balances to enable them to grant more loans or to make other additional investments in a credit "crunch" of short duration. A reverse "repo" is initiated to create the opposite effect of a "repo." rates are usually set by the local Fed. Operating details are similar to non-Fed R/Ps.

Credit Same as non-Fed R/Ps, as well as local Fed's confidential appraisal of participating bank.

Liquidity R/P - member bank - extremely high. Reverse R/P - member bank - considerably reduced.

Maturities Determined by local Fed; usually overnight, sometimes up to two weeks.

Payment Federal funds.

Denominations Usually over $1,000,000.

Tax Features "Repo" interest is considered as expense and "reverse repo" interest is considered as income to member bank; the net is subject to federal, state, and local income tax treatment.

Certificates of Deposit (CDs)

Definition Negotiable time deposits made at a bank at a higher than usual rate of interest.

Denominations $100,000 is the usual minimum but CDs are generally for larger amounts ($1,000,000 or more).

COLLATERALIZED MORTGAGE OBLIGATIONS - CMOs

A traditional mortgage-backed security ("MBS") represents an ownership interest in a pool of specific mortgages. As homeowners make monthly payments of interest and principal on their mortgages, these payments are passed through monthly on a pro rata basis to investors who own the mortgage-backed securities. Investors receive principal payments with the very first monthly payment, and they continue to receive principal payments each month that the underlying mortgages are outstanding, which may be as long as 30 years. The principal portion includes both scheduled principal payments as well as unscheduled principal prepayments that result when mortgages are paid off, in full or in part, ahead of time.

Mortgages are generally prepaid because homeowners refinance their loans at lower rates, because they move, or because they default and their loans are foreclosed. Because homeowners can prepay their mortgages at any time, traditional mortgage-backed securities offer no call protection against earlier than expected return of principal, and investors can never be certain of the exact term of their investment or the amount of their monthly payments.

Furthermore, when homeowners refinance high interest rate mortgages because rates have fallen, investors who purchased traditional mortgage-backed securities have their principal returned earlier than anticipated. They are often left with no alternative but to reinvest at interest rates that are not nearly as attractive as when the mortgage-backed securities were originally purchased.

The innovative structure of collateralized mortgage obligations ("CMOs") helps to minimize the risk of untimely return of principal that is associated with traditional mortgage-backed securities. The first CMO appeared in June 1983 with a current approximate value in excess of $200 billion.

The general purpose of the agencies that insure MBSs is to provide liquidity to the mortgage market, enabling lenders to find potential buyers for the mortgages that they hold. There are three credit agencies that purchase mortgages from the lenders and shape them into MBSs which are sold to investors:

Federal Home Loan Mortgage Corporation (Freddie Mac) A federally sponsored corporation that purchases conventional (nongovernment-guaranteed) mortgages from federally chartered thrift institutions.

Federal National Mortgage Association (Fannie Mae) Originally chartered under the National Housing Act of 1938. Fannie Mae was designed to provide a secondary market for mortgage loans guaranteed by the U.S. government (FHA and VA) as well as some selected conventional mortgages. Although Fannie Mae is sponsored by the government, it is a publicly owned corporation.

Government National Mortgage Association (Ginnie Mae) A government-owned corporation formed in 1968. It operates as a division of the Department of Housing and Urban Development (HUD). Ginnie Mae purchases and packages FHA and VA mortgages from private lenders to strengthen the mortgage market and encourage construction of new housing. Ginnie Maes (unlike Fannie Maes and Freddie Macs) are guaranteed by the full faith and credit of the U.S. government.

CMOs are basically corporate bonds that are secured by quality mortgage-backed securities issued by Ginnie Mae, Fannie Mae, and Freddie Mac. Although they are structured differently from traditional MBSs, they usually obtain an AAA rating due to the quality of the underlying collateral. The stability of the collateral makes CMOs less subject to credit risks than similarly rated corporate bonds.

Unlike MBSs of the traditional type, which pay interest and principal to all bondholders on a pro rata basis, CMOs issue various classes of bonds designed to meet the needs of particular investors. Each class, or "tranche," has its own individual characteristics, such as projected life, average life, and yield.

CMOs are issued by government-sponsored entities such as Fannie Mae or Freddie Mac or by broker/dealers, banks, or other nongovernmental organizations. Those issued by nongovernmental groups are solely the obligation of those groups with no other guarantees. However, the quality of the underlying collateral generally earns these obligations an AAA rating.

There are many ways to structure a CMO offering, but by studying a typical example we will understand the characteristics of these securities.

EXAMPLE

When the issuer places the underlying mortgages in the pool, he begins to sell bonds against the portfolio. However, unlike an MBS, which offers only one class of security, CMOs will offer several tranches, each having a different maturity. In a given situation an investor may be able to choose among 2-year, 10-year, and 30-year maturities. The average life of each bond may well be less than the stated maturity. Based on anticipated prepayments, the 30-year tranche may have an average life of only 20 years, which means that roughly half the bonds in this tranche will have been paid off in 20 years.

The determination of anticipated prepayments is often done by the research staff of the issuer. The Public Securities Association (PSA) has also produced a model based on prior prepayment experience of typical mortgages. By determining a standard annual percentage for prepayments this model can assign a PSA speed for each issue. The lower the PSA speed the longer it will take for the issue to be repaid.

Let's designate the 2-year bonds as tranche A, the 10-year bonds as tranche B, and the 30-year bonds as tranche C.

As interest is paid on the mortgages in the pool, it is distributed (usually monthly) to all tranches. However, principal payments would first accrue to tranche A until that class has been fully paid off. When tranche A is retired the principal payments are moved to the tranche B holders. When tranche B is retired principal payments are used to retire tranche C.

The yields on the various tranches are projected based upon the cash flow produced by the mortgages, allowing for anticipated prepayments. The yield can vary if the actual prepayments vary from the projected schedule just as the maturities may vary due to this same factor.

The structure used in our example is often referred to as a "vanilla CMO." However, in some CMOs a more complex design is created in which special tranches are offered. Some examples of these special classes are:

PAC (Planned Amortization Class) This class has an average life and maturity planned within a specific time range using the PSA model.

TAC (Targeted Amortization Class) This class has an average life that can be extended but not shortened. This provides the bondholder with a degree of call and prepayment protection. If interest rates decline the prepayment will be paid to other tranches.

Companion Class Companion class CMOs are paid after the conditions in the PAC and TAC classes have been met. As this class would be more sensitive to interest rate changes due to its longer average life, it will generally offer a higher yield than the PAC and TAC classes.

Factor Factor is the decimal representation of the ratio of the current balance of the original balance. In other words, the amount of principal still outstanding of the original face amount of the bond.

WAC Weighted average coupon of the collateral.

WAM Weighted average maturity of the collateral.

Z Bond Class in a CMO structure that, up to a point, compounds interest instead of paying out. Then at a particular point, it becomes a passthrough security, paying both interest and principal until it is completely retired.

Lockout A specified period of time during which principal payments cannot be diverted from one class to another to satisfy PAC guarantees.

The versatility of CMOs allows the investor to choose from a number of structures the one that best suits her investment needs. It is not even necessary to limit investment to a single maturity as some CMOs offer staggered maturities in which portions of the investment mature at different time intervals.

CMOs provide investors with a vehicle that lessens the concern regarding the uncertain life of a traditional MBS. The CMO holder can look forward to a steady flow of income and a high level of safety of principal due to the AAA rating generally assigned to the bonds.

Despite these positive features CMOs do have some negatives. During a period of rising interest rates prepayments would be expected to decline, which could lead to an average life beyond that originally projected. Alternative investments at the higher rates might provide more attractive yields than those offered by previously issued CMOs. As with all debt securities that make payments based on fixed rates, the market value of CMOs would decline in periods of rising interest rates.

Due to the tremendous growth of the CMO market, the National Association of Securities Dealers ("NASD") described the advertising practices to be used by dealers in selling the product. Advertisements must specify that the yield on a CMO is an estimate based on assumed prepayments and that the actual yield may vary from this estimate. It would also be deemed misleading to state in advertising the CMOs are "government-guaranteed securities." Only those securities issued by a government agency may be said to be "government agency guaranteed." If a CMO is a private issue by a dealer, bank, or other entity, this relationship may be described. As with all securities, CMOs are subject to market risk. Prospective investors must be made aware of this fact. The NASD has also advised members to avoid describing yields for bonds with maturities longer than ten years as being predictable. Any such reference should include the prepayment expectations associated with these securities.

ANSWER SHEET FOR CHAPTER 2 EXAMINATION

1. Ⓐ Ⓑ Ⓒ Ⓓ
2. Ⓐ Ⓑ Ⓒ Ⓓ
3. Ⓐ Ⓑ Ⓒ Ⓓ
4. Ⓐ Ⓑ Ⓒ Ⓓ
5. Ⓐ Ⓑ Ⓒ Ⓓ
6. Ⓐ Ⓑ Ⓒ Ⓓ
7. Ⓐ Ⓑ Ⓒ Ⓓ
8. Ⓐ Ⓑ Ⓒ Ⓓ
9. Ⓐ Ⓑ Ⓒ Ⓓ
10. Ⓐ Ⓑ Ⓒ Ⓓ

11. Ⓐ Ⓑ Ⓒ Ⓓ
12. Ⓐ Ⓑ Ⓒ Ⓓ
13. Ⓐ Ⓑ Ⓒ Ⓓ
14. Ⓐ Ⓑ Ⓒ Ⓓ
15. Ⓐ Ⓑ Ⓒ Ⓓ
16. Ⓐ Ⓑ Ⓒ Ⓓ
17. Ⓐ Ⓑ Ⓒ Ⓓ
18. Ⓐ Ⓑ Ⓒ Ⓓ
19. Ⓐ Ⓑ Ⓒ Ⓓ
20. Ⓐ Ⓑ Ⓒ Ⓓ

21. Ⓐ Ⓑ Ⓒ Ⓓ
22. Ⓐ Ⓑ Ⓒ Ⓓ
23. Ⓐ Ⓑ Ⓒ Ⓓ
24. Ⓐ Ⓑ Ⓒ Ⓓ
25. Ⓐ Ⓑ Ⓒ Ⓓ
26. Ⓐ Ⓑ Ⓒ Ⓓ
27. Ⓐ Ⓑ Ⓒ Ⓓ
28. Ⓐ Ⓑ Ⓒ Ⓓ
29. Ⓐ Ⓑ Ⓒ Ⓓ
30. Ⓐ Ⓑ Ⓒ Ⓓ

31. Ⓐ Ⓑ Ⓒ Ⓓ
32. Ⓐ Ⓑ Ⓒ Ⓓ
33. Ⓐ Ⓑ Ⓒ Ⓓ
34. Ⓐ Ⓑ Ⓒ Ⓓ
35. Ⓐ Ⓑ Ⓒ Ⓓ
36. Ⓐ Ⓑ Ⓒ Ⓓ
37. Ⓐ Ⓑ Ⓒ Ⓓ
38. Ⓐ Ⓑ Ⓒ Ⓓ
39. Ⓐ Ⓑ Ⓒ Ⓓ
40. Ⓐ Ⓑ Ⓒ Ⓓ

41. Ⓐ Ⓑ Ⓒ Ⓓ
42. Ⓐ Ⓑ Ⓒ Ⓓ
43. Ⓐ Ⓑ Ⓒ Ⓓ
44. Ⓐ Ⓑ Ⓒ Ⓓ
45. Ⓐ Ⓑ Ⓒ Ⓓ
46. Ⓐ Ⓑ Ⓒ Ⓓ
47. Ⓐ Ⓑ Ⓒ Ⓓ
48. Ⓐ Ⓑ Ⓒ Ⓓ
49. Ⓐ Ⓑ Ⓒ Ⓓ
50. Ⓐ Ⓑ Ⓒ Ⓓ

To remove answer sheet, cut along dotted line.

CHAPTER 2 EXAMINATION

1. Commercial paper is typically issued with a maturity date not exceeding:

   (A) 90 days
   (B) 6 months
   (C) 270 days
   (D) one year

2. Government National Mortgage Association (Ginnie Mae) bonds are quoted in:

   (A) $\frac{1}{8}$
   (B) $\frac{1}{4}$
   (C) $\frac{1}{16}$
   (D) $\frac{1}{32}$

3. The minimum denomination for U.S. treasury notes and bonds is:

   (A) $100
   (B) $1,000
   (C) $5,000
   (D) $10,000

4. The least active secondary market exists for:

   (A) treasury bills
   (B) banker's acceptances
   (C) certificates of deposit
   (D) commercial paper

5. Which of the following can be classified as a money market instrument?

   I.   American Depository Receipts
   II. banker's acceptances
   III. commercial paper
   IV. treasury bills

   (A) I and II only
   (B) III and IV only
   (C) II, III, and IV only
   (D) I, II, III, and IV

6. Bonds of the Federal Intermediate Credit Bank (FICB) are:

   (A) a direct obligation of the U.S. government
   (B) issued by the Federal Farm Credit Banks
   (C) designed to help promote residential housing sales
   (D) exempted from federal taxation for interest paid to holders

7. Treasury bills enjoy all of the following characteristics, EXCEPT:

   (A) they are quoted in percentages on a yield-to-maturity basis
   (B) their payments are exempt from state taxation
   (C) the bid price is numerically higher than the associated offer price
   (D) they mature from one to three years from the date of their issuance

8. The purpose of the Federal National Mortgage Association is to:

   I.   provide money for mortgages to qualified veterans
   II. purchase selected mortgages and loans from qualified holders of these investments
   III. promote liquidity in the secondary mortgage market
   IV. fix mortgage rates for certain mortgage banks, life insurance companies, and savings and loan associations

   (A) I and III only
   (B) II and III only
   (C) II and IV only
   (D) I, II, III, and IV

9. Which of the following U.S. government securities quotations represents a T-bill?

    (A) 98.9–100
    (B) 96–96⅛
    (C) 5.78–5.73
    (D) 5.55–5.75

10. Interest payments to holders of CMOs are generally paid

    (A) weekly
    (B) monthly
    (C) annually
    (D) at maturity

11. A CMO issue consists of three tranches; one has an average life of 2 years, the second an average life of 10 years, and the third an average life of 30 years. Initially, interest payments received will be distributed:

    (A) first to the holders of the 2-year tranche
    (B) first to the holders of the 10-year tranche
    (C) first to the holders of the 30-year tranche
    (D) equally to all the bondholders

12. Which of these U.S. government securities have a stated rate of interest on the face of their certificates?

    I.   treasury bonds
    II. treasury notes
    III. treasury bills

    (A) I and II only
    (B) II and III only
    (C) I only
    (D) III only

13. Interest paid on U.S. treasury bonds is:

    (A) subject to federal and state income taxes
    (B) exempt from federal and state incomes taxes
    (C) subject to state income tax but exempt from federal income tax
    (D) subject to federal income tax but exempt from state income tax

14. Debt securities of each of the following issuers trade freely in the open market EXCEPT for those of the:

    (A) Federal National Mortgage Association (Fannie Mae)
    (B) Federal Land Banks
    (C) Banks for Cooperative
    (D) Federal Reserve Banks

15. Characteristically, obligations of U.S. government agencies:

    I.   can be issued in coupon form
    II. can be issued in registered form
    III. are not guaranteed by the federal government
    IV. are exempt from SEC registration requirements

    (A) I and IV only
    (B) II and III only
    (C) I, II, and IV only
    (D) I, II, III, and IV

16. When depositors withdraw their money from savings institutions to invest in higher yielding U.S. treasury securities, it is called:

    (A) the multiplier effect
    (B) disintermediation
    (C) reverse repo
    (D) open market operations

17. A corporation has cash it intends to use in six months for the purchase of equipment. The most prudent investment it could make during the six-month period would be in:

    (A) common stock
    (B) preferred stock
    (C) treasury bills
    (D) treasury bonds

18. The newspaper shows that U.S. treasury 7⅜ of 2010 closed yesterday at 98.12. Which statement is correct with regard to the tax status of this issue?

    (A) Interest is exempt from state taxation.
    (B) Interest is exempt from federal taxation.
    (C) Interest is subject to taxation by both state and federal governments.
    (D) Interest is subject to taxation by all government entities but realized capital gains are not.

19. Classify the debt securities listed below, in ascending order according to the stability of their principal value:

    I.   a Federal National Mortgage Association bond
    II. a guaranteed corporate bond
    III. a Series EE savings bond
    IV. a U.S. treasury bond

       (A) I, II, III, IV
       (B) II, I, IV, III
       (C) IV, III, II, I
       (D) III, IV, I, II

20. Which of the following mortgage-backed securities is guaranteed by the U.S. government as to the timely payment of principal and interest?

    (A) Federal National Mortgage Association issues
    (B) Government National Mortgage Association issues
    (C) Federal Home Loan Association issues
    (D) Private issue guaranteed securities

21. A debt instrument identifiable as funded debt is a:

    (A) U.S. treasury bond
    (B) Series EE savings bond
    (C) corporate bond
    (D) Fannie Mae discount note

22. A typical money market instrument would carry a:

    (A) serial bond maturity date
    (B) long-term maturity date
    (C) medium-term maturity date
    (D) short-term maturity date

23. An offering price of 102 plus accrued interest could apply to:

    (A) Treasury bills
    (B) banker's acceptances
    (C) commercial paper
    (D) CDs (certificates of deposit)

24. A U.S. government security that may be tendered at par value in the payment of corporate taxes is known as a:

    (A) term bond
    (B) tax anticipation bill
    (C) special tax bond
    (D) pre-issue bond

25. Advertisements regarding CMO securities by firms that are members of the NASD should disclose:

    (A) the exact yield to be paid to investors
    (B) that the yield is based on the prevailing discount rate
    (C) that the stated yield is an estimate and may vary based on prepayments and market factors
    (D) that the yield may be greater than the stated percentage but never less

26. Which of the following comments incorrectly describes U.S. securities markets?

    (A) It is a capital market comprised of long-term debt and equity issues.
    (B) It is a money market comprised of short-term debt and equity issues.
    (C) It is a municipal market comprised of tax-exempt issues of state and local governments.
    (D) It is a government and agency market comprised of both short-term and long-term debt issues.

27. What rate of return takes into account appropriate appreciation or depreciation of market value in relating it to a debt security's par value?

    (A) current yield
    (B) nominal yield
    (C) yield to maturity
    (D) basis yield

28. Which of the following attributes is not a feature of U.S. treasury bills?

    (A) This security has an unusually high degree of liquidity in the marketplace.
    (B) It always sells at a discount from face value.
    (C) It is most often issued with three-month, six-month, or one-year maturities.
    (D) Interest received from this investment is exempt from federal income taxes.

29. Under which of the following conditions would homeowners be most likely to refinance existing mortgages?

    (A) when interest rates are stable
    (B) when interest rates are falling
    (C) when interest rates are rising
    (D) when the yield curve is inverted

30. Which of the following comments regarding U.S. treasury bills is not true?

    (A) They are offered at a discount reflecting their yield to maturity.
    (B) They are issued in denominations ranging from $1,000 to $1,000,000.
    (C) They are broadly classified as money market instruments.
    (D) Although issued by the Treasury Department, they are general obligations of the U.S. government.

31. Which issue(s) represent a direct obligation of the U.S. government?

    I.   Federal Home Loan Bank bonds
    II. U.S. treasury savings bonds (Series EE)
    III. Tax Anticipation Bills
    IV. Federal National Mortgage Association bonds

        (A) I, II, III, and IV
        (B) II only
        (C) II and III only
        (D) III and IV only

32. CMOs are sold and priced based on their:

    (A) expected average life
    (B) stated maturity
    (C) current yield
    (D) par value

33. Under NASD advertising standards a dealer may state that a CMO has an implied AAA rating if the securities are issued:

    (A) with an average life no longer than ten years
    (B) by a private issuer who has applied for but has not received a rating
    (C) in amounts less than $1,000,000
    (D) by a U.S. government agency

34. A class of CMO securities that has its own stated maturity, average life, and estimated yield is referred to as a:

    (A) bracket
    (B) tier
    (C) tranche
    (D) flow

35. The Public Securities Association (PSA) provides a model relating the prepayment experience of all mortgages. Generally speaking:

    (A) the lower the PSA speed the longer the issue will remain outstanding
    (B) the higher the PSA speed the longer the issue will remain outstanding
    (C) the PSA speed is the same for all CMO issues
    (D) the PSA speed applies only to CMO issues with an average life of less than ten years

36. If a Federal Home Loan Bank issue is offered at 95.22, about how much will it cost to purchase only one bond?

    (A) $95.22
    (B) $951.63
    (C) $952.20
    (D) $956.88

37. In terms of currency, how much is one mill worth?

    (A) $\frac{1}{10}$ of 1¢
    (B) $\frac{1}{10}$ of 10¢
    (C) $\frac{1}{10}$ of $1
    (D) $\frac{1}{10}$ of $1,000

38. Which one of the following debt instruments pays its holder interest on his investment only at maturity?

    (A) a corporate serial bond
    (B) U.S. treasury bills
    (C) income bonds
    (D) U.S. Series H bonds

39. Which of these securities would have the greatest amount of market risk for investors?

    (A) U.S. treasury bills
    (B) U.S. treasury certificates
    (C) U.S. treasury notes
    (D) savings bank deposits

40. All of the following securities are marketable EXCEPT:

    (A) tax anticipation bonds
    (B) municipal bonds
    (C) treasury bonds
    (D) Series EE bonds

41. A quote in the newspaper reads as follows:

Bid	Asked
4.72	4.68

    This quote is for a:

    (A) treasury note
    (B) treasury bill
    (C) treasury bond
    (D) Series HH bond

42. A treasury bill is sold at a discount basis that determines its:

    (A) face value
    (B) nominal yield
    (C) rate of return
    (D) yield to call

43. A treasury obligation that has no fixed rate of interest with a 30-day maturity due April 22 is most likely a:

    (A) treasury note
    (B) tax anticipation bill
    (C) term bond
    (D) Series EE bond

44. Which of the following securities would have the greatest risk for the investor?

    (A) a guaranteed corporate bond
    (B) a GNMA bond
    (C) a Series HH bond
    (D) a treasury bill

45. A quote for a treasury bond is 97.28 bid, 98.2 asked. This quote was established:

    (A) by the terms of the indenture
    (B) by the Federal Reserve Board
    (C) by the NASD
    (D) by competitive bidding

46. The International Bank for Reconstruction and Development is more commonly referred to as:

    (A) the Inter-American Bank
    (B) the World Bank
    (C) the Export-Import Bank
    (D) the Banks for Cooperatives

47. Which issues represent direct obligations of the United States?

    I.   Export-Import Bank bonds
    II. Series EE savings bonds
    III. treasury bonds
    IV. Federal National Mortgage Association bonds

    (A) II only
    (B) II and III only
    (C) III and IV only
    (D) I, II, and III only

48. An institution requesting a quote on a block of 100 bonds from a government securities dealer receives a response of 98.02 bid, 98.06 asked. What is the dollar amount the institution will receive if the bonds are sold to the government securities dealer?

    (A) $98,062.50
    (B) $98,187.50
    (C) $98,250.00
    (D) $98,750.00

49. Which of the following government securities have no collateral value?

    (A) Series EE savings bonds
    (B) treasury notes
    (C) treasury bonds
    (D) treasury bills

50. From the standpoint of safety of principal, which of the following is most secure?

    (A) FHLMC Collateralized Mortgage & Obligation
    (B) FNMA pass-throughs
    (C) GNMA pass-throughs
    (D) Farm Credit System Bonds

CHAPTER 2 EXAMINATION ANSWERS

1. **C** A characteristic of the security.
2. **D** Most government securities are quoted in 32nds, except treasury bills, which are quoted on a yield-to-maturity basis.
3. **B** Please note that this is the minimum denomination. Normally, they are issued in denominations much larger than this.
4. **D** Bills have the most active secondary market, next would be banker's acceptances and after that, negotiable certificates of deposit. There is a small secondary market for commercial paper.
5. **C** American Depository Receipts are traded in lieu of foreign certificates and their purpose is to facilitate transfer of ownership in foreign securities. They are not money market instruments.
6. **B** The other choices have no application whatsoever.
7. **D** The most popular maturity for treasury bills is 90 or 91 days. They do not have maturities of longer than one year.
8. **B** Choices II and III adequately describe the purpose of Fannie Mae.
9. **C** Since treasury bills are quoted in terms of yield, the bid will exceed the offer. These are percentage figures, not dollar figures.
10. **B** Interest to holders of CMOs is generally paid monthly, but in some cases the payments are made quarterly or semiannually.
11. **D** Interest payments are distributed to all holders on an equal basis. Principal payments are directed to the tranche holders in time sequential order.
12. **A** Treasury bills are always sold at a discount from par. Notes and bonds have coupons.
13. **D** Interest on government securities is taxed at the federal level but is exempt from state and local taxes. On the other hand, municipal bond interest is exempt from federal income tax, but subject to state and local taxes, except in the state of issuance.
14. **D** The Federal Reserve Banks do not issue negotiable securities.
15. **D** All of these items describe U.S. government agency securities.
16. **B** By definition (there must be an easier word).
17. **C** Clearly, common stock and preferred stock would not be a suitable short-term investment. T-bills, by their very nature, are short term in scope. Please note, however, that a treasury bond with only six months or less remaining to maturity might be a suitable investment as well.
18. **A** Interest on U.S. government securities is exempt from state and local income taxation.
19. **B** The key here is "ascending," which means from lowest stability to highest stability.
20. **B** Only Government National Mortgage Association securities (Ginnie Maes) carry the direct guarantee of the U.S. government.
21. **C.** All of the other choices are securities of the U.S. government or agencies.
22. **D** By definition, money market means up to one-year maturity.
23. **D** Only CDs trade "and interest."
24. **B** These specifically designated securities may be used at face value in payment of corporate taxes,

although they may have a later maturity.

25. **C** The stated yield on a CMO is an estimate based on expected prepayments. This figure is only an estimate and may vary due to market and prepayment fluctuations.

26. **B** The money market is the market for short-term, high-grade debt securities. Equity securities are not traded in the money market.

27. **C** The premium or discount is a consideration in computing the yield to maturity.

28. **D** Choices (A), (B), and (C) correctly describe treasury bills.

29. **B** When interest rates are declining, homeowners would be most likely to refinance high interest rate mortgages with new borrowings at the new lower rates.

30. **B** The minimum certificate issued for a treasury bill is $10,000.

31. **C** Federal Home Loan bonds and Federal National Mortgage Association bonds are indirect obligations of the U.S. government.

32. **A** The average life of a CMO is the length of time that each dollar of invested principal is expected to remain outstanding. Pricing of the securities is based on this factor.

33. **D** Government agencies usually do not seek a rating so it is permissible to state that they have an "implied AAA rating." Privately issued CMOs cannot be referred to as being rated until the rating is actually received.

34. **C** The term "tranche" is used to describe a separate class of CMO securities that are part of an issue.

35. **A** The PSA speed measures the anticipated prepayment of mortgages. The lower speed indicates a smaller percentage of prepayment and, therefore, a longer time period from issuance until redemption.

36. **D** 95.22 means 95 and $^{22}/_{32}$. A 32nd is .3125 in dollars. Multiplying .3125 times 22 gives approximately $6.88. $950 (95) plus $6.88 equals $956.88.

37. **A** By definition. Note that on a bond a point equals $10.

38. **B** U.S. treasury bills do not have coupons, but rather are surrendered at par value at maturity. The other choices, when they are paying interest, pay currently.

39. **C** Treasury bills and certificates are short-term securities and subject to much less market risk than treasury notes, which are longer term securities. Savings bank deposits are not subject to market risk.

40. **D** Series EE savings bonds are not tradable securities; they are purchased and held to redemption.

41. **B** Treasury bills are quoted on a discount yield basis. Treasury notes and bonds are quoted on a price basis as a percentage of face value.

42. **C** Treasury bills have no coupon or fixed rate of return. The investor's rate of return is determined by the difference between the discounted price at which the bills are purchased and the price at which they are redeemed at maturity.

43. **B** Tax anticipation bills (TABs) are non-interest-bearing treasury obligations whose maturities come after corporate tax payment dates. They are accepted for redemption at face value prior to maturity on corporate tax payment dates to encourage their use by corporations.

44. **A** A guaranteed corporate bond would have the greatest risk to the investor. All of the other instruments are either direct obligations of the U.S.

government or are guaranteed as to interest and principal by the U.S. government.

45. **D** The price at which treasury bonds are quoted, as with all negotiable securities, is determined in the market by competitive bidding among government securities dealers.

46. **B** The official name is the International Bank for Reconstruction and Development, but in more recent years it has been referred to as the World Bank.

47. **B** Series EE savings bonds and treasury bonds are direct obligations of the U.S. government; the others are not.

48. **A** If the bonds are sold to the dealer, the institution will receive the bid price of 98.02 (98²⁄₃₂). On $100,000 this translates to $98,062.50.

49. **A** Series EE are nonnegotiable and have no collateral value. They may be sold back only to the government.

50. **C** GNMA (Government National Mortgage Association) pass-through obligations are guaranteed as to principal and interest by the United States government.

Municipal Securities

The general Securities Registered Representative examination places heavy emphasis on municipal securities. Because of this the successful candidate is qualified to deal in municipal securities with no additional exam requirement.

In order to properly prepare you for this important area of municipal securities, our coverage will be quite extensive. Careful study of the following material will be an important part of your work.

Municipal securities are issued by states, cities, and other political subdivisions including municipal authorities, which construct and maintain facilities such as bridges and tunnels for public use. Municipals are generally divided into two categories: general obligation bonds and revenue bonds.

TYPES OF MUNICIPAL SECURITIES

General Obligation Bonds

Unlimited Tax Bonds
Secured by full faith and credit and taxing power of the issuer without limit as to rate and amount.

Limited Tax Bonds
Secured by full faith and credit and taxing power of the issuer but limited as to rate and amount.

Limitations on Issuance
By voter approval, statutory, or constitutional restrictions:

Voter Approval Submitted by referendum to the voters for approval.

Statutory A limit imposed by laws of the state, which can be changed only by action of the state legislature.

Constitutional A limit imposed by the constitution of the state, which can only be eliminated by a constitutional amendment.

Revenue Bonds

- Generally payable from the revenue of the project or facility financed.
- Usually not subject to debt limitations since they are not secured by full faith and credit and taxing power of the state or municipality.

No.

UNITED STATES OF AMERICA
STATE OF ALASKA

NORTH SLOPE BOROUGH

GENERAL OBLIGATION BOND, SERIES Q

NORTH SLOPE BOROUGH, a municipal corporation and political subdivision of the State of Alaska (hereinafter called the "Borough"), for value received, hereby promises to pay the bearer hereof, or, if this bond be registered in accordance with the provisions endorsed hereon to the then registered owner hereof,

ON THE TWENTIETH DAY OF JUNE,

2006

without option of redemption prior to maturity, the principal sum of

FIVE THOUSAND DOLLARS ($5,000),

upon the presentation and surrender hereof, and to pay interest on such principal sum from the date hereof at the rate of

eight and fifty hundredths per centum (8.50%)

per annum, payable semiannually on the twentieth day of June and the twentieth day of December in each year until the maturity hereof, commencing on the twentieth day of June, 1983, but in the case of the interest due on or before maturity, only upon the presentation and surrender of the respective interest coupons representing such interest hereto attached as they severally mature. Both principal of and interest on this bond are payable at the principal office of Rainier National Bank, in the City of Seattle, State of Washington, Paying Agent and Registrar, in such coin or currency of the United States of America which at the time of payment is legal tender for public and private debts.

This bond is one of a duly authorized issue of bonds of like designation herewith aggregating One Hundred Million Dollars ($100,000,000) in principal amount. This bond and the issue of bonds of which it forms a part are issued under and pursuant to the authority of Resolution Serial No. 43-82, adopted by the Assembly of the Borough on November 9, 1982, (hereinafter referred to as the "Resolution"), and the ordinances referred to therein ratified by the qualified voters of the Borough (hereinafter referred to as the "Ordinances"), and under the authority of and in full compliance with the Constitution and laws of the State of Alaska and the Charter of North Slope Borough, for the purpose of paying part of the cost of certain capital improvements in the Borough as more fully described in the Resolution and the Ordinances.

The bonds of the issue of bonds of which this bond is a part are general obligations of the Borough. The full faith and credit of the Borough are pledged to the payment of the principal of and interest on said bonds as the same become due and payable.

This bond is transferable by delivery except when registered otherwise than to bearer. It may be registered as to principal only in accordance with the provisions endorsed hereon.

It is hereby certified, recited and declared that all acts, conditions and things required by the Constitution and laws of the State of Alaska and the Charter of North Slope Borough to exist, to happen and to be performed precedent to and in the issuance of this bond do exist, have happened and have been performed in due time, form and manner as required by law, and that the amount of this bond, together with all other indebtedness of the Borough, does not exceed any constitutional, statutory or charter limitation of indebtedness.

IN WITNESS WHEREOF, **North Slope Borough** by its Assembly has caused this bond to be signed by the manual or facsimile signature of its Mayor and its corporate seal to be imprinted or reproduced hereon and attested by the manual or facsimile signature of its Director of Administration and Finance, provided that at least one signature on the face hereof shall be a manual signature, and has caused the interest coupons hereto attached to be authenticated with the facsimile signature of said Mayor and this bond to be dated as of the Twentieth day of December, 1982.

NORTH SLOPE BOROUGH

ATTEST: SPECIMEN

By ....MEN

12-2(

Eugene Brower

Director of Administration
and Finance

NORTH SLOPE BOROUGH
INCORPORATED
SEAL
JULY 1, 1972
STATE OF ALASKA

Mayor

- Usually issued as obligations of a legally created authority or commission of a state or municipality for a specific project or facility, such as the New Jersey Sports Authority.

Sources of Revenue

- Charges to the users of the facility in the form of tolls or fees, such as toll roads, bridges, or sewer systems.
- Special taxes levied by a state or municipality to provide additional revenue to an authority within certain limitations.
- Rental or lease payments: contractual agreements for a definite amount over a definite period of time. Either a public agency such as a state or municipality or a private agency such as a corporation could be a tenant or leasee.
- Legislative appropriation: either a state or municipality could assign a portion of its general funds to supplement revenue, particularly if the facility is of special benefit to the area.

Security for Revenue Bonds

Protective Covenants Agreements entered into between the issuer and the bondholder for the latter's protection.

Rate Covenant Issuer to establish and maintain rates of revenue sufficient to meet operations and maintenance, annual debt service, and certain reserves to cover all contingencies.

Insurance Covenant Issuer to maintain insurance in an amount sufficient to cover all contingencies.

Maintenance Covenant Issuer to keep the facility in good repair and working order.

Nondiscrimination Issuer to give no free service except in the case of public emergency.

Engineering Reports Issuer to retain services of a reputable engineer to oversee the facility.

Records and Reports At least one annual audit by CPA mandatory, with an update to principal underwriter recommended.

Additional Bonds Indenture should allow for them. Debt may be an equal or junior lien to outstanding bonds. Earnings should be sufficient to support all debt if the lien is equal.

- Closed-end Indenture: No parity lien bonds except to complete facility. All others added must be junior lien.
- Open-end Indenture: Permits additional bonds under a formula that covers debt service requirements to include new bonds. Usually based on prior year's net revenue.
- Project Completion: Provision to issue bonds necessary to complete facility to protect original bondholders.

Application of Revenue Revenues are generally applied in this order:

Operation and Maintenance Fund Provides funds to keep facility in proper condition to produce revenue.

Bond Service and/or Sinking Fund Monthly allocations of revenue sufficient to meet current principal and interest of serial bonds. Deposits in sinking fund to meet future principal payment on term bonds.

Debt Service Reserve Funds allocated to provide for next year of principal and interest on serials and two years' interest on terms.

Reserve Maintenance Fund Funds allocated to provide for next year of principal and interest on serials and two years' interest on terms.

Renewal and Replacement Fund Contribution made only if excess funds are available.

Surplus Fund From excess funds left after contributions to above funds. May be used to retire bonds or make improvements or extensions to the facility. Also could be used for any other lawful purpose.

New Housing Authority Bonds

These bonds, often called public housing authority bonds, are issued by local housing authorities. Secured by annual net rentals of facility and an annual contribution contract with the Public Housing Administration. Unconditional pledge to provide balance of funds sufficient to pay principal and interest. Faith of United States is pledged, which gives the bondholder the tax benefit of a municipal security plus a U.S. government guarantee.

Other Bonds

Special Tax Bonds
Payable only from special fund, not full faith, credit, and taxing powers.

Excise Tax Tax levied on a particular item or items, usually semiluxury items, proceeds of which are pledged to debt service. For example, Puerto Rico has issued "rum tax" bonds backed solely from revenues produced by that tax.

Special Assessment Levied against those who primarily benefit from the facility. Usually limited improvements in an area.

Lease Rental
Proceeds to an authority sufficient to cover principal and interest requirements. This method has been used to build sports and exposition facilities.

Moral Obligations
State or municipality does not provide full faith, credit, or taxes. Payable from a special source with no legal obligation.

Industrial Development
Revenue bonds secured by a lease or contracts for use of facilities.

Pollution Control
Revenue bonds issued to construct contamination facilities to meet ecological requirements. Generally secured by leases for use of facilities.
   Note: the quality of the lessees are the real basis for evaluating these securities.

Refunding Bonds
Issued to redeem outstanding bonds, usually to provide a specific advantage to the issuer, such as a lower net interest cost.

Advanced Refunding Bonds
Issued to redeem outstanding bonds, usually with the intent of obtaining a better rate or relieving the issuer from certain restraints in the outstanding issue.

Double-Barreled
Secured primarily by revenue with supplemental taxing power to provide for deficiencies in debt service.

Notes

Project Notes (PN)
Issued by local housing projects (for short-term temporary financing). Tax exempt federally and in state of issue. These securities are secured by local issuer and full faith and credit of U.S. pledge. Interest paid at maturity-bearer from 60 days to one-year maturity.

Tax Anticipation Notes (TAN)
Issued short term to provide funds for general operations of municipalities. Tax collections are usually due at various times of the year, which may not coincide with when expenses are due and payable.

Bond Anticipation Notes (BAN)
Issued short term for interim financing pending issuance of permanent bonds. Usually for some public project.

Revenue Anticipation Notes (RAN)
Issued short term to provide temporary funds needed before the cash inflow is due from sources other than taxes.

Construction Loan Notes (CLN)
Issued short term to provide temporary funds during construction period of facilities.

Tax Treatment

Interest Income
Under existing statutes and as a result of numerous test cases, interest derived from bonds of the various states, territories, commonwealths, political subdivisions of each, including

authorities and the District of Columbia, are exempt from federal income tax. This doctrine of mutual immunity from taxation is founded on the concept of inherent separation of powers of the various states and the federal government with each reserving the right to conduct its own operations. The formation of the union of states for the benefit of the group did not take away the rights of the states to govern themselves and to independently raise funds by means of debt securities to finance their operations. The Supreme Court has held that to accomplish this end, it is necessary, under our system of government, that there be reciprocal immunity from federal taxation of states and state taxation of the federal. However, the Tax Reform Act of 1986 distinguishes between municipal bonds issued before August 15, 1986 and those issued after that date. Any municipal bond issued prior to this date retains any of the tax-exempt features that they offered before. Any municipal bond issued after this date falls into one of three categories, depending on its purpose.

Public Purpose Bonds Issued directly by the state or local authority and used for traditional municipal projects such as new schools or highway improvement programs. These municipal bonds are tax exempt.

Private Activity Bonds Although issued by the state or local government, they supply funds for private projects, such as a sports arena, shopping mall, or civic center. These bonds are subject to federal taxation, but may be exempt from state and local taxation.

Nongovernment-purpose Bonds These bonds raise funds for nongovernmental uses such as housing or student loans. These are tax exempt. As far as this chapter is concerned, consider all bonds under discussion as tax exempt.

There is no reciprocal agreement between the various states with regard to the taxation on the interest of each others' bonds, with one notable exception, namely, the territories or commonwealths located geographically outside the continental United States. They enjoy exemption from both federal and state taxation including the political subdivisions of same. Thus, at this time, municipal securities issued by Puerto Rico, the Virgin Islands, and Guam are exempt from all state and local income taxes as well as federal income taxes. As a general rule, the securities of multistate authorities enjoy tax exemption within each state. It has been the policy of each state to exempt from taxation within the state bonds of its own and its political subdivisions and to subject the income from bonds of other states and their political subdivisions to income taxes. Therefore, a New York City resident purchasing a municipal security issued by any municipality or authority within that state (e.g. Buffalo, Nassau County, City of Yonkers, Municipal Assistance Corp.) would gain "triple exemption" from federal, New York State, and New York City income tax.

Value of Tax Exemption To estimate the value it is necessary to determine how much greater yield would be necessary to return the same result after the payment of taxes. This will vary, dependent upon the tax bracket of the investor. As a convenience, tax equivalent yield tables have been published showing the relationship to federal taxes. By extending the state and/or local tax rate factor into the computation, it is simple to derive the overall taxable yield necessary to attain the same results gained from tax-exempt securities.

To compute the comparable taxable yield required to equal a tax-free yield you divide the tax-free coupon by the difference between the client's federal tax bracket and 100%.

EXAMPLE _____

A client in the 28% federal tax bracket is offered a tax-free municipal with a yield of 9%. What yield would he require in a fully taxable bond to retain the same number of dollars after taxes?

$$1.00 - .28 \text{ (federal tax bracket)} = .72$$

$$\frac{9.00}{.72} = 12.5\%$$

_____

Further savings may accrue to the investor due to savings on local taxes.

Premiums and Discounts

Ideally, from the investor's side, if all bonds remained at par for their entire life, it would simplify the tax exempt computation and eliminate all gains and losses. However, the general market varies regularly and as a result, the principal price of bonds varies to reflect these changes; hence, it is necessary to treat each situation in a different light.

Amortization of Premiums

Simply stated, a premium must be written off over the life of the bond. It has the effect of reducing the net tax-exempt yield since it is a reflection of the current market yield on a bond. Since the coupon rate on the bond is always a constant, any lowering of the yield must be accomplished by a rise in the principal price. From a tax standpoint, the investor, therefore, must adjust his cost by amortizing it as a nondeductible expense or loss. Indirectly, this has the effect of reducing his tax-exempt income. Any profit or loss after the appropriate cost adjustment resulting from the sale of the securities would then be a principal nature.

EXAMPLE _____

A client purchases a municipal security at a price of 110 ($1,100). The bond will mature in exactly ten years. The client must amortize the $100 premium paid over the life (ten years) of the bond. We simply divide the premium ($100) by the number of years until maturity (ten) and arrive at the annual amount to be amortized ($10). Thus, if the client holds the bond for six years his cost will be reduced to 104 (6 years at $10 each equals $60). A sale at 105 ($1,050) at that point would result in a long-term gain of $10 per bond.

_____

Accretion of Bond Discounts

Conversely, it is necessary to accrete bond discounts and adjust the cost over the life of the investment.

Original Issue Discount

When bonds are purchased on an original issue at a discount, the discount is considered to be part of the interest paid to the bondholder for the use of his money. This interest amount is federally tax exempt and increases the yield on the investment. Recent use of zero coupon bonds has taken advantage of this factor. An investor might buy

$100,000 face amount of "zeros" for an investment of perhaps $35,000. If bought on the original issue and held to maturity, the $65,000 additional received is considered income under the tax law. As it is municipal bond income, it is federally (and, perhaps, locally) exempt from income tax.

MARKET FOR MUNICIPAL SECURITIES

Indicators

Blue Lists
A daily publication for bond dealers listing all munibond offerings by dealers. Contents are listed alphabetically by states and maturities in chronological order. The offering yield or dollar price is included. The total volume of offerings is listed daily.

Bond Buyer
A daily publication for bond dealers. News relevant to municipals is printed for the information of its dealer subscribers. In addition, it provides a summary of recent bond underwritings showing the percentage of new offerings sold or taken down from the accounts.

Indices Each Thursday an average yield of 20 long-term bonds is published. This index reflects the general trend of the market for the previous week. Additionally, an 11-bond GO index and an index of 30-year revenue bonds is provided. The 20-bond index is composed of bonds with a 20-year maturity and a rating equivalent to A. The 11-bond index is composed of bonds with a 20-year maturity and a rating equivalent to AA.

Visible Supply Most issuers provide the *Bond Buyer* with details of coming sales, which are then compiled into a total amount representing the number of bonds that will be offered by underwriters usually in the next 30 days. The *Bond Buyer* is only available on the Internet.

Dow Jones Municipal Index
A weekly average of leading state and major city tax-exempt bond yields.

Primary Market

Types of Underwritings

Competitive Bids
Most general obligation bonds are sold under the sealed bid procedure. Each underwriter or group thereby places a bid for the issue with the best combination of price and interest rate being the winner.

Negotiated Sales
In many cases it is advantageous to the issuer to retain the services of an experienced municipal dealer to set up proposed bond issue and do the underwritings. Therefore, they enter into a contract to provide all of the financial services from inception to marketing. Although most negotiated sales are offered to the public, some are offered privately to institutional investors.

Sources of Information on Proposed Issues

Daily Bond Buyer

This publication is the main source of advertising sales of coming issues. It also provides worksheets with all pertinent information necessary for the prospective bidder.

Munifacts

A wire service for dealers listing coming sales without the detailed information.

Newspapers and Publications

Issuers often also take ads in local papers for coming bond sales. In some areas of the country, information on sales is submitted to a limited publication that sends the information to all local dealers.

Direct Mail

Issuers often send notices of sale, bid forms, and financial statistics to all dealers who had bid on prior issues. In some areas, the approving attorney mails this information to all dealers who are on the mailing list of the attorney. This procedure is particularly used for issues that are local and have no national appeal.

Official Notice of Sale and Official Statement

Most notices are in the same general format and most statements contain the same pertinent financial information for the bidder to determine the general condition of the issuer. The notice spells out the following information:

Date, Time, and Place of the Sale

Complete Description of the Issue Includes par value, purpose, maturities, and so on.

Manner of Bid While there are occasional oral bids, or auctions, generally most sales are conducted by the sealed bid process.

Authority for Sale To be acceptable to an underwriter, bonds must be issued under some constitutional or statutory power that will make them legal and valid obligations.

Type of Bond Various types of bonds, including general obligation, unlimited tax, limited tax, special tax, and revenue.

Interest Rate Limitations Some issuers specify a maximum rate of interest, others specify a limited interest difference on multiple-coupon rates, some specify multiple-coupon rates, and some even specify multiples of $\frac{1}{20}$ and $\frac{1}{8}$ of one percent of the acceptable rate unit.

Interest Payment Dates Interest is generally payable semiannually and usually one payment date corresponds to the maturity month of the bond. Often the first coupon may be more or less than six months depending on the date of issue.

Denominations and Registrations Virtually all bonds are issued in $5,000 pieces. Most bonds have provisions for registration as to principal or principal and interest.

Amount of Bid Some issuers specify that no bid for less than par will be accepted. Others may place a limit on the discount from par that will be acceptable. Still others specify a maximum limit above par.

Expense Liabilities The cost of printing and attorney fees is usually borne by the issuer as is the cost of the paying agent. Most issuers will deliver to the buyer free at the nearest major city, elsewhere, at cost of purchase. Cost of insured bonds will be specified at time of sale.

Good Faith Deposit Most issuers require a deposit to accompany the bid, ranging from a set amount or a percentage of par value, usually ½% to 5%. This is to protect the issuer in case the buyer does not take up and pay for the bonds. Some municipalities do not require a deposit. The deposit is held in escrow until delivery, when it may be applied to the purchase price or returned to buyer directly.

Name of Approving Attorney The bidders depend upon the attorney for protection to insure that the bonds are validly issued and require that the attorney be generally recognized in the industry.

Bid Form Bid forms vary dependent on the conditions of the award. In general, they will provide for the par value of bonds, total principal to be paid, interest rate or rates per maturity, total interest, and net interest cost. Some forms may not require all of the above if there is only one interest rate permitted.

Method of Place of Settlement The place of settlement is mutually agreed upon by the issuer and seller but is generally in a major city. Large issues are signed by machine. The recognized attorney is located in the issuer's city. Convenient banking is available. Payment is made in one of three ways: bank cashier's check, certified check, or federal funds. After count and examination by purchaser, examination of executed bond by attorney, closing papers and legal opinion by attorney, payment by buyer to issuer, a closing is completed.

Right of Rejection It is common practice for the issuer to reserve the right to reject all bids. He is then protected in the case of a sale with only one bid, which is, in effect, noncompetitive.

Basis for Award Generally speaking, awards are made on the lowest net interest cost to the issuer on competitive bidding. There may be slight variations in procedures but the net results are the same.

Functions of Bond Attorney

Establishes Eligibility for Tax Exemption

As previously stated, not all interest income on all municipal bonds is exempt from federal income taxes under the Internal Revenue Code. The approving attorney so states in his final legal opinion, although he is careful to state that the exemption only holds under existing law.

Authority for Issues

Before a proposed bond issue can be put up for sale, it must be established that there is a legal basis and power to issue bonds. There must be statutory power and no violation of the state constitution under the statute by which the bonds will be issued. In addition, all the necessary steps as required by the common laws of the state must be complied with in full. The judiciary of the various states have rendered decisions in the past on the legality of procedures for bond issues, and it is the approving attorney who ultimately reviews the entire transcript of proceedings to be certain that the issuer has followed every procedure necessary to bring into being a legal and valid bond issue.

Examines Executed Bonds

The attorney examines not only the executed bond but also the proof submitted to him before printing. He gives final approval to the printer when he is satisfied that the contents of the proof are in proper form. Prior to the formal closing and payment, the attorney again examines an executed bond and states in his final opinion that all the requirements for a legal and proper negotiated instrument have been completed.

Issues a Written Legal Opinion

There are three basic documents necessary to complete a closing on a bond issue:

1. treasurer's receipt
2. signature and no-litigation certificate
3. legal opinion

While the format of each document may vary slightly, the contents are basically the same. The purchaser receives a receipt for his full payment to the issuer, usually specifying the total principal and interest and total money transmitted. The signature and no-litigation papers give specimens of signatures of all the issuer's officials plus a statement by the local attorney that there is no litigation existing or pending at the time of the closing that would affect the validity of the issue. Usually stated is the fact that the officials are in office at that time and that the signatures are guaranteed to be authentic by a local bank.

Legal opinions vary greatly in length. General obligation issues are relatively brief but revenue bond legals usually are quite long, and often there is insufficient space to have them printed on the bonds. Generally, they are composed of a complete description of the issue, including the date of issue, coupon rate or rates, and call features, if any, and they cite the authority under which the bonds are issued. In some cases, the fact that a legal opinion is on file with the trustee or paying agent is printed on the bonds, and they are accepted as good delivery form. Even then the purchaser is entitled to an original signed by the approving attorney.

Formation of Underwriting Account (Syndicate)

Account Formation Procedures

Most dealers and bank dealers have at least one individual, and in many cases, an entire department, exclusively devoted to underwriting of new issues. As a result, they all subscribe to the *Bond Buyer* and follow the coming scheduled bond sales. On issues of national interest, management has historically been in the hands of major firms or banks. On local issues, which are usually much smaller, the management of the bid rests with local dealers. Over the years, syndicates have been formed to bid jointly on certain issues. Therefore, when notice is published of a new issue by that issuer, an invitation is extended by the manager to all members of prior accounts. It is usually a form letter outlining all pertinent details including proposed participations and the fact that the participant is willing to accept all of the usual duties and responsibilities involved. By signing and returning the letter to the manager, the member has indicated his desire to participate in the underwriting.

Competitive bidding generally creates a number of syndicates and opens the way for most bond firms to receive invitations to bid jointly. As a result of mergers and terminations, the makeup of accounts does change and provides openings for new firms to gain acceptance. In many cases, there are co-managers and often a rotation of the management from issue to issue. It is customary to permit firms to withdraw from one account and join another, provided the decision is made in advance of any discussion of pricing and bidding. In general, and particularly in large accounts, the pricing is governed by a poll of the major members of the group at a preliminary meeting. However, the lower bracket members are invited to attend all meetings. The final meeting is generally scheduled about one hour before sale time. The manager then gives a run of maturity yield, coupons, tentative spread, and sometimes presale interest. About this time, the members are polled as to their desire to remain or withdraw. If they stay, they have the option of limiting their participation or being willing to accept more bonds. Many out-of-town members use proxies who have received specific instructions to act for that member. In cases where the member is not present and has not proxied, the manager uses the original signed syndicate letter to the member as authority for commitment.

The manager exclusively has the responsibility to submit the bid. As agent for the group, he provides the required good faith deposit. He may have a personal representative at the sale or use an agent to submit the bid. There is a set time for opening bids and none will be accepted after the deadline. However, the terms of the syndicate agreement afford him protection from liability by reason of a late bid or any other unintentional error. When bid time arrives, it is customary for the competing groups to check bids and thus determine which group has won the issue subject to the official award by the issuer. As in most businesses and, particularly in the securities industry, time is of the essence when reoffering new issues. When the award becomes official, the manager sends out a confirmation of purchase letter containing the following information:

1. Complete description of securities, including par value, coupon, maturity, and net reoffering scale
2. Average unit dollar production of the scale
3. Profit spread
4. Net dollar bid to the issuer
5. Dealer concession per maturity
6. Member takedown per maturity
7. Request for proportionate share of good faith based on revised participation
8. Duplicate of letter signed and returned

Customarily, the manager establishes an order period at the final meeting ranging from one or more hours during which time all orders will have some priority. Upon the filling of these orders, the balance of unsold bonds are available to all members on a first come basis. To summarize the role of the manager, the members confer upon him extensive authority to act on their behalf from the formation of the joint account until the final settlement including the banking and carrying of unsold bonds.

Allocation Procedures

Orders that are submitted to the manager on a firm basis prior to the sale have the top priority. It is only proper and equitable that these orders should have preference because they provide the manager with additional strength to support the bid. The second priority after the award is given to group net orders for the benefit of the account as a whole. The third priority could be twofold, group and designated less concessions. The fourth would be designated less the takedown and the final preference would be members at the take-down. The manager, at his discretion, usually decides on the priorities for the last groups based on the overall account benefit. In many cases, it is a very difficult decision, particularly if the account has a potential sellout possibility.

Types of Accounts

There are two types: Eastern, or undivided, and Western, or divided. In the first type, all of the bonds are pooled in the hands of the manager and each member's performance benefits all other members on their remaining liability, which is in the same proportion as their original percentage. Of course, it is the sellers who still make the most profit since they benefit by the normal takedown on sales. Even in a divided account, it is often customary to have the earlier maturities undivided and the balance divided by maturity bracket. The divided account provides a greater profit potential to the member with selling ability plus it reduces his remaining liability regardless of the performance of his co-members. Initially, he is capable of making the takedown on his deal and within the various brackets discharging his liability. In addition, he receives additional compensation for oversales charged to the underseller for discharging that member's liability.

EXAMPLE

In a $10,000,000 offering, a member of the syndicate may, in a Western account, underwrite $1,000,000 of the issue. Should that member sell that amount of bonds, he has no further liability (although he may sell additional bonds). In a $10,000,000 offering done as an Eastern account, the member may underwrite 10% of the issue. In this case, he is liable for 10% of whatever balance remains in the account. The member may sell $3,000,000 of the issue to his clients. However, if an unsold balance of $2,000,000 still remains in the account, he would be liable for $200,000 (10% of $2,000,000) of that account.

Each type of account has certain advantages. In Eastern accounts, remaining unsold bonds are divided among the members in direct proportion to their original participation, regardless of the member's sales. In Western accounts, unsold bonds are allocated based on the sales performance of the member.

To summarize the pros and cons of each type of account, the business must be viewed as it exists today. In general, accent is placed on selling or distribution. Therefore, only a very small portion of the spread after normal account expenses is left to the underwriting group. Profit checks are minimal in relation to original liability. As a result, except for the old-line firms, which still place a value on their position in the business and their ability to formulate the actual bid, the real moneymakers are the sellers. Merely having access to the bonds satisfies most of the smaller firms and definitely contains their liability in the unsuccessful accounts.

Determination of Syndicate Bid

A short time prior to the sale, the manager and the major bracket members run an offering scale by yield per maturity converted into dollar prices. They arrive at a unit price. From this price, they deduct their profit spread and the net result is the dollar price principal bid to the issuer.

The coupon or coupon rates are projected over the life of the issue and converted into a unit interest cost. Any premium or discount on the principal will be added or deducted to attain a net interest cost figure. Most awards are made on this basis. On issues where only one coupon is permitted, the lowest interest rate receives the award. On duplicate rate bids, the highest principal price wins.

Profit or Loss Allocation

Settlement of accounts vary between Eastern and Western. In both types, all proper expenses are charged to the account. All net proceeds of sales are credited. The result leaves the net profit available for distribution to the members in proportion to their original participations. The procedure is the same in divided accounts except for the over-seller-underseller factor.

Payment and Delivery

It is usual in the notice of sale to state the approximate delivery date. As a general guide, it is from three to five weeks after the sale. The reason for this delay is usually attributed to the volume of bonds relative to the limited number of banknote companies available for printing. However, the issuer and buyer settle upon a mutually agreeable time and place to close the issue. The purchaser makes banking arrangements to make payment by certified or bank check for the bonds. In the rare case of federal funds checks, the buyer provides those funds. Before closing, the purchaser counts and examines all bonds to ascertain that they have been properly executed. Thus satisfied, he checks the signature and no-litigation certificates. Next, he reads the opinion of the approving attorney. Finally, the buyer checks the treasurer's receipt and, all being in order, makes payment and takes up the issue. The final money represents the principal bid plus accrued interest to date of delivery.

Public Offering

After the award by the issuer to the purchaser, all bonds are offered for sale by the members to investors. Initially, all bonds held by the group can only be offered at set scale price and in the case of sales to other nonmember dealers at the concession set by the group. All sales must be cleared for takedown by the manager. Subsequent offerings may be made at reduced prices with the concurrence of the majority of the account members. Upon occasion, lower bids may be offered for some or all of the remaining bonds, and the account may be polled for acceptance or rejection of the bid. All of these factors make it necessary to give the manager certain discretionary authority within certain limits.

CALCULATIONS

All municipal bonds yields and interest are computed on a 360-day basis. Municipal notes are generally computed on a 360-day basis, but many are issued on a 365-day basis.

Basis Book

Before the advent of the computer, the Financial Publishing Company published a variety of basis books. Under each separate coupon rate was a series of tables representing both the dollar price and the yield every month until maturity. Yields were listed vertically on the page and dollar prices per month were horizontal. Any yield or dollar price not listed had to be interpolated, which was possible because of the 30-day constancy of the scales. There is an inverse relationship between price and yield: The higher the price, the lower the yield, and the lower the price, the higher the yield.

Accrued Interest

A new issue is usually figured on a 360-day basis from the date of issue to settlement date. Occasionally, there are long and short coupons when the dated date differs from the month of maturity. In the secondary market, the accrued interest is computed from the previous coupon maturity to the settlement date.

Interest on municipal bonds is computed up to but not including the settlement date of the trade. The buyer pays to the seller accrued interest from the date of the last coupon. In municipal bond interest computations, all months are given 30 days and the year is considered to have 360 days.

EXAMPLE

On Monday, June 6, a client purchases $5,000 of municipal bonds with a 6½% interest rate, paying interest January and July 1 (J & J1). The trade is made "regular way." To compute interest we must first determine the settlement date of the trade. Regular way trades in municipals settle on the third business day after the trade. Therefore, our settlement date would be Thursday, June 9. The buyer would pay the seller eight days' interest for June plus 30 days for each preceding month:

January	30 days
February	30 days
March	30 days
April	30 days
May	30 days
June	8 days
	158 days' interest

We then use the formula for computing interest, which is

$$Principal \times Rate \times Time = Interest$$
$$\$5,000 \times \frac{6.5}{100} \times \frac{158}{360} = \$142.63$$

We know the principal is $5,000 and the interest rate is 6.5 (6½%) As we have calculated our days at 158 our calculation is complete. The buyer pays the agreed price of the transaction plus the $142.63 interest to the seller. (Note: Interest on U.S. government securities is computed differently. Here we use a 365-day year and assign each month its exact number of days.)

Some bonds pay interest on a day other than the first of the month. In our example above, if the bonds paid interest on January and July 15 (J & J 15) we would use 16 days' interest for January. The buyer would pay interest for January 15 plus the remaining 15 days of the 30-day month.

Net Yield Capital Gains Tax

This is applicable to bonds selling at a discount. Institutions do not receive the benefit of the capital gains rate since the accretion is taxable as ordinary income regardless of duration of holding. Individuals meeting the time requirement receive the benefit of the long-term capital gains tax rate. Keep in mind that long-term capital gains are taxed the same as ordinary income for institutions.

Taxable Equivalent Yield

This is the rate of return on a taxable basis needed to produce an equivalent yield after taxes to equal a tax-exempt yield.

Current Yield

This is the rate of return in relation to the dollar price and coupon rate. It is computed by dividing the coupon rate by the dollar price. No consideration is given to the amortization of the premium or accretion of the discount.

The term "yield" on a debt security defines the percentage return that the purchaser receives on his investment. Yield can be expressed in three different ways:

1. nominal yield
2. current yield
3. yield to maturity

Nominal Yield

The nominal yield is simply the annual rate of interest stated on the bond. Thus, a bond carrying a 6% stated interest rate has a nominal yield of 6%. This is based on the face value ($1,000) of the bond and does not take into consideration the current market price, which most often will be other than $1,000. Nominal yield also ignores the fact that bonds, unlike stock, have a maturity date at which time the bondholder will receive $1,000 from the issuer, which may be more or less than his actual purchase price.

Current Yield

Current yield is computed in the same manner as one would calculate the yield on a stock. If we were told that General Motors common stock was trading at $61 per share and paid an annual dividend of $2.50 per share, we would compute the yield by dividing the dividend ($2.50) by the market price ($61). The result would be a current yield of 4.10%.

$$\frac{2.50}{61} = 4.10$$

Current yield on a bond is figured in exactly the same manner. Were we told that a client owned a 6% general obligation bond trading at the market price of 82 (82% of $1,000 face value, or $820) we would determine the current yield on the bond by dividing the annual yield $60 by the current market price of $820 (82% of $1,000). The result would be a current yield of 7.3%.

Yield to Maturity (Average Yield)

This takes into consideration the fact that the bond may be purchased above or below the $1,000 face value. As the investor will be paid $1,000 at maturity, he will receive more or less than his original investment. Bonds purchased above face value ($1,000) are said to be purchased at a "premium." Those purchased below face value are said to be purchased at a "discount." In computing yield to maturity we consider this premium or discount in our calculation.

EXAMPLE

A client purchases one State of Kentucky 8% GO bond at a price of 91 (910). The bond will mature in exactly 9 years.

Step I
Determine the total discount by subtracting the purchase price ($910) from the face value ($1,000) that will be paid to the holder at maturity.

$$\begin{array}{r} \$1,000 \\ - \ \$ \ \ 910 \\ \hline \$ \ \ \ \ 90 \ \text{(Total Discount)} \end{array}$$

Step II
We must now annualize this discount by dividing the total discount ($90) by the number of years until maturity (9). This procedure is known as "accretion." The $90 total discount divided by 9 years equals $10 annualized (accreted) discount.

Step III
We now add the annual accretion ($10) to the annual interest received by the bondholder, which is $80 (8% of the $1,000 face value). The $10 accretion plus $80 annual interest equals $90. This would be the average annual return received by the bondholder ($80 of interest plus $10 of accretion).

Step IV
We now divide the $90 (interest plus accretion) by the average of the bond's current price ($910) and the bond's eventual price at maturity ($1,000).

$$\begin{array}{r} \$ \ \ 910 \\ + \$1,000 \\ \hline \$1,910 \end{array}$$

$$\frac{1,910}{2} = 955$$

Our answer is 9.42% ($90 ÷ 955 = 9.42%) yield to maturity.

This is called the "rule of thumb" method and may be used as a guide for determining yield to maturity.

Let's try another example of a bond trading at a "premium."

A client purchases a 6% revenue bond at a price of 107.5 ($1,075 = 107.5% of $1,000 face value). The bond will mature in exactly 15 years.

Nominal yield, as shown earlier, is the interest rate on the bond, 6%.

Current yield is again determined by dividing the annual interest ($60, 6% of $1,000) by the market price ($1,075). This equals 5.5% current yield.

Yield to maturity is determined in the same way as bonds trading at discount except in this case we are dealing with a premium bond. This bond is trading at $1,075 while its face (par) value is only $1,000. The $75 difference is the "premium." Again we must annualize this premium by dividing it by the number of years remaining until maturity (15). This process is known as "amortization."

The total premium of $75 divided by 15 years equals $5 annual amortization.

At maturity the client will receive $75 less than he paid for the bond ($1,075 cost - $1,000 face value). This averages out to $5 per year over the 15 years.

We now determine the true annual return by subtracting the $5 annual amortization from the $60 (6% of $1,000) annual interest.

$$\begin{array}{r} \$60 \\ - \ \$\ 5 \\ \hline \$55 \end{array}$$

We again divide this "true" return ($55) by an average of the current price $1,075 (107.5) and the eventual price $1,000 (100) to determine our yield to maturity.

$$\begin{array}{r} 1,075 \\ + \ 1,000 \\ \hline 2,075 \end{array}$$

$$\frac{2,075}{2} = 1,037.50 \text{ (average price)}$$

$55 (true annual return) ÷ $1,037.50 (average price) = 5.30% (yield to maturity)

Amortization of the Premium

Premiums must be written off annually and are not deductible for tax purposes. In effect, they represent a reduction of coupon income to the holder even though the whole coupon is fully tax-exempt income.

Accretion of Discount

Discounts are accreted on an annual basis but are not taxable until sale or maturity. For individuals they are capital gains; for institutions they are ordinary income. The coupon interest is fully tax exempt.

Debt Service Computations

Debt service is the funds required to pay principal and interest over the life of the issue. Annual debt service is the funds necessary to pay maturing principal and interest on all outstanding bonds each year. Level debt service is the funds necessary each year to pay even amounts of principal and interest over the life of the issue.

Dollar Value of Points and Fractions

The basic unit in municipal bonds is $1,000 and dollar prices are figured as they relate to that unit. One point represents $10 and the fractional points are portions of $10; for example, ½ point is $5 and each ⅛ point is $1.25. For example, the price of 98⅝ in dollars is $986.25. At the present time, the vast majority of municipal bonds are traded on a decimal basis.

Relationship of Bond Prices to Changes

Maturity
As a general rule, the longer the life of the bond to maturity the greater the tendency for prices to vary. The reason for this is the degree to which the future can be predicted. As a result fixed income securities are subject to the effects of changes in various unpredictable financial, economic, and political factors. As a result of this uncertainty, and particularly for the fact that negative changes could occur, the bondholder is rewarded for his risk in the form of lower prices.

Coupon
As a general rule, the higher the coupon the higher the price and the lower the coupon the lower the price.

Yield
As a general rule, yields are related to the risk involved. As a result, they relate to the life of the bond; the shorter the life, the lower the yield and the longer the life, the higher the yield. However, all three are interrelated in the price, with the yield being the ultimate determining factor, since most bonds are traded on a yield basis. As a result, there is an inverse relationship that can be summarized as the higher the yield, the lower the price, and vice versa.

Yield to Call
A bondholder may be exposed to the possibility of having his bond redeemed prior to maturity. Even though such redemption is not a certainty, he is afforded some protection to insure that he will receive his return in yield in that eventuality. Since all calls are at a price of par or higher, bonds selling at a discount are not affected. The holder is certain to receive his yield since the discount dollar price is lower to maturity than it is to a call date. Conversely, premium price bonds are higher figured to maturity than to call date. As a result, the bondholder may not receive his expected yield return if the bonds are called. To afford him protec-

tion in this eventuality, the price is figured on the premise that a call could occur. When there are multiple call options, the yield is figured to the call that will produce the lowest dollar price. As a result, the holder is assured of a worst case scenario yield.

Flat - Without Interest

When settlement date and coupon date are simultaneous, bonds are traded ex-interest. When bonds are in default, they are traded without interest, or flat. In that case, the seller must specify that past due unpaid coupons are attached to the bond.

Basis Points

A basis point represents one hundredth of one percent in yield. This is equivalent to ten cents—$.10.

Value of a Mill

$\frac{1}{10}$ of a cent. The reason we mention the value of a mill is because some municipalities still use this amount when applying taxes. The State of Connecticut is one example.

FEDERAL LEGAL CONSIDERATIONS

Issuance and Distribution of Municipal Securities

Municipal Securities Are Currently Exempt from Registration Requirements of the Securities Act of 1933 and the Reporting Requirements of the Securities Exchange Act of 1934.

Municipal Securities Rulemaking Board (MSRB) Regulation of Underwriting under Securities Act Amendments of 1975.

Disclosure of Capacity Every municipal securities dealer who submits an order to a syndicate or to a member of a syndicate for the purchase of municipal securities held by the syndicate shall disclose at the time of submission of such order if the securities are being purchased for its dealer account, for the account of a related portfolio of such municipal securities dealer, for a municipal securities investment trust sponsored by such municipal securities dealer, or for an accumulation account established in connection with such a municipal securities investment trust.

Confirmation of Sale Sales of securities held by a syndicate to a related portfolio, municipal securities investment trust, or accumulation account referred to in the section above shall be confirmed by the syndicate manager directly to such related portfolio, municipal securities investment trust, or accumulation account to the municipal securities dealer submitting the order.

Disclosure of Group Orders Every syndicate shall establish the priority to be accorded to different types of orders for the purchase of securities from the syndicate during the underwriting period and, if such priority may be changed, the procedure for making changes.

Priority of Orders Every syndicate shall establish the priority to be accorded to different types of orders for the purchase of securities from the syndicate during the underwriting period and, if such priority may be changed, the procedure for making changes.

Communications Relating to Priority of Orders and Order Period Prior to the first offer of any securities by a syndicate, the senior syndicate manager shall furnish in writing to the other members of the syndicate (1) the priority to be accorded to different types or orders for securities to be distributed by the syndicate; (2) the procedure, if any, by which such priority may be changed; (3) if the senior syndicate manager or managers are to be permitted on a case-by-case basis to deviate from the agreed upon order of priority, the fact that they are permitted to do so; and (4) if there is to be an order period, whether orders may be confirmed prior to the end of the order period.

Disclosure of Syndicate Expenses At or before the final settlement of a syndicate account, the senior syndicate manager shall furnish to the other members of the syndicate an itemized statement setting forth the nature and amounts of all actual expenses incurred on behalf of the syndicate.

Regulation of Municipal Market Professionals

MSRB

The Municipal Securities Rulemaking Board (MSRB) is an independent, self-regulated organization designed to establish rules for regulation of the municipal securities industry. The board consists of 15 members drawn equally from three areas: (1) securities firms, (2) bank dealers, and (3) public members.

Under the Securities Act Amendments of 1975, enforcement of MSRB rules is accomplished by the Securities and Exchange Commission (SEC), the National Association of Securities Dealers (NASD), the Federal Reserve Board, the Comptroller of the Currency, and the Federal Deposit Insurance Corporation.

Registration of Brokers, Dealers, and Bank Dealers

Under the Securities Exchange Act of 1934, all brokers and dealers are required to register with the SEC.

Banks

A separately identifiable department or division of a bank is that unit of the bank that conducts all of the activities of the bank relating to the conduct of business as a municipal securities dealer as such activities are hereinafter defined, provided that:

1. Such unit is under the direct supervision of an officer or officers designated by the board of directors of the bank as responsible for the day-to-day conduct of the bank's municipal securities dealer activities, including the supervision of all bank employees engaged in the performance of such activities; and,
2. They are separately maintained in or separately extractable from such unit's own facilities or the facilities of the bank, all of the records relating to the bank's municipal securities dealer activities, and further provided that such records are so maintained or otherwise accessible as to permit independent examination thereof and enforcement of

applicable provisions of the 1934 act; the rules and regulations thereunder are the rules of the Board.

For the purpose of this rule, the activities of the bank that shall constitute municipal securities dealer activities are as follows:

1. underwriting, trading, and sales of municipal securities
2. financial advisory and consultant services for issuers in connection with the issuance of municipal securities
3. processing and clearance activities with respect to municipal securities
4. research and investment advice with respect to municipal securities
5. any activities other than those specifically enumerated above that involve communication, directly or indirectly, with public investors in municipal securities.
6. maintenance of records pertaining to the activities described in items (1) through (5), above.

SEC Rules

All municipal brokers and dealers are required to maintain a minimum net capital as stated in SEC Uniform Net Capital Rule (Rule 15C 3-1). This rule is not applicable to bank dealers. All municipal brokers and dealers, including banks, are bound by SEC antifraud rules.

MSRB Rules

The following is an outline of the MSRB rules to guide municipal securities representatives and enhance their knowledge of the business. The ultimate implementation rests with the officers and principals of the broker and dealer.

Historically, the municipal bond business was not regulated until Congress passed the Securities Act Amendments in 1975. It created the MSRB to develop rules for the business, and the board has been steadily submitting rules for the approval of the SEC, which governs all phases of the securities business. Necessarily, it has been a slow process because municipal securities have a unique position in the securities industry. They are authorized and issued by states and political subdivisions of states, which zealously guard their freedom from federal control.

As a result, the SEC, as a federal agency, is limited to regulation of the business as it relates to investments but has no direct control over the issuers, who do not have to clear their issue with any federal agency as in the cases of corporate equity or debt securities.

Standards of Professional Qualification

No municipal securities broker or municipal securities dealer shall effect any transaction in, or induce or attempt to induce the purchase or sale of, any municipal security unless such municipal securities broker or municipal securities dealer and every natural person associated with such municipal securities broker or municipal securities dealer is qualified in accordance with the rules of the board.

Keeping and Preserving of Records

Books and records to be made by municipal securities brokers and dealers: MSRB Rules G8–G9 and G10; SEC Rules 17a-3 and 17a-4.

ANSWER SHEET FOR CHAPTER 3 EXAMINATION

1. Ⓐ Ⓑ Ⓒ Ⓓ

2. Ⓐ Ⓑ Ⓒ Ⓓ

3. Ⓐ Ⓑ Ⓒ Ⓓ

4. Ⓐ Ⓑ Ⓒ Ⓓ

5. Ⓐ Ⓑ Ⓒ Ⓓ

6. Ⓐ Ⓑ Ⓒ Ⓓ

7. Ⓐ Ⓑ Ⓒ Ⓓ

8. Ⓐ Ⓑ Ⓒ Ⓓ

9. Ⓐ Ⓑ Ⓒ Ⓓ

10. Ⓐ Ⓑ Ⓒ Ⓓ

11. Ⓐ Ⓑ Ⓒ Ⓓ

12. Ⓐ Ⓑ Ⓒ Ⓓ

13. Ⓐ Ⓑ Ⓒ Ⓓ

14. Ⓐ Ⓑ Ⓒ Ⓓ

15. Ⓐ Ⓑ Ⓒ Ⓓ

16. Ⓐ Ⓑ Ⓒ Ⓓ

17. Ⓐ Ⓑ Ⓒ Ⓓ

18. Ⓐ Ⓑ Ⓒ Ⓓ

19. Ⓐ Ⓑ Ⓒ Ⓓ

20. Ⓐ Ⓑ Ⓒ Ⓓ

21. Ⓐ Ⓑ Ⓒ Ⓓ

22. Ⓐ Ⓑ Ⓒ Ⓓ

23. Ⓐ Ⓑ Ⓒ Ⓓ

24. Ⓐ Ⓑ Ⓒ Ⓓ

25. Ⓐ Ⓑ Ⓒ Ⓓ

26. Ⓐ Ⓑ Ⓒ Ⓓ

27. Ⓐ Ⓑ Ⓒ Ⓓ

28. Ⓐ Ⓑ Ⓒ Ⓓ

29. Ⓐ Ⓑ Ⓒ Ⓓ

30. Ⓐ Ⓑ Ⓒ Ⓓ

31. Ⓐ Ⓑ Ⓒ Ⓓ

32. Ⓐ Ⓑ Ⓒ Ⓓ

33. Ⓐ Ⓑ Ⓒ Ⓓ

34. Ⓐ Ⓑ Ⓒ Ⓓ

35. Ⓐ Ⓑ Ⓒ Ⓓ

36. Ⓐ Ⓑ Ⓒ Ⓓ

37. Ⓐ Ⓑ Ⓒ Ⓓ

38. Ⓐ Ⓑ Ⓒ Ⓓ

39. Ⓐ Ⓑ Ⓒ Ⓓ

40. Ⓐ Ⓑ Ⓒ Ⓓ

41. Ⓐ Ⓑ Ⓒ Ⓓ

42. Ⓐ Ⓑ Ⓒ Ⓓ

43. Ⓐ Ⓑ Ⓒ Ⓓ

44. Ⓐ Ⓑ Ⓒ Ⓓ

45. Ⓐ Ⓑ Ⓒ Ⓓ

46. Ⓐ Ⓑ Ⓒ Ⓓ

47. Ⓐ Ⓑ Ⓒ Ⓓ

48. Ⓐ Ⓑ Ⓒ Ⓓ

49. Ⓐ Ⓑ Ⓒ Ⓓ

50. Ⓐ Ⓑ Ⓒ Ⓓ

To remove answer sheet, cut along dotted line.

CHAPTER 3 EXAMINATION

1. An investment banker participating in an Eastern account underwriting of $10,000,000 municipal bonds agrees to underwrite 10% of the issue. One week later $4,000,000 remains unsold, but this firm has distributed $1,500,000 of bonds. What would be this firm's remaining liability in the account?

   (A) – 0 –
   (B) $400,000
   (C) $600,000
   (D) $1,000,000

2. If, in the previous question, the underwriting were a Western account, what would be the firm's initial liability in the account?

   (A) – 0 –
   (B) $400,000
   (C) $600,000
   (D) $1,000,000

3. From what source of revenues do "double-barreled" municipal issues have their debt service guaranteed?

   (A) one specific project plus a federal subsidy
   (B) at least two specific projects
   (C) all projects sponsored by that municipality
   (D) one specific project plus that municipality itself

4. Which of the following terms are most often associated with dollar bonds?

   I. serial
   II. term
   III. callable
   IV. limited tax

   (A) I and IV only
   (B) II and III only
   (C) I and III only
   (D) II, III and IV only

5. Revenue bonds are least likely to provide construction funds for:

   (A) a toll highway
   (B) an airport
   (C) a public school
   (D) a pollution control facility

6. Municipal bond broker's brokers generally:

   I. trade for dealer banks
   II. trade for nonbank dealers
   III. underwrite new issues
   IV. position bonds for their own account

   (A) I and II only
   (B) II only
   (C) III and IV only
   (D) I, II, III, and IV

7. The rate covenant on a revenue bond issued to finance a muncipal toll facility provides that the rates be set to cover about what percentage of the facility's maintenance charges and debt service requirement?

   (A) 75%
   (B) 100%
   (C) 120%
   (D) 150%

8. Dealer A has given a workable bid to Dealer B. If market conditions change, Dealer A may:

   (A) not change his bid
   (B) not change his bid unless he first notifies Dealer B
   (C) change his bid only with the prior approval of Dealer B
   (D) change his bid

9. Municipalities are most likely to issue notes for which of the following purposes?

   (A) short-term cash needs
   (B) federal income tax payments
   (C) repairs in the infrastructure
   (D) long-term financing

10. A municipal dealer knowingly mails confirmations of purchase to customers who have not placed orders for the bonds. What do MSRB rules prescribe for this practice?

    I.   It is considered a violation of rule G-17 which requires fair dealing with customers.
    II. It is an unethical procedure known as using "wooden tickets."
    III. No violation of rules occurs if customer accepts delivery of bonds confirmed.

    (A) I only
    (B) I and II only
    (C) II and III only
    (D) III only

11. A revenue bond is issued by a state agency. The state legislature is granted the authority to apportion money to support the debt service if necessary, but is not legally obligated to do so. What type of bond is described?

    (A) limited tax
    (B) double-barreled
    (C) Series 8
    (D) moral obligation

12. A group net order is one that benefits municipal syndicate members:

    (A) equally
    (B) according to their percentage participation in the account
    (C) according to the number of designated orders they've received
    (D) according to the number of presale orders they've received

13. A syndicate manager has just been informed that its bid has been accepted and all syndicate members are duly notified. Public information on the award will be most quickly available from:

    (A) the *Blue List*
    (B) the daily *Bond Buyer*
    (C) the *Wall Street Journal*
    (D) *Munifacts*

14. Under what circumstances may a municipal securities dealer guarantee a customer against loss in market value of bonds?

    (A) only if the agreement is in writing
    (B) only if the bonds are rated AAA or Aaa
    (C) only if the bonds are insured by MBIA, AMBAC, BIG, or FGIC
    (D) under no circumstances

15. When pricing callable municipal bonds on a yield basis, the "price to call" is based on:

    I. in-whole calls
    II. partial calls
    III. sinking fund calls
    IV. catastrophe calls

    (A) I only
    (B) II and III only
    (C) III or IV only
    (D) I or IV only

16. Feasibility studies and engineering surveys would be MOST necessary prior to a new offering of:

    I. general obligation bonds
    II. limited tax bonds
    III. revenue bonds
    IV. corporate debentures

    (A) I and IV only
    (B) III only
    (C) II, III and IV only
    (D) I and II only

17. Of the information below, which does not appear in the official notice of sale?

    (A) the type of bond
    (B) the amount of required good faith check
    (C) the names of underwriting syndicate members
    (D) the method and place of settlement

18. An individual investor buys a municipal bond at 102 and holds it ten years until it matures. For tax purposes how must that premium be treated?

    (A) recorded as a long-term capital loss
    (B) an ordinary loss taken as a deduction from taxable income
    (C) amortized over the life of the bond and results in no loss at maturity
    (D) carried forward as a premium loss and applied against profits realized on future municipal transactions

19. If you buy a ten-year municipal bond at 102 and sell it five years later at 101, what is the result for tax purposes?

    (A) a $10 long-term capital loss is realized
    (B) the $10 loss is applied against ordinary income reducing it
    (C) no capital loss or income deduction is recognized
    (D) the $10 loss is applied against future profits in municipal securities transactions

20. Which of the following municipal securities carries the full faith and credit of the U.S. government for payment of interest and principal if the issuer's funds are insufficient to meet its requirements?

    (A) general obligation bonds issued by cities and states
    (B) special tax bonds issued by municipalities
    (C) revenue bonds issued by a municipal port authority
    (D) new housing authority bonds issued by a public housing authority

21. If a customer buys a municipal bond at a discount and holds it to maturity the:

    (A) interest is taxable as ordinary income
    (B) the capital gain is tax exempt
    (C) interest is tax exempt, but the capital gain is taxable as short or long term
    (D) the capital gain is tax exempt, but the interest is taxable as ordinary income

22. What document relating to procedures should be consulted by prospective bidders for a municipal bond about to be sold by its issuer?

    (A) the Eastern account agreement
    (B) the official notice of sales
    (C) the offering circular
    (D) the SEC Registration Statement

23. All of the following information appears in the official notice of sale EXCEPT:

    (A) method and place of settlement for the bonds
    (B) denominations and registration privileges
    (C) an offering scale of serial maturates
    (D) amount of good faith check required

24. All of the following information appears in a municipal syndicate letter to underwriters EXCEPT:

    (A) the specific bid and offering terms of the issue
    (B) the amount of each member's participation
    (C) the extent of the manager's authority in directing the offering
    (D) the duration of the syndicate account

25. Which of the following sources of information provide news of prospective municipal securities sales to underwriters?

    I.   the *Blue List*
    II. the daily *Bond Buyer*
    III. the *SEC News Digest*
    IV. *Munifacts*

    (A) I and II only
    (B) II and IV only
    (C) I, III, and IV only
    (D) I, II, III, and IV

26. A municipal bond that is backed by the full faith and credit of the U.S. government as to principal and interest is a:

    (A) revenue bond
    (B) general obligation bond
    (C) port authority bond
    (D) public housing authority (PHA) bond

27. Under a leaseback arrangement used to finance construction of local schools, who is the issuer of these municipal bonds?

    (A) the state in which the schools are located
    (B) the local school district itself
    (C) a legal authority created for this purpose
    (D) a public housing authority commissioned by the federal government

28. Who usually employs and pays the municipal bond attorney rendering a legal opinion about the validity of the issue?

    (A) the purchaser of the bonds
    (B) the underwriter of the bonds
    (C) the issuing municipality
    (D) the issuing municipality's financial advisor

29. Which of the following municipal bonds may be grouped under the broad classification of "revenue bonds"?

    (A) special tax
    (B) new housing authority
    (C) general obligation
    (D) limited tax

30. A municipal corporation formed to operate public facilities is:

    I. the Port Authority of New York and New Jersey
    II. the Golden Gate Bridge Authority
    III. the Pennsylvania Turnpike Commission
    IV. the Massachusetts Port Authority

    (A) III only
    (B) I and IV only
    (C) II and III only
    (D) I, II, III, and IV

31. In what order of priority does the trustee of a municipal revenue bond apply income and revenues derived from the underlying toll facility?

    I. renewal and replacement fund
    II. operation and maintenance fund
    III. bond service account fund
    IV. reserve maintenance fund

    (A) I, II, III, IV
    (B) II, III, IV, I
    (C) II, IV, III, I
    (D) III, II, IV, I

32. Into what broad category of municipal security would a "limited tax" bond be placed?

    (A) general obligation
    (B) special tax
    (C) revenue
    (D) new housing authority

33. What do we call the rate of discount from the list price that is paid to a municipal securities underwriting group member for its sale participation?

    (A) commission
    (B) concession
    (C) spread
    (D) takedown

Questions 34–36 are based on the following information:

A 5% municipal bond maturing in exactly 15 years is trading at a market price of 85.

34. What is the nominal yield?

    (A) 5.88%
    (B) 5.10%
    (C) 5.00%
    (D) cannot be determined

35. What is the current yield?

    (A) 5.00%
    (B) 5.88%
    (C) 6.49%
    (D) 5.10%

36. Compute the yield to maturity using the "rule of thumb" method:

    (A) 5.00%
    (B) 5.88%
    (C) 5.10%
    (D) 6.49%

37. Which of these bond buyer indexes reflects the lowest average yield for municipal bonds?

    (A) the 50-bond index
    (B) the 20-bond index
    (C) the 11-bond index
    (D) the weekly unsold bond index

38. What does the bond buyer placement ratio represent?

    (A) the amount of municipal bonds held by banks and insurance companies as a percentage of municipal bonds outstanding
    (B) the amount of municipal bonds distributed weekly as a percentage of each week's new issue accounts of more than $1,000,000
    (C) the amount of municipal bonds offered in the daily *Blue List* as a percentage of the day's new issue accounts of $1,000,000 or more
    (D) the par value amount of municipal bonds offered in the *Blue List* as a percentage of the 30-day visible supply for competitive and negotiated issues

39. How much money is a concession of ⅜ worth for one municipal bond?

    (A) $ 0.375
    (B) $ 3.75
    (C) $ 37.50
    (D) $375.00

40. In a competitive underwriting of municipal bonds, which two of these factors determines which bidder gets the issuer's award?

    I.   the highest rate of interest
    II. the lowest rate of interest
    III. the highest premium
    IV. the lowest premium

    (A) I and III only
    (B) I and IV only
    (C) II and III only
    (D) II and IV only

41. A customer concerned about the liquidity of a possible municipal bond purchase would probably be most interested in the rating supplied by:

    (A) the bond buyers
    (B) Moody's
    (C) White's
    (D) Dow Jones

42. Which of the following forms of underwriting is *least* likely for an offering of municipal bonds?

    (A) negotiated
    (B) competitive bid
    (C) firm commitment
    (D) best efforts

43. A new municipal bond is offered for sale on May 7 to settle on May 9. The bond is dated May 1. A buyer will pay the principal amount:

    (A) only
    (B) plus accrued interest from May 1 to May 7
    (C) plus accrued interest from May 7 to May 14
    (D) plus accrued interest from May 1 to May 8

44. A municipal dealer buys 100M of 7% 20-year GO bonds at par. The bonds are marked up and immediately reoffered for sale. Which of the following reoffering prices would probably be deemed excessive?

    (A) 6.8% net
    (B) 6.9% less .5
    (C) 100.75
    (D) 5.00% net

45. Municipal bonds would be the least attractive investment for:

    (A) an insurance company
    (B) a pension fund
    (C) a commercial bank
    (D) the executive officer of an industrial corporation who is in a maximum tax bracket

46. If a municipality had funds available to make a partial call of an issue of outstanding serial bonds, which bonds would they call first?

    (A) the shortest maturity
    (B) the maturity with the largest number of bonds
    (C) the longest maturity
    (D) the maturity bearing the lowest interest rate

47. Which of the following are considered "advertisements" under MSRB rules?

    I.   market letters
    II.   research reports
    III. offering circulars
    IV. abstract from preliminary official statement

        (A) I and II only
        (B) III and IV only
        (C) I, II, and IV only
        (D) I, II, III, and IV

48. Which of the following would be least relevant in evaluating the safety of a general obligation bond?

    (A) per capita debt
    (B) total GO debt/market value of property
    (C) total GO debt/assessed value of property
    (D) total debt service/net operating revenues

49. Municipal syndicate allocation procedures are described in which of the following?

    (A) underwriting agreement
    (B) syndicate account letter
    (C) agreement among the underwriters
    (D) official statement

50. What expression is used to describe the application of income and revenues derived from the operation of a facility financed from proceeds of a revenue bond?

    (A) debt service
    (B) flow of funds
    (C) revenue funding
    (D) disbursement of priorities

CHAPTER 3 EXAMINATION ANSWERS

1. **B** In an Eastern account, liability remains open until the syndicate is closed. Thus, the investment banker would have a liability of 10% of the unsold portion, or $400,000.

2. **D** In a Western account, each underwriter has divided liability and is responsible only for the portion that he agreed to underwrite. In this example, the underwriter's liability is $1,000,000 (10% of $10,000,000).

3. **D** Double-barreled bonds are first payable from the revenues of a specific project, but are further guaranteed by a municipality.

4. **B** Dollar bonds are so-called because they are not quoted on the yield-to-maturity basis customary for GO serial bonds. Rather they are quoted on a percent-of-par basis much like corporate bonds. They are typically revenue term (single maturity date) bonds and are usually callable.

5. **C** Schools are occasionally constructed through the use of rental leaseback bonds, which may be considered a type of revenue bond. Much more frequently, however, they are built with the proceeds of regular GO bonds. The other choices are typical examples of revenue bond financing.

6. **A** Broker's brokers act in a purely agency capacity. They attempt to locate the other side of the trade for municipal dealers and charge a commission when successful. They do not trade from position, underwrite, or deal directly with individual investors.

7. **C** Approximately 120% is the usual rate coverage on a toll facility.

8. **D** A workable bid indicates a price level where a dealer is willing to negotiate business. It is, however, not a firm bid and may be changed before becoming firm.

9. **A** In general, notes are used to generate cash for short-term needs. BANs may be issued to fund the initial stages of a highway or bridge repair program, but the intent is to replace them with more permanent funding as soon as the bond issue is sold.

10. **B** This unethical practice would rarely work with astute investors but might be attempted with large trust department or institutional investors who buy large quantities of bonds from many dealers.

11. **D** The lack of a legally binding obligation removes such as issue from the general obligation category. Although defaults are possible, it is usually held that no state legislature would allow a moral obligation issue to default because of the adverse credit repercussions and damage to the state's credibility, if not its credit.

12. **B** For instance, if the group net order produces $3,000 in fees and a syndicate member has a 10% overall participation, it receives $300 in fees.

13. **D** *Munifacts* is the wire service provided by the daily *Bond Buyer*. It displays information of particular interest to municipal traders, underwriters, and other participants in the fixed-income markets.

14. **D** No guarantees may be made against loss of market value because no one can guarantee where the market may go. Insured bonds are protected against loss of principal and interest, but not against market depreciation.

The nearest thing to a guarantee against market loss would be a "put bond" allowing the holder to sell the bond back to the issuer at par if prices declined.

15. **A** "Price to call" computations are based on in-whole calls only. These calls will result in all bondholders being called at once, thus guaranteeing a certain minimum yield to all. Partial or sinking fund calls do not affect all bondholders, and catastrophe calls are so rare as to be considered unlikely under normal conditions.

16. **B** The security for a revenue bond depends on the revenues produced by the use of the facilities. Engineering estimates of construction costs and potential traffic flow are critical.

17. **C** At the time the notice of sale is published the syndicate has generally not been formed. All other information is required.

18. **C** For tax purposes, premiums are amortized over the life of the bond on an annual basis.

19. **C** The $20.00 premium is amortized over a ten-year period ($2.00 per year); after five years the bond has been written down $10.00 to 101. The sale at 101 results in no loss.

20. **D** By definition.

21. **C** Note that this presumes that the investor bought the municipal bonds in the secondary trading market.

22. **B** All details of bid requirements are found in the official notice of sale.

23. **C** The scale is set by the successful bidder.

24. **A** Bid and offering terms are determined later.

25. **B** The *Blue List* shows current offerings. Municipals are not registered with the SEC and therefore do not appear in the SEC News Digest.

26. **D** PHAs are one of the few municipal issues backed by the full faith and credit of the U.S. government.

27. **C** By definition.

28. **C** The issuer pays the bond attorney.

29. **A** A very general grouping but the only answer available.

30. **D** All named are municipal corporations.

31. **B** Operation and maintenance are the first priority followed by debt service, maintenance reserves, and lastly renewal and replacement.

32. **A** A limited tax bond is generally classified as a general obligation.

33. **D** Takedown is an additional allowance on bonds sold by a member.

34. **C** Nominal yield is equal to the coupon on the bond, 5.00%.

35. **B** To determine current yield we divide the annual interest ($50) by the market price ($850), which equals 5.88%.

36. **D** First we take the total discount from par ($150) and divide by the number of years to maturity (15) to determine the annual discount ($10). This is then added to the coupon rate ($50) to find the true annual return. The resulting figure ($60) is then divided by an average of the current price (85) and par (100). The result: 60 divided by 92.5=6.49% yield to maturity.

37. **C** This is the highest quality index and would, therefore, reflect the lowest average yield.

38. **B** By definition.

39. **B** ⅜ of $10.00, which is $3.75.

40. **C** The lowest interest rate and highest premium to the issuer would be the determining factors in the bidding for a municipal bond issue.

41. **C** White's ratings are based on trading market data as opposed to the financial data underlying the issue. The latter criteria are used by Moody's and S&P to determine credit risk.

42. **D** Best efforts deals are most often associated with small corporate stock or limited partnership offerings. Municipal securities are usually competitive bid (GO) or negotiated (revenue). Both types are firm commitment—the syndicate buys the entire issue.

43. **D** The dated date is the date from which interest begins to accrue. Interest accrues up to but does not include the settlement date. Hence, the buyer will pay 8 days of accrued interest in addition to the principal amount.

44. **D** The first three quotes indicate moderate markups over cost. A quote of 5% net, however, indicates a pretty hefty markup and a price not "reasonably related to the market." The dollar price would be about 125, a 25% markup over the dealer's cost.

45. **B** Since the pension fund does not pay income taxes, the tax freedom would not be appealing to them.

46. **C** The longest maturity is called first as the municipality would save the cost of interest payment for the longest possible period of time.

47. **D** The term "offering circular" is used here to describe an interdealer informational bulletin on an upcoming new issue (note that the same term may be used to describe the brief document that accompanies a corporate Regulation A offering). Market letters and research reports are likewise dealer prepared and thus subject to MSRB rules. Although the preliminary official statement is published by the issuer and beyond MSRB rules, any excerpt or abstract of this document is considered "advertising" for regulatory purposes.

48. **D** This ratio is applicable to revenue bonds, not to GO bonds. The other three are all used in measuring credit risk in a GO bond.

49. **B** This letter is sent by the manager of a competitive bid syndicate to the other members. The priority and other procedures, including allocation amounts, are specified. Members signify acceptance by signing the letter and returning it to the manager.

50. **B** By definition.

The Securities Act of 1933–Underwriting

NASD ESTABLISHED

There are two major federal securities laws in the United States. The Securities Act of 1933, our topic in this section, covers the offering of new securities and related matters. The Securities Exchange Act of 1934 covers virtually all other matters. For example, the 1934 act established the Securities and Exchange Commission. It requires stock exchanges to register with the SEC; under an amendment it established the NASD to regulate the over-the-counter market; it authorizes the Federal Reserve to establish margin requirements for securities transactions; and it covers many other regulatory areas.

The Securities Act of 1933 was enacted to prevent fraud in the issuance of securities. It is sometimes called the full-disclosure law as it requires that a registration statement be filed with the SEC that contains all information available regarding the issuing company and the details of the particular offering. This information is then given to the prospective purchaser in the form of a prospectus.

With exceptions that will be discussed later, the registration statement must be filed by a company wishing to offer securities (called the "issuer") and by those considered to be "affiliated persons" of that issuer. An affiliated person is one who has the ability to influence the policies of that corporation, such as the chairman, president, or controlling stockholder.

The SEC never approves an issue nor do they generally disapprove one. They attempt to see that the information provided in the prospective is sufficient to permit investors to determine the suitability of the investment for their particular portfolios.

Many securities offerings are exempt from the filing requirements of the act. Among them are:

- U.S. government securities
- municipal securities
- offerings by charitable institutions
- intrastate offerings
- commercial paper
- banker's acceptances
- certificates of deposit
- securities that must register with other government agencies (e.g. railroad equipment trust certificates which must register with the Interstate Commerce Commission)
- insurance policies and fixed annuities

Not exempt from registration with the SEC, but requiring a briefer, less expensive form of registration, are offerings made under Regulation A of the act. These offerings may not exceed a total value of $5,000,000 and are made under an offering circular rather than a prospectus. The $5,000,000 limit under Regulation A covers all offerings made by an issuer over a 12-month period. Other exempted offerings are "private placements" and offerings made under SEC Rules #144, 144A, 145, 147, and 237.

The exceptions are a group of entities defined as "accredited investors" in SEC Rule 505. Private placements may be distributed to any number of accredited investors, but to no more than 35 nonaccredited investors during any 12-month period.

The term "accredited investor" includes:

1. financial institutions (investment companies, banks, insurance companies, etc.)
2. nonprofit organizations with assets of $5,000,000 or more
3. any purchaser of at least $150,000 of the securities being offered
4. individuals with net worth in excess of $1,000,000
5. individuals with income in excess of $200,000 in each of the last two years, with the exception that this level will be achieved in the year of purchase

Rule 144

Rule 144 states that stock acquired privately or as compensation must be held for a minimum of two years on a fully paid basis before it is eligible for sale under this rule. Stock acquired in the open market by affiliated persons is not subject to the two-year requirement.

Suppose the president of Acme Engine, Inc., wished to sell 25,000 shares of the company stock without registering the sale with the SEC. She might approach Goldman Sachs Group, Inc., to assist her with the sale. Assume that Acme Engine stock is listed on the New York Stock Exchange.

Step I
Goldman Sachs would check the SEC to see that Acme Engine was a reporting company. As the buyers of these shares will not receive a prospectus, the information regarding the company must be available to them.

Step II
If the amount to be sold is more than 500 shares or more than $10,000 in value, notification of the sale must be given to the SEC. This notice (Form 144) allows the sale to take place over a period of 90 days so as not to depress the price of the shares by a forced sale. Seldom would this much time be needed.

Step III
How much can this person sell? In any three-month period a person can sell up to 1% of the outstanding stock or, if the shares are listed on an exchange, the average weekly volume for the last four weeks, whichever is greater. Suppose that Acme Engine had 2,000,000 shares outstanding. One percent would be only 20,000 shares, so a sale of 25,000 would be excessive. However, as Acme stock is listed on the NYSE, Goldman would check the volume for the previous four weeks on consolidated Network A. Suppose they found the volume to be:

4 weeks ago –	40,000 shares
3 weeks ago –	48,000 shares
2 weeks ago –	30,000 shares
1 week ago –	52,000 shares

The sum of the four weeks' volume is 170,000 shares. We divide this by 4 to obtain the average volume, 42,500 shares. Thus, we could sell up to 42,500 shares, making our sale of 25,000 well within the limit of Rule 144.

Keep in mind this covers sales of unregistered shares over a three-month period, allowing our client to make four such sales a year. In computing the amount that may be sold under Rule #144, we consider only unregistered sales of the same security. Thus, if the president of Acme Engine had sold shares in a registered offering last month that would not be counted. She may also have sold convertible bonds or convertible preferred stock of the company, but that would not affect her limit on sales of the common stock under Rule 144.

Step IV

In general the dealer (Goldman Sachs Group, Inc.) handling the Rule 144 sale cannot solicit buy orders for the shares. They are sold in the general market on an exchange or over the counter in the normal manner. Goldman could buy some or all of the shares themselves acting as *principal* or can sell them for the client acting as *agent*. The firm handling the sale *cannot* charge more than their normal commission for a trade of this size despite the fact that some additional work on their part may have been necessary.

Step V

The details of the sale would be reported to the SEC.

Rule 144A

This rule allows for the purchase of restricted stock by organizations classified as "qualified institutions." A "qualified institution" is defined as having a minimum of $100 million invested in securities not affiliated with the entity. These "qualified institutions" may trade among themselves without regard to the provisions of Rule 144 outlined above.

Rule 145

Rule 145 allows for the sale of unregistered stock acquired through merger or acquisition. Perhaps you owned a factory in Ohio that you sold to Acme Engine and received unregistered Acme Engine Stock as part of the payment. After holding the shares for two years you could sell them under this rule. The details such as permissible amounts and time factors are the same as in Rule 144. In short, these two rules are the same except for the manner in which the stock was acquired.

Rule 147

This rule covers "intrastate offerings" and allows sales that meet the limits of the rule to be made without registration with the SEC. (Note: the offering must comply with the laws of the particular state.)

A company wishes to offer shares of stock in Texas. To qualify as an intrastate offering the following requirements must be met:

1. The offering may be made only to bona fide Texas residents.
2. The buyers may not sell these shares to non-Texas residents for a period of nine months.

3. The principal office of the issuing company must be in Texas (although it may be incorporated elsewhere).
4. Eighty percent of the proceeds of the offering must be used in Texas.
5. Eighty percent of the corporate assets must be in Texas.
6. Eighty percent of the corporation's revenue must be earned in Texas.

Intrastate offerings are rare as few corporations would meet these stringent requirements.

Rule 237

This infrequently used rule permits the limited sale of unregistered securities of a company that has not filed the necessary reports with the SEC. The holder may sell the lesser of up to 1% of the outstanding stock or $50,000 in value in a 12-month period provided:

1. The SEC is notified ten days before the sale.
2. The corporation has been in existence for five years.
3. The seller has owned the securities for five years.
4. The sale price is negotiated without the service of a broker or dealer.

REGISTERED OFFERINGS

We have devoted much study to issues that can be offered without SEC registration. Let us now turn our attention to offerings that require registration. A requirement for issuance of debt securities is found in the Trust Indenture Act of 1939, which is an amendment to the Securities Act of 1933. In order to provide investors with necessary information, this law requires that an offering of debt securities in the amount of $1,000,000 or more be made under a trust indenture. The indenture is the contract between the issuing corporation and the investors and contains all necessary information regarding the issue (amount, interest rate, collateral, etc.). This indenture must appoint one or more trustees who have no conflict of interest. As additional protection for the bondholders, the trustees must make an annual report to the SEC showing that they continue to act in this capacity.

The most effective way to understand the procedure of making a public offering of securities is to take a hypothetical deal from step one to its conclusion.

Suppose ten years ago you and three friends established the Acme Toy Company, Inc., to manufacture, sell, and distribute dolls, stuffed animals, and other toy products. You would probably have had a small amount of authorized stock, perhaps 1,000 shares, and would have issued perhaps 400 shares, 100 shares for each of the four founders. You would each have owned 25% of the equity of the corporation.

ACME TOY COMPANY, INC. COMMON STOCK	
Authorized	1,000 shares
Issued and Outstanding	400 shares

After ten years of growth you may now wish to expand your business by constructing a new factory in California. You estimate the cost to be about $10,000,000. As your company needs long-term capital, you would approach an investment banker (had you required short-term financing, you would have used a commercial bank, such as Citibank or Harris Trust).

You approach Goldman Sachs Group, Inc. and detail your needs. Goldman Sachs would research your company, as well as the toy industry and general market conditions, and make a recommendation as to how the needed capital could be raised. They might suggest that Acme Toy would be worth a total value of $20,000,000 in the marketplace and that the $10,000,000 could be raised by selling half the company. Although the four founders would own only half the stock, the company would be larger, Also, there would be a public market for the shares, allowing them to sell some of their holdings should they so desire. To implement the sale, the capitalization would have to be increased and the current stock split accordingly. By amending the charter the new capital structure might look like this:

ACME TOY COMPANY, INC.
COMMON STOCK

Authorized	3,000,000 shares
Issued and Outstanding	1,000,000 shares

The four founders would each now own 250,000 shares, still representing 25% of the total. However, with the assistance of Goldman Sachs, the company would now make a public offering of an additional 1,000,000 shares. After the offering there would be 2,000,000 shares outstanding and our founders would own a total of 50% of this now larger publicly held company. This offering would be a primary offering as the shares are being sold by the issuing company. Should the founders wish to sell some of their shares, that would be a secondary offering and the proceeds of the sale would go to the shareholders not the issuer. Many offerings are part primary and part secondary.

Goldman Sachs would be the managing underwriter of the offering and would proceed as follows:

Step I - Registration

A registration statement covering the issue would be filed with the SEC for a minimum of 20 days until the effective date. This is the date on which the SEC tells the issuer that the registration statement is effective and that the public offering may commence. In fact the time could be longer, but the minimum period is 20 days.

Note: In February 1982 the SEC enacted Rule 415, which permits major companies to file what are called "shelf" registrations. This rule permits the larger public companies to file a single registration statement covering anticipated financing needs for a two-year period. The securities can be brought to market at any time during that period in whole or in part as the company desires. This rule, by not requiring a separate filing for each offering, allows issuers to move quickly when market conditions are advantageous.

Step II - Issuance of Red Herring

Part of the registration statement is a preliminary prospectus called the "red herring" because of the red legend on the cover that notes the incomplete nature of the information. Red herrings contain much information regarding the offering, but seldom contain the price, which is normally determined on the offering date based on then current market conditions. This preliminary prospectus can be used to familiarize potential investors with many facts about the issuing company.

Step III - Formation of the Underwriting Group (Syndicate)

Goldman Sachs, the manager, would invite other investment bankers to participate in this offering. Perhaps 30 or 40 firms would be asked to participate in order to give broad distribution to the shares and create interest in the company in the financial community. Goldman Sachs would take the largest amount, perhaps 200,000 shares, and would offer participation to the other firms in varying amounts known as "brackets." Our syndicate might include, in part, the following firms:

Firms	Shares to Be Underwritten
Goldman Sachs Group, Inc.	200,000
Bear Stearns Companies, Inc.	50,000
Deutsche Bank Securities, Inc.	50,000
Keefe, Bruyette & Woods, Inc.	50,000
Merrill Lynch & Co.., Inc.	50,000
Swiss American Securities, Inc.	50,000
A.G. Edwards	40,000
William Blair & Co.	40,000
Legg Mason, Inc.	40,000
Prudential Securities, Inc.	40,000

Other firms would be invited to underwrite smaller amounts. Note that in each bracket the firms are listed alphabetically. Firms are quite conscious about the bracket in which they appear and would seldom accept a position they felt to be below their dignity.

The underwriters do not sign any final commitment but do sign an agreement among underwriters which gives the manager, Goldman Sachs, complete authority to make the decisions regarding the offering.

Step IV - Due Diligence Meeting

This is a meeting between the issuing corporation and the underwriters to discuss the offering. Although the offering price is not set at this meeting, it gives the underwriters the opportunity to further investigate the issuer and protect the interests of their clients.

Step V - "Blue-skying" the Issue

"Blue sky" laws are the security laws of the various states. In order to offer new issues in a state you must comply with its requirements. The manager provides the underwriters with a "blue sky list," which informs them of the status in each state. The issue may not be blue-skied in all states and, therefore, the sale of shares in those states would constitute a violation.

Step VI - The Public Offering

The manager would be in constant touch with the SEC and might be told, for example, that the registration statement will be effective next Wednesday. The manager would call a meeting of the underwriters on that morning, at which time the price would be determined. Perhaps the agreement would call for the underwriters to purchase the securities from the corporation at $10 per share and offer them to the public at $11 per share. This would allow a gross profit—called the "gross spread"—of $1 per share on the 1,000,000 shares. Those under-writers agreeing to the terms would sign an underwriting agreement in which each firm would agree to purchase their portion of the issue and reoffer it to the public. Each underwriter acts severally but not jointly, meaning each is responsible only for its own stock. Thus, William Blair & Co. agrees to purchase 40,000 shares from the company at $10 each but is not liable for the shares underwritten by the other firms.

Goldman Sachs would take a management fee, perhaps $0.10 on all shares underwritten, so our offering to this point would appear:

$11.00	Offering Price to Public
– $10.00	Paid to Ace Toy
$ 1.00	Gross Spread
– $ 0.10	Management Fee
$ 0.90	Underwriter's Fee

The final prospectus would now be published and sent to any purchasers of the shares. Any omission or misrepresentation of fact in this document would bring about liability to those responsible under the 1933 act. A "tombstone ad" might appear in the newspapers the next day announcing the offering. This ad is not an offering to sell the shares but a matter of record only.

If the demand for these shares is so great that they are immediately sold, the manager would terminate the offering, and the shares would begin to trade in what is called the "after-market," which is the over-the-counter market after the public offering has been completed.

On May 23, 2004, Rule 2790 of the NASD became effective. This rule seeks to protect the integrity of the public offering process by regulating how Initial Public Offerings (IPOs) are allocated regardless of secondary-market pricing. There are two significant changes in the Rule. First, firms must receive from each person and account, within 12 months prior to any allocation of an IPO, a representation that the person or account is eligible as a non-restricted person to receive new issue securities.

The definition of a "restricted person" covers several categories. The Rule defines the term to include members or other broker/dealers. This includes broker/dealer personnel. This is further defined to include any officer, director, general partner, associated person, or employee of a member or any other broker/dealer. Agents of a member or any other broker/dealer are "restricted persons" if they are engaged in the investment banking or securities business. "Restricted persons" also include immediate family members, as well as anyone employed by or associated with the member or an affiliate of the member. It also includes anyone who has the ability to control the allocation of the new issue.

The Rule went even further to include finders and fiduciaries as "restricted persons." Those acting in a fiduciary capacity would include managing underwriters, including but not limited to attorneys, accountants, and financial consultants. The Rule also treats as a "restricted" person an immediate family member of a finder or fiduciary if the finder or fidu-ciary materially supports, or receives support from, the immediate family member. The Rule defines as a "restricted person" any person who has the authority to buy or sell securities for a bank, savings and loan institution, insurance company, investment company, investment advisor, or collective investment account. Rule 2790 excluded a person who has authority to buy or sell securities for an investment club or a family investment vehicle.

The second change allows restricted persons who hold an interest in a collective investment, such as a private investment fund, that receives an IPO allocation provided such restrictions to hold no more than 10% of the account's beneficial interest.

The term "immediate family member" is defined as a person's parents, mother-in-law or father-in-law, spouse, brother or sister, brother-in-law or sister-in law, son-in-law or daughter-in-law, children, and any other individual to whom the person provided material support. Notably absent are aunts, uncles, and cousins.

Since the restrictions apply to all IPOs, the old term "Hot Issues" is no longer viable.

As with any Rule or Regulation, there are exceptions and/or exemptions. The following is a list of the general exemptions:

1. An investment company registered under the Investment Company Act of 1940.
2. A common trust fund or similar fund as described in Section 3(a)(12)(A)(iii) of the Securities Exchange Act of 1934, provided that: (i) the fund has investments from 1,000 or more accounts, and (ii) the fund does not limit beneficial interests in the fund principally to trust accounts of restricted persons.
3. An insurance company general, separate, or investment account, provided: (i) account is funded by premiums from 1,000 or more policyholders or if a general account, the insurance company has 1,000 or more policyholders, and (ii) the insurance company does not limit the policyholders whose premiums are used to fund the account principally to restricted persons, or if a general account, the insurance company does not limit its policyholders principally to restricted persons.
4. An account, including a fund, limited partnership, joint back office broker-dealer or other entity, if the beneficial interests of restricted persons do not exceed in the aggregate 10% of the account.
5. A publicly traded entity (other than a broker-dealer authorized to engage in the public offering of new issues either as a selling group member or underwriter, or an affiliate of such a broker-dealer) that is: (i) listed on a U.S. national securities exchange, (ii) traded on the NASDAQ National Market, or (iii) a non-U.S. issuer whose securities meet the quantitative designation criteria for listing on a national securities exchange or trading on the NASDAQ National Market.
6. An investment company organized under the laws of a non-U.S. jurisdiction, provided that: (i) the investment company is listed on a non-U.S. exchange or authorized for sale to the public by a non-U.S. regulatory authority, and (ii) no person owning 5% or more of the shares of the investment company is a restricted person.
7. An ERISA benefits plan that is qualified under Section 401(a) of the Internal Revenue Code, provided that the plan is not sponsored solely by a broker-dealer.
8. A state or municipal government benefits plan that is subject to state or municipal regulation.
9. A tax-exempt charitable organization under Section 501(c)(3) of the Internal Revenue Code.
10. A church plan under Section 414(e) of the Internal Revenue Code.

We have had a successful offering. How did it come about? Let's give large credit to the manager, Goldman Sachs, that handled the deal. Goldman Sachs had full authority over the syndicate and told the members how much of the stock they were underwriting they could retain for their own sales. Perhaps they were told that they had 50% retention. Therefore, Goldman Sachs though responsible for 200,000, shares retained only 100,000. Bear Stearns and the other firms underwriting 50,000 had only 25,000 to sell, and the 40,000 share bracket retained only 20,000. The balance, 500,000 shares (50% of the 1,000,000), is put into the "pot," which the manager attempts to distribute on behalf of the underwriting syndicate. If the manager succeeds, the deal is half sold and the offering is on its way to a happy conclusion.

The manager distributes the pot in two ways:

Group Sales

These are large sales made normally to financial institutions on behalf of the group. Dreyfus Fund wishes to purchase 30,000 shares of Ace Toy. Rather than contact each underwriter separately, they go to Goldman Sachs and request 30,000 shares. If Goldman Sachs gives them the shares, the credit is allocated to each underwriter in proportion to its position in the deal. (At times the institution is permitted to designate the credit to those firms that it wishes to repay for financial services rendered.)

Selling Group This consists of other investment bankers who wish to receive a portion of the issue for their clients. Perhaps Fidelity Brokerage requests 3,000 shares for its clients. As Fidelity is not an underwriter of this issue, Goldman Sachs Group, Inc. may give them the shares in the selling group. They would be sold to Fidelity at $11, less a selling concession of perhaps $0.30 per share. Fidelity must offer the shares at $11 and cannot engage in free-riding or withholding. They will earn a profit of $0.30 per share, which is, of course, less than the underwriter's profit because the selling group member does not bear the underwriting risk.

If there was no stock left in the pot, Fidelity could have contacted any of the underwriters and attempted to buy shares less the reallowance. The reallowance is set by the manager and in this case may be $0.20 per share. If American Swiss Securities, Inc., had some unsold shares they might sell them to Fidelity at $11 less $0.20 reallowance. Fidelity would not make as much as they would have with the selling concession, but they will have filled their customers' orders. The breakdown of our offering now looks like this:

$11.00	Offering Price to Public
− $10.00	Price to Ace Toy
$ 1.00	Gross Spread
− $ .10	Management Fee
$ .90	
− $ .30	Selling Concession ($0.20 Reallowance)
$ .60	Underwriting

The $.60 underwriting is the minimum profit received by the members of the syndicate if the offering succeeds.

The manager also keeps in close touch with the underwriters and might take stock away from one that is not moving it and give it to another who has demand. Note: Dealers cannot sell a security until the effective date. Prior to that time they may only accept "indications of interest" from clients and must contact the person again when the securities are offered.

The manager has other methods at his disposal to assist the offering.

Overallotting

This is in fact the short selling of the issue. The manager causes more shares to be sold than the total amount of the deal. Thus, with no securities left in the pot, Goldman Sachs continues to give stock to institutions for group sales and to dealers in the selling group. They build up an overallottment, or short position, of 70,000 shares that they will have to buy back in the aftermarket, thereby giving support to the offering. If they are wrong in their assessment of the offering, a large loss could result. If the manager shorted 70,000 shares and the stock began trading at $15, the short position would have to be covered at the higher price. The resulting loss would be shared by the underwriters in proportion to their position.

Often a new issue contains a "green shoe" clause, which allows the manager an option to increase the size of the offering generally by 10% to 15% under the same terms and condi- tions. If our Ace Toy offering of 1,000,000 shares had a 10% green shoe, Goldman Sachs could have increased the offering to 1,100,000 shares. They could then have overallotted up to 100,000 shares without concern, and, if the stock did begin trading at $15, they could exercise the green shoe option to cover the short. (The term "green shoe" comes from the first offering that used this marketing device, Green Shoe Manufacturing Co.)

Stabilization

This is artificially supporting the price of a new issue in the aftermarket. Though it would appear to violate usual SEC policy, which prohibits market manipulation, it is permitted as it may prevent a new issue from declining in value to the detriment of the investors. If, on the offering date of our Ace Toy shares, the manager felt that the deal was not fully sold it would employ a securities dealer to make a bid in the open market at or below (never above) the public offering price, thus holding the price at or near the offering level. By bidding $11 or perhaps 10.85 the offering price would be reasonable and the underwriters could continue to make sales at $11. They would have to sell the shares remaining in the syndicate plus those repurchased in the course of the stabilization. The procedure may not succeed as the syndicate may buy shares back faster than the underwriters are selling them. In that case, the manager will cease the stabilization and let the price fall. The underwriters will lose money, but that is the risk they have been paid to take.

Stabilization is often made with a syndicate penalty bid, which means that underwriters will be penalized their profit on any shares that their clients resold to the syndicate during stabilization. As the purchaser did not hold the securities, the underwriter did not do a proper job of distribution. The loss of profit to the underwriter is not as disturbing as the harm done to the firm's reputation as an effective distributor of securities.

Had our offering been successful, the underwriters would have made a gross profit of $1,000,000. Management fees, expenses, and selling concessions would have been deducted from this, but the net profit would have been substantial. Sometimes an underwriter is given warrants for the company stock as further compensation. Warrants given to underwriters cannot have a life longer than five years and cannot be exercisable below the public offering price. On our Ace Toy deal, the underwriter could have received five-year warrants exercisable at $11 per share.

Best Efforts Offering

We have been discussing a "firm" underwriting in which the investment bankers actually buy the shares from the company guaranteeing the price ($10 per share in our example). Some offerings do not contain this guarantee and are called "best efforts" offerings. In this case the investment banker pledges to use his best efforts but makes no guarantee. In a best efforts offering the banker works as an agent and is paid a commission for whatever he sells but has no liability for the unsold portion.

Frequently, a best efforts offering is done on an "all or none" basis, meaning that no sales are final unless the entire issue is sold. The banker might attempt to sell 500,000 shares "all or none." As clients purchase shares their money is placed in escrow. At the end of an agreed period, usually 30 days, the money is given to the issuer if all shares have been sold or returned to the investor if less than the agreed amount was placed.

Mini-Max Offering

A further variation is a "mini-max" offering. This type of offering will be for a minimum number of shares but may reach a higher maximum. For example, a mini-max of 200,000 to 400,000 shares requires that at least 200,000 shares be placed but that the total could grow to as much as 400,000 shares.

Underwriters prepare for unexpected negative developments through a "market out" clause. This permits the offering to be canceled if some adverse event occurs with the issuing company or should market conditions not permit the offering to be made successfully.

Standby Offerings

These are done in connection with rights offerings made by a corporation to its shareholders. Should the Long Island Power Authority (LIPA) offer rights to its shareholders to purchase additional stock at $13 per share, the company might employ investment bankers to insure the success of the offering. If the LIPA stock remains above $13, the rights would be attractive. However, should the price fall below the subscription level, the new shares would not be purchased. The investment bankers are paid a fee to stand by and agree to purchase any unsubscribed shares. The bankers will buy rights from holders who do not wish to use them and will sell the shares represented by these rights to their clients. In this way the issuing company is guaranteed that they will receive the money for the new shares.

ANSWER SHEET FOR CHAPTER 4 EXAMINATION

1. Ⓐ Ⓑ Ⓒ Ⓓ   11. Ⓐ Ⓑ Ⓒ Ⓓ   21. Ⓐ Ⓑ Ⓒ Ⓓ
2. Ⓐ Ⓑ Ⓒ Ⓓ   12. Ⓐ Ⓑ Ⓒ Ⓓ   22. Ⓐ Ⓑ Ⓒ Ⓓ
3. Ⓐ Ⓑ Ⓒ Ⓓ   13. Ⓐ Ⓑ Ⓒ Ⓓ   23. Ⓐ Ⓑ Ⓒ Ⓓ
4. Ⓐ Ⓑ Ⓒ Ⓓ   14. Ⓐ Ⓑ Ⓒ Ⓓ   24. Ⓐ Ⓑ Ⓒ Ⓓ
5. Ⓐ Ⓑ Ⓒ Ⓓ   15. Ⓐ Ⓑ Ⓒ Ⓓ   25. Ⓐ Ⓑ Ⓒ Ⓓ
6. Ⓐ Ⓑ Ⓒ Ⓓ   16. Ⓐ Ⓑ Ⓒ Ⓓ   26. Ⓐ Ⓑ Ⓒ Ⓓ
7. Ⓐ Ⓑ Ⓒ Ⓓ   17. Ⓐ Ⓑ Ⓒ Ⓓ   27. Ⓐ Ⓑ Ⓒ Ⓓ
8. Ⓐ Ⓑ Ⓒ Ⓓ   18. Ⓐ Ⓑ Ⓒ Ⓓ   28. Ⓐ Ⓑ Ⓒ Ⓓ
9. Ⓐ Ⓑ Ⓒ Ⓓ   19. Ⓐ Ⓑ Ⓒ Ⓓ   29. Ⓐ Ⓑ Ⓒ Ⓓ
10. Ⓐ Ⓑ Ⓒ Ⓓ   20. Ⓐ Ⓑ Ⓒ Ⓓ   30. Ⓐ Ⓑ Ⓒ Ⓓ

31. Ⓐ Ⓑ Ⓒ Ⓓ   41. Ⓐ Ⓑ Ⓒ Ⓓ
32. Ⓐ Ⓑ Ⓒ Ⓓ   42. Ⓐ Ⓑ Ⓒ Ⓓ
33. Ⓐ Ⓑ Ⓒ Ⓓ   43. Ⓐ Ⓑ Ⓒ Ⓓ
34. Ⓐ Ⓑ Ⓒ Ⓓ   44. Ⓐ Ⓑ Ⓒ Ⓓ
35. Ⓐ Ⓑ Ⓒ Ⓓ   45. Ⓐ Ⓑ Ⓒ Ⓓ
36. Ⓐ Ⓑ Ⓒ Ⓓ   46. Ⓐ Ⓑ Ⓒ Ⓓ
37. Ⓐ Ⓑ Ⓒ Ⓓ   47. Ⓐ Ⓑ Ⓒ Ⓓ
38. Ⓐ Ⓑ Ⓒ Ⓓ   48. Ⓐ Ⓑ Ⓒ Ⓓ
39. Ⓐ Ⓑ Ⓒ Ⓓ   49. Ⓐ Ⓑ Ⓒ Ⓓ
40. Ⓐ Ⓑ Ⓒ Ⓓ   50. Ⓐ Ⓑ Ⓒ Ⓓ

CHAPTER 4 EXAMINATION

1. A managing underwriter could stabilize a new stock issue offered at 21 by bidding:

   I.   20.85
   II. 21
   III. 21.50
   IV. 22.50

   (A) I and II only
   (B) II only
   (C) II and III only
   (D) I and IV only

2. In the distribution of a new issue, a dealer acting as an underwriter is said to have a:

   (A) firm market
   (B) divided account
   (C) free ride
   (D) firm commitment

3. In a best efforts distribution of a new nonexempt issue, a broker/dealer:

   (A) may allow a selling concession to a bank or trust company
   (B) agrees to buy the issue at a specified price
   (C) is not required to use an offering circular or prospectus
   (D) acts as an agent for the issuer

4. An issuer who has sold securities that have been registered under the Securities Act of 1933 may state which of the following?

   I.   The securities have been approved by the SEC.
   II. The SEC has passed on the accuracy of the information in the prospectus.
   III. The SEC has passed on the adequacy of the information in the prospectus.
   IV. The SEC has passed on the merits of the securities as an investment.

   (A) I only
   (B) I and II only
   (C) II, III, and IV only
   (D) None of the above

5. Assuming that the information contained in a registration statement is complete and accurate, the registration statement will become effective:

   (A) 10 days after it is received by the SEC
   (B) 20 days after it is received by the SEC
   (C) 30 days after it is received by the SEC
   (D) only after the SEC specifically clears the issue in writing to the principal underwriter

<u>Questions 6 and 7 are based on the following information:</u> A company is offering stock to the public for the first time. The registration statement lists 150,000 shares to be sold at $400 per share. The company conducts business in a 100-mile radius that includes towns in two neighboring states.

6. The preliminary prospectus for this offering must contain all of the following information EXCEPT:

   (A) a notice in red ink to the effect that the prospectus has not been approved by the SEC
   (B) a section describing how the funds from the sale are to be used
   (C) a statement of the company's assets and liabilities
   (D) the price at which the issue is being offered

7. If the underwriter decides to offer the issue to the public in the two neighboring states, which of the following is (are) true?

   I.   The issue must be registered only in the company's home state.
   II. The issue can be sold only by registered representatives licensed in the states in which the issue is sold.
   III. The underwriter must publish a tombstone ad in all three states.
   IV. The issue must meet any existing blue sky requirements of all three states.

   (A) I only
   (B) II and IV only
   (C) IV only
   (D) III and IV only

8. Goldman Sachs offers 3,000,000 shares of Class Clothing Corp. common stock at $27 per share. The next day an advertisement appears in the *Wall Street Journal* announcing the offering and listing the names of some of the underwriting firms. This ad is commonly referred to as a:

   (A) public offering
   (B) tombstone ad
   (C) sales directive
   (D) syndicate announcement

9. For what period of time does a Form 144 remain in effect?

   (A) 30 days
   (B) 60 days
   (C) 90 days
   (D) one year

10. A corporation has 3,500,000 shares of common stock outstanding and its trading volume over the last few weeks has been as follows:

    Week 1 – 43,000
    Week 2 – 30,900
    Week 3 – 37,500
    Week 4 – 42,600
    Week 5 – 33,000 (most recent week)

    If an affiliated person wanted to liquidate some of his holding of 100,000 shares pursuant to SEC Rule 144, how many shares could he sell?

    (A) 35,000
    (B) 36,000
    (C) 37,400
    (D) 38,500

11. A trust instrument drawn pursuant to the Trust Indenture Act of 1939 sets forth:

    I. the duties of the trustee
    II. the rights of the stockholders
    III. the obligations of the issuing corporation
    IV. the regulation of the NASD

    (A) I and II only
    (B) III and IV only
    (C) I and III only
    (D) I, II, III, and IV

12. The free-riding and withholding rules apply to:

    (A) any OTC security
    (B) any new issue that sells at a premium
    (C) any new issue that sells at a discount
    (D) no longer applicable

13. In a firm commitment offering, any shares that are not sold are:

    (A) returned to the issuing corporation
    (B) listed in the over-the-counter market
    (C) transferred to treasury stock
    (D) owned by the members of the syndicate

14. In a securities underwriting a participating firm is said to be liable severally but not jointly. This type of underwriting is called:

    (A) a Western account
    (B) an Eastern account
    (C) a best efforts offering
    (D) an all or none offering

15. In the offering of new securities, members of the syndicate are permitted to sell to other dealers less the reallowance. The amount of the reallowance is determined by the:

    (A) NASD
    (B) issuing corporation
    (C) syndicate manager
    (D) SEC

16. Under Rule 415 a corporation may file a single registration statement with the SEC covering its anticipated financing need for the next:

    (A) one year
    (B) two years
    (C) three years
    (D) five years

17. A client who has been classified as a restricted person according to Rule 2790 of the NASD may purchase equity securities of an IPO except:

    (A) to purchase securities to avoid dilution
    (B) the new issue of securities are purchased pursuant to a stand-by agreement
    (C) the transaction is exempt by an order of the NASD
    (D) the new issues of securities are purchased pursuant to a best effort basis

18. An ERISA benefits plan qualified under Section 401(a) of the Internal Review Code may:

    (A) purchase any IPO security provided the plan is not sponsored solely by a broker/dealer
    (B) apply for an exemption
    (C) only purchase securities rated "A" or better
    (D) purchase only securities issued by the state or federal government

19. The term "secondary market" refers to:

    (A) trading in issues of low quality
    (B) trading in outstanding issues
    (C) issues that banks are not permitted to underwrite
    (D) private placements

20. An issuer is most likely to request an investment letter from the purchaser in connection with an offering of:

    (A) a hot issue
    (B) a mutual fund
    (C) a private placement
    (D) an exempt security

21. In distribution of a new issue underwriters or selling group members are prohibited from:

    (A) selling to the public at the so-called public offering price
    (B) selling to another broker or dealer so that the other broker or dealer can fill an accommodation order
    (C) withholding blocks of a new issue in the member's account
    (D) doing all of the above

22. Generally, the purpose of the Securities Act of 1933 is to:

    (A) regulate the activities of investment advisors
    (B) regulate the sale of securities on national exchanges
    (C) provide for disclosure of information about new securities offerings
    (D) provide for disclosure of the financial condition of underwriters

23. Provisions of SEC Rule 145 would normally apply to an exchange of one security for another as a result of:

    (A) a stock split
    (B) a change in par value
    (C) a merger
    (D) a "no-sale" ruling issued by the SEC

24. Which of the following would not be subject to the holding period restrictions under Rule 144?

    (A) restricted stock acquired via investment letter
    (B) restricted stock acquired via stock option plan
    (C) restricted stock acquired via private placement
    (D) restricted stock acquired via open market purchase

25. Which of the following does not describe an underwriting procedure?

    (A) best efforts
    (B) all or none
    (C) standby
    (D) fill or kill

26. If a new issue is being offered in a corporation's home state and two neighboring states:

    I.   the issue must be registered in all three states
    II. registered representatives soliciting purchase must be registered in any state where they ask for orders
    III. the underwriters must publish a tombstone in all three states
    IV. registration with the SEC under the 1933 act makes state registration unnecessary

    (A) I and II only
    (B) I, II, and III only
    (C) III and IV only
    (D) II and IV only

27. The registration requirements of the federal securities acts protect the public interest by providing for a prospectus on new issues and its review by the SEC before publication. This:

    (A) provides the SEC with adequate information on which to base its approval of new issues
    (B) does not imply SEC approval of the issue
    (C) guarantees purchasers against an untrue statement of material fact or an omission of material fact
    (D) relieves participating underwriters from any further responsibility for checking essential facts before recommending purchase to their customers

28. In order for an offering to qualify as an intrastate offering under Rule 147:

    (A) 80% of the proceeds of the offering must be used in that state
    (B) 80% of the corporation's assets must be located in that state
    (C) 80% of the corporate revenues must be earned in that state
    (D) all of the above are required

29. Under what conditions may an NASD member firm sell an IPO to an employee of another broker/dealer?

    (A) if the amount of the purchase is small and the transaction accords with the employee's normal investment practice
    (B) if the member firm notifies the other broker/dealer of the transaction
    (C) if the employing broker/dealer guarantees that resale of the securities acquired by its employee will be restricted for two years
    (D) under no circumstances

30. A provision under which an underwriter can cancel a proposed public offering due to some unforeseen occurrence is known as a:

    (A) blue sky provision
    (B) contra-market clause
    (C) fill or kill provision
    (D) market-out clause

31. In stabilizing a new issue, the manager may make a "syndicate penalty bid." This means that:

    (A) the underwriter will be penalized his profit on any securities repurchased from his clients
    (B) all stock purchased will be returned to the issuing corporation
    (C) the manager will charge the syndicate the value of the shares
    (D) any shares repurchased will be added to the treasury stock of the issuing corporation

32. The Securities Act of 1933 provides for:

    (A) extension of credit in the securities industry
    (B) establishment of the Securities and Exchange Commission
    (C) regulation of new issues of securities
    (D) all of the above

33. The gross spread in a new issue depends upon:

    I.   the amount of the issue
    II. the business of the corporation
    III. the type of industry it is engaged in
    IV. the past record of the company

    (A) I and III only
    (B) II only
    (C) II and IV only
    (D) I, II, III, and IV

34. In a registered public offering of 500,000 shares at $36, 300,000 shares were authorized but unissued and 200,000 shares were sold on behalf of an affiliated person. From this information, it is evident:

    I.   the entire proceeds of the offering accrue to the corporation
    II. 300,000 shares are identified as a primary distribution
    III. 60% of the proceeds are paid to the corporation while the balance accrues to the affiliated person
    IV. the entire offering is a primary distribution

    (A) I and IV only
    (B) I and III only
    (C) II and III only
    (D) II and IV only

35. Blue sky laws provide for all of the following EXCEPT:

    (A) registration of representatives
    (B) registration of securities to be offered in the state
    (C) interstate mail fraud in securities offerings
    (D) registration of securities dealers

36. An excerpt from a recent tombstone ad reveals bonds offered publicly at 101. Why were they priced at a premium?

    (A) to enable investors to establish a tax loss when the bonds are redeemed at maturity
    (B) to reflect prevailing credit ratings and market conditions for an issuer of this quality
    (C) to provide the issuer with a larger deduction from pretax earnings for higher than usual interest payments
    (D) to comply with SEC rules mandating such pricing for debt issues maturing in the year 2000 and thereafter

37. Securities may be sold under SEC Rule 144 provided:

    I.   they have been owned one year prior to the sale
    II. they are sold in agency transactions only
    III. they are sold in principal transactions only
    IV. the company files regular financial data with the SEC

    (A) I only
    (B) I and IV only
    (C) I and II only
    (D) III and IV only

38. The agreement between the members of a syndicate and the manager is known as the:

    (A) agreement among underwriters
    (B) underwriting agreement
    (C) standby agreement
    (D) selling agreement

39. Details of a new stock offering state that between 1,000,000 and 1,500,000 shares will be sold depending upon market conditions. This offering is a:

    (A) best efforts
    (B) standby
    (C) mini-max
    (D) market potential

40. Each of the following is found in the final prospectus EXCEPT:

    (A) a statement as to possible stabilization by the manager
    (B) the public offering price
    (C) a copy of the underwriting agreement
    (D) a statement that the SEC neither approves nor disapproves of the issues

41. A registered representative of a firm that is an underwriter of a new offering of common stock can send to a client a copy of his firm's recent research report on that stock:

    (A) if it is accompanied by a red herring
    (B) if he has permission of his employer
    (C) if his firm is not the managing underwriter
    (D) under no conditions

42. With respect to the public offering of securities by an underwriting syndicate, which of the following is true?

    (A) the underwriting spread is greater than the selling concession
    (B) the reallowance is greater than the selling concession
    (C) the selling concession is greater than the underwriting spread
    (D) the reallowance is greater than the underwriting spread

43. Regulation A permits a short form of filing for offerings of new securities provided the total amount of the offering does not exceed:

    (A) $1,000,000
    (B) $5,000,000
    (C) $2,000,000
    (D) $2,500,000

44. Which of the following would not normally be a function of an investment banker?

    (A) providing short-term capital needs of industry
    (B) underwriting new issues of securities
    (C) providing long-term capital needs of industry
    (D) assisting in large secondary offerings of securities

45. A public offering by an investment banker in which any securities not sold are returned to the issuer is known as a(n):

    (A) firm commitment
    (B) best efforts offering
    (C) all or none offering
    (D) contingency offering

46. To qualify as an intrastate offering under SEC Rule 147, the issue:

    I.   must be approved by the SEC
    II. must be sold only to bona fide residents of one state
    III. cannot exceed $1,500,000 in value
    IV. must consist of common stock only

    (A) I, II, III, and IV
    (B) I and II only
    (C) II only
    (D) II and IV only

47. All of the following affect the public offering price of a new issue, EXCEPT:

    (A) anticipated earnings of the issuer for the next year
    (B) dividend projections for this year
    (C) the book value of the issuer
    (D) the selling group's determination of value in the prevailing market climate

48. Only one of the following holders of unregistered stock is precluded from sale of that stock under Rule 144. Who is it?

    (A) an institutional investor
    (B) an officer of the issuing corporation
    (C) a broker/dealer organization
    (D) a holder of more than 10% of the outstanding stock

49. In a registered public offering of 750,000 shares @ 40, an underwriter of 30,000 shares is advised by the manager its retention will be 70%. How many shares may the underwriter sell to its own customers?

    (A) 30,000
    (B) 21,000
    (C) 9,000
    (D) as many as it can up to a maximum of 51,000 shares

50. In a competitive bidding for mortgage bonds of a large public utility the winning underwriter is determined by:

    (A) the highest dollar amount paid to the issuer
    (B) the lowest net interest cost to the issuer
    (C) the shortest maturity date for the bonds
    (D) the refunding and sinking fund terms in the indenture

CHAPTER 4 EXAMINATION ANSWERS

1. **A** Only bids at or just below the public offering price stabilize an offering. A bid of 21.50 or 22.50 is destabilizing as it would force the price of the issue up.

2. **D** The term "underwriting" means a guarantee to the issuing corporation. The underwriter makes a firm (solid) commitment to purchase the securities. In best efforts offerings no such guarantee is made.

3. **D** Question 2 discusses a "firm" offering. In a best efforts offering the investment banker acts as agent for the issuer and makes no guarantee that the securities will all be sold.

4. **D** The SEC attempts to see only that the material provided is sufficient for a reasonable investment decision to be made by the potential investor.

5. **D** A registration statement becomes effective—meaning that the securities may now be offered to the public—when notice is received from the SEC.

6. **D** The offering price is usually determined on the offering date and does not usually appear in the preliminary prospectus.

7. **B** The state laws must be complied within any state in which the offering is to be made. These laws are usually referred to as "blue sky" laws.

8. **B** Tombstone ads are used to announce new issues, office openings, personnel additions, and the like. They do not offer to buy or sell securities, they just state the facts. The name "tombstone" indicates that they are informational only, just like a grave marker (Born 1915 - Died 1988 - Rest in Peace).

9. **C** To avoid a forced sale, stock may be sold under Rule 144 over a 90-day period.

10. **B** Under Rule 144 you can liquidate 1% of the outstanding shares or the average weekly volume for the preceding four weeks, whichever is greater. The total volume for the last four weeks was 144,000 shares. By dividing this figure by 4 we determine the average volume is 36,000 shares, which is greater than 1% of the outstanding 3,500,000 shares (35,000).

11. **C** The trust indenture does not define rights of stockholders and makes no mention of NASD regulations.

12. **D** Rule 2790 of the NASD replaced free-riding, withholding, and so-called hot issues.

13. **D** In a firm commitment the underwriter actually buys the securities from the issuing corporation. If they don't sell them, they own them and may suffer a loss.

14. **A** In a Western account each underwriter has a divided liability and is responsible only for his portion of the issue. In Eastern accounts, generally used in municipal bonds, the underwriter is responsible for a percentage of any unsold portion. This is called undivided liability.

15. **C** The reallowance as well as the selling concession given to selling group members are determined by the managing underwriters.

16. **B** The corporation can then offer these securities in whole or in part for the ensuing two years.

17. **D** All the others are exempt as listed in the general exemptions.

18. **A** An ERISA benefits plan that is qualified under Section 401(a) of the

Internal Revenue Code may purchase any IPO security, provided that the plan is not sponsored by a broker/dealer.

19. **B** "Secondary market" refers to transactions in securities after the original issue has been made. When an issuer offers new securities to the public it is referred to as a "primary offering."

20. **C** Normally, private placements are done with an investment letter.

21. **C** This practice is prohibited under NASD Rule 2790.

22. **C** The 1933 act is concerned with offerings of new securities and related matters.

23. **C** Rule 145 basically applies to mergers, consolidations, and acquisitions.

24. **D** The two-year holding period does not apply when the security was acquired in the open market. However, if the security is owned by a control person, the other provisions of Rule 144 apply.

25. **D** "Fill or kill" is an order qualifier, requesting immediate execution of the whole order or immediate cancellation. Best efforts underwritings, frequently linked to all or none, are usually seen on small new issues. Standby underwritings are utilized to guarantee the success of a rights offering.

26. **A** Underwriters aren't required to publish a tombstone anywhere, although they usually do so for prestige purposes. Also, while some states permit "registration by coordination" with an SEC filing, the SEC registration in itself does not qualify a security in any state.

27. **B** The SEC never approves an issue. They only attempt to see that sufficient information has been provided

from which a proper investment determination can be made.

28. **D** All of the choices are required for an offering to qualify as intrastate.

29. **D** An NASD member firm may not allocate shares of a hot issue to itself, to any of its employees, or to any employee of a firm that underwrites securities.

30. **D** It is used only in the case of some unusual occurrence.

31. **A** As the client sells the shares back to the syndicate shortly after the offering, the underwriter has not made a proper distribution. He, therefore, may be penalized his profit.

32. **C** Choices (A) and (B) are covered in the Securities and Exchange Act of 1934.

33. **D** The underwriting spread (or gross spread) depends upon all of the items.

34. **C** The 200,000 shares were sold on behalf of an affiliated person, so the proceeds go to that person. This makes that portion a secondary. A primary distribution is where the proceeds benefit the issues.

35. **C** Blue sky laws are state security laws and would not cover interstate regulations.

36. **B** Premiums or discounts are used in bond offerings to bring the yield on the investment in line with current market conditions.

37. **B** An overly simplified recap of Rule 144. Because either principal or agency methods may be used, II and III are clearly false. IV is always true, and I is true in the case of restricted stock. There is no holding period for control stock if acquired in an open market purchase.

38. **A** The agreement among underwriters authorizes the manager to handle

the offering, including execution of the final contract with the issuer, which is called the "underwriting agreement."

39. **C** These offerings state the minimum and maximum number of shares to be offered.

40. **C** The underwriting agreement is the formal legal contract between the issuer and the underwriting syndicate. It may be quite lengthy and is not reproduced in the prospectus, although a number of specified details usually appear in summary form. Among these are: the members of the syndicate, the portion purchased by each, the amount of underwriter's compensation, and the proceeds to the company.

41. **D** The registered representative may send the red herring but not a firm research report.

42. **A** The underwriting spread (gross spread) is the difference between the price paid to the issuer and the public offering price. The selling concession is the amount that the managing underwriter gives to dealers in the selling group. The reallowance is the amount that underwriters may give to other dealers and is less than the selling concession.

43. **B** As stated in Regulation A.

44. **A** Providing short-term capital needs of industry is normally the function of the commercial banker, not the investment banker.

45. **B** The best efforts offering is very similar to a consignment sale. The investment banker does not make any guarantee as to the success of the offering and pays for only those securities that are actually sold. Naturally, the unsold shares are returned to the issuer.

46. **C** Under Rule 147 intrastate offerings can be sold only to residents of one state and cannot be sold outside that state for nine months. All other choices are incorrect.

47. **D** The selling group has no voice in price determination.

48. **C** By definition under Rule 144. A broker/dealer cannot use Rule 144 when selling stock.

49. **B** 70% of 30,000 is retained by the dealer for their own sales. The balance, 9,000 shares, is kept in the pot by the manager.

50. **B** This is the basis for all competitive bids, which are often used for debt securities.

Direct Participation Programs and Limited Partnerships

A direct participation program is any ownership interest in a business that permits the owner to include both income and business losses on his tax form without an intervening tax. The majority of tax shelter investments are found in oil and gas, real estate, and equipment leasing. In this section, we will cover the basic concepts and characteristics of direct participation programs and the possible advantages to investors for whom this form of investment is suitable. Please note that for the Series 7 exam, "direct participation programs" and "limited partnerships" are synonyms.

LIMITED PARTNERSHIPS

A limited partnership is any syndicate, group, pool, or joint venture that is not a corporation, trust, or estate through which business is carried on. It is composed of at least one general partner who manages the day-to-day activity and who is financially responsible for the unpaid debts of the partnership. In addition, there must be at least one limited partner who shares in the profits of the partnership but whose losses are limited to the amount invested in the venture.

Limited partnerships provide tax benefits by having all profits and losses flow through to the individual partners. The partnership itself pays no taxes. The personal tax returns of the individual partners reflect the activity of the limited partnership. Some, but not all, partnerships are registered with the Securities and Exchange Commission and publish a prospectus. Others remain private and file no information with the SEC. These usually require much larger investments and are appropriate only for more affluent, knowledgeable investors.

Formation of Limited Partnerships

Limited partnerships are chartered very much like a corporation via a set of public and private documents. The document that is most like the corporate charter is called the "certificate of limited partnership." It contains:

1. the business purpose of the partnership and identifies the partnership by name, and by the name, address, and status of each general partner and each limited partner

2. financing, including contributions of money or property, by whom the contributions are made, and circumstances under which any additional contributions may be made or contributions may be returned.
3. sharing arrangements—allocation of expenses as well as profits and income
4. term of the partnership's life (the usual span is ten years)
5. provisions for changes in membership, including:
   - if interests in the partnership may be transferred and how;
   - under what circumstances new partners may be admitted; and
   - provision of continuing or dissolving business in the event of the death of a general partner.

This certificate must be signed by at least one general partner and one limited partner and filed with the state in which the partnership is organized. The certificate becomes official on the date it is filed. If there are substantial changes in the partnership, the certificate must be amended to reflect them or to reflect any error it is discovered to contain. Amendments must be filed within 30 days of the change or discovery of the error. Partnerships organized in any state must, of course, comply with the laws of that state.

The agreement of limited partnership is a contract stipulating the rights, obligations, and limitations of both the general and the limited partners. This agreement need not be filed publicly.

The subscription agreement is evidence of purchase of an interest in a limited partnership by a limited partner. It contains name, address, and social security number (or tax ID number) of the limited partners. This document also contains the limited partner's statement that he or she qualified as to net worth, and that he or she has read the prospectus and is familiar with and can accept the risks inherent in the nature of the partnership business. It grants power of attorney to the general partner to act for the limited partner in matters of the partnership.

A most important point, it is the responsibility of the registered representative to verify that a limited partner is in fact financially qualified and informed as to the risks and nature of the partnership's business.

Powers, Obligations, and Limitations on General Partners

The general partner's right to share in the rewards of the business is spelled out in detail in the partnership agreement. His obligations are to manage the business of the partnership, and to act as a fiduciary on behalf of the limited partners and in the best interest of the partnership.

The limitations placed on the general partner (sometimes called the sponsor or syndicator) shed some light on the way in which he must discharge his obligations. The general partner may never act in any way that would prevent the ordinary business of the partnership; may never buy or sell any asset of the partnership for any purpose but the partnership's business; and may never compete with the partnership for personal gain.

Specific written permission of the partnership is required before a new general or limited partner may be admitted to the partnership; before partnership business may be continued after the death, retirement, or incompetency of another general partner; before any compensation may be received from the partnership beyond that specified in the partnership agreement.

In rare cases when a general partner must act for the partnership outside of the agreement of limited partnership, a special form of permission called a "partnership democracy" is created. In the case of a legal action, for example, the notification of judgment against the partnership is required through the partnership democracy before the general partner may accept the judgment. This acceptance is called "confessing the judgment."

Rights, Obligations, and Limitations on Limited Partners

- The right to share in the profits as outlined in the certificate of limited partnership, plus the return of their capital contributions, if any remain, when the partnership is dissolved.
- Access to the books and records of the partnership.
- Periodic information about the partnership and the status of their ownership interest.
- The right to sue the general partner or to dissolve the limited partnership in certain circumstances.
- The circumstances under which the limited partner may transfer ownership interest to another person. Death transfers the limited partnership's interest to the deceased partner's estate, which now has all the rights and obligations of an owner of the partnership.

Causes of Dissolution of Limited Partnerships

The partnership agreement specifies the date on which the partnership is to be dissolved. The partnership can be dissolved prior to that date by:

- a majority vote of the limited partners
- the sale of the partnership assets
- the death or incompetency of the general partner, unless the partnership agreement provides for a replacement

In the event a limited partnership is terminated, it is the responsibility of the general partner to report the termination to the state where the partnership was formed, so that the limited partnership certificate may be canceled.

When a limited partnership is terminated, there will also be a distribution of the assets as follows:

1. secured creditors
2. general creditors
3. return of investment to limited partners
4. general partners
5. distribution of profits

If the assets are not sufficient to meet the credit obligations of the partnership, it is the responsibility of the general partners to meet these debts.

Federal Tax Qualifications for Limited Partnerships

We mentioned earlier that limited partnerships are not tax-paying entities as corporations are. Consequently, a limited partnership must differ from a corporation in at least two of six fundamental characteristics in order to meet the basis of federal tax qualification as a limited partnership.

Corporations have these six characteristics:

1. engage in business for profit
2. are associations of two or more individuals
3. have central management
4. provide limited liability
5. have perpetual life
6. are freely transferable

The first two (business for profit and two or more associates) are unavoidable in a limited partnership; the second two are too precious to give up thus most limited partnerships provide a definite term to their life and restrict transfer of assets, and in that way secure for themselves status as a limited partnership.

Federal Tax Treatment of Limited Partners

The details of the tax payment are well beyond the Series 7 exam. However, there are a number of terms that apply to partnerships and their taxation.

Basis is the partnership owner's adjusted purchase price. The total cost is comprised of any lump-sum cash contributions to the partnership, plus any periodic contributions, plus any recourse loans for which individual partners are responsible. (Nonrecourse loans, that is, loans taken out by the partnership and for which the partners are not personally responsible, may or may not be part of the basis. Tax advice is needed.)

A partner's basis is *adjusted upward* by income left in the partnership or by excess percentage depletion. This latter term will be reviewed when we talk about oil and gas programs and the kinds of depletion allowances. A partner's basis is *adjusted downward* by distributions made from partnership assets, for example, cash or property paid out, expenses that are not amortized, depletion allowances, and for losses.

Crossover describes a partnership that generates taxable income for the partners. For example, in the beginning, income is offset by depreciation and depletion; later there is an excess of income that becomes taxable. This is an example of crossover.

Phantom income is income that is taxable but not represented by any cash flow. For example, a partner gives away an ownership interest and in doing so is relieved of a debt on the interest. This debt relief is considered income by the IRS—and it is taxable.

Recapture refers to the fact that a premature sale of a partnership interest may cause certain deductions and tax credits on housing rehabilitation to be recaptured as taxable income. Since these deductions were previously used to offset otherwise taxable income, this can place quite a tax burden on the owner. Tax advice is needed.

The tax laws are quite specific about basis. Basis cannot be a negative number; thus, any tax benefits based on a partnership interest are limited to the amount "at risk" (the basis).

Deductions, depreciation, depletion and tax credits are the four most common tax benefits associated with limited partnerships. Deductions are expenses that reduce income in the year the expense occurs; depreciation and depletion represent intangible cost paid back over a period of time. Tax credits are outright deductions from the tax bill. At the present time, tax credits are limited to: (1) rehabilitations of historic buildings, and (2) low-income housing.

Deductions

Deductible items include:

- interest paid during the tax year
- real estate and sales tax
- professional fees (such as those for attorneys, accountants)
      Fees may include management or other fees paid to a general partner, but such fees may be disallowed if they are "excessive" or "not usual and necessary."
- costs of finding minerals and evaluating probable profitability of mining efforts and, naturally, general operating expenses

Some deductions cannot be taken in the year they occur, but rather must be taken in small pieces, amortized, over the life of the venture or some other period. Such a deduction is prepaid interest, in which next year's interest paid now is deductible next year, the following year's the same, and so on. For construction period and tax, the same principle applies; however, a table determines the period over which these are amortized. Prepaid fees are amortized over the life of the service they buy. Financing fees (like points) are amortized over the life of the loan, as are loan standby and loan commitment fees. Partnership organization fees (which do not include commissions and cost of sales) are amortized over 60 months.

Syndication fees are expenses that cannot be deducted at all. These are commissions and other costs of sales of a partnership: printing, legal, underwriting expense. These remain a part of the cost of the partnership, and as such reduce the taxable gain if there is any.

These deductions, either taken in the year they occur or amortized, reduce basis or shelter all or a portion of income from limited partnerships. The point at which the income from a limited partnership venture exceeds the deductible expenses is called the "crossover point."

Depreciation

Depreciation is an accounting term describing the fact that certain corporate assets simply wear out. The depreciation charge is deducted from both the value of the asset on the balance sheet and, correspondingly, from net income on the income statement.

EXAMPLE _____

Here is a business asset that costs $200,000, and has an estimated life of ten years; the depreciation is straight-line.

Balance Sheet		Income Statement	
Fixed Assets		Revenue from Sales	$850,000
Equipment:		Cost of Goods Sold	– $600,000
Cost	$200,000	Depreciation	– $ 20,000
Depreciation	– $ 20,000	Income before	
	$180,000	Interest & Taxes	$230,000

In practice, the balance sheet entry will represent accumulated depreciation; that is, the total depreciation since the asset was placed in use, whereas the income statement will represent only this year's depreciation. However, the total of the annual depreciations listed on the income statement will total the accumulated depreciation on the balance sheet.

The Tax Reform Act of 1986 (TRA of 1986) established two kinds of depreciation: straight-line and accelerated cost recovery system (ACRS). In general, straight-line must be used for real estate. Other assets permit the owner to use either straight-line or ACRS, with the amount of time and the method of ACRS defined by the IRS. In general, the General Securities Exam (GSE) does not probe into such matters because they are terribly complex—even for experts!

Two things that should be noted about depreciation: the amount that is depreciable is no longer limited to scrap value—100% of the cost is now depreciable; land is never depreciable.

The term "cost basis" is the technical expression for the amount that is depreciable. For example, the cost basis on an acquisition of a piece of developed real estate would start with the cost *plus* commissions, fees, and other acquisition charges *minus* the value of the land (which cannot be depreciated). This resulting cost basis would then be depreciated on an annual straight-line basis over the next 31.5 years (the ACRS time for real estate).

Depletion

Natural resources such as coal, oil, timber, and so on do not wear out, they get used up. The accounting term to describe the value of the resources thus used up is "depletion." Depletion allowance is the tax accounting method of providing systematic deductions for the decreasing value of an asset like a mine or a well while the minerals from it are being used up.

There are two ways of computing depletion: cost depletion and percentage depletion. *Cost depletion* is very simple. It permits the owner to deduct a portion of the money received from the sale of the products, for example, oil, until the entire cost is recovered. *Percentage depletion* is more complex. Under this accounting method, it is possible to recoup more than the original cost. The excess percentage depletion is added back to the cost of the program.

It is obvious that percentage depletion is more advantageous than cost depletion. However, it is only permitted on new oil programs. It is not permitted if the partnership also refines or markets the oil products, and it is only permitted on small wells (those with less than 1,000 barrels of oil per day).

REAL ESTATE LIMITED PARTNERSHIPS

Most real estate partnerships are sponsored by developers or brokers who become the general partner. They are compensated by commissions, management fees, and other monies associated with the management of the properties. These partnerships may invest in a variety of properties: residential (apartments, duplexes, etc.) or commercial (office buildings, warehouses, shopping centers). Large partnerships usually own a portfolio of buildings, sometimes consisting of both residential and commercial.

Investors enter real estate limited partnerships for a few basic reasons:

- to diversify some of their investment capital into an area other than stocks and bonds
- to participate in the benefits of owning the kind of real estate they have neither the capital nor the business acumen to purchase or operate on their own
- as shelter from taxes

The typical limited partnership goes through a life cycle that lasts from four to ten years, although there are no hard and fast rules on this. The typical partnership goes through this cycle:

1. The sponsor raises capital from investors.
2. The partnership is formally established, with the sponsor as general partner and the investors as limited partners.
3. The general partner purchases one or more buildings and operates them on behalf of the partnership.
4. When many of the tax benefits have been used up, and/or when the buildings have appreciated significantly, the general partner will sell the properties and distribute the proceeds according to an agreed-upon formula. The partnership ends at this point.

Generally, the return to investors comes from four sources: cash distributions, tax benefits, property appreciation, and reduction of the mortgage. Every partnership has different objectives and will stress some of these sources of benefits more than others.

Cash Distributions

Limited partnerships that buy existing income properties with tenants already in place usually generate the most cash distributions. After collecting the rents and making payments for taxes, utilities, maintenance, and the mortgage, the property may have funds left over to pay out directly to the limited partners.

Tax Benefits

Like other business enterprises, operators of real estate may deduct the costs of operations from their revenues in determining taxable income. These deductions include cash expenses like mortgage interest, salaries to building managers, maintenance expenses, and taxes. They also include a noncash expense: depreciation. Depreciation deductions very often result in the real estate operation showing a loss for tax purposes while still having cash to distribute to the partners. The partners can use the loss to shelter some of their other income.

Property Appreciation

During the life of the partnership the properties it owns may increase in resale value because of inflation, improvements to the buildings, good management, or all three.

Reduction of Mortgage Loans

Most mortgages on property are structured so that each monthly payment is part interest and part repayment of the loan principal. After five to ten years of mortgage payments the limited partnership has increased its equity in the property to a considerable extent.

All investments carry risk, and real estate tax shelters can experience problems due to interest rate changes, poor occupancy levels, costs of operations, or changes in the tax code. The key to success is the ability of the general partner to buy right, manage right, and sell right.

REAL ESTATE PROGRAMS

Real estate programs offer a wide range of benefits including tax savings, price appreciation, and income. Each type of program contains its own combination of risk elements, which add up to its degree of risk.

New construction programs provide great appreciation potential and some potential for tax savings but little or no potential for income. They do not qualify for any special category of tax savings, and the elements of risk include cost overruns, construction delays, location risk, zoning and negotiation risk, and a period of no income. If, however, these risks are avoided, the appreciation potential may be enormous.

Existing properties provide some potential for tax savings, income, and appreciation. In existing properties, tax savings arise from investment tax credits (ITCs) for rehabilitation of old or historic buildings, income potential from rents, and appreciation potential from the gain in value that has characterized real estate over the past years. Risks in existing properties are generally confined to vacancies or lease restrictions and zoning and regulatory risks.

Government-assisted housing provides little or no income or appreciation potential but can provide sizable tax savings. These savings are the result of high leverage and multiple writeoffs combined with a special schedule for accelerated depreciation and little risk of recapture. While there is the risk that government policy or tax law may change this, there is reduced risk of audit by the IRS.

Sale and Leaseback

Many real estate programs begin with sales of a property to the partnership, which then leases it back to the seller. This arrangement is called a "user leaseback" and the seller-lessee occupies the property. If the seller-lessee rents to others the arrangement is called an "operator leaseback." The usual contract in either case is a triple-rent lease, that is, a lease in which the lessee is responsible for property taxes, insurance premiums, and maintenance costs.

The benefits to the seller-lessee in such an arrangement may include the liquidity from the sale and its resulting improvement of the balance sheet as well as the ability to deduct rent as an operating expense. These are traded for the obligation represented by a long-term lease and the loss of any appreciation value in the property.

The buyer-lessor benefits through depreciation and interest deductions on any financing, which enables them to distribute cash, which is tax-free or nearly so. The lease itself and the quality of the tenant provide for ease in financing in many cases, but also represent the greatest risk—default. Appreciation potential is also retarded by the long-term lease.

Condominiums as Securities

Condominiums may be classed and regulated as securities if there is investment intent, or the part of the management is conducted by a third party or a rental pool, or if a roster exists for rental of the unit.

As a direct investment (rather than a partnership interest) condominiums are evidenced by the following documents:

- The master deed establishes the project as a whole and its purpose. It defines unit size, common areas, cost-sharing arrangements, and type of management.
- Bylaws describe management procedure, how members are elected, and the limits of their authority.
- Regulations establish rules for occupancy such as restrictions on children, animals, and noise.
- The purchase and sale agreements define the terms of the sale: what unit, what price, and how financed.
- The rental agreement establishes rental management fee and restrictions on the owner's use of the property. If owners use a condominium as a residence for more than the greater of 14 days or 10% of the number of days it is rented the IRS may declare it a residence and the owner may lose the right to claim interest and depreciation as business deductions.
- The unit deed defines what the buyer owns (the unit) and what spaces are to be shared with other investors on what terms.

Benefits of condominium securities include tax savings in the form of deductions for depreciation, management fees, interest, and operating expense. Income may result from the rental, but in most cases is subordinated to appreciation potential, which can be significant. Risks include erosion of property value, cost of management, and possible loss of business status if the venture is classed a hobby by the IRS and tax savings are disallowed.

Raw Land

Raw land provides no tax relief, no income, and is held largely for its appreciation potential. It usually generates a negative cash flow in the form of property taxes. Because it contains more uncertainties and fewer immediate rewards than other ventures, it is considered highly speculative and risky.

OIL AND GAS PROGRAMS

Oil and gas limited partnerships gained popularity with investors as oil and gas prices increased sharply in the mid 1970s. But enthusiasm for this form of investment has dampened lately in response to a softening in the price of oil. Still, owing to the long-term nature of oil and gas ventures, these partnerships may be excellent investments for some individuals.

Oil and gas partnerships usually take one of the following forms:

- drilling programs: these drill a number of test wells in hopes of discovering commercially viable resources
- income programs: these buy the rights to proven, producing wells

Of the two types, drilling programs are the most popular, despite higher risks. Registered drilling programs became available to small investors in the late 1960s, with minimum investments of $5,000 to $10,000. These programs are usually sponsored by operating oil companies, which act as the general partner. Once the sponsor raises a large pool of capital from limited partners, it typically will expend that capital over a one- to two-year period on a number of test wells. Test wells that prove productive give the partnership a stream of income over the life of the wells (which may be 10 to 25 years).

There are different types of drilling partnerships: Exploratory partnerships are wildcat ventures that explore for new fields. These are the riskiest forms of drilling, but the most profitable if successful. Developmental partnerships concentrate their test wells adjacent to areas of proven reserves. These are the least risky—and also the least rewarding. Balanced partnerships do both exploratory and developmental drilling.

Limited partners in drilling programs look to two sources of investment benefits, the extent of which depends on the success of test wells and good management practices by the general partner.

- *Tax deductions*: The investors' capital is expended in a way that allows the individual limited partner to deduct most of his investment from his personal taxable income over the first two years.
- *Tax-advantaged income*: Income from sales of oil and gas is not fully taxed due to the "oil depletion allowance."

Oil and gas programs also offer potential for appreciation, income, and tax savings. Exploratory programs provide tax savings through ITCs and, if successful, may provide income sheltered by the depletion allowance, a large potential appreciation. These are in essence "wildcatters," who drill for new discoveries or to extend existing fields. High initial expenses, dry holes, long delays before return, and recapture of investor depreciation cost (IDCs) upon sale are the risks such programs face.

Developmental programs seek to add to proven reserves in an existing field. They provide the benefits of tax relief from IDCs and good probability of income, sheltered partially by the depletion allowance. Their risks include high base costs, delays before return, and recapture of IDCs on sales.

Income programs sell oil or gas from properties bought or leased. They provide as a benefit income partially sheltered, but, because they don't drill, there is little or no tax savings and little appreciation potential (unless the price of the natural resource rises). The risks lie largely in inaccurate estimates of proven reserves and subsequent overpriced leases or properties.

Combined, or balanced, programs structure themselves as percentages of exploratory, developmental, or income to provide the mix of benefits and or risks suited to a particular set of objectives.

Allocating Costs and Revenues; Sharing Arrangements

These are methods of dividing costs and profits, and, if you will, are incentives for the limited partner to risk capital and the general partner to succeed. A purchased interest is one in which the general partner pays all or part of the expenses. More usual is a carried interest in which someone else (the limited partner) pays the lease or purchase price of the property and the expenses of exploration and production.

The overriding royalty interest is a carried interest in which the general partner (sponsor) takes ⅛ or ¹⁄₁₆ of revenue off the top (overriding royalty) leaving the rest for the limited partners (and expenses).

In the revisionary working interest, also a carried interest, limited partners recover expenses before the distribution of ⅛ or ¹⁄₁₆ to the general partner. All other revenues revert to the limited partners.

The net operating profits interest is carried also, but production expenses are deducted from gross revenues before anything goes to the general partner. The remainder, of course, goes to the limited partners.

The disproportionate sharing interest is purchased normally at 25% of the costs of the program. It's "disproportionate" because the general partner takes 50% of the revenues.

In functional allocation the general partner pays nondeductible costs like organization of the partnership, capitalized and amortized costs like leases and equipment, and 1% of IDCs; the limited partners pay 99% of IDCs and half the operating costs. The split is usually 40/60 or 50/50 of the revenues, with the general partners receiving the larger portion. The limited partners, however, get all the juicy tax savings while sharing in income and capital appreciation.

EQUIPMENT LEASING PROGRAMS

In the past, equipment leasing programs have been popular where there is a need for the equipment and when it is economically more advantageous to the company to lease rather than buy the equipment. Almost all forms of equipment have been the subject of leasing agreements.

It is beyond the scope of this supplement to concentrate on the reasons why companies choose to lease. In short, they save the capital cost of the equipment, spread out the lease payments over time, and avoid the "headaches" of ownership.

The buyer-lessor of the equipment does so because the cash flow is partially tax sheltered by depreciation, the cash-on-cash return is high, and because there may be residual value for the equipment that partially (or totally, in some cases) recoups the cost of the equipment. Except for technological obsolescence (e.g., a brand new computer technology makes other computers obsolete), equipment leasing is generally not high risk.

Of course, it is important in limited partnerships that center on equipment leasing to have the right general partner and the right lessee. Failure to do so may result in cost inefficiencies, inadequate leasing, and other situations that lose income for the partnership. If the right lessee is not obtained, there is always the danger of default, idle use periods, and obsolescence.

Two terms are used in conjunction with equipment leasing:

- *Full payout leases:* the total lease payments are net to the lessor; that is, the lessee pays all operating costs, and the total of the payments equals or exceeds the cost of the equipment plus financing. Obviously, such a lease arrangement has little risk, totally recoups costs, and provides a minimum income.
- *Operating leases:* These are for a shorter period of time (often one half or less of the expected life of the equipment), leave the owner-lessor with the risk of rerental and the resale of the equipment for its salvage value. The cash flow is higher, and the depreciation at an accelerated rate is higher, but there are added risks.

Factors in Evaluating the Economic Soundness of a Partnership

- Can the venture produce gains or income?
- Are the assets (land, rights or equipment) fairly priced?
- Is the financing adequate? Consider debt; recourse or nonrecourse installment payments assessments voluntary or mandatory letters of credit?
- Is the general partner honest and capable? Consider his or her business history, track record of success, stability, financial soundness.
- How are other programs done?

We have touched on the major vehicles for tax-sheltered limited partnership investments. Many other opportunities exist. In recent years, the cable TV industry has provided outlets for limited partnerships, and the growth of that industry will require substantial capital investment. A limited partnership can be expected to provide much of that capital in exchange for the tax savings available from depreciation and tax credits.

Conflicts of Interest with the General Partners

Adjacent leases held by a general partner may indicate exploration of the field at the expense of the partnership.

Co-mingling of partnership funds with other funds, especially those of the general partner, is bad business. So is lending or borrowing between the partnership and the general partner. General partners' service to the partnership should be fair and reasonable, not "favorable" to the general partner.

Finally, because the general partner handles day-to-day management he or she should probably receive some incentive for good performance during this portion of the program. At liquidation or termination, however, most programs defer returns to the general partner until some return is realized by the limited partners. When evaluating return on a program either cash-on-cash or internal rate of return is normally used.

Cash-on-cash simply divides dollars received by dollars invested. Internal rate of return is slightly more accurate (and complicated) because it takes into account the time value of money.

Investor Selection of a Program

Investors should be sure expenses of the partnership will not be considered "abusive," which could cause tax benefits to be "disallowed."

Investors should understand their obligations to commit funds initially as well as any installment or staged payments, assessments, and all debt recourse and nonrecourse as well as letters of credit.

Investors need to understand the term of the commitment and relative illiquidity of the investment as well as the risk of loss of entire principal, nature of projections concerning income, change in tax law, and increased risk of audit. Investors need to assess these risks against their resources, their objectives in the light of current and future tax, and their understanding of the venture.

THE SECURITIES INVESTOR PROTECTION ACT AND SIPC

In the latter part of the 1960s the securities industry began to experience internal problems that had not existed since the Great Depression of the 1920s and 1930s. Securities firms found themselves in financial difficulties and many of them failed. Customers of these firms who had cash balances or securities positions at the firms were subject to losses. In an effort to protect these clients, the New York Stock Exchange set up a fund to provide protection for customers of troubled firms. All NYSE members were assessed and the monies used to partially indemnify customers. As conditions worsened, the fund was discontinued after expending an amount estimated at $120,000,000.

In 1970 Congress passed the Securities Investor Protection Act, which established the Securities Investor Protection Corporation (SIPC). SIPC is not a U.S. government agency but is a federally chartered, nonprofit corporation. Its purpose is to provide protection for the accounts of customers of broker/dealers that become insolvent. All broker/dealers, except bank dealers, must become members of SIPC and must display evidence of membership in each office. When SIPC came into being all members were assessed based on their gross revenues until the fund totaled $150,000,000. SIPC also has a line of credit at the U.S. Treasury of $1 billion should the fund itself prove to be inadequate.

Should an SIPC member firm fail, trustees are sent in to handle the liquidation. Values are determined on the day that these trustees arrive. For instance, if a client's account contained 100 shares of Telephone (AT&T), which was trading at $65 that day, that value would be used in determining the client's protection. When the client receives a distribution sometime later, the stock may be trading at a much higher or much lower price, but the $65 value would be used. Creditors are given six months to present their claims, after which the trustees will begin distribution.

SIPC protects clients to a maximum of $500,000 per customer. However, no more than $100,0000 of this can be applied to cash balances. For example, if client Jones has $500,000 of securities in his account, he would be fully protected by SIPC. Client Smith has a $500,000 credit balance (cash) in her account, so she would be protected only to a maximum of $100,000. Client Brown has $250,000 of securities and $250,000 cash in his account. He would receive maximum protection under SIPC of $350,000 ($250,000 security value and $100,000 cash).

Should a client have an account with a value in excess of $500,000, she would become a general creditor of the firm. She may recover more than $500,000 from other sources, but not from SIPC.

SIPC coverage is per customer not per account. John Jones may well have a cash account, margin account, and income account, but his total coverage is limited to $500,000. Mary Smith may have portions of her account separately designated as an A account, B account, C account, and so on, but as she is one individual, her protection will not exceed $500,000. However, if Fred Brown has an individual account, his wife, Ruth, has an individual account, and they have a joint account, each would be separately covered under SIPC to the $500,000 maximum.

As this organization is the *Securities* Investor Protection Corporation, commodity accounts receive no protection. Commodities are not considered securities under this definition.

TAXATION: CHANGES TO THE IRA RULES

Regulatory changes and the Economic Growth and Tax Relief Reconciliation Act of 2001 have changed many of the rules that govern IRAs. Here is an overview of the changes:

- The maximum contribution for traditional IRAs and Roth IRAs was increased from $2,000 to $3,000 through 2004. For the years 2005 through 2007, the maximum contribution will increase to $4,000. For the year 2008 and thereafter, the maximum contribution will increase to $5,000.

- For people 50 and over, an additional IRA contribution may be made. This additional contribution is referred to as "Catch-up." Through the year 2004, an extra $500 may be added for a total contribution of $3,500. The "Catch-up" amount for 2005 remains the same at $500 plus your maximum contribution of $4,000 for a total contribution of $4,500. For the years 2006 and 2007, the "Catch-up" increases to $1,000, for a total contribution of $5,000. For the year 2008 and thereafter, the "Catch-up" is $1,000, for a total contribution of $6,000.

- Separate five-year holding period was established for traditional IRA-to-Roth IRA conversions. A separate five-year holding period applies with respect to the portion of a distribution that is properly allocable to a traditional IRA-to-Roth IRA conversion. For this portion of a distribution, the five-year period starts with the year in which the conversion contribution was made (which may be later than the year for which your first Roth IRA contribution was made). Even though the distribution of amounts attributable to the conversion may not be subject to income tax, they are subject to a 10% penalty tax if made during the five-year holding period.

Five-year Holding Period for Roth IRA Distributions

In order for your Roth IRA distributions to be "qualified distributions," you must have held your Roth IRA for at least five years prior to the distribution. This five-year holding period is generally measured by counting five years beginning with the earlier of the first year from which your first regular Roth IRA contribution relates (not necessarily the year in which your first regular Roth IRA contribution is made) or the first year in which you made a conversion contribution.

Individual Retirement Accounts (IRAs)

Keeping the above changes in mind, an individual who receives compensation in the form of wages, salaries, professional fees, and commissions may open an IRA. Excluded from contributions are dividends, interest, and capital gains. Individuals covered by an employer retirement plan are now permitted to have an IRA.

The maximum contribution is $3,000 or 100% of annual compensation, whichever is the lesser (see above for "Catch-up" provisions). For contributions in excess of the limit, a 6% penalty is charged on the excess. In addition, the excess is not tax deductible, and the income earned is not deferred.

For individuals not covered by a qualified retirement plan, the traditional IRA contributions are deductible from your current income. For individuals covered by a qualified retirement plan, the IRS has established limits on the amount you may deduct. The actual amounts are not tested on the Series 7 Exam. Just be aware that there is a certain amount and as income exceeds this amount, the amount that you can deduct from income is reduced until no longer deductible.

Husbands and wives who are both employed may have two separate IRAs using the maximum contributions. In the event they file a joint return, a maximum deduction of $8,000 per year would be allowed. ("Catch-up" provisions are also permitted). In the event one or both of the individuals are covered by a qualified retirement plan, the same restrictions mentioned in the preceding paragraph apply.

Should an individual have a non-working spouse (husband or wife), the individual may contribute an additional $4,000 to a separate account on behalf of the spouse. Again, "Catch-up" provisions apply.

Contributions must be made in cash and may be deposited as late as April 15 for the previous year. The IRA may be opened at a bank, mutual fund company, or brokerage firm, which will act as a custodian for your investments. Keep in mind that the bank, mutual fund company, or brokerage firm is only safekeeping your investments. The owner of the IRA determines the investment, which may be in stocks, bonds, and investment companies. REITs and annuity items such as artwork, stamp collections, and collectibles are not permitted. In addition, the investments must be paid for in full. Margin accounts are not permitted; consequently, there is no short selling. IRA investments and contributions are tax-deferred until distributions are made.

Funds in an IRA may be distributed without penalty starting at age 59½ and must start to be withdrawn on April 1 of the following year that the owner reaches age 70½. The amount that must be distributed in a year is determined by the IRS based on the owner's life expectancy. The life expectancy is determined by the IRS as well.

Early withdrawals from an IRA are subject to a 10% penalty in addition to the taxes to be paid. However, the IRS allows early distributions under certain situations (e.g., death, incompetence of the IRA owner, certain medical expenses, higher education expenses, and purchase of a first-time home).

The owner of an IRA may transfer his/her investment from one retirement plan to another with no tax liability. The transfer goes from one institution to another. If the owner withdraws the investment and reinvests it with another institution, he has carried out a transaction known as a "rollover" as opposed to a transfer. While there is no restrictions on the number of transfers, a rollover may only be done once every 12 months. In addition, the rollover must be done within 60 days.

Roth IRAs

Contributions to a Roth IRA are not deductible for income tax purposes. However, earnings on contributions to a Roth IRA will accumulate on a tax-deferred basis and may ultimately be tax-free if the earnings are part of a "qualified distribution."

A qualified distribution would be a distribution made after a five-year holding period and made after age 59½, death, or disability or for the first $10,000 of a qualified first-time home purchase. Contributions to a Roth IRA are the same as traditional IRAs as well as the "Catch-up" provisions and spouse provisions. Mandatory withdrawals at age 70½ does not apply.

Simplified Employee Pension Plans (SEPs)

An SEP is a qualified retirement plan and the word "simplified" says it all. It was originally designed for small business owners. The employees open their own IRAs and the employer makes contributions on their behalf. Employers may make their contributions into the same account. Employers must include all employees that have worked three of the last five years, earned at least $450 (adjusted for cost of living), and are at least 21 years of age. The maximum amount an employer may contribute is 25% of an employee's salary with a cap of $41,000 for 2004. The employee is fully vested for the full amount.

Education IRA–Coverdell Education Savings Account

Originally called an Education IRA, it was not a retirement account. Consequently, the name was changed to better identify the purpose. They are now known as Coverdell Education Savings Accounts. It was designed to save money for a child's education. An individual may contribute after taxes up to $2,000 for children under the age of 18, depending on the income of the owner. Distributions and accumulations are tax free if the funds are used for higher education.

Other Types of Retirement Plans

Retirement Plans can be broken down into two categories—qualified and non-qualified. A qualified plan is one in which the contributions are tax deductible due to the fact that the plan meets the requirements set forth by the Employee Retirement Income Security Act of 1974 (ERISA) and the various IRS Rules. The tax on the accumulation is deferred until it is withdrawn, which is usually at a lower tax rate since income is normally lower at retirement. In addition, the plan cannot discriminate, which means the plan must generally be for all full-time employees. The assets of the plan are held by a trust. Any withdrawals are taxed as ordinary income.

A defined contribution plan provides an individual account for each participant. The benefits are based on the amount contributed and are also affected by income, expenses, gains, and losses. For 2004 the annual contributions in a defined contribution plan cannot exceed the smaller of $41,000 or 100% of the participant's compensation. An employer may deduct up to 25% of eligible compensation for each plan participant. Some types of defined contribution plans include 401(K) plans, 403(b) plans, employee stock ownership plans (ESOPs), and profit-sharing plans.

A defined benefit plan promises the participant a specific monthly benefit at retirement and may specify this as an exact dollar amount. Monthly benefits could also be calculated through a formula that considers a participant's salary and years of service.

One type of qualified plan would be a profit-sharing plan. This plan allows employees to share in the profits of the company. The amount of the contribution by the employer will vary from company to company.

401(K) plans allow employees a percentage of their salaries before taxes. Employers may match the contributions in various percentages according to the plan. The employer's contribution with respect to vesting is again varied according to the plan. However, employee contributions are fully vested immediately. Normally, the employee is provided a menu of investment options to invest in ranging from speculatively to conservative with mixtures of in-between.

Employee Stock Ownership Plan (ESOP)

In this plan, the employee is investing in the stock of his/her employer. The employer receives a tax deduction based on the market value of the stock without a cash outlay. Many employees suffered substantial losses in these plans in the early 2000s.

403(b) Plans

The 403(b) is similar to the 401(K), but it is only available to employees of non-profit organizations such as approved charitable organizations, churches, and fraternal organizations. The approval is under section 501(c)(3). They are sometimes referred to as Tax Sheltered Annuity (TSA) or Tax Deferred Annuity (TDA). Contributions are deductible from income.

Section 529 Plans

A Section 529 plan is not a retirement plan but a savings plan to meet post-high school educational needs. Like the Educational IRA (Coverdell Education Savings Accounts), contributions are made after taxes, but some plans provide a deduction from state taxes. These are state-run plans and vary from state to state. Just know that it exists. The previously described IRAs, Roth IRAs, Keogh (HR-10) Plans, and SEPs are all qualified. A non-qualified plan is almost the exact opposite of a qualified plan in all respects. The contributions are not tax deductible; the plan does not meet the standards of ERISA and can discriminate, which usually means the plan is designed to take care of highly paid executives. In addition, the plan is usually not established as a trust.

A Deferred Compensation Plan is a non-qualified plan. In this plan, the employee agrees to defer receipt of current income in favor of payment at retirement. This is popular with professional ball players and top executives. It assumes that persons will be in a lower tax bracket at retirement.

A Payroll Deduction Plan is another non-qualified plan. Employees allow the employer to deduct a specific amount after taxes. This deducted amount may be invested in a number of investments such as mutual funds, life insurance, and variable annuities.

TAXATION

This section will address the area of taxation that is included in The General Securities Registered Representative Examination. Keep in mind that the Series #7 Exam is designed to test the knowledge that is necessary for an "entry level" broker.

With this in mind, there are several definitions that will assist you in this section.

Earned Income Income most commonly in the form of wages and salaries; however, providing goods or services, collecting a pension, or cashing in an annuity is also classified as earned income.

Progressive Tax A graduated tax. Your tax rate will increase as your income increases. Gifts and inheritances are subject to Progressive Taxes.

Flat Tax Tax in which all pay the same rate such as sales tax, gasoline tax, and taxes on liquor and cigarettes. In addition, some states also have a flat tax rate.

Passive Income Income received where the taxpayer does not take an active role such as a limited partnership or rental real estate. (See section on Direct Participation Programs and Limited Partnerships.) Passive Income is taxed the same as earned income.

Passive Losses Passive Losses may only be deducted from Passive Income.

Deferred Income Income that is earned; no taxes are paid on the income until some time in the future. (See section on IRAs and Keogh.)

Investment/Portfolio Income Income received as a result of owning securities such as dividends, interest option premiums, and capital gains on stocks, bonds, options, and futures; sometimes referred to as unearned income.

Interest Income Interest income received on debt issues differs according to the issuer. (See Chapters 2 and 3.)

Cash Dividends Dividends that are taxable in the year they are paid. Shareholders pay tax on the full amount received. Many shareholders elect not to receive the dividends but to have the dividends reinvested; nevertheless, they must pay taxes on those dividends since they have the option of receiving them in cash.

Jobs and Growth Tax Relief Reconciliation Act of 2003 Act that changed the taxes on qualified dividends to a maximum of 15% in the 25% bracket or above (the highest tax bracket is currently 35%) and a maximum of 5% for those in the 10 to 15% brackets. Effective 2008, the 5% rate drops to 0.

Qualified Dividends This generally applies to dividends received on U.S. stocks held for more than 60 days during a 120-day period. Otherwise, it will be treated as ordinary income.

Alternative Minimum Tax (AMT) Tax designed to make sure that wealthy individuals pay at least some form of income tax. Just be aware that certain individuals are subject to the AMT. Please note that this is an increasing problem that Congress will likely have to address in the near future.

Real Estate Investment Trusts (REITs) Trusts that do not pay federal taxes (see Chapter 7). Consequently the dividends are not qualified and are taxed as ordinary income.

Dividends on Foreign Securities Reciprocal dividends on foreign securities are subject to the requirements of domestic dividends. However, foreign taxes are often withheld. In this case, the recipient still owes U.S. income tax on the net dividend. The amount of foreign tax withheld may be claimed as a deduction against income or may be applied as a credit against U.S. income tax.

Stock Dividends and Splits Stock dividends are not taxable at the time they are received. However, you must adjust the cost basis of your position in the security.

	Shares	Total Cost	Cost Per Share
January 15, 2004	200	6,000	30
June 30, 2004			
10% Stock Dividend	20	-0-	-0-
Total Shares	220	6,000	27.27

A stock split is treated the same as a stock dividend (see below).

	Shares	Total Cost	Cost Per Share
January 15, 2004	200	6,000	30
June 30, 2004			
2-for-1 Stock Split	400	-0-	15

Capital Gains and Losses Gains or losses that are a result of transactions in capital assets. For purposes of this part, we are limiting them to stocks, bonds, and options, even though there are many others. Capital losses are deductible from capital gains. Capital losses and gains are further broken down into long term and short term. If the holding period exceeds one (1) year, it is long term. If it is less than one (1) year, it is short term.

EXAMPLE

In 2004 a client had long-term capital gains of 7,000 and long-term capital losses of 4,000.

Capital Gain	$7,000
Capital Loss	– $4,000
Net Capital Gain	$3,000

Tax Due   450 ($3,000 × 15% = 450)

Long-term capital gain tax as of 2003 is 15%.

Should an investor experience net capital losses for the year, they can be employed to produce tax savings. Net losses may be used to offset up to $3,000 of taxable income in any tax year. Should the losses exceed $3,000, the balance can be carried over to be applied against capital gains in the future or to affect additional amounts of income of up to $3,000.

EXAMPLE

In 2004 a client has $10,000 of capital losses and $3,000 of capital gains. Prior to consideration of these capital transactions, the client had taxable income of $65,000.

Capital Loss	$10,000
Capital Gain	– $ 3,000
Net Capital Loss	$ 7,000
Taxable Income	$65,000
Less $3,000 of Net Loss	– $ 3,000
Taxable Income	$62,000

The client would save the tax that otherwise would be due on the $3,000 of taxable income and can carry the remaining $4,000 of the loss into 2005.

If in 2005 he has net capital gains of $8,000, he could offset $4,000 of this amount and be taxed on only the remaining $4,000. If he had no capital gains in 2005, he can offset $3,000 of that year's taxable income and carry the remaining $1,000 forward for use in 2006.

Wash-Sale Rule

The tax law includes a "wash-sale rule" to prevent taxpayers from using losses to offset gains while, in effect, continuing to hold the same or similar asset that resulted in the loss. Thus, if securities are sold at a loss and the investor acquires substantially identical securities within a period beginning 30 days before the sale and ending 30 days after the sale, the loss is disallowed and is added to the cost basis of the new securities.

EXAMPLE

> A client owns 10M New City 5½, 1/1/15 bonds purchased on June 1, 2005, at 92. On December 1, 2005, he buys an additional 10M bonds of the same description at 87. On December 7, 2005, he sells the original 10M at 86. What is his tax situation?
>
> The client cannot use the $600 loss on the bonds originally purchased as it is nondeductible under the wash-sale rule. He purchased identical securities within the 30-day period. The loss of $600 (92 – 86) is added to the cost of his second purchase giving him a tax cost basis of 93 (87 + $600 nonallowable loss) on the new securities.

Please note that the wash-sale rule considers purchases of the security made both 30 days before and after the sale. If, on November 6, 2005, a customer sold 500 shares of Texas Instruments at a loss and wished to use that loss in his tax calculation, he could not repurchase Texas Instruments before December 7, 2005, (31 days later), nor could he have purchased it after October 6, 2005, (31 days earlier). This causes the investor to be exposed to market fluctuations for the 30-day period. Perhaps our customer sold the stock on November 6 at $26 per share. On December 7, the first day he can repurchase, the stock might be at $37. He would have his tax loss but would probably not be smiling.

Tax Swaps

Investors can avail themselves of tax losses by swapping currently owned items for others (usually bonds) that do not fall under the substantially identical securities interpretation of the wash-sale rule.

Thus, a client might sell New York State 4¼ bonds due 6/11/15 at a loss and buy New York State 4½ bonds due 6/1/17. As he has changed both the coupon and maturity, the loss would be allowable.

At year end, clients wishing to swap make their lists available, and broker/dealers can provide swap ideas. Often, the client might improve his maturity and/or coupon while getting a tax advantage from the loss.

In stocks, the client might sell one security, in which she shows a loss, and purchase a similar security in the same industry. For example, sell one major oil company stock at a loss and purchase a different major oil company stock. Swaps are more generally used in bonds, as the similarities between items are greater than in stocks. Two AA-rated bonds with similar interest rates and maturity dates would tend to fluctuate about the same amount. This might not be true of two common stocks, even though they are in the same industry.

Accrued Interest

Normally, when a buyer purchases a bond, he pays accrued interest to the seller. In the case of municipals, the interest is considered to have been paid by the issuer and retains its tax-exempt status to both buyer and seller.

Multiple Positions

Often clients accumulate securities over a period of years. Perhaps your client bought IBM over a period of time as follows:

April 7, 2003 – 100 shares at $ 68
April 10, 2004 – 100 shares at $ 60
April 17, 2005 – 100 shares at $125

In January 2006, she wishes to sell 100 shares of ABC at $103 per share. The sale will be applied against the first purchase made on April 7, 2003, unless she designates otherwise. The FIFO (first-in, first-out) principle is used as a rule. Perhaps the client would prefer to apply the sale against the last purchase made on April 17, 2005, at $125. By doing this, she will show a loss of 22 points rather than a gain of 35 points. To accomplish this, the sell order would be marked "sale versus purchase made April 17, 1986." This legend would also appear on her trade confirmation, and she would be able to avail herself of a better tax situation.

Corporate Taxation

Under present law, a tax is imposed on the taxable income of corporations. The maximum rate is 35%.

When a corporation distributes its after-tax earnings to individual shareholders as dividends, a tax is imposed on the shareholders at rates up to 15%.

If a corporation receives a dividend from another corporation, the receiving corporation is entitled to a deduction that excludes a significant part of the dividend from taxable income. The percentage of a dividend received that is deducted varies from 70 to 100%, depending on the level of ownership of the receiving corporation in the distributing corporation.

If the receiving corporation owns less than 20% of the distributing corportion, the dividend received deduction is 70%. If the receiving corporation owns less than 80% but at least 20% of the distributing corporation, the dividend received deduction is 80%. If the receiving corporation owns 80% or more of the distributing corporation, the dividend received deduction is generally 100%.

If a corporation invested in common and preferred stocks of less than 20% of the issue and received $100,000 in dividends in 1995, it would pay tax on only $30,000 of this amount. If a corporation owns 20% or more, 80% of the dividend is received. Your corporate clients have good reason to purchase high-yielding stocks. Municipal bonds would also be suitable, as that interest is exempt from federal income tax.

Gift and Estate Taxes

Gift taxes were imposed in the United States to prevent wealthy individuals from avoiding the federal estate taxes. In past years, people of means could give away all of their assets to family and friends prior to death. When they died there would be no assets in their estate, thus no tax due.

A person can make gifts of up to $11,000 per year per person with no tax ramification. A wealthy woman can give up to $11,000 a year to each of her children, grandchildren, friends, neighbors, in fact to anyone, and the gifts would not be subject to tax. For husbands and wives making joint gifts, the amount increases to $22,000. Gifts in excess of the $11,000 are applied against a unified credit that may be used to defray the tax on excess gifts or to reduce the person's estate value for tax purposes. If the woman above gives her daughter a $50,000 gift in one year, $11,000 would not be considered, but $39,000 would be applied against her unified credit. When she dies, the estate value would be $39,000 greater than if she had not made a gift of this size. This unified credit offsets up to $194,200 in gift and/or estate taxes.

A significant change made by the Economic Growth and Tax Relief Reconciliation Act of 2001 gradually increase the amount that may be exempted using the unified credit. The following is the timetable:

Year	Amount Excluded
2002–2003	$1,000,000
2004–2005	$1,500,000
2006–2008	$2,000,000
2009	$3,500,000
2010	Repealed (subject to sunset provisions)
2011	$1,000,000

When a person dies, the estate is evaluated on the date of death and again six months from the date of death. The estate can use either value for determining estate taxes due. The remaining unified tax credit is then deducted, and the tax due is determined. This tax, like income tax, is a progressive tax. The greater the value, the higher the percentage of tax. While the estate can use the value on date of death or six months later, any securities sold are valued at the sale price, no matter when the sale was made.

Gifts of Securities

As a happy birthday gesture, your grandmother gives you $10,000 of stock that she purchased many years ago. The gift does not affect her unified credit, and you are certainly willing to accept it. Six months later, you sell the stock for $13,000. What is your tax situation? First, it is a long-term trade, as you pick up Grandma's holding period, and she has owned the stock for many years. However, your cost on the stock is the donor's cost or the value at the time of the gift, whichever is less. Your smart grandmother bought that stock many years ago for $100. You, therefore, have a long-term gain of $12,900 ($13,000 sale price - $100 cost). Had Grandma bought the stock for $15,000, you would take the $10,000 value on the date of the gift and report a $3,000 long-term capital gain ($13,000 sale price - $10,000 value on the date of the gift). This would not have been a smart move on Grandma's part. She should have sold the stock for $10,000 and taken a $5,000 tax loss for herself. She then could make a gift to you of $10,000 in cash.

The Taxpayer Relief Act of 1997 and the Tax Relief Act of 2001 gradually increased the Estate Tax Credit. At the same time, the top tax rate will be decreasing until 2010, when estate and gift taxes are fully repealed. However, in 2011, estate taxes return to their 2002 levels.

Following is a breakdown of the new Estate and Gift Taxes for each year:

Calendar Year	Maximum Estate Tax Rate	Maximum Estate Tax Exclusion Amount	Maximum Estate Tax Unified Credit	Maximum Gift Tax Unified Credit	Gift Tax Exclusion Amount
2001	55% (plus 5% surcharge)	$675,000	$220,550	$220,550	$675,000
2002	50%	$1 million	$345,800	$345,800	$1 million
2003	49%	$1 million	$345,800	$345,800	$1 million
2004	48%	$1.5 million	$555,800	$345,800	$1 million
2005	47%	$1.5 million	$555,800	$345,800	$1 million
2006	46%	$2 million	$780,800	$345,800	$1 million
2007	45%	$2 million	$780,800	$345,800	$1 million
2008	45%	$2 million	$780,800	$345,800	$1 million
2009	45%	$3.5 million	$1,455,800	$345,800	$1 million
2010	35% (gift tax only)	Estate tax repealed	Estate tax repealed	$345,800	$1 million
2011	55% (plus 5% surcharge)	$1 million	$345,800	$345,800	$1 million

In 2005, an estate holder who dies can pass $1.5 million of their estate tax free. Any excess is subject to estate taxes.

As the table indicates, the Gift Tax Credit is not as large as the Estate Tax Credit. For gifts made in 2002 or later, the gift tax maximum exclusion is fixed at $1 million. Only in 2011, when the Estate Tax Credit returns to $1 million, will both credits be equal (and "unified").

KEOGH (HR-10) PLANS

In 1962 Congress passed the Self-Employed Individual Tax Retirement Act. As the legislation was sponsored by Congressman Keogh of Brooklyn, New York, the investments made under this law are commonly referred to as "Keogh Plans." The law was designed to allow self-employed persons to establish a tax shelter to set aside funds to provide for their eventual retirement.

Under provisions of the law, effective January 1, 1984, a self-employed person may deposit up to 20% of earned income to a maximum of $40,000 annually into any investment approved by the Internal Revenue Service. Most usual investment programs, such as bank deposits (CDs), investment company shares, securities, life insurance, variable annuities, and mortgages can be used for these plans. The person may even establish a self-administered plan, which permits him in effect to trade in the account.

A person does not have to be exclusively self-employed to be eligible for a Keogh. Perhaps a client of yours earn $50,000 per year as an employee of a major corporation, but earns additional monies, perhaps $20,000 a year, from a part-time, self-employed activity. The client might devote weekends to selling real estate, landscape gardening, or consulting on an independent basis. The $20,000 so earned could be used as the basis for a Keogh Plan, allowing up to 20% of this amount ($4,000) to be sheltered.

A self-employed doctor earning $100,000 annually could deposit the maximum of 20% into a Keogh. The $20,000 would be deducted from gross income for tax purposes, saving whatever amount of tax would have been due. Additionally, any earnings on the investment would accumulate tax-free until retirement. Perhaps the doctor invested in a long-term corporate bond fund yielding 8%. That income would not be subject to tax in the year it was earned. Upon retirement, when the money is withdrawn from the plan, it would be taxed as regular income, perhaps at a lower bracket.

The maximum deductible contribution is $41,000. Suppose an author earned $300,000 per year from writing mystery novels. She could not deposit 20% into her Keogh, as that would amount to $60,000. She would be limited to contributions of $41,000 annually.

If a person establishes a Keogh Plan, they must also provide a plan for any full-time employees, defined as those who have been employed for a minimum of three years and who work a minimum of 1,000 hours per year. Thus, an accountant who has worked for our writer for ten years but only works one week a year preparing her taxes would not be eligible. He has the three-year minimum but not the minimum number of annual hours required. The author may also employ a full-time secretary, who has been in her employ for five years. This person is eligible and must be provided with a Keogh Plan at the same percentage as her employer's. In our example, the employer has a 13% Keogh (earnings of $300,000 with $41,000 deposited in the plan). Should the secretary earn $30,000 per year, the employer would have to deposit $3,900 (13% of $30,000) in the employee's Keogh. Unlike many other retirement plans, the eligible employee in a Keogh Plan is immediately vested. That is, should she leave her current employment the plan goes with her. It is her property.

If the employer's earned income is extremely high, the percentage figure that she could deposit in a Keogh would be quite small. For example, if our author earned $2,000,000 per year, she would still be limited to a maximum deposit of $41,000 into her plan. This works out to 2%. The law now states that high-earning employers cannot discriminate against employees. They must make a reasonable contribution to the eligible employee's plan.

Money deposited in a Keogh Plan for the benefit of either the employer or employee can be withdrawn without penalty beginning at age 59½. Withdrawal must begin at age 70½ in amounts related to the person's life expectancy.

Should a person have a need to withdraw money prior to age 59½, a penalty equal to 10% of the amount withdrawn is assessed. Should any person need to withdraw $10,000 at age 55, a penalty of $1,000 would be levied. Additionally, the entire $10,000 would be subject to income tax that year. If the need to withdraw is caused by disability, the penalty could be waived by the IRS.

There are many similarities between Keoghs and IRAs. The penalty for withdrawal before age 59½ and the requirement to withdraw beginning at age 70½ are identical. As in a Keogh plan, the amount contributed to an IRA is a pretax deduction from the person's income.

ANSWER SHEET FOR CHAPTER 5 EXAMINATION

1. Ⓐ Ⓑ Ⓒ Ⓓ   11. Ⓐ Ⓑ Ⓒ Ⓓ   21. Ⓐ Ⓑ Ⓒ Ⓓ

2. Ⓐ Ⓑ Ⓒ Ⓓ   12. Ⓐ Ⓑ Ⓒ Ⓓ   22. Ⓐ Ⓑ Ⓒ Ⓓ

3. Ⓐ Ⓑ Ⓒ Ⓓ   13. Ⓐ Ⓑ Ⓒ Ⓓ   23. Ⓐ Ⓑ Ⓒ Ⓓ

4. Ⓐ Ⓑ Ⓒ Ⓓ   14. Ⓐ Ⓑ Ⓒ Ⓓ   24. Ⓐ Ⓑ Ⓒ Ⓓ

5. Ⓐ Ⓑ Ⓒ Ⓓ   15. Ⓐ Ⓑ Ⓒ Ⓓ   25. Ⓐ Ⓑ Ⓒ Ⓓ

6. Ⓐ Ⓑ Ⓒ Ⓓ   16. Ⓐ Ⓑ Ⓒ Ⓓ   26. Ⓐ Ⓑ Ⓒ Ⓓ

7. Ⓐ Ⓑ Ⓒ Ⓓ   17. Ⓐ Ⓑ Ⓒ Ⓓ   27. Ⓐ Ⓑ Ⓒ Ⓓ

8. Ⓐ Ⓑ Ⓒ Ⓓ   18. Ⓐ Ⓑ Ⓒ Ⓓ   28. Ⓐ Ⓑ Ⓒ Ⓓ

9. Ⓐ Ⓑ Ⓒ Ⓓ   19. Ⓐ Ⓑ Ⓒ Ⓓ   29. Ⓐ Ⓑ Ⓒ Ⓓ

10. Ⓐ Ⓑ Ⓒ Ⓓ   20. Ⓐ Ⓑ Ⓒ Ⓓ   30. Ⓐ Ⓑ Ⓒ Ⓓ

31. Ⓐ Ⓑ Ⓒ Ⓓ   46. Ⓐ Ⓑ Ⓒ Ⓓ

32. Ⓐ Ⓑ Ⓒ Ⓓ   47. Ⓐ Ⓑ Ⓒ Ⓓ

33. Ⓐ Ⓑ Ⓒ Ⓓ   48. Ⓐ Ⓑ Ⓒ Ⓓ

34. Ⓐ Ⓑ Ⓒ Ⓓ   49. Ⓐ Ⓑ Ⓒ Ⓓ

35. Ⓐ Ⓑ Ⓒ Ⓓ   50. Ⓐ Ⓑ Ⓒ Ⓓ

36. Ⓐ Ⓑ Ⓒ Ⓓ   51. Ⓐ Ⓑ Ⓒ Ⓓ

37. Ⓐ Ⓑ Ⓒ Ⓓ   52. Ⓐ Ⓑ Ⓒ Ⓓ

38. Ⓐ Ⓑ Ⓒ Ⓓ   53. Ⓐ Ⓑ Ⓒ Ⓓ

39. Ⓐ Ⓑ Ⓒ Ⓓ   54. Ⓐ Ⓑ Ⓒ Ⓓ

40. Ⓐ Ⓑ Ⓒ Ⓓ   55. Ⓐ Ⓑ Ⓒ Ⓓ

41. Ⓐ Ⓑ Ⓒ Ⓓ

42. Ⓐ Ⓑ Ⓒ Ⓓ

43. Ⓐ Ⓑ Ⓒ Ⓓ

44. Ⓐ Ⓑ Ⓒ Ⓓ

45. Ⓐ Ⓑ Ⓒ Ⓓ

To remove answer sheet, cut along dotted line.

CHAPTER 5 EXAMINATION

1. Who is responsible for verifying that limited partners meet the net worth and income requirements?

   (A) the limited partners
   (B) the general partner
   (C) the sponsor
   (D) the registered representative

2. Which of the following is (are) in the subscription agreement?

   I. identification of the limited partners
   II. qualification of the limited partners for subscription
   III. granting of power of attorney to the limited partners
   IV. a record of sale of the partnership interests

   (A) I, II, and III only
   (B) II, III, and IV only
   (C) I, III, and IV only
   (D) I, II, and IV only

3. Which of the following is available BOTH to owners of stock and owners of limited partnership participations?

   (A) deduction of business expenses from income
   (B) a share in the profits from earnings
   (C) tax credits
   (D) deductions for losses in excess of income earned

4. Which of the following activities by a limited partner may subject the partner to unlimited liability?

   I. participate in management
   II. commit the partnership in any manner
   III. lend his or her name to the partnership
   IV. make loans beyond those specified in the agreement

   (A) I, II, III, and IV
   (B) II and III only
   (C) III and IV only
   (D) II and IV only

5. Partnership democracy is:

   (A) a prohibition against control by a single partner
   (B) the sharing of management by all partners
   (C) permission granted to the general partner to act outside the partnership agreement
   (D) a synonym for silent partner

6. The general partner is prohibited from all of the following EXCEPT:

   (A) acting in such a way as to impede the orderly business of the partnership
   (B) buying or selling assets of the partnership except to foster the business of the partnership
   (C) competing in any way with the partnership
   (D) accepting compensation from any other partnership

7. As a general rule, when a partnership is terminated, in what order are assets distributed?

(A) general creditors, secured lenders, limited partners, general partners
(B) secured lenders, limited partners, general creditors, general partners
(C) secured lenders, general creditors, limited partners, general partners
(D) general creditors, general partners, limited partners, secured lenders

8. Each of the following will result in the termination of a limited partnership EXCEPT:

(A) transfer of ownership of a limited partnership interest
(B) the sale or transfer of partnership assets
(C) majority vote of the limited partners to end the partnership
(D) arrival of the termination date established in the agreement

9. Creditors whose claims are not settled upon the dissolution of a limited partnership may seek recourse from:

(A) the general partner's profits
(B) the general partner's personal assets
(C) the partnership's gross revenues
(D) the limited partner's personal assets

10. Crossover is best defined as:

(A) the point at which the program becomes profitable
(B) the point at which income exceeds deductions
(C) the fact that there are more general than limited partners
(D) limited partners profit more than general partners

11. Which of the following pairs of corporation characteristics are the easiest for a partnership to avoid?

(A) business objective and centralized management
(B) continuity of life and limited liability
(C) two or more associates and free transferability of assets
(D) continuity of life and transferability of assets

12. Which of the following best describes depreciation?

(A) a tax credit available to investors in heavy equipment
(B) deductions from gross income to offset lower value of equipment
(C) return of principal from real estate investments
(D) capitalized and amortized maintenance costs

13. On which of the following is depreciation not permitted?

(A) rental property whose value is falling
(B) residential property not used for business
(C) property whose maintenance exceeds the investment credit
(D) equipment subject to recapture

14. In terms of depletion, percentage depletion is better than cost depletion because it:

(A) permits recovery of more than the original cost
(B) is limited to production
(C) is more widely available
(D) is not subject to recapture

15. Which of the following is NOT an intangible drilling cost?

    (A) salaries
    (B) supplies and fuel
    (C) machinery and pipe
    (D) repairs

16. Limited partnerships try to avoid recapture because:

    (A) it turns potential capital gains into current taxable income
    (B) it may subject the partnership to the add-on tax
    (C) it increases the risk of a tax audit
    (D) it always increases the investor's tax bracket

17. If recaptured deductions are added to income, recaptured investment tax credits are added to:

    (A) income
    (B) basis
    (C) gains
    (D) taxes

18. All of the following decrease basis EXCEPT:

    (A) cash or property paid out
    (B) depletion of real property
    (C) losses
    (D) income from extraordinary sources

19. The importance of the "at risk" rule is that:

    (A) it limits deductions to the amount at risk
    (B) it limits liability to the amount at risk
    (C) deductions for interest may not exceed investment income
    (D) it prevents carryforward of disallowed interest deductions

20. The possible reward for investing in raw land is:

    (A) deferred income
    (B) large deductions
    (C) potential for capital appreciation
    (D) the lack of investment risk

21. In a triple net lease, the tenant is not responsible for:

    (A) taxes
    (B) financing charges
    (C) insurance premiums
    (D) maintenance

22. A deed to a condominium can qualify as a security in each of the following cases EXCEPT:

    (A) the seller intends to profit
    (B) there is management by other than the owner
    (C) there is a time and space rental pool
    (D) there is a 14-day owner usage provision

23. For condominiums, which of the following sets out the details of the management board, their powers, and their limitations?

    (A) master deed
    (B) bylaws
    (C) rental agreement
    (D) loan agreement

24. Phantom income is best described as:

    (A) income from deductions and tax credits
    (B) the nontaxable portion of a distribution
    (C) income received but not reported
    (D) income reported but not received

25. Which of the following oil and gas programs does not directly involve drilling?

    (A) exploratory
    (B) developmental
    (C) balanced
    (D) income

26. Which of the following are sources of funding for limited partnerships?

    I.   the proceeds of the offering
    II. periodic assessments on the partners
    III. installment payments
    IV. nonrecourse loans

        (A) I and IV only
        (B) I and II only
        (C) II and III only
        (D) I, II, III, and IV

27. Which of the following are primary considerations in evaluating the worth of a limited partnership?

    I.   the cost of the assets
    II. the adequacy of the funding
    III. the competence of management (general partner)
    IV. the size of the tax deductions

        (A) I, II, and III only
        (B) IV only
        (C) II and III only
        (D) III and IV only

28. Which of the following is associated with an income oil and gas partnership?

    (A) capital appreciation
    (B) the risk of dry holes
    (C) high intangible drilling costs
    (D) cash flow and depletion allowance

29. Which of the following is a benefit of Section 8 low-income-housing partnerships?

    (A) high, reliable income
    (B) large deductions
    (C) potential for capital appreciation
    (D) low risk

30. In order to determine the amount of estate tax, if any, due, the assets of a decedent's estate are valued as of the date of death. A second evaluation is then made:

    (A) three months from date of death
    (B) six months from date of death
    (C) one year from date of death
    (D) at any time up to six months from date of death

31. SIPC was established under:

    (A) Securities Act of 1933
    (B) Securities Exchange Act of 1934
    (C) Securities Investor Protection Act of 1970
    (D) Securities Exchange Reform Act of 1975

32. Under Keogh Plan provisions, contributions for employees must be fully vested:

    (A) at the time of the contribution
    (B) after three years of service
    (C) after five years of service
    (D) after ten years of service

33. Under the provisions of the Keogh Plan, all of the following are eligible to establish self-retirement funds EXCEPT:

    (A) a doctor whose income is derived solely from the practice
    (B) a salaried advertising executive who makes an additional $5,000 a year from freelance work
    (C) a salaried securities analyst who make an additional $2,000 from giving talks to clubs
    (D) a salaried corporate executive who receives each year a bonus of approximately $5,000 worth of securities of the firm

34. Under the terms of the 1970 Securities Investor Protection Act, what is the status of a customer whose account assets exceed SIPC Insurance coverage when his broker/dealer becomes insolvent?

    (A) The U.S. Treasury is pledged to make up the deficiency.
    (B) All broker/dealers are assessed to fully satisfy customer asset deficiencies.
    (C) The customer becomes a general creditor of the insolvent concern for the amount of difference involved.
    (D) SIPC will issue a debenture to guarantee eventual repayment of any unsatisfied customer claims.

35. A self-employed person with a Keogh Plan must include all full-time employees in the plan no later than:

    (A) immediately after employment
    (B) after one year of employment
    (C) after two years of employment
    (D) after three years of employment

36. An employee participant in a Keogh Plan becomes fully vested in that plan:

    (A) immediately
    (B) after one year
    (C) after two years
    (D) after three years

37. Which of the following persons is ineligible to have a Keogh Plan for retirement income purposes?

    (A) a doctor whose income is derived from the practice of medicine
    (B) an advertising agency executive whose income is derived from a salary plus $5,000 in outside consulting fees
    (C) a member firm employee whose income results from a salary plus a year-end bonus
    (D) an artist whose annual income comes from a salary plus monies earned from sales of personal paintings at staged exhibitions

38. Distribution from an IRA can begin at age 59½ and must begin at age:

    (A) 70½
    (B) 65
    (C) 68
    (D) whenever the individual wants to retire

39. All of the following taxes are recognized as flat rate taxes EXCEPT:

    (A) excise tax
    (B) gasoline tax
    (C) gift tax
    (D) general tax

40. For a self-employed individual's Keogh Plan, ERISA permits an investment in:

    (A) a unit investment trust
    (B) a variable annuity
    (C) a U.S. treasury bond
    (D) all of the above

41. An investor owns shares individually in a mutual fund that pays $250 in dividends annually. Which statement is true with regard to federal tax liability?

    (A) He pays tax at his regular rate on the entire $250.
    (B) He is liable for the tax on those dividends over the $100.
    (C) If he files a joint tax return, he is entitled to a $200 annual deduction from liability for those dividends.
    (D) If the dividends are automatically reinvested in additional fund shares, he need not pay tax until the year in which those monies are actually received.

42. A Keogh Plan can be described as a:

    I.   tax shelter
    II. retirement plan
    III. tax-free trust

    (A) II only
    (B) II and III only
    (C) I, II, and III
    (D) I and II only

43. If federal excise taxes were increased by the government, what would you suggest the typical investor do about his portfolio?

    (A) sell his treasuries and invest in municipal bonds
    (B) sell his corporate bonds and invest in treasuries
    (C) sell his municipal bonds and invest in good quality growth stocks
    (D) take no action as a result of this tax news

44. A tax-free rollover of assets between qualified retirement plans for the benefit of a specific individual is permitted so long as it is accomplished within:

    (A) 30 days
    (B) 60 days
    (C) 90 days
    (D) one year

45. Which of the following accounts that a customer has at a brokerage firm will be covered under SIPC if the brokerage firm should go bankrupt?

    I.   individual account
    II. joint account with spouse
    III. commodities account
    IV. joint account with daughter

    (A) I only
    (B) I and II only
    (C) I, II, and IV only
    (D) I, II, III, and IV

46. Under the Self-Employed Retirement Act (Keogh Plan), voluntary contributions are:

    (A) prohibited
    (B) penalized at a rate of 10%
    (C) permitted after three years of plan opening
    (D) permitted but not deductible

47. A Keogh Plan employee participant wants to quit his job and establish a qualified IRA. With respect to the assets in his Keogh Plan, this person may:

    I.   roll over the assets to an IRA within 60 days tax-free
    II. distribute the assets from taxes, immediately
    III. forfeit his right to Keogh Plan assets if he quits before 59½ years of age
    IV. distribute the assets and pay an IRS penalty as a result

       (A) I and IV only
       (B) II and III only
       (C) I and III only
       (D) none of the above

48. A tax shelter specifically designed for self-employed individuals is:

    (A) an individual retirement account
    (B) a Keogh Plan
    (C) a subsidized deferral account
    (D) a Shelter Island plan

49. An employer earning $300,000 and contributing the maximum employs a research assistant who is eligible for a Keogh. If this person earns $12,000 per year, how much must be deposited in her plan?

    (A) $600
    (B) $1,200
    (C) $1,500
    (D) $1,800

50. John Smith, age 54, has a Keogh Plan with investments valued at $104,500. He withdraws $25,000 to open a retail clothing store in his area. Which of the following statements is true regarding this situation?

    (A) The entire plan is terminated and $104,500 becomes immediately taxable
    (B) A penalty of 10% of the amount withdrawn is assessed.
    (C) A penalty of 10% of all assets in the plan is assessed.
    (D) No contribution can be made to the plan for six years.

51. Which best describes a Coverdell ESA?

    I.   A savings account that is set up to pay the qualified education expenses of a designated beneficiary.
    II. It may be opened at any bank in the United States or other IRS approved entity.
    III. Any beneficiary under 21 years of age.
    IV. The trustee must be an individual.

       (A) I and IV
       (B) II and III
       (C) I and II
       (D) III and IV

52. An SEP-IRA may be converted to a Roth IRA:

    (A) without restriction
    (B) only after the two-year holding period
    (D) not eligible for conversion
    (D) after the 90-day holding period

53. In order for your Roth IRA distribution to be qualified, you must have held your Roth IRA for at least:

    (A) 90 days
    (B) 1 year
    (C) 2 years
    (D) 5 years

54. The maximum dollar amount an employer may make to an SEP IRA is:

    (A) $2,000
    (B) $2,500
    (C) $5,000
    (D) $41,000

55. In a 401(K) Plan, the employee's contribution is vested at what point:

    (A) after 2 years
    (B) immediately
    (C) after 5 years
    (D) the same as the employer's contribution

CHAPTER 5 EXAMINATION ANSWERS

1. **D** It is the responsibility of the registered representative to make sure the limited partners meet the net worth and income requirements

2. **D** III is an incorrect answer. You do not grant power of attorney to a limited partner, only to a general partner.

3. **B** Both shareholders and limited partners will share in the profits from earnings.

4. **A** All of the answers mean taking an active part in the role of management, causing you to lose your limited liability.

5. **C** An example may best explain this answer. A building with only a 60% occupancy is up for sale and it is a good deal. However, the agreement specifies a 70% occupancy is necessary to purchase. If the limited partners approve the purchase, this would be a partnership democracy.

6. **D** Many times the general partner in one limited partnership is the general partner in another limited partnership.

7. **C** This is the normal order of payment in a liquidation.

8. **A** Transfer of ownership would cause the termination unless provisions were provided for in the agreement. In addition, upon the death of a limited partner, transfer is automatic.

9. **B** When the partnership runs out of assets and debt is still there, you can look to the assets of the general partners.

10. **B** By definition.

11. **D** The other characteristics are far too important to give up.

12. **B** Equipment has a so-called life expectancy. If a machine costs $60,000 and its life expectancy is ten years,

you would depreciate $6,000 each year.

13. **B** Only on income-producing property, such as a two or three-family house, is depreciation permitted.

14. **A** This is only allowed for small producing oil wells.

15. **C** By definition.

16. **A** The other answers are just not true. Keep in mind that partnerships don't pay taxes, the partners do.

17. **D** Nondeductible expenses have no effect on basis.

18. **D** This is a one-time event, the writeoff of a loss on the sale of property.

19. **A** Deductions may not exceed your contributions.

20. **C** While the reward can be substantial, the risk is also great.

21. **B** In a triple leaseback arrangement the tenant is responsible for taxes, insurance, and maintenance.

22. **D** The 14-day usage provision allows the owner to deduct depreciation but has nothing to do with the classification as a security.

23. **B** Bylaws in general detail management's responsibility, powers, and restrictions.

24. **D** A recourse loan that is forgiven is considered phantom income.

25. **D** On an income program, the well is already producing oil. The risk is falling prices.

26. **D** All are sources for funding of limited partnerships.

27. **A** Notice that the use of the word "primary" is the key. Tax deductions are a definite consideration but not a primary one.

28. **D** Remember, income programs are already producing oil wells.

29. **D** The low risk is due to the fact of government guarantee and/or subsidiaries.

30. **B** The second evaluation is made six months from the date of death. The estate may then use either value in determining the taxes due.

31. **C** This is the law that established SIPC.

32. **A** Keogh Plan requires immediate vesting upon becoming a participant.

33. **D** Keogh accounts are available to persons whose income in whole, or in part, is earned on a self-employed basis. A bonus to a salaried person (D) does not meet this test.

34. **C** Once the coverage under SIPC is exhausted, the customer then becomes a general creditor in the amount of the difference. Since all the assets have already been exhausted, the odds of this customer receiving restitution are nil.

35. **D** The provisions of the Keogh Plan are such that all full-time employees must be covered no later than three years after they have been employed. Please note that the plan-holder can establish a shorter time interval, should they desire.

36. **A** From the standpoint of the employer, this is a disadvantage, but is a requirement under the Keogh Plan act. In corporate plans, it sometimes takes many years for an employee to become fully vested.

37. **C** An individual may establish a Keogh Plan for self-employed income. (This does not include investment income.) Thus a salary or bonus would not qualify, as this is not self-employed income.

38. **A** Under the IRA (and the Keogh), this is the age at which withdrawals must begin.

39. **C** By definition, a gift tax is a progressive tax, whereas all of the others are "level" percentage charges, sometimes referred to as "regressive."

40. **D** All of these investments would qualify for Keogh Plans or IRAs.

41. **B** If the securities were owned jointly, then $200 could be deducted on a joint return. Since this was an individual return, he gets only $100 exclusion.

42. **C** The Keogh Plan provides tax shelter for current income and is designed to provide a retirement plan for self-employed individuals. While the monies are in the plan, dividends, interest, and capital gains are tax-free.

43. **D** Excise taxes normally are not important to the typical investor. They generally have little effect on security prices.

44. **B** Under the provisions of ERISA.

45. **C** Commodities accounts are not covered by SIPC, as commodities are not considered to be securities. The others would all be covered as there is different beneficial ownership. However, if a customer had a cash account and a margin account, the individual would still be considered to have only one account, since there was only one beneficial owner.

46. **D** A person can make limited voluntary contributions to a Keogh, but they do not qualify as a tax deduction.

47. **A** Choices II and III are clearly wrong, but choices I and IV are correct

48. **B** Keoghs are for the self-employed, IRAs for employed persons. Choices (C) and (D) do not exist.

49. **B** As the employer is making a 10% contribution to her Keogh ($30,000

is 10% of $300,000) the minimum Keogh deposit for an eligible employee is 10% or $1,200.

50. **B** Withdrawal from a Keogh Plan prior to age 59½ results in a penalty of 10% of the amount withdrawn.

51. **C** I and II are correct by definition. The beneficiary must be under 18 years old, and the trustee or custodian must be a bank or entity approved by the IRS.

52. **A** An SEP-IRA may be converted to a Roth IRA without restriction. The two-year holding period applies to Simple IRAs.

53. **D** It is a five-year holding period.

54. **D** The employer may make a contribution of 25% of the employee's salary with a cap of $41,000.

55. **B** Immediately as far as the employer's contribution that will vary according to the plan.

NYSE and Over-the-Counter Transactions/NASD

CHAPTER 6

OPENING AND HANDLING OF ACCOUNTS

When a prospective customer seeks to open a new securities account with a NYSE member firm, the registered representative ("RR") is required to use "due diligence" in ascertaining relevant personal and financial information about that person's means, needs, and abilities. Usually called the "Know Your Customer Rule" (Rule 405), this requirement can be summed up in one word: *Suitability*. No RR should solicit or accept, and no member firm should permit, any transaction which, based on this customer information, is not "suitable."

Base Information Required

There is general agreement among brokers as to the minimum information necessary to satisfy NYSE Rule 405. There may be considerable variances between firms as to the amount of this information that must be on the new account form prior to its approval by an office manager. Large firms tend to enforce fairly rigid policies; smaller firms tend to be more flexible, especially in small communities.

As the amount and type of information necessary in new accounts reports is left to the compliance department of each firm, it would appear to be an easy rule to live with. Quite the contrary is true. You are required to know your customer. Despite the great care taken, should something go amiss with the account, you and your firm would be considered in violation of this very general rule. As an industry, we would prefer more specific requirements no matter how demanding. Some areas of our industry, such as options and municipals, do have particular information standards, but the NYSE and NASD are more general, leaving final judgment to the firm and their representatives.

Full Name and Address If a post office box is used as a mailing address, the actual home and business addresses must appear on the form. A post office box alone is not acceptable.

Social Security or Taxpayer ID Number Under federal law, brokers must report dividends paid to customer accounts as well as other relevant tax information.

Age Customers must be of legal age to transact business and to enter into binding contracts.

Employment Status Status, such as employer, self-employed, retired, is required. NYSE rules require special permission for certain types of accounts and employers (see below).

Marital Status Spouse's name, if married, is required.

Dependents Number of dependents you declare on your income tax.

Investment Objective Objective such as speculation, long-term growth of capital, and income, is required. This is necessary to match security recommendations to the suitability requirements of the customer.

Net Worth This is required if an option account. Net worth is everything other than principal residence; liquid net worth; annual income; investment experience. Net worth is useful to know under any circumstances, but is specified by the options exchanges due to the additional risk inherent in many options transactions.

Other information that the NASD required:

- Customer's name and address. If correspondence is to be sent to a P.O. Box, the actual address of the customer must be on file.
- That the customer is of legal age.
- Signature of the RR opening the account.
- Signature of the principal approving the opening of the account.

Additional information that should be obtained:

- Taxpayer's ID number
- Citizenship of customer
- Occupation of the customer

Special Employment Considerations

Because of potential conflicts of interest, accounts for employees of members, member organizations, and the NYSE require additional care. Any account for any employee of NYSE or its subsidiaries, including officers, requires the prior written consent of the exchange. Accounts for employees of other NYSE member firms require *prior written consent of the employer* and *duplicate confirmations and account statements* forwarded to the employer.

Documentation

There is no standard policy on cash accounts. Most firms request a sample of the customer's signature on a signature card, but a cash account can be opened and traded with no documentation (other than the new account form) of any kind.

On a margin account, the customer must sign the "hypothecation" (margin or customer) agreement to collateralize any loan he may use. Most firms also ask the customer to sign a "stock loan consent" form allowing the broker to lend the customer's margin securities to others. This document is often included on the same sheet as the hypothecation agreement.

Federal law requires the broker to provide the margin customer with a "truth-in-lending" statement describing loan terms and rates. This document need not be signed by the customer.

Additional documentation is required for most of the accounts below and is discussed in each section.

Third-Party Accounts

Normally, orders may be accepted only from the principal (owner) of the account. Occasionally, a customer may delegate trading decisions to another person, often an investment advisor, by signing a "power of attorney" in favor of that party. This allows the holder of the power of attorney to enter orders directly with the RR without prior consultation with the customer. The most common type is the limited power of attorney, usually called a "trading authorization," which is limited to securities transactions. The more comprehensive "full power of attorney," which also allows funds and/or securities to be withdrawn from the account by the holder, is being seen more often these days.

To accept an order from an unauthorized party is a serious violation of NYSE rules and could cause the RR to be liable for any losses suffered. Sometimes a problem arises involving married couples. It is not uncommon for a customer to phone the RR and say: "Buy me 200 GM and put 100 in my wife's (husband's) account." Unless the spouse has power of attorney, this order is illegal and should be refused unless the RR first confirms the order with the other spouse. While this may be embarrassing to the RR, it is better than having the spouse disavow the trade, leaving the RR responsible for any loss.

Discretionary Accounts

If a trading authorization is made out in favor of an employee of a member firm (generally an RR), the account is considered "discretionary." Because of an inherent potential conflict of interest, many members do not allow such accounts while others specialize in discretionary accounts. For those that do allow them, NYSE rules require:

1. Prior written request for discretion from the customer.
2. Acceptance of the account in writing by a member or allied member of the exchange.
3. Marking each order "Discretion" and getting approval in writing (by initialing) of each order by a member, allied member, or branch office manager.
4. Frequent supervisory reviews to protect against churning or unsuitable recommendations.

Time and price of execution may be orally delegated by the customer without regard to this rule. Hence, an order to "Buy 500 KQB sometime today if the market weakens" is acceptable even without a signed power of attorney. Because of the potential for misunderstanding, most firms do not permit such orders as a matter of house policy.

Numbered or Coded Accounts

To protect the confidentiality of customer accounts, NYSE rules permit carrying accounts under code names, numbers, or aliases. The customer must provide a written acknowledgment of ownership of the account and provide all normal information for the broker's records. Then the customer's confirms and statements will be printed with the coded title.

Custodial Accounts

While minors may own securities and receive them in a variety of ways, their ability to enter into binding contracts to acquire or dispose of such property is strictly limited. For this reason, most securities transactions involving minors and brokerage firms are effected through custodial accounts under the Uniform Gifts to Minors Act. A number of states have passed a very similar version called the Uniform Transfers to Minors Act (UTMA). In these accounts, an adult acts on the minor's behalf until the age of majority is reached.

Account Title One custodian per one minor per account. The use of joint custodians or joint recipients is not permitted. A typical account title would be: "Jane Doe, custodian for Thomas Doe UGMA, State of Minnesota (the legal residence of the minor)."

Type of Account Cash ONLY—no margin.

Type of Gift Securities, cash, or insurance policies are permitted. All gifts are irrevocable and become the permanent property of the minor. When bearer certificates are donated, the donor and custodian may not be the same person. Also, this type of certificate must be accompanied by an irrevocable deed of gift.

Permissible Investments and Activities All states permit "reasonably prudent" investments on behalf of the minor. The prohibition of margin transactions rules out short sales, commodities, and many types of options trading.

The custodian may (1) buy and sell custodial property when deemed best; (2) subscribe to rights offerings, liquidate rights, or deposit additional cash to "round up" new shares in such an offering; (3) liquidate all or part of the custodial property to finance major benefits for the minor (college tuition, e.g.).

Prohibited Activities The custodian may not (1) pledge or lend custodial property; (2) co-mingle personal and custodial funds; (3) use custodial property to answer margin calls or make temporary loans to personal accounts; or (4) use custodial property for financing normal out-of-pocket costs associated with raising children.

Fees Ordinarily, a custodian may charge a reasonable fee for services. When the custodian is also the donor of the property, however, fees are not permitted. A few states (New York, e.g.) limit the payment of fees to a bank or trust company, but such limitations are unusual.

Tax Consequences All tax liabilities for such custodial property belong to the minor. For this reason, the minor's social security number must be on the account. It is generally preferable for a parent not to act as custodian for offspring if substantial gifts are involved because custodial property donated by a parent will be included in the parent's estate should he or she die before the minor reaches majority.

Death of a Minor or Custodian If the minor dies prior to reaching majority, any custodial property becomes part of the minor's estate and will be probated. If the custodian dies prior to the minor's majority, the legal guardian normally becomes the new custodian.

Reaching Majority Upon attaining majority in the state of legal residence, the minor assumes legal responsibility for contracts and the custodial relationship ceases. The former minor may then present the security certificates to the transfer agent, who will then reregister ownership in the new name. Although the custodian's authority ceases on the minor's majority birthdate, the new adult may then legally delegate a power of attorney to this person.

Joint Tenancy Accounts

These are accounts where property is jointly owned by two or more parties. The two most common are "joint tenancy with rights of survivorship" (WROS) and "tenancy in common" (TIC). In either case, all tenants are equally empowered to transact business in the account. In order to transfer property, all tenants must endorse the certificates. Upon death of any tenant, the tenancy is dissolved. In the case of WROS accounts, the surviving tenant is sole owner of the account. In the case of TIC accounts, the deceased tenant's portion becomes part of that tenant's estate. The surviving tenant(s) may either distribute the remaining assets or establish a new tenancy.

Corporate Accounts

When an account is opened in the name of a corporation, the corporation must furnish: (1) a corporation resolution—a document signed by the directors and empowering certain persons to act on behalf of the corporation, for example, enter orders, sign certificates; and (2) the corporate charter or an excerpt from the charter that authorizes securities transactions. All usual new account information must be on record.

Death of a Customer

Upon learning of a customer's death, the RR's first step is to cancel all open orders. The next step is to change the account title to, for example, "John Jones, deceased" and to block the account from any further trades pending receipt of appropriate documents. These include:

- copy of the death certificate
- copy of the will
- copy of the court appointment of executor or administrator, which establishes either the executor's or administrator's right to act for the estate (letters testamentary)
- estate tax waivers, which establish that there are no further estate tax claims against the property (requirements in this area have been eased in recent years)
- affidavits of domicile, which establish the state of legal residence at time of death and whose laws apply to the settlement of the estate

EXCHANGE REGULATIONS

Under NYSE rules, registered representatives are expected to devote full time to the job and any outside employment requires the prior written consent of the employer. Firms are not allowed to hire an RR in a nominal capacity solely because of the business obtained by such a person; for instance, a firm could not appoint a practicing physician as an RR merely as a funnel for orders directed by his colleagues.

Other important regulations covering the activities of registered representatives include:

Keeping a Book

An RR is expected to keep a record of all customer transactions listed by date and including the number of shares, the name of the security, and the price. Transactions should be posted on the day that the RR receives confirmation of the trade. This book is the property of the firm and should the RR leave, these records remain with the firm.

Speaking and Writing Activities

In the development of a clientele, a retail RR will almost certainly be involved in these endeavors in order to become more widely known to prospective customers. Care must be taken to ensure that NYSE rules on "suitability" of recommendations are strictly observed.

If a speaking engagement is arranged so that an RR is invited to speak before a general audience (the Masons, VFW, Elks, etc.), the talk must be general in nature. No specific security recommendations may be made and any literature to be distributed must be on a "pick-up" only basis. All speaking engagements must be recorded in the firm's log.

If the prospective clients are invited by the brokerage firm to attend an investment discussion or seminar, specific recommendations may be made and literature may be distributed to each participant. Thus, if a firm advertises a seminar on investing in high-risk special situations, an investor who accepts the invitation to attend may be handed copies of research reports and other literature, as well as receive verbal recommendations.

Teaching Activities

An RR may teach a course in a recognized educational establishment (university, community college, adult education center, etc.). Prior permission of the employer is required. The RR must also file a copy of the course outline or synopsis in the firm's log. The teaching must not interfere with the regular business day of the RR, and any compensation must be the normal rate paid for regular academic duties of similar nature.

Correspondence

All incoming correspondence, including personal mail, received at a branch office must be opened by the office manager or an authorized delegate. Should an RR receive business-related correspondence at home, it should be immediately turned over to the manager.

Outgoing correspondence must also be reviewed and approved by the office manager or delegate. An exception to this rule is a brief note, often accompanying a research report or sales literature, which does not specifically recommend a security or course of action. ("Here's our report on the microchip industry, as promised–Regards, Jim.")

If an RR wishes to write a letter illustrating the success of her investment selections, all other recommendations made in the past 12 months must be shown, including date and price when recommended for purchase and/or sale, current values if position is still extant, and all costs. The letter must also contain a statement to the effect that "past performance may not be indicative of future results."

Any testimonial letters used must indicate if fees or gratuities were paid to the person providing the testimonial.

Advertising At all large firms and many smaller ones, individual RRs are not allowed to place advertisements independently. Where allowed, however, all copies must first be submitted to the firm's authorized party (e.g., advertising director or compliance officer) for prior approval. If options are involved, the firm's Compliance Registered Options Principal must give prior approval and the copy must be submitted to an options exchange at least ten days prior to first use.

When a firm is an NASD-only member, regular advertising must be submitted to the NASD not later than five days after first use, but three days after if the topic is investment company shares.

Outside Directorships An RR may, with the employer's prior approval, hold up to 3 directorships in nonfinancial corporations and one directorship in a bank. Any directorship in a financial organization, or any directorship in excess of the limits above, requires prior approval of the NYSE.

Order Tickets When entering an order the registered representative is responsible for seeing that all required information is included on the order at time of entry. Necessary information includes:

- name and/or number of account
- number of shares
- market (NYSE, ASE, OTC, etc.)
- buy or sell (if sell, long or short)
- security description (name or symbol)
- type of order (market, limit, stop)
- time qualification (day or good until cancelled)

Any other necessary information, such as payment or delivery instructions, must also be included.

Many firms no longer use the hard copy order ticket. The buy or sell is accomplished via a computer. However, the above information is required on both the ticket and the screen.

EXCHANGE MARKETS

Trading on stock exchanges in the United States began in the latter part of the eighteenth century. The predecessor of the New York Stock Exchange, the nation's largest exchange, was founded in May 1792. It began as an outdoor market and was founded by a group of men who were primarily commodity brokers. They met each day and traded the few securities available at that time and then returned to their major business, commodities. The exchange was founded under the "Buttonwood Tree Agreement" as the original location was under a tree on Wall Street. Although the tree no longer exists, a plaque commemorates the location of this historic event. The evolution of trading on exchanges has resulted in what is known as an "auction market." In this form of trading there is continuous bidding and offering during the trading day (9:30 A.M.–4:00 P.M. EST or EDT). This competition between both buyers and sellers results in transactions at the most equitable price at any given moment.

Although the New York Stock Exchange is by far the largest, there are six other exchanges registered with the Securities and Exchange Commission. They are the American Stock Exchange (New York), the Boston Stock Exchange, the Philadelphia Stock Exchange, the

Chicago Stock Exchange, the Cincinnati Stock Exchange, and the Pacific Exchange (Los Angeles and San Francisco).

Trading on each of the exchanges is quite similar. A firm that is an exchange member receives an order to buy 100 shares of General Motors "at the market" (market orders are to be executed at the best price available at the time). This order is transmitted to the "floor" of the exchange and given to a "member" of that exchange (usually called a "broker"). The member may be employed by the firm entering the order or may be an independent broker who executes orders for others, receiving a fee ("floor brokerage") for those efforts. The independent brokers are called "two-dollar brokers," as that was the fee originally charged for each 100 shares. Since then these fees have been negotiated by the parties, but the name "two-dollar broker" remains.

The broker holding the order will proceed to a particular location on the floor, known as the "trading post." Each security is assigned to only one post so that all orders to buy and sell that security will converge at this one location. At the post the broker will find another exchange member known as the "specialist," whose function is to provide an orderly market in the securities assigned to him. He will provide our broker with a current quotation on General Motors, saying, perhaps, that "GM is 47 to 47.50." This quotation tells our broker that the highest price anyone is willing to pay (the "bid") is $47 per share and the lowest price at which anyone is willing to sell (the "offer," or "asked price") is $47.50 per share. The specialist will also tell our broker the "size" of the market by saying 700 by 900. This means that $47 per share will be paid for 700 shares and that 900 shares are offered for sale at $47.50 per share. Our broker could buy the 100 shares immediately at $47.50 or he could make a bid higher than the best current bid of $47 in the hope that some other firm might accept this bid and sell him the 100 shares of stock. This bidding and offering in competition with others provides us with a continuous auction market.

Some orders contain specific price limitation. For example, "sell 100 IBM at 99." This indicates that the stock can be sold at $99 per share or higher but not any any price lower than $99 per share. Often these limit orders are placed at prices that are not feasible at the time that they are entered. Perhaps IBM is trading at $95 per share when our order to sell at $99 reaches the floor. In this case, the firm may give the order to the specialist to handle for them. He will note this order on his "book" and, should IBM rise in price to $99, he will sell the stock for us. He will, of course, charge us a fee, but, by giving him the order, it frees our broker to handle other more immediate business.

By employing this auction process, exchange trading insures the best available price at any given moment. Prices change continually, but by channeling all orders in a particular security to one location, all buyers and sellers can compete with equality.

Electronic trading has increased dramatically; however, the concept described above is the same. Consequently, the speed and volume of trades has also increased dramatically as well. In addition, increased use of electronic trading will allow for future growth.

Types of Securities Orders

Market

A market order (MKT) requires immediate execution at the best available price. Thus, an order to buy 100 shares of Ford Motor at the market instructs the broker handling the order to purchase the shares at the best current offering. Should the stock be quoted "8 to 8.30," the best current offering is 8.25 and the broker would purchase the shares at that price. Should he attempt to buy at a lower price, he runs the risk of "missing the market." Should he be forced later to buy the shares above 8.25, he would be responsible to the customer for the difference in price.

Limit

Limit orders to buy specify the maximum price a buyer is willing to pay. Limit orders to sell specify a minimum price a seller is willing to accept. A limit order contains a specific price. Thus, an order to buy 300 ABC @ 30 instructs the broker to buy 300 shares of ABC at any price up to and including (BUT NEVER MORE THAN) 30.

Stop

The stop order to buy or sell is used to make a transaction only after a certain price is reached. If the "stop" price is touched or passed, the order is said to be "elected" ("triggered" or "activated"). The order then becomes a market order and will be executed at once, or as soon as possible. Sell stop orders are used to: (1) liquidate long positions, either to protect profits or stop a loss (hence, the obsolete and inaccurate but common reference to "stop-loss" orders); or (2) initiate a short position. Buy stop orders are used mainly to: (1) cover short positions, or (2) establish long positions on charting "breakouts."

Stop-Limit

The stop-limit order is essentially the same as a stop order, except that it becomes a limit order (not a market order) upon being elected (triggered). The order may specify the same stop and limit prices or split them. For example, "sell 100 V @ 29 stop limit" (or 29 STP-LMT) would require a sale at 29 or below to elect the order but a minimum price of 29 would be necessary to execute. On the other hand, an order to "buy 200 X @ 45 STP-LMT 46" would be elected by a sale at 45 or higher, and the order filled at any price not higher than 46. Note: On the American Stock Exchange, round-lot stop orders are not permitted. An order entered with a stop must also contain a limit at the same price: "sell 200 MTT @ 33 STP-LMT." Other exchanges do not require this procedure.

Examples of Execution of Securities Orders

Market Order

Buy 100 LMN @ mkt. After receipt of the order LMN trades occur at 85–85.25–85.50. Order executed @ 85, as it was the first one to occur after entry of the market order.

Limit Order (Sell)

Sell 100 TIR @ 32. After entry of the order TIR trades occur at 31.25–31.85–32.12. The order is executed at 32.12 as the client would sell at 32 or better.

Limit Order (Buy)

Buy 100 DOD @ 12. After entry of the order DOD trades occur at 12.50–12.25–12.12–12.25. Market closes.

The order is not executed as no trade took place at 12 (the customer's limit) or lower.

Stop Order

Buy 100 XDO @ 30 stop. After entry of the order XDO trades occur at 29.50–29.75–30–30.25–30.50. Order is executed at 30.25. The transaction at 30 elected (triggered) the stop, making it a market order. The client is entitled to the next transaction, which was 30.25.

Stop-Limit Order

Sell 100 NXR @ 45 stop limit. After entry of the order NXR trades at 45.50–45–44.50–44.75. The order is not executed. The trade at 45 elected the stop but it then became a limit order to sell at 45, and no transactions occurred at that price or higher.

Classification of Exchange Members

There are 1,366 memberships (often called "seats") on the NYSE. The men and women who own these seats are entitled to execute orders on the exchange floor where they generally perform one of four functions:

Specialist A member of the exchange responsible for maintaining an orderly market in a security.

Commission House Broker A member who primarily handles orders for his own firm's clients. Large firms would have many brokers on their staff.

"Two-Dollar Broker" An independent member who executes orders for others. He may receive the overflow business that commission house brokers can't handle or do the floor business for a firm whose own member is not on the floor.

Registered Trader A member who buys and sells solely for his own account.

Order Qualifications and Instruction

Time Instructions Orders that bear no time designation are presumed to be "day" orders and expire if not filled on that day. Orders may also be entered GTC ("good till canceled"), meaning they remain entered until canceled. Sometimes such orders are called "open" orders. On the NYSE, only day or GTC orders may be placed on the specialist's book. Orders entered with some other designation (GTW, "good through the week," e.g.) are entered at the responsibility of the entering broker. That is, a GTW order is put on the book as GTC. If unexecuted at the end of the week, the entering broker is responsible for canceling the order, and the specialist has no further responsibility.

Once an order has been entered as a "day," an attempt to extend its duration to GTC will be treated as if a new order is being entered. The significance of this is that any position established on the specialist's book is thereby lost and there may now be substantial "stock ahead" of this order.

Special Execution Instructions There are several special instructions that may be added to an order in addition to those thus far discussed. These direct the floor broker handling the order to execute in some manner other than a normal trade.

AON, "all or none" As the name implies, the order is to be executed in its entirety or not at all. Such orders are fairly common in bond trading and may also be used on OTC stocks. On the NYSE, AON has no standing (cannot be voiced) on the floor. This does not mean that it cannot be used for NYSE stocks but that brokers accept such orders at their peril. If an attempt is made to execute AON, it might result in a partial fill for which the broker would be liable.

Contingent Orders, "either/or" Two orders are entered simultaneously on the same stock with the execution of one side, either partial or complete, causing a corresponding cancelation on the other. Suppose a customer had sold short 500 IKX @ 100 and the shares appeared to be encountering some technical "support" around 83. The customer might enter an order to either "buy 500 IKX @ 80" or "buy 500 IKX @ 85 STOP/GTC." Execution of either side would, of course, close out ("cover") the short position. Should the stock drop to 80 or below, the limit side of the order would be executed and the stop portion canceled. On the other hand, if the stock first rose in price to 85, the stop portion would be elected and its execution would cancel the limit side. If a partial execution had occurred at either price, the executed portion would be deducted from both sides of the order. For example, if 300 shares had been purchased @ 80 and subsequently the market rose above 80 (but stayed below 85), the remaining part of the order would still be unexecuted. The order would be amended to read "buy 200 IKX @ 85 STOP/GTC."

FOK, "fill or kill" This is the same an AON except it must be done immediately or canceled. An order is entered to "buy 500 T @ 61 FOK." The floor broker asks the specialist for a size and quote on T, and the specialist responds "60.75–61, 3 by 2." This means only 200 shares can be purchased @ 61 at once. The order cannot be filled and it will be canceled with the customer being informed of such at once.

IOC, "immediate or cancel" This is like FOK except that a partial execution is acceptable. Given the same circumstances as above, an order to buy "500 T @ 61 IOC" would result in the purchase of the 200 available shares and the cancellation of the remainder.

NH, "not held" This designation on a market order frees the floor brokers to use their judgment as to when an execution should take place. The broker is "not held" to the tape, meaning the usual immediate execution of a market order may be delayed if the broker feels a better price may be obtained later. Other designations with the same meaning as "not held" are DRT ("disregard tape") or TAKE TIME. Note that the judgment only extends to time and price of execution, not the selection of security or the decision to buy or sell. FULLY DISCRETIONARY ORDERS MAY NOT BE PLACED WITH A FLOOR MEMBER.

Ex-Dividend Reduction On the day a stock goes "ex" a cash dividend, the price is marked down by the amount of the dividend. For instance, if XYZ closed yesterday at 34 and today was "ex" a 27-cent dividend, today's opening price would most likely be 33.73 (34 minus

.27 for the dividend). Orders entered below the market could thus be executed as a result of the stock price going down because of such reductions, not because of market action. To protect against this possibility, the specialist will reduce the price on such orders proportionately unless expressly told not to. Thus, buy limit and sell stop orders will be reduced by the amount of the cash dividend. Should the customer wish no such reduction, he or she tells the registered representative to add to the order the designation DNR ("do not reduce"). Orders above the market (buy stops, buy stop-limits, and sell limits) are not reduced for cash dividends, and the use of DNR on these orders is not necessary.

Special Methods for Handling Large Blocks of Stock

Normally, members of the exchange must execute their orders to buy or sell stock on the exchange floor. On occasion an order may be too large to be filled using the normal auction procedure. In these cases the NYSE may permit the member firm to execute the order using one of several special methods.

Specialist Block Purchases or Sales These are private transactions made directly with the specialist off the floor, usually at a price slightly above or below the current level prevailing on the floor. For example, suppose your firm had an order to sell 500,000 shares of General Motors at the market. Perhaps the most recent sale of General Motors shares took place at $48. However, the market may not be able to absorb a block this large and to sell 500,000 shares it might be necessary to see the stock down to $42 per share. With exchange permission your firm contacts the specialist in General Motors and asks him if he would like to make a specialist block purchase. Should the specialist wish to buy the stock he might make a bid of 47.50. Because this is .5 point below the current price the trade could not take place on the floor as it would distort the trading in the stock. Therefore, a private transaction takes place in which you sell the stock for your client to the specialist off the floor at 47.50. No publicity is given to the trade as it does not show on the tape displaying floor transactions and is not included in the trading volume for the stock.

If your firm wished to buy a large block of stock it might also be done off the floor. This would be known as a specialist block sale. These transactions are quite rare as the specialist would normally prefer to purchase or sell large blocks on the floor in the normal course of trading.

Exchange Distributions and Exchange Acquisitions These transactions are usually best accomplished by a firm having a large retail branch office system (Merrill Lynch, UBS, General Motors, Painewebber, etc.). Again, with the 500,000 shares of General Motors to sell, the firm—with exchange approval—informs its branches that they plan to make an exchange distribution. The offices now solicit buy orders from their many clients. When the orders to buy total 500,000 shares, they are placed on the floor together with the large sell order. The firm's broker then crosses (buys and sells as agent) the 500,000 shares of General Motors. The trade will appear on the tape identified as an "exchange distribution":

GM DIST
500,000 s 48

The advantage to the buyers of the stock is that they would pay a net price of 48 with no commission added. The seller is pleased as he sells the stock at its current price level rather than forcing the price down with his large block. He would pay a larger than usual commission allowing the firm to compensate those who solicited the buy orders.

If the order were to buy a large block the procedure is called an "exchange acquisition" and would be identified on the tape display by the letters ACQ.

Special Offers and Special Bids A "special offering" allows a member firm to employ the sales abilities of all other member firms to distribute a large block of stock. Suppose a firm had 600,000 shares of Dow Chemical to sell for a large institutional client. It might, with exchange approval, elect to make a special offering of these shares on the NYSE floor. An announcement would appear on the tape stating, "Bear, Stearns & Co. is making a Special Offering of 600,000 shares of Dow Chemical at $40 less a special commission of $.80 per share." As a registered representative of some other firm seeing this notice, you might obtain an order from one of your customers to purchase 200 shares. The order would be given to your broker, who would go to the post where DOW is traded and buy the 200 shares from the Bear Stearns broker at 80 net. Your client would pay no commission and your firm would receive $.80 per share from Bear, Stearns. The transaction would appear on the tape as:

DOW SPEC. OFF.

2 s 40

Each transaction would be displayed until the block was all sold or was withdrawn for lack of interest. The seller would obtain the current market price rather than forcing the stock down and would pay a larger than usual fee for this service.

If the order was to buy a large block the procedure used would be a "special bid."

Secondary Distributions A "secondary distribution" is the sale of a large block of stock off the exchange floor, generally after the close of the market, in which exchange members and nonmembers may participate. The secondary is the most often used method for distributing large blocks. Depending on the identity of the seller, the offering may have to be registered with the SEC before the sale can be made. If the seller is an affiliated person, one who can influence the corporation's policies, SEC registration would be necessary (Note: Rule 144, which was discussed in detail in an earlier section, permits some sales by these persons to be made without registration.) Thus, a secondary may be registered or nonregistered depending on the particular case.

An investment banking firm would handle the secondary distribution for the seller of the block and, in the case of an extremely large block, may put together a group of firms to underwrite the offering (called the "syndicate"). This group could and usually would include firms that were not members of the NYSE. The secondary would be announced on the tape as:

"Goldman Sachs Group, Inc. is making a Secondary Distribution of 1,000,000 shares of IBM at 91 less a special commission of $1.00 per share"

Unlike the special offering, which was done on the NYSE floor, this would be handled off the floor at the Goldman Sachs Group, Inc. office. Those interested would contact Goldman Sachs Group, Inc. and attempt to buy shares at 91 net to their clients less a dollar per share concession for the firm originating the order. Secondary distributions are usually done after the market closes but are sometimes done during regular market hours. These are called "spot secondaries."

The Role of the Specialist As noted earlier, the specialist is a member of the exchange responsible for maintaining an orderly market in a security. The term "specialist" is used to indicate the firm itself as well as the individual members who handle the trading of the shares in which the firm specializes. Specialist firms are large, well-capitalized organizations. As they do not often deal with the public their names are not as well known nationally as, for instance, UBS, Painewebber, Merrill Lynch, and Morgan Stanley. However, large specialist firms such as LaBranche & Co. and Spear, Leeds & Kellogg are major financial organizations. They will handle a number of different securities as specialist and will control many individual exchange memberships.

In performing his functions the specialist acts in two capacities: as broker (agent), where he executes orders entrusted to him by other firms; and as principal (dealer), where he buys and sells for his own firm's account.

When acting as agent the specialist accepts orders from member firms that are away from the current price. Thus, if Fahnstock and Co. had an order to buy 2,000 shares of General Motors at $48 when the last sale of General Motors was $50, it would not pay them to waste their broker's valuable time by having him stand at the post waiting for a decline in price. They would send the order to the specialist, who would place the order on his "book." Should the stock decline to $48, the specialist would buy the shares and report the purchase to Fahnstock and Co. At the end of the month the specialist would send a bill for the floor brokerage charged for executing the order. Many limit orders as well as virtually all stop orders are given to the specialist. In busy markets the specialist might also be given market orders that firms find themselves unable to handle.

When acting as a broker the specialist can do anything that the originating firm can do in executing an order. However, when acting as a principal some restrictions are placed on his activities. As the specialist is privy to information that the rest of us do not have, such as the number and size of orders on his book, he would otherwise have an unfair advantage over us.

Restrictions on Specialist Acting as Principal

- Specialist cannot bid or offer on the same side as a market order he is holding. If a firm gave the specialist an order to buy 200 shares of Scott Paper at the market, the specialist could not bid at any price for his own account until that order was completed. He could, however, sell stock while holding the buy order, as that would be the opposite "side" of the market.
- Specialist cannot bid or offer on the same side at the same price as a limit order he is holding. Suppose the specialist was quoting Eastman Kodak "25.50, 1,000 up." That means that the best bid for Kodak was 25 for 1,000 shares and the best offer was $25.50 for 1,000 shares. Assume that the buy order at $25 was given to the specialist by Bear, Stearns & Co. and the sell order at 25.50 was given to him by Morgan Stanley. While he holds those limit orders he cannot bid 25 or offer $25.50 for his own account as this would be competing with customers' orders. Note: The specialist can bid or offer between these prices as that would improve the market. Thus, in our example the specialist would be free to bid or offer at any price between 25.01 and 25.24.

- Specialist cannot cause the election of a stop order. As noted earlier stop orders are memorandum orders that become market orders if the stated price is reached or surpassed. With IBM trading at 91 a customer places an order to "Sell 100 IBM @ 85 stop." This order is placed on the specialist book as a memorandum. Should IBM decline in price and trade at 85 or lower the stop would be elected (triggered), and the specialist would now sell the 100 shares at the best price available. As only the specialist knows the existence of the stop orders he could take advantage of the situation.

  If there were many thousands of shares to buy or sell stop at a particular price he could elect these orders simply by buying or selling 100 shares for his own account. He would execute these orders at the market and receive the floor brokerage. He might even adjust his position ahead of time to take advantage of the market's reaction to the elected stop orders. Therefore, he cannot be the cause of the electing of a stop order. In our example, "Sell 100 IBM @ 91 stop," the specialist could not bid or offer for his own account at 91 or lower as success in this bid or offer would elect the stop.

  Note: Stop orders tend to collect at the same price as they are frequently used by technical analysts whose studies lead to the same conclusion. Thus, when too many stop orders are entered at the same price their election could disrupt the market. For this reason the exchange often bans stop orders to prevent their disturbing the orderliness of the market.

- Specialist cannot be broker and/or dealer on the same transaction. If the specialist wishes to buy or sell for his own account he cannot also act as agent for the firm on the other side of the trade. If the specialist were given an order to buy 100 Exxon at the market and wished to fill the order by selling stock for his own account, he would have to summon the broker for the firm with the buy order and return the order to him. He could then sell the stock as dealer (principal) while the other firm's broker would represent it on the buy side.

- Specialist cannot stop stock for his own account. Stopping stock is a procedure in which the specialist guarantees to reserve stock at a price giving the broker an opportunity to improve the price. For example, a broker for Prudential Securities has an order to sell 100 XYZ at the market. Upon arriving at the post he is told by the specialist that the stock is quoted 78-79. The broker notes on the indicator above the post that the last sale of XYZ was at 79. The broker has a problem. The best price (bid) at which he can sell the stock is 78, which is one point below the last sale. This will not please the client but if the broker attempts to better the price he runs the risk of missing the market. Should the broker later be forced to sell below 78, he will be responsible for any difference in price.

In an attempt to solve the problem, he says to the specialist, "Will you stop me at 78?" If the specialist agrees the Prudential broker can relax. The specialist has guaranteed him that he will not sell below 78, which is the best price currently available. The specialist will then be given the order and he will offer the stock above 78 (perhaps at 78.50). If a buyer comes to the post the Prudential order may be filled at 78.50 but in no case will the shares be sold below 78. The specialist has guaranteed this by stopping the stock. To fulfill the guarantee the specialist may have to buy the stock himself, but he will stop stock on many occasions to prevent, if possible, large variations in prices of transactions.

Note: When "stopped stock" trades it is printed on the tape with an identifier $\frac{s}{t}$, which shows that this transaction was at a price previously guaranteed by the specialist. This is done to prevent some other client from feeling that he was entitled to that transaction. Should the stock in our example above eventually be sold at 78, it would show on the tape as:

XYZ

s
78 t

Short Sales A short sale is defined by the Securities Exchange Commission "as a sale of a security which you do not own, or if you own it you do not intend to deliver it." (The mechanics of a short sale are discussed in detail in Chapter 8 "The Federal Reserve and Margin.") A short sale is when the investor sells borrowed securities with the hope of buying them back in the future at a lower price. However, there are a few prerequisites before a short sale can be completed.

1. It may only be executed in a customer's margin account.
2. The order must be market short.
3. He must be able to borrow the securities he is selling short (his broker will provide this service).

NYSE Bond Activity

The exchange recognizes that the market for bonds is often better in the over-the-counter market. For this reason it permits member firms to execute orders for $10,000 face value of bonds off the floor of the exchange. Orders calling for amounts from $1,000 to $9,000 can also be executed over the counter under the exchange's "Nine-Bond Rule" if one or more of the following conditions exist:

- The customer instructs the firm to execute his order off the floor (in this case the firm can act only as agent).
- The order is for U.S. government or municipal bonds.
- The bonds have been called or are within one year of maturity.
- After careful check it is apparent that a fair market does not exist on the floor.

Tape Displays Transactions in stocks are shown continually during the trading day on what are commonly called "ticker tapes." This name goes back to the earlier days of the tape, invented by Thomas Edison, when the tape made a clicking sound as it progressed. Thus each transaction was called a "tick" (e.g., General Electric just ticked at 38.24).

Today's tape is broken into two separate systems. Consolidated Tape A shows transactions in stocks that are listed on the New York Stock Exchange. However, it shows trades in these stocks wherever they may occur. Thus, trades in GM on the tape may well have taken place on the NYSE but also could have occurred on any other stock exchange as well as in the "third market," which is the over-the-counter trading of exchange-listed stocks. Consolidated Tape B shows transactions in stocks listed on the American Stock Exchange that occur on that exchange or in any other market.

When a trade occurs in a stock it is shown on the tape by the symbol for the stock, the transaction price, and an indication of the volume of the trade. A transaction of 100 shares shows only the symbol and the trade price. For example, a trade of 100 shares of Texas Instruments at 37.50 would appear:

TXN

37.50

Trades of 200–9,900 shares use only the first digit or digits of the volume with the letter "s" appearing between. A trade of 700 TXN at 37.50 would appear:

TXN

7 s 37.50

A trade of 9,500 TXN at 25.50 would appear:

TXN

95 s 37.50

Trades of 10,000 shares or more show the full volume figure, again with the letter "s" between. A trade of 10,700 TXN at 37.50 would appear:

TXN

10,700 s 37.50

Should the volume of trading cause the tape to run late (generally, five minutes or more) the announcement "digits deleted" will appear. The tape will then print only the last digit of the price. Our 1,700-share trade of TXN at 37.50 would appear:

TXN

1,700 s 7.50

Further delays will cause "volume digits deleted" to be announced and that trade would appear:

TXN

7.50

Although most stocks trade in 100-share units (round lot) some stock on the NYSE use a 10-share round lot. These stocks are primarily those listed at "Post 30" where inactive stocks are traded. Round-lot trades in 10-share unit stocks are identified by the letters "$\frac{s}{s}$" appearing between the volume and price. A trade of 400 shares of XYZ PR at 165 (PR is the symbol denoting a preferred stock) would appear:

XYZ PR

40 $\frac{s}{s}$ 165

A trade of 60 shares of XYZ PR would appear:

XYZ PR

6 $\frac{s}{s}$ 165

The exchange attempts to print transactions on the tape in the order in which they occurred. Sometimes this is impossible due to mechanical or human error. In that case, the out-of-sequence trades are identified as "sold sales" by use of the letters "SLD." If the following trades in U.S. Steel were shown on the tape,

X	X SLD	X
113	113.35	113.12

we would know that the second transaction was not shown in proper order and no conclusions should be drawn from this sequence.

When the market opens each day transactions begin to be shown on the tape. If a particular stock opens late (more than a half hour after the opening) or opens at a price sharply up or down from the previous close the opening trade will be identified by the letters "OPD" (opened). The price change that would call for the use of this symbol is as follows: for stocks closing below $20 per share, a change at the next morning's opening of 1 point or more; for those closing at $20 or higher, a change of 2 points or more.

Suppose Teledyne (TDY) closes tonight at 44. Should it open tomorrow morning at 42 or lower or 46 or higher the symbol OPD will be used. Let's say tomorrow 2,700 shares of Teledyne open at 46.50. It would appear on the tape:

TDY OPD
27 s 46.50

This calls our attention to the stock and may lead us to make an inquiry to better service our clients.

Note: Stocks listed on exchanges have symbols of no more than three characters. IBM is as long as they get. Symbols for over-the-counter stocks, which will be discussed later, have four or more characters in their symbol; for example, Fidelcor - FICR.

THE NASD AND THE OVER-THE-COUNTER MARKET

The NASD was founded under the Maloney Act Amendment to the Securities and Exchange Act of 1934. The amendment, passed by Congress in 1938, allowed for the establishment of a securities association to regulate the over-the-counter market. The National Association of Securities Dealers was formed in 1939. It has authority in the over-the-counter market similar to that of the stock exchanges in regulating their members and markets.

Any broker or dealer who transacts any branch of the investment banking or securities business in the United States is eligible to join the NASD, unless subject to one of the following:

- where the broker/dealer has been suspended or expelled from a national securities exchange for violating just and equitable principles of trade.
- where the SEC or any stock exchange has an order revoking or denying the registration of the broker/dealer.
- where the individuals do not meet the training or experience or other standards that the NASD Board of Governors may feel necessary.
- where the individuals have been convicted in the last ten years of a felony or misdemeanor involving embezzlement, misappropriation or funds, or abuse of a fiduciary relationship.

This takes on added importance because only NASD members have the advantage of price concessions, discounts, and other underwriting allowances.

The NASD rules require registration of all principals and representatives. The main classes of principals are: general securities principal; and financial and operations principal.

The NASD requires that all corporations and partnerships have least two persons registered as principals. The following individuals must be registered as principals: persons engaged in management or supervision of the firm's investment banking or securities business; persons involved in the training of principal personnel of the member. Thus, these would normally have to register as principals: sole proprietors, partners, officers, managers or officers of supervisory jurisdiction, directors, managers of investment banking activities, and training directors responsible for training the above.

Since September 1, 1972, every broker/dealer must designate a financial principal who will be responsible for the preparation and approval of financial statements and net capital computations. To qualify as a financial principal, a person must pass a written examination unless specifically exempted by the NASD.

The term "registered representative" is defined by the NASD as every partner, officer, or employee of a member engaged in any of the following activities:

1. solicitation or handling of listed or unlisted securities business
2. sales of listed or unlisted securities on an agency or principal basis
3. solicitation of subscriptions to service provided on a fee basis, such as investment management or advisory services
4. training registered representatives

The NASD also has certain limited categories of registration for persons who sell only certain investment products or engage in specific areas of activity. The limited categories include:

1. investment company and variable products representative
2. direct participation programs representative
3. real estate securities representative

These individuals are exempt from registration:

- Foreign associates if they are not U.S. citizens or residents and do not transact business with U.S. citizens or residents
- Other employees who are exempt, such as those engaged in clerical or ministerial functions, those whose participation is nominal (money partners), those who work on the floor of an exchange, and those who handle only exempt securities or commodities.

If a person associated with the member voluntarily resigns, a formal resignation must be addressed to the NASD in writing. The NASD will immediately notify the member and such resignation will not take effect until 30 days after receipt of the resignation by the NASD or so long as any complaint or action is pending against the person. However, the NASD may, at its discretion, declare the resignation effective at any time. An NASD member must also give written notice to the NASD when a registered representative is terminated, not later than 30 calendar days after the termination.

Further, anyone guilty of submitting a membership or registration application that is misleading or any member that fails to register an employee who should be registered is subject to disciplinary action by the NASD.

NASD regulations can be separated into four categories: Conduct Rules, Code of Procedure, Code of Arbitration, and Uniform Practice Code.

Conduct Rules

The Conduct Rules are concerned with the day-to-day operations of a securities firm and contain many important sections.

The Conduct Rules are numerous, but they are not covered in their entirety here. The reason being is that in the Series #7 Exam, the questions are designed to assess the knowledge for an entry level Registered Representative. Please do not take this statement to mean that you can take this section lightly. On the contrary, the items discussed below will be tested.

There are various sections of the Conduct Rules, and even though their rule numbers are not tested, their content must be understood and applied.

One section deals with business conduct of members and touches on advertising. It requires that all advertising be submitted to the NASD for approval within five days after first use. One exception to this states that advertising regarding investment companies must be submitted within three days after first use. Advertising includes any material prepared for use in the media such as newspapers, magazines, radio, television, recorded telephone reports, and motion picture advertising. Excluded from the definition of advertising are the so-called "tombstone ads," which announce new issues, office openings, and personnel changes. Sales literature includes research reports, market letters and such and need not be submitted to the NASD for approval but must be approved by a principal of the firm. The firm must also maintain a separate file of advertising and sales literature for three years after its use.

Purchase and sale of equity IPOs, discussed in our coverage of new issues, are also included in this section of the Conduct Rules. Please review the provisions of Rule 2790 in Chapter 4.

Another section requires that you have reasonable grounds for believing that a recommendation is suitable for a customer based upon facts disclosed by the customer concerning his other security holdings and his financial situation and needs, providing he has furnished such information to you. Further, it prohibits the following practices under its policy of fair dealings:

- recommending speculative low price securities without regard for suitability
- churning
- trading of mutual fund shares
- fraudulent activity
- recommending purchases beyond the customer's financial means

This section prohibits a member or any person associated with a member from directly or indirectly giving a gratuity or gift in excess of $100 per individual per year to any person who is a representative of another person, if the payment or gratuity is in relation to the business of the employer of the recipient of the gift. This section further requires that a separate record of all payments or gratuities in any amount be retained by the member.

It is a violation of the Conduct Rules for anyone vested with discretion over a client's account to churn that account. It also prohibits the use of discretion in a customer's account unless the customer has given prior written authorization and the account has been accepted by the member and approved in writing by the member, partner, officer, or manager designated by the member. Further, the member or the person designated by the member must approve each discretionary order promptly and must review all discretionary accounts frequently in order to protect them from transactions that might be considered churning. With regard to this rule, discretion as to price or time only does not apply.

It is also prohibited to use of manipulative, deceptive, or other fraudulent devices to induce the purchase or sale of a security by a client.

This section prohibits a member from guaranteeing a customer against loss in his account. However, the main thrust of this section is to prohibit members from making improper use of a customer's securities or funds. Without the written consent of the client, the firm may not borrow or lend the customer's securities. Normally, they may pledge or hypothecate (use as collateral for loans to brokers or dealers) no more of a customer's securities than might be considered fair and reasonable in view of the indebtedness of the customer to the firm, unless such member receives the prior written authorization of the client designating the particular securities to be loaned.

Further, this section prohibits any person associated with a member from sharing in the profits or losses of any customer account except with prior written permission of his member firm and providing that he shares only in direct proportion to the financial contribution he has personally made to that account.

Another section requires each member to keep and preserve books, records, and documents in conformity with all applicable rules, laws, regulations, and policies of the NASD. Each member must also maintain records of customers to show the following information:

- name
- address and whether the customer is legally of age
- signature of the registered representative and of the individual accepting the account for the member
- if the customer is associated with another member, that fact must be noted
- if the account is discretionary, the age or approximate age and occupation of the customer

Finally, this section requires that a member keep and preserve in each office of supervisory jurisdiction a separate file or record of all written complaints of customers and action taken by the member, if any, to satisfy the complaint.

Members are required to allow a bona fide regular customer to inspect, upon request, the information relative to the member's financial condition as disclosed in its most recent balance sheet.

Members may grant or receive selling concessions, discounts, and other allowances in connection with the sale of securities that are part of a fixed-price offering only as consideration for services rendered in the distribution and only to brokers or dealers actually engaged in the investment banking or securities business. It also states that a member is not prohibited from selling securities at the stated public offering price to persons to whom it provides bona fide research. In order to grant a selling concession, discount, or other allowance to another person, a member must obtain a written agreement from that person that he will comply with the provisions of Rule 2790. If the member grants such a concession, discount, or other allowance to a nonmember broker/dealer in a foreign country, he must also obtain from that broker or dealer a written agreement to comply with the various provisions as if that foreign broker/dealer were a member of the NASD.

This section prohibits a member from dealing with a nonmember on any terms other than it would deal with the public. The provisions of this section do not apply to any nonmember broker/ dealer in a foreign country who is not eligible for membership in the NASD.

This applies exclusively to the activities of members in connection with the sale of open-end investment company shares. No member may offer or sell the shares of any open-end investment company if the public offering price includes a sales charge that is excessive, taking into consideration all relevant circumstances. Sales charges will be considered excessive if they do not conform to the following provisions:

1. The maximum sales charge in any transaction cannot exceed 8½% of the offering price.
2. If a fund does not offer dividend reinvestment, the maximum sales charge is 7¼%.
3. If rights of accumulation are not made available, the maximum sales charge is:

   - 8% of the fund if it offers dividend reinvestment; and
   - 6¾% if it does not.

   Rights of accumulation permit reduced sales charges on future purchases after a new breakpoint is reached.
4. If quantity discounts (breakpoints) are not made available on single purchases, the maximum sales charge is:

   - 7¾% if the fund offers dividend reinvestment and rights of accumulation.
   - 7¼% if it offers dividend reinvestment but not rights of accumulation.
   - 6½% if it offers rights of accumulation, but not dividend reinvestment.
   - 6¼% if it offers neither rights of accumulation nor dividend reinvestment.

The rule further prohibits a member from withholding a customer's order for any investment company security so as to profit himself as a result of such withholding. A member may only purchase shares of an investment company if he already has a purchase order in his possession or if it is for his own investment account.

A mutual fund shareholder may have his shares redeemed by the investment company at net asset value. Some funds charge a redemption fee of 1% or 2%. With some technical exceptions, shares must be redeemed by the fund within seven days after they are tendered.

Further, no member is permitted to favor or disfavor the distribution of a particular investment company shares on the basis of the brokerage commissions received or expected to be received from any source including the investment company. However, members who sell investment company shares are permitted to execute transactions for that investment company as long as such orders are not obtained on the basis of their sales of the investment company shares.

This section of the Conduct Rules sets forth supervisory requirements. Each member must establish, maintain, and enforce written procedures that enable it to supervise properly the activities of each registered representative. In addition to registered representatives, associated personnel are required to comply with all appropriate securities laws, regulations, and rules. The responsibility for proper supervision rests with the member who must designate a partner, officer, or manager in each office of supervisory jurisdiction to carry out the written procedures.

This section of the Conduct Rules states that complaints may be brought against an NASD member or any person associated with an NASD member by:

- a public customer
- the District Business Conduct Committee of the NASD
- the Board of Governors of the NASD
- the Securities and Exchange Commission

A member or person associated with a member may be required by the District Business Conduct Committee, the board of governors, or duly authorized agents of either committee to report orally or in writing concerning any matter under investigation or to testify at any hearing. The NASD may also investigate the books and records of any member relating to any investigation or hearing. No member or person associated with a member may refuse to permit an inspection of books and records. A failure to furnish reports when requested by the NASD constitutes grounds for suspension. After 15 days' notice in writing and continued failure to furnish the information requested, the president of the NASD is authorized on behalf of the board of governors to suspend the member or person associated with the member.

This section of the Conduct Rules states that a member or person associated with a member can be censured, be fined up to $15,000, be suspended from membership or registration, expelled, have his registration revoked, be barred from association with a member, or be given any other penalty appropriate under the circumstances. The member is also prohibited from paying any salary or commission that results from any security transaction earned during a period of suspension of an associated person.

Every member is responsible for keeping and preserving appropriate records for carrying out the member's supervisory procedures. A member or his authorized representative must review and endorse in writing, on an internal record, all transactions and correspondence of its registered representatives pertaining to the solicitation or execution of any securities transactions. Each member organization, through the member of another registered principal, must also review the activities of each office, including the periodic examination of customer accounts to detect and prevent any irregularities or abuses and, at least once a year, must conduct an inspection of each office of supervisory jurisdiction.

Under this section of the NASD rules, the board of governors has issued an interpretation covering "private securities transactions." For the purposes of this interpretation, private securities transactions means securities transactions not sponsored by the firm that involve a limited number of purchasers or sellers (as contrasted with public offerings registered with the SEC), and other investment transactions involving associated personnel that may mislead customers into believing the transactions are sponsored by the member. Obviously, these types of transactions are prohibited.

The Conduct Rules also require that if an employee of one member seeks to open an account with another member, the second member must notify the person's employer promptly in writing. The member carrying the account must exercise reasonable diligence to determine that the transactions will not adversely affect the interest of the employing member. Additionally, this rule requires that the employer receive duplicate copies of the confirmations and/or monthly statements of the carrying member relating to the transactions of that employee.

This section prohibits a member from offering or selling a variable annuity if the payment includes a sales charge that is unfair, taking into consideration all relevant circumstances. A variable annuity may not be offered or sold other than at a value that is determined after receipt of payment in accordance with the provisions of the contract. Payment is not considered to have been received until the contract has been accepted by the insurance company.

This section also requires that a member promptly transmit to the issuer all applications for variable annuities and at least that part of the purchase payment that will be credited toward the contract (as opposed to that part applied to the sales load).

Lastly, this rule provides that a member may not participate in selling a variable annuity unless the insurance company makes prompt payment of the amounts requested and payable under the contract when presented with a proper request for either a partial or total redemption.

The Code of Procedure

The NASD has established a Code of Procedure for handling trade practice complaints regarding violations of the Conduct Rules adopted thereunder. This code provides for the District Business Conduct Committee of the NASD to hear and pass upon all complaints regarding violations of these rules. The Board of Governors of the NASD acts as an appeals court and review body but does not handle the original complaint. Any initial complainant or initial respondent to a complaint may request a hearing before the District Business Conduct Committee and is entitled to such a hearing. In the absence of such a request for a hearing, the committee itself may order a hearing if it deems such action necessary or appropriate. If a hearing is held, both the complainant and the respondent are entitled to be heard in person, to be represented by counsel, and to submit any relevant matter which they may desire to present.

In any case in which the District Business Conduct Committee believes that the facts of the matter are not in dispute; that the acts, practices, and conduct involved do constitute a violation of the Conduct Rules; and that following the regular complaint procedure does not appear to be appropriate, the committee may offer the respondent an opportunity to waive a hearing and accept a summary complaint procedure. In the case of the summary complaint procedure, the penalty for all violations alleged cannot exceed censure and/or a fine of $2,500.

A respondent in a hearing before a District Business Conduct Committee may at any time propose in writing to the district secretary an order of settlement. The district secretary must submit such an offer to the committee. An initial cap offer of an initial cap settlement may be made at any time during the course of a proceeding, but must be made in conformance with the provisions of the Conduct Rules. The offer may not be frivolously made or propose a penalty inconsistent with the seriousness of the violations to be found. Any action taken by the District Business Conduct Committee is subject to review by the board of governors on its own motion within 45 days after the date of notice, or upon the motion of any aggrieved person providing such motion is filed within 15 days after the date of notice. In any case where either the complainant or the respondent feels aggrieved by any disciplinary action taken or approved by the board of governors, either party may make application for review to the Securities and Exchange Commission in accordance with Section 15A of the Securities Exchange Act of 1934.

Code of Arbitration

The NASD's Code of Arbitration procedure was adopted for the arbitration of controversies arising out of the securities or related business of any member. The Code of Arbitration procedure handles disputes or controversies: between or among members; between members and public customers; and between members, the clearing corporation, and clearing banks or associated banks. Any disputed claim or controversy subject to arbitration under this code must be submitted to arbitration under the circumstances:

- at the insistence of a member against another member
- at the insistence of a public customer against a member and/or person associated with a member
- at the insistence of a member, the NCC division of the Depository Trust Clearing Corp., a clearing bank or associated bank, against the other
- at the insistence of a member against a person associated with a member or a person associated with a member or a person associated with member against member
- at the insistence of a person associated with a member against another person associated with a member

Uniform Practice Code The Uniform Practice Code of the NASD is designed to standardize the practices employed by dealers in making and settling transactions. The code, which is supervised by the Uniform Practice Committee, exempts certain securities, including U.S. government securities and municipal bonds. Let us look at the important sections of the code.

Delivery Dates

There are four types of trades under the Uniform Practice Code.

Regular Way "RW" trades settle on the third business day after the trade. Thus, if a broker sells securities to another broker on Monday, May 7, on a regular way basis, the seller delivers those securities on Thursday, May 10, at which time the buyer must be prepared to make payment. (Note: Regular way trades in U.S. government securities are settled on the first or next business day after the trade.)

Seller's Option Seller's option trades settle from the third business day to the sixtieth calendar day after the trade. The conditions of the trade must be agreed upon at the time the trade is made. For example; a client of a broker wishes to sell some stock today but does not have physical possession of the certificates. Perhaps they are at his daughter's home some distance away and he cannot get them for three weeks or so. The selling broker could offer his securities "seller 25." If a buyer accepted these terms, delivery would not be required of the selling broker until the twenty-fifth calendar day after the trade. Thus, the client has sold his shares today but has 25 days to deliver. Suppose the client unexpectedly obtained possession of the securities sooner than he had anticipated, perhaps on the tenth day after the trade. In this case, the selling broker could deliver the securities earlier than stated in the original trade by giving the buying dealer one day written notice.

Cash Trades These trades settle on the day of the trade. A client may have an emergency and need money immediately. His broker could offer the securities for "cash." Should someone accept the offer under those terms, delivery and payment would occur the same day. This would allow the client to obtain his needed funds that day. Naturally, the securities must be in good deliverable form for a cash trade to be made. It is possible that in both seller's option and cash trades the seller may have to make a sacrifice on the price. The buyer is accommodating the seller and may charge for that accommodation by dropping his bid.

When Issued "WI" trades (the actual name is "When As and If Issued") are settled on some undetermined future date. Perhaps a new issue of stock or bonds is made. At the time of the offering, the actual certificates may not have been printed. (This is particularly true in bond offerings when the coupon rate is often not determined until the offering date.) In this case we will begin to trade the stock "when issued" until the manager of the syndicate can provide us with a settlement date. WI may also occur when a stock splits. We begin to trade the stock WI until the NASD Uniform Practice Committee can give us a final settlement date.

A close relative of when issued is when distributed ("WD"). This is the result of a spinoff. Company A owns Company B and decides to give the B shares to the holders of A stock. This is known as a spinoff. We begin to trade the Company B stock as soon as the arrangement is final but again the physical certificates may not yet be available. We trade WD until the new shares are ready.

Ex-Dividends. Ex-Rights. Ex-Warrants.

When a corporation declares a cash dividend or issues rights or warrants to their shareholders that corporation determines the "record date" for the distribution. The record date is the date on which you must be on the books (records) of the corporation to be entitled to the dividend. A buyer of securities becomes the record owner on the settlement date of the trade. Therefore, a regular way trade must be made three business days prior to the record date in order for the buyer to be entitled to a distribution. If you purchased stock two business days prior to the record date, you would be too late to receive the dividend as settlement date is three business days later and would be after the record date. Trades made on the "ex" date permit the seller to retain the dividend as it is too late for the buyer to receive it. This is also true for distribution of rights, warrants, and other items. Cash trades settle on the same day as the trade. Therefore, a security bought for cash on the record date would entitle the buyer to receive the dividend. Thus, cash trades are ex-dividend on the business day following the record date. It should be kept in mind that the "ex" dates for rights and warrants under normal circumstances is the day after the payable date.

Good Delivery

A "good delivery" is one that the buying dealer is required to accept. When securities are delivered in settlement of a transaction the buyer inspects them. If they comply with the Uniform Practice Code, they are good delivery and the buying dealer must pay for them. There are a number of elements that are necessary for a good delivery.

I am including the various denominations of bond and stocks that constitute a good delivery. The reason being is that they are still on the books of the NASD and according to the current outline for the General Securities registered Representative Examination (Test Series #7) Section 6.2.1 page 19; they can still test on them. However, physical delivery of securities is almost non-existent these days. Therefore, know they exist, but don't spend too much time on this area.

When a dealer makes a delivery to settle a trade, it must conform to certain requirements as to the denomination of the certificates used. In bond transactions, delivery must be in denominations of $1,000 or multiples thereof. Also acceptable would be bonds in $500 denominations. For example, Morgan Stanley sells $10,000 XYZ debentures to Bear, Stearns & Co. Morgan Stanley could deliver any combination of $1,000 denomination bonds or multiples of $1,000 or $500 face-value bonds. For example, all of the following would be good delivery on this $10,000 bond (10M) trade.

1 × $10,000
10 × $ 1,000
2 × $ 5,000
9 × $ 1,000 and 2 × $500
20 × $ 500
2 × $ 4,000 and 4 × $500

There are many other possible combinations, but these are all good delivery. Bonds in denominations other than those mentioned are not a good delivery and need not be accepted by the purchasing dealer.

Here are a few examples of deliveries on our 10M bond trade that would not be a good delivery.

10 × $750 and 10 × $250
30 × $300 and 5 × $200
10 × $600 and 10 × $400

These odd denominations are called "baby bonds" and when sold must be designated as such. The price paid is usually below the bid for bonds of acceptable denominations.

In stock trades, good delivery for a round lot would be 100-share certificates or multiples of 100. If A.G. Edwards & Sons sells 400 shares of stock to Morgan Stanley, A.G. Edwards could deliver one 400-share certificate, two 200-share certificates, four 100-share certificates. Also considered good delivery on round-lot stock trades would be odd-lot certificates which can be assembled into 100-share amounts. This means the buyer must take odd-lot pieces if they can be "piled up" into 100-share piles. For example, on our 400-share trade, Edwards could deliver eight 50-share certificates, twenty 20-share certificates, or 400 one-share certificates. All of these can be assembled (piled up) into 100-share amounts. Any proper combination of round-lot or odd-lot certificates is good delivery. For example, on our 400-share trade, all of the following would be acceptable:

4 × 100
2 × 200
1 × 200 and 4 × 50
8 × 50

It would not be a good delivery if the seller delivered five certificates for 80 shares. Although this certainly totals 400, 80-share certificates cannot be combined into 100-share amounts.

In an odd-lot stock trade the seller may deliver any number of certificates as long as the total exactly matches the trade. If a transaction of 40 shares took place, the seller could deliver one 40-share certificate, four 10-share certificates, or two 20-share certificates. However, the buyer need not accept a delivery of 50 shares on the 40-share trade nor a 30-share partial delivery. The delivery must be for precisely 40 shares.

Suppose we had a combination of a round lot and an odd lot for, say, a trade of 440 shares. The easiest way to approach this is to separate it into 400 shares and 40 shares. To be good delivery you must be able to segregate the odd lot (40). The remaining certificates must satisfy the requirements for the round lot (400). All of the following would be good delivery on a trade of 440 shares:

$$4 \times 100 \text{ and } 2 \times 20$$
$$8 \times 50 \text{ and } 4 \times 10$$
$$4 \times 50, 2 \times 100 \text{ and } 40 \times 1$$
$$4 \times 95 \text{ and } 12 \times 5$$

Note: On the above we use 8 of the share certificates for the odd lot. Each of the remaining 5 shares when combined with a 95 share piece results in 100.

The following would not be good delivery on a 440-share trade :

$$4 \times 110$$
$$5 \times 80 \text{ and } 4 \times 10$$
$$10 \times 30 \text{ and } 3 \times 50$$

Registered Versus Bearer Securities

Securities in "bearer" form are those that do not include the name of the owner. A bearer security is like a $100 bill. Whoever has it, owns it. Delivery of bearer securities is considered good as long as they are not mutilated. A bearer bond with some of the remaining interest coupons torn off is not good. A bearer stock certificate with ink stains obliterating some of the details is not good. On rare occasions, a mutilated certificate can be good delivery if it is authenticated by the issuing company or its agent (transfer agent, registrar, etc.).

Registered securities are those bearing the name of the registered owner. These require a properly completed "assignment and power of substitution." This is the proper name for the back of the certificate, which must be completed and signed by the registered owner. We often use a separate assignment and power of substitution, which we call a "stock power" or "bond power." This is simply a facsimile of the back of the certificate and is used for purposes of safety and convenience. The assignment must be signed by the owner exactly as his or her name appears on the certificate. A certificate registered "Roger T. Jones" should be signed "Roger T. Jones." If it is signed "R.T. Jones," the dealer delivering the certificate must place a stamp under the signature guaranteeing that this is "one and the same person" and the dealer must sign the guarantee. Often the name of the person has changed since the certificate was issued, usually due to marriage or divorce. A certificate registered "Mary A. Jones" might now be owned by Mary A. Smith, the woman's married name. She would sign both names and the dealer handling her delivery would guarantee her "to be one and the same person." Securities registered in joint accounts must be signed by all tenants. Should you have a security registered in the names of five co-tenants, all five must endorse in order for the certificate to be a good delivery.

In any case, the signature or signatures on an assignment must be guaranteed by a broker/dealer or a bank. Keep in mind that the buying dealer does not know the person to whom the certificate is registered. By having the signature guaranteed, the buying dealer is safe should there be a forgery or other impropriety.

Bearer securities are still around, but corporations and municipalities haven't used them in several years. Eventually they will disappear when the last ones mature.

"Legal" Items

A "legal" item is one that requires supporting documentation. Perhaps the securities being sold were registered in the name of a deceased person. To accomplish transfer of these securities, many documents would be needed. The needs of transfer agents vary to some degree, but we would expect that an appointment of the estate's executor or administrator from the court of jurisdiction would be a necessity. In addition, tax waivers, an affidavit of domicile, and instructions regarding the disposition of the assets from the executor or administrator would be required for transfer of ownership of the securities. It would not be proper to place the burden of this problem on the dealer purchasing the securities. The selling dealer should accomplish the transfer and deliver the securities in "street name" (broker/dealer name) to the buyer. In brief, the buyer should not be expected to accept delivery of securities that present any transfer problems. Those problems should be solved by the agent for the seller, and the securities delivered to the buyer should be in readily transferable form.

Other examples of legal items would be those in the name of an executor, administrator, trustee, receiver, or any other registrar that would place an unnecessary burden on the buyer, who bought only the stock, not any problems associated with it.

Due Bills and Due Bill Checks

A "due bill" is similar to an IOU. It is used when the selling dealer delivers the securities too late to accomplish transfer to the name of the buyer when a cash dividend or other distribution is imminent. For example, on April 4, a corporation declares a cash dividend that is payable to stockholders of record on Wednesday, April 11. A buyer of the stock on April 4 would be entitled to this dividend as the trade would settle three business days later (April 9), before the record date. It would be most unlikely that the stock, even if delivered on April 9, could be transferred in time to have the dividend paid to the rightful recipient, the buyer. To avoid unnecessary paperwork, the seller will deliver the securities accompanied by a due bill for the amount of the dividend. On payment date, the buyer simply presents the due bill to the seller and collects the amount to which he is entitled. To save even further problems, the seller might use a "due bill check." This is simply a check for the amount due to the buyer, carrying a date that coincides with the payment date of the dividend.

Due bills can be used as a substitute for any item to which the buyer is entitled but which the seller is unable to deliver. For example, they are used as a substitute for stock dividends, stock splits, rights, warrants, and other distributions that are due to the buyer, but that the seller is not in a position to deliver.

Due bills and due bill checks are rare indeed. This is occasioned by the Automated Clearing of transactions via Depository Trust Clearing Corporation (DTCC).

Buy-Ins and Sell-Outs

When two dealers are party to a securities transaction they assume obligations under the Uniform Practice Code. They are required to complete settlement of the transaction under the terms of the contract. As an example, in a regular way transaction in stock, the seller is required to deliver the securities on the third business day following the transaction and the buyer must be prepared to make proper payment on that day. Should either party to the trade fail to perform their obligation, the other party has access to procedures that protect their rights. Should a selling dealer fail to deliver as required, the buyer can implement a procedure known as a "buy-in." If delivery is not made as required, the buying dealer, after giving 24 hours' notice, can repurchase the securities and charge any price difference (loss) to the defaulting seller. For example, a trade occurred on 100 shares of Acme Fashion stock at $22. If the seller does not deliver on time, the buyer sends him a "buy-in notice." If no response is received in 24 hours, the buyer simply repurchases the stock, perhaps at $23 per share, and charges the difference to the seller.

On the other hand, if the seller makes a proper delivery and the buyer refuses to pay, the seller has a procedure called a "sell-out." When delivery has been refused, the seller immediately (no 24-hour notice required) resells the stock and charges any difference in price (loss) to the buying dealer who did not live up to the contract terms.

Please note that these procedures are available to dealers who are party to a trade. They are usually not used at the first opportunity but are available should a dealer have concern regarding completion of a transaction.

Mark to the Market

A "mark to market" is used to adjust the value of securities borrowed or owed. For example, Dealer A buys 100 shares of stock from Dealer B at $50 per share. The trade is made on a when issued basis, meaning that Dealer B cannot deliver the stock as it has not yet been made available. During the time that this contract remains uncompleted, the stock might rise in value to $60 per share. In this case Dealer A could send Dealer B a mark to market for $1,000 ($10 per share × 100 shares). The mark to market allows Dealer A to be safe from loss should Dealer B fail to deliver the shares. Dealer A has a contract with his client at $50 per share. Should Dealer B fail to make delivery, Dealer A would have to replace the shares at $60 in the open market, resulting in a 10-point loss on 100 shares. By marking to the market, Dealer A receives the $1,000 that is at risk and cannot suffer a loss. Conversely, had the shares dropped in value from $50 to $40 in the open-market when issued trading, Dealer B could send a mark to market for $1,000 to Dealer A. As the shares are trading $10 below the contract price, it is Dealer B who is now at risk. The mark to market relieves that problem.

Reclamation

In a "reclamation," a dealer requests that another dealer reclaim an improper delivery. For instance, Dealer A purchases 100 shares of United Apple Cider Co. stock from Dealer B. On settlement date, Dealer B delivers 100 shares of United Apple Butter Co. stock and Dealer A accepts it and pays for it. The next day Dealer A notices that they have received the wrong stock and sends Dealer B a reclamation notice requesting that Dealer B pick up the improper delivery and return the payment until the proper security is delivered. Normally, a dealer has 15 days to send a reclamation notice, but, if the delivered securities later prove to be stolen or counterfeit, the dealer has 30 months to demand reclamation.

THE OVER-THE-COUNTER MARKET

The term "over the counter" (OTC) defines any transaction that does not take place on a registered stock exchange. Numerically, most securities are traded over the counter, as only some 4,000 securities are traded on the exchanges. Virtually all new issues trade over the counter, as do most bonds. The common stock of most banks, insurance companies, and smaller companies that would not meet the requirements for exchange listing trade in the OTC market. The OTC market includes the "third market," which is the over-the-counter trading of securities that are listed on exchanges. For example, there is a market for IBM, General Motors, and other major corporations shares made over the counter by dealers who are not exchange members. There is also a "fourth market" in which large institutional clients trade directly with each other without utilizing the services of a broker.

When we discussed the trading of securities on exchanges, we stated that the listed market is an "auction market." The OTC market, on the other hand, is called a "negotiated market." Here the dealers negotiate with each other in an attempt to obtain the best price available at a given moment.

A major difference between listed and OTC trading is that in the listed market firms generally act only as agents for their clients. For example, a member organization receives an order to buy 10,000 shares of General Motors for a client. The member organization sends the order to the floor of the NYSE, where its floor member executes it as the trading post. When completed, the member will send a confirmation to its client charging a commission on the transaction. In the OTC market firms also act as agents, but more frequently they act as principal or dealer in that they buy and/or sell securities for their own account. In this function, called "market-making," the firm owns the securities and buys from or sells to their clients as principal.

Let us look at the agency function first. A member organization receives an order to buy 100 shares of Last Chance Saloon Corp. common stock at the market. Last Chance shares trade over the counter. If the broker does not make a market in these shares, it would execute the order as agent for the customer. The broker is expected to make a reasonable effort to obtain the best price available. The broker might consult a trade publication called the "pink sheets" in an effort to execute the order (we will discuss NASDAQ further on).

The pink sheets are published by an independent company, now called the Pink Sheets. They contain an alphabetical listing of the OTC stocks together with the name and telephone number of firms that have an interest in trading these shares. The SEC requires that, to list in the pink sheets, the shares must have been issued under an effective registration statement and the company must be current in its required reports to the commission. The Pink Sheets also publishes the "yellow sheets," which list bonds trading in the OTC market.

When the brokerage firm's clerk who is responsible for executing the order to buy 100 Last Chance Saloon Corp. opens the pink sheets, she might see the following:

pink sheets
Electronic Messaging
1-800-LIST-OTC

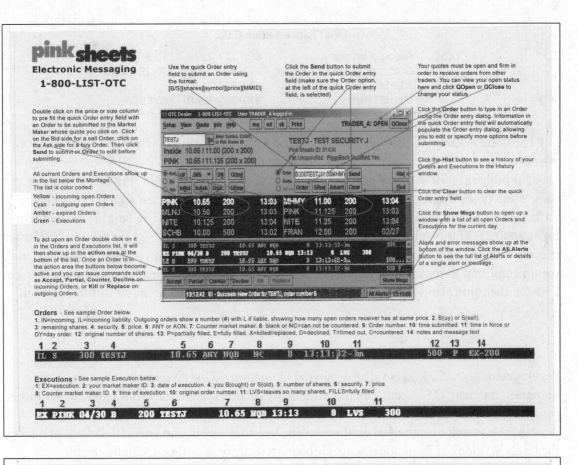

Use the quick Order entry field to submit an Order using the format:
[B/S][shares][symbol][price][MMID]

Click the **Send** button to submit the Order in the quick Order entry field (make sure the Order option, at the left of the quick Order entry field, is selected)

Your quotes must be open and firm in order to receive orders from other traders. You can view your open status here and click **QOpen** or **QClose** to change your status.

Double click on the price or size column to pre fill the quick Order entry field with an Order to be submitted to the Market Maker whose quote you click on. Click on the Bid side for a sell Order, click on the Ask side for a buy Order. Then click **Send** to submit or **Order** to edit before submitting.

Click the **Order** button to type in an Order using the Order entry dialog. Information in the quick Order entry field will automatically populate the Order entry dialog, allowing you to edit or specify more options before submitting.

Click the **Hist** button to see a history of your Orders and Executions in the History window.

All current Orders and Executions show up in the list below the Montage. The list is color coded:
- Yellow - incoming open Orders
- Cyan - outgoing open Orders
- Amber - expired Orders
- Green - Executions

Click the **Clear** button to clear the quick Order entry field.

Click the **Show Msgs** button to open up a window with a list of all open Orders and Executions for the current day.

To act upon an Order double click on it in the Orders and Executions list, it will then show up in the **action area** at the bottom of the list. Once an Order is in the action area the buttons below become active and you can issue commands such as **Accept, Partial, Counter, Decline** on incoming Orders, or **Kill** or **Replace** on outgoing Orders.

Alerts and error messages show up at the bottom of the window. Click the **All Alerts** button to see the full list of Alerts or details of a single alert or message.

Orders - See sample Order below.
1: IN=incoming, IL=incoming liability. Outgoing orders show a number (#) with L if liable, showing how many open orders receiver has at same price. 2: B(uy) or S(sell). 3: remaining shares. 4: security. 5: price. 6: ANY or AON. 7: Counter market maker. 8: blank or NC=can not be countered. 9: Order number. 10: time submitted. 11: time in force or DY=day order. 12: original number of shares. 13: P=partially filled, E=fully filled, X=killed/replaced, D=declined, T=timed out, C=countered. 14: notes and message text

1	2	3	4	5	6	7	8	9	10	11	12	13	14
IL	S	300	TESTJ	10.65	ANY	NQB	NC	8	13:13;32-3m		500	P	EX-200

Executions - See sample Execution below.
1: EX=execution. 2: your market maker ID. 3: date of execution. 4: you B(ought) or S(old). 5: number of shares. 6: security. 7: price. 8: Counter market maker ID. 9: time of execution. 10: original order number. 11: LVS=leaves so many shares, FILLS=fully filled

1	2	3	4	5	6	7	8	9	10	11
EX	PINK	04/30	B	200	TESTJ	10.65	NQB	13:13	8	LVS 300

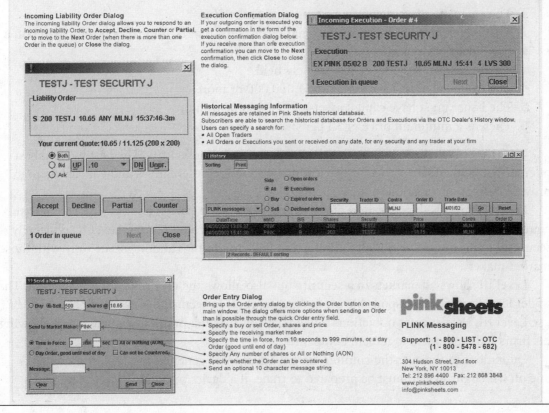

Incoming Liability Order Dialog
The incoming liability Order dialog allows you to respond to an incoming liability Order, to **Accept, Decline, Counter** or **Partial**, or to move to the **Next** Order (when there is more than one Order in the queue) or **Close** the dialog.

Execution Confirmation Dialog
If your outgoing order is executed you get a confirmation in the form of the execution confirmation dialog below. If you receive more than one execution confirmation you can move to the **Next** confirmation, then click **Close** to close the dialog.

Historical Messaging Information
All messages are retained in Pink Sheets historical database.
Subscribers are able to search the historical database for Orders and Executions via the OTC Dealer's History window.
Users can specify a search for:
- All Open Traders
- All Orders or Executions you sent or received on any date, for any security and any trader at your firm

Order Entry Dialog
Bring up the Order entry dialog by clicking the Order button on the main window. The dialog offers more options when sending an Order than is possible through the quick Order entry field.
- Specify a buy or sell Order, shares and price
- Specify the receiving market maker
- Specify the time in force, from 10 seconds to 999 minutes, or a day Order (good until end of day)
- Specify Any number of shares or All or Nothing (AON)
- Specify whether the Order can be countered
- Send an optional 10 character message string

pink sheets
PLINK Messaging

Support: 1 - 800 - LIST - OTC
(1 - 800 - 5478 - 682)

304 Hudson Street, 2nd floor
New York, NY 10013
Tel: 212 896 4400   Fax: 212 868 3848
www.pinksheets.com
info@pinksheets.com

	Last Chance Saloon Corp.		
LCSC	Allen & Company	800-221-2246	30.5
	Goldman Sachs Group, Inc.	212-902-1006	30.25–30.75
	A.G. Edwards & Sons	212-943-2510	
	Merrill Lynch	212-449-1000	OW BW

The daily pricing of Pink Sheet Stocks are now electronically transmitted (see exhibit on previous page).

Our broker's clerk will now make a reasonable effort to obtain the best price by phoning some or all of the dealers. Let us assume that the quotes in the sheets are accurate. As our broker wants to buy, the best offer shown is by Allen & Co. at 30.50. The best bid is Goldman Sachs at 30.25. This best bid and best offer is called the "inside market." In our example the inside market is 30.25–30.50. Our broker would buy 100 shares at 30.50 from Allen & Company and would confirm it to the client at that price, adding on a fair and reasonable commission, let's say $50. On the confirmation our broker would disclose that it acted as agent on this transaction.

NASDAQ

In recent years, the job of dealing in the OTC market has been simplified through the development of NASDAQ (NASD Automated Quotation). This system allows us to obtain quotation on many OTC securities through an automated system that eliminates the far more cumbersome approach of the pink sheets.

NASDAQ service is provided on three levels: Level I, Level II, and Level III. Before discussing the levels, let's look at the requirements for listing a security in NASDAQ. To be eligible:

1. The company must currently be reporting to the SEC.
2. There must be a minimum of four market-makers, that is, four dealers who maintain a two-sided (bid and offer) market.
3. There must be 300,000 shares publicly held.
4. The company must have assets of $4,000,000 or more.
5. The issuer must have capital assets of $2,000,000 or more.
6. There is a minimum price of $3 per share.

NASDAQ Level I service provides the inside market on a security. The best bid and best offer at that moment are shown. It is used by registered representatives and enables them to provide current information to their clients.

Level II provides the quotation of all market makers in a particular security. The over-the-counter order clerk who executes the firm's agency orders would use the Level II service. By seeing all of the quotes he can identify the best bids or offerings and negotiate only with those market-makers.

Level III shows all markets in a security but also allows the user to input information. The trader for a firm who is responsible for making markets in securities—as principal—would use Level III. He can enter quotations and change his existing prices instantaneously, allowing his firm's bids and offers to remain competitive.

Quotations in the over-the-counter market are of three general types. A "firm quote" is one on which the dealer must be prepared to trade. If a dealer responds to a request for a quote by saying "19 to 19.50," that is a firm (as in solid) quote, and the dealer must buy or sell a minimum of 100 shares at those prices. All quotations on NASDAQ must be firm quotation.

A "subject quote" is one that is subject to confirmation. Perhaps a dealer in New York City is making a market, but the firm's interest in the stock is from their office in Chicago. When asked for a quote the New York person may respond by saying "19 to 19.50 subject," meaning he is not prepared to trade at that moment. He would first want to check with Chicago.

A "workout quote" is an approximate quote. Perhaps the security trades infrequently and the dealer is not certain of the exact level. He might quote the stock "20 to 22 workout," meaning that this is the approximate area where he feels he might work out a firm quotation. When identifying quotes as "subject" or "workout" the dealer is not required to buy or sell at the stated prices.

OTC Trading: Markups and Markdowns

Let's return to our client, who wished to buy 100 shares of Last Chance Saloon Corp. In the earlier example, the order was given to a broker who executed it acting as agent. Let us now suppose that the order is given to Allen & Company, a market-maker in the security. Allen & Company will act as principal in this trade, that is, it will sell the shares directly to the client from its own inventory. Allen's quote on the stock is 30–30.50, but this is a wholesale quotation, for dealers only.

Allen is not required to sell stock to a client at 30.50 but is entitled to what is known as a "markup." The markup is based on the current offering price, not on the dealer's cost. Markups are not synonymous with profits. The dealer may have a profit in the trade that is more or less than the markup or may in fact show a loss on the position.

The amount of markup is based on standards of reasonableness, as was the case with the commission on agency trades. The dealer looks to the conditions involved in the trade, such as:

1. Availability of the security—active stocks carry a lesser markup than inactive ones.
2. Price of the security—the higher the price the smaller the percentage of mark-up.
3. Type of security—bonds, due to their higher price, generally have a smaller markup than stocks.
4. Service to the client—if the firm provided some extraordinary service, the markup can be larger than usual.

The NASD does have a 5% Guideline Policy which covers both commissions and markups. What this does not say is that dealer can charge commissions and markups of 5%. This would normally be too high and would be deemed unreasonable. The guideline says that markups or commissions in excess of 5% would normally be deemed unreasonable on their face. It is the factors involved in the trade, mentioned above, that determine what is reasonable.

Perhaps a reasonable markup on our trade of Last Chance Saloon Corp. would be .75 per share, which is approximately 2.5% (.75 mark up divided by 30.50 offering price). Allen & Company would add that amount to the offering price of 30.50 and would confirm the trade to the client at 31.25 net ($3,125). They would state on the confirmation that they acted as principal on the transaction. In our example, the client buying through our broker, acting as agent, paid a total of $3,100 (30.50 plus .50 commission) while the total cost of the purchase from Allen & Company was $3,125 (30.50 plus .75 markup). In the real world this would generally not be the case. The client would usually obtain a better price from a firm acting as principal. The example is used to show that it could happen and still not be unreasonable. A price can be fair and reasonable and still not be the best price.

In our example we used markups. When a customer is selling stock to a dealer, as principal, that dealer may mark down the price, that is, reduce the wholesale bid by a reasonable amount when dealing with a customer. The standards for markdowns are the same as for markups.

There are two situations when a dealer is expected to charge less than a normal markup (or markdown).

Proceeds Transactions

In a proceeds transaction the client sells a security through a dealer as agent and reinvests the proceeds in an item from the dealer's inventory. For example an RR calls a client and suggests that she buy 100 shares of Last Chance. The RR's firm makes a market in the security. The client agrees with the idea, but as she has no cash available, she instructs the RR to sell 100 shares of XYZ stock and use the proceeds to purchase the Last Chance stock. On the sale of XYZ the dealer charges a commission of .50 ($50). From the allowable markup on the purchase of the Last Chance (.75) the dealer must subtract the commission received on the sale of the XYZ (.50) and mark up only the difference—.25. Remember, we are using allowable markups. You may find in your career that actual markups and markdowns are usually less than what is allowable under NASD regulations due to the competitive nature of our industry.

Rascals, or Simultaneous Transactions

A rascal, or simultaneous transaction, is one in which the dealer had the order before taking the position. Using our original example, suppose the customer gave the order to buy the 100 shares of Last Chance to our broker but instructed them to report the trade at a net (no commission) price. As our broker does not make a market in the shares, they might buy 100 shares from Allen & Company at 30.50 for our broker's firm account. They would then mark up the price and confirm to the client at a net price. As our broker had no risk as a market-maker, they are not permitted a markup as high as the market-maker, Allen & Company. Blair & Company is permitted to mark up an amount equivalent to the allowable commission (.50) and not the amount allowed the market maker (.75).

Interpositioning

This is an illegal practice in the over-the-counter market. It is the introduction of a dealer to a trade unnecessarily at the customer's expense. For example, a customer of Dealer A enters an order to buy 100 shares of Glittering Gold Corp. stock at the market. The order clerk at Dealer A checks the situation and finds he can buy the stock at 41.50 from a market marker, Dealer B. Instead of executing the order in this manner, the clerk calls his friend Dealer C, who does not make a market in the stock, and tells him that he needs 100 shares. Dealer C buys the 100 shares from Dealer B at 41.50 for his own account and then sells it to Dealer A at 41.75. The customer of Dealer A pays 41.75 plus commission, when she would have paid only 41.50 plus commission had the order been executed properly. Of course, the clerk at Deal A meets his friend at Dealer C later and they divide up the $25 that Dealer C made by being "interposed" in the trade. Since the advent of NASDAQ, interpositioning has been easier to detect and has become less frequent, but the possibility of this violation occurring still exists.

It would not be interpositioning if a dealer used others to assist him with an order as a means of helping the client. For example, a client wishes to buy 100,000 shares of an over-the-counter stock. The dealer executing the order might use other firms to assist him in accumulating this large block so that the true size of the order does not become known. This knowledge would cause market-makers to raise their offering prices and result in the client paying a higher price.

ANSWER SHEET FOR CHAPTER 6 EXAMINATION

1. Ⓐ Ⓑ Ⓒ Ⓓ   11. Ⓐ Ⓑ Ⓒ Ⓓ   21. Ⓐ Ⓑ Ⓒ Ⓓ

2. Ⓐ Ⓑ Ⓒ Ⓓ   12. Ⓐ Ⓑ Ⓒ Ⓓ   22. Ⓐ Ⓑ Ⓒ Ⓓ

3. Ⓐ Ⓑ Ⓒ Ⓓ   13. Ⓐ Ⓑ Ⓒ Ⓓ   23. Ⓐ Ⓑ Ⓒ Ⓓ

4. Ⓐ Ⓑ Ⓒ Ⓓ   14. Ⓐ Ⓑ Ⓒ Ⓓ   24. Ⓐ Ⓑ Ⓒ Ⓓ

5. Ⓐ Ⓑ Ⓒ Ⓓ   15. Ⓐ Ⓑ Ⓒ Ⓓ   25. Ⓐ Ⓑ Ⓒ Ⓓ

6. Ⓐ Ⓑ Ⓒ Ⓓ   16. Ⓐ Ⓑ Ⓒ Ⓓ   26. Ⓐ Ⓑ Ⓒ Ⓓ

7. Ⓐ Ⓑ Ⓒ Ⓓ   17. Ⓐ Ⓑ Ⓒ Ⓓ   27. Ⓐ Ⓑ Ⓒ Ⓓ

8. Ⓐ Ⓑ Ⓒ Ⓓ   18. Ⓐ Ⓑ Ⓒ Ⓓ   28. Ⓐ Ⓑ Ⓒ Ⓓ

9. Ⓐ Ⓑ Ⓒ Ⓓ   19. Ⓐ Ⓑ Ⓒ Ⓓ   29. Ⓐ Ⓑ Ⓒ Ⓓ

10. Ⓐ Ⓑ Ⓒ Ⓓ   20. Ⓐ Ⓑ Ⓒ Ⓓ   30. Ⓐ Ⓑ Ⓒ Ⓓ

31. Ⓐ Ⓑ Ⓒ Ⓓ   41. Ⓐ Ⓑ Ⓒ Ⓓ

32. Ⓐ Ⓑ Ⓒ Ⓓ   42. Ⓐ Ⓑ Ⓒ Ⓓ

33. Ⓐ Ⓑ Ⓒ Ⓓ   43. Ⓐ Ⓑ Ⓒ Ⓓ

34. Ⓐ Ⓑ Ⓒ Ⓓ   44. Ⓐ Ⓑ Ⓒ Ⓓ

35. Ⓐ Ⓑ Ⓒ Ⓓ   45. Ⓐ Ⓑ Ⓒ Ⓓ

36. Ⓐ Ⓑ Ⓒ Ⓓ   46. Ⓐ Ⓑ Ⓒ Ⓓ

37. Ⓐ Ⓑ Ⓒ Ⓓ   47. Ⓐ Ⓑ Ⓒ Ⓓ

38. Ⓐ Ⓑ Ⓒ Ⓓ   48. Ⓐ Ⓑ Ⓒ Ⓓ

39. Ⓐ Ⓑ Ⓒ Ⓓ   49. Ⓐ Ⓑ Ⓒ Ⓓ

40. Ⓐ Ⓑ Ⓒ Ⓓ   50. Ⓐ Ⓑ Ⓒ Ⓓ

CHAPTER 6 EXAMINATION

1. When a customer buys an OTC stock from a firm that is a market-maker in that stock, the price the customer pays:

   (A) does not include a markup
   (B) includes a markup
   (C) includes a commission and a markup
   (D) includes a special fee

2. A market-maker has purchased a particular stock over a period of time for prices as high as $9 per share and as low as $3 per share. His average cost is approximately $6 per share. The current NASDAQ quote for the stock is 5 to 5.25. According to the NASD Conduct Rules, the dealer's offering price to the public should be based on:

   (A) the current market for the stock
   (B) $3
   (C) $9
   (D) the dealer's average cost of $6

3. Which of the following stock exchanges is not registered with the SEC?

   (A) Cincinnati Stock Exchange
   (B) Boston Stock Exchange
   (C) Chicago Stock Exchange
   (D) Honolulu Stock Exchange

4. Level III of NASDAQ provides which of the following?

   (A) representative quotations
   (B) firm quotations
   (C) subject markets
   (D) workout markets

5. A registered representative wishes to buy shares of a new issue his firm is distributing. Under NASD Conduct Rules, the RR may:

   I. not do so under any circumstance
   II. do so if he has a history of buying hot issues
   III. not do so for his own account, but may purchase shares for member of his immediate family
   IV. do so if his allotment is insubstantial, not disproportionate to public orders, and constitutes his normal investment practice.

   (A) I only
   (B) III only
   (C) IV only
   (D) II and IV only

6. When a member firm buys or sells securities directly, as principal, with a public customer, it is acting as:

   (A) a dealer
   (B) a broker
   (C) an agent
   (D) none of the above

7. A buy-in of a customer's sale transaction is mandated if the securities have not been received by the broker/dealer within how many business days following the settlement date?

   (A) 5
   (B) 10
   (C) 20
   (D) 30

8. An individual opens a new account with a broker/dealer and asks for a copy of the firm's financial statement. If the firm had not been subject to a formal audit by an independent public accountant for quite some time, what should it do in response to this request?

(A) give the customer its latest available statement

(B) wait until after the next audit is completed before providing a statement to the customer

(C) delay sending a statement until the customer has had an account with the firm for at least six months

(D) refuse to provide its financial statement

9. A registered bond with "Happy Birthday" scrawled across the face of the certificate is delivered to a broker/dealer in satisfaction of sale by another member firm. Assuming it is accompanied by an authentic assignment, power of substitution form, and tax stamps, if appropriate, this is a good delivery only if

(A) the certificate is validated by the transfer agent

(B) the certificate is validated by the registered owner

(C) the marking did not cover the name of the registered owner or the principal amount of the bond

(D) this is *not* a good delivery under any circumstances

10. Martin Smith maintains an individual cash account as well as a joint account with his wife at your firm. While he is out of town on a business trip his wife calls you with an order to buy 100 ABD at the market for Mr. Smith's individual account. It is a stock Mr. Smith had previously been interested in buying, but only at the "right price." What would you do?

(A) Refuse to accept the order unless you have a signed trading authorization in favor of Mrs. Smith in your possession.

(B) Execute the order as requested.

(C) Enter the order only after receipt of written instructions to do so from Mrs. Smith.

(D) Buy the stock in the joint account and, after verification from Mr. Smith, journal the security to his individual account.

11. If a wealthy investor gives a friend discretion to invest $50,000 for him any way he sees fit, the person so empowered must:

(A) be registered with the SEC under the Investment Advisors Act of 1940

(B) conform to the prudent man requirements in that state

(C) furnish written documents of authority to the brokerage firm executing the orders

(D) be registered with the NYSE and NASD as a representative.

12. A registered representative just accepted a customer's instructions to buy a specific stock in the over-the-counter market with the credit balance in his account. Which of these orders for that issue can be entered and executed on a single ticket in a typical broker/dealer organization?

    (A) buy 150 XYZ at the market
    (B) buy 150 XYZ at 17.50 or better
    (C) buy $2,500 worth of a mutual fund XYZ Corp.
    (D) all of these orders

13. An individual opens an account at a broker/dealer organization with instructions to "transfer and ship." This means that:

    (A) all correspondence to the customer must be sent by registered mail
    (B) each trade report must note the customer's certificate registration instructions
    (C) securities purchased must be registered in the name of the customer and then delivered to him
    (D) transactions for that customer will be transferred to another broker for processing purposes

14. According to the NASD Conduct Rules, a party judged guilty of an infraction of a rule by the District Business Conduct Committee may then appeal to:

    (A) the Securities and Exchange Commission
    (B) the NASD Board of Governors
    (C) the public court system
    (D) the NASD Board of Arbitration

15. To accommodate a customer's order to buy an over-the-counter stock, a NASD broker/dealer is permitted to:

    I.   sell him those shares from his firm's inventory
    II. sell these shares short to the customer
    III. enter into a riskless, or simultaneous, transaction
    IV. act as agent on this transaction

    (A) I and IV only
    (B) II and III only
    (C) I and II only
    (D) I, II, III, and IV

16. An investor purchasing a corporate bond regular way will have to pay the contract price plus accrued interest:

    (A) up to and including the trade date
    (B) up to but not including the trade date
    (C) up to but not including the settlement date
    (D) up to and including the settlement date

17. Service charges by a NASD dealer for transfer and safekeeping of customer securities held in street name:

    (A) may not be levied under NASD Conduct Rules
    (B) may not be levied unless there is no trading in the account for more than six months
    (C) may be levied only if the security value is less than $5,000
    (D) may be levied only if the charge is fair, reasonable, and nondiscriminatory

18. Acme Corporation issued bonds that pay interest on January 15 and July 15 each year until maturity. An investor purchasing these bonds on Monday April 12 must pay the contract price plus accrued interest for:

    (A) 87 days
    (B) 89 days
    (C) 93 days
    (D) 90 days

19. Most publicly owned securities are:

    (A) listed
    (B) over the counter
    (C) unregistered
    (D) exempt from SEC registration requirements

20. A registered representative privately assured a customer a certain stock would double in price within 18 months. During this period the stock performed as he predicted. Which of the following statements concerning this is true?

    (A) The commentary was permissible because the stock advanced as the RR forecast.
    (B) This was a violation because the SEC requires all information about stock prices to be publicly announced.
    (C) The statement constituted a form of fraud prohibited under the Securities Exchange Act of 1934.
    (D) The comment to the customer would be permitted only if the representative had been registered with the SEC under the Investment Advisors Act of 1940.

21. The NASD markup policy requires that over-the-counter transactions with a customer be at:

    (A) prices reasonably related to the current market price of the security
    (B) a markup not to exceed 5% of the current offering price
    (C) prices reasonably related to the dealer's cost
    (D) a markup based on previous activity in that customer's account

22. The return by the receiving party of securities previously accepted for delivery or a demand by the delivering party for return of securities that have been delivered is called:

    (A) rejection
    (B) close-out
    (C) reclamation
    (D) redelivery

23. A four-letter symbol assigned to an issue is characteristic of an equity security:

    (A) authorized for inclusion in the NASDAQ system
    (B) listed on the NYSE
    (C) admitted to unlisted trading privileges on a regional stock exchange
    (D) trading in less than 100-share units on the American Stock Exchange

24. The NASD Conduct Rules permits a transaction made "seller's option" to be delivered earlier than the expiration of the contracts:

    (A) if the buyer is given one day's notice in writing
    (B) if the seller is located in New York City
    (C) if the client requests it
    (D) if the buyer is a nonclearing member

25. In regard to discretionary accounts, which of the following statements are correct?

    I.   The customer must approve each transaction in writing before the order is entered.
    II. The customer must grant written authorization to the member firm to exercise discretion in the account.
    III. The account must be accepted in writing by a partner, officer, or designated official of the member firm.
    IV. Each discretionary order must be approved prior to entry by a partner, officer, or designated official of the member firm.

    (A) I, II, III, and IV
    (B) II, III, and IV only
    (C) II and III only
    (D) II and IV only

26. Which of the following are considered to be discretionary orders under the NASD Rules of Fair Practice?

    I.   A customer instructs her RR to purchase XYZ Corporation whenever the RR deems the price to be right.
    II. A customer instructs her registered representative to sell 300 shares of ABC Company that is long in her account when the RR thinks the time and price is appropriate.
    III. A customer gives a member firm a check for $25,000 and instructs the firm to purchase bank stocks and insurance company stocks when the prices appear to be favorable
    IV. A customer instructs her RR to buy 1,000 shares of Acme Corporation at a time and price that the RR determines are favorable.

    (A) I, II III, and IV
    (B) I and III only
    (C) III only
    (D) II and IV only

27. A dealer buys 100 shares of BD common, an actively traded stock, at 23.50. Three days later, when BD common is quoted at 19.50–19.75, he sells the 100 shares to a customer. The basis for the dealer's markup is:

    (A) 10⅛
    (B) 19⅞
    (C) 23½
    (D) 5% above his cost

28. The practice of positioning stock in response to a customer's order and immediately marking it up for resale to the customer is:

    (A) a factor to consider in the NASD guideline
    (B) a simultaneous transaction
    (C) a riskless transaction
    (D) all of the above

29. Which of the following would be considered a firm quotation in the over-the-counter market?

    (A) 27.50
    (B) 27.50 workout
    (C) 27.50 subject
    (D) both (A) and (B)

30. Which of the following securities is traded only in the over-the-counter market?

    (A) corporate bonds
    (B) preferred stocks
    (C) open-end investment companies
    (D) closed-end investment companies

31. The 5% markup policy applies to:

    (A) riskless transactions
    (B) primary distributions
    (C) registered secondaries
    (D) mutual funds

32. The NASD markup policy applies to:

    I.   agency sales OTC
    II. principal transactions in municipal bonds
    III. mutual fund sales
    IV. new issues of corporate securities

    (A) I only
    (B) I, II, and III only
    (C) II and III only
    (D) I and IV only

33. In considering the fairness of a firm's markup, the NASD considers:

    (A) dealer's cost of the security
    (B) financial condition of the client
    (C) profitability of the member
    (D) amount of the transaction

34. For a member to exercise discretionary power in any customer's account requires written authorization by that customer:

    (A) except when the customer is a spouse of the registered representative
    (B) except when the customer has given an oral approval after the transaction
    (C) except when only time and price of execution are involved
    (D) in all cases

35. All of the following would be good delivery, broker-to-broker, on a sale of 470 shares of stock EXCEPT:

    (A) 47 10-share certificates
    (B) 4 100-share certificates and one 70-share certificate
    (C) 8 50-share certificates, one 40-share certificate and one 30-share certificate
    (D) 2 100-share certificates and 3 90-share certificates

36. A NYSE floor member executing an order for a public customer asks the specialist in the stock to guarantee her a price while giving the customer an opportunity to obtain a better price. This procedure is known as:

    (A) a stop order
    (B) stopping stock
    (C) floor protection
    (D) a special deal

37. When opening a brokerage account for a customer, a registered representative must determine the customer's:

    I.   investment objectives
    II. financial resources
    III. financial requirements
    IV. prior investment results

    (A) I only
    (B) I and II only
    (C) I, II, and III only
    (D) I, II, III, and IV

38. With regard to the brokerage accounts described below, all of these comments are true EXCEPT:

    (A) In a community property state, for a married woman to open a brokerage account, she must do it jointly with her husband.
    (B) Stock purchased in a custodian account may not be purchased on margin or held in bearer form.
    (C) Numbered accounts are permissible provided there is a record kept on file at the brokerage firm attesting to the actual ownership of the account.
    (D) If a fiduciary intends to buy stocks in a margin account, the trust agreement authorizing margin transactions must be kept on file at the brokerage firm.

39. Merrill Lynch announces through its wire system that it has a large block of stock for sale. Customers purchasing the stock will not pay a commission. The block is crossed on the NYSE floor and is printed on the NYSE tape. This is:

    (A) a special offer
    (B) an exchange distribution
    (C) a secondary distribution
    (D) a specialist block purchase

40. John Jones and his wife, Mary Jones, maintain a joint account with your firm as "joint tenants in common." Mary Jones calls you and places an order to sell 100 shares of U.S. Steel common stock, which is long in their account. Which of the following statements is correct regarding this order?

    (A) You may enter the order.
    (B) You may enter the order only after confirming with John Jones.
    (C) This order must be approved by your manager prior to entry.
    (D) This order may not be accepted.

41. A limit order can best be described as an order:

    (A) to buy at a specific price or lower
    (B) to sell at a specific price or higher
    (C) to be executed at a specific price or better
    (D) that is in effect for only one day

42. Maintaining a fair and orderly market and acting as a broker's broker are dual functions of the:

    (A) competitive trader
    (B) odd-lot dealer
    (C) specialist
    (D) two-dollar broker

43. The stock exchange's ticker tape just printed

    MST. SLD
    98¼

    What does it mean?

    (A) One hundred shares of MST traded on the exchange and appear out of order on the ticker tape.
    (B) Trading was suspended in MST pending dissemination of news.
    (C) The last sale of MST was for 100 shares at 98.25.
    (D) The preceding transaction in MST was two or more points different than 98.25.

44. A customer entered an order to sell long 100 shares of PDQ @ 38.75 stop limit. Thereafter, the following round-lot transactions occurred, 38.75, 38.65, 38.50. At what price was this order executed?

    (A) 38.75
    (B) 38.65
    (C) 38.50
    (D) it was never executed

45. The CG Insurance Agency is not incorporated. It is comprised of three general partners who maintain an active securities account identified as "The CG Insurance Company." If one of those partners should die suddenly, what course of action should be undertaken by the registered representative servicing that account?

    (A) Freeze the account from further activity until a death certificate and new partnership agreement are furnished to your firm.
    (B) No special action is required because the death of a single partner does not terminate the partnership agreement.
    (C) Distribute the assets in the account to the surviving partners in the insurance agency.
    (D) Execute sell orders but do not accept buy orders or distribute assets from the account until a new partnership agreement is given to your firm.

46. A customer wants to buy 500 shares of NYSE listed stock at 38.87, but he wants to buy them at one time, right away, or else forget it. What kind of an order should the RR enter to accommodate this customer?

    (A) fill or kill
    (B) all or none
    (C) immediate or cancel
    (D) now or never

47. A registered representative is given a limited trading authorization by a client. This permits her to:

    (A) withdraw money from the account
    (B) enter orders for the account at her discretion
    (C) withdraw securities from the account
    (D) all of the above

48. A customer wants to buy stock in a closely held corporation with a small amount of outstanding shares. The RR should advise him:

    (A) it is probably a good investment
    (B) he will have a greater percentage ownership in that concern as a result
    (C) of the probability of wide price fluctuations and possible difficulties in selling the stock
    (D) about the profit possibilities in a rising market

49. In opening a new account for a customer, a registered representative should:

    I.   inquire about his age
    II. investigate his credit rating
    III. verify "street name" stocks in his possession if he wants to sell them
    IV. determine what is "suitable" for the customer based upon his financial background

    (A) all of the above
    (B) II and IV only
    (C) I and II only
    (D) I and III only

50. If a customer dies, the registered representative would be required to:

    I.   cancel all open (GTC) orders
    II. sell out the account
    III. await instructions and necessary papers from the executor of the estate
    IV. execute all open (GTC) orders

    (A) I and II only
    (B) I and III only
    (C) III and IV only
    (D) I, II, and III only

CHAPTER 6 EXAMINATION ANSWERS

1. **B** The market-maker must act as principal; hence, the customer would pay a markup and not be charged a commission.

2. **A** As required under the NASD markup policy as set out in the Conduct Rules.

3. **D** Because of its small trading volume, the Honolulu Stock Exchange is exempt from SEC registration.

4. **B** All NASD Level III quotations are firm. This means the dealer must buy and sell a minimum of 100 shares at these prices.

5. **A** By definition. New issues may not be distributed by an NASD firm to any of its employees.

6. **A** When a firm does business *directly* with a customer, it is acting as a dealer. When it *represents* a customer, it is acting as a broker.

7. **B** By definition. If a customer fails to deliver securities within ten days after settlement, the broker must repurchase the securities.

8. **A** Customer must be provided with the most recent available information.

9. **A** This is a mutilated bond and must be validated before it can be a good delivery. The validation can be made by the issuer of the security or its authorized agent. The transfer agent would be so authorized.

10. **A** Unless Mrs. Smith has been given written trading authorization over Mr. Smith's account, we cannot accept orders from her or any other person.

11. **C** The investor has simply given his friend discretion. When he enters orders, the brokerage firm must be assured that he has the authority to do so for the account of another.

12. **D** In the OTC market, all of the orders depicted would be possible. A mutual fund is considered OTC.

13. **C** By definition. This means transferred to the customer's name and delivered to the customer.

14. **B** The next appeal after the board of governors would be to the SEC and, from there, to the federal courts.

15. **D** All of the choices are permissible and normal ways for a firm to handle a customer's order.

16. **C** On accrued bond interest, it is always figured up to but not including the settlement date. The exception is seller's option contracts, which are figured as though the trades took place on a regular-way basis. Please note that interest accrual begins on and includes the coupon date.

17. **D** As set out in the Conduct Rules.

18. **D** Interest accrues up to but not including the settlement date. Corporate bonds are figured on a 30-day month (irrespective of the number of days in the month) and a 360-day year (irrespective of the number of days in a year). Interest begins on and includes the coupon date. A regular way purchase on April 12 would settle regular way on April 15. Hence, there are 14 interest days in April. In January, there are 16 days (the 15 days remaining plus the coupon date, January 15), February and March are figured at 30 days each. Hence, 16 + 30 + 30 + 14 = 90 days.

19. **B** The OTC market is much larger than the listed markets in number of securities traded.

20. **C** Such predictions are inherently fraudulent even though they may later turn out to be true.

21. **A** Under the markup policy. All markups must be based upon the current market rather than inventory costs.

22. **C** In a reclamation a dealer requests that another dealer reclaim an improper delivery.

23. **A** Stocks listed on an exchange have no more than three characters in their symbol. IBM is as long a symbol as possible.

24. **A** A contract made on a "seller's options" basis may be terminated by the seller at an earlier date, providing that he gives the buyer one day's written notice. However, such a contract may never be settled earlier than the fourth business day following the trade date.

25. **C** Obviously, I is incorrect, as this would not constitute discretion. Choice IV looks plausible; however, each order entered for a discretionary account must be approved promptly, not necessarily before execution.

26. **B** In I, the customer did not tell the registered representative what quantity to purchase, hence this is discretionary. In III she did not identify any securities or amounts, hence, this is discretionary. Choices II and IV constitute time and price discretion only.

27. **B** The markup is always based on the current market price not on cost. Therefore, we would base the markup on the offering side of the current quotation.

28. **D** Riskless, or simultaneous, transactions call for a smaller than usual markup under the guidelines.

29. **A** Anytime that there is qualifying language attached to a quotation it is not considered to be firm.

30. **C** As open-end investment company's shares are a continuous offering of new securities; they cannot be traded on a stock exchange. They trade only in the over-the-counter market. The other choices, corporate bonds, preferred stocks, and closed-end investment companies, can trade either on exchanges or in the over-the-counter market.

31. **A** The markup policy applies to everything except securities sold under a prospectus which would be the case in choices (B), (C), and (D).

32. **A** Please note that the markup policy applies to basically all securities other than governments and municipals except where the security is being offered under a current prospectus. Mutual funds and new issues of corporate securities are sold under a prospectus, so would not be covered by the markup policy. Municipal bonds, as an exempt security, are not covered either. Please note that the Municipal Securities Rulemaking Board (MSRB), however, is very interested in markups on municipal bonds.

33. **D** The dollar amount of the transaction is one of the factors in considering the fairness of markup. Other factors include the kind of security (equity or debt), the amount and kind of service rendered, the unit price of the security, and the general availability.

34. **C** The exception to the discretionary rule is where the customer has specified whether he wishes to buy or sell the security involved and the amount (the number of shares), and

he gives discretion only as to time or price of execution.

35. **D** Three 90-share certificates are not good delivery as you cannot combine 90-share certificates into 100-share amounts.

36. **B** This is the process of "stopping stock."

37. **C** It is mandatory that the registered representative understand and know the first three items. It is not necessary that the RR know the fourth item, although this would be desirable.

38. **A** All of the other choices are true. Please note that in a community property state, some transfer agents still require the husband's signature when securities are registered in the wife's name and are to be transferred.

39. **B** An exchange distribution is a large block sold internally by one firm and crossed on the floor. The trade would print on the tape identified by the letters "DIST."

40. **A** In a joint account any tenant is empowered to enter orders. This is an inclusion in the joint account agreement.

41. **C** Choice (A) describes only a buy limit order. Choice (B) describes only a sell limit order. Choice (C) is a proper description of all limit orders.

42. **C** This basically defines the functions of a specialist.

43. **A** The ticker symbol SLD means that the print is out of sequence.

44. **D** The first transaction at 38.75 elected the order, but since it was both a stop order and a limit order, there was never another transaction at 38.75, so the order was never executed.

45. **D** When this question is missed, normally the choice selected is (A) because this is the policy of many firms in our business. Curiously, the account is frozen as to buy orders or distribution of cash and securities from the account, but sell orders may be accepted from a general partner in the account pending receipt of proper legal documentation.

46. **A** This adequately describes a fill or kill order.

47. **B** A limited trading authorization only allows for the entering of orders. A full trading authorization would also permit the holder to withdraw money and securities from the account.

48. **C** This corporation, since it is closely held, will have a small "float." This means that the shares available for trading are few in number. Hence, price fluctuations will tend to be wide, and liquidity will tend to be poor.

49. **A** This is as required in Rule 405 of the NYSE and under suitable requirements in the Rules of Fair Practice of the NASD.

50. **B** Basically, choices II and IV are ridiculous. Choices I and III describe at least two activities that must be undertaken upon the death of a customer.

Investment Companies

INVESTMENT COMPANY ACT OF 1940

The Investment Company Act of 1940 defines an investment company as either a corporation or a trust through which investors pool their funds in order to obtain diversification and supervision of their investments.

The management company directs the investments and makes the portfolio decisions. This professional service is not available individually to small investors, but can be obtained by this method of investing. The management company charges a fee of approximately ½% to 1% of the assets for their service. (In recent years, the level has come closer to the lower end of that range.) The management contract must be renewed by the shareholders of the investment company each year. No long-term contracts are permitted under the law.

There are three classifications of investment companies under the 1940 act.

Face-Amount Certificate Companies

These issue face-amount certificates, which are purchased by investors via a single payment or through a series of installments. The face value of the certificate is payable at the end of a particular time period. Interest is paid during the life of the certificate and is guaranteed by the investment company. The guarantee is often backed by real estate or some other asset.

Unit Investment Trusts

These issue redeemable units. Each unit represents a specific interest in a portfolio of securities. Some trusts purchase shares of a particular investment company. Investors then purchase shares of the trust under a contractual plan. Most contractual plans use the unit investment trust vehicle.

Management Companies

These manage a diversified portfolio of securities and seek to attain a specified investment objective. Management companies may be either open end or closed end. It is the open-end management-type investment company that is commonly known as a "mutual fund."

Real Estate Investment Trusts (REITs)

REITs were established to supply capital for the real estate industry by providing money for mortgages, construction, and other similar enterprises. They are comparable in many ways to closed-end investment companies. REITs are required to distribute a minimum of 90% of net investment income to their beneficial owners (shareholders). Capital gains may be retained by the REIT or distributed to owners, as the trust desires. Additionally, the REIT must concentrate its investment in real estate–related ventures. At least 75% of its assets must be invested in this manner.

Open-End Versus Closed-End Investment Companies

There are three basic differences between open-end and closed-end investment companies.

Capitalization

The open-end investment company is an unusual form of security. It is a continuous offering of new shares. When an open-end company is started, a new issue is offered to the public. However, unlike other new issues, this one does not end. The "fund" continues to offer shares (there is no limit on the amount that can be offered) at a public offering price determined by a formula described in the prospectus. The prospectus must be reissued at least every 16 months.

Closed-end investment companies have a fixed number of shares. Their shares are traded on stock exchanges and in the over-the-counter market. Some well-known closed-end companies are Pimco Funds and Alliance N.Y.

Determination of the Market Price

The market price of an open-end company is based on the net asset value of the shares. Once each business day the fund must determine the net asset value per share. (They may make the calculation more than once a day for marketing purposes, if they wish.) They value their portfolio holdings and determine the total assets. Liabilities are then subtracted, leaving total net assets. This total is then divided by the number of shares outstanding at that moment, yielding the net asset value per share.

Let us suppose that the calculator showed a per share net asset value of $27.60. This would be the bid side of the quotation. To obtain the offering price, we would then factor in the sales charge, or load, which can be as much as 8.5% of the offering price (9% on contractual plans).

Some funds have no sales charge and are called "no-load funds." Were this the case, the bid and offering price would be the same figure. Our quotation would be $27.60–$27.60.

Let us suppose that our fund has a maximum sales charge of 8%. (Note: The maximum sales charge is always used in this calculation. Volume discount rates are not considered.) Keep in mind that the stated sales charge is a percentage of the offering price, not of the asset value. Thus, given an asset value of $27.60 and a maximum sales charge of 8%, we simply take the difference between the sales charge and 100% and divide that figure into the net asset value per share.

$$
\begin{array}{r}
100\% \\
-\ \underline{\ 8\%\ \text{Maximum Sales Charge}} \\
.92
\end{array}
$$

$27.60 divided by .92 = $30.00 offering price. Our quotation, therefore, is $27.60–$30.00.

Let's check to see if our calculation is correct. We have stated that the sales charge was 8% of the offering price:

$$\$30.00 \times 8\% = \$2.40$$

The difference between the bid, $27.60, and the offering, $30.00, is $2.40. We appear to be correct. This quotation will remain until the next computation a day later.

All orders for mutual fund shares must be executed on the next price after the order is entered. If a fund sets its price at 4:00 P.M. each day, orders received up to that time will be executed at that price. Those received after 4:00 P.M. must wait for the next day's price. This rule is known as "forward pricing" and was instituted some years ago to eliminate abuses of the old method, which permitted orders to be executed based on the price established prior to the order being entered.

The market price of the shares of a closed-end investment company is determined by supply and demand. They may sell at asset value, above asset value, or below asset value, depending on the condition of the marketplace.

Redemption

Open-end investment company shares are redeemed by selling the shares back to the fund, normally at net asset value. If an order had been entered to sell shares and the next established quotation was $27.60–$30.00, the shares would be redeemed by the fund at the asset value of $27.60. Occasionally, there is a small redemption charge, but this has not been prevalent in recent years. In general, an investment company must redeem shares within seven days after the holder submits a request to redeem.

Closed-end shares are sold in the open market. Again, the price is determined by supply and demand and may not necessarily be related directly to the net asset value.

Diversified Versus Nondiversified Companies

Management-type investment companies may be either diversified or nondiversified. A diversified company must adhere to certain investment standards. Seventy-five percent of its assets must be invested in such a way that:

- Not more than 5% of total assets are invested in the securities of any one company; and
- The investment company cannot purchase more than 10% of the voting stock of any one corporation.

For example, an investment company with total assets of $100,000,000 must invest $75,000,000 (75%) of those assets so that not more than $5,000,000 (5% of $100,000,000) are invested in the securities of any one company. In addition, this investment may not represent ownership of more than 10% of the voting stock of any corporations.

These standards assure diversification of risk for the investors and prevent investment companies from taking controlling positions in public corporations.

Types of Investment Companies by Objective

The Investment Company Act of 1940 requires that investment companies state their investment objectives and policies in their prospectus. Any change in these policies must be approved by a majority of the fund's shareholders. Here are some of the different types of funds, based on their objectives:

Common Stock Funds

These funds invest most of their assets in common stocks. Within this general grouping there may be many varieties. Some may stress investments in "growth companies," while others may concentrate on high grade common stocks, often referred to as "blue chips." Some common stock funds state that their intention is to select more speculative stocks for better than average growth potential. These, of course, carry a high degree of risk.

Bond and Preferred Stock Funds

These have been a greater factor in recent years with the increase in interest rates pending. They invest in fixed-income securities, which provide greater than usual current return for the holder.

Balanced Funds

These funds vary their investments among common stocks, preferred stocks, and bonds. They are said to be the most conservative type of funds as they can shift their holdings depending on market conditions. Often these balanced funds will state in their prospectus what portion of the portfolio may be invested in each type of security. For example, 40% in common stock, 20% in preferreds, and 40% in bonds.

Growth Funds

These are funds where their investment objective is capital appreciation. They invest in securities they believe have above average growth potential. These securities usually have a higher market risk. It is the old story: the greater the risk, the greater the reward.

Government Bond Funds

These funds only invest in treasury securities.

Municipal Bond Funds

These funds only invest in municipal securities. In fact, some municipal bond funds only invest in a particular state's securities; such as New York or Florida giving resident's of those states complete tax-free income.

Index Funds

They invest in securities that match those of a particular index such as Standard and Poor. These investors feel that their investment will at least keep up with the market.

International Funds

These funds invest in foreign securities and make it easy for Americans to invest overseas. Many of these specialize in a particular country such as Japan Fund and Korea Fund. Another type of international fund is the emergency market funds. These funds invest in securities of so-called third-world countries.

Exchange Traded Funds

Similar to a mutual fund in that investors pool their funds to obtain professional management and diversification. However, these funds are not purchased or redeemed from the issuer. They are purchased on the various exchanges and NASDAQ. Many of these funds are comprised of the various indices. In addition, these securities may be purchased on margin and limit; stop and market order may be utilized in their purchase and sale. They have become extremely popular in recent years.

Income Funds

These attempt to provide greater than usual income. While these funds often invest in good quality bonds, they may seek to provide a greater return by purchasing bonds of low quality. While these so-called "junk bonds" can provide a very high return, they also entail greater than usual risk.

Specialized Funds

These funds concentrate their investments in a particular industry or group of related industries. Perhaps they will invest only in chemical and drug stocks, or public utilities or airlines. Some even specialize by investing only in companies in a particular geographic area such as the southwestern United States, feeling that that area may experience an economic growth surpassing other parts of the country.

Dual-Purpose Funds

These came into existence in the 1960s. They are closed-end companies that offer two classes of stock, generally called "income" shares and "capital" shares. The two classes are issued in equal amounts. Holders of the "income" shares receive all the income generated by the entire portfolio, while holders of the "capital" shares receive all the capital gains generated by the entire portfolio. This type of fund is called "leveraged," as each shareholder receives $2 of benefit for every $1 invested.

Money Market Funds

These funds became very popular when interest rates began to rise sharply in the late 1970s. These funds invest in short-term "money market" securities (generally U.S. treasury securities and bank certificates of deposit). Shareholders of these funds receive the current short-term rates and have a very low risk investment. Many of these money market funds provide other services, such as check-writing privileges.

Distribution of Open-End Investment Company Shares

As we have noted earlier, closed-end investment company shares are bought and sold in the open market with their price being determined by supply and demand. Open-end company shares and mutual funds are distributed using four different methods:

Fund - Underwriter - Selling Group Member - Investor

The most usual method utilizes an underwriter and a selling group much as in other offerings of new securities. With open-end investment companies, however, the offering is continuous. An investor wishing to purchase shares of ABC Fund would place an order with a securities dealer who has signed a selling agreement with the fund. The dealer would place the order with the fund underwriter, who would purchase the shares from the fund at the next pricing. The underwriter would purchase the shares at the offering price less the total sales charge. The underwriter would then sell to the selling group member (the dealer) at the offering price less a portion of the sales charge. The selling group member then sells to the client at the public offering price. Let's say that ABC Fund has an asset value of $27.60 and a maximum sales charge of 8%. The offering price would, therefore, be $30 (27.60 divided by .92). The customer's order would be executed as follows:

- ABC Fund to underwriter at $27.60 ($30 minus 8%)
- underwriter to selling group member at $27.90 ($30 minus 7%)
- selling group member to client at $30 (offering price)

Note that the fund receives $27.60, the asset value, for each share issued, thus experiencing no dilution. The underwriter keeps 1% of the 8% sales charge for his efforts and the selling group member earns the other 7%. The client pays the offering price of $30 per share as stated in the prospectus. Our figures are for illustrative purposes only but are in line with those generally in use in the industry.

Fund - Underwriter - Investor
Some fund underwriters employ their own sales force and do not employ a dealer selling group. In this case, the distribution would be: fund to underwriter to investor.

Fund - Investor
Many funds have no sales charge, and the shares are bought and sold at net asset value. In this case, the investor buys directly from the fund. As there is no "load" (sales charge), no underwriter or selling group is used. These are referred to as no load funds.

Fund - Underwriter - Plan Company - Investor
Mutual fund shares are often offered under periodic payment, or contractual, plans. These are usually offered by dealers known as "plan companies." In these cases the fund sells the shares to the underwriter who, in turn, sells to the plan company. That company then distributes to the investor under the terms of the contract. Note that in these contractual plans the maximum sales charge that may be charged is 9%.

Restrictions on Distribution of Investment Company Shares

The regulatory authorities require distributors of investment company shares to comply with many regulations not required in the distribution of other products. They feel that the purchasers of these shares are often small investors who are not sophisticated in investment techniques and who, therefore, require more than usual protection. Some of the special restrictions are:

No special deals can be offered by the underwriter of mutual fund shares. For example, the underwriter could not contact a securities dealer and offer gifts or prizes such as vacation trips to salespersons selling a minimum amount of shares to their clients. This special incentive might cause some less than ethical salespeople to induce their clients to purchase products not suitable to their investment purposes. Should the underwriter wish to host a luncheon or cocktail party to explain their operation to a firm's sales force, this would not be a violation of the "special deal" prohibition.

Broker/dealers may not "trade" open-end investment company shares. That is, they may not buy them for the firm's inventory in the hopes of selling them at a higher price at a later date. The fear is that some unscrupulous dealer may attempt to force the shares on some clients who should not own them. Therefore, a broker/dealer may not "take down" shares of a mutual fund from the underwriter except to fill an order previously received or for the firm's own investment account. This rule is applicable only to trading mutual funds. It is quite usual in the investment business for dealers to buy stocks and bonds for firm inventory in anticipation of a rising market.

Dealers in mutual fund shares are required to maintain the public offering price. While competition causes much price-cutting by securities dealers, this practice cannot be applied to sales of open-end shares. In our example, the selling group member would earn a 7% sales charge in selling the fund shares. He purchased them at $30 less 7% and sells them to the investor at $30. He might be willing to offer a 2% discount to clients in order to develop sales, as this would still leave a fine 5% profit. However, while this may be done on sales of other products, it cannot be done with fund shares. The dealer must maintain the public offering price. These front end load shares are referred to as Class A.

Contingent Deferred Sales Charge (CDSC)

This is commonly referred to as Bank-End Loads and permit the investor to buy shares at the NAV. However, a sales charge is imposed at the time of redemption of the shares. Under normal circumstances, the sales charge is reduced the longer you hold the shares, and if you hold them long enough, the sales charge is eliminated, hence the name contingent deferred sales charge. These shares are referred to as Class B shares.

Class C Shares

These shares have a so-called 12b-1 annual fee referred to as a level load, which is currently equal to 1% of the fund's assets. In addition, not all, but some, funds charge a front end sales charge of 1%. Further, some funds impose a contingent deferred sales charge if the shares are sold before 18 months have passed.

Methods of Purchasing Open-End Investment Company Shares

Regular Account

In a "regular account," a client purchase shares just as he would purchase shares of other securities. He simply places an order for a specific number of shares and makes payment in the normal manner. The shares can either be sent to him or held for him in his account. Although this is the usual manner in which other securities are purchased, it is most unusual in mutual funds. The purchasers of this product generally are attempting to build their investments to attain some future goal and tend to use an accumulation-type account.

Letter of Intent

In a "letter of intent," the customer states her plan to purchase shares over a period of time. This is done to take advantage of the breakpoints in sales charges usually offered. For example, our fund might apply an 8% load on amounts under $10,000, but the charge might be only 7% on amounts between $10,000 and $20,000. The charge would continue to decline to a point where, for investments of $1,000,000 or more, the charge might drop to 1%. These levels at which the charge is reduced are called "breakpoints."

As we have stated, purchasers of mutual funds are usually small investors and seldom have large amounts of dollars to invest at one time. They might consider signing a letter of intent in which the total amount invested over a period not to exceed 13 months would be considered when determining the sales charge. Thus, if the investor sent in $1,000 per month for the 13 months, she would be charged 7% rather than 8% on a retroactive basis.

Letters of intent can also be backdated for up to 90 days to take advantage of deposits made prior to signing the letter. Letters of intent are available to individuals or to groups of related people such as pension and profit-sharing plans. They are not available to groups of unrelated people such as investment clubs.

A distant relative of a letter of intent is called a "right of accumulation." Here, the total value of the client's investment is considered when determining the sales charge. Thus, a small investor may reach the $10,000 breakpoint after seven years of investing in the funds shares. From that point on her sales charge could be reduced to 7% rather than the 8%. While the reduction is not retroactive, it can provide a savings in the future.

Voluntary Accumulation Plan

A "voluntary accumulation plan" is best described by the word "voluntary" in its title. In this plan, the client makes an initial purchase (a minimum amount is usually required) and makes subsequent deposits (again, usually a minimum requirement) on a voluntary basis. Thus, a client may start a plan with a deposit of perhaps $250 and make subsequent deposits of $50 or more whenever the funds are available. Frequently, the client may reinvest income and capital gains distributions at net asset value, saving the sales charge. Please note that although the client may elect to reinvest these distributions, they would nonetheless be taxable to him that year. The client using this voluntary plan will reap the benefits of professional management of his portfolio while, hopefully, building the investment value.

The fund employs a bank or trust company to act as the fund custodian. Among the duties of the custodian are:

- functioning as either registrar or transfer agent for fund shares
- acting as dividend disbursing agent
- receiving and investing payments from clients
- maintaining custody of securities owned by the fund
- bookkeeping and recordkeeping

Dollar-Cost Averaging

The investment technique of "dollar-cost averaging" calls for the periodic investment of equal dollar amounts in a security, perhaps an investment company. If the plan is properly followed, it will result in the investor obtaining an average cost on his shares that is lower than the average price paid. For example, a person invests $200 per month in an investment company for four consecutive months as follows:

Month	Investment	Share Price	Number of Shares Purchased
May	$200	$ 4	50
June	$200	$ 5	40
July	$200	$ 4	50
August	$200	$ 8	25
Total	$800	$21	165

The investor has purchased 165 shares at a total cost of $800; therefore, his average cost per share is $4.85. ($800 divided by 165). However, the average price paid for the shares was $5.25, which is the sum of the prices paid (21) divided by the number of purchases (4).

This in no way guarantees a profit as the shares could well be trading below our client's cost of $5.25. By keeping the dollar amount of the investment consistent, the investor buys more shares when the price is low (50 shares for $200 at a price of $4) and fewer shares at higher price levels (only 25 shares for $200 when the price is $8).

REGULATIONS GOVERNING THE SALE OF INVESTMENT COMPANY SECURITIES

Securities Act of 1933

The Securities Act of 1933 governs the offering of new issues of securities and related matters. Investment companies must file a registration statement with the Securities and Exchange Commission prior to the original offering of the shares. The "full disclosure" of all material information is required in this registration statement. The SEC does not approve the issue, but only attempts to see that all information is made available to the prospective investors.

As with other new issues, the fund must publish a prospectus that must be provided to the investor prior to or at least with the solicitation of an order. Some of the items required in the prospectus are:

- type of company (open end or closed end, etc.)
- investment objectives
- investment policies
- management fees
- sales charges
- redemption features

The Investment Company Act of 1940 (and 1970 Amendments)

We have discussed many parts of this law in our prior study of investment companies. Some additional provisions that those studying this topic should know follow.

- In order to make a public offering of its shares, a registered investment company must have a net worth of at least $100,000.
- Not more than 50% of the directors of an investment company may be affiliated with the investment company's underwriter or its investment advisors.
- Registered investment companies may not purchase securities on margin. (They may under certain conditions make short sales, however, which are made in margin accounts).
- Dividends paid to shareholders must be paid from the fund's net income (amounts received from dividends on stocks and interest on bonds).
- The maximum sales charge on contractual plans may not exceed 9%.
- Open-end companies may issue only one security, which must be "voting stock." They may not issue senior securities such as bonds or preferred stock. This prohibition does not apply to closed-end companies.

- The fund may not purchase securities of any company if any of the fund's officers or directors own more than 5% of that company's securities or if, collectively, the fund's officers or directors own more than 5% of that company's securities.
- A majority of the shareholders must approve any major change in the fund's policies.

Internal Revenue Code Subchapter M

An investment company that is registered under the 1940 act can qualify as a regulated investment company under the Internal Revenue Code Subchapter M. This registered-regulated company will be relieved of the problem of double taxation. Income and capital gains, which are distributed to the shareholders, will not be taxable to the investment company. This "conduit," or "pipeline," theory of taxation allows the fund to avoid much of the direct taxation that would inhibit its investment program. To qualify for this favored tax treatment, the investment company must meet certain requirements:

1. The investment company must be a domestic concern.
2. It must be registered as a management company or as a unit investment trust under the Investment Company Act of 1940.
3. A minimum of 90% of gross income annually must be received from interest on bonds or dividends on stocks in the fund's portfolio.
4. The fund must distribute a minimum of 90% of its net income from interest and dividends to its shareholders. (Note: Most companies distribute all investment income, as the shareholders generally reinvest these monies; this leaves the fund free from any tax liability.)

Capital gains are not considered to be investment income. The investment company can distribute these to shareholders in whole or in part as they see fit. Those capital gains that are distributed are taxable to the shareholder, those that are retained by the fund are taxable to the fund. There is no requirement to distribute capital gains under the Internal Revenue Code as there is with investment income.

The holding period of the fund determines if a capital gain distribution is to be treated as a short-term or a long-term gain by the recipient shareholder. Thus, if the fund held a security long enough to qualify for long-term tax treatment (currently, more than one year), and sold the security at a profit, any distribution of this profit to shareholders would qualify as a long-term gain to that shareholder. It is possible then for an individual to hold the fund's shares for a short-term period and still receive a capital gain distribution.

Capital gains distributions are made no more than once each year and must be made in the year taken. Distributions from investment income, however, are usually made quarterly by the investment companies to their shareholders.

COMPUTATIONS OF YIELD

Great care must be taken when expressing the "yield," or rate of return, on investment company shares so as not to deceive the potential investor. Yield can only be expressed on a twelve month basis. It would be improper to tell a client that "the fund had a yield of 7% over the last six months," implying a 14% annual return—which may not be the case. Further, yield can be expressed only in one of two ways: current yield or historic (average) yield.

Current Yield

Current yield is determined by using the current offering price and adding to it any capital gains distributions made over the most recent 12 months. This addition reflects the fact that had the fund not made the distribution, the offering price would be higher by that amount. This "new" offering price is then divided into the total of all income distributions made during the last 12 months. The result is current yield.

EXAMPLE _____

Current Quotation	$9.20 – $10.00
Capital Gains Distribution (12 months)	$ .50
Income Distribution (12 months)	$ .50

Offering Price ($10) plus Capital Gains ($.50) = $10.50
Income Distribution ($.50) divided by $10.50 = Current Yield (4.76%)

Historic (Average) Yield

Historic (average) yield is determined by using the average monthly offering price over the past 12 months. This figure is then divided into the income distributions for the period, resulting in the historic yield. Capital gains distributions are not considered in this calculation because by using the average monthly offering price those distributions have been factored in.

EXAMPLE: _____

Average monthly offering price (12 months)	$12.80
Income distribution (12 months)	1.20
Capital gains distribution (12 months)	.76

Income Distribution ($1.20) divided by Average Offering Price ($12.80) =
Historic (Average) Yield (9.38%)

Exchange Traded Funds (ETF)

The first Exchange Traded Fund (ETF) came into being in 1993. The SPDR 500 Trust (SPY) was traded on the American Stock Exchange (AMEX). They are becoming common investment vehicles for both individual and institutional investors. As of this writing, there are hundreds of U.S. ETFs with assets in excess of $200 billion.

ETFs are similar to an open-end mutual fund as well as a stock. They represent a fractional ownership in an underlying portfolio of securities that trade a specific market index. However, ETFs are traded on the American Stock Exchange, the Chicago Board Options Exchange, and the New York Stock Exchange. Mutual funds, on the other hand, are purchased and redeemed directly with the fund itself. Consequently, mutual funds cannot be purchased in a margin since they are classified as a new issue. (Mutual funds may be carried on margin for 30 days after the purchase.) Since ETFs are listed securities, they may be purchased in a margin account.

Another difference is that mutual funds are priced once a day after the closing of the market. The prices of ETFs fluctuate according to changes in their underlying portfolios and according to changes in market supply and demand. The normal response to the statement is that ETFs are just like a closed-end fund. However, unlike closed-end funds, ETFs are permitted to continuously offer shares, which changes the number of outstanding shares, which in fact can be changed daily to meet demand. Consequently, there are no large discounts or premiums to their Net Asset Value (NAV). As you know, closed-end funds usually trade at a discount to its NAV and sometimes at premium to their NAV.

Some of the more popular ETFs are the NASDAQ-100 (QQQ), iShares Russell 3000 (IWV), iShare Russell (IWM), Ishare S&P 500 (IVV), and SPOR (SPY).

The following is a brief description of the characteristics of ETFs:

- Continuous Pricing. ETFs have the same intraday pricing as other securities. The estimated NAV, also called Indicative Optimized Portfolio Value (IOPV), for the basket of securities is repriced for market makers and specialists every 15 seconds. It is this process that keeps premiums and discounts to the NAV at a minimum.
- Diversification. Much like mutual funds ETFs, they eliminate the single stock risk that occurs when an investor invests primarily in a favorite sector.
- Fees. ETFs are subject to brokerage commissions; however, the savings from lower annual fees can affect these costs for long-term holders. The annual fees of ETFs are lower than most mutual funds.
- Settlement. Trades settle in three business days. All shares are book entry held in Depository Trust Company (DTCC).
- Trading Unit. A round lot is 100 shares. Odd lots less than 100 shares trades as well.

PROHIBITED PRACTICES

"Selling Dividends"

"Selling dividends" is inducing a customer to purchase shares based on an imminent dividend. For example, an open-end investment company is quoted $9.20–$10. The fund has announced that a dividend of $.50 will be paid in the near future. A salesperson attempts to induce a client to buy the shares by saying, "Hurry up and place your order. You will receive a $.50 dividend on a $10 purchase price. That's 5% of your money."

In fact, the investor would gain nothing, since when the shares trade "ex-dividend" the price will decline by the $.50. If the investor waits, he will buy the shares at a lower price and will not incur a tax liability for the dividend. To prevent "selling dividends" investment companies often use a special date declared by the directors as the "ex-dividend" date rather than the generally used ex-date in our industry, which is two business days prior to the record date. Any investment prior to a large distribution can cause a tax liability.

"Twisting"

Twisting is causing an investor to sell one investment company to purchase another similar company solely to create a new sales charge for the benefit of the registered representative. In other areas of our business we call this improper treatment of customers "churning," but with investment companies the term "twisting" is used. Note: It would not be twisting to suggest a switch from one investment company to another if it suited the needs of the client. For example, a change from a "growth fund" to an "income fund" for a recently retired person might represent sound investment advice.

Breakpoint Sales

A "breakpoint sale" is a device used to cause a client to pay a sales charge larger than might be necessary. A particular investment company has a schedule of charges that calls for an 8% load for investments of less than $10,000, but only 7% for investments from $10,000 to $20,000. A salesperson recommends a purchase of $9,900 of the fund to a client so that he might obtain the higher sales charge. This is a flagrant breakpoint sales violation since by investing an additional $100 the client would save $100 in sales charge (1% of $10,000). The violation can be more subtle such as breaking up an investment into several similar type companies when the client could achieve a saving in cost by placing his dollars in a single investment.

ADVERTISING AND SALES LITERATURE

SEC Rule 158 replaced the statement of policy on sales literature of investment companies. It does not specify exact requirements, but is aimed at providing guidance in the preparation of investment company advertisements. The term "sales literature" includes any communication, whether in writing or otherwise, used by any person to offer to sell or induce the sale of any securities of any investment company. The use of sales literature in connection with the sale of investment company shares is unlawful if that information is materially misleading, contains an untrue statement of material fact, or omits a material fact. Information may be considered misleading if it lacks proper explanations, qualifications, or limitations; presents past performance in a way that implies similar future performance; or misrepresents the investment company or its management. Sales literature is covered whether it is used by an issuer, an underwriter, a dealer, or a registered representative if it can be reasonably expected to be used with prospective clients. Sales literature may not represent or imply that the person's investment will increase, be preserved, or be protected against loss. A discussion of the advantages of the investment must be balanced with a discussion of the risks.

FIXED AND VARIABLE ANNUITIES

To make a proper study of variable annuities, we must first look at the annuity contract as an overall product. For many years the life insurance industry in the United States has offered a fixed annuity contract. This policy was designed to supplement other forms of insurance, which began to pay out only upon the death of the insured person. The fixed annuity, on the other hand, allows for the payment of a fixed dollar amount periodically to the annuitant during his lifetime. It provided a source of retirement income that would supplement other benefits such as company retirement plans and social security. The fixed annuity would begin to pay at a certain time, perhaps when the annuitant reached the age of 65. There is a minimum age of 59½ to avoid any penalties. It would pay a fixed amount, perhaps $200 per month, for a fixed period or, more usually, for the life of the annuitant. Often the contract was set up to include a "joint or survivor" provision. In this case, the payments would continue to be paid after the death of the survivor, usually to the spouse, for the remainder of that person's life. The fixed annuity can be purchased by a single lump-sum payment or by the payment of periodic premiums over a period of years.

Mortality Risk

Insurance companies base their payment guarantees on a continuing study of life expectancy. Thus, payments on a fixed annuity are calculated on the finding that the annuitant will "go to his reward" on a fixed date. Should the insured person outlive that expectancy, the insurance company must continue to make the agreed payments. Thus, the mortality risk is borne by the insurance company, not by the purchaser of the fixed annuity contract.

Investment Risk

The investment risk in a fixed annuity contract is also borne by the insurer. As stated earlier, the annuitant may live beyond his expectancy, causing payments to continue past the anticipated time. Additionally, the insurance company's investment experience may not be as favorable as expected.

The company invests its reserves in securities and mortgages. If the return on these investments declines, they are still obliged to make the agreed payments. However, if the income on investments is greater than anticipated, this excess is passed on to the annuitant. Naturally, careful study is given to the investment program and the fixed annuity payments are geared to conservative expectations. However, the investment risk in a fixed annuity contract belongs to the insurance company.

Variable annuity contracts generally allow for unused units to be paid to a beneficiary in case the annuitant dies before receiving payment of his entire holding (called by insurance people an "adverse mortality experience"). Thus, the decedent's spouse might receive payment for remaining units or they might become an asset of the decedent's estate. Should the annuitant live beyond the expected time, he would exhaust his 12,000 units. However, he would continue to be paid the value of 150 units each month for his lifetime. The mortality risk is, therefore, borne by the variable annuity company.

Assumed Investment Return (AIR)

In determining the initial monthly payments for variable annuities, the calculation considers more than the amount invested by the contract holder. The Assumed Investment Return (AIR) is also recognized. This additional amount is usually figured to be 5% per year. By including this in the calculation, the annuitant may receive a monthly payment of $8 for each $1,000 invested at age 65. Without the AIR factor, the rate might only $6 per $1,000 making the contract unattractive. By using AIR, we assume this 5% annual growth rate will occur. Should the return for a period be greater than the AIR, the dollar value of the annuity unit will increase, as will the payment to the contract holder. Should the AIR not be achieved, both unit value and payout will decrease.

AIR is not a guarantee. It is possible that the anticipated rate will not occur. However, as the AIR is generally conservative, the annuity company expects to meet its goal and, therefore, includes it in its calculations.

ANSWER SHEET FOR CHAPTER 7 EXAMINATION

1. Ⓐ Ⓑ Ⓒ Ⓓ   11. Ⓐ Ⓑ Ⓒ Ⓓ   21. Ⓐ Ⓑ Ⓒ Ⓓ

2. Ⓐ Ⓑ Ⓒ Ⓓ   12. Ⓐ Ⓑ Ⓒ Ⓓ   22. Ⓐ Ⓑ Ⓒ Ⓓ

3. Ⓐ Ⓑ Ⓒ Ⓓ   13. Ⓐ Ⓑ Ⓒ Ⓓ   23. Ⓐ Ⓑ Ⓒ Ⓓ

4. Ⓐ Ⓑ Ⓒ Ⓓ   14. Ⓐ Ⓑ Ⓒ Ⓓ   24. Ⓐ Ⓑ Ⓒ Ⓓ

5. Ⓐ Ⓑ Ⓒ Ⓓ   15. Ⓐ Ⓑ Ⓒ Ⓓ   25. Ⓐ Ⓑ Ⓒ Ⓓ

6. Ⓐ Ⓑ Ⓒ Ⓓ   16. Ⓐ Ⓑ Ⓒ Ⓓ   26. Ⓐ Ⓑ Ⓒ Ⓓ

7. Ⓐ Ⓑ Ⓒ Ⓓ   17. Ⓐ Ⓑ Ⓒ Ⓓ   27. Ⓐ Ⓑ Ⓒ Ⓓ

8. Ⓐ Ⓑ Ⓒ Ⓓ   18. Ⓐ Ⓑ Ⓒ Ⓓ   28. Ⓐ Ⓑ Ⓒ Ⓓ

9. Ⓐ Ⓑ Ⓒ Ⓓ   19. Ⓐ Ⓑ Ⓒ Ⓓ   29. Ⓐ Ⓑ Ⓒ Ⓓ

10. Ⓐ Ⓑ Ⓒ Ⓓ   20. Ⓐ Ⓑ Ⓒ Ⓓ   30. Ⓐ Ⓑ Ⓒ Ⓓ

31. Ⓐ Ⓑ Ⓒ Ⓓ   41. Ⓐ Ⓑ Ⓒ Ⓓ

32. Ⓐ Ⓑ Ⓒ Ⓓ   42. Ⓐ Ⓑ Ⓒ Ⓓ

33. Ⓐ Ⓑ Ⓒ Ⓓ   43. Ⓐ Ⓑ Ⓒ Ⓓ

34. Ⓐ Ⓑ Ⓒ Ⓓ   44. Ⓐ Ⓑ Ⓒ Ⓓ

35. Ⓐ Ⓑ Ⓒ Ⓓ   45. Ⓐ Ⓑ Ⓒ Ⓓ

36. Ⓐ Ⓑ Ⓒ Ⓓ   46. Ⓐ Ⓑ Ⓒ Ⓓ

37. Ⓐ Ⓑ Ⓒ Ⓓ   47. Ⓐ Ⓑ Ⓒ Ⓓ

38. Ⓐ Ⓑ Ⓒ Ⓓ   48. Ⓐ Ⓑ Ⓒ Ⓓ

39. Ⓐ Ⓑ Ⓒ Ⓓ   49. Ⓐ Ⓑ Ⓒ Ⓓ

40. Ⓐ Ⓑ Ⓒ Ⓓ   50. Ⓐ Ⓑ Ⓒ Ⓓ

CHAPTER 7 EXAMINATION

1. The net asset value of a mutual fund was $9.27 last month. This month it is calculated to be $9.85. What is this change in value called?

   (A) yield
   (B) asset revaluation
   (C) appreciation
   (D) capital gain

2. Which of the following types of investment companies pays out 90% of its net investment income to its shareholders?

   (A) diversified
   (B) registered
   (C) regulated
   (D) balanced

3. Your customer wishes to invest $50,000 in three mutual funds offered by different underwriters with growth as a main objective. A recommendation to purchase only one such fund for $50,000 might be more suitable to the investor:

   (A) if the growth in one fund will be greater than the combined growth in three
   (B) if the income from one fund will be greater than the combined income in three
   (C) if a withdrawal plan would be easier to employ using a single fund
   (D) if the purchase of one fund would probably be made at a breakpoint allowing more dollars to be invested in fund shares

4. Which of the following may occasionally be purchased at a *discount* from net asset value?

   I.   no-load funds
   II. closed-end funds
   III. open-end funds
   IV. contractual plans

   (A) I and II only
   (B) II only
   (C) III only
   (D) I, II, III, and IV

5. What type of mutual fund would invest in equities and bonds?

   (A) dual purpose
   (B) balanced
   (C) technology
   (D) growth

6. Each of the following statements about a letter of intent are true EXCEPT:

   (A) a letter of intent has a maximum duration of 13 months
   (B) a shareholder may not redeem any shares for 13 months
   (C) a letter of intent may be backdated by 90 days
   (D) a certain portion of shares purchased are held in escrow until the terms of the letter are met

7. A bank or trust company, when acting as *custodian* for a mutual fund:

   (A) guarantees investors' loss on investments
   (B) provides investment advice to the fund's managers
   (C) redeems and issues fund shares
   (D) physically protects the fund's assets

8. The cost of *maintaining* an investment in a mutual fund is best reflected in the:

   (A) custodial fee
   (B) sales charge
   (C) expense ratio
   (D) net investment income

9. An "accumulation unit" of a variable annuity is used to determine:

   (A) the value of the annuitant's contract before annuity payments begin
   (B) the amount of annuity payments to be made to the owner
   (C) the amount to be passed to the annuitant's beneficiary
   (D) the amount returned to the annuitant upon redemption of the account

10. Which of the following are true about mutual funds?

    I.   The maximum sales charge is 7%.
    II. Investors can receive a reduced sales charge if they sign a ten-month letter of intention to purchase a certain dollar amount of shares.
    III. Under a "right of accumulation" privilege, investors receive a reduced sales charge on new purchases when a breakpoint level is reach.
    IV. No-load funds may charge a liquidation fee when an investor sells the shares.

       (A) I only
       (B) III only
       (C) III and IV only
       (D) I, II, and IV only

11. All of the following are investment companies within the terms of the Investment Company Act of 1940 EXCEPT:

    (A) a holding company dealing in mineral leaseholds
    (B) a face-amount certificate company
    (C) a unit investment trust company
    (D) a management company

12. A mutual fund's custodial bank is often all of the following EXCEPT:

    (A) its transfer agent
    (B) its investment advisor
    (C) its registrar
    (D) its dividend disbursing agent

13. A management group may serve an investment company as its:

    I.   underwriter
    II. investment advisor
    III. custodian bank
    IV. plan company

       (A) II only
       (B) I and III only
       (C) II and IV only
       (D) I, II, and IV only

14. Which of the following organizations usually plays a prominent role in guiding investment policies of mutual funds?

    (A) the plan company
    (B) the management group
    (C) the custodian bank
    (D) the underwriter

15. A mutual fund's custodian may engage in each of the following practices EXCEPT:

    (A) changing shareholder registrations on the fund's records
    (B) disbursing dividends and/or capital gains to the fund's shareholders
    (C) lending the fund's securities to banks or broker/dealers
    (D) maintaining sales records for the fund's underwriter

16. To change its investment objective from income to growth, a registered investment company must obtain approval from:

    (A) the NASD
    (B) the SEC
    (C) a majority of the shareholders
    (D) all of the above

17. Under the Investment Company Act of 1940, the minimum net worth of a registered investment company must be:

    (A) $100,000
    (B) $50,000
    (C) $25,000
    (D) $5,000

18. Which of the following pairs of terms are synonyms in connection with most mutual funds?

    (A) net asset value and offering price
    (B) selling price and bid price
    (C) net asset value and redemption price
    (D) bid price and management fee

19. Under what circumstances may a registered investment company change its investment objective?

    I.   It must gain the prior approval of the SEC.
    II. It must obtain a new charter from the state secretary.
    III. It must be voted upon and approved by the shareholders of the company.
    IV. Prior public notice of the company's intention must be recorded in the *Federal Register*.

    (A) III only
    (B) I and IV only
    (C) II and III only
    (D) I, II, III, and IV

20. A mutual fund's custodian bank is paid according to which of the following specifications when it receives deposits from a shareholder's reinvestment plan?

    (A) a commission for each share purchased
    (B) a percentage of the sales charge
    (C) a processing fee
    (D) a percentage of the fund's net asset value

21. If a mutual fund has invested its assets, allocating about one third each for bonds, preferred, and common stocks, it is identified as:

    (A) an income fund
    (B) a specialized fund
    (C) a balanced fund
    (D) a unit investment trust fund

22. A mutual fund with an 8% load and a 1% redemption fee carries a current quote of $6.25–$6.79. If an investor has tendered his shares for redemption on that basis, the per share price he will receive is approximately:

(A) $6.79
(B) $6.72
(C) $6.25
(D) $6.19

23. The net investment income of an open-end investment company represents:

(A) net profits from the investment company operation
(B) net gains on sales of portfolio securities
(C) dividends, interest, and net gains on sales of securities
(D) net income from dividend and interest paid on securities in a fund portfolio

24. Which of these statements is pertinent to closed-end investment companies?

(A) They are continuously issuing new shares.
(B) They are prohibited from issuing any securities other than common stock.
(C) Their shares are traded in the open market at prices determined by forces of supply and demand.
(D) Their shares are redeemable at net asset value.

25. What percentage load is associated with a mutual fund quoted 16.60–18.04?

(A) 8.7%
(B) 9%
(C) 8%
(D) cannot be determined from information presented

26. Which of the following registered investment companies normally sells with an appropriate commission added to its contract price?

(A) an open-end management company
(B) a unit investment trust company
(C) a face-amount certificate company
(D) a closed-end investment company

27. Which of the following statements about the bank or trust company serving as a custodian of an open-end mutual fund is correct?

(A) The custodian performs all management, supervisory, or investment functions.
(B) The custodian may perform an essential clerical type service for the fund and its shareholders.
(C) The custodian takes part in the sale or distribution of the fund shares.
(D) The custodian affords protection against possible decline in the value of the fund shares.

28. The XYZ Fund, a load fund, offers a reinvestment plan. This means that:

(A) purchasers of fund shares must agree to make regular investments over a period of years, usually ten
(B) income, dividend, and capital gains distributions are automatically used to purchase shares of the fund
(C) holders of fund shares are permitted to regularly purchase additional shares at the bid price
(D) no federal income taxes must be paid on dividends and capital gains distributions from the fund.

29. A mutual fund letter of intent may permissibly be predated for a period of time up to:

    (A) 5 business days
    (B) 10 calendar days
    (C) 90 calendar days
    (D) 13 months

30. Which of the following statements regarding mutual funds is true?

    (A) The custodian bank can also be the fund's transfer agent.
    (B) The sponsor receives a management fee based on the fund's total assets.
    (C) The terms "management company" and "investment advisor" are interchangeable when speaking of mutual funds.
    (D) The management company receives a portion of the sales load for managing the fund assets.

31. Which of the four sets listed below is that of a closed-end investment company?

Net Asset Value	Asked Price
(A) $7.50	$8.10
(B) $10.10	$11.00
(C) $28.14	$27.75
(D) $20.15	$21.85

32. An investment company incapable of issuing a long-term debt instrument is:

    (A) a face-amount certificate company
    (B) a unit investment trust company
    (C) a closed-end management company
    (D) an open-end investment company

33. The term "mutual fund" is the popular name for which of the following?

    (A) all investment companies
    (B) pension funds
    (C) open-end investment companies
    (D) closed-end investment companies

34. Which of the following statements concerning mutual fund fees is accurate?

    (A) The management group receives a fee based upon the amount of assets in the fund.
    (B) The sponsor (underwriter) receives a management fee for buying and selling the fund's portfolio securities.
    (C) The management group receives part of the sales charge in addition to the management fee.
    (D) The custodian bank receives part of the management fee in addition to a fee for safekeeping the fund's securities.

35. Each of the following statements about mutual funds and variable annuities is true EXCEPT:

    (A) Each is regulated under the Investment Company Act of 1940.
    (B) The holder of each must pay income taxes on the dividends received each year.
    (C) The registered representative must have an NASD registration to solicit either one.
    (D) The payout of each depends on the performance and investment result of the securities owned in the portfolio.

36. A customer's purchase order with a dealer for investment company shares must be executed at a price based on the net asset value of the shares:

    (A) next computed after receipt of the order by the dealer
    (B) last computed before receipt of the order by the dealer
    (C) computed the previous day at the close of the New York Stock Exchange
    (D) computed the same day the order was received by the dealer

37. A mutual fund characterized by a modest sales charge and an investment in a fixed portfolio of municipal securities is a:

    (A) face-amount certificate company
    (B) unit investment trust company
    (C) management company
    (D) open-end or closed-end company

38. A "front-end" load mutual fund plan is most applicable for:

    (A) a voluntary accumulation plan
    (B) a contractual plan
    (C) an automatic withdrawal plan
    (D) an optional withdrawal plan

39. An investor's pledge to purchase a specified dollar amount of a mutual fund within a specified period of time is called:

    (A) a promissory note
    (B) a letter of intent
    (C) an investment letter
    (D) a stock power

40. An investment company acting as a conduit in the distribution of net investment income, pursuant to IRS rules, is called:

    (A) balanced
    (B) diversified
    (C) regulated
    (D) dual-purpose

41. Mutual fund salespersons may not represent that their product is like or safer than:

    I.   an insurance policy
    II. a fixed annuity
    III. a corporate debt instrument
    IV. a U.S. government bond

        (A) IV only
        (B) I and III only
        (C) II and IV only
        (D) I, II, III, and IV

42. All sales literature and advertising having to do with investment company shares prepared by members of the NASD must be filed for review with the:

    (A) Anti-Trust Division of the Justice Department
    (B) SEC
    (C) Federal Reserve Board
    (D) NASD

43. Reinvestment of dividends and distributions from investment company shares:

    (A) accomplishes all of the following
    (B) results in compounding of shares, which can be an important factor in making an investment account grow
    (C) permits deferment of all federal income taxes on dividends and distributions until the plan is liquidated
    (D) makes possible the purchase of fund shares at a price below net asset value

44. The principal underwriter of an open-end investment company is frequently called the:

    (A) participating investment advisor
    (B) sponsor
    (C) selling group member
    (D) investment counselor

45. The public offering price of the securities of an open-end management investment company is:

    (A) determined by a method set forth in the prospectus of the issuing company
    (B) based upon net asset value of the securities underlying the shares of the issuing company plus the standard 10% sales charge
    (C) determined by the relative demand for the shares of the issuing company
    (D) the price used by distributors in determining "sales incentive" discounts to individual purchasers

46. The net investment income of an open-end investment company represents:

    (A) net income from dividends and interest paid on securities in the fund's portfolio
    (B) net gains on sales of portfolio securities
    (C) dividends, interest, and net gains on sales of securities
    (D) net profits from the investment company operation

47. Registration of open-end investment company shares with the SEC implies that the:

    (A) shares have investment merit
    (B) SEC approves the issue
    (C) SEC guarantees the accuracy of the disclosures in the registration statement
    (D) prospectus contains the significant facts about the issue

48. In the sale of open-end investment company shares, the dollar amount at which the sales charge is reduced on quantity transactions is referred to as the:

    (A) margin
    (B) breakpoint
    (C) split
    (D) spread

49. The amount closed-end investment company securities are selling above net asset value is known as the:

    (A) premium
    (B) discount
    (C) commission
    (D) sales charge

50. Investment companies must issue financial statements to shareholders:

    (A) monthly
    (B) quarterly
    (C) semiannually
    (D) annually

CHAPTER 7 EXAMINATION ANSWERS

1. **C** By definition. Had you been the owner of the mutual fund, then you would have had what is called "unrealized appreciation."

2. **C** Investment companies regulated by the Internal Revenue Code Subchapter M are required to pay out a minimum of 90% of their net income annually to their shareholders.

3. **D** There is nothing inherently unsuitable about recommending three different funds to a customer with $50,000 to invest. However, in most cases, a single well-chosen fund offers satisfactory diversification and could normally be purchased at a significant reduction in sales charge.

4. **B** Mutual funds may be purchased at NAV (no load) or NAV plus a sales charge but never at less than NAV (a discount). Closed-end fund pricing has no direct link to NAV, thus making possible a price at a significant discount to NAV.

5. **B** A balanced fund invests for growth, common stocks, and income preferred stocks and bonds.

6. **B** Redemptions are permissible at any time. However, since "escrow shares" are set aside to cover the difference in sales loads based on terms of the letter, a partial or total redemption prior to 13 months may liquidate part or all of the escrow account and the investor may thus not receive back 100% of net asset value.

7. **D** This is what the "custodian" does when acting in that role. If the same bank were also acting as transfer agent, it would provide the services noted in (C).

8. **C** While the sales charge is a one-time expense and the custodial fees are negligible, the operating expenses of a fund are continuing costs as long as the fund is held.

9. **A** Payouts, on the other hand, are made in a number of annuity units. The holder is entitled to a set number of annuity units monthly.

10. **C** No-load funds may charge a liquidation fee when an investor redeems his shares. The right of accumulation is a privilege granted by some mutual funds wherein an investor receives a lower sales charge on additional purchases if the value of the shares he already owns plus the contemplated new money addition reaches or exceeds a breakpoint.

11. **A** Choices (B), (C), and (D) identify the three classifications of investment companies under the 1940 act.

12. **B** This function is generally performed by an outside advisor or the management company.

13. **D** The custodian for an investment company must be independent of the company.

14. **B** Obviously, the management group will have an important role in guiding investment policy. The management group is actually made up of the management company, which includes the principal underwriter or sponsor, and the investment advisor.

15. **C** This is not permissible under federal law.

16. **C** As required in the 1940 Investment Company Act. The shareholders must also approve liquidation of assets, change of name, and any other factor that would materially affect the interests of the shareholders.

17. **A** As required in the 1940 act. Keep in mind that this was a considerable sum of money in 1940.

18. **C** This is the only pair of synonyms.

19. **A** Anything that vitally affects the interests of the shareholders must be subject to approval by a vote of the shareholders.

20. **C** Please note that some custodian banks do not charge the processing fee to the individual account, but rather to the mutual fund itself.

21. **C** This is the manner in which a balanced fund typically invests its assets. It varies its investments among various types of securities.

22. **D** The fund has a redemption fee of 1%. One percent of the bid price would be about 6 cents. Therefore, on a redemption, you would receive approximately $6.19. Note: The load is paid when the shares are purchased.

23. **D** By definition. Net investment income does not include gains from sales of securities.

24. **C** None of the other choices are true relative to a closed-end company. Rather, the other choices describe an open-end company.

25. **C** The sales charge in this case is $1.44. Divide 1.44 by the offering price of $18.04.

    NAV   OP
    16.60 18.04   difference = 1.44
    $$\frac{1.44}{18.04} = 8\%$$

26. **D** Note that an open-end management company includes a sales charge, not a commission.

27. **B** The custodian bank holds the money and securities of the investment company as well as performing the bookkeeping and recordkeeping functions. It does not perform in a supervisory or advisory role.

28. **B** This properly describes the mechanics of a reinvestment plan.

29. **C** An investor has up to 90 days from the date of original purchase to sign a letter of intent. Please note that the maximum time span of a letter of intent is 13 months from initial purchase, and this 90-day grace period does not extend the 13-month interval.

30. **A** It has become increasingly common for the transfer function (issuing and redeeming shares, disbursing dividends, and distributions) to be performed by a satellite "shareholder-serving agent" affiliated with the sponsor, while the custodial function (holding the funds and cash and securities) continues in the hands of a bank or trust company. However, banks sometimes perform both functions.

31. **C** In this case, the asked price is at a discount from net asset value. This could never be the case in an open-end company.

32. **D** By definition. Open-end management companies may not issue any senior securities. They may only issue "voting stock."

33. **C** "Mutual fund" is the term generally used in referring to open-end management-type investment companies.

34. **A** The management fee is based upon the assets in the fund. Choices (B) and (D) are clearly wrong, but to the extent that the principal underwriter may be considered part of the management group (in some cases), choice (C) could come fairly close.

35. **B** Mutual fund shareholders incur a tax liability on the cash value of each income dividend and capital gains distribution, whether received in cash or reinvested. The tax is due in the return for the tax year when distributed. Holders of variable annuity contracts are not taxed until withdrawals are made. The insurance

company, in fact, makes no distributions during the accumulation period.

36. **A** This is as per the investment company rule in the Conduct Rules. This is called "forward pricing" as opposed to what used to be the case, "back pricing." Basically, the price is computed as of the close of the market. If an order is received after the computation, then it is executed based on the net asset value computed on the next business date.

37. **B** This would be an example of a fixed trust, which is one of the subdivisions of a unit investment trust.

38. **B** This is the only real possibility here. In the voluntary accumulation plan, the load is "level." In an automatic withdrawal plan or an optional withdrawal plan, a sales charge is paid only upon the acquisition of the shares. In the contractual plan, the load is said to be "front-end" since the bulk of the sales charge is taken out in the early life of the plan.

39. **B** This describes the letter of intent, which may run as long as 13 months.

40. **C** The term "regulated" refers to tax status under Subchapter M of the Internal Revenue Code. This simply means that if a mutual fund or other investment company qualifies for regulated status, the threat of triple taxation is eliminated.

41. **D** This is a rule that was required by the statement of policy. The statement of policy has been abandoned in favor of using a simple fraud interpretation. Basically, under today's interpretation, a broker/dealer must be prepared to demonstrate that what he or she says or prints is not fraudulent. Representing a mutual fund as being safer than any of these products would probably constitute fraud.

42. **D** Sales literature regarding investment company shares must be filed with the NASD within three days after first use.

43. **B** By reinvesting dividends and capital gains the number of shares owned will increase. These programs often permit purchases at, but not below, the net asset value. The shareholder does not avoid tax liability on the amount invested.

44. **B** The principal underwriter is often called the sponsor or the distributor of the shares of the open-end investment company.

45. **A** The method uses the net asset value and, to this, programs in the sales charge, if any.

46. **A** Income consists of interest on bonds and dividends on stocks in the portfolio. Profits on sales of securities are capital gains.

47. **D** The SEC never approves or guarantees any issue. It only attempts to verify that sufficient information is provided to the potential investor.

48. **B** The "breakpoint" is the dollar value at which the sales charge is reduced. A customer using a letter of intent often is able to take advantage of this privilege.

49. **A** Closed-end investment companies trade in the open market and their price is determined by supply and demand. Often the market price is higher than the net asset value per share. This amount is called the "premium."

50. **C** Investment companies are required to issue financial reports to their holders semianually. They may, of course, report more frequently if they wish.

The Federal Reserve and Margin

In discussing purchasing of securities on margin, or credit, some background information on the Federal Reserve System is appropriate, since it regulates the amount of credit outstanding in the United States.

FEDERAL RESERVE SYSTEM

The Federal Reserve System is divided into 12 different districts throughout the country. If you look at the face of a dollar bill, on the left side you will see a large letter. This letter indicates which Federal Reserve Bank distributed the money, "A" is from Boston, "B" is from New York, "C" is from Philadelphia, etc. The Federal Reserve Banks do not print the money, they simply distribute it.

Remember that the Federal Reserve Bank is not a government agency. It is a bank, but a very special one. It is often called "the banker's bank." Though there is no connection to the federal government, there is some governmental influence, as discussed below.

At the top level of the Federal Reserve System is a board of governors. There are seven governors, each appointed by the president of the United States for a 14-year term. The only restriction on appointing a member to the board of governors is that no two governors may come from the same Federal Reserve district. In addition, since the terms are for 14 years, the governors are politically insulated from day-to-day pressures. The president normally appoints a governor every two years. Consequently, many members of the board are appointed by different presidents and political parties, and many varying economic viewpoints are represented.

The level below the board of governors is the board of directors. Each of the 12 Federal Reserve districts has its own board of directors. Each board of directors consists of nine individuals, three of whom are appointed by the board of governors. However, the remaining six are elected by the member banks in each district. As you can see, two thirds of each board of directors is controlled by the member banks themselves. Each district also has a slate of officers.

The primary purpose of the Federal Reserve is to regulate the amount of credit outstanding in the United States. Although there are approximately 14,000 commercial banks in the United States today, only 5,000 of these are members of the Federal Reserve System. How can a mere one third of the banks be so powerful? These 5,000 member banks are responsible for 75 percent of the available credit in the United States.

How does the Federal Reserve control credit? There are three major and several lesser ways.

Reserve Requirements

As a member of the Federal Reserve System, a bank is required to deposit a percentage of its deposits, which are of three basic types.

DDA, or Demand Deposits Accounts

This is a fancy name for checking accounts. The bank has no idea when a customer is going to write a check or for what amount. For this reason, the monies in a customer's checking account require the highest percentage to be left with the Federal Reserve. There is a complex sliding scale formula, but for our use, the percentage is approximately 10%.

Time Deposits, or CDs

These require a far smaller percentage deposit, because the bank knows when it must return the borrowed funds and can make the necessary arrangements.

Savings Deposits

These require about the same reserves as time deposits, because savings accounts deposits have a tendency to remain for longer periods of time than checking accounts. In addition, the bank has the right to require 30 days' notice prior to any withdrawal. This right is seldom used, but it could become necessary if there was a "run" on the bank. Most people are unaware of this condition, but just read the first page of your passbook.

As a member of the Federal Reserve, a bank is required to compute its reserve requirements daily. With the banking industry so highly computerized this task is easily completed.

If, at the end of the day, the bank has a $20,000,000 reserve requirement, this is recorded and set aside until Wednesday, which is the end of the bank week. At this point, the member bank would look at its daily reserve requirement for the previous two weeks and take an average. If it came up with a requirement of $25,000,000 and there was only $15,000,000 on deposit with the Federal Reserve, it would have to deposit $10,000,000 by the end of the day to be in compliance with the reserve requirement. Under normal circumstances, it would be very difficult to attract sufficient deposits to satisfy the $10,000,000 requirement. However, other member banks are making the same computation, and some will have excess funds. Note: No interest is paid on Federal Reserve deposits, which is one disadvantage in being a member of the Federal Reserve System.

Since there is no advantage to leaving excess funds at the Federal Reserve, they become available to be lent to those banks requiring additional deposits. Hence, we get the term "federal funds," or, more commonly, "fed funds."

Members of the Federal Reserve have access to the Federal Reserve wire system, which can move funds from one bank to another in a matter of seconds. So, while the original (and current) meaning of fed funds were those funds to meet reserve requirements, fed funds also have the broader meaning of immediately usable funds, as opposed to clearinghouse funds.

"Clearinghouse funds" are funds that the average person uses when writing a check to the landlord or the store owner, or a birthday check to someone. The funds are not usable by the recipient until the check clears. The check you wrote goes through the clearinghouse system, back to the originating bank, which moves the amount out of your account and into the account of the person to whom you wrote the check. If the banks are in the same Federal

Reserve district, the check will usually clear the next business day. Checks between districts will take longer, depending on the distance between them.

The federal funds rate is the amount one bank will pay another for the use of funds overnight. This rate is determined by supply and demand. If more banks require funds than have excesses, the fed funds rate will increase. A classic example of this supply and demand function occurred on December 31, 1986, which also happened to be a Wednesday, the end of the banking week. On this particular day, the fed funds rate hit a high of 25% and a low of .25%. This unusual situation was occasioned by the banks wishing to make some cosmetic changes in the balance sheet for the end of the year. However, the end of the year happened on a Wednesday, and because of these accounting moves, most banks found themselves buyers of fed funds, which drove the rate to this unusually high rate. By the end of the day, when the banks had settled their requirements with the Federal Reserve, there was no demand for these funds, thus the drop to .25%.

With this brief background of reserve requirements and federal funds, let us look at some of the main ways in which the Federal Reserve regulates credit in the United States.

Increase Reserve Requirements

If the Federal Reserve decided to increase the reserve requirements from 10% to 15%, this would be a very severe action. All member banks would come under the new additional requirement, and there would be no excess funds to borrow. To attract additional deposits, higher rates would have to be paid. If additional deposits were not attracted fast enough, demand loans would be called, causing liquidations, foreclosures, and so on. There is no doubt that increasing the reserve requirements tightens credit. The reverse, lowering reserve requirements, causes the member banks to have excess funds, thereby reducing interest rates and easing credit restraints. Tightening too much causes recession; easing too much causes inflation. The Federal Reserve strives to strike a balance.

Discount Rate

This is the rate the Federal Reserve charges its member banks to borrow money. The discount rate is historically lower than all other money rates, because the proceeds of the loan are restricted as to use. The member bank may only borrow at the discount rate if the proceeds are used exclusively for meeting the Federal Reserve requirement. In addition, this loan is a secured loan. The Federal Reserve is willing to help a bank out and lend it money to meet its reserve requirement, but the loan must be collateralized by the very best securities, that is, treasury bills, notes, and bonds, or those securities issued by certain government agencies that are guaranteed as to principal or interest. Increasing or decreasing the discount rate has only a very minor effect on the amount of credit available.

Federal Open Market Committee

The actions and decisions of this committee have the most immediate effect on credit availability. The severity of this effect falls somewhere between increasing reserve requirement and changing the discount rate.

The Federal Open Market Committee (FMOC) comprises the seven governors of the Federal Reserve Board and five of the twelve presidents of the various districts throughout the country, one of whom is always the president of the Federal Reserve Bank of New York. The other presidents rotate on and off the committee periodically. This committee meets once a month (more often if needed) and decides the day-to-day credit policy that will be followed. Should the committee decide to tighten credit, this would be accomplished by selling various government obligations to the member banks and charging the banks' respective reserve requirement accounts. This would cause most banks to be below reserve requirements, and monies must be found to replenish their account. Attracting additional deposits requires higher interest rates, which in turn means credit will cost the borrower more.

If the Federal Open Market Committee decides that looser credit policies are in order, the Federal Reserve will start buying the various government bills, notes, and bonds and will pay the banks by crediting their reserve accounts. Then there would be excess reserves in the vast majority of the member banks. With no interest being paid on the funds left with the Federal Reserve, the member banks will withdraw the excess and put it in the hands of the public in the form of loans. To entice the consumer to borrow when there is a surplus of funds, the bank must lower its rate, and the competition must follow. When the FOMC buys, it eases credit and lowers interest rates. The Federal Reserve prefers this method to ease and tighten credit because it is readily reversible.

Other ways the Federal Reserve affects credit are related to the securities industry.

- Regulation T: Regulates the amount of money that a broker may lend on securities.
- Regulation U: Regulates the amount of money that a bank may lend on securities.
- Regulation G: Regulates the amount of money that organizations other than banks and brokers may lend on securities.

MARGIN ACCOUNTS AND SHORT SALES

The extension of credit to customers in securities transactions is regulated by three entities: Federal Reserve Board, NYSE, NASD, and individual firms.

The Federal Reserve, under Regulation T, limits the amount that a broker may lend to a customer wishing to purchase securities and also dictates the amount a customer must deposit when selling securities short. Regulation T is an initial requirement and is only employed when a client makes a purchase or sale in his account.

The NYSE establishes maintenance requirements, which set the level to which an account may deteriorate before some action must be taken by the customer. These rules are designed to protect the broker. Should the customer fail to take action, the broker is empowered to liquidate the account. This authority is granted in the customer's agreement, which is signed by the customer before the account is opened.

Virtually all broker/dealers establish house rules, which are generally more stringent than the maintenance requirements of the NYSE and often more strict than the federal requirements. For example, Regulation T permits any listed security to be bought on margin, but most firms will not permit credit to be allowed on low-priced stocks (perhaps under $10 per share). You will, of course, have to know your own firm's house rules thoroughly. They could not be a subject of this exam, as they may differ from firm to firm.

Let us concentrate our efforts on Federal Reserve and maintenance requirements.

Federal Reserve Requirements

Federal Reserve Regulation T sets the amount that a client must deposit to purchase or sell short securities. Similar limits are placed on banks by Regulation U and on other lenders (factors, finance companies, etc.) by Regulation G.

In a cash account the client is required to deposit 100% of the cost of each purchase. No credit can be allowed. Accounts that permit the extension of credit are called "margin" accounts. Equity securities as well as listed corporate bonds, convertible bonds, municipals, and direct obligations of the U.S. government are bought and sold in a margin account. Regulation T not only sets the amount the customer must deposit, it mandates when the required payment must be made. In both cash and margin accounts payment must be made promptly, but no later than two business days after the settlement date, which is currently three business days after the trade date, often referred to as "T+3." As industry standards require the broker/dealer to pay the seller's broker on the third business day, the client's confirmation will show this as the settlement date of the trade. However, the client does not violate Regulate T if she pays by the fifth business day following the trade.

Should a client be unable to pay on time for a valid reason, such as illness or mail delivery problems, the dealer can request an extension of time for payment. This extension can be granted by any registered stock exchange or by any district office of the NASD. A client may receive only five extensions in any twelve (12)-month period, regardless of the reasons.

All too often customers refuse to pay for transactions. In this case the broker must liquidate the transaction. If your firm experiences a loss, they may sue the client, but this is not the concern of the Federal Reserve.

Customers sometimes make payment in an improper manner. For example, on Monday a client buys 1,000 shares of Ford Motor Company. On Wednesday he instructs you to sell 1,000 of Eastman Kodak to provide payment for the purchase of Ford. This is improper payment. In order to pay for a purchase of securities by selling other securities, the transactions should take place on the same day. In our example, the client owned both the Ford and Eastman Kodak shares for two days while having sufficient funds to hold only one of these positions.

In another instance, should a customer purchase a security in a cash account and sell that same security prior to making full cash payment, that account would become frozen for 90 calendar days. This 90-day freeze requires the customer to have the funds in advance of any purchase for the next 90 days.

In requiring payment from customers, Regulation T does allow a small amount of leeway. A broker is permitted to overlook an amount due in an account up to $1,000. This amount is not forgotten. The client still owes it to his broker, but no Regulation T violation occurs if this amount is not deposited. Again, this waiver is purely at the discretion of the broker.

Long Margin Accounts

The term "long" simply means that the investor has purchased the security or otherwise acquired the security. Margin is the amount that a client must deposit when he purchases securities. If margin is set at 50%, a client purchasing securities must deposit 50% of the cost. The broker may lend the customer the difference between the cost of the purchase and the current margin requirements (CMR). This amount is called the Loan Value (LV). Long margin account contains these long positions. Thus, if the current margin requirement is 50%, the current loan value is also 50%.

Suppose a customer opens a new margin account and purchases $60,000 of marginable stocks. He would deposit a minimum of $30,000 (50%) and the broker would lend him the remaining $30,000 (50%):

$60,000	Market Value (MV)
$30,000	Debit (DR)
$30,000	Equity (EQ)

The value of the account is $60,000, and the customer owes the broker $30,000, so his equity in the account is $30,000, the amount he deposited. This is the same as buying a house worth $60,000 if you put up $30,000 and take a $30,000 mortgage from a bank. The house is worth $60,000, but your equity is the $30,000 that you put up. The bank's loan is secured by the property and should you default in payment, the house may be sold to repay your debt. In our example, the securities in your account are the collateral for your loan from the broker and if problems arise, the firm can sell those securities to protect itself from loss. As securities in margin accounts are collateral, they are kept by the broker in "street name" (the name of the broker). This enables a sale to be made rapidly should later conditions so require.

This client owes the broker $30,000. The broker generally acquires the money, which they lend to clients by making a "call loan" at a bank. A call loan is a loan made by a broker using securities as collateral. The collateral that the broker supplies will come from the account of the customer who is the end borrower. The term for this is "hypothecate," which is a synonym for "pledge." The customer hypothecates (pledges) his securities to the broker, who then rehypothecates (repledges) them at the bank to secure the call loan.

The broker cannot use all the securities in the customer's account, as this would not usually be necessary to make the required loan. The current limit permits the broker to rehypothecate securities in the account with a value up to 140% of the client's debit balance.

In our account the client's debit is $30,000. The broker could pledge up to $42,000 (140% of $30,000) of securities at the bank to secure the loan for this client. The remaining securities in the account, $18,000 ($60,000 MV minus $42,000 pledged), must be segregated and clearly identified as this customer's property. If the bank requires less than 140% collateral, we pledge only that amount. The maximum amount that may be used is 140%.

Once the account has been established we may expect the value to change as the market moves up or down. Let's look at the account again. Suppose the securities in the account appreciated by $10,000. This increased value would show in the market value and in the equity. The debit would not change. (As with the $60,000 house that you bought, if it increased in value by $10,000, you would not owe the bank any more money but would add to your equity in the house.) After the increase, our client's account would appear as follows:

$70,000 MV
$30,000 DR
$40,000 EQ

As you can see, the broker is merely financing this transaction. The broker does not partake of any profits and/or losses.

At this point the account has excess equity. With Regulation T at 50%, an account with $70,000 market value requires equity of $35,000 (50%). The account has $40,000 equity, which is $5,000 in excess of the requirement. The excess equity could be withdrawn by the client in cash. If the excess was sent to the client, it would increase his debit by $5,000 and reduce his equity by the same amount. After withdrawing his excess equity the account would show:

$70,000 MV
$35,000 DR
$35,000 EQ

Here is an easy method to calculate excess equity: Subtract the 50% requirement of current market value from the equity; this equals excess.

$40,000	Equity
− $35,000	Requirement
$5,000	Excess over Regulation T

We are in compliance with Regulation T. Our equity, $35,000, is 50% of the market value, and the debit (loan), $35,000, is also 50% of the market value.

On the other hand, when a customer develops excess equity in his account he might wish to use this excess to purchase additional securities. As new purchases require only a partial payment (we are using 50%), the excess equity translates into a greater amount of what is called "buying power." To determine buying power we divide the excess equity by the current margin requirement (CMR).

In our example we have $5,000 excess. We divide this by .50 (CMR) and the result is $10,000 of buying power in this account. If the client used this buying power and purchased $10,000 worth of stock, the market value and the debit would be increased by $10,000 and the account would now show:

$80,000 CMV
$40,000 DR
$40,000 EQ

Note that the equity is not increased as the client did not deposit any funds for these additional purchases. (If you added a $10,000 wing to that $70,000 house but borrowed the money from the bank, your equity in the house would not increase. The value would increase and the loan would increase, but your equity would be the same. You would just have a bigger house. Our client has a bigger account.)

When value increases in a long margin account, excess equity is created. This amount can be withdrawn in cash or can be used to create buying power, which increases the account's value but not the equity. (Note: When Regulation T is 50%, buying power is excess equity multiplied by two.)

We have demonstrated the result if value in the account increases. Let us now look at the results of a decrease in market value. Suppose our original $60,000 of securities declined to $56,000. The result would be a $4,000 decline in both the market value and the equity. The debit stays the same. (If that house you bought declined in value, it would not change the amount of your mortgage.) The account would now show:

$56,000 MV
$30,000 DR
$26,000 EQ

This account is not in any trouble as the broker has $56,000 in collateral for a $30,000 loan. However, the equity of $26,000 is below the requirements of Regulation T. In an account with $56,000 MV, the equity should be $28,000 (50%). Or looking at it another way, in an account with $56,000 of MV, the loan value is $28,000 (50%). This client is borrowing $30,000. Regulation T never requires additional deposits when an account declines. (Those requirements will be discussed later under maintenance requirements.) However, when an account falls below Regulation T requirements, it becomes a "restricted account" and certain limitations are placed on future trading by that client. Remember, "restricted" does not necessarily mean that the account is in dire trouble (in our example it certainly is not), it just means that it is below the requirements of Regulation T. In a restricted account, the client may continue to trade but must do so in a controlled manner.

If a customer wishes to make a purchase in a restricted account, he must deposit 50% of the cost of that purchase. Our client wishes to purchase $2,000 of additional stock. He must deposit $1,000 (50%) of that amount. Now the account appears:

$58,000 MV
$31,000 DR
$27,000 EQ

The market value is increased by $2,000, but the debit by only $1,000 (client deposited $1,000 into the account). This deposit also increases his equity. Note that the client did not have to bring the entire account up to 50% equity, but was only required to deposit 50% of the cost of the new purchase. The overall account has improved. Prior to this purchase his debit was 53.6% of the market value ($30,000 DR divided by $56,000 MV). After the purchase his debit represents only 53.4% of the market value ($31,000 DR divided by $58,000 MV).

Suppose in this example the client wished to deposit securities in lieu of cash. As the amount of cash required was $1,000, he must deposit securities with a loan value of that amount. We simply divide the amount of cash needed, $1,000, by the current loan value (.50) of the securities and find that $2,000 in security value would be required. (Again, with margin at 50% we could take the cash needed, $1,000, and multiply by two, but with margin at other levels we need the more cumbersome formula that we have used.) After the deposit of $2,000 in securities the account would show a market value increase of $4,000, the securities purchased plus the securities deposited. The debit and the equity would each be increased by $2,000. Here is our account:

$60,000 MV
$32,000 DR
$28,000 EQ

Again, the account has been improved as the debit has been reduced from 53.6% to 53.3% ($32,000 DR divided by $60,000 MV).

Should a customer with a restricted account sell securities he may withdraw 50% of the proceeds of the sale. With our account as shown above:

> $60,000 MV
> $32,000 DR
> $28,000 EQ

The customer sells securities with a value of $3,000. He may withdraw $1,500 (50%) of that amount in cash. Should he do so the account would appear:

> $57,000 MV
> $30,500 DR
> $26,500 EQ

The $3,000 sale has reduced his market value by that amount and has reduced his equity and debit by $1,500, as 50% of the proceeds were withdrawn in cash.

If the client did not wish to withdraw the $1,500, but rather left it in the account, the market value and debit balance would each be reduced by the entire $3,000, as follows:

> $57,000 MV
> $29,000 DR
> $28,000 EQ

The account would still be restricted, as under Regulation T an account with $57,000 in market value requires $28,500 (50%), and our client has only $28,000 equity.

SMA (Special Memorandum Account)

To protect monies that become available in customers' margin accounts we are permitted to set up a special memorandum account (SMA). When a client sells securities, or market values increase resulting in excess equity, we note this availability in the client's SMA. This amount is now available for the client's later use in the purchase of additional securities or for cash withdrawals. The SMA does not contain money, but is simply a record of funds that may be used by the client. It is much like an available line of credit. In our example, when the client made the $3,000 sale, let's assume that he did not withdraw the cash. The account would appear:

> $57,000 MV   SMA $1,500
> $29,000 DR
> $28,000 EQ

Note that both the market value and the debit have been reduced by $3,000. The $1,500 credit to the SMA is just a memorandum entry that the client has that amount available. He may withdraw it in cash or use it toward payment for future purchases. Suppose two weeks later the client requests a check for $1,500. The account would then show:

```
$57,000 MV    SMA 0
$30,500 DR
$26,500 EQ
```

When we sent him the check for $1,500, we increased his debit and decreased his equity by that amount.

Suppose, instead of withdrawing the $1,500 in cash, the customer called two weeks later and wished to purchase $5,000 of additional securities. The $1,500 in the SMA could be used in partial payment of that purchase. Ordinarily, he would have to deposit $2,500 (50%) of the $5,000, but with $1,500 available in the SMA, only $1,000 of additional funds would be required. After this trade we would show:

```
$62,000 MV    SMA 0
$33,000 DR
$29,000 EQ
```

The $5,000 purchase increases the market value by that amount. The $1,000 deposited is added to his equity. The $4,000 additional cost of the purchase is added to his debit.

The SMA can be used for purchases or cash withdrawals with one limitation. It cannot be used if such use would bring the account below the minimum maintenance requirements prescribed by the NYSE and the NASD. These requirements, to be discussed in detail later in this section, are employed when the account has reached a dangerous level. We are not permitted to use the SMA to bring the account below these levels. Examples of this prohibition will be shown in our later discussion.

Short Accounts

The Regulation T requirement for selling securities short is currently the same as for long positions. The customer must deposit 50% of the proceeds of the short sale into his account. Should a client of a broker wish to sell 1,000 shares of ABC short at $120 per share, she must deposit $60,000 (50% of $120,000) into her account. This deposit is required under Regulation T as a credit control instrument. This client, by selling short, has created 1,000 shares of ABC. Her deposit reduced the effect of that additional value in our economy. In addition, her deposit protects the broker from loss should ABC rise in value. When a client sells short she does not borrow any money, she borrows stock. Therefore, there is never a debit balance in a short account, always a credit balance. Initially we take the proceeds of the sale and add the margin deposited to determine the credit in the account. In our example it would be:

```
$120,000    Sale of 1,000 ABC @ $120
$ 60,000    50% Margin Deposited
$180,000    Credit Balance
```

To determine the equity in the account we subtract the current market value of the stock from this credit:

```
  $180,000    Credit Balance
– $120,000    Short Market Value
  $ 60,000    Equity
```

The credit balance does not change, but the equity in the account will change as the market value of ABC rises or falls.

Before looking further into short margin accounts, we must discuss the mechanics of short selling.

Before entering an order to sell short, the broker must ascertain his ability to borrow the stock. When the transaction is made, the stock must be delivered to the buyer. As our short seller does not have the stock, it must be borrowed. If our broker were handling the short sale, a first attempt would be made to borrow the shares from another client of our broker who owned them and had signed a "consent to loan securities." Failing that, our broker would approach other firms and ask them to lend the stock. Perhaps Broker A would agree to lend 1,000 shares of ABC to our broker. Broker A would take the stock from a client who had agreed to allow shares to be used for this purpose. Assured of borrowing the stock, our broker would now enter an order to "sell 1,000 ABC @ market short" on the NYSE floor. Our broker might sell the stock to Broker B at $120 per share. Broker A would lend the stock to our broker for delivery to Broker B, the buyer. Broker B would pay our broker $120,000 for the ABC, which our broker would give to Broker A as security for the loan of the stock.

When the trade is settled the parties' positions are:

- Broker B: bought 1,000 ABC @ 120, received the shares from our broker and paid us $120,000.
- Broker A: loaned 1,000 shares of ABC to our broker and received $120,000 as collateral for the loan.
- Our broker: has only an open contract. The money, $120,000, is at Broker A and the stock, 1,000 ABC, is at Broker B. Our broker does have the $60,000 deposit (50%) required to be made by the short seller under Regulation T.

The incentive for Broker A to lend the stock to our broker is the money received as collateral. Broker A can use these funds in the operation of business, lending it at current interest rates to clients who have debit balances. Our broker can use the $60,000 margin deposit in the same manner. If you have the opportunity to look at the annual reports of the large retail brokerage firms, you will find that this use of "money float" is often their largest source of revenue.

Stocks are sometimes lent at a "premium." Should a stock be difficult to borrow due to a merger, takeover, or some other unusual event, the borrower may have to pay a fee to the lender for the use of the stock. This fee, of course, is passed on to the client who sold the stock short.

In periods of high interest rates stocks may lend at "rate." This means that the lender pays the borrower interest on the money. Remember, Broker A has $120,000 that is being lent at perhaps 10% interest. Broker A may pay our broker interest on the money at a lower rate and still realize a fine profit on the transaction.

If neither a premium nor a rate is involved, the securities are said to be "lending flat."

As stated earlier, the client who sold the 1,000 ABC shares short has effectively created those shares. There are two owners of the same 1,000 shares, the Broker A client whose shares were loaned and the Broker B client who bought them. When ABC pays a cash dividend or stock dividend or splits its stock, it will make the payments to Broker B, who is in possession of the stock. Who takes care of Broker A's client? The short seller, of course. Our broker's client must pay to the lender any distributions made by ABC. The only privilege that the lender of the stock loses is the voting rights on the shares. ABC will allow only 1,000 shares to vote. Broker B will receive these voting rights. Broker A's client will surrender this privilege.

Getting back to our original example:

$120,000	Sold 1,000 ABC @ $120 short
+ $60,000	Margin Deposited
$180,000	Credit Balance (Cr)
$180,000	Credit Balance (Cr)
− $120,000	Current Short Market Value (CSMV)
$ 60,000	Equity (EQ)

The equity will increase if ABC declines in price and will decrease if ABC rises in price.

ABC Declines to $110 Per Share	
$180,000	Credit Balance (Cr)
− $110,000	Current Market Value (CMV)
$70,000	Equity (EQ)

ABC Rises to $130 Per Share	
$180,000	Credit Balance (Cr)
− $130,000	Current Market Value (CMV)
$ 50,000	Equity (EQ)

Short selling is a high-risk market technique as there is no limit to the potential loss. If you bought ABC at $120 per share it can only go down 120 points (unlikely, but possible). If you short at $120 it can go up to $200, $300, $400, or more. In addition, you will be liable for any cash dividends or other distributions that are paid during the period you are short. Short selling has a place in our markets. It should, however, be a place reserved for the sophisticated investor who can fully understand the unlimited risk involved.

Maintenance Requirements

The NYSE and the NASD impose regulations on margin accounts called "maintenance requirements," which we will divide into four categories.

U.S. Government and Municipal Securities

U.S. government and municipal securities are exempt from Regulation T of the Federal Reserve. The NYSE, however, does require a minimum maintenance as follows:

U.S. Governments These are on a sliding scale, requiring less as the instrument approaches maturity. The following table gives the requirements for treasury bills and interest-bearing notes and bonds:

Years to Maturity	NYSE Requirement
Less than 1 year	1%
1 year but less than 3 years	2%
3 years but less than 5 years	3%
5 years but less than 10 years	4%
10 years but less than 20 years	5%
20 years or more	6%

Municipal Securities These are classified as exempt securities, and no maintenance requirement is imposed by the Federal Reserve under Regulation T. However, the NYSE has initial and maintenance requirements, which are 15% of the market value or 7% of the principal, whichever amount is greater. If a customer purchased 10M (10,000) NYC 8½ of 25 @87, a requirement is established for 15% of the market value ($1,305) or 7% of the principal ($700), whichever is greater (in this case $1,305).

The requirement for municipals will usually be 15% of the market value. This is because in order for the 7% requirement to be the larger of the two, the market value of the bond would have to be 46.625 or lower.

Other Governments In addition to the above initial and maintenance requirements, requirements on zero coupon government obligations are:

Years to Maturity	NYSE Requirement
5 years or more	3% of principal
More than 5 but less than 10	3% of principal or 4% of market whichever is greater
More than 10 but less than 20	3% of principal or 5% of market whichever is greater
More than 20	3% of principal or 6% of market whichever is greater

Maintenance for Long Positions

The minimum maintenance for a long position is 25% of the market value. Under Regulation T, the initial equity was 50%, so to reach maintenance levels the account must decline substantially. The NYSE wants to protect the broker from loss and, therefore, requires this minimum equity for long positions. A client with a long position valued at $60,000 must maintain a minimum equity of $15,000 (25%).

$60,000 MV
$45,000 DR
$15,000 EQ (Minimum Required)

Note that when the equity ($15,000) reaches 25% of the market value, it is also one third of the debit ($45,000). We can, therefore, express the minimum requirement as 25% of the market value or one third of the debit balance. This second method should be used in projecting the point to which a client's account could decline before requiring action under maintenance requirements.

EXAMPLE

A client's long margin account appears as follows:

$70,000 MV
$51,000 DR
$19,000 EQ

To what amount can the equity decline before requiring action under maintenance requirements?

Answer: $17,000. We simply take one third of the debit balance to determine the minimum equity required. One third of $51,000 is $17,000. If the equity declined to this point the account would appear:

$68,000 MV
$51,000 DR
$17,000 EQ

At this point the equity ($17,000) is 25% of the market value ($68,000) and is also one third of the debit balance ($51,000).

Try this question to test yourself on a point discussed earlier in this section.

EXAMPLE

A client's long margin account appears as follows:

$40,000 MV   SMA $3,100
$28,000 DR
$12,000 EQ

The client asks you to send him a check from his SMA for "as much as you can." How much can you send him?

Answer: $2,000. This is the difference between current equity, $12,000 and minimum maintenance requirement, $10,000. If this amount is sent the account will look like this:

$40,000 MV   SMA $1,100
$30,000 DR
$10,000 EQ

At this point the equity ($10,000) is 25% of the market value ($40,000). We stated earlier that the SMA cannot be used to bring the account below maintenance requirements.

Maintenance for Short Positions

This is more demanding than for long positions as the potential loss in a short position cannot be accurately measured. While a long position requires minimum maintenance of 25%, in a short account the minimum equity must, in general, be 30% of the market value. Thus, a client short 1,000 shares of XYZ trading at $140 per share ($140,000) must have a minimum equity of $42,000 (30% of $140,000) in his account.

The maintenance rules on short positions are even more stringent on low-priced stocks. The obvious reason is that a low-priced stock can't go down very far, but has an unlimited upside potential. The minimum maintenance on short positions is:

Stock Under $5 Per Share $2.50 per share or 100% of the current market value, whichever is greater. For example, a client short 1,000 shares of a stock trading at $2 per share must have minimum equity of $2,500 ($2.50 per share). A client short 1,000 shares of stock trading at $4 per share must have minimum equity of $4,000 (100% of market value).

Stock Trading at $5 Per Share or Higher $5 per share or 30% of the market value, whichever is greater. For example a client short 1,000 shares of a stock currently trading at $10 per share must have minimum equity of $5,000 ($5.00 per share). A client short 1,000 shares of a stock currently trading at $80 per share must have minimum equity of $24,000 (30% of $80,000).

Note: For stocks trading at $16.87 or higher, the minimum equity for a short position under maintenance requirements is 30% of the market value. For stocks trading below $16.87 per share, the more stringent $5.00 per share equity requirements would apply.

$2,000 Minimum Equity

To discourage small investors from going into debt through margin trading, the maintenance rules state that the minimum equity in an account must be $2,000 or 100% of market value, whichever is less.

EXAMPLE

As an initial purchase in her margin account, a client buys 100 shares of XYZ at $24 per share. How much must she deposit?

Answer: $2,000. While Regulation T would only require a deposit of $1,200 (50%), the maintenance rules are more stringent in this case. They require $2,000 or 100% ($2,400), whichever is less. The $2,000 requirement would prevail.

Suppose the initial purchase by this client was 100 shares at $16. In this case the required deposit would be $1,600 (100%), as this would be less than the $2,000.

Note: On short sales the minimum is always $2,000 as we do not know at what price the customer will repurchase the stock to cover the short.

Let's look at another case where this $2,000 minimum would apply.

EXAMPLE

A customer's long margin account appears as follows:

$5,000 MV	SMA $700
$2,800 DR	
$2,200 EQ	

Question: How much cash can the customer withdraw from his SMA?

Answer: $200. If we sent this client a check for $200 the account would look like this:

$5,000 MV	SMA $500
$3,000 DR	
$2,000 EQ	

The equity has been reduced to the minimum allowed under maintenance requirements, $2,000. As demonstrated earlier, the SMA cannot be used to bring an account below these minimum maintenance requirements. Often a client will have both long and short positions in his account. The longs and shorts must be computed separately as the requirements differ. However, it is considered as one account in determining its compliance to margin requirements.

Our discussion of margins has focused on federal and maintenance requirements. Your firm's own house rules will be most important in the future. Be sure to be thoroughly familiar with those requirements.

ANSWER SHEET FOR CHAPTER 8 EXAMINATION

1. Ⓐ Ⓑ Ⓒ Ⓓ   11. Ⓐ Ⓑ Ⓒ Ⓓ   21. Ⓐ Ⓑ Ⓒ Ⓓ

2. Ⓐ Ⓑ Ⓒ Ⓓ   12. Ⓐ Ⓑ Ⓒ Ⓓ   22. Ⓐ Ⓑ Ⓒ Ⓓ

3. Ⓐ Ⓑ Ⓒ Ⓓ   13. Ⓐ Ⓑ Ⓒ Ⓓ   23. Ⓐ Ⓑ Ⓒ Ⓓ

4. Ⓐ Ⓑ Ⓒ Ⓓ   14. Ⓐ Ⓑ Ⓒ Ⓓ   24. Ⓐ Ⓑ Ⓒ Ⓓ

5. Ⓐ Ⓑ Ⓒ Ⓓ   15. Ⓐ Ⓑ Ⓒ Ⓓ   25. Ⓐ Ⓑ Ⓒ Ⓓ

6. Ⓐ Ⓑ Ⓒ Ⓓ   16. Ⓐ Ⓑ Ⓒ Ⓓ   26. Ⓐ Ⓑ Ⓒ Ⓓ

7. Ⓐ Ⓑ Ⓒ Ⓓ   17. Ⓐ Ⓑ Ⓒ Ⓓ   27. Ⓐ Ⓑ Ⓒ Ⓓ

8. Ⓐ Ⓑ Ⓒ Ⓓ   18. Ⓐ Ⓑ Ⓒ Ⓓ   28. Ⓐ Ⓑ Ⓒ Ⓓ

9. Ⓐ Ⓑ Ⓒ Ⓓ   19. Ⓐ Ⓑ Ⓒ Ⓓ   29. Ⓐ Ⓑ Ⓒ Ⓓ

10. Ⓐ Ⓑ Ⓒ Ⓓ   20. Ⓐ Ⓑ Ⓒ Ⓓ   30. Ⓐ Ⓑ Ⓒ Ⓓ

31. Ⓐ Ⓑ Ⓒ Ⓓ   41. Ⓐ Ⓑ Ⓒ Ⓓ

32. Ⓐ Ⓑ Ⓒ Ⓓ   42. Ⓐ Ⓑ Ⓒ Ⓓ

33. Ⓐ Ⓑ Ⓒ Ⓓ   43. Ⓐ Ⓑ Ⓒ Ⓓ

34. Ⓐ Ⓑ Ⓒ Ⓓ   44. Ⓐ Ⓑ Ⓒ Ⓓ

35. Ⓐ Ⓑ Ⓒ Ⓓ   45. Ⓐ Ⓑ Ⓒ Ⓓ

36. Ⓐ Ⓑ Ⓒ Ⓓ   46. Ⓐ Ⓑ Ⓒ Ⓓ

37. Ⓐ Ⓑ Ⓒ Ⓓ   47. Ⓐ Ⓑ Ⓒ Ⓓ

38. Ⓐ Ⓑ Ⓒ Ⓓ   48. Ⓐ Ⓑ Ⓒ Ⓓ

39. Ⓐ Ⓑ Ⓒ Ⓓ   49. Ⓐ Ⓑ Ⓒ Ⓓ

40. Ⓐ Ⓑ Ⓒ Ⓓ   50. Ⓐ Ⓑ Ⓒ Ⓓ

CHAPTER 8 EXAMINATION ◣━━━ ━ ━ ━ ━━━

<u>Questions 1–7 are based on the following information:</u> Regulation T is set at 50%. A customer's account contains the following long position:

	Price
100 N.Y. Times	30
200 Met Life	70
200 Con Edison	40
200 Equity One	25

Total Market Value	$30,000
Debit	– $12,000
Equity	$18,000

1. What is the customer's excess equity in this account?

   (A) $3,000
   (B) $18,000
   (C) $12,000
   (D) -0-

2. What is the buying power in the account?

   (A) $3,000
   (B) $6,000
   (C) $11,000
   (D) -0-

3. If the customer wished to purchase 100 shares of Hasbro at $30 per share, how much additional money must be deposited in the account?

   (A) $3,000
   (B) $1,500
   (C) $2,000
   (D) -0-

4. If, in addition to the 100 shares of Hasbro, the client wished to purchase 100 shares of IBM at $120, how much money must be deposited in the account?

   (A) $6,000
   (B) $7,000
   (C) $4,500
   (D) $1,500

5. Under Regulation T, when must the money due in question 4 be deposited in the account?

   (A) no later than the fifth business day after the trades
   (B) no later than the seventh business day after the trades
   (C) on the day the trades are made
   (D) on the next business day following the trades

6. If the customer wished to deposit securities in lieu of cash to meet the margin call, how much in security value must be deposited?

   (A) $3,000
   (B) $6,000
   (C) $9,000
   (D) $15,000

7. If the client refused to make payment as required for the trades, what would the firm carrying the account do?

   (A) request an extension from the NYSE
   (B) liquidate the positions
   (C) advance the money to the customer
   (D) freeze the account for 90 days

8. Which of the following is the least important method of money control exercised by the Federal Reserve?

   (A) reserve requirements
   (B) open market operations
   (C) discount rate
   (D) Regulation T

9. When it lowers reserve requirements, the Federal Reserve Board is attempting to:

   (A) ease credit
   (B) raise interest rates
   (C) counter inflation
   (D) increase the rediscount rate

10. In your monthly review of customer's statements, you note that one client has paid for seven purchases five days late.

    (A) This situation is acceptable provided payment was received before the securities were sold.
    (B) The firm must ascertain that the client had a sufficient bank balance on settlement date.
    (C) This late payment is no violation provided the securities in question were not listed on the NYSE.
    (D) You must ascertain that extensions had been obtained under Federal Reserve Regulation T.

11. A client purchases 100 shares of Met Life in his margin account at $70 per share. The total cost of the purchase is $7,068 (including commissions). With a current requirement of 50%, which of the following payments would be acceptable under Regulation T?

    I. $7,068
    II. $3,534
    III. $3,000
    IV. $3,400

       (A) I only
       (B) I and II only
       (C) I, II, and IV only
       (D) I, II, III, and IV

12. If the Federal Reserve wished to ease credit, which of the following steps would it take?

    I.   raise the discount rate
    II. purchase securities in the open market
    III. lower reserve requirements
    IV. increase margin requirements under Regulation T and Regulation U

       (A) I and II only
       (B) II, III, and IV only
       (C) II and III only
       (D) I, II, III, and IV

13. Hypothecation usually refers to:

    (A) none of the following
    (B) forecasting the market on the basis of past performances
    (C) pledging securities as collateral for a loan
    (D) determining a reasonable offering price for a new security issue

14. A customer's long margin account reflects the following:

Security	Market Value
Stock A	$ 20,000
Stock B	50,000
Stock C	40,000
Stock D	70,000
Total	$180,000
Debit Balance	$ 60,000

If the current margin requirement is 60%, then the firm may rehypothecate from this account the following amount of securities at market value:

(A) $108,000
(B) $180,000
(C) $60,000
(D) $84,000

15. Exemption from compliance with Regulation T would be granted to:

(A) none of the following
(B) a broker or dealer who does not handle margin accounts
(C) a broker or dealer handling business only in fully registered securities
(D) a broker or dealer transacting less than 10% of his business through the medium of a member of a national securities exchange.

16. The initial FRB margin requirement is set at 60%. A customer purchases 100 ABC at $100 per share ($10,000) and deposits $6,000 in the account. If ABC increased in value to $150 per share, how much excess equity would the customer have in the account?

(A) $1,000 excess
(B) $1,500 excess
(C) $2,000 excess
(D) $3,000 excess

17. Under initial federal requirements of 70%, an investor purchasing 100 shares of a listed stock at $40 wants to satisfy the resulting margin call by delivering other listed stocks into his account. He may do so by depositing stocks with a current market value of:

(A) $9,333
(B) $5,714
(C) $4,000
(D) $2,800

18. A customer is opening a margin account with a member organization. If he wishes to purchase 100 shares of XYZ at $15, the amount of his initial deposit of cash must be:

(A) $375
(B) $1,050
(C) $1,500
(D) $2,000

19. Call loans made by banks to brokers and dealers are generally for the purpose of:

(A) expansion of office facilities
(B) meeting operating expenses
(C) carrying margin accounts
(D) financing securities held in inventory

20. A customer having a cash account fails to make full and prompt payment for a purchase. The broker liquidated the transaction. Two weeks later the customer telephones to place a buy order for 100 shares of XYZ common. The broker/dealer:

    (A) must refuse the order since Regulation T requires that under the circumstances the account must be frozen for 90 days
    (B) may handle the order if he obtains a firm promise from the customer to the effect that the settlement will be made promptly
    (C) must require under Regulation T a 25% down payment before the order can be executed
    (D) may handle the transaction at his own risk

21. A customer sells short 100 VJX @ 60 and makes the required Regulation T deposit. VJX then rises in price to 65. At this point the credit balance is:

    (A) $2,500
    (B) $3,500
    (C) $6,000
    (D) $9,000

22. An investor purchases 100M XYZ Corp. 8s of 2015 convertible bonds in a margin account. If the bonds were purchased at 110, what is the minimum deposit required by Regulation T?

    (A) $25,000
    (B) $27,500
    (C) $50,000
    (D) $55,000

23. On the same day, an investor buys $8,500 worth of OTC marginable stock and sells $7,800 of listed stock. If the account had no SMA, a Regulation T call:

    (A) would be issued for $350
    (B) would be issued for $700
    (C) would be issued for $3,900
    (D) would not be issued

24. With no other positions, an investor sells short 2,000 FYI @ $2 per share. The required minimum deposit is:

    (A) $1,000
    (B) $2,000
    (C) $4,000
    (D) $5,000

25. Under Regulation T of the Federal Reserve, extensions of time for payment in a client's account may be obtained from:

    (A) the New York Stock Exchange
    (B) the NASD
    (C) the Chicago Stock Exchange
    (D) any of the above

26. Under Regulation T of the Federal Reserve, a broker may overlook an amount due in a customer's account:

    (A) if it does not exceed $1,000
    (B) if the client request it in writing
    (C) if the value of a trade is less than $1,000
    (D) under no conditions

27. As an initial transaction in a margin account, a customer sells short 1,000 shares of a listed stock at $2. At the time Regulation T requirements are fixed at 50% margin. How much money will the broker ask this customer to deposit?

    (A) $1,000
    (B) $2,000
    (C) $2,500
    (D) $3,000

28. In a frozen account a customer:

    (A) may not trade corporate securities under any circumstances
    (B) may make purchases but not sales of corporate securities
    (C) must deposit the full purchase cost before the order may be executed
    (D) must deposit sufficient cash for each transaction no later than the settlement date

29. A client sells short 100 shares of ABC Corp. at $18 in a new margin account. The Regulation T requirement is 50%. The customer must deposit:

    (A) $900
    (B) $1,800
    (C) $2,000
    (D) $2,500

30. What Federal Reserve Board regulation governs the extension of securities-related credit by banks?

    (A) Regulation G
    (B) Regulation T
    (C) Regulation U
    (D) Regulation X

31. Which of the following clients could not open a margin account?

    (A) an uncovered option writer
    (B) a corporation
    (C) a husband and wife (joint account)
    (D) a custodian under the UGMA

32. Which of the following is an acceptable deposit to answer an NYSE maintenance call?

    (A) U.S. savings bond
    (B) SMA
    (C) U.S. treasury notes
    (D) any of the above

33. An investor buys $100,000 (principal amount) of municipal bonds @ 89 on margin. Presuming the account has no cash or securities, what is the minimum required deposit?

    (A) $5,080
    (B) $13,350
    (C) $22,500
    (D) $50,000

34. An investor buys $100,000 U.S. Treasury 10⅛s of 31 on margin. If the current market price is 92.16, the customer's minimum deposit is:

    (A) $4,625
    (B) $5,550
    (C) $10,000
    (D) $25,000

35. Which of the following are methods of money control exercised by the Federal Reserve in its pursuit of a sound monetary policy?

    (A) adjusting reserve requirements
    (B) the purchase and sale of U.S. government securities in the open market
    (C) the discount rate
    (D) all of the above

36. A customer's margin account has a $1,000 SMA balance. If the customer buys $20,000 of listed securities, how much fully paid margin stock must the customer deposit to answer the Regulation T call? Presume that Regulation T is set at 50%.

    (A) such a deposit would not satisfy the call
    (B) $9,000
    (C) $10,000
    (D) $18,000

37. A customer's margin account has an SMA of $2,000. If $10,000 in new securities are purchased, how much additional cash must be deposited?

    (A) $3,000
    (B) $4,800
    (C) $5,000
    (D) $6,000

38. The primary responsibility for a member firm's credit policies rests with:

    (A) the New York Stock Exchange
    (B) its controller
    (C) members and allied members of the firm who are experienced in this area
    (D) the Federal Reserve System

39. In an economic period of "easy money" circumstances, which of the following would likely reflect this condition?

    I.   an increase in the discount rate
    II. a decease in the discount rate
    III. an increase in bank reserve requirements
    IV. a decrease in bank reserve requirements

    (A) I and III only
    (B) II and IV only
    (C) I and IV only
    (D) II and III only

40. A broker/dealer must "buy in" a customer who has failed to deliver securities:

    (A) 10 days after settlement date
    (B) 15 days after settlement date
    (C) 30 days after settlement date
    (D) 40 days after settlement date

41. A customer has a mixed margin account. If the equity in his long position increases by $10,000 and the equity in his short position decreases by $10,000, what will be the effect on the total equity in the account?

    (A) increase
    (B) decrease
    (C) no change
    (D) cannot be determined

42. A customer's margin account has securities valued at $20,000 and an $8,000 credit balance. What is his equity in the account?

    (A) $8,080
    (B) $12,800
    (C) $20,000
    (D) $28,000

43. With Regulation T set at 50%, a firm wishes to impose house rules that require a minimum equity of 40% to be maintained by its clients.

    (A) This cannot be done as this level is below Regulation T requirements.
    (B) This cannot be done as maintenance requirements only require minimum equity of 25% for long positions.
    (C) This is permissible.
    (D) This action must be approved by the Federal Reserve and the NASD.

44. A short sale can be made in which of the following type of account?

    (A) special cash account
    (B) a custodian account
    (C) margin account
    (D) special memorandum account

45. Which of the following statements regarding a special memorandum account is incorrect?

    (A) A balance in the account can be used to purchase additional securities.
    (B) A balance in the account can be withdrawn if it would not bring account below maintenance requirements.
    (C) Funds in the account are not available if the account is restricted.
    (D) A sale in a restricted account could result in a credit to the SMA.

46. Hypothecation in customer accounts is permissible only if:

    (A) all of the following are observed
    (B) the customer's securities are pledged with the firm's securities in a commercial bank as protection
    (C) written consent of each customer is obtained
    (D) the value of securities pledged exceeds the aggregate indebtedness of those customer accounts

47. With listed stocks valued at $70,000 in a customer's margin account versus a debit balance of $20,000, a member firm may normally lend to itself or other dealers securities worth:

    (A) $20,000
    (B) $28,000
    (C) $50,000
    (D) $70,000

48. In a margin account, when a customer sells stock which of the following happens?

    I.   The debit balance declines.
    II. Equity declines.
    III. The SMA balance remains the same.
    IV. Equity remains the same.

    (A) I and IV only
    (B) II and III only
    (C) I and II only
    (D) III and IV only

49. If a customer fails to pay for securities purchased in a cash account, the member firm:

    (A) may grant an extension for a bona fide reason
    (B) may place the securities temporarily in a general account
    (C) must purchase the securities for the firm's error account
    (D) must liquidate the securities or otherwise cancel the transaction

50. All of the following are generally descriptive of the federal funds rate EXCEPT:

    (A) It is higher than the discount rate.
    (B) It fluctuates based upon supply and demand.
    (C) It is a leading indicator of short-term rates.
    (D) It moves up and down directly with fluctuations in long-term yields.

CHAPTER 8 EXAMINATION ANSWERS

1. **A** With Regulation T set at 50%, the customer's equity should be 50% of the market value. With market value of $30,000, the equity should be $15,000. As the actual equity is $18,000, the client has an excess of $3,000.

2. **B** To determine buying power, we divide the excess equity, $3,000, by the current margin requirement (.50); the result is $6,000. Note: When margin is set at 50% the same result would be obtained if you multiply the excess equity (3,000) by 2; the result is $6,000.

3. **D** The purchase of 100 Hasbro at 30 would require $1,500 (50%). As we determined in question 2, the client has $6,000 in buying power; therefore, no additional deposit would be required.

4. **C** The Hasbro purchase ($3,000) and the IBM purchase ($12,000) would require $7,500 (50%). As the client has $3,000 excess equity, a deposit of $4,500 would satisfy Regulation T.

5. **A** Under Regulation T, payment is due promptly, but no later than the fifth business day after the trade.

6. **C** The required cash is $4,500. If the client wished to deposit securities in lieu of cash, he must deposit securities whose loan value (50%) is $4,500. To determine the amount we divide the cash required ($4,500) by the current loan value (50%): $9,000.

7. **B** If the client refuses to make payment in an account, the firm is required to liquidate the positions.

8. **D** Regulation T regulates brokers extending credit to customers on security transactions. It is important to the securities industry, but does not have the overall importance of the other functions.

9. **A** If the Fed lowers reserve requirements, the member banks will have more money available for loans. This would result in an easing of credit.

10. **D** If valid reasons exist, extension of time for payment can be obtained from any registered stock exchange or from any NASD office.

11. **B** Choices I, full payment, and II, 50% margin, are certainly acceptable.

12. **C** Buying in the open market injects funds into the economy and lowering reserve requirements gives banks more available funds. The other choices would tend to tighten the money supply.

13. **C** The term "hypothecate" is synonymous with "pledge." In a margin account, the customer hypothecates (pledges) his securities with the broker. The broker then rehypothecates (repledges) some of the securities as collateral at the bank. (See question 14.)

14. **D** A firm may rehypothecate securities in a margin customer's account in an amount up to 140% of the customer's debit balance. In this question the debit is $60,000, and 140% of $60,000 is $84,000.

15. **A** Regulation T covers both cash and margin accounts as part of its credit regulation function. No one is exempt from this regulation.

16. **C** The customer started out with a $6,000 equity (the amount of the margin deposit). This left the customer, initially, with a debit balance of $4,000. If the market value of Xerox increased to $15,000, the cus-

tomer's equity would have increased to $11,000 (market value less debit balance). The customer need have an equity of only 60%; 60% of $15,000 is $9,000. Since the amount of equity the customer has, $11,000, is greater than the amount he needs at 60%, $9,000, there is an excess of $2,000.

17. **A** If the customer were putting up cash, he would need to put up 70% of $4,000, or $2,800. However, the customer wishes to deposit securities. With margin requirements at 70%, loan values are at 30%. He would have to deposit securities whose loan value was $ 2,800. To arrive at this figure, we divide the amount of cash required, $2,800, by the current loan value, 30%, to get $9,333.

18. **C** Under NYSE maintenance requirements the minimum equity in an account must be $2,000 or 100%, whichever is less. In this case 100% of the cost ($1,500) is the lesser figure.

19. **C** A call loan is a loan made to a broker who uses securities as collateral. They are usually made to finance the debits in margin accounts.

20. **A** In a frozen account payment must be made in advance of any trade for 90 days after the freeze occurs.

21. **D** Credit balances in short accounts do not change because of market action. A short sale of $6,000 and a Regulation T deposit of $3,000 create a credit balance of $9,000. The balance will remain at that level unless there is a transaction, a deposit, or a withdrawal.

22. **D** The current requirement is the same 50% as for margin accounts: $110,000 × 50% = $55,000.

23. **D** While technically a net purchase of $700 requires a 50% Regulation T

deposit, brokers may waive a Regulation T call for under $1,000 at their discretion.

24. **D** If stocks are sold short at low prices, the NYSE maintenance requirement may well supersede Regulation T. The requirement for shares under $5 is the greater of $2.50/per share or 100% of the market value. In this case, $2.50 per share exceeds the market value of $2, so the requirement is $2.50 × 2,000 = $5,000. For shares over $5 in value, the requirement is the greater of $5 per share or 30% of the market value.

25. **D** In addition to the NASD and organized exchanges, it should be pointed out that you request extensions from the organization that audits you.

26. **A** In a cash account, we do not need to take action against the customer if the net amount due is $1,000 or less.

27. **C** Here we encounter the minimum maintenance requirement. On shares that have a market value below 5, the requirement is 100% of the market value or $2.50 per share, whichever is higher.

28. **C** This refers to an account that had to be sold out for nonpayment by settlement day. The account must be "frozen," or restricted to full cash payment, in advance of any purchase for a period of 90 days.

29. **C** In a short account, the minimum equity that must exist to transact any business is $2,000. It may be considerably higher depending upon house margin requirements and/or minimum maintenance requirements.

30. **C** Regulation T refers to the extension of credit by broker/dealers. Regulation U refers to extension of credit by banks on securities.

31. **D** Under the Uniform Gifts to Minors Act (UGMA), the securities must be registered in the name of the custodian for the benefit of the minor for the gift to have constructive receipt. Obviously, in a margin account, all securities are held in street name, so this would not constitute a valid gift. Hence, margin accounts are inappropriate for custodians under the UGMA.

32. **C** A maintenance call requires the infusion of new funds or new negotiable securities, if a sellout or buy-in is to be avoided. Treasury notes meet this standard, but neither of the others does. Savings bonds are not negotiable and thus not good collateral. They would first have to be cashed in. Use of the SMA increases the debit balance and cannot improve the equity in the account.

33. **B** Munis are not subject to Regulation T. The NYSE maintenance requirement thus becomes both the initial and the maintenance requirement for such bonds. For municipals, the requirement is 15% of the market value or 7% of the principal amount whichever amount is greater.

34. **B** The NYSE maintenance requirement on securities issued or guaranteed by the U.S. government with a maturity of 20 years or more is 6% of the market value. $92,500 \times 6\% = \$5,550$.

35. **D** These are the three major methods of money control exercised by the Fed.

36. **D** Fully paid marginable stock equal to the dollar value of a purchase (or short sale) satisfies the Regulation T requirement. This account already has $1,000 SMA, which is worth $2,000 in buying power. A stock deposit of $18,000 would cover the remaining Regulation T requirements.

37. **A** A $10,000 purchase requires $5,000 initial margin under Regulation T. The existing SMA of $2,000 is applicable against this on a dollar-for-dollar basis. One could also say that a $10,000 purchase exceeds the "buying power" ($4,000).

38. **C** Firms are expected to implement house rules to protect them against losses in margin accounts. This responsibility rests with the firm's upper management, who are experienced in this area.

39. **B** Choices I and III would have the effect of tightening money, not easing it.

40. **A** This is the required time at which a customer must be bought in.

41. **C** The increase in the long position is offset by the decrease in the short position.

42. **D** Market value plus credit balance equals the equity.

43. **C** Firms may establish house rules as they see fit as long as they are at least as strict as the minimum maintenance requirements. A firm could literally require 100% equity. Regulation T is an initial requirement and does not dictate minimum equity.

44. **C** The exact cost of the purchase to cover the short cannot be calculated at the time the short sale is executed. For that reason all short sales must be made in margin accounts.

45. **C** SMA funds are available for use if the account is restricted as long as their use does not violate maintenance requirements.

46. **C** This refers to the general agreement or margin agreement.

47. **A** When lending customer's securities to itself or to other brokers, a firm may only use an amount equal to

the customer's debit balance. In this case that equals $20,000.

48. **A** A sale results in a credit entry; hence, the debit balance declines. Equity would remain the same after a sale, assuming no withdrawal.

49. **D** Regulation T requires the position to be closed (bought in or sold out) if the customer fails to comply with rules. Note that an "extension" of time to pay or deliver may indeed be granted for a bona fide reason, but not by the member. Only an exchange or the NASD may grant such.

50. **C** Federal funds move (and sometimes lead) short-term rates.

Options

EQUITY OPTIONS

Call

An option giving the holder the right to buy stock at a fixed price any time during the lifespan of the option.

Put

An option giving the holder the right to sell stock at a fixed price any time during the lifespan of the option.

Type

All listed options are of either of two types: puts or calls.

Class

All options of the same type on the same underlying security, for example, all IBM calls (regardless of expiration months or striking prices), form the IBM call class. Puts on IBM would thus be a different class than IBM calls.

Series

All options of the same class with the same strike price and same expiration month. For example, MSA April 50 calls for one series in the MSA call class of options and MSA April 60 calls for another.

Holder or Buyer

The purchaser of an open option position.

Writer

The seller (creator) of an option position. As such, the writer may also be said to be "short" the option.

Opening Transactions

Opening purchases create (or increase) long positions. Opening sales create (or increase) short positions.

Closing Transactions

Closing purchases reduce (or eliminate) short positions. Closing sales reduce (or eliminate) long positions. If a client with no other position bought 1 IBM January 120 call @ 11, it would be an opening purchase.

Trading Cycles
Each class of listed option may trade in only one of three cycles, each cycle distinguished by its expiration month. The cycles are occasionally referred to by the first month in each.

Striking Price
Also termed "exercise price." The price per share the buyer of a call agrees to pay the seller should the call be exercised, or the price per share the seller of a put option agrees to pay the buyer if exercised. Listed options have standardized striking prices, usually multiples of five or ten points.

"In the Money"
On a call, current market price of the stock is higher than the striking price; on a put, current market price of the stock is lower than the striking price. Thus, if IBM is trading at $98 per share an IBM October 90 call would be "in the money" by eight points. An IBM July 100 put would also be "in the money" by two points.

In determining which options are in the money no consideration is given to the premium paid by the holder. In the money does not mean that the option is necessarily profitable to the holder at that point.

"Out of the Money"
On a call, current market price of the stock is lower than the striking price; on a put, current market price of the stock is higher than the striking price.

Thus, if XRX is trading at $35 per share, an XRX April 40 call is out of the money by five points. Although neither of these options has any intrinsic value, they may still command a premium based on the amount of time remaining until expiration.

Intrinsic Value
If the option is in the money, intrinsic value is the difference between the market price of the stock and the exercise price of the option. For example, when BLY stock is at 43, the intrinsic value of the BLY August 35 call is $800 regardless of the actual market price of the option. Out of the money options, therefore, have no intrinsic value.

Premium
The amount the buyer of the option pays to the seller for the option. In other words, the option's market price. (For purposes of the exam, confine use of "premium" to this definition.)

Aggregate Exercise Price
The striking price of the option times the number of shares in the contract, normally 100 (though not always). Thus, the aggregate exercise price of an April 80 call is $8,000.

Open Interest
The total number of contracts in a given class or series capable of being offset by closing transactions. In other words, either the total number outstanding short positions or the total number of outstanding long positions (not the total of both). Open interest in a given series may be zero, or it may be in thousands, depending on the activity and popularity of the underlying stock. There is no rule limiting open interest on the number of shares outstanding.

Spread

A simultaneous long and short position in different series of the same class. For instance, long 1 DD April 35 call and short 1 DD April 40 call.

Straddle

A put and a call (either both long or both short) on the same stock, with the same exercise price and the same expiration month, for example, long 1 NOM June 40 call and long 1 NOM June 40 put.

Combination

A put and a call (either both long or both short) on the same stock, with either different exercise prices and/or different expiration months, for example, long 1 XON October 30 call and long 1 XON October 35 put.

Note: In our examples of a straddle and a combination we used "long" positions. Should an investor sell options rather than go long (buy), the position created would be a short straddle, or short combination.

"Covered"

Calls are covered when the short option position is protected by a simultaneous long position in: (1) the underlying stock; (2) a convertible security, (3) an "escrow receipt," (4) a warrant (plus any cash necessary for exercise), or (5) a call with an equal or lower striking price and an expiration date no sooner than that of the short option.

Puts are covered when *and only when* the account is long a put with a striking price equal to or higher than the short put and an expiration date no sooner than that of the short option. A put writer is not considered covered if he is short the underlying stock.

Uncovered or Naked

This position is where the buyer or the seller has an underlying position as described above in "Covered." Naked options are very risky; however, they may be very profitable. If the underlying stock or index moves as the investor anticipated, the profit can be high because the investor would only have to put down a small amount of money. On the other hand, if the stock or index moves the other way, the seller of the naked option could suffer large losses.

Uses of Options

A number of questions will be asked about various option strategies. Most such questions deal with breakeven points upon expiration of the option. That is, if the option (and any related stock position) were liquidated immediately prior to expiration, at what point would the transactions net out to zero profit or loss? Further questions may ask for maximum profit and loss possible from a given position. Commissions may be ignored for all questions on this exam.

Long Option Positions

For all long option positions, the maximum possible loss is the amount paid in premiums. The maximum profit on a long put is the difference between zero and the aggregate exercise price of the put (less the premium paid). The maximum profit on a long call position cannot be computed.

Call Purchase Breakeven point is the striking price plus the premium paid. For example, an investor buys 1 HOI March 30 call for $300 and breaks even at 33. (If the option were exercised at 30 and the stock so acquired were sold immediately at 33, the $300 profit would exactly offset the cost of the call.) Any lower stock price on expiration would show a loss. Any stock price higher than $33 would represent a profit to the holder.

Put Purchase Breakeven point is the striking price less the premium paid. For example, an investor buys 1 DEC April 110 put for $700. He breaks even if the market price of DEC is $103. Stock purchased at $103 and put to the writer at $110 would exactly recapture the $700 premium price.

Long Straddle Breakeven points are the striking price plus the combined premiums on the upside and the striking price minus the combined premiums on the downside. For example, an investor buys 1 KO April 65 call at $400 and 1 KO April 65 put at $200. At expiration, KO must be higher than 71 (65+6) or lower than 59 (65 – 6) for a net profit to be realized. Naturally, the market might move far enough in both directions for both sides to be exercised or closed out profitably, but at expiration any previously unexercised straddle must have one side out of the money while the other side is in the money (excluding the possibility, certainly not strong, that the stock closes precisely on the striking price).

Long Combination Breakeven points are the call striking price plus the combined premiums on the upside and the put striking price less the combined premiums on the downside. For example, an investor buys 1 CAT July 80 put at $100 and 1 CAT July 90 call at $350. At expiration, CAT must be higher than 94.50 or lower than 75.50 for a net profit to be realized. The total premium cost is $450. With the put exercisable at 80, he would break even if the stock were at 75.50 (buy at 75.50, put at 80 = $450 profit). Breakeven on the call would occur if the stock were trading at 94.50 (call at $90, sell at 94.50 = $450 profit).

Short Option Positions

Writing strategies differ from buying strategies in that the position must be evaluated in conjunction with a long or short position in the underlying stock, which the writer may be compelled to purchase or sell. When calculating breakeven points on covered calls, assume the investor sells the stock upon expiration of the option, although this may happen infrequently in the real world.

Basic Writing Strategies

Sell a Covered Call "At the Money" Breakeven point is the acquisition cost of the stock less the premium received. The maximum profit is the premium. For example, an investor buys 100 BA at 50, simultaneously selling 1 BA May 50 call for $550. Breakeven is 44.50; maximum profit is $550.

The $550 premium protects the stock bought at $50. Should the investor be forced to sell his position at 44.50, the loss in the stock is equal to the premium received. However, should the stock rise, let's say to $60, he will be called at $50 the cost of the stock. His profit will be limited to the $550 premium.

Sell a Covered Call "Out of the Money" Breakeven point is the acquisition cost of the stock less the premium. The maximum profit is the premium plus the out of the money amount. For example, an investor buys 100 EK at 34 and sells 1 EK October 40 call for $300. Breakeven point is 31 and maximum profit is $900. That is, the option will be exercised at any price higher than 40, leaving the investor with a $600 profit on the purchase and sale of the stock (34 to 40) plus the $300 premium.

Sell a Covered Call "In the Money" Breakeven point is the acquisition cost of the stock less the premium. Maximum profit is the option premium less its intrinsic value (upon establishment of the position). For example, an investor buys 100 MCD at 58, simultaneously selling 1 MCD July 50 call for $1,000. Breakeven is at 48 (58 – 10) and the maximum profit is $200 ($1,000 premium less the $800 loss on the stock position, which is the intrinsic value of the call).

Sell a Naked Call Breakeven is the striking price plus the premium received. Maximum profit is the premium. Maximum loss is unlimited. For example, with no stock position, an investor sells 1 EK August 35 call at $250 (EK stock at 33.50). Breakeven is 37.50 and there will be a loss above this price that is potentially unlimited. Maximum profit is $250 and is realized if EK stock is 35 or below upon expiration of the option.

Sell a Naked Put Breakeven is the striking price less the premium received. Maximum profit is the premium. Maximum loss is the difference between the aggregate exercise price (less the premium) and zero. For example, an investor sells 1 HOM August 100 put at $950. Breakeven is 90.50. Maximum profit is $950 if HOM is above 100 at expiration. If exercised, HOM is purchased at 90.50 (100 exercise price less 90.50 premium received) and, thus, $9,050 is the maximum possible loss.

Note: An investor who felt the market was about to rise could use options in one of two ways: (1) go long calls, or (2) go short puts. For instance, an investor feeling that IBM trading at $90 per share was about to rise might go long (buy) IBM October 90 calls at $6. Once IBM rose above $96 per share, he would begin to profit.

He might also short (sell) IBM 90 puts at $5. Should IBM be above $90 the owner of the put will not deliver the stock to him at $90 (it could be sold for more in the open market), and he will profit by retaining the $500 premium.

An investor who felt the market was about to go down also has two strategies available (1) go long puts, or (2) go short calls. For example, an investor feeling that Danaher Corp. trading at $110 per share will fall in price could go long (buy) DHR April 110 puts at $4. Once DHR drops below $106 per share he will profit by buying the stock, perhaps at $102, and exercising his $110 put. After subtracting the $4 cost of the put he will still have a $4 profit per share.

He might also sell (short) DHR April 110 calls at $7. Should DHR be below $110 at expiration, the call will not be exercised, and he profits by retaining the $700 premium.

From a standpoint of market direction, being long calls is equivalent to being short puts (rising market), and being long puts is the same as being short calls (declining market).

Spreads

"Spread" refers to the difference in premiums paid and received in the simultaneous purchase and sale of two (or more) series in the same class of option. The spreader hopes that this difference will either widen or narrow as the stock price fluctuates and the options approach expiration. In other words, the spreader's goal is to make money on one side faster than it is lost on the other. The simultaneous long/short position reduces the risk of pure long or short positions, but at the same time precludes the larger profit potential associated with such positions.

While there are numerous variations, most spreads may be categorized as being established as either "credits" or "debits." In a credit spread, the option sold produces more premium than the cost of the option purchased; in a debit spread, the option purchased costs more than the premium received on the option sold. Credit spreads are profitable when the spread narrows or when both sides expire unexercised. Debit spreads are profitable when the spread widens or when both sides may be exercised.

Example 1: Call Bull Spread This is also referred to as "money," "vertical," or even—though rarely—"perpendicular" spread.

An investor buys 1 XOM April 60 call at $800 and sells 1 XOM April 70 call at $400 when XOM stock is at 64. The maximum profit occurs when XOM is at 70 or any higher price. At this price the spread would have widened to $1,000. The (long) April 60, which costs $800, could be closed at $1,000 for a $200 profit. The (short) April 70, however, will expire worthless for a $400 profit. Each leg of the spread, therefore, contributes to the total profit of $600. Note that the spread cannot produce more profit than $600 because every point XOM rises above 70 produces a point of loss (or reduced profit) on the 70 call, erasing each additional point of profit on the 60 call. Thus, the maximum profit is the difference between the striking prices less the debit. The maximum possible loss is the $400 debit, which would occur if XOM were below 60 at expiration. Then, both options would expire worthless and the $800 loss on the long option is partially offset by the $400 profit on the expired short option.

Example 2: Call Bear Spread

Had the spreader been bearish on XOM and taken the opposite side of the market, that is, sold the April 60 call and bought the April 70 call, a $400 credit would have resulted. If the stock then fell below 60, both options would have expired worthless and the spread would have narrowed to its minimum possible (zero). Therefore, the initial credit of $400 is the maximum profit. The maximum loss had the spread widened against the investor would have been the difference between the striking prices less the credit.

Example 3: Put "Horizontal" Spread This is also called a "time" spread.

The investor buys 1 APD October 50 put at $500 and sells 1 APD July 50 put for $400. As the striking prices are the same so must be the intrinsic values. However, the October 50 put premium is greater than that for the July 50 because it has a 90-day longer life. As July approaches, the July 50 will begin to lose any time value it has, and the option will revert to its intrinsic value, if indeed it has any. The October 50 put, however, still has 90 days to run and its premium should not contract as much. Hence, if APD were at $400 upon expiration, the July 50 put could be closed out for $200, yielding a $200 profit over the opening sale at $400. The October 50 put, of course, would also have an intrinsic value of $200 but might be priced at $400 because of the potential for appreciation over the remaining 90 days of its life. If so, it could be closed out for about that price, leaving a $100 loss (on cost of $500). The spread as whole, therefore, had been profitable by widening out from the initial premium difference of $100 ($500 versus $400) to the closing difference of $200 ($400 versus $200).

The terms "vertical" and "horizontal" come from the system that the newspapers once used in listing options activity. Horizontal spreads use different expiration months and the months were listed across the paper. Vertical spreads use different strike prices, which were listed from top to bottom in the press.

Taxation

Long Options

When opening purchases are followed by closing sales, the taxable result is a capital gain or loss. For example, on 2/22/08 an investor buys 1 GWW April 60 call at $450 and sells it at $700 on 3/31/08. The result is a $250 gain.

The "expiration" of either a long put or a long call is treated as a closing sale (for no consideration) on the expiration date. Hence, the entire premium is a capital loss.

The "exercise" of a long call option represents the purchase of the underlying security. The premium paid is added to the aggregate exercise price of the option (which is the price paid for the stock) to establish the cost basis for the stock. The holding period commences on the date of exercise. The holding period of the option is irrelevant. For example, on 1/24/08 an investor buys 1 ABM May 15 call for $275 and exercises the option on April 15. The investor has thus purchased 100 ABM on 4/15/08 for $1,775 ($1,500 exercise price+$275 premium).

The exercise of a put option, on the other hand, results in the sale of a security. In this case, the premium is subtracted from the aggregate exercise price of the option to determine the selling price of the stock. This price is then compared to the acquisition cost of the stock put to the writer to determine the extent of the profit or loss realized. The holding period is based upon the date the stock was originally purchased and the date the put was exercised. For example, on 6/18/07 an investor buys 1 CX October 30 put for $125. On 9/9/07 the put is exercised and the investor delivers 100 CX originally purchased on 5/3/95 for $2,600. The result is a $275 capital gain ($3,000 – $2,600 = $400 – $125 = $275).

Note: The acquisition of a put against a long position in the stock cancels the holding period for any stock not already held long term. The holding period of such stock commences again upon the elimination of the put position.

Short Options

When opening sales are followed by closing purchases, the taxable result is always a capital gain or loss, *never ordinary income or loss*. For example, on 6/10/07 an investor sells 1 SGP August 40 put for $550 and on 8/5/07 buys it back for $250, resulting in a $300 capital gain.

The "expiration" of either a short put or a short call is treated as if a closing purchase (for no consideration) had been made on expiration date. Hence, the entire premium is a capital gain.

The "exercise" of a short call option results in the sale of the underlying security by the writer. The premium received is added to the aggregate exercise price of the option to determine the sale proceeds. The exercise date is considered the sale date. The cost basis and actual holding period of the stock delivered determine the nature and extent of the gain or loss. For example, on 2/15/07 an investor wrote 1 TFX October 45 call for $1,000. On 3/28/07 the investor receives an exercise notice and delivers TFX stock originally purchased for $2,900 in 1962. Thus the investor realizes a $2,600 capital gain ($4,500 – $2,900 = $1,600+$1,000 = $2,600).

The exercise of a short put option results in the purchase of stock by the writer and thus is devoid of tax consequences until the security is actually sold. The writer subtracts the premium received from the aggregate exercise price to determine the cost basis of the stock. The holding period for the stock commences on the put's exercise date. For example, on 4/18/07 an investor writes 1 TFX June 45 put for $500 and on 6/2/07 the put is exercised. The investor thus buys 100 TFX for $4,000 ($4,500 less $500 premium) with the holding period starting on 6/2/07.

Summary of Key Dates and Times

Hours of Trading 8:30 A.M. to 3:10 P.M. (CT) except on the business day prior to expiration when trading ceases at 3:00 p.m. (CT).

Premium Due to Clearing Corporation 9:00 A.M. (CT) on business day following report of matched trade. Normally matched trades are reported on trade date and, thus, premium is due next business day following trade date.

Option Issued ("Transaction Effective") Normally noon (CT) the business day after trade date, as above.

Exercise Cutoff Time 4:30 P.M. (CT) on the business day prior to expiration. A customer must notify broker carrying account of intent to exercise prior to that time or option will expire.

Exercise Notices Acceptable at Clearing Corporation (Other than Last Trading Day) 9:00 A.M. to 3:30 P.M. (CT). Note that "cutoff time" is one hour later but only on the business day prior to expiration.

Exercise Settlement Date Noon (CT) on the third business day following the date an exercise notice is tendered to the clearing corporation.

Expiration 10:59 P.M. (CT) on the Saturday following the third Friday of the expiration month.

LEAPS

Long-Term Equity Anticipation Securities (LEAPS)

The listing of equity options on exchanges began in the early 1970s. Since that time an increasing number of strategies that employ this product have been developed. In addition to creating bullish, bearish, and neutral positions, options can be used to protect existing long and short positions.

One drawback in the use of options has been their limited life. In the past, exchanges listed options with an approximate maximum of nine months until expiration. The time factor increased the risk to the option's holder because, with each tick of the clock, a portion of the option's value vanished.

This negative aspect was reduced to some degree in 1992 when the Securities and Exchange Commission approved the listing of options with as much as 39 months of life before expiration. Referred to as LEAPS, these *Long-Term Equity Anticipation Securities* are similar to the traditional shorter options in their trading methods and strategic applications, although the increased time factor does allow for some expanded uses.

LEAPS are available in both puts and calls and allow investors to protect against a decline in a stock or to take advantage of an upward move for an extended period of time. They are more closely related to an actual position in the underlying security than the shorter options. The extended time provided by LEAPS will command a greater premium than on similar options of less duration, but the cost will still be only a fraction of the amount required to purchase the underlying security.

For example, with Yahoo stock trading at $50 a share the purchase of 100 shares would cost $5,000 (plus expenses). At the same time a Yahoo 50 call with two months until expiration was available for a premium of 4.60 ($460). However, a Yahoo 45 LEAPS with two years until expiration commanded a premium of 10.20 ($1,020). Purchase of the LEAPS would give the holder a call on the stock for nearly two years at a price less than 20% above the current market price. LEAPS are traded American style—that is, the holder has the right to exercise at any time prior to expiration.

While LEAPS offer certain strategic advantages they cannot be considered equivalents to a position in the underlying stock. Although issued with longer durations, they do in time expire. There is a continuing erosion of the option's premium that works against the holder. An additional factor for investors to consider is that option holders do not receive any dividends while stockholders generally do receive quarterly payments.

LEAPS can be found listed in the financial pages each day. In May 2004 the following listing appeared:

Option/Strike		EXP	Call Vol Last	Put Vol Last	
Yahoo					
50	45	Jan 05	130./0.20	16042	4.60

This listing provides a complete description of the previous day's trading: the underlying stock (Yahoo), the expiration month and year (January 2005), the strike price (45), and the type of option. Information as to trading volume and last sale is also provided.

All usual strategies are available using LEAPS. Long or short positions can be established as with the shorter contracts and straddles and spreads can also be created. The only distinguishing feature of LEAPS is the time factor.

Investors must weigh the advantages of using LEAPS as opposed to using shorter options and rolling them over as each expiration approaches. As options are not suitable for all investors, great care must be exercised before recommending their use.

The basic facts for the trading of LEAPS are as follows:

Trading Unit	100 share per contract
Trading Hours	9:30 A.M. to 4:10 P.M. Eastern Time
Settlement	The underlying stock
Exercise	American style
Expiration	The Saturday following the third Friday of the expiration month
Premium Quotation	Minimum fluctuation on series with a premium below $3 is ($6.25 per contract) for series.

Effective January 2000, the SEC approved a 25 percent loan value of the current market value on listed options having a life of more than 9 months.

For OTC options, the loan value is 25 percent of the In-the Money or the intrinsic value. Consequently, when both listed and OTC options get to the point that their lives are less than 9 months, no loan value may be extended.

Adjustments in Contract Terms

A significant difference between listed and unlisted options is the effect of cash dividends on their exercise price. The striking price of a "conventional" (OTC) option is normally the market price of the underlying stock at the time of the sale. Should the stock go ex-dividend, the striking price is reduced by the exact amount of the cash dividend. For example, a 95-day call on KWR has a $25.625 striking price. Upon KWR going ex a $0.44 cash dividend, the striking price would be reduced to $25.185. Therefore, should the call be exercised the coverage call writer "loses" the dividend through lower sale proceeds.

On the other hand, listed option striking prices are not reduced for cash dividends. The covered call writer thus retains all dividends on the stock unless the call holder submits an exercise notice to the Clearing Corporation prior to the ex-dividend date. This increases the appeal of covered writing, especially on relatively high-yielding, low-volatility stocks that typically do not command large premiums (e.g., public utilities).

Stock dividends, splits, rights offerings, or spinoffs, however, do cause adjustments in listed option contracts. If the distribution results in less than one new share for each outstanding share (e.g., three for two split, 15% stock dividend) the number of shares per contract is increased to account for the new amount of shares and the striking price is lowered accordingly.

If the distribution results in one or more new shares for each outstanding share, new contracts are issued for 100 shares each at the new strike price. For example, STI goes ex a 6% stock dividend. An STI March 80 call would be adjusted to 106 shares and the striking price reduced to 75.50. The new striking price ($75.47) is found by dividing the old aggregate exercise price ($8,000) by the new number of shares (106) and rounding to the nearest $\frac{1}{16}$ (not necessarily the next higher, as with other ex-dividend reductions). Another example: CME splits four for one. A CME July 120 put would be adjusted to 4 CME July 30 puts, 100 shares each.

Rights offerings and other noncash distributions usually result in the reduction of striking prices but no additional shares per contract. The Clearing Corporation reserves the right to make whatever adjustments are fair and equitable.

Note: Premiums are quoted in price per share. Investors typically make an automatic mental adjustment by multiplying a given quotation times 100 to find the cost of an option. For instance, the quote shows UN July 60 calls at 2.50, meaning it could have been bought or sold for $250. However, suppose UN had split three for two (or paid a 50% stock dividend). This would result in an adjusted (150 shares) UN July 40 call. On this contract a quotation of 2.50 would thus represent $375, not $250 (150 shares × $2.50) per adjusted contract.

Floor Procedures

AMEX and CBOE floor procedures have some marked difference. On the exam be careful to note to which exchange a particular question refers. For instance:

On the CBOE, limit orders are placed on the book of the:

(A) specialist
(B) order book official
(C) market-maker
(D) registered trader

Answer (B) is correct (see **Order Book Official**), but the same question prefaced by "On the AMEX" would have to be answered (A).

Order Book Official

The CBOE member who is charged with handling the "book" for open orders in a specific class of options. Accepts public orders only! May not accept orders for: spreads, straddles, proprietary accounts, market-makers, or contingencies (including stops and stop limits). You may thus only enter limit and market orders on the book. *Makes no principal trades.*

Market-Maker

The CBOE member registered to make competitive bids and offers in specific classes of options. Intention is to increase liquidity. *Does not have any book function.*

Floor Broker

The CBOE member who handles public orders; acts only as agent. Frequently also registered as market-maker but may act in only one of these capacities on any given day in a particular stock.

Specialist

The AMEX member who has both book and principal function in a particular option class.

Registered Options Trader

The AMEX member with function similar to CBOE market-maker.

Trading Rotation

Brief period during which bids and offers are accepted on only one specific series per class. The order book official starts with the nearest expiration month and lowest striking price (calls) or highest striking price (puts), opening the various series in sequence and proceeding to the next expiration month. The process is repeated until all series are opened. Used on openings and at other times when deemed necessary for a fair and equitable market.

Accommodation Liquidations ("Cabinet Trades")

A worthless option may be liquidated by placing an order to sell it at $.01 per share with an order book official. An execution produces a confirmation showing the liquidation for a gross sum of $1.00, which is sometimes useful for tax records.

"Off Floor" Transaction
Only permissible when the member has made an attempt to execute on the floor and has reasonably ascertained that a better price may be obtained off the floor.

Options Clearing Corporation

Assignment of Exercise Notices
The Options Clearing Corporation (OCC) assigns exercise notices tendered to it on a random selection basis. An exception occurs when the notice involves *block size* (25 or more contracts). In this case the Options Clearing Corporation will attempt to assign such notices to member accounts short an equal number of contracts in order to reduce clearances to a minimum.

    Note: In choosing which of its customers is allocated an exercise notice, a member firm may use random selection or FIFO ("First In, First Out," meaning the oldest shorts are exercised first).

Issuance of Options
The Options Clearing Corporation (not the exchange and also *not* the writer) is the issuer of a listed option. The option is issued at noon (CT) on the business day following the trade date. (See Summary of Key Dates and Times.)

Reports
Prior to 9:00 A.M. (CT) the OCC reports daily to its members:

1. Positions: All exchange transactions for any member accounts that settle that day and any net premium due the member or the OCC. Includes all opening, closing, and exercise transactions.
2. Margins: The margin required that day for all short positions and contracts exercised in accounts of members.

    The senior Registered Options Trader (ROP) or delegate must make a daily review of these reports.

Automatic Exercise
The OCC will automatically exercise any long position which, on expiration date, is "in the money" by .75 point (customer account) or .25 point (firm account).

Regulation and Supervision of Customer Accounts

New Account Data
A member opening an account for a new customer must obtain and record the following data on the new account document:

- investment objectives
- total estimated annual income and estimated liquid net worth
- age, marital status, and number of dependents
- previous securities investment experience
- employment status

A copy of the completed document must be verified, signed, and returned by the customer within 15 days after the approval of the account.

OPTIONS INFORMATION FORM AND AGREEMENT

Account # _____

Dear Client:

Exchange rules require us to request the following information from all customers who intend to effect transactions in options. The information is intended to assist us in making recommendations that are appropriate to your investment objectives. We would appreciate your completing the form. Bear Sterns Securities may, on the basis of the information provided, decline to accept any account for option activity or may limit such account to specific activities.

NAME _____

ADDRESS _____ PHONE # _____

IF ACCOUNT IS IN NAME OF MORE THAN ONE INDIVIDUAL, PLEASE SUPPLY INFORMATION FOR ALL OWNERS.

OCCUPATION _____ EMPLOYER _____

TYPE OF BUSINESS _____ YEARS THERE _____

AGE _____ MARITAL STATUS _____ DEPENDENTS _____

APPROXIMATE INCOME _____ SPOUSE'S INCOME _____

APPROXIMATE NET WORTH   APPROXIMATE LIQUID NET WORTH
(Do not Include Residence) _____ (Cash, Securities, Other) _____

CHECK BOX

OTHER INVESTMENTS: ☐ REAL ESTATE ☐ TAX SHELTERS ☐ SAVINGS

INVESTMENT OBJECTIVES: ☐ INCOME ☐ GROWTH ☐ TRADING PROFITS

PAST INVESTMENT EXPERIENCE: _____ ACTIVITY _____

	YEARS EXPER.	NONE	LIMITED	MODERATE	EXTENSIVE
STOCK/BONDS	_____	☐	☐	☐	☐
OPTIONS	_____	☐	☐	☐	☐
COMMODITIES	_____	☐	☐	☐	☐

INVESTORS SHOULD NOT PURCHASE PUT OR CALL OPTIONS UNLESS THEY ARE ABLE TO SUSTAIN A TOTAL LOSS OF THE PREMIUM AND TRANSACTION COSTS, OR WRITE UNCOVERED OPTIONS UNLESS THEY ARE ABLE TO SUSTAIN SUBSTANTIAL FINANCIAL LOSS.

PLEASE CHECK (SELECT) ONE OR MORE OF THE OPTIONS STRATEGIES YOU MAY WISH TO EMPLOY:

COVERED CALL WRITING ☐

PUT/CALL SPREADS PUT/CALL BUYS (SPECULATIVE) ☐

PUT WRITING (SPECULATIVE) ☐

UNCOVERED CALL WRITING
(THIS IS A HIGHLY SPECULATIVE ACTIVITY) ☐

ATTENTION CLIENT: PLEASE SIGN THIS FORM ON THE BOTTOM RIGHT HAND SIDE AFTER READING THE AGREEMENT. THANK YOU.

Date _____ _____
                          R.R. Signature

Date _____ Approved Equity Options _____
                          BOM/ROP

Date _____ Approved For Currency Options _____
                          BOM/ROP

Date _____ Approved Init. Rate Options _____
                          BOM/ROP

Date _____ Approved _____
                          Registered Options Principal

Special Options Agreement

Within 15 days after the approval of an account for options trading, a customer must sign and return to the member a "special options agreement" in which the customer agrees to abide by exchange and OCC rules (see "position" and "exercise limits.")

Statement of Account

A member must send any customer a statement of account at least quarterly if the account had a money or security position in the preceding quarter, and at least monthly to all accounts with an entry in the preceding month. Customer statements must include a notice recommending the customer notify the firm of any material changes in investment objectives or financial situation and, *if margin account*, must also show:

- market value of each option and security position
- total market value of all securities in the account
- margin equity
- total annual commissions derived from options transactions

Note: If aggregate commissions paid are not set forth on the account statement, there must be a statement to the effect that information with respect to commissions and other charges incurred in connection with the execution of option transactions has been included in confirmations of these transactions previously furnished to the customer, and that a summary of this information will be made available to the customer promptly upon request.

Records

All documents discussed above, plus any options confirmations, must be maintained for a minimum of three years. A branch office must also retain its own copies of such documents for the most recent six months.

Approval of Accounts

Prior to any transactions a new customer options account must be approved by a registered options principal who is also an officer or partner of the member. Every member must also qualify each branch office manager as an ROP. In addition, every member must designate a Senior Registered Options Principal (SROP) to supervise all customer accounts. The SROP must be either a general partner or executive officer of the member. Also, each member must also have a Compliance Registered Options Principal (CROP), who is responsible for implementation and enforcement of compliance policies.

Discretionary Accounts

The customer must first authorize discretion in writing and the account must be approved in writing by an ROP officer or partner. Every order entered must be identified as "discretionary" and approved on the day of entry (not necessarily *prior to* entry) by an ROP. The account is then to be subject to frequent supervisory reviews. The member must keep records of all customer discretionary transactions, including customer name, time and date of execution, premiums, and number of transactions involved.

Judgment as to *time and price only* is not considered discretion and may be orally delegated by the customer to a registered representative. For example, if a client calls a registered representative and tells him to "sell my XON calls, but watch the market, maybe it will rally later today," such an order would not require discretionary authority. The client has ordered the specific options to be sold leaving only the time and price of the execution to the registered representative.

Sharing in Profits or Losses

While NYSE categorically prohibits sharing of profits and losses between a customer and a registered representative, it is permissible under CBOE rules. The member firm employer must approve such accounts in writing. The sharing agreement must be in writing and any sharing agreement must be proportional (not necessarily equal) to each party's equity. Naturally, where firms belong to both CBOE and NYSE, the more restrictive NYSE rule applies.

Suitability

Besides the new account data specified above, every registered representative must have "reasonable grounds" for every recommendation made to a customer. In the case of a recommendation involving either an uncovered call or any put, the customer must be "reasonably expected" to be capable of evaluating the risks involved.

A prudent maximum of 15% to 20% of the customer's investible assets may be committed to an options buying program.

Position Limits and Exercise Limits

Effective March 1985 position and exercise limits for all options were expanded in accordance with a "three tiered" increase approved by the Securities and Exchange Commission. The limits are:

1. 8,000 contracts on the same side of the market for those options whose underlying stock meets either of the following tests:

   - Trading volume of at least 30,000,000 shares during the most recent six-month trading period and a minimum of 120,000,000 shares outstanding; *or*
   - Had trading volume of at least 40,000,000 shares in the most recent six-month trading period without regard to the total number of shares outstanding.

2. 5,500 contracts on the same side of the market for those options whose underlying stock meets *either* of the following tests:

   - Trading volume of at least 15,000,000 shares during the most recent six-month trading period and a minimum of 40,000,000 shares outstanding; *or*
   - Had trading volume of 20,000,000 shares during the most recent six-month trading period without regard to the number of shares outstanding.

3. 3,000 contract on the same side of the market for all other options.

The exchanges will review the volume and outstanding share information of all underlying stocks every six months to determine which limit applies. Note: "Acting in concert" may include an investment advisor or a registered representative with discretionary powers over customer accounts, as well as those banding together to exert manipulative pressures.

No investor or group of investors "acting in concert" may have a position in excess of the permitted amount on the same side of the market.

The "bull" side of the market would be long calls and short puts; the "bear" side; long puts and short calls. Thus, no combination of either of those "bull" or "bear" positions can exceed the permitted amount.

	EK Stock
Bull	Bear
Long calls	Long puts
Short puts	Short calls

Any combination on either side of the line may equal but not exceed the permitted amount.

Advertising and Sales Literature

All options advertising of a member firm must first receive the approval of the CROP and must be submitted to the exchange at least ten days prior to first use. Any form of media, including radio, TV, and telephone recordings, constitutes "advertising." Copies must be retained by the firm for at least three years.

In general, advertising and sales literature may not contain:

- untrue or misleading statements
- omissions of material fact
- promises of specific results
- illegible disclaimers or hedge clauses
- exaggerated statements; for example, "All of our clients made fortunes last year."
- overpromissory statements, for example, "You can't lose if you follow our system."
- flamboyant statements, for example, "We can't do anything wrong."

In short, advertising and sales literature should meet high standards of good taste and truthfulness.

INDEX OPTIONS

Exchange-traded options on stock indexes (index options) are based on the same principles as listed stock options and may be used for similar purposes. The main difference from an investment standpoint is that index options are designed to permit investors to profit from, or to protect against, general price movements in the stock market rather than in individual stocks.

The stock index is a method of reflecting in a single number the market values of many different stocks. Stock indexes are compiled and published by various sources, including securities exchanges. An index may be designed to be representative of the stock market as a whole, or a broad market sector (e.g., industrials), or of a particular industry (e.g., computers). An index may be based on the prices of all the stocks or only a sample of the stocks in the universe it is intended to represent.

A stock index, like the cost of living index, is ordinarily expressed in relation to a "base" established when the index was originated. The base may be adjusted from time to time to reflect such events as capitalization changes in component stocks or to maintain continuity when stocks are added to or dropped from the index group. The adjustments are generally designed to ensure that the index level will change only as a result of price changes resulting from trading.

Different stock indexes are calculated in different ways. One method is to "value weight" the index. That is, in calculating the index level, the market price of each component stock is multiplied by the number of shares outstanding. Value weighting is thus also called "capitalization weighting." Because of this method of calculation, changes in the stock prices of large corporations will generally have a greater influence on the level of the index than price changes of small corporations.

Another popular method to calculate a stock index is to simply add up the prices of the stocks in the index and divide by the number of stocks, disregarding number of shares outstanding. Still another method measures daily percentage movements of stock prices by averaging the percentage price changes of all stocks included in the index.

Like other options listed on U.S. securities exchanges, all index options are issued by the Options Clearing Corporation (OCC). As of the date of this course, index options are traded or approved for trading on the American Stock Exchange, the Chicago Board Options Exchange, the NASD, the Pacific Stock Exchange, and the Philadelphia Stock Exchange. As stated earlier, index options are traded in basically the same manner as stock options. However, there is a substantial difference in the way exercises are settled.

When an index option is exercised, the exercise is settled by a payment of cash, not by the delivery of stock or some other security. The assigned writer is obligated to pay the exercising holder cash in an amount equal to the difference (expressed in dollars) between the closing level of the underlying index on the exercise date and the exercise price of the option, multiplied by a specified index (multiplier).

For example, assume that a holder of a June S&P 180 call on CBOE's S&P 100 Stock Index chooses to exercise it on the date when the index closes at 185. Since the multiplier for the S&P 100 Index is 100, the assigned writer would be obligated to pay, and the exercising holder would be entitled to receive, $500 in cash ($185 − $180 = $5 × 100 = $500).

The multiplier for an index option performs a function similar to the unit of trading for a stock option. It determines the total value of each point difference between the exercise price of an in-the-money option and the current level of the underlying index. A multiplier of 100 means that a one-point difference will yield $100 of intrinsic value. The multiplier for options on a particular index is fixed by the exchange when the options are first opened for trading.

INTEREST RATE OPTIONS

The exam questions in this area deal with the details about the options contracts themselves. Because the options on the three treasury securities have several features in common, these will be addressed first. After this, features particular to each specific option will be discussed.

Options on Treasury Securities

Features in common include:

Issuer

As with all listed options (both debt and equity) the issuer is the Options Clearing Corporation (OCC).

Trading Hours

9:00 A.M.–3:00 P.M. (ET)
8:00 A.M.–2:00 P.M. (CT)

Settlement Date for Options Trades

Next business day.

Exercise Settlement Method

Securities are transferred by wire via Federal Reserve wire system. Payment is made in federal funds; that is, funds on deposit with the Federal Reserve and usable the same day.

Treasury Bill Options (AMEX)

Contract Size

$1,000,000—13-week T-bills.

Expiration Cycle

March—June—September—December. The nearest three expiration months trade at one time.

Expiration Date

The second business day prior to exercise settlement date (normally Tuesday).

Exercise Settlement Date

The day of issue of new 13-week T-bills within the expiration week (normally Thursday).

Expiration Weeks

The first week in the expiration month in which a T-bill originally issued.

Striking Prices

T-bill option striking prices are determined by an index system familiar to those who trade financial futures. With equity options, of course, holders of long calls profit when prices rise. T-bills, however, are quoted on a yield basis and, because of the inverse relationship between price and yield, decline in price as yields rise. By subtracting the bill's discount from 100%, an index can thus be developed showing price appreciation in a fashion more familiar to option traders.

For example, if 13-week bills were currently @ 8%, the index price would be 92 (100% – 8%). If yields declined to 7%, the index price rises to 93 (100% – 7%), and the holder of a call with a 92 striking price would have a more valuable asset than previously. Striking prices are added at 20-basis-point intervals, usually on either side of the current bill quote. If 13-week T-bill rates were now 8.20%, strikes would be introduced at 91.60 and 91.80 and 92.00 to bracket the index price of −91.80 (100% − 8.20%). Depending on market conditions, strike prices may also be introduced at 50-basis-point intervals.

Quotation

Quotes are in basis points, each equal to $25. A premium of .75 is thus worth $1,875 (75 × $25), and one of 2.95 is worth $7,375 (295 × $25).

In- and Out-of-the-Money Amounts

Calls are in the money when the market price of the security is higher than the striking price of the option, and out of the money when the market price is lower than the strike. Naturally, the definitions are reversed for puts.

For example, assume a current 13-week bill yields 8.5%. To determine if a May 90 call is in the money, convert the yield to an index price (100% − 8.50% = 91.50). If this index price is higher than the strike, the option is in the money by whatever that amount is, in this case 1.50 points (91.50 − 90.00 = 1.50).

If the premium for this call had been 3.85, its composition would have been 1.50 points of intrinsic value and 2.35 points of time value (or net premium). For an in-the-money option, the amount by which the premium exceeds the intrinsic value is called the "time value." If the strike price had been 92 and the premium 1.05, the option would have been out of the money, and the entire premium (2,625) would represent new premium. In other words, out-of-the-money options have no intrinsic value.

Aggregate Exercise Price

Because striking prices are derived from an annualized rate of return, the discount must be "deannualized" to reflect the maturity of the particular bill underlying the option. For example, suppose one were asked how much cash would be required to exercise a May 90 call. A 90 striking price is a 10% annualized discount. Only 1/4 of that discount is applicable to a 90-day bill, so we can find the discount first as a percentage by this formula 100% − (10% × 90/360) = 97.5%. The percentage is then applied to the 1,000,000 face value of the contract to produce an aggregate exercise price of $975,000 ($1,000,000 × 97.5%).

Treasury Note Options (AMEX and CBOE)

Contract Size

$100,000 principal amount of the specific note listed. Note: The AMEX currently lists options on ten-year notes. The CBOE currently lists options on five-year notes.

Expiration Cycle

AMEX T-note options trade on the February-May-August-November cycle, with two expirations generally trading at one time. CBOE T-note options trade on either the January-April-July-October cycle or the March-June-September-December cycle.

Expiration Date

Saturday following the third Friday of the expiration month.

Striking Prices
One-point intervals bracketing the current market price of the note, for example, 98–99–100.

Quotations
Points and 32nds of a point. Each point equals $1,000 (1% of $100,000), and each 32nd equals $31.25. A premium quoted @ 3.16 or 3-16 would thus be $3\frac{16}{32}$ or $3\frac{1}{2}$% of $100,000 = $3,500.

Treasury Bond Options (CBOE)

Contract Size
$100,000 principal amount of the specific bond listed.

Expiration Cycle
March-June-September-December, with three expiration months trading at one time.

Expiration Date
Saturday following the third Friday of the expiration month.

Striking Prices
Two-point intervals bracketing the current market price of the bond, for example, 98-100-102.

Quotations
Same as T-notes.

In- and Out-of-the-Money Amounts
Same as T-notes.

Aggregate Exercise Price
Same as T-notes.

Exercise and Settlement
Same as T-notes.

FOREIGN CURRENCY OPTIONS

In 1982 the Philadelphia Stock Exchange introduced trading in options on six currencies: deutschemarks, Swiss francs, French francs, Canadian dollars, British pounds, and Japanese yen. Recently the Chicago Board Options Exchange began trading options on these same currencies. The contract specifications for those currencies are listed on the following chart. These currencies account for the largest share of the interbank foreign exchange trading and for the bulk of the foreign currency futures contracts, which were the only two foreign exchange markets in existence prior to the introduction of foreign currency options.

U.S. Listed Foreign Currency Options		
Contract Specifications	Contract Size (units of currency)	Options Style
Options on spot currencies		
Australian dollars	50,000	American
British pound	31,250	American
Canadian dollar	50,000	American
European currency (Euro)	62,500	American
Japanese yen	6,250,000	American
Swiss franc	62,500	American

ANSWER SHEET FOR CHAPTER 9 EXAMINATION

1. Ⓐ Ⓑ Ⓒ Ⓓ
2. Ⓐ Ⓑ Ⓒ Ⓓ
3. Ⓐ Ⓑ Ⓒ Ⓓ
4. Ⓐ Ⓑ Ⓒ Ⓓ
5. Ⓐ Ⓑ Ⓒ Ⓓ
6. Ⓐ Ⓑ Ⓒ Ⓓ
7. Ⓐ Ⓑ Ⓒ Ⓓ
8. Ⓐ Ⓑ Ⓒ Ⓓ
9. Ⓐ Ⓑ Ⓒ Ⓓ
10. Ⓐ Ⓑ Ⓒ Ⓓ

11. Ⓐ Ⓑ Ⓒ Ⓓ
12. Ⓐ Ⓑ Ⓒ Ⓓ
13. Ⓐ Ⓑ Ⓒ Ⓓ
14. Ⓐ Ⓑ Ⓒ Ⓓ
15. Ⓐ Ⓑ Ⓒ Ⓓ
16. Ⓐ Ⓑ Ⓒ Ⓓ
17. Ⓐ Ⓑ Ⓒ Ⓓ
18. Ⓐ Ⓑ Ⓒ Ⓓ
19. Ⓐ Ⓑ Ⓒ Ⓓ
20. Ⓐ Ⓑ Ⓒ Ⓓ

21. Ⓐ Ⓑ Ⓒ Ⓓ
22. Ⓐ Ⓑ Ⓒ Ⓓ
23. Ⓐ Ⓑ Ⓒ Ⓓ
24. Ⓐ Ⓑ Ⓒ Ⓓ
25. Ⓐ Ⓑ Ⓒ Ⓓ
26. Ⓐ Ⓑ Ⓒ Ⓓ
27. Ⓐ Ⓑ Ⓒ Ⓓ
28. Ⓐ Ⓑ Ⓒ Ⓓ
29. Ⓐ Ⓑ Ⓒ Ⓓ
30. Ⓐ Ⓑ Ⓒ Ⓓ

31. Ⓐ Ⓑ Ⓒ Ⓓ
32. Ⓐ Ⓑ Ⓒ Ⓓ
33. Ⓐ Ⓑ Ⓒ Ⓓ
34. Ⓐ Ⓑ Ⓒ Ⓓ
35. Ⓐ Ⓑ Ⓒ Ⓓ
36. Ⓐ Ⓑ Ⓒ Ⓓ
37. Ⓐ Ⓑ Ⓒ Ⓓ
38. Ⓐ Ⓑ Ⓒ Ⓓ
39. Ⓐ Ⓑ Ⓒ Ⓓ
40. Ⓐ Ⓑ Ⓒ Ⓓ

41. Ⓐ Ⓑ Ⓒ Ⓓ
42. Ⓐ Ⓑ Ⓒ Ⓓ
43. Ⓐ Ⓑ Ⓒ Ⓓ
44. Ⓐ Ⓑ Ⓒ Ⓓ
45. Ⓐ Ⓑ Ⓒ Ⓓ
46. Ⓐ Ⓑ Ⓒ Ⓓ
47. Ⓐ Ⓑ Ⓒ Ⓓ
48. Ⓐ Ⓑ Ⓒ Ⓓ
49. Ⓐ Ⓑ Ⓒ Ⓓ
50. Ⓐ Ⓑ Ⓒ Ⓓ

CHAPTER 9 EXAMINATION

1. A customer with no existing position writes 1 XYZ July 60 put and 1 XYZ July 60 call. The position established is a:

   (A) short combination
   (B) long combination
   (C) long straddle
   (D) short straddle

2. A client purchases 100 shares of ABC at 78. On the same day he writes 1 ABC October 80 call for a premium of 4. If the option expires unexercised what is the client's profit on the 100 shares of stock?

   (A) $200
   (B) $400
   (C) $600
   (D) cannot be determined

3. The loan value of a call option held in a customer's margin account is:

   (A) -0-
   (B) 25%
   (C) 30%
   (D) the complement of the FRB's initial margin requirement for listed stocks

4. An uncovered call option writer will profit if:

   I.   the price of the underlying stock increases
   II. the price of the underlying stock decreases
   III. the option expires
   IV. the option is exercised

   (A) I and III only
   (B) II and IV only
   (C) II and III only
   (D) I and IV only

5. At the time its underlying stock is trading at 48 an investor buys a listed call option with a $50 striking price for a $300 premium. At what minimum price must that stock trade for this person to recover his investment? (Ignore commissions, transfer taxes, and the ability to sell this option itself for a greater premium.)

   (A) $45
   (B) $48
   (C) $51
   (D) $53

6. The price an investor pays for a listed option is called the:

   (A) striking price
   (B) spread
   (C) premium
   (D) exercise price

7. The expiration date of a listed option is:

   (A) the last day of the expiration month
   (B) the third Saturday of the expiration month
   (C) the Saturday following the third Friday of the expiration month
   (D) the third Friday of the expiration month

Questions 8–10 are based on the following information: In June a customer bought 100 shares of Safeway at $35. In November he then bought a listed Safeway put option with a $35 strike price and a July expiration for a $600 premium.

8. If the option expires without being exercised, how is the premium expense treated by that investor?

   (A) as a $600 capital loss
   (B) as a $600 capital gain
   (C) $600 is added to the investor's acquisition cost for the stock
   (D) $600 is held in abeyance until the stock is eventually sold

9. If the investor sells the stock at $45 in July 2007, what is his resulting tax liability for that transaction?

   (A) no liability established until the offsetting option position is sold or exercised
   (B) a $400 gain
   (C) a $1,000 gain
   (D) a $400 capital loss

10. If in April this customer exercises the put option and uses his stock to satisfy the obligation, what is the resulting tax consequence?

   (A) a $600 capital loss
   (B) neither profit nor loss on this transaction
   (C) cannot be determined without knowledge of Safeway's current market price at the time of exercise
   (D) defined as a "wash sale" and may not be included in the investor's tax considerations for the year

11. An investor buys one RFQ October 80 put and sells one RFQ October 70 put. This position is a:

   (A) calendar spread
   (B) money spread
   (C) straddle
   (D) combination

12. An investor buys one TNT June 40 call for $1,000 and sells one TNT March 40 call for $600. Later, the June call is closed out for $1,200 and the March call for $900. The net result is a:

   (A) $100 loss
   (B) $100 profit
   (C) $200 loss
   (D) $200 profit

13. A call option is in the money when the market price of the underlying security is:

   (A) lower than the striking price of the option
   (B) the same as the striking price of the option
   (C) higher than the striking price of the option
   (D) higher than the striking price plus the premium

Questions 14–15 refer to the following information: A trader buys 1 XYZ September 50 call @ 7 and sells 1 XYZ September 60 call @ 3. At that time, XYZ stock is @ 55, and the investor has no stock position.

14. The customer breaks even when XYZ is at:

   (A) 54
   (B) 55
   (C) 57
   (D) 60

15. The maximum possible profit is:

    (A) $500
    (B) $600
    (C) $1,000
    (D) unlimited

16. To profit from an expected market decline, an investor with a cash account only could:

    I. sell short
    II. write a naked call
    III. buy a put
    IV. write a "covered" put

        (A) I and IV only
        (B) III only
        (C) III and IV only
        (D) I, II, III, and IV

17. In comparing the premium cost of a LEAPS option with the premium cost for a traditional option on the same security with the same strike price, it can be generally stated that:

    (A) the premium will be approximately the same
    (B) the LEAPS option premium will be greater than the traditional option premium
    (C) the premium for the traditional option will be greater than the LEAPS option premium
    (D) LEAPS premiums do not consider time value

18. In comparing the premium cost of a LEAP option with the premium cost for a traditional option on the same index with the same strike price it can be generally stated that:

    (A) the premiums will be approximately the same
    (B) the LEAP premium will be greater than the traditional options premium
    (C) the premium for the traditional option will be greater than the LEAP option premium
    (D) LEAP premiums are determined by the Options Clearing Corporation

19. An option that permits the holder to exercise the contract only at expiration is referred to as:

    (A) European style
    (B) American style
    (C) Nordic style
    (D) Asian style

20. An investor buys 1 ABC Nov. 65 call @ 3 and 1 ABC Nov. 65 put @ 2. At expiration, ABC is trading at 72. The put expires and the call is closed out at its intrinsic value. What is the resulting profit?

    (A) $200
    (B) $300
    (C) $500
    (D) $700

21. A customer is long spot Canadian dollars @ .7400. If she buys 1 XCD July 74 put @ .35, at what price does she break even?

    (A) .4900
    (B) .7365
    (C) .7400
    (D) .7435

22. Which of the following would affect the amount of premium paid for a listed option contract?

    I.   the volatility of the underlying stock
    II. the market price of the underlying stock
    III. the time remaining until the option expires

    (A) I only
    (B) II only
    (C) I and II only
    (D) I, II, and III

23. In early September a customer buys 100 shares of ABC stock for $83 per share and simultaneously writes 1 ABC March 90 call for $4 per share. The customer will break even when ABC stock is at:

    (A) $94
    (B) $87
    (C) $86
    (D) $79

24. Which of the following options positions is characteristic of a short straddle?

    (A) long one put and short one call
    (B) long one call and short one put
    (C) short one put and short one call
    (D) long one call and long one put

25. All of the following statements are true of *exchange* traded options EXCEPT:

    (A) They are adjusted for stock dividends.
    (B) They are adjusted for stock splits.
    (C) They are adjusted for cash dividends.
    (D) They are adjusted for reverse splits.

26. If a writer sells a covered call option he may have to:

    (A) buy the underlying stock if the call is exercised
    (B) deposit margin into his account to serve as collateral
    (C) purchase a put option to hedge against an unlimited loss potential
    (D) sell a security he already owns

27. Under no circumstances may a customer or group of customers acting in concert hold or write contracts in a class of listed options to exceed how many contracts?

    (A) 4,000
    (B) 5,000
    (C) 7,000
    (D) 8,000

28. How are *long* listed call options valued in a margin account?

    (A) at the same market price as the underlying stock
    (B) at the striking price of the option plus the amount of difference in the money, less the difference out of the money
    (C) at the current premium value trading on the exchange
    (D) listed call options have no value for margin account purposes

29. A customer buys 100 shares of XYZ stock at $40 per share and sells a listed July call at 45 for a $2 premium. As a result his maximum loss potential is:

    (A) $3,800
    (B) $4,000
    (C) $4,200
    (D) $4,500

30. Which of these options positions by an investor is indicative of the same class of option?

    (A) long one XYZ July 70 put and one XYZ July 70 call
    (B) long one PDQ Oct. 20 call and one PDQ Jan. 30 call
    (C) short one FRB Feb. 60 put and one TUG Feb. 60 put
    (D) short one CBO June 40 call and one PSE June 20 call

31. A member firm may allocate option assignment notices to customers using which of the following methods?

    I.   random selection basis
    II. a first in, first out basis
    III. giving preference to the largest writer
    IV. any equitable basis

    (A) I and II only
    (B) I, II, and IV only
    (C) II, III, and IV only
    (D) II and IV only

32. An investor held one XYZ July 30 listed call option when the underlying stock split 2 for 1. As a result, his position on the Option Clearing Corporation's record would appear:

    (A) long one XYZ July 30 call
    (B) long one XYZ July 30 call and short one XYZ July 30 call
    (C) long two XYZ July 30 calls
    (D) long two XYZ July 15 calls

33. If a customer bought a stock at $50 and wrote a covered call option for an $8 premium, to what price can that stock decline for that person to break even?

    (A) $42
    (B) $50
    (C) $58
    (D) $60

34. In December a customer bought 100 shares of a listed stock at $27 and soon after sold a covered call on that security with a $30 strike price for a three-point premium. Assuming the option expires unexercised two months later, what will be his investment result?

    (A) realized ordinary income of $300
    (B) a $300 capital gain
    (C) a $600 capital gain
    (D) gain or loss cannot be determined until the customer sells the stock

35. The execution of which of the following would create a "spread"?

    I.   buy one EK October 50 call
    II. sell one EK October 50 put
    III. sell one EK October 60 call
    IV. buy one EK October 50 put

    (A) I and II only
    (B) I and III only
    (C) III and IV only
    (D) I and IV only

36. On October 25 a customer buys five listed XYZ Corp. July 50 calls and pays a $3 premium for each call. The current market price of XYZ Corp. is $48 per share. How much money will the customer have to deposit?

    (A) $500
    (B) $1,000
    (C) $1,500
    (D) $2,000

37. What would the breakeven point be for the buyer of the calls in question 36 (disregarding commissions)?

    (A) $48
    (B) $45
    (C) $53
    (D) $58

38. The holder of a listed call option is entitled to a dividend payable on the underlying stock:

    (A) always
    (B) only if he submits an exercise notice to OCC *prior* to the ex-dividend date
    (C) only if he submits an exercise notice to OCC *after* the ex-dividend date
    (D) never

39. When does a call option provide the most value for its holder?

    (A) when the underlying stock is extremely volatile
    (B) in the month prior to its expiration date
    (C) when there is a large open interest in that class of options
    (D) when the underlying stock price is rising

40. In mid-September, an option writer sold a CBS February 50 covered call at 6. It subsequently expired without being exercised. How is the premium treated?

    (A) The writer's acquisition cost of the underlying stock is reduced by $600.
    (B) The $600 premium is a capital gain.
    (C) The $600 premium constitutes ordinary income.
    (D) The $600 premium is rolled over into another CBS call with the next longest expiration date.

41. As far as prices of options are concerned:

    (A) premiums on listed stocks are usually greater than on unlisted stocks
    (B) premiums on higher-priced stocks are usually greater than on lower-priced stocks
    (C) premiums on well-known companies are usually larger than on less well-known companies
    (D) premiums on volatile stocks are usually larger than on less volatile stocks

42. With regard to listed options, the Options Clearing Corporation sets all of the following EXCEPT:

    (A) premium amount
    (B) contract size
    (C) striking price
    (D) expiration

43. A customer buys 100 shares of stock and then decides to write a listed call option involving that security. How would the registered representative identify the customer's intentions on that option order ticket?

    (A) sell uncovered in an opening transaction
    (B) sell covered in an opening transaction
    (C) sell uncovered in a closing transaction
    (D) sell covered in a closing transaction

44. Assume you owned ten listed call option contracts with a $60 exercise price at the time the issuer of the underlying stock split its common stock 3 for 2. How would your holdings be reflected on the records of the Options Clearing Corporation on the day the stock began trading ex-dividend?

    (A) 10 contracts with a $90 exercise price
    (B) 10 contracts with a $40 exercise price
    (C) 15 contracts with a $40 exercise price
    (D) 15 contracts with a $60 exercise price

45. After the ex-dividend date, each call option contract in question 44 would be equal to how many shares of that stock?

    (A) 50
    (B) 75
    (C) 100
    (D) 150

46. To maintain a listed options account at a member firm, customers must sign an options agreement and return it to the member:

    (A) within 15 days after the account is approved for options trading
    (B) within 30 days after the account is approved for options trading
    (C) within 60 days after the account is approved for options trading
    (D) at or prior to the time the account is approved for options trading

47. When an index option is exercised, settlement is made by:

    (A) delivery of the underlying securities
    (B) delivery of a futures contract
    (C) cash
    (D) any of the above

48. Options on foreign currencies are traded on the Philadelphia Stock Exchange. Which of the following currencies are represented by these contracts?

    I.   Japanese yen
    II. British pounds
    III. Canadian dollars
    IV. Swiss francs

    (A) II and III only
    (B) I and IV only
    (C) I, II, and IV only
    (D) I, II, III, and IV

49. An investor buys $100M U.S. treasury bonds at 101-00 and sells one U.S. treasury bond February 100 call on the same security for a premium of 3-24. If the option is exercised, what will be the economic result?

    (A) profit of $2,750
    (B) loss of $1,000
    (C) profit of $3,750
    (D) loss of $3,240

50. The premium for a deutschemark 65 call increases from 0.95 to 1.55. How much profit does a holder make (DM contract = 62,500)?

    (A) $155
    (B) $375
    (C) $1,550
    (D) $3,750

CHAPTER 9 EXAMINATION ANSWERS

1. **D** A straddle consists of a put and a call on the same stock with the same strike price and the same expiration month. As this customer wrote both a put and a call this is a short straddle.

2. **D** The client has not sold the stock; therefore, we cannot determine any profit or loss on that position. He does have a $400 profit on the expired option.

3. **A** Options do not have loan value, except long-term LEAPS.

4. **C** The option writer hopes that the option will never be exercised (it will expire) or that the price of the underlying stock decreases, which would make exercise unlikely.

5. **D** We get our breakeven price on a call option by adding the premium to the striking price. Had this been a put, we would get our breakeven price by subtracting the premium from the striking price.

6. **C** By definition. The premium.

7. **C** By definition. Watch out for answers like choice (B).

8. **A** The investor lost the amount he paid in premium, hence he has a loss by that amount ($600).

9. **C** The investor realized a $1,000 gain on the stock.

10. **A** Since the striking price is the same as the amount paid for the stock, the investor loses the premium he paid for the option, which in this case is $600.

11. **B** The use of different striking prices in a spread position may be called a "money," "vertical," or "price" spread.

12. **A** The long position (June 40) was bought at $1,000 and sold at $1,200 for a $200 profit. However, the short March 40 call was sold at $600 and repurchased for $900, a $300 loss. In other words, while the spreader had expected the spread to widen, in fact it narrowed—from $400 to $300 on closing—showing a $100 overall loss.

13. **C** Note that the amount of premium paid or received is not relevant, nor is the fact that one is either a long or short option. For example, if XYZ is at 55, an XYZ June 50 call is 5 points in the money even though a seller might have to pay (and a writer receive) $800 in premiums.

14. **A** The position is a bull (money or price) spread placed at a debit. The breakeven point is found by adding the debit to the lower of the striking prices. The debit is $400 ($700 – $300), making the breakeven point 54. At that level the 50 call has an intrinsic value of $400 versus a $700 cost—a $300 loss. However, the September 60 call expires for a $300 profit, balancing the loss on the long call. At any price higher than 54, the spread will have widened to produce a profit.

15. **B** In a price or money (debit) spread, the maximum profit may be computed by subtracting the debit from the difference between the striking prices. Thus, (60 – 50) – 4=$6, or $600.

16. **B** Selling short, writing naked calls, and writing covered puts (put spreads) would all prove profitable if an investor's forecast of declining prices were correct. However, all must be done in margin accounts. Only the outright put purchase may be done in a cash account.

17. **B** As LEAPS have a longer time until expiration than traditional options, the premium for a LEAPS would usually be greater than for a similar standard option.

18. **B** LEAP options allow for a greater profit potential. As traditional options do not have the longer life, they command a greater premium.

19. **A** European-style options can only be exercised at expiration while American-style options can be exercised at any time during their life. The terms "Nordic style" and "Asian style" are not used in options trading.

20. **A** If ABC is at 72, a November 65 call has an intrinsic value of $700. A sale at that value versus a cost of $300 produces a $400 profit. From this, subtract the $200 loss on the expired put to yield an overall profit of $200.

21. **D** The put protects against a deterioration in the exchange rate of the Canadian dollar, but the cost of the put raises the breakeven point. If the spot Canadian dollar rises to .7435 (original spot price .7400 plus the put premium $.0035) the expired put premium cancels the appreciation. Above that level, the appreciation of the spot price will be profitable. If the dollar declines, on the other hand, the maximum possible loss is $.0035, the put premium.

22. **D** Logically, one must expect a greater reward for a greater risk. The option writer therefore will demand a higher premium for a stock more likely to move sharply in price than for one whose price is expected to remain fairly steady; for example, calls on growth stocks or trading favorites are typically more expensive than those on public utilities. Naturally, the market price of the stock determines whether the option is in or out of the money and whether the option will reflect any intrinsic value. Finally, the time value of an option premium is greater for a longer maturity option than a shorter one on the same stock, regardless of the implied volatility of the underlying security.

23. **D** Cost of the stock ($83) less the premium received ($4) would allow the decline to $79 in the stock before a loss would be experienced.

24. **C** The position defines a short straddle. If the client were long one put and one call it would be a long straddle.

25. **C** No adjustment is made on listed options for cash dividends.

26. **D** Writing covered means that you own the underlying security. If the call is exercised, this means you will have to sell a security owned.

27. **D** By definition (effective March 1985).

28. **D** By definition. Although options may be purchased in a margin account, they must be paid for in full as they have no loan value, unless they have a maturity of more than 9 months (LEAPS).

29. **A** Should the stock decline to zero, he would lose $4,000 on his long position, less $200 premium received.

30. **B** A class of options is a put or a call covering the same underlying security.

31. **A** Firms may use only random selection or "first in, first out" under OCC rules.

32. **D** On stock splits and distributions, the strike price is reduced proportionately and the number of shares (or contracts) is increased accordingly.

33. **A** Since he received an $8 premium, the stock can fall to $42 without his losing money (other than the transactions costs).

34. **B** His profit will be the premium received.

35. **B** Since a spread is a simultaneous long and short position in two different series in the same class of option, II and IV would also be a spread, but this is not one of the answer choices.

36. **C** Since options do not have loan value other than long-term LEAPS, they must be paid for in full. Since each option carries a $300 premium and the customer bought five contracts, he must deposit $1,500.

37. **C** We determine this by adding the premium to the striking price.

38. **B** Under the OCC rules.

39. **D** By definition. If the question had been relative to a put then the answer would have been when the underlying stock price was declining.

40. **B** Under the provisions of the tax law.

41. **D** The more volatile (wide and frequent price swings) a security, the more likely it is that an option would be exercised. Hence, a writer demands a higher premium.

42. **A** The premium is determined by the forces of supply and demand in an auction market on the exchanges.

43. **B** Clearly, this is an opening transaction. Since the writer of the call owns the stock, he is also covered.

44. **B** The number of shares represented in each contract is increased proportionately and the strike price is reduced proportionately. Each contract now represents 150 shares.

45. **D** The strike price is now 40 ($6,000/150 shares).

46. **A** As required by the rules of the various exchanges, particularly the CBOE and the AMEX.

47. **C** Exercise of an index option is settled by payment of cash.

48. **D** Options on all of these currencies are traded. In addition, trading is conducted in Euros and Australian dollars.

49. **A** The premium received is $3,750 ($3^{24}/_{32} \times \$100,000$). If the call is exercised, bonds purchased at $101,000 will be sold at $100,000, the striking price, producing a $1,000 loss. This offsets part of the premium received and results in an overall profit of $2,750 ($3,750 – $1,000).

50. **B** Premiums are quoted in cents per unit of underlying currency. This premium increased by .60 cents ($.006), so $.006 \times 62,500 = \$375$.

Securities Analysis

The Securities Exchange Act of 1934 (Section 13) requires corporations that have issued securities to the public to file financial statements with the commission annually. These statements are furnished to the stockholder and are published shortly after the end of the business year. A corporation may use any predetermined 12-month period and, therefore, may have its year end in any given month. A reporting year ending in December is called a "calendar year," while one ending in any other month is referred to as a "fiscal year."

A basic knowledge of the components of corporate financial statements is required for all professionals in the investment industry. Our study of this topic will be confined to the general information needed. A more detailed study would be necessary for candidates pursuing careers in securities analysis, corporate finance, or similar areas.

FINANCIAL STATEMENTS

Corporations issue two types of financial statements: (1) the balance sheet and (2) the income and retained earnings statement.

The balance sheet shows the condition of a corporation at a given point in time. Thus, the balance sheet of Acme Furniture Manufacturing Corp., as of December 31, 2006, would show the assets—things of value—held by that corporation as of that date. These assets would be shown on the left side of the balance sheet. On the right side of the balance sheet would be the liabilities—amounts to be paid—of that corporation. As the assets should exceed the liabilities, the right side will also show the stockholder's equity (net worth) of the corporation. This is the amount by which the assets exceed the liabilities and represents the value of the owners' (stockholders') interest.

The left side is equal in value to the right side, hence the name, and the overall picture gives us the balance sheet equation: total assets equal total liabilities plus stockholder's equity.

BALANCE SHEET	
TOTAL ASSETS	TOTAL LIABILITIES
	STOCKHOLDER'S EQUITY

The Balance Sheet

Assets

Corporate assets on the balance sheet are divided into three categories: current assets, fixed assets, and intangible assets.

Current Assets These are assets that can be converted to cash in one year or less. Among such items would be cash itself. Also considered current are marketable securities. In our industry a sale of securities in the usual manner, regular way, is settled in three business days. For sales of U.S. government securities made regular the settlement would be much sooner, only one business day. As this certainly meets the one-year-or-less test, marketable securities are current assets. Due to the rapidity with which these securities can be sold, they are also considered to be a cash equivalent. So, should the term "cash and equivalents" arise, it refers to the actual cash and marketable securities shown as assets on the balance sheet.

Accounts Receivable

These are amounts due from clients who have purchased the corporation's products. We certainly hope that they will pay their bills within a year, so accounts receivable are a current asset. Our business experience may have taught us that a certain percentage of these receivables are never paid for any of a number of reasons (death, bankruptcy, etc.). We, therefore, may reduce the receivables by an amount called "reserve for doubtful accounts."

Inventories

The inventories of a corporation include finished goods that are ready for sale as well as work in progress and materials on hand that will be used to produce the company's products. As a rule of thumb, a manufacturing corporation should turn over its inventory between five and six times each year. This certainly qualifies inventories as a current asset that can be converted to cash in one year or less.

Inventories are usually the largest current asset of a manufacturing company. They are, however, subject to questions should cash be needed rapidly to meet an emergency. Perhaps they are seasonal in nature and could not be sold or would have to be sold at a sacrifice price that would not reflect their true value. For that reason we will later test the company's balance sheet by removing the inventory from the current assets. The result will be called quick assets (current assets minus inventory).

Let us begin to construct the balance sheet of our hypothetical company, Acme Furniture Manufacturing Corporation.

ASSETS		LIABILITIES
Current Assets		Current Liabilities
Cash	$ 750,000	
Marketable Securities (at cost)	2,500,000	
Accounts Receivable (less reserve for doubtful accounts)	1,750,000	Long-Term Liabilities
Inventories	3,000,000	
Total Current Assets:	$8,000,000	

ASSETS (continued)	LIABILITIES (continued)
Fixed Assets	Stockholder's Equity (Net Worth)
Intangible Assets	

Fixed Assets These are assets that are held for use or investment and not for sale over the near term. The usual fixed assets are land, buildings, machinery, furniture, and fixtures. Fixed assets, other than land, are amortized over their lifetime.

Amortization is simply the written-down value of the capital expenditure for the asset. There are three types of amortization:

- Depreciation: The amount written off due to the expected wearing out of buildings, machinery, furniture, and fixtures. The depreciation taken each year is a pretax deduction on the corporation's income statement that results in a meaningful tax savings.
- Depletion: The loss arising from the wasting away of a natural resource such as a coal mine or oil well. Depletion is also a tax deduction for the corporation.
- Obsolescence: A form of amortization that is caused by changes in technology. When someone builds a better mousetrap, ours may become obsolete.

Intangible Assets These are assets to which a true value cannot be assigned. They may well have great worth and may produce income for the corporation, but the value is not determinable. For example, trademarks are intangible assets. Such trademarks as "Coke" or "Kleenex" are certainly valuable tools for product sales, but their dollar value would be impossible to determine. We therefore label them as "intangibles." Other intangibles would be copyrights, good will, and patents.

Let's add fixed assets and intangible assets to our balance sheet:

ASSETS		LIABILITIES
Current Assets		Current Liabilities
Cash	$ 750,000	
Marketable Securities (at cost)	2,500,000	
Accounts Receivable (less reserve for doubtful accounts)	1,750,000	
Inventories	3,000,000	Long-Term Liabilities
Total Current Assets	$8,000,000	
Fixed Assets		
Land	$1,250,000	
Buildings	2,450,000	
Machinery	800,000	
Furniture/Fixtures	200,000	
Less: Accumulated Depreciation	1,200,000	STOCKHOLDER'S EQUITY (Net Worth)
Net Fixed Assets	$3,500,000	
Intangible Assets		
Patents and Trademarks	$ 100,000	
Total Assets	$11,600,000	

We have now completed the asset side of our balance sheet. Let's move over to the right-hand side.

Liabilities

Current Liabilities These include all items that will be due for payment in one year or less. Examples are wages, loan payments, business expenses, accounts payable to suppliers, taxes, debt securities due within the year, and interest on all debt payable in the year. Please note that interest is an obligation of a corporation and is a liability. Failure to pay can cause the holders of the debt instruments to force liquidation. Dividends on stock, however, are not required to be paid. They represent a reward to stockholders, not an obligation. They become a current liability only from the time they are declared by the corporation until the time they are actually paid.

Long-Term Liabilities These consist of the outstanding bonds issued by the corporation, not including, of course, those due in one year or less, which would be current liabilities.

Another look at our balance sheet with current and long-term liabilities added:

ASSETS		LIABILITIES	
Current Assets		Current Liabilities	
Cash	$ 750,000	Accounts Payable	$2,500,000
Marketable Securities		Taxes Payable	280,000
(at cost)	2,500,000	Accrued Expenses	500,000
Accounts Receivable		Interest Payable	220,000
(less reserve for doubtful accounts)	1,750,000	Total Current Liabilities	$3,500,000
Inventories	3,000,000		
Total Current Assets	$8,000,000	Long-Term Liabilities	
Fixed Assets		8% Mortgage Bonds due 2019	$1,000,000
		7% Debentures due 2012	1,000,000
Land	$1,250,000	Total Long-Term Liabilities	$2,000,000
Buildings	2,450,000		
Machinery	800,000	Total Liabilities	$5,500,000
Furniture/Fixtures	200,000		
Less: Accumulated Depreciation	1,200,000	STOCKHOLDER'S EQUITY	
Net Fixed Assets	$3,500,000	(Net Worth)	
Intangible Assets			
Patents and Trademarks	$ 100,000		
Total Assets	$11,600,000		

Stockholder's Equity

We have detailed the assets and liabilities of our corporation. The amount by which the assets exceed the liabilities is the stockholder's equity (net worth). You could put your personal financial situation to this same test. Add up your assets (house, car, bank account, securities, furniture, etc.) and subtract your liabilities (mortgage on the house, car loan, credit card balances, etc.) and the difference is what you are worth.

Corporations may have a number of types of stock outstanding, but let us assume that ours has preferred stock and common stock.

The preferred stock is carried on the balance sheet at stated (par) value. Thus, 100,000 shares of $10 par preferred would show as $1,000,000 (100,000 shares×$10 par).

The common stock is also carried at par, so given the same number of shares and par value (100,000 shares at $10 par) the common would also be carried at $1,000,000. However, all other items listed on the balance sheet below the stated value of the common stock are considered part of the total value of that issue. There are two such items that could be listed: retained earnings and capital surplus.

Retained Earnings Also known as "earned surplus," this is the amount of money earned in our previous business history. In effect, each year we add to our balance sheet the amount of our bottom line. Should we show a profit of $150,000 from the operation, we would have added that amount to the current assets as cash. To make a compensating entry on the right side we would add $150,000 to our retained earnings. This total will change as each year's business experience is recorded.

Retained earnings are also useful in making the sheet balance when the entries being recorded would seem to indicate otherwise. For example, suppose our company issued $1,000,000 of additional long-term debentures. It would not be unusual to have those bonds priced at a premium over face value. Therefore, the $1,000,000 issue may produce $1,100,000 proceeds to the corporation. This could be caused by the interest rate on the bonds being higher than current market requirements.

Let's show the result of the bond issue on our balance sheet:

ASSETS		LIABILITIES	
Cash	+$1,100,000	Fixed Liabilities	+$1,000,000
		STOCKHOLDER'S EQUITY	
		Retained Earnings	+ $100,000

Balance has been achieved.

Should the bond sale have resulted in the corporation receiving a discount from face value we would charge the retained earnings. For example: $1,000,000 of bonds sold for proceeds of $900,000 would be reflected as follows:

ASSETS		LIABILITIES	
Cash	+$900,000	Fixed Liabilities	+$1,000,000
		STOCKHOLDER'S EQUITY	
		Retained Earnings	-$ 100,000

Balance has been achieved again.

Retained earnings are also used to attain balance when a corporation pays a stock dividend. Unlike a stock split, we must make a balance sheet adjustment when a stock dividend is paid. Suppose our corporation split its stock 2 for 1. This would result in our having 200,000 shares outstanding rather than the previous 100,000 shares. However, with a stock split we would inversely change the par value resulting in no change in the stated balance sheet value. Let's look at our balance sheet before and after the split:

- Before: 100,000 Shares Common Stock ($10 par): $1,000,000 (100,000×$10)
- After: 200,000 Shares Common Stock ($5 par): $1,000,000 (200,000×$5)

In reverse splits, the number of shares is decreased (1 for 2 split). In this case, the par value would be increased proportionately to produce the needed results.

When stock dividends are paid, the par value of the stock remains unchanged. Thus, should our corporation pay a 100% stock dividend the result would be a new total of 200,000 shares of $10 par stock, or $2,000,000 total stated value. Here again, we would use retained earnings to achieve balance by reducing them an amount equal to the increased stated value of the stock. Let's try our before and after experiment again.

Before	
100,000 Shares Common Stock ($10 Par)	$1,000,000
Retained Earnings	3,100,000
Total:	$4,100,000
After	
200,000 Shares Common Stock ($10 Par)	$2,000,000
Retained Earnings	2,100,000
Total:	$4,100,000

Capital Surplus Also known as paid-in capital, this represents the amount that a company receives for its stock in excess of par value. We have noted that the par value of a common stock may in no way reflect its value in the marketplace. Thus, a corporation may sell additional stock to the public at a price well above its par value. For example, suppose a corporation sold 100,000 shares of common stock $10 par but was paid $20 per share by the buyers. The result on our balance sheet would initially be:

Left Side
Cash=$2,000,000 (100,000 shares×$20)
Right Side
Stated Value of Common+$1,000,000 (100,000 shares×$10 Par)

Since this surely does not balance, we add a capital surplus of $1,000,000. The result is:

Left Side	
Cash=$2,000,000 (100,000 shares×$20)	
Right Side	
Stated Value of Common + $1,000,000 (100,000 shares×$10)	
Capital Surplus	$1,000,000
Total	$2,000,000

We can now complete our balance sheet by adding the stockholder's equity (net worth) section.

ACME FURNITURE MANUFACTURING CO.
BALANCE SHEET - DECEMBER 31, 2006

ASSETS		LIABILITIES	
Current Assets		**Current Liabilities**	
Cash	$ 750,000	Accounts Payable	$2,500,000
Marketable Securities		Taxes Payable	280,000
(at cost)	2,500,000	Accrued Expenses	500,000
Accounts Receivable		Interest Payable	220,000
(less reserve for doubtful accounts)	1,750,000	**Total Current Liabilities**	**$3,500,000**
Inventories	3,000,000	**Long-Term Liabilities**	
Total Current Assets	**$8,000,000**	8% Mortgage Bonds due 2019	$1,000,000
Fixed Assets		7% Debentures due 2012	1,000,000
Land	$1,250,000	**Total Long-Term Liabilities**	**$2,000,000**
Buildings	2,450,000		
Machinery	800,000	**Total Liabilities**	**$5,500,000**
Furniture/Fixtures	200,000	**STOCKHOLDER'S EQUITY**	
Less: Accumulated Depreciation	1,200,000	(Net Worth)	
Net Fixed Assets	**$3,500,000**	Preferred Stock, 8%	
Intangible Assets		cumulative ($10 par)	
Patents and Trademarks	$ 100,000	100,000 shares	$1,000,000
		Common Stock $10 par	
		(authorized 250,000 shares;	
		issued and outstanding	
		100,000 shares)	$1,000,000
		Retained Earnings (earned surplus)	3,100,000
		Capital Surplus (paid-in capital)	1,000,000
		Total Stockholder's Equity	**$6,100,000**
Total Assets	**$11,600,000**	**Total Liabilities & Stockholder's Equity**	**$11,600,000**

Financial Tests Using the Balance Sheet

Using our completed balance sheet we can now put the corporation to some tests to see if it shows sufficient strength to warrant investment consideration.

Net Working Capital

This is the amount by which the current assets exceed the current liabilities. It tells us the amount in dollars the corporation would have to work with in the likely event that all items that could be converted to cash in one year (current assets) were in fact so converted, and that all items to be paid in one year (current liabilities) were, in fact, paid. Our formula would be:

Net Working Capital=Current Assets – Current Liabilities

Using our balance sheet, the net working capital of Acme is $4,500,000: ($8,000,000 current assets – $3,500,000 (current liabilities).

Current Ratio

This shows the ratio of the current assets to the current liabilities. As in all computations of ratios, the solution is gained by dividing. For example, the ratio of A to B is determined by dividing A by B. The answer is expressed as *x* to 1. A ratio might be 3.7 to 1 or .85 to 1 or 9 to 1, and so on. For a manufacturing company, the standard states that the current ratio should be at least 2 to 1. The formula:

$$\text{Current Ratio} = \text{Current Assets} \div \text{Current Liabilities}$$

Our current ratio is 2.29 to 1: $8,000,000 (current assets) ÷ $3,500,000 (current liabilities). It is safely above the minimum standard.

Quick Assets

These take into consideration our earlier statement that, although inventories are a large current asset, they may not be possible to liquidate quickly in the event of an emergency. We, therefore, do not consider them in determining this formula:

$$\text{Quick Assets} = \text{Current Assets} - \text{Inventories}$$

Our quick assets total $5,000,000: $8,000,000 (current assets) – $3,000,000 (inventories).

Net Quick Assets

These are the same as net working capital except that in this calculation we eliminate the inventory.

Our net quick assets are $1,500,000: $8,000,000 (current assets) – $3,000,000 (inventories – $3,500,000 (current liabilities).

Quick Assets Ratio

This is also called the "acid test ratio." As with other ratios, we know that our answer will result from division. This ratio is similar to the current ratio but again we eliminate the inventory. The formula:

$$\text{Quick Assets Ratio (Acid Test Ratio)} = (\text{Current Assets} - \text{Inventories}) \div \text{Current Liabilities}$$

Our result shows a ratio of 1.43 to 1: $8,000,000 (current assets) – $3,000,000 (inventories) ÷ $3,500,000 (current liabilities).

This result, 1.43 to 1, is again safely above the minimum quick assets ratio for manufacturing companies, which is set at 1 to 1.

Net Tangible Assets Value per Share This is commonly called "book value." It tells us how many dollars of net tangible assets stand behind each of the outstanding shares of a corporation's common stock. It does not show the true value of the shares or the probable value in the event of liquidation but just the amount of muscle in the form of asset dollars that are at work for each share. The formula:

$$\text{Book Value} = (\text{Balance Sheet Value of Common} - \text{Intangible Assets}) \div \text{Number of Issued and Outstanding Common Shares}$$

Be careful when determining the balance sheet value of the common not to overlook the retained earnings and capital surplus should they be shown. They are, as stated earlier, a part of a common stockholder's equity. Thus, our balance sheet value of common is

$5,100,000: $1,000,000 (stated value) + $3,100,000 (retained earnings) + $1,000,000 (capital surplus).

Our book value is $50 per share: $5,100,000 (balance sheet value of common) – $100,000 (intangible assets) ÷ 100,000 (shares of common stock issued and outstanding).

Capitalization Ratios These are designed to show the ratio of one part of the company's capitalization to the total capitalization. Note: Capitalization of a corporation includes the long-term debt, the preferred stock, and the common stock values. Short-term debt securities, those due within one year, are not included in this calculation. From our balance sheet we can see that our total capitalization is $8,100,000. Broken down it consists of:

- $2,000,000 long-term debt
- $1,000,000 preferred stock
- $5,100,000 common stock (includes retained earnings and capital surplus)

To compute the capitalization ratio for any part of the corporation's capitalization, we simply divide its value by the total value (a ratio, remember). For example:

- Capitalization Ratio for Long-Term Debt = .25 to 1 (25%)
  $2,000,000 (long-term debt) ÷ $8,100,000 (total capitalization)
- Capitalization Ratio for Preferred Stock = .12 to 1 (12%)
  $1,000,000 (preferred stock value) ÷ $8,100,000 (total capitalization)
- Capitalization Ratio for Common Stock = .63 to 1 (63%)
  $5,100,000 (common stock value) ÷ $8,100,000 (total capitalization)

Why would one be interested in these capitalization ratios? They might be of aid in determining if the corporation has the type of capitalization suitable to a particular investor's needs.

A "conservative capitalization" is one with little or no debt. As interest on debt is an obligation of a corporation, one with only a small amount could ride out a bad earnings period more comfortably. Dividends on stock, both common and preferred, could be cut or eliminated until the earnings picture improved. With heavy debt obligations, the corporation would face great problems in these lean periods.

On the other hand, a "leveraged capitalization" has a larger than usual amount of debt. The investor in this type of company feels that in periods of rising earnings, the interest on the debt does not increase, allowing the increased earnings to reflect more dramatically on the proportionately smaller amount of common stock. The danger, of course, is that in poor earnings periods the interest on the debt must be paid and could cause a sharp drop in the earnings per share of common stock.

Income and Retained Earnings Statement

We can put Acme Furniture Manufacturing to no further financial tests without first looking at its statement of income and retained earnings. Then we will describe and apply some additional formulas.

The income and retained earnings statement shows the result of a period of operation for the corporation. Its basic components are the amounts received by the corporation from sales of goods, investments, and other sources; the amount paid out for expenses such as sales and administrative costs, taxes, interest, depreciation, dividends, and so on; and the amount retained at the end of the period covered—the well-known "bottom line." Most publicly held companies report this information on both a quarterly and annual basis, and a careful study of changes can be a valuable tool for the investment professional.

ACME FURNITURE MANUFACTURING CO.
STATEMENT OF INCOME AND RETAINED EARNINGS
YEAR ENDED DECEMBER 31, 2006

Net Sales		$20,000,000
Cost of Sales (Expenses)		
Labor & Materials	$6,500,000	
Selling & Administrative Costs	4,500,000	
Manufacturing Costs	3,000,000	
Depreciation	780,000	
Interest on Debt	220,000	$15,000,000
Operating Income		$ 5,000,000
Investment Income		400,000
Total Income		$ 5,400,000
– Federal Income Tax		2,000,000
Net Income		3,400,000
– Preferred Dividend ($.80 per share)		80,000
Net Earnings		3,320,000
– Common Dividend ($10.00 per share)		1,000,000
Retained Earnings (Year)		2,320,000
Retained Earnings (Prior Years)		780,000
Total Retained Earnings (as of 12/31/06)		$ 3,100,000

Net sales represent the gross sales less any items returned or any discounts granted. We then subtract the cost of sales, or expenses, required to produce those sales. The resulting figure is called operating income, which is the amount left from our sales after expenses. It shows the results of the operation of the business for the time period covered.

Net Sales	$20,000,000
Less: Expenses	15,000,000
Operating Income	$ 5,000,000

We would now add any other income received during the period to give us total income. On our sample statement we have used only investment income, which represents interest or dividends on securities or bank accounts owned by the corporation. There are other items called "nonrecurring," or "extraordinary," which we will address at a later point.

Operating Income	$5,000,000
Plus: Investment Income	400,000
Total Income	$5,400,000

Next, we must deduct federal taxes (and local taxes should they apply). We have used an arbitrary amount of $2,000,000, which is about 37% of total income. After deduction of taxes we arrive at net income.

Total Income	$5,400,000
Less: Federal Income Tax	2,000,000
Net Income	$3,400,000

Net income is the income to the corporation after all items required to be paid have been paid. What remains is for the corporation to reward stockholders through dividend payments and to add to their retained earnings for further use in corporate affairs. The preferred dividend is paid first (that is one of the reasons it is called "preferred"). After deducting it, we arrive at net earnings.

Net Income	$3,400,000
Less: Preferred Dividend	80,000
Net Earnings	$3,320,000

Our final item is the payment of a dividend to our common stockholders if we so choose. As we had a good year, let's pay them each $10.00 per share. After that payment what remains is retained earnings for the year.

Net Earnings	$3,320,000
Less: Common Dividend	1,000,000
Retained Earnings	$2,320,000

The retained earnings for the year are added to those from previous years to arrive at total retained earnings. Please note that we showed a fine profit for the year. In some years we may lose money but the corporation might elect to pay dividends to their shareholders from previous years' retained earnings.

Retained Earnings (Year)	$2,320,000
Plus: Retained Earnings (Prior Years)	780,000
Total Retained Earnings	$3,100,000

Now that we have our income statement put together, let us continue our tests of our corporation.

Financial Tests Using the Statement of Income and Retained Earnings

Operating Margin of Profit
This shows the percentage of each sales dollar that the company retained after expenses. It measures the efficiency of the management operating the business. The formula:

$$\text{Operating Margin of Profit} = \text{Operating Income} \div \text{Net Sales}$$

Our margin is 25%: $5,000,000 (operating income) ÷ $20,000,000 (net sales)

Operating Ratio

This shows the opposite of the operating margin of profit. It details the ratio of expenses to net sales. The formula:

$$\text{Operating Ratio} = \text{Cost of Sales (Expenses)} \div \text{Net Sales}$$

Our operating ratio is .75 to 1: $15,000,000 (expenses) ÷ $20,000,000 (net sales)

Cash Flow

This takes into consideration a most interesting aspect of depreciation, depletion, and amortization. They are called "noncash" charges, meaning that although we deducted them prior to paying taxes, we did not, in fact, expend any of our cash on them. Therefore, our net income does not reflect the true amount of cash available to us until we add back these noncash items. On our statement we show only depreciation, but depletion and amortization would also be added, if shown. The formula:

$$\text{Cash Flow} = \text{Net Income} + \text{Noncash Charges}$$

Our cash flow is $4,180,000: $3,400,000 (net income) + $780,000 (depreciation)

Were we asked the cash flow per share, we would divide the cash flow of $4,180,000 by the number of common shares issued and outstanding (100,000), giving us $41.80 cash flow per share.

Earnings per Share of Common

On a primary basis, this is computed by dividing the net earnings by the number of shares of stock issued and outstanding. This shows us how much earning power stands behind each share of stock. The formula:

$$\text{Primary Earnings per Share} = \text{Net Earnings} \div \text{Number of Shares Issued and Outstanding}$$

We show primary earnings per share of $33.20: $3,320,000 (net earnings) ÷ 100,000 (shares).

Often corporations have income in a year that cannot be expected to appear every year. Such items as the sale of a factory, a tax rebate, and profit on a sale of securities are called "extraordinary," or "nonrecurring" items. They are included in our computation of primary earnings per share. However, they are deleted when we compute earnings per share excluding nonrecurring Items. These items could have resulted in profits or losses to the corporation; therefore, their elimination could either increase or decrease earnings. Please note that although a profit on sale of securities is considered a nonrecurring item, investment income is deemed to be usual and expected and is not deducted when excluding the "extraordinary" amounts.

A third method of computing earnings per share of common is known as "fully diluted earnings." This recognizes the existence of convertible securities in the corporation's capitalization. Should they be converted into common stock by their owners it would result in additional shares of common outstanding and lower earnings per share.

For example, suppose the 100,000 shares of preferred stock of Acme Furniture Manufacturing Corp. were convertible into common stock on a share-for-share basis. This conversion would add 100,000 shares of common, making the total outstanding 200,000 shares. Of course, once the preferred was converted there would be no further payment of a dividend on these shares. The net earnings would, therefore, increase by the amount of the preferred dividend. Net earnings would now be $3,400,000 ($3,320,000 plus $80,000 preferred dividend). We would divide that number by 200,000 shares of common giving us fully diluted earnings of $17 per share.

Price-Earnings Ratio

This shows the relationship between the earnings per share of common and the market price of the shares. By comparing the ratios of companies in similar industries one might discover a security that appeared out of line with its competitors on a market price basis.

For example, if we were told that Acme common stock was trading at $166 per share, we could readily compute the price-earnings ratio. The formula:

Price-Earnings Ratio=Market Price of Common÷Earnings per Share of Common

Our stock is trading at a 5 to 1 ratio: $166 (market price)÷$33.20 (earnings per share)

Divided Payout Ratio

This tells us what portion of the monies available for dividend payments to common stockholders was actually paid out. The formula:

Dividend Payout Ratio=Common Dividend÷Amount Available for Dividends

Acme had a dividend payout ratio of .30 to 1: $1,000,000 (common dividend)÷ $3,320,000 (net earnings).

Growth companies tend to pay out a small portion of their earnings in dividends, preferring to retain the earnings for enhancement of the growth. As earnings increase, the percentages of payment may remain the same but the dollar payment may increase sharply. Public utilities, on the other hand, tend to pay a large portion of their earnings to shareholders in the form of dividends. These so-called "defensive" securities will provide a greater current yield than would growth company shares.

Inventory Turnover

This shows us the record of movement of a company's inventories. A manufacturing company should make such a turnover between five and six times each year. A smaller turnover may indicate too large an inventory when compared to the company's net sales. The formula:

Inventory Turnover=Net Sales÷Year-End Inventory

Inventory turnover for Acme was: 6.7 × $20,000,000 (net sales)÷$3,000,000 (inventory from the balance sheet)

Collection Ratio

This enables us to determine the speed with which the corporation's customers pay their bills. We would find no merit in a company that showed huge sales but had very slow paying clientele. The firm would suffer severe expenses in carrying their receivables with little cash coming in.

First, we determine one day's average sales by dividing the net sales by 365 days. The resulting figure is then divided into the accounts receivable, showing us the number of days of sales that are outstanding at this point and thus the average number of days required for an account to pay its bill. The formula:

Collection Ratio = Accounts Receivable ÷ (Net Sales ÷ 365)

Our collection ratio would be .32 to 1, or approximately 32 days to collect our bills: $20,000,000 (net sales) ÷ 365 (days) = $54,800. $1,750,000 (accounts receivable) ÷ $54,800 = 32.

While many other tests may be used to evaluate the financial conditions of a corporation, the ones we have used are the basic formulas. They will be listed again on the last page of this section for your review.

Depreciation

We have stated earlier that depreciation is the writing down of the value of a fixed asset. The amount of depreciation each year is a pretax deduction on the corporation's income statement. Thus, the corporation saves the percentage of this amount that would normally be paid in tax. A corporation in the maximum bracket would, therefore, realize a large tax savings. Depletion and other noncash charges are also eligible for this treatment.

There are three main methods that a corporation may employ in determining each year's depreciation.

Straight-Line Depreciation

Straight-line depreciation writes off equal amounts each year. Let's say that our corporation purchases a machine at a cost of $50,000. The machine will have an estimated usable lifetime of ten years. At the end of the ten years, we are told that it will have a salvage value of $5,000, perhaps as scrap metal. To compute the depreciation, using the straight-line method, we would subtract the salvage value from the $50,000 cost and divide the resulting figure by the number of years of useful life:

$50,000   Cost
− $5,000   Salvage value
$45,000   Depreciable value

$45,000 divided by 10 years = $4,500 per year

Each year for the ten years we would take a $4,500 deduction on our income statement, saving the tax that we would normally have paid on that amount.

Remember, this is a noncash charge in that the deduction did not require us to actually spend any money.

Accelerated Methods

The other two methods of depreciation are called "accelerated methods." Although they result in the same amount of deductions over the ten years, they allow for greater deductions in the early years than in later years. A corporation would choose one of these if they had a desire to save more on taxes immediately and let later years be assisted by new acquisitions of fixed assets.

Double Declining Balances

In this accelerated method we do not consider salvage value. Begin by treating the entire cost as though you were using the straight-line method.

$$\text{\$50,000 cost divided by 10 years}=\text{\$5,000}$$

This figure, $5,000, is then expressed as a percentage of the cost:

$$\text{\$5,000 divided by \$50,000}=10\%$$

We then double the percentage to 20% and apply that each year on a decreasing value.

> Year 1 – $50,000×20%=$10,000 depreciation
> Year 2 – $40,000 ($50,000 – $10,000)×20%=$ 8,000 depreciation
> Year 3 – $32,000 ($40,000 – $8,000)×20%=$ 6,000 depreciation
> ⋮

We continue this until the end of the ten years or until we have depreciated the machine to the $5,000 salvage value. We can never depreciate below the salvage value.

Sum of the Years' Digits

Here again, in this second accelerated method called "Sum of the Years' Digits (SOYD)," we determine the amount to be depreciated by subtracting salvage value from cost.

$$
\begin{array}{r}
\$50,000 \\
-\ \$5,000 \\
\hline
\$45,000
\end{array}
$$

We then multiply that amount each year by a fraction, the denominator of which is found by adding the digits of the years of life of the machine. In this case:

$$1+2+3+4+5+6+7+8+9+10=55$$

To this point we have found part of our formula:

$$\$45,000\times ?/55$$

For the numerator we start with the number representing the last year of the depreciation schedule, in this case 10. Each year we move back one year, as follows:

> Year 1 – $45,000×$10/55$=$8,182 depreciation
> Year 2 – $45,000×$9/55$=$7,364 depreciation
> Year 3 – $45,000×$8/55$=$6,545 depreciation
> ⋮

We continue this until the end of the tenth year, when we have:

$$\text{Year 10} - \$45,000 \times \tfrac{1}{55} = \$818 \text{ depreciation}$$

We have depreciated a total of $45,000, as in the other methods, but have had greater deductions early and very little at the end.

The difference in methods can be sharply seen just using the first year computed in our examples for each type:

First-Year Depreciation	
Straight-Line Method	$4,500
Double Declining Balances	$10,000
Sum of the Years' Digits	$ 8,182

At the end, the result is depreciation of $45,000 in total. Only the methods differ. Our corporation chooses the one that suits it best.

Evaluation of Inventory

The method by which corporations value their inventory can sharply affect their reported earnings. For example, suppose our Acme Furniture Manufacturing Corp. produces a small table that at one time cost it $8 to manufacture. As prices rose so did its costs, to $9, $10, and now $11. As costs rose Acme, of course, raised its prices. Originally, it may have sold the table for $14, but now it charges $18.

When they sell a table for $18, what do they use as their cost? They might simply average the cost of their inventory and use that figure ($9.50) for each sale ($8+9+10+11=38÷4= $9.50 average). They might, however, use the first in, first out ("FIFO") method meaning the oldest inventory is used against the sale. Hence, our sale at $18 would be applied against our oldest (first) inventory ($8), giving us a profit of $10 per table. In periods of rising prices, FIFO results in higher profits but also in higher taxes.

A more conservative method of inventory evaluation is the last in, first out ("LIFO") method. Here our sales are applied against our most recent (last) inventory ($11). Thus, the sale of a table at $18 produces a profit of $7, which results in less profit and less tax liability for the corporation that year.

The corporation may use whichever method they find best and may even choose to change methods when conditions warrant.

On the following pages we will show again the Balance Sheet and Statement of Income and Retained Earnings that we created earlier in this section.

ACME FURNITURE MANUFACTURING CO.
BALANCE SHEET – DECEMBER 31, 2006

ASSETS		LIABILITIES	
Current Assets		**Current Liabilities**	
Cash	$ 750,000	Accounts Payable	$2,500,000
Marketable Securities		Taxes Payable	280,000
(at Cost)	2,500,000	Accrued Expenses	500,000
Accounts Receivable		Interest Payable	220,000
(less reserve for doubtful accounts)	1,750,000	Total Current Liabilities	$3,500,000
Inventories	3,000,000		
Total Current Assets	$8,000,000	**Long-Term Liabilities**	
		8% Mortgage Bonds due 2019	$1,000,000
Fixed Assets		7% Debentures due 2012	1,000,000
Land	$1,250,000	Total Long-Term Liabilities	$2,000,000
Buildings	2,450,000		
Machinery	800,000	Total Liabilities	$5,500,000
Furniture/Fixtures	200,000		
Less: Accumulated Depreciation	1,200,000	**STOCKHOLDER'S EQUITY**	
Net Fixed Assets	$3,500,000	(Net Worth)	
		Preferred Stock, 8%	
Intangible Assets		cumulative ($10 par)	
Patents and Trademarks	$ 100,000	100,000 shares	$1,000,000
		Common Stock $10 par	
		(authorized 250,000 shares;	
		issued and outstanding	
		100,000 shares)	$1,000,000
		Retained Earnings (earned surplus)	3,100,000
		Capital Surplus (paid-in capital)	1,000,000
		Total Stockholder's Equity	$6,100,000
Total Assets	$11,600,000	Total Liabilities & Stockholder's Equity	$11,600,000

ACME FURNITURE MANUFACTURING CO.
STATEMENT OF INCOME AND RETAINED EARNINGS
YEAR ENDED DECEMBER 31, 2005

Net Sales		$20,000,000
Cost of Sales (Expenses)		
Labor & Materials	$6,500,000	
Selling & Administrative Costs	4,500,000	
Manufacturing Costs	3,000,000	
Depreciation	780,000	
Interest on Debt	220,000	
		$15,000,000
Operating Income		$ 5,000,000
Investment Income		400,000
Total Income		$ 5,400,000
– Federal Income Tax		2,000,000
Net Income		3,400,000
– Preferred Dividend ($.80 per share)		80,000
Net Earnings		3,320,000
– Common Dividend ($10.00 per share)		1,000,000
Retained Earnings (Year)		2,320,000
Retained Earnings (Prior Years)		780,000
Total Retained Earnings (as of 12/31/05)		$ 3,100,000

FINANCIAL STATEMENT FORMULAS

1. Net Working Capital = Current Assets − Current Liabilities
2. Current Ratio = Current Assets ÷ Current Liabilities
3. Quick Assets = Current Assets − Inventories
4. Net Quick Assets = Current Assets − Inventories − Current Liabilities
5. Quick Assets Ratio (Acid Test Ratio) = (Current Assets − Inventories) ÷ Current Liabilities
6. Net Tangible Asset Value per Share (Book Value) = (Balance Sheet Value of Common − Intangible Assets) ÷ Number of Common Shares Issued and Outstanding
7. Capitalization Ratios
   a. Long-Term Debt = Long-Term Debt ÷ Total Capitalization
   b. Preferred Stock = Value of Preferred ÷ Total Capitalization
   c. Common Stock = Value of Common ÷ Total Capitalization
8. Operating Margin of Profit = Operating Income ÷ Net Sales
9. Operating Ratio = Cost of Sales (Expenses) ÷ Net Sales
10. Cash Flow = Net Income + Noncash Charges
11. Earnings per Share of Common = Net Earnings ÷ Number of Shares Issued and Outstanding
12. Price-Earnings Ratio = Market Price Common ÷ Earnings per Share of Common
13. Dividend Payout Ratio = Common Dividend ÷ the Amount Available for Dividends
14. Inventory Turnover = Net Sales ÷ Year-End Inventory
15. Collection Ratio = Accounts Receivable ÷ (Net Sales ÷ 365)

TECHNICAL ANALYSIS

The art of technical analysis is a study of past price movements, volume, and trends. With thorough knowledge of these elements technicians feel they can read the future strength or weakness of markets in general and of particular securities. Technical analysts do not rely on earnings and dividend payments as do fundamental analysts, since they feel they are reflected in the price movement and volume changes. Technical analysis is broken down into three basic areas of study: averages and indices; market theories; and the study of chart patterns. We will look into these areas briefly as a thorough study of technical analysis would fill many volumes.

Averages and Indices

Dow Jones Averages
There are four averages compiled by Dow Jones on a continuing basis:

- 30 Industrial Stocks
- 20 Transportation Stocks
- 15 Utility Stocks
- 65 Stocks (a composite of the three above)

All of the Dow averages are share-weighted to allow for stock splits and stock dividends paid by the corporations over the years. Thus a movement of one point in a company with 300,000,000 shares outstanding will have more effect on the average than the same change in a company having only 100,000,000 shares outstanding. The Dow Jones Industrial Average (DJIA) of 30 stocks is the most often cited gauge of market movement. When one says "the market is down three points" one is referring to a three-point drop in the DJIA. In fact, a one-point move in the Dow Industrials represents a change of about five cents in the price of a representative share. Though it contains less components than other barometers, it has shown price movements remarkably similar to those of the broader indicators.

Standard & Poor's Composite Index
The Standard & Poor's Composite Index uses 500 stocks representing all major sectors of the economy. It contains:

- 400 Industrials
- 20 Transportations
- 40 Utilities
- 40 Financial Companies

Each of the four components is published separately to give insight into the movements of the specific area. The S&P indices are weighted just as are the Dow Jones averages to give consideration to the number of shares outstanding for each company.

The S&P 500 is called an "index." The Dow Jones Industrials is called an "average." An average contains a small number of components, while an index uses a larger number of components and is measured against a base year or value.

Here are a few of the more popular indexes.

The Wilshire Associates Equity Index
This index is the broadest of all the averages and indexes. It is market weighted and represents the market value of the securities trades on the NYSE, AMEX, and OTC issues.

Amer Major Market Index
Even though this index was created by the American Stock Exchange, it is composed of stocks listed on the NYSE, 15 of which are on the DJIA.

Value Line Composite Index
Made up of 1700 NYSE, AMEX, and OTC, this index is watched by Value Line Investment Survey.

The Russell 3000 Index
This index is made up of the largest capitalized U.S. securities.

The Russell 2000 and 1000
The 2000, which is the most popular of the three known as the Russell 2000 Small Stock Index, is a benchmark of the stock price performance of small companies. The Russell 1000 measures the so-called Mid Cap stocks.

New York Stock Exchange Market Index

The NYSE Index is based on all common stocks listed on the New York Stock Exchange. This index multiplies the price of each common stock by the number of its shares outstanding. This weighting results in those companies with larger capitalizations having a greater effect on the index than those with smaller capitalizations.

MARKET THEORIES

Dow Theory

This theory holds, in part, that there are three trends in a market that can be measured: the long-term trend, which measures overall market direction, the intermediate trend, which is useful for trading purposes; and the day-to-day fluctuations, which are important only to day traders. Proper measurement of the long-term trend is most important as it can show, the theory asserts, a change in direction of the market. Should a bull market reverse itself, few if any stocks will be spared and the theorist would tend to liquidate all positions. As the old Wall Street adage holds, "When the house burns down both the good and the bad people jump out the window."

Advance-Decline Theory

This theory, also called the "breadth of the market theory," records the number of stocks that go up in a day compared with the number that go down. Proper measurement of these figures can show the strength of a market and can signal a change in market direction. Although the general market might be rising, more individual stocks might be declining. The overall rise could well be due to a sharp price increase in a relatively small number of components. This could indicate that the market lacks underlying strength and may soon experience a decline. The same may be true when in a declining market the advances outnumber the declining shares. Again, a change in direction may be forthcoming.

Odd-Lot Theory

This theory measures the activity of the odd lot (1–99 shares) customers. It takes the position that the small customers are generally wrong in their trading. Thus, if odd-lot purchases exceed odd-lot sales, the market should decline. If the "odd-lotter" is selling it might be time to buy because the little guy is usually on the wrong side. As this theory takes a view opposite to the view of a group, it is sometimes referred to as a contrarian theory. In recent years the percentage of trading volume attributable to odd-lot customers has declined sharply, giving this theory less support than it had in the past.

Short-Interest Theory (Cushion Theory)

This theory is also contrarian as it proposes taking action opposite to the feeling of a group of investors, in this case, the short sellers. An increase in short sales is considered to be a bullish factor for two reasons. First, short sellers at some point must repurchase the shares. Should the market decline the buying will support the market—that is, provide a cushion.

Secondly, should the short seller be wrong and the market rise, he will be forced to cover his shorts. These purchases will accelerate the pace of a rising market.

Barron's Confidence Index

Barron's Confidence Index records the yields on high-grade bonds versus those on low-grade bonds. The yields on high-grade bonds will, of course, be lower, but as investor confidence grows the spread will narrow. It is felt that this increased confidence will move to the stock market in ensuing months, causing an increase in the value of equities. Naturally, a widening of this yield spread shows a waning of confidence, which might later cause a selloff in stocks.

Chart Patterns

Study of past performance through the use of charts can provide insight into future price movements. The technician feels, among other things, that history does repeat itself, and that by patiently following chart patterns one will be rewarded. There are literally thousands of theories that utilize charts. Let us look at two of them.

Support Levels and Resistance Zones

Let's suppose that in recent months a stock sold as high as $60 per share and as low as $35 per share. The current price is $47.

Should the stock return to its former high ($60) sellers who missed it the last time might offer stock for sale. This supply will make it difficult for the stock to penetrate its former high. However, a penetration of the former high could lead to a further rise as the resistance formed by the supply of stock has been exhausted. On the downside, a drop to $35, the former low, should awaken buyers in this security. The buy orders will provide support at this level, perhaps preventing a further decline and making for an attractive purchase. Should the stock, however, drop below this support level, the security should be temporarily avoided.

Head and Shoulders Formations

A "head and shoulders" pattern would look like this:

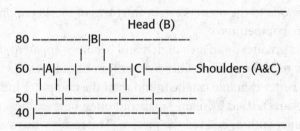

This is a bearish pattern. The stock rose from a base of 40 to a high of 60 (left shoulder). Fell back to the neck (50) then rose to a new high of 80 (head). It retreated again to the neck (50) before rising to a level of 60 (right shoulder) for the second time. A retreat back to the base of 40 would indicate a decline in the stock to still lower levels.

On the other hand, a "reverse head and shoulders" pattern is bullish. In this formation the stock declines, rises to a base, declines to a lower level and rises again to the base. Another decline ensues to the level of the first decline followed by a rally to the base. Penetration of this base would indicate a significant rise in the value of the stock might lie ahead. This pattern would look like this:

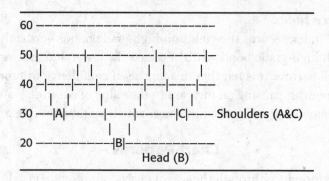

Industry Analysis

The industries that comprise the economy of the United States can be classified into three types: defensive, growth, and cyclical.

Defensive industries are those that are least vulnerable to economic change. Companies in the defensive class would be those providing goods and services that are necessary to the consumer—the last things cut out of a person's budget should economic conditions worsen. The industry generally cited as being most "defensive" is the public utility industry. Aside from providing a basic necessity, utilities are not subject to the competitive factor generally associated with the American way of life. A particular utility serves a geographic area. There is no need for price-cutting to defeat the competition, as there is none. Rates are set by a utility commission that historically allows a reasonable return to the company. The food industry can also be considered defensive as the consumer would certainly buy bread and meat before buying a new suit or car.

Growth industries are those in areas of increasing demand or public acceptance. More often than not growth industries commit a large portion of revenues to research and development and consequently do not pay large dividends to shareholders. Earnings are used to foster continued growth. Rewards to the owners are in the form of market appreciation. Growth industries by nature are competitive.

As the potential of a product or an area of demand becomes apparent, new companies will attempt to capture a share of the market. This competition usually results in the failure of some of the participants. No better example can be found than the computer industry. Early in its history the industry was characterized by many small and often new entities. As the growth potential became obvious, larger entities entered the picture. The result—many small companies were forced out of the business and even major suppliers "threw in the towel" due to narrowing or nonexistent profit margins. Success breeds more success but it also breeds competition. Growth industries require continued vigilance by investors and investment professionals.

Cyclical industries are those that are most subject to economic changes, or "cycles." They may be engaged in areas that would be affected by recession, such as luxury items. The best example of a cyclical industry is automobiles. In addition to being adversely affected by a lessening of consumer buying power, U.S. auto sales were in at one time severely damaged by foreign competition. In the early 1980s Ford and General Motors saw earnings drop sharply, resulting in severe dividend reductions, and Chrysler barely avoided bankruptcy. By late 1983, however, U.S. auto sales were so improved that Chrysler, which had traded at $3½ per share in 1982, traded above $35 per share. In the same period, Ford had a low of $16½ and a high of $70, and General Motors rose from a 1982 low of $34 to $80 per share. As taste and economic conditions change, the automobile industry suffers or prospers. That's cyclical. A perfect example occurred during the recession in 1991, when the automobile industry again fell on hard times.

SOURCES OF INDUSTRY STATISTICS

Many of the statistics used by the financial analyst are provided by the U.S. government. The Department of Labor supplies a monthly figure of unemployment levels in our nation. Changes in this level, as well as long-term trends, provide the student with information regarding the overall health of the economy. A lowering of the number of unemployed could represent an increase in industrial production and a more vibrant economy. Increases in unemployment are a detriment to economic growth due to lost consumer buying power and the drain placed on the government in supporting necessary social programs. The U.S. Department of Commerce reports the gross domestic product on a quarterly basis as well as the Index of Leading Indicators each month.

Gross domestic product (GDP), which shows the estimated total value of all goods and services produced in the United States, is considered the most accurate indicator of overall business activity in the nation. GDP shows the total amount earned by the nation. The Index of Leading Indicators includes 10 components ranging from money supply and stock prices to new business formations and the layoff rate in the manufacturing industry. Generally, some of the indicators are up while others are down, but the total trend of this index is useful in analyzing the business cycle. The Federal Reserve reports weekly on the money supply. The most often quoted item is M1, which includes the total amount of currency in circulation as well as the value of demand deposits at commercial banks. Increases in money supply tend to be inflationary and could lead the Fed to tighten credit. A lessening of supply might presage an easing of credit restrictions, which generally is positive for both the stock and bond markets.

ANSWER SHEET FOR CHAPTER 10 EXAMINATION

1. Ⓐ Ⓑ Ⓒ Ⓓ   11. Ⓐ Ⓑ Ⓒ Ⓓ   21. Ⓐ Ⓑ Ⓒ Ⓓ

2. Ⓐ Ⓑ Ⓒ Ⓓ   12. Ⓐ Ⓑ Ⓒ Ⓓ   22. Ⓐ Ⓑ Ⓒ Ⓓ

3. Ⓐ Ⓑ Ⓒ Ⓓ   13. Ⓐ Ⓑ Ⓒ Ⓓ   23. Ⓐ Ⓑ Ⓒ Ⓓ

4. Ⓐ Ⓑ Ⓒ Ⓓ   14. Ⓐ Ⓑ Ⓒ Ⓓ   24. Ⓐ Ⓑ Ⓒ Ⓓ

5. Ⓐ Ⓑ Ⓒ Ⓓ   15. Ⓐ Ⓑ Ⓒ Ⓓ   25. Ⓐ Ⓑ Ⓒ Ⓓ

6. Ⓐ Ⓑ Ⓒ Ⓓ   16. Ⓐ Ⓑ Ⓒ Ⓓ   26. Ⓐ Ⓑ Ⓒ Ⓓ

7. Ⓐ Ⓑ Ⓒ Ⓓ   17. Ⓐ Ⓑ Ⓒ Ⓓ   27. Ⓐ Ⓑ Ⓒ Ⓓ

8. Ⓐ Ⓑ Ⓒ Ⓓ   18. Ⓐ Ⓑ Ⓒ Ⓓ   28. Ⓐ Ⓑ Ⓒ Ⓓ

9. Ⓐ Ⓑ Ⓒ Ⓓ   19. Ⓐ Ⓑ Ⓒ Ⓓ   29. Ⓐ Ⓑ Ⓒ Ⓓ

10. Ⓐ Ⓑ Ⓒ Ⓓ   20. Ⓐ Ⓑ Ⓒ Ⓓ   30. Ⓐ Ⓑ Ⓒ Ⓓ

31. Ⓐ Ⓑ Ⓒ Ⓓ   41. Ⓐ Ⓑ Ⓒ Ⓓ

32. Ⓐ Ⓑ Ⓒ Ⓓ   42. Ⓐ Ⓑ Ⓒ Ⓓ

33. Ⓐ Ⓑ Ⓒ Ⓓ   43. Ⓐ Ⓑ Ⓒ Ⓓ

34. Ⓐ Ⓑ Ⓒ Ⓓ   44. Ⓐ Ⓑ Ⓒ Ⓓ

35. Ⓐ Ⓑ Ⓒ Ⓓ   45. Ⓐ Ⓑ Ⓒ Ⓓ

36. Ⓐ Ⓑ Ⓒ Ⓓ   46. Ⓐ Ⓑ Ⓒ Ⓓ

37. Ⓐ Ⓑ Ⓒ Ⓓ   47. Ⓐ Ⓑ Ⓒ Ⓓ

38. Ⓐ Ⓑ Ⓒ Ⓓ   48. Ⓐ Ⓑ Ⓒ Ⓓ

39. Ⓐ Ⓑ Ⓒ Ⓓ   49. Ⓐ Ⓑ Ⓒ Ⓓ

40. Ⓐ Ⓑ Ⓒ Ⓓ   50. Ⓐ Ⓑ Ⓒ Ⓓ

CHAPTER 10 EXAMINATION

1. Which of the following would be least useful to an analyst making a technical market report?

    (A) advances and declines
    (B) new highs and lows
    (C) the short interest
    (D) predictions of recession in the economy

2. An advance-decline line plotted by market technicians is intended to gauge:

    (A) the quality of the market
    (B) the volatility of the market
    (C) the direction of the market
    (D) the volume of activity in the market

3. In a corporation's financial statements, earned surplus is also recognized to be its:

    (A) gross profit
    (B) operating income after payment of interest expense
    (C) earnings retained after payment of dividends to shareholders
    (D) net income

4. Choose the only statement below that is true:

    (A) If its earnings are sufficient, a corporation is required to pay a cash dividend to its common stockholders.
    (B) A growth company would be more likely to pay a cash dividend than a stock dividend.
    (C) A stock split and a stock dividend are reflected in exactly the same manner on a corporation's balance sheet.
    (D) The amount of dividends paid by a corporation can have a significant influence on the market price of its stock.

5. Which of the following balance sheet items is affected by a stock split?

    (A) shareowner's equity
    (B) working capital
    (C) par value
    (D) capital surplus

6. Based upon these selected figures from a corporation's income statement, determine its operating income

Cost of Goods Sold	$ 820,000
Sales	1,200,000
Selling & Administrative Expenses	95,000
Depreciation	7,000
Returns, Discounts, etc.	100,000
Net Sales	1,100,000

    (A) $85,000
    (B) $178,000
    (C) $285,000
    (D) $380,000

7. The total assets of an industrial corporation amount to $840,000, of which $350,000 are current items. Its total liabilities are $460,000, of which $290,000 are fixed obligations. How much is this corporation's working capital?

    (A) $60,000
    (B) $110,000
    (C) $180,000
    (D) $380,000

8. ABC Corp. earned $2 per share last year and is selling at $20. If it earns $3 per share this year and its price-earnings ratio stays the same, it should sell at:

    (A) $20
    (B) $25
    (C) $30
    (D) $60

9. A blue chip stock with a P/E of 17 is now selling at 74.50. From this we may deduce that the company's earnings per share in its last twelve months were:

   (A) about $4.38
   (B) $6.20
   (C) $1.70
   (D) impossible to calculate from this information

10. If M1 has dropped, then:

    (A) currency and demand deposits have risen
    (B) currency and demand deposits have declined
    (C) checking and savings account balances have declined
    (D) reserve requirements have declined

11. Issuance of a nonconvertible debenture at par by an industrial corporation will have what effect upon its net worth?

    (A) increase it
    (B) lower it
    (C) leave it unchanged
    (D) none of the above

12. The accounting statement that represents the financial position of a business at a particular point in time (rather than over a period of time) is the:

    (A) income statement
    (B) balance sheet
    (C) profit and loss statement
    (D) earnings statement

13. If a corporation selects a 12-month period ending other than on December 31 as the basis for computing and reporting profits, this period is known as the corporation's:

    (A) earnings period
    (B) financial year
    (C) calendar year
    (D) fiscal year

14. Which of the following statements concerning theories about the technical analysis of stocks is correct?

    (A) The advance-decline index is a good measure of the direction of a bull or bear market.
    (B) The odd-lot theory states it is a good time to buy stocks when investors are buying odd lots on balance
    (C) Trading volume is bullish when heavy on a decline and light on an advance.
    (D) The short-interest theory states that a small short interest makes the market technically strong.

15. A technical analyst's chart pattern known as a "head and shoulders" pattern is a reversal of:

    (A) an upward trend
    (B) a downward trend
    (C) a trendless market condition
    (D) investor confidence in the government securities futures market

16. Which of these persons would consider annual reports of a corporation to be the most important factor in making an investment decision?

    (A) a technical analyst
    (B) a chartist
    (C) a follower of the Dow theory
    (D) a fundamental analyst

17. The Dow Jones Industrial Average is based on:

    (A) 30 industrial stocks
    (B) 65 industrial, transportation, and utility stocks
    (C) 400 industrial stocks
    (D) all NYSE-listed common stocks

18. The market theory that states that the small investor is usually wrong is called the:

    (A) advance-decline theory
    (B) odd-lot theory
    (C) Dow theory
    (D) short-interest theory

19. After an extended period of backing and filling, a stock moves up sharply through a resistance level on heavy volume. A technical analyst would likely call this a:

    (A) buy-in
    (B) technical rally
    (C) buying climax
    (D) breakout

20. Technical analysts are normally interested in each of the following EXCEPT:

    (A) the advance-decline ratio
    (B) the 200-day moving average line
    (C) the price-earnings ratio
    (D) the odd-lot theory

21. The New York Stock Exchange Market Index is comprised of:

    (A) all securities listed on the NYSE
    (B) all common stocks listed on the NYSE
    (C) all common and preferred stocks listed on the NYSE
    (D) all convertible preferred and common stocks listed on the NYSE

22. Technical analysts believe that the development of a chart pattern showing a reverse head and shoulders indicates an issue whose next market movement will be:

    (A) higher
    (B) lower
    (C) sideways
    (D) extremely volatile

23. A leveraged company can be described as one that has a small portion of its capital represented by:

    (A) common stock
    (B) preferred stock
    (C) debentures
    (D) convertible bonds

24. The best description of a balance sheet's concept would be:

    (A) assets=stockholder's equity
    (B) assets=liabilities and profits
    (C) total assets=total liabilities and profits
    (D) total assets=total liabilities and net worth

25. A technical analyst comparing the number of stocks that rose in value to the number of stocks that fell on a particular day would be charting:

    (A) the purchase versus sales indicator
    (B) the market trendline
    (C) the advance-decline line
    (D) up volume versus down volume

26. From a market technician's viewpoint, which of these statements is true?

    (A) Heavy volume in a declining market is a bullish indicator.
    (B) Once a trendline is established the price of the stock will follow it closely.
    (C) Odd-lot purchases on balance are a bullish indicator.
    (D) Light volume in a rising market is a bullish indicator.

27. Over the past six months, the country had experienced a mild increase in unemployment, a mild decline in security prices, and a slowdown in economic activity. This would be commonly referred to as:

    (A) a technical adjustment
    (B) inflation
    (C) a recession
    (D) deflation

28. Which of the following best describes depreciation?

    (A) a tax credit available to investors in heavy equipment
    (B) deductions from gross income to offset lower value of equipment
    (C) return of principal from real estate investors
    (D) capitalized and amortized maintenance costs

29. On which of the following is depreciation *not* permitted?

    (A) rental property whose value is falling
    (B) vacant land
    (C) property whose maintenance exceeds the investment credit
    (D) equipment

30. The Dow Jones Industrial Average:

    (A) depicts the market value of 30 component stock issues
    (B) is an average price of 30 component stock issues
    (C) is a figure derived by dividing market values of 30 component stocks by a constant number
    (D) is calculated by dividing market value of 30 component stocks by a continuously changing denominator

31. A company earns $6 per share and pays out 20% in common stock dividends. What does the stock yield if it sells at $30 per share?

    (A) 10.00%
    (B) 4.00%
    (C) 2.50%
    (D) 6.00%

32. The value of a trademark will appear on the balance sheet under:

    (A) fixed assets
    (B) current liabilities
    (C) current assets
    (D) intangible assets

33. All of the following are true of stockholder's equity EXCEPT:

    (A) It consists of capital stock, capital surplus and retained earnings.
    (B) It is carried on the asset side of the balance sheet.
    (C) It includes the value of the preferred stock.
    (D) It is also known as net worth.

34. Inflation tends to do all of the following EXCEPT:

    (A) increase prices of manufactured goods
    (B) decrease the value of fixed-income investments
    (C) decrease purchasing power
    (D) decrease bond yields

35. A corporation with 1,000,000 shares of $50 par common stock outstanding splits the stock 4 for 1. After the split is effective the company will have outstanding:

    (A) 1,000,000 shares of $ 50.00 par
    (B) 4,000,000 shares of $ 12.50 par
    (C) 4,000,000 shares of $ 50.00 par
    (D) 1,000,000 shares of $100.00 par

36. Which of the following items would be considered to be an intangible asset?

    (A) marketable securities
    (B) trademarks
    (C) accounts receivable
    (D) furniture

37. When are dividends on common stock considered to be a current liability of a corporation?

    (A) after they have been paid
    (B) from the time they are declared until they are paid
    (C) when they exceed the corporation's retained earnings
    (D) at no time

38. Which of the following statistics is published by the Commerce Department?

    (A) short-interest ratio
    (B) balance of payments
    (C) index of indicators
    (D) gross national product

39. The annual interest on a corporation's long-term debt is a:

    (A) current liability
    (B) pretax deduction
    (C) corporate obligation
    (D) all of the above

40. A technical analyst would probably be most interested in which of the following ratios?

    (A) acid test ratio
    (B) stock ratio
    (C) short-interest ratio
    (D) quick ratio

41. Marketable securities are a:

    (A) current asset
    (B) fixed asset
    (C) intangible asset
    (D) all of the above

42. Book value of a corporation is also known as:

    (A) net tangible asset value per share
    (B) intangible value
    (C) par value
    (D) dilution value

43. Which of the following items would *not* be included in the net worth section of a corporation's balance sheet?

    I.   long-term debt
    II. retained earnings
    III. capital surplus
    IV. accounts receivable

        (A) II and III only
        (B) I and IV only
        (C) III and IV only
        (D) I and III only

44. Which of the following items is deducted after the calculation of a corporation's net income?

    (A) taxes
    (B) dividends
    (C) interest
    (D) all of the above

45. A corporation has net income of $4,200,000. It has outstanding 100,000 shares of 8% preferred stock ($100 par) and 400,000 shares of common stock ($10 par). What are the earnings per share of common?

    (A) $8.50
    (B) $6.00
    (C) $4.20
    (D) $10.50

46. Which of the following is normally the largest current asset of a manufacturing company?

    (A) sales
    (B) inventory
    (C) accounts receivable
    (D) notes receivable

47. Depletion allowances are used by:

    (A) machine tool companies
    (B) manufacturing companies
    (C) insurance companies
    (D) natural resource companies

48. The XYZ Corporation has 900,000 shares of common outstanding and holds 100,000 shares as treasury stock. At the end of the third quarter $450,000 is to be distributed as a dividend on the common. The dividend per share would be:

    (A) $0.45
    (B) $0.50
    (C) $2.00
    (D) $2.22

49. A large manufacturing company has current assets of approximately $9,400,000 and current liabilities of about $4,900,000. With respect to the standard minimum, the current ratio is:

    (A) substantially below the standard minimum
    (B) somewhat below the standard minimum
    (C) about the standard minimum
    (D) somewhat above the standard minimum

50. According to the short-interest theory (cushion theory), if there were a major decline in short positions this would be a:

    (A) bullish factor
    (B) bearish factor
    (C) neutral factor
    (D) buy signal

CHAPTER 10 EXAMINATION ANSWERS

1. **D** Economic news of forecasts is of less importance to a "technical analyst" than indicators derived from the actual market itself. Some technicians ignore "fundamental" economic data. The general premise of technical analysis is that "the tape tells all." That is, market prices reflect a consensus view of all known and applicable fundamental data.

2. **C** The advance-decline theory measures the direction of a market and may even indicate that a change in direction is near.

3. **C** By definition, and also because the other choices are clearly incorrect. Please note that earned surplus, which is also referred to as retained earnings, does not necessarily represent a fund of cash, but rather, earnings that have been retained in the business since its inception after the payment of all expenses, taxes, and dividends. Normally, this money has been reinvested in other capital assets.

4. **D** Earnings are usually the dominant force in influencing market prices. However, dividend payments (the amount of the dividend) can have a tremendous influence on the market price also.

5. **C** The other items listed remain unchanged, whereas par value is reduced in proportion to the split.

6. **B** Operating income is determined by taking net sales and subtracting total operating expenses. In this case, net sales were $1,100,000. Total operating expenses would include cost of goods sold, selling & administrative expenses, and depreciation.

7. **C** We get this by subtracting current liabilities from current assets. To get current liabilities, we must subtract fixed liabilities from total liabilities.

8. **C** The company has a price-earnings ratio of 10. If the ratio remains the same, and earnings go up, then 10×3 equals 30.

9. **A** You divide 74½ (market price) by 17 (P/E ratio).

10. **B** "Demand deposits" are checking account balances. Newer developments such as NOW accounts, money market funds, and large CDs have made this gauge of the "money supply" too restrictive for many economists, who have developed further measurements.

11. **C** We simply add an asset (cash) and add a liability (a nonconvertible debenture) in equal amounts. Thus, net worth is unchanged.

12. **B** The balance sheet shows the condition of a corporation at a given point in time (e.g., year ending December. 31, 1993) while the income statement shows the result of a period of operation.

13. **D** If a corporation reports its results based on a year ending in December, it is known as calendar-year reporting. If any other month represents the corporate year end, it is known as a fiscal year.

14. **A** Advance-decline theory supposedly signals a change in market direction.

15. **A** A "head and shoulders" pattern is bearish and signals a downward trend.

16. **D** Fundamental analysts are concerned with computations made from a corporation's financial reports.

17. **A** The less widely followed Dow Jones Composite Average has 65 issues (30 industrials, 20 transportation, and 15 utilities). The 500 Stock Standard & Poor's Composite, on the other hand, is more familiar than the S&P 400 industrials.

18. **B** This is sometimes referred to as the "theory of contrary opinion," and sometimes as "Drew's odd-lot theory."

19. **D** An upward move through a resistance level or a downward move through a support level is called a breakout.

20. **C** The price-earnings ratio is considered a fundamental factor, just like yield, book value, current ratio, and so on. The technician is not interested in fundamental factors.

21. **B** By definition.

22. **A** When the head is upright, it frequently indicates a downward move in the market. When the head and shoulders are upside down, as in this case, it normally means that the market will move higher.

23. **A** The term "leverage" means that there are securities with charges senior to the common stock in the capitalization. There can be debt leverage, where the senior securities are bonds or debentures. Also, there can be equity leverage, where preferred stocks are senior to the common. Naturally, there can be a combination of both debt and equity leverage. A company whose capitalization had a small percentage of common stock must, therefore, have other senior securities outstanding.

24. **D** This is sometimes called the "balance sheet equation."

25. **C** Basically, by definition.

26. **B** This is the basis for "trend" analysis. Please notice that this is a viewpoint rather than a truism. Choices (A), (C) and (D) are all incorrect.

27. **C** A mild increase in unemployment, a decrease in stock prices, and a slowdown in economic activity are indicative of a period of recession. Were these severe downturns it would indicate a depression.

28. **B** Depreciation is the writing down of the value of an asset. The amount so depreciated is a pretax deduction.

29. **B** Land is not a depreciable asset.

30. **C** Although we use a "constant," this figure does change when changes occur in the average either through the stock dividends or splits.

31. **B** The payout is $1.20 (20% of $6). We divide this by the market price ($30) to give us the yield (4%).

32. **D** Intangible assets are those to which a true value cannot be assigned. A trademark would fall into that category.

33. **B** Net worth is carried on the liability side of the balance sheet. It is not a true liability, but rather only a contingent liability to owners.

34. **D** Inflation tends to result in higher interest rates, which would cause outstanding bond prices to decline. This would increase the yield on outstanding bonds and cause new bond offerings to be made at higher returns.

35. **B** We will increase the number of outstanding shares four times and inversely change the par value by dividing the old par ($50) by four.

36. **B** Intangible assets are those whose true value cannot be determined. Trademarks as well as copyrights, patents, goodwill, and so on, would fit this definition.

37. **B** Once the dividend is declared it becomes a current obligation of the corporation.

38. **C** Gross domestic product and the Index of Leading Indicators are published by the Commerce Department.

39. **D** Bond interest fits all of these definitions.

40. **C** The short-interest ratio compares that total number of shares sold to the average daily trading volume. It is a technical measure of the market as opposed to a "fundamental" ratio, as are choices (A), (B), and (D). If the total short interest exceeds the average daily trading volume by more than 1.5 times, the indicator is considered bullish.

41. **A** Current assets are those that can be converted to cash in one year or less. Marketable securities certainly fit this definition.

42. **A** This is a usual way of expressing book value.

43. **B** Net worth includes the stated value of the preferred and common stock plus the retained earnings (earned surplus) and capital surplus (paid-in surplus). Long-term debt (a long-term liability) and accounts receivable (a current asset) are not included in net worth.

44. **B** Dividends on both preferred and common are paid from net income or retained earnings. Taxes and interest are deducted before the net income is calculated.

45. **A** From the net income of $4,200,000 we subtract the preferred dividend of $800,000 ($8 per share on 100,000 shares), giving us net earnings of $3,400,000. This is then divided by the 400,000 shares of common. Answer: $8.50 per share.

46. **B** Inventory is normally the largest current asset of a manufacturing company. Note: Sales would usually be larger than inventory, but they are not a current asset.

47. **D** Depletion is the wasting away or use of a natural resource.

48. **B** Treasury stock does not receive dividends. In this case the $450,000 would be distributed among 900,000 shares, resulting in a dividend of $.50 per share.

49. **B** The minimum current ratio of a manufacturing company should be 2 to 1. The current ratio of this company is 1.92 to 1 (9.4 divided by 4.9).

50. **B** A decrease in shorts is bearish. There are now fewer open positions to be covered should the market decline, giving less support (cushion) to the market.

General Securities Registered Representative Examination: Series 7

CHAPTER 11

Practice Examinations

ANSWER SHEET FOR PRACTICE EXAMINATION 1

Part 1

1. Ⓐ Ⓑ Ⓒ Ⓓ	26. Ⓐ Ⓑ Ⓒ Ⓓ	51. Ⓐ Ⓑ Ⓒ Ⓓ	76. Ⓐ Ⓑ Ⓒ Ⓓ	101. Ⓐ Ⓑ Ⓒ Ⓓ
2. Ⓐ Ⓑ Ⓒ Ⓓ	27. Ⓐ Ⓑ Ⓒ Ⓓ	52. Ⓐ Ⓑ Ⓒ Ⓓ	77. Ⓐ Ⓑ Ⓒ Ⓓ	102. Ⓐ Ⓑ Ⓒ Ⓓ
3. Ⓐ Ⓑ Ⓒ Ⓓ	28. Ⓐ Ⓑ Ⓒ Ⓓ	53. Ⓐ Ⓑ Ⓒ Ⓓ	78. Ⓐ Ⓑ Ⓒ Ⓓ	103. Ⓐ Ⓑ Ⓒ Ⓓ
4. Ⓐ Ⓑ Ⓒ Ⓓ	29. Ⓐ Ⓑ Ⓒ Ⓓ	54. Ⓐ Ⓑ Ⓒ Ⓓ	79. Ⓐ Ⓑ Ⓒ Ⓓ	104. Ⓐ Ⓑ Ⓒ Ⓓ
5. Ⓐ Ⓑ Ⓒ Ⓓ	30. Ⓐ Ⓑ Ⓒ Ⓓ	55. Ⓐ Ⓑ Ⓒ Ⓓ	80. Ⓐ Ⓑ Ⓒ Ⓓ	105. Ⓐ Ⓑ Ⓒ Ⓓ
6. Ⓐ Ⓑ Ⓒ Ⓓ	31. Ⓐ Ⓑ Ⓒ Ⓓ	56. Ⓐ Ⓑ Ⓒ Ⓓ	81. Ⓐ Ⓑ Ⓒ Ⓓ	106. Ⓐ Ⓑ Ⓒ Ⓓ
7. Ⓐ Ⓑ Ⓒ Ⓓ	32. Ⓐ Ⓑ Ⓒ Ⓓ	57. Ⓐ Ⓑ Ⓒ Ⓓ	82. Ⓐ Ⓑ Ⓒ Ⓓ	107. Ⓐ Ⓑ Ⓒ Ⓓ
8. Ⓐ Ⓑ Ⓒ Ⓓ	33. Ⓐ Ⓑ Ⓒ Ⓓ	58. Ⓐ Ⓑ Ⓒ Ⓓ	83. Ⓐ Ⓑ Ⓒ Ⓓ	108. Ⓐ Ⓑ Ⓒ Ⓓ
9. Ⓐ Ⓑ Ⓒ Ⓓ	34. Ⓐ Ⓑ Ⓒ Ⓓ	59. Ⓐ Ⓑ Ⓒ Ⓓ	84. Ⓐ Ⓑ Ⓒ Ⓓ	109. Ⓐ Ⓑ Ⓒ Ⓓ
10. Ⓐ Ⓑ Ⓒ Ⓓ	35. Ⓐ Ⓑ Ⓒ Ⓓ	60. Ⓐ Ⓑ Ⓒ Ⓓ	85. Ⓐ Ⓑ Ⓒ Ⓓ	110. Ⓐ Ⓑ Ⓒ Ⓓ
11. Ⓐ Ⓑ Ⓒ Ⓓ	36. Ⓐ Ⓑ Ⓒ Ⓓ	61. Ⓐ Ⓑ Ⓒ Ⓓ	86. Ⓐ Ⓑ Ⓒ Ⓓ	111. Ⓐ Ⓑ Ⓒ Ⓓ
12. Ⓐ Ⓑ Ⓒ Ⓓ	37. Ⓐ Ⓑ Ⓒ Ⓓ	62. Ⓐ Ⓑ Ⓒ Ⓓ	87. Ⓐ Ⓑ Ⓒ Ⓓ	112. Ⓐ Ⓑ Ⓒ Ⓓ
13. Ⓐ Ⓑ Ⓒ Ⓓ	38. Ⓐ Ⓑ Ⓒ Ⓓ	63. Ⓐ Ⓑ Ⓒ Ⓓ	88. Ⓐ Ⓑ Ⓒ Ⓓ	113. Ⓐ Ⓑ Ⓒ Ⓓ
14. Ⓐ Ⓑ Ⓒ Ⓓ	39. Ⓐ Ⓑ Ⓒ Ⓓ	64. Ⓐ Ⓑ Ⓒ Ⓓ	89. Ⓐ Ⓑ Ⓒ Ⓓ	114. Ⓐ Ⓑ Ⓒ Ⓓ
15. Ⓐ Ⓑ Ⓒ Ⓓ	40. Ⓐ Ⓑ Ⓒ Ⓓ	65. Ⓐ Ⓑ Ⓒ Ⓓ	90. Ⓐ Ⓑ Ⓒ Ⓓ	115. Ⓐ Ⓑ Ⓒ Ⓓ
16. Ⓐ Ⓑ Ⓒ Ⓓ	41. Ⓐ Ⓑ Ⓒ Ⓓ	66. Ⓐ Ⓑ Ⓒ Ⓓ	91. Ⓐ Ⓑ Ⓒ Ⓓ	116. Ⓐ Ⓑ Ⓒ Ⓓ
17. Ⓐ Ⓑ Ⓒ Ⓓ	42. Ⓐ Ⓑ Ⓒ Ⓓ	67. Ⓐ Ⓑ Ⓒ Ⓓ	92. Ⓐ Ⓑ Ⓒ Ⓓ	117. Ⓐ Ⓑ Ⓒ Ⓓ
18. Ⓐ Ⓑ Ⓒ Ⓓ	43. Ⓐ Ⓑ Ⓒ Ⓓ	68. Ⓐ Ⓑ Ⓒ Ⓓ	93. Ⓐ Ⓑ Ⓒ Ⓓ	118. Ⓐ Ⓑ Ⓒ Ⓓ
19. Ⓐ Ⓑ Ⓒ Ⓓ	44. Ⓐ Ⓑ Ⓒ Ⓓ	69. Ⓐ Ⓑ Ⓒ Ⓓ	94. Ⓐ Ⓑ Ⓒ Ⓓ	119. Ⓐ Ⓑ Ⓒ Ⓓ
20. Ⓐ Ⓑ Ⓒ Ⓓ	45. Ⓐ Ⓑ Ⓒ Ⓓ	70. Ⓐ Ⓑ Ⓒ Ⓓ	95. Ⓐ Ⓑ Ⓒ Ⓓ	120. Ⓐ Ⓑ Ⓒ Ⓓ
21. Ⓐ Ⓑ Ⓒ Ⓓ	46. Ⓐ Ⓑ Ⓒ Ⓓ	71. Ⓐ Ⓑ Ⓒ Ⓓ	96. Ⓐ Ⓑ Ⓒ Ⓓ	121. Ⓐ Ⓑ Ⓒ Ⓓ
22. Ⓐ Ⓑ Ⓒ Ⓓ	47. Ⓐ Ⓑ Ⓒ Ⓓ	72. Ⓐ Ⓑ Ⓒ Ⓓ	97. Ⓐ Ⓑ Ⓒ Ⓓ	122. Ⓐ Ⓑ Ⓒ Ⓓ
23. Ⓐ Ⓑ Ⓒ Ⓓ	48. Ⓐ Ⓑ Ⓒ Ⓓ	73. Ⓐ Ⓑ Ⓒ Ⓓ	98. Ⓐ Ⓑ Ⓒ Ⓓ	123. Ⓐ Ⓑ Ⓒ Ⓓ
24. Ⓐ Ⓑ Ⓒ Ⓓ	49. Ⓐ Ⓑ Ⓒ Ⓓ	74. Ⓐ Ⓑ Ⓒ Ⓓ	99. Ⓐ Ⓑ Ⓒ Ⓓ	124. Ⓐ Ⓑ Ⓒ Ⓓ
25. Ⓐ Ⓑ Ⓒ Ⓓ	50. Ⓐ Ⓑ Ⓒ Ⓓ	75. Ⓐ Ⓑ Ⓒ Ⓓ	100. Ⓐ Ⓑ Ⓒ Ⓓ	125. Ⓐ Ⓑ Ⓒ Ⓓ

Part 2

1. Ⓐ Ⓑ Ⓒ Ⓓ	26. Ⓐ Ⓑ Ⓒ Ⓓ	51. Ⓐ Ⓑ Ⓒ Ⓓ	76. Ⓐ Ⓑ Ⓒ Ⓓ	101. Ⓐ Ⓑ Ⓒ Ⓓ
2. Ⓐ Ⓑ Ⓒ Ⓓ	27. Ⓐ Ⓑ Ⓒ Ⓓ	52. Ⓐ Ⓑ Ⓒ Ⓓ	77. Ⓐ Ⓑ Ⓒ Ⓓ	102. Ⓐ Ⓑ Ⓒ Ⓓ
3. Ⓐ Ⓑ Ⓒ Ⓓ	28. Ⓐ Ⓑ Ⓒ Ⓓ	53. Ⓐ Ⓑ Ⓒ Ⓓ	78. Ⓐ Ⓑ Ⓒ Ⓓ	103. Ⓐ Ⓑ Ⓒ Ⓓ
4. Ⓐ Ⓑ Ⓒ Ⓓ	29. Ⓐ Ⓑ Ⓒ Ⓓ	54. Ⓐ Ⓑ Ⓒ Ⓓ	79. Ⓐ Ⓑ Ⓒ Ⓓ	104. Ⓐ Ⓑ Ⓒ Ⓓ
5. Ⓐ Ⓑ Ⓒ Ⓓ	30. Ⓐ Ⓑ Ⓒ Ⓓ	55. Ⓐ Ⓑ Ⓒ Ⓓ	80. Ⓐ Ⓑ Ⓒ Ⓓ	105. Ⓐ Ⓑ Ⓒ Ⓓ
6. Ⓐ Ⓑ Ⓒ Ⓓ	31. Ⓐ Ⓑ Ⓒ Ⓓ	56. Ⓐ Ⓑ Ⓒ Ⓓ	81. Ⓐ Ⓑ Ⓒ Ⓓ	106. Ⓐ Ⓑ Ⓒ Ⓓ
7. Ⓐ Ⓑ Ⓒ Ⓓ	32. Ⓐ Ⓑ Ⓒ Ⓓ	57. Ⓐ Ⓑ Ⓒ Ⓓ	82. Ⓐ Ⓑ Ⓒ Ⓓ	107. Ⓐ Ⓑ Ⓒ Ⓓ
8. Ⓐ Ⓑ Ⓒ Ⓓ	33. Ⓐ Ⓑ Ⓒ Ⓓ	58. Ⓐ Ⓑ Ⓒ Ⓓ	83. Ⓐ Ⓑ Ⓒ Ⓓ	108. Ⓐ Ⓑ Ⓒ Ⓓ
9. Ⓐ Ⓑ Ⓒ Ⓓ	34. Ⓐ Ⓑ Ⓒ Ⓓ	59. Ⓐ Ⓑ Ⓒ Ⓓ	84. Ⓐ Ⓑ Ⓒ Ⓓ	109. Ⓐ Ⓑ Ⓒ Ⓓ
10. Ⓐ Ⓑ Ⓒ Ⓓ	35. Ⓐ Ⓑ Ⓒ Ⓓ	60. Ⓐ Ⓑ Ⓒ Ⓓ	85. Ⓐ Ⓑ Ⓒ Ⓓ	110. Ⓐ Ⓑ Ⓒ Ⓓ
11. Ⓐ Ⓑ Ⓒ Ⓓ	36. Ⓐ Ⓑ Ⓒ Ⓓ	61. Ⓐ Ⓑ Ⓒ Ⓓ	86. Ⓐ Ⓑ Ⓒ Ⓓ	111. Ⓐ Ⓑ Ⓒ Ⓓ
12. Ⓐ Ⓑ Ⓒ Ⓓ	37. Ⓐ Ⓑ Ⓒ Ⓓ	62. Ⓐ Ⓑ Ⓒ Ⓓ	87. Ⓐ Ⓑ Ⓒ Ⓓ	112. Ⓐ Ⓑ Ⓒ Ⓓ
13. Ⓐ Ⓑ Ⓒ Ⓓ	38. Ⓐ Ⓑ Ⓒ Ⓓ	63. Ⓐ Ⓑ Ⓒ Ⓓ	88. Ⓐ Ⓑ Ⓒ Ⓓ	113. Ⓐ Ⓑ Ⓒ Ⓓ
14. Ⓐ Ⓑ Ⓒ Ⓓ	39. Ⓐ Ⓑ Ⓒ Ⓓ	64. Ⓐ Ⓑ Ⓒ Ⓓ	89. Ⓐ Ⓑ Ⓒ Ⓓ	114. Ⓐ Ⓑ Ⓒ Ⓓ
15. Ⓐ Ⓑ Ⓒ Ⓓ	40. Ⓐ Ⓑ Ⓒ Ⓓ	65. Ⓐ Ⓑ Ⓒ Ⓓ	90. Ⓐ Ⓑ Ⓒ Ⓓ	115. Ⓐ Ⓑ Ⓒ Ⓓ
16. Ⓐ Ⓑ Ⓒ Ⓓ	41. Ⓐ Ⓑ Ⓒ Ⓓ	66. Ⓐ Ⓑ Ⓒ Ⓓ	91. Ⓐ Ⓑ Ⓒ Ⓓ	116. Ⓐ Ⓑ Ⓒ Ⓓ
17. Ⓐ Ⓑ Ⓒ Ⓓ	42. Ⓐ Ⓑ Ⓒ Ⓓ	67. Ⓐ Ⓑ Ⓒ Ⓓ	92. Ⓐ Ⓑ Ⓒ Ⓓ	117. Ⓐ Ⓑ Ⓒ Ⓓ
18. Ⓐ Ⓑ Ⓒ Ⓓ	43. Ⓐ Ⓑ Ⓒ Ⓓ	68. Ⓐ Ⓑ Ⓒ Ⓓ	93. Ⓐ Ⓑ Ⓒ Ⓓ	118. Ⓐ Ⓑ Ⓒ Ⓓ
19. Ⓐ Ⓑ Ⓒ Ⓓ	44. Ⓐ Ⓑ Ⓒ Ⓓ	69. Ⓐ Ⓑ Ⓒ Ⓓ	94. Ⓐ Ⓑ Ⓒ Ⓓ	119. Ⓐ Ⓑ Ⓒ Ⓓ
20. Ⓐ Ⓑ Ⓒ Ⓓ	45. Ⓐ Ⓑ Ⓒ Ⓓ	70. Ⓐ Ⓑ Ⓒ Ⓓ	95. Ⓐ Ⓑ Ⓒ Ⓓ	120. Ⓐ Ⓑ Ⓒ Ⓓ
21. Ⓐ Ⓑ Ⓒ Ⓓ	46. Ⓐ Ⓑ Ⓒ Ⓓ	71. Ⓐ Ⓑ Ⓒ Ⓓ	96. Ⓐ Ⓑ Ⓒ Ⓓ	121. Ⓐ Ⓑ Ⓒ Ⓓ
22. Ⓐ Ⓑ Ⓒ Ⓓ	47. Ⓐ Ⓑ Ⓒ Ⓓ	72. Ⓐ Ⓑ Ⓒ Ⓓ	97. Ⓐ Ⓑ Ⓒ Ⓓ	122. Ⓐ Ⓑ Ⓒ Ⓓ
23. Ⓐ Ⓑ Ⓒ Ⓓ	48. Ⓐ Ⓑ Ⓒ Ⓓ	73. Ⓐ Ⓑ Ⓒ Ⓓ	98. Ⓐ Ⓑ Ⓒ Ⓓ	123. Ⓐ Ⓑ Ⓒ Ⓓ
24. Ⓐ Ⓑ Ⓒ Ⓓ	49. Ⓐ Ⓑ Ⓒ Ⓓ	74. Ⓐ Ⓑ Ⓒ Ⓓ	99. Ⓐ Ⓑ Ⓒ Ⓓ	124. Ⓐ Ⓑ Ⓒ Ⓓ
25. Ⓐ Ⓑ Ⓒ Ⓓ	50. Ⓐ Ⓑ Ⓒ Ⓓ	75. Ⓐ Ⓑ Ⓒ Ⓓ	100. Ⓐ Ⓑ Ⓒ Ⓓ	125. Ⓐ Ⓑ Ⓒ Ⓓ

To remove answer sheet, cut along dotted line.

PRACTICE EXAMINATION 1

PART 1

NUMBER OF QUESTIONS: 125   TIME: 3 HOURS

Directions: Each of the questions or incomplete statements below is followed by four suggested answers or completions. Select the one that is best in each case and then blacken the corresponding space on the answer sheet.

1. Under NYSE rules, what action must a member firm take when it receives a complaint from a client regarding the handling of an account?

    (A) Notify the Securities and Exchange Commission.
    (B) Respond in writing to the client and keep a record of any action taken.
    (C) Fine the registered representative who handles the account.
    (D) Close the client's case.

2. Which of the following items would be important considerations when recommending municipal bonds to a client?

    (A) the legal residence of the client
    (B) the total portfolio of the client
    (C) the client's tax bracket
    (D) all of the above

3. A registered representative (RR) of a NYSE firm wishes to open an account with another firm. This would require written permission from:

    (A) the RR's employer
    (B) the NYSE
    (C) the SEC
    (D) all of the above

4. A common stock's book value is also known as:

    (A) liquidation value
    (B) exchange value
    (C) net tangible asset value per share
    (D) net worth

5. Which of the following accounts would not be allowed to grant trading authorization to an RR?

    (A) a corporation account
    (B) a husband and wife joint account
    (C) a custodian under the UGMA
    (D) an account for an employee of a broker/dealer

6. A customer enters an order to sell 500 shares of XYZ common stock, which is traded over the counter. A trader quotes the stock 27–27.25. Which of the following statements is correct?

    (A) The trader must buy the 500 shares at 27.
    (B) The trader must buy 100 shares at 27.
    (C) The trader need not buy any of the stock.
    (D) The trader must buy the 500 shares at 27.25.

7. A client who places an order on the NYSE to buy at the close will receive an execution:

(A) at the closing price
(B) at a price as close as possible to the closing price
(C) at the closing bid
(D) at the closing offer

8. Which of the following powers is not extended to the SEC under the Securities Act of 1933?

(A) power to require "full disclosure" on new corporate issues
(B) power to require filing of a registration statement for corporate new issues
(C) power to deny registration where legal requirements are not met
(D) power to regulate the offering of a new bank stock sold intrastate

9. Municipal securities would be purchased by all of the following types of accounts EXCEPT:

(A) individual investors
(B) corporations
(C) commercial banks
(D) corporate pension funds

10. During a period of stable interest rates which of the following types of securities would be most likely to experience volatile price changes?

(A) convertible bonds
(B) non-convertible bonds
(C) U.S. treasury securities
(D) general obligation bonds

11. Government National Mortgage Association (GNMA) pass through securities pay interest and principal:

(A) monthly
(B) quarterly
(C) semiannually
(D) annually

12. The confirmation of a municipal securities transaction to a client must include all of the following EXCEPT:

(A) taxable equivalent yield
(B) the par value of the bonds
(C) the accrued interest
(D) the total amount of the transaction

13. An open-end investment company with a maximum sales charge of 8% is currently quoted $15 bid – $16.30 offered. The sales charge is reduced to 5% for purchases of $50,000 to $74,999. Approximately how many shares would be purchased by a client investing $60,000?

(A) 3,680
(B) 3,800
(C) 4,000
(D) 3,953

14. Which of the following best describes municipal dollar bonds?

I.   term
II. serial
III. series
IV. callable

(A) I and II only
(B) I and IV only
(C) II and IV only
(D) III and IV only

15. Geographical diversification of municipal investments can protect against all of the following EXCEPT:

    (A) adverse legislation in one area
    (B) economic decline in one region
    (C) increasing interest rates
    (D) default by one particular issuer

16. Federal Reserve Board Regulation T applies to customer transactions of all of the following securities except:

    (A) U.S. treasury securities
    (B) convertible bonds
    (C) listed options
    (D) listed warrants

17. Regarding the over-the-counter market, which of the following statements are correct?

    I.   The Federal Reserve Board regulates which OTC securities are marginable.
    II. The NASD regulates trading practices in the OTC market.
    III. The SEC regulates OTC transactions.

    (A) I and II only
    (B) II and III only
    (C) I and III only
    (D) I, II, and III

18. Which of the following are true regarding a recourse loan of limited partnership?

    I.   Limited partners assume responsibility for the loan's repayment.
    II. Limited partners do not assume responsibility for the loan's repayment.
    III. Principal repayment lowers the limited partner's basis.
    IV. Any principal repayment increases the limited partner's basis.

    (A) I and II only
    (B) I and III only
    (C) II and III only
    (D) II and IV only

19. Net asset value of a mutual fund will be affected by:

    (A) appreciation
    (B) amortization
    (C) annualization
    (D) disintermediation

20. The most complete information regarding a new issue of municipal securities would be found in the:

    (A) *Bond Buyer*
    (B) Blue List
    (C) White's Ratings
    (D) official statement

21. The least important factor in the diversification of a municipal bond portfolio is:

    (A) rating
    (B) location of issuer
    (C) denomination of bonds
    (D) maturity schedule

22. A customer sells short 500 XYZ at $56 per share. The market price of XYZ declines to $34 per share. To protect his profit on XYZ, the customer should:

    (A) buy 5 XYZ puts
    (B) buy 5 XYZ calls
    (C) sell 5 XYZ puts
    (D) sell 5 XYZ calls

23. Which of the following securities will generate the greater current return with moderate risk?

    (A) common stock
    (B) a convertible bond
    (C) a nonconvertible mortgage bond
    (D) an income bond

24. Under Regulation T, the 90-day restriction of a frozen account would apply to a customer who purchases and sells:

    (A) different stocks in different accounts
    (B) stock in different accounts
    (C) stock in a margin account without fully paying for the purchase
    (D) stock in a cash account without having first fully paid for the purchase

25. According to MSRB rules, when may a municipal dealer share in profits or losses of a customer's account?

    (A) if the dealer effected the transaction for the customer's account
    (B) if the dealer receives compensation
    (C) if pursuant to a written guarantee made to the customer
    (D) under no condition

26. Which of the following sign the agreement among underwriters?

    (A) members of the syndicate
    (B) MSRB
    (C) attorney
    (D) issuing municipality

27. The priority of orders for a municipal bond offering is established by the:

    (A) notice of sale
    (B) prospectus
    (C) official statement
    (D) agreement among underwriters

28. White's Ratings for municipal securities are based on:

    (A) maturity
    (B) marketability
    (C) yield
    (D) interest rates

29. Which statement regarding bearer bonds is correct?

    (A) Interest payments are made directly to the owner.
    (B) They lack marketability.
    (C) Coupons are attached to the bonds.
    (D) The bond's rating is significantly lowered by the lack of registration.

30. Under SEC Rule 144, permission for sale of unregistered shares by an unaffiliated person is dependent upon other sales of that stock by this person over the preceding:

    (A) 60 days
    (B) 90 days
    (C) three months
    (D) two years

31. All of the following orders can be accepted for a custodial account under the Uniform Gifts to Minors Act EXCEPT:

    (A) purchase of a U.S. treasury security
    (B) purchase of a common stock
    (C) short sale of a listed common stock
    (D) sale of a corporate bond

32. An investor in a limited partnership has established a basis, for tax purposes, of $25,000. During the year, his share of the partnership losses was $8,000 and he received a cash distribution of $20,000. How much of the loss can be used to offset his other ordinary income?

    (A) $20,000
    (B) $8,000
    (C) $5,000
    (D) $12,000

33. In the reporting of last-sale information for NASD OTC stock, which of the following statements is correct?

    (A) Last-sale price information is available on all over-the-counter stocks.
    (B) Last-sale price information is available on OTC transactions in the National Market System.
    (C) Last-sale price information is available on NASDAQ National List OTC stocks.
    (D) Last-sale price information is not available on any NASDAQ OTC stocks.

34. Which of the following statements is true concerning option sales literature?

    (A) It may not project future performance.
    (B) It cannot include supporting documentation.
    (C) It must be preceded or accompanied by an OCC disclosure document.
    (D) It must disclose the firm's past experience based on the firm's recommendations.

35. If the syndicate manager of a new issue of municipal bonds wishes to allocate the bonds in a manner different from the priority established in the agreement among underwriters, the manager must:

    (A) obtain permission of all underwriters
    (B) forfeit his management fee
    (C) increase the takedown
    (D) be prepared to justify his allocation

36. A customer has written one ABC Feb 50 call at 4 in a cash account. Which of the following cannot be used to cover the call?

    (A) securities that are convertible into 100 shares of ABC
    (B) 100 shares of ABC
    (C) an escrow receipt for 100 ABC common shares
    (D) a long position of 1 ABC Feb 55 put

37. Which of the following industries is most cyclical?

    (A) retail stores
    (B) public utilities
    (C) oil stocks
    (D) appliance manufacture

38. Which of the following would generally not be a benefit received by investors in an equipment-leasing direct participation program?

    (A) income from rental payments
    (B) deductions for loan interest
    (C) cost recovery deductions
    (D) appreciation of investment

39. All of the following would be considered conflicts of interest for the general partner in a limited partnership EXCEPT:

    (A) accepting a fee for agreeing not to compete with the limited partnership
    (B) selling his existing office building to the limited partnership
    (C) acting as an agent for the partnership
    (D) accepting loans from the partnership

40. A customer is exercised on an S&P 100 Index 310 put. The index closed at 300. The client who was exercised would:

    (A) deliver cash
    (B) receive cash
    (C) delivery securities
    (D) receive securities

41. Which of the following statements concerning commercial paper is correct?

    (A) The corporation guarantees the payment of interest and principal.
    (B) Maturity is 270 days or less.
    (C) It can be issued directly by the corporation.
    (D) all of the above.

42. A registered representative must obtain written verification on an investor's net worth when recommending which of the following investments?

    (A) a direct participation program
    (B) an open-end investment company
    (C) a convertible bond
    (D) purchase of a preferred stock

43. With AMX trading at 55, an investor buys 1 AMX Oct 50 put at 3 and sells 1 AMX Oct 60 put at 11. The investor would want any of the following to occur EXCEPT:

    (A) the stock to rise
    (B) the premiums to narrow
    (C) the premiums to widen
    (D) both options to expire

44. Which of the following types of accounts could not be handled on a discretionary basis?

    (A) corporation account
    (B) joint account
    (C) options account
    (D) custodial account

45. Limited partners have which two of the following rights in a DPP?

    I. right to inspect partnership books
    II. right to sue the general partner for damages
    III. right to fix the compensation of the general partner
    IV. right to all of the tax benefits from the project

    (A) I and II
    (B) I and IV
    (C) II and III
    (D) III and IV

46. Which of the following orders for treasury bills will be filled first in the weekly auction?

    (A) orders from commercial lenders
    (B) orders from the federal open market account
    (C) noncompetitive bids
    (D) orders from primary market makers

47. For income tax purposes, a capital gain from the sale of a municipal bond can be offset against a capital loss from which of the following investments?

    I.   common stock
    II. GO bond
    III. real estate
    IV. corporate bond

    (A) II only
    (B) I and IV only
    (C) I, II, and IV only
    (D) I, II, III, and IV

48. An Eastern account has been formed to issue $2,000,000 in municipal securities. A syndicate member has a 25% participation and has sold $200,000. If there is a total of $800,000 remaining unsold, what is the member's liability?

    (A) $75,000
    (B) $150,000
    (C) $200,000
    (D) $300,000

49. A customer buys one XYZ Jun 90 put at 7 and sells one XYZ Jun 85 put at 3. Which of the following describes the spread?

    (A) credit-bearish
    (B) debit-bearish
    (C) credit-bullish
    (D) debit-bullish

50. Which of the following option positions would contain the greatest risk?

    (A) long a call
    (B) long a put
    (C) short an uncovered put
    (D) short an uncovered call

51. If a customer opened an account with you and instructed you to buy $15,000 worth of securities, what type of account would this be?

    (A) omnibus
    (B) discretionary
    (C) third party
    (D) disclosed

52. Which of the following is the order routing system used on the floor of the NYSE?

    (A) CQS
    (B) Are ub a book entry
    (C) DOT
    (D) AON

53. Which of the following must be licensed to sell securities in a particular state?

    I.   resident broker/dealer
    II. nonresident broker/dealer
    III. resident broker
    IV. nonresident broker

    (A) II and III only
    (B) I and III only
    (C) II and IV only
    (D) I, II, III, and IV

54. Which of the following bonds would most likely be paid by taxes on cigarettes and liquor?

    (A) special tax bonds
    (B) general obligation bonds
    (C) double-barreled bonds
    (D) special assessment bonds

Use the information in the following
NASDAQ display to answer questions 55–56.

LCSC
L 11.25 O 11.25 C   11
B 11   H 11.25 NC +.38
A 11.25 L 10.75 V   258 T 11:02

55. The quote on LCSC is:

(A) 11.12 workout
(B) 10.75–11.25
(C) 11–11.25
(D) 10.75–11

56. A customer placed an order to sell
LCSC at 11.125. When the trade price
was 11.25, which of the following
would be a valid reason for not having
executed the trade?

(A) the last trade was by another
market-maker
(B) the order was entered late
(C) the last trade at 11.25 was for
yesterday
(D) the firm missed the market

57. If an investor purchases 6½% revenue
bonds at 96 (subsequent to the original
issue, which was at par) and holds
them to maturity, the difference
between 96 and par is:

(A) a capital gain
(B) a capital loss
(C) taxable income
(D) nontaxable income

58. The primary purpose of ERISA is to
protect:

(A) against a registered representative's
mishandling of a client's IRA
account
(B) employees of the federal government from mismanagement of their
pension funds
(C) all employees from the employer's
mishandling of retirement funds
(D) pensioners from investment
advisor's mismanagement of their
portfolios

59. A client might be advised to buy index
calls if she believed which of the
following was likely to occur?

(A) interest rates were going to rise
(B) interest rates were going to fall
(C) the market was going to turn
bullish
(D) the market was going to turn
bearish

60. All of the following securities would be
good for delivery EXCEPT:

(A) securities registered in a corporate
name signed by an officer listed on
the corporate resolution
(B) custodial securities signed by the
minor
(C) securities registered to and signed
by a legal guardian
(D) trust securities signed by the trustee

Questions 61–62 are based on the following information:

	NAV	Offer Price	NAV Chg
DEF	7.33	8.09	.05
UVW	8.28	9.00	.08

61. A purchase of 200 shares of DEF will cost:

    (A) $1,618
    (B) $1,618+sales charge
    (C) $1,466
    (D) $1,466+sales charge

62. What is the sales charge percentage on UVW?

    (A) 7
    (B) 7½
    (C) 8
    (D) 8½

63. What is the function of the Federal National Mortgage Association?

    (A) buy and sell FHA-insured mortgages and VA-guaranteed mortgages
    (B) issue mortgages
    (C) provide financing for government housing bonds
    (D) guarantee the timely payment of interest and principal on government securities

64. A customer buys one ABC June 60 call at 5 when the market price is $60. The stock moves to $85 and the customer exercises his contract. The tax consequence of these transactions is a:

    (A) cost basis of ABC stock of $65
    (B) gain of $500
    (C) loss of $500
    (D) cost basis of ABC stock of $60

65. The following transaction is reported on the NYSE ticker tape:

    DNC Pr
          88 s 66¼

    This report shows a transaction of:

    (A) 88 shares of DNC preferred
    (B) 880 shares of DNC preferred
    (C) 8,800 shares of DNC preferred
    (D) a special offering of DNC preferred

66. A control relationship would exist between a municipal broker/dealer and an issuer if:

    (A) officers of the municipal dealer wish to purchase the bonds
    (B) the firm recently underwrote an issue of bonds for the municipality
    (C) a partner of the underwriter is in a position of authority over the issuer of the municipal bonds
    (D) the dealer trades other bonds of the municipality

67. If NYSE halts trading in a stock on which there are listed options, who would determine if the trading in those options would also be halted?

    (A) the SEC
    (B) the NASD
    (C) the OCC
    (D) the exchange on which the options trade

68. A municipal security trader employed by a broker/dealer participating in a joint account may do all of the following EXCEPT:

    (A) sell more than half of the bonds
    (B) provide quotes indicating more than one market for the security
    (C) effect a transaction for a related portfolio
    (D) purchase bonds for an accumulation account

69. A technical analyst calculating the number of securities advancing and declining would be following which of the following market theories?

    (A) short-interest theory
    (B) random walk theory
    (C) Drew's odd-lot theory
    (D) breadth of the market theory

70. Which of the following statements is true regarding the activities of a municipal securities broker's broker?

    (A) The broker maintains the anonymity of the clients using his services.
    (B) The broker charges no fees.
    (C) The broker bids only for large blocks.
    (D) The broker must be a member of the NYSE.

71. Holders of U.S. treasury securities would be most concerned about:

    (A) purchasing power risk
    (B) financial risk
    (C) default
    (D) credit risk

72. A 60-year-old man needs $30,000 for his son's college education and withdraws the funds from his IRA. Doing so, he must pay:

    (A) a 10% penalty
    (B) a capital gains tax on the amount withdrawn
    (C) a 10% penalty and income tax
    (D) no penalty, but income tax on the amount withdrawn

73. A client with a non-tax-qualified variable annuity withdraws funds prior to the contract being annuitized. Which of the following tax consequences would result?

    (A) all of the funds are taxable
    (B) the income is deferred until termination
    (C) a capital gain
    (D) the amount in excess of basis is considered to be ordinary income.

74. The operating expenses of a mutual fund divided by the fund's average net asset value is known as:

    (A) current ratio
    (B) expense ratio
    (C) price-earnings ratio
    (D) acid test ratio

75. Which of the following terms refers to a variable annuity?

    (A) discretionary account
    (B) syndicate account
    (C) separate account
    (D) joint account

76. A specialist may function as all of the following EXCEPT:

    (A) agent
    (B) broker
    (C) underwriter
    (D) principal

77. If the investor owns 100 shares of stock that split 2 for 1, how will the investor obtain the additional 100 shares?

    (A) receive a certificate for 100 shares from the company
    (B) send a due bill for 100 shares to the company
    (C) redeem the old certificate for two new 100-share certificates
    (D) redeem the old certificate for a new one issued for 200 shares

78. To which of the following does the 5% markup policy apply?

    (A) nonexempt securities
    (B) mutual funds
    (C) new issues
    (D) government securities

79. Stock index options expire:

    (A) weekly
    (B) monthly
    (C) quarterly
    (D) annually

80. Which of the following must be disclosed by a municipal securities dealer to a customer on request?

    (A) manager's fee
    (B) syndicate members' names
    (C) identity of any person for whom the order is being placed within the group
    (D) syndicate order priority

81. Advertisements prepared for use by a municipal securities broker/dealer must be approved by:

    (A) the MSRB
    (B) a municipal principal of the firm
    (C) the SEC
    (D) all of the above

82. A customer's option account has been approved, and positions have been established. The option agreement has not been returned by the customer within the required 15 days. What action should the firm take?

    (A) the account must be frozen
    (B) existing option positions must be closed out
    (C) only orders for closing transactions will be accepted
    (D) no specific action is required

83. An investor is long 1 ABC Nov 50 put and 1 ABC Nov 55 call. The position is a:

    (A) short straddle
    (B) long straddle
    (C) long combination
    (D) short combination

84. A manager of a GNMA fund writes covered calls against the portfolio to enhance the fund's investment return. For tax purposes, distributions by the fund would be categorized as:

    (A) ordinary income
    (B) capital gains
    (C) capital losses
    (D) capital gains and ordinary income

85. Which of the following would a customer examine to evaluate the creditworthiness of a new municipal security?

    (A) official statement
    (B) legal opinion
    (C) agreement among underwriters
    (D) notice of sale

86. If, at expiration, the market price of the underlying stock is the same as the exercise price of the option, which of the following positions would result in a profit?

    (A) long call
    (B) short call
    (C) long put
    (D) long combination

87. A registered representative registered to solicit orders of municipal securities only may solicit orders for all of the following EXCEPT:

    (A) water revenue bonds
    (B) general obligation bonds
    (C) special tax bonds
    (D) municipal bond funds

88. Early debt retirement provisions are met by:

    (A) a sinking fund
    (B) sale of a new bond issue
    (C) treasury borrowings
    (D) refunding of debt

89. Which of the following sequences of transactions illustrates zero plus tick?

    (A) 38.50–38.50–38.625
    (B) 50.25–50.50–50.50
    (C) 17.25–17.50–17.75
    (D) 24.50–24.50–24.50

90. Which of the following market indicators contains the smallest number of components?

    (A) the Value Line Index
    (B) the NYSE Composite Index
    (C) the Dow Jones Composite
    (D) the Dow Jones Industrial Average

91. The chairman of the board of a major corporation wishes to sell stock under Rule 144. The stock was given to him as employment compensation. Which of the following statements regarding the sale are correct?

    I.   The broker/dealer can act as principal or agent.
    II. The securities must have been paid for in full for two years.
    III. The broker/dealer can solicit buy orders.
    IV. The broker/dealer can charge an additional fee for his services.

    (A) I and II only
    (B) I and III only
    (C) II and III only
    (D) I, III, and IV only

92. MSRB rules permit a registered representative to:

    I.   guarantee a customer a profit
    II. offer to personally repurchase the bond in the future or a set price
    III. sell municipal bonds at par
    IV. sell a repurchase agreement

    (A) I and IV only
    (B) II and III only
    (C) III and IV only
    (D) I, II, III, and IV

93. Which of the following is not considered to be a member of an RR's immediate family according to NASD rules?

    (A) mother
    (B) daughter
    (C) aunt
    (D) father-in-law

94. Which of the following is not one of the leading economic indicators as published by the Department of Commerce?

    (A) inventory changes
    (B) orders for new equipment
    (C) consumer price index
    (D) index of industrial production

95. What is an underwriter's maximum sales compensation, including wholesaling costs, in a DPP offering?

    (A) 8½%
    (B) 3%
    (C) 15%
    (D) 10%

Questions 96–97 are based on the following information: A limited partner invests $20,000 in a DPP program and signs a recourse loan for $20,000.

96. What is the investor's maximum potential loss?

    (A) $20,000
    (B) $40,000
    (C) $50,000
    (D) unlimited

97. Using the information in question 96, what is the investor's cost basis?

    (A) $20,000
    (B) $40,000
    (C) $50,000
    (D) $80,000

98. Which of the following are affected when a company buys a machine for cash?

    (A) shareholder's equity
    (B) total assets
    (C) total liabilities
    (D) net working capital

99. Which of the following are affected when the company pays a cash dividend?

    (A) shareholder's equity
    (B) total assets
    (C) intangible assets
    (D) long-term liabilities

100. A municipal syndicate is preparing a bid on a new municipal issue. The first step in preparing their bid would be to determine the:

    (A) gross spread
    (B) concession
    (C) takedown
    (D) offering scale

101. Which of the following statements regarding REITs is correct?

    (A) They trade only in the over-the-counter market.
    (B) They trade on exchanges only.
    (C) They are traded at redemption value.
    (D) They trade both in the over-the-counter market and on exchanges.

102. Generally warrants are issued in connection with which of the following types of offerings?

    (A) mortgage bonds
    (B) debentures
    (C) income bonds
    (D) convertible bond issues

103. The most important aspect of a DPP would be:

    (A) management
    (B) economic viability
    (C) savings
    (D) liquidity

104. A direct participation program that does not have a legitimate business purpose is called:

    (A) a limited shelter
    (B) an abusive shelter
    (C) a crossover shelter
    (D) a nonparticipatory shelter

Questions 105–107 are based on the following information: A client writes 10 XYZ Jun 40 puts at 4.75 when ABC is trading at $42 a share. The customer has no other position.

105. What is the investor's maximum possible gain?

    (A) $44,700
    (B) $40,000
    (C) $4,750
    (D) unlimited

106. What is the investor's maximum possible loss?

    (A) $35,250
    (B) $40,000
    (C) $4,750
    (D) unlimited

107. XYZ stock rises to 50, and the customer closes the position by purchasing the options at .25. What is his gain?

    (A) $250
    (B) $4,500
    (C) $40,000
    (D) $39,750

108. When DML is trading at 52.25, a customer buys 100 shares of DLM and 1 DML Jan 50 put at 1.50. At expiration in January, DML is trading at 38.375. The customer lets the option expire, and sells the stock at the market. The result is a gain of:

    (A) $862.50
    (B) $150.00
    (C) $612.50
    (D) $462.50

109. Which of the following persons cannot be allocated shares of a "hot issue"?

    (A) employees of insurance companies that deal in securities
    (B) officers of banks
    (C) employees of an underwriting firm
    (D) the wife of an employee of an underwriting firm

110. An employee of a NYSE firm wishes to accept a part-time job on weekends to increase his income. To do so, the employee must have written permission from:

    (A) the NYSE
    (B) the NASD
    (C) his employer
    (D) all of the above

111. Which of the following are reasons to sell securities short?

    (A) arbitrage
    (B) hedge
    (C) profit from a price decline
    (D) all of the above

112. A person associated with a municipal bond dealer may do all the following during his apprenticeship EXCEPT:

    (A) offer bonds to other dealers
    (B) sell bonds to public clients
    (C) sell new issue municipal bonds to security dealers
    (D) provide quotations to other dealers

113. RFM closed at 83, a plus tick, on the NYSE on May 3. (May 4 is the date that the security will trade "ex" dividends. The dividend is in the amount of $.75.) What is the lowest price that you could execute a short sale at the opening of trading May 4?

    (A) 83
    (B) 82¼
    (C) 82⅜
    (D) any price

114. Which of the following best describes gross domestic product (GDP)?

    (A) total income of all U.S. companies
    (B) total value of all goods and services produced in the United States
    (C) total value of all real estate in the United States
    (D) total of all bank deposits in the United States

115. A broker/dealer purchased ABC stock at 39 for his inventory position. One month later the interdealer market for ABC was 37.50–37.75 and the broker/dealer sold the stock to a customer. The basis for the dealer's markup was:

    (A) 37.50
    (B) 39
    (C) 37.75
    (D) 37.625

116. The "additional bonds test" in a municipal revenue bond indenture states that:

    (A) no additional bonds can be issued for twelve months
    (B) subsequent bonds would have no claim on project revenue
    (C) new bonds must have a lower coupon
    (D) bonds having an equal claim on project revenue can only be issued if debt service coverage is adequate

117. A trader purchased euros in the spot market for .380. To protect his position, he also bought a euro September 38 put .0087. Above what price would his position be profitable?

    (A) .3713
    (B) .3714
    (C) .3880
    (D) .3887

118. Investment bankers perform all of the following functions EXCEPT:

    (A) accept time deposits
    (B) underwrite new issues
    (C) distribute blocks of stock to investors
    (D) purchase corporate bonds for resale

119. A customer with no other position writes one uncovered ABC Jun 80 call for a premium of 5. What is the customer's maximum loss potential on this position?

    (A) unlimited
    (B) $8,000
    (C) $7,500
    (D) $500

Questions 120–125 are based on information in the following chart.

Fund	Year Offered	Total Net Assets Mar. 31 '03 (MIL.$)	Max. Sales Chg. %	Invest. Income 2003	Invest. Income 2004	Security Profits 2003	Security Profits 2004	$10,000 Invested 12-31-98 Now Worth	% Yield From Inv. Inc.
AIM Aggressive Growth Fund	'84	1976.0	5.5	....	....	....	....	10,961	....
AIM Balanced Fund Cl.A	'78	1275.0	4.75	0.451	....	....	....	9,822	1.8
AIM Charter Cl.A	'67	1934.0	5.5	0.024	....	....	....	8,589	0.2
AIM Constellation Cl.A	'66	8642.0	5.5	....	....	....	....	9,342	....
AIM High Yield Fund Cl.A	'78	612.0	4.75	0.347	....	....	....	8,501	7.5
AIM Income Cl.A	'88	411.0	4.75	0.379	....	....	....	10,808	5.5
AIM Intermed. Govt. Fund Cl.A	'87	481.0	4.75	0.417	....	....	....	11,871	4.4
AIM Intl. Equity Cl.A	'92	1236.0	5.5	0.022	....	....	....	10,093	0.1
AIM Limited Maturity Treas. Shs.	'87	429.0	1.0	0.154	....	0.17	....	11,531	1.5
AIM Municipal Bond Cl.A	'77	303.0	4.75	0.372	....	....	....	12,085	4.4
AIM Select Growth Cl.A	'67	293.0	5.5	....	....	....	....	9,702	....
AIM Value Cl.A	'84	4986.0	5.5	....	....	....	....	8,507	....
AIM Weingarten Cl.A	'66	2129.0	5.5	....	....	....	....	6,224	....
Alger Small Cap. Portfolio Cl. B	'86	88.0	ERF	....	....	....	....	8,561	....
Alliance Americas Govt. Inc. Trust Cl. B	'92	608.0	ERF	0.582	....	....	....	12,602	8.0
Alliance Growth Fund Cl.B	'87	943.0	ERF	....	....	....	....	7,459	....
Alliance Growth & Income:Cl A	'32	3135.0	4.25	0.03	....	....	....	10,717	0.8
Alliance High Yield Cl.B	'97	261.0	ERF	0.463	....	....	....	8,633	7.6
Alliance Global Strategic Income Trust Cl.A	'96	34.0	4.25	0.589	....	....	....	11,814	6.4
Alliance Muni Income:Cal.Cl.A	'86	626.0	4.25	0.551	....	....	....	11,983	5.0
Alliance Muni Income:Insur.Cal.Cl.A	'86	122.0	4.25	0.182	....	....	....	11,000	1.1
Alliance Muni Income:N.Y. Cl.A	'86	284.0	4.25	0.51	....	....	....	11,582	5.0
Alliance Muni Bond:Insur.Natl.Cl.A	'77	135.0	4.25	0.427	....	....	....	11,056	4.1
Alliance Muni Bond:Natl. Cl.A	'86	362.0	4.25	0.546	....	....	....	10,088	5.3
Alliance New Europe Fund Inc.	'90	71.0	4.25	....	....	....	....	9,213	....
Alliance Premier Growth Cl.B	'92	2297.0	ERF	....	....	....	....	8,159	....
Alliance Quasar Fund Cl.B	'90	184.0	4.25	....	....	....	....	8,691	....
Alliance Real Estate Invest. Cl.B	'98	119.0	ERF	0.448	....	....	....	16,225	3.1
Alliance Technology Cl.B	'93	1361.0	None	....	....	....	....	7,045	....
Alliance Worldwide Fund Cl.A	'94	211.0	4.25	0.64	....	....	....	13,122	0.3
Amer. Century Cal. High Yield Muni Fund	'87	340.0	None	0.519	....	....	....	11,648	5.3
Amer. Century Cal. Long Term Tax Free	'83	493.0	None	0.538	....	....	....	10,978	4.7
Amer. Century GNMA Fund	'85	1673.0	None	0.519	....	....	....	12,354	5.0
Amer. Century Growth Fund	'58	4429.0	None	....	....	....	....	8,491	....
Amer. Century Select Fund	'58	3007.0	None	....	....	....	....	8,802	....
Amer. Century Short Term Govt.	'82	995.0	None	0.198	....	....	....	11,599	2.1
Amer. Century Target 2005 Fund	'85	330.0	None	4.29	....	2.09	....	14,440	4.3
Amer. Century Target 2010 Fund	'85	232.0	None	4.39	....	5.03	....	16,352	5.3
Amer. Century Target 2015 Fund	'86	149.0	None	3.99	....	2.39	....	15,988	6.0
Amer. Century Target 2020 Fund	'90	175.0	None	3.08	....	3.29	....	16,708	6.5

120. Which of the following is a no-load fund?

(A) AIM Aggressive Growth Fund
(B) Alliance Growth Fund CIB
(C) Alliance Technology CIB
(D) Alliance Worldwide Fund CLB

121. Which of the following funds has shown the greatest increase in value since 12/31/98?

(A) Alliance American Govt., Inc. Trust CLB
(B) Alliance Worldwide Fund CIA
(C) American Century Target 2010 Fund
(D) American Century Target 2020 Fund

122. Which of the following funds shows the greatest yield from investment income?

    (A) Aim High Yield Fund CIA
    (B) Alliance Americas Govt., Inc. Trust CIB
    (C) American Century GNMA Fund
    (D) American Century Target 2020 Fund

123. Which of the following funds has the lowest maximum sales charge?

    (A) AIM Aggressive Growth Fund
    (B) AIM High Yield Fund C1.A
    (C) AIM Limited Maturity Treas. Shs.
    (D) AIM Select Growth C1.A

124. Which of the following funds has the highest maximum sales charge?

    (A) AIM Intl. Equity C1.A
    (B) AIM Municipal Bond C1.A
    (C) Aim Value C1.A
    (D) Alliance New Europe Fund, Inc.

125. Which of the following funds did not make a capital gains distribution in 2003?

    (A) AIM High Yield Fund C1.A
    (B) AIM Municipal C1.A
    (C) Alliance Mun Income Cal. C1.A
    (D) Amer. Century Growth Fund

PART 1 ANSWERS

1. **B** The firm must respond to the complaint in writing and maintain a file recording the handling of the complaint.

2. **D** All of these items are important considerations when recommending municipal securities to a client.

3. **A** Under NYSE rules an employee of a member firm must have written permission from his employer to open an account at another firm. The employer must also receive copies of all confirmations and statements.

4. **C** The book value is often called net tangible asset value per share.

5. **C** Under the UGMA a custodian cannot delegate authority to handle an account and thus could not grant a trading authorization.

6. **B** A trader is only required to buy or sell 100 shares at his quoted price.

7. **B** Orders to be executed "on the close" are executed as close as possible to the closing price, but the exact closing price cannot be guaranteed.

8. **D** In most cases, the SEC has no regulatory authority over intrastate offerings of new issues. Such would usually fall under the jurisdiction of the state securities and/or banking commission. SEC Rule 147 more clearly defines just what constitutes "intrastate" for certain offerings.

9. **D** Municipal securities are generally purchased to provide tax-exempt income. As pension funds do not pay taxes, these securities would not be attractive to them.

10. **A** The price movement of convertible securities is largely influenced by the action of the common stock into which they are convertible. Therefore, the stability of interest rates would not be a major factor in the price movement.

11. **A** This monthly payment schedule is unique to GNMA passthroughs.

12. **A** Taxable equivalent yield can only be determined if the client's tax bracket is known. It is not shown on the client's trade confirmation.

13. **B** The purchase price for investments of $60,000 would be $15.79 (bid of 15 divided by 95%) as the sales charge is only 5%. The amount invested, $60,000, divided by $15.79 a share equals approximately 3,800 shares.

14. **B** Dollar bonds are term issues, which are quoted on a dollar basis. Term bonds are callable prior to maturity.

15. **C** Geographical diversification cannot protect against a loss of value due to an increase in interest rates.

16. **A** The Federal Reserve is empowered to establish margin requirements under the Securities Exchange Act of 1934. As U.S. treasury securities are exempt from this legislation, they are not included in the Fed's margin regulations.

17. **D** Statements I, II, and III are all correct.

18. **B** In a recourse loan, the lender does have recourse to the limited partners to satisfy the debt. Resource loans are included in the limited partners' tax basis.

19. **A** Net asset value per share is increased by portfolio appreciation. The other choices are not relevant to mutual funds.

20. **D** The official statement on a municipal security is similar to the prospectus on an offering of corporate securities. It contains all of the important information.

21. **C** The denomination in which the bonds are issued would not be a factor in diversifying a portfolio. The other choices would be important considerations.

22. **B** As the customer is short the stock, he wishes to protect himself against an increase in price. The purchase of calls would accomplish this.

23. **C** Both the common stock and the convertible bond contain a considerable risk factor. The mortgage bond would best suit this customer's needs.

24. **D** Purchases in cash account must be paid for in full prior to the time of sale. Full payment is not required in a margin account.

25. **D** A municipal dealer may not, under any condition, share in the profits or losses in a customer's account.

26. **A** The agreement among underwriters is signed by the dealers that form the underwriting syndicate.

27. **D** The order priority is found in the agreement among underwriters.

28. **B** The degree of marketability for a municipal security is measured by White's Ratings.

29. **C** Bearer bonds have interest coupons attached. Interest payments are mailed to the holders of registered bonds.

30. **C** The amount permitted to be sold under Rule 144 is measured over a three-month period.

31. **C** The Uniform Gifts to Minors Act does not permit the use of margin accounts. As all short sales must be executed in margin accounts, they could not be accepted for a UGMA account.

32. **C** The $20,000 cash distribution reduces the partner's basis to $5,000. Losses are then applied, but cannot exceed the basis. Thus only $5,000 of the loss could be taken in that year.

33. **B** Last-sale transactions are available only on stocks that are included in the National Market System.

34. **C** Option sales literature must be preceded by or accompanied by a disclosure document.

35. **D** The priority of allocation of orders on a municipal issue are established in the agreement among underwriters. The manager may change this order, however, if he feels it is in the best interest of the syndicate. The manager must be prepared to justify this change.

36. **D** A call can be written in a cash account if it is covered by the underlying security, a convertible security, or an escrow receipt from a bank.

37. **D** Manufacturers of appliances generally show a more erratic pattern of earnings than the industries mentioned in the other choices.

38. **D** The value of equipment will usually decline over its usable life. This would preclude an investor's receiving any capital appreciation.

39. **C** The function of the general partner is to manage the business of the partnership and would not be deemed a conflict of interest. The other activities would be conflicting.

40. **A** Settlement of index options is made in cash. As the customer is being put at 310 when the index is

trading at 300, he must deliver cash equal to the difference in strike prices.

41. **D** All of these statements are correct regarding commercial paper.

42. **A** As the registered representative is responsible for determining the suitability of investing in a DPP he must verify the client's net worth.

43. **C** If the difference between the premiums widens beyond its current 8 points both options would be exercised, resulting in a loss of $200.

44. **D** Under the Uniform Gifts to Minors Act, custodians cannot delegate their responsibility to others.

45. **A** The limited partners have the right to inspect partnership records and the right to sue a general partner acting outside the partnership agreement. The general partner's compensation is determined in the original agreement, and as the general partner must receive some of the profits and tax benefits, they do not go entirely to the limited partners.

46. **C** All noncompetitive bids are filled first at the weekly T-bill auction. They are given the average price of all bids accepted.

47. **D** A gain from the sale of a capital asset can be offset by a loss from the sale of any other capital asset.

48. **C** The syndicate member has a 25% participation. Since this is an Eastern account, he is responsible for 25% of all bonds remaining unsold, $25\% \times \$800,000 = \$200,000$.

49. **B** As the customer paid (7) more premium than he received (3), the spread is established at a debit. As he will profit if the stock declines, it is a bearish position.

50. **D** This is tantamount to being short the stock. The uncovered call writer will lose if the stock goes up beyond the strike price of the option, and there is no ceiling on how high up it could go.

51. **B** This would be discretionary, since the specific securities and amounts were being left to your judgment.

52. **C** The DOT system (designated order turnaround) is used to route orders on the Exchange floor and speed the execution and reporting.

53. **D** The securities laws of each state, known as Blue Sky laws, require licensing for any firm or individual representing a firm engaged in the sale of securities in that state.

54. **A** Principal and interest on special tax bonds are paid only from special taxes on items such as tobacco, liquor, and gasoline.

55. **C** The quote is 11 (bid) – 11.25 (ask). The machine is telling us the following:

Last 11.25	Open 11.25	Close	10.88
Bid 11	High 11.25	Net change	+.38
Ask 11.25	Low 10.75	Volume	258 Time

56. **A** The over-the-counter market is a decentralized market consisting of competing market-makers. Limit orders are usually not entered on the screen since they are away from the current market. A trade at a price above the customer limit could well have been made by another market maker.

57. **A** The difference between purchase price of a municipal purchased in the secondary market (after original issue) at a discount and either sale price or maturity is a capital loss. In this question, it is a capital gain.

58. **C** ERISA's primary purpose is to protect participants in union and

corporate pension plans from discriminating pension practices and misappropriation of and mis-management of pension plan assets. The law is very stringent in its investment reporting requirements.

59. **C** Index calls reflect the market in general and have nothing to do with interest rates. If we are bullish on the market in general we buy calls.

60. **B** Securities registered in the name of a custodian would be good delivery only if they were endorsed by the custodian not the minor who was the recipient of the gift.

61. **A** This is an open-end investment company. Since the NAV is lower than the offer price, it is a load fund. The sales charge is built into the offer price, which investors have to pay to purchase its shares. Therefore, the investor would pay $1,618 (200×8.09=$1,618).

62. **C** The formula is

$$\frac{\text{sales charge}}{\text{offer price}} = \frac{9.00 - 8.28}{9.00} = \frac{0.72}{9.00} = 8\%$$

63. **A** FNMA buys FHA, VA, and conventional mortgages and uses mortgages to back the issuance of debt securities.

64. **A** Exercise of a call option to acquire stock position does not generate a taxable gain or loss. We add the premium to the strike price to determine the client's cost of the stock.

65. **C** The 88s indicates 88 lots of 100 shares each, for a total of 8,800 shares.

66. **C** A control relationship exists when a dealer or one of its principals is in a position to exercise influence over the issuer of municipal securities.

67. **D** A trading halt in the underlying stock generally leads to a halt in trading for the options. That decision is made by the exchange on which the options trade.

68. **B** When acting in a joint account the dealers may not issue quotations that falsely indicate more than one market for the joint account securities.

69. **D** The breadth of the market theory, sometimes referred to as the "advance-decline" theory, attempts to predict future market direction by measuring the change in the number of securities advancing compared to the number declining in price.

70. **A** A "broker's broker" does not disclose the identity of the dealers who utilize his services. He is, of course, paid for his services and deals in large or small amounts of bonds.

71. **A** There is little or no financial or credit risk with U.S. treasury securities. However, a loss of purchasing power due to inflation could be a concern.

72. **D** Withdrawals from an IRA after reaching the age of 59½ do not incur a penalty but are subject to income tax. Withdrawals made prior to age 59½ incur a penalty of 10% of the amount withdrawn.

73. **D** The contributions are made to a non-tax-qualified variable annuity and are not taxable upon withdrawal. However, an amount above the contribution or basis is considered to be ordinary income.

74. **B** The expense ratio of a mutual fund is determined by dividing the operating expenses by the total net assets.

75. **C** The portfolio of securities of a variable annuity is held apart from the insurance company's other assets. These securities are deposited in a separate account.

76. **C** Stock exchange specialists may trade as brokers or agents (executing orders for others) or principals trading for their own accounts. The specialist's job is to maintain a fair and orderly market. Underwriting activities are not a part of the specialist's function as they do not take place on stock exchanges.

77. **A** All that happens after a split is that the company sends you the additional shares.

78. **A** The 5% markup policy of the NASD does not apply to securities offered by prospectus (new issues and mutual funds) or to exempt securities (governments and municipals).

79. **B** Stock index options trade with monthly expiration intervals, with only the closest two or three months trading at any time.

80. **D** Of the items listed, only the order priority must be disclosed to customers upon request.

81. **B** MSRB rules require that all advertising be approved by a principal of the firm prior to use.

82. **C** As the requirement to return the documents within 15 days has not been met, the firm can only enter orders to close out the current position.

83. **C** As both the strike price and the expiration month are different the position is a combination. The customer is long both options so it is a long combination.

84. **D** Any interest distributed will be considered ordinary income, but any profits generated by trading the portfolio will be considered capital gains.

85. **A** The official statement contains all the important information regarding a municipal security. It is similar to the prospectus used in corporate issues.

86. **B** If the stock price is the same as the exercise price at the time of expiration the writer of a short call will not be called. He will profit by retaining the premium.

87. **D** A person with a limited registration for municipal securities can sell only those products. Municipal bond funds are investment companies and would require additional registration.

88. **A** A sinking fund is established to retire (sink) bonds prior to maturity.

89. **B** A "Zero+Tick" is a transaction at the same price as the last sale, but higher than the last different sale. Only answer (B) shows such a sequence.

90. **D** Although it is the most quoted market indicator, the Dow Jones Industrial Average contains only 30 stocks. The Dow Composite has 65, the NYSE Composite about 1,550, and the Value Line Index about 1,725.

91. **A** Under Rule 144 the broker/dealer can act as principal or agent. Securities received as employment compensation must have been held for two years on a fully paid basis. However, the broker/dealer cannot solicit orders nor may he charge more than his usual commission.

92. **C** A registered representative cannot guarantee a profit to a customer or indemnify him against a loss. She can, however, sell municipal securities or repurchase agreements.

Under MSRB interpretation, a repurchase agreement is not deemed to be a guarantee against loss.

93. **C** Under NASD rules the immediate family of a registered representative includes his parents, spouse, children, brother, sisters, parents-in-law, and brothers- and sisters-in-law. Not deemed part of his immediate family are aunts, uncles, nieces, and nephews. This definition is important in the allocation procedures of hot issues to avoid free riding.

94. **D** Industrial production is classified as a coincident indicator of the economy as it measures a broad sector of the economy. The other, more narrow measurements, are considered to be economic indicators.

95. **D** Under NASD rules, the maximum sales compensation for the underwriter of direct participation programs is 10%. This includes the associated selling cost.

96. **B** As the partner is liable for the $20,000 recourse loan, it increases her potential liability to $40,000— The investment of $20,000 plus the loan.

97. **B** As the partner is liable for the loan it is considered to be part of her basis.

98. **D** The purchase of the machine reduces a current asset (cash) and therefore reduces net working capital (current assets minus current liabilities). The other items are not affected.

99. **B** Payment of a cash dividend reduces a current asset (cash) and reduces a current liability (dividend declared). Thus, total assets are reduced, but the other items are not changed.

100. **D** The first step in determining the bid on a municipal bond issue would be to "write the scale" of offering prices. Profit and other determinations are made later.

101. **D** REITs are much like closed-end investment companies and can trade on exchanges or in the over-the-counter market.

102. **B** Warrants are most often included with an offering of debentures. Their inclusion may lead to a lower interest rate.

103. **B** Economic viability is the most important factor in choosing a DPP. If that is not present, the other factors are inconsequential.

104. **B** Abusive shelters are those formed only to create tax deductions and have no legitimate purpose. They can be subject to legal attack by the Internal Revenue Service.

105. **C** When a customer writes an uncovered put, his maximum profit is the premium received. In this case he received $475 for each put or a total of $4,750.

106. **A** The customer could be required to purchase 1000 shares of XYZ stock at $40 a share. If XYZ stock was worthless he would lose $40,000 less the $4,750 premium received for writing the puts.

107. **B** The customer received $4,750 to write the puts. If he repurchased them for $25 each, a total of $250, his profit would be $4,500.

108. **D** The customer makes 6.125 points on the stock or $612.50. He loses 1.50 points, or $150, on the expired put. His net gain is 4.625 points, or $462.50.

109. **C** An employee of a securities firm that underwrites securities cannot be allocated shares of a hot issue. Employees of financial institutions

and members of the immediate family of a broker/dealer can be allocated hot issues under certain conditions.

110. **C** Under NYSE rules any outside employment must be approved by the member firm employer.

111. **D** All of the choices would be possible reasons for selling stock short.

112. **B** During the 90-day period of apprenticeship a municipal representative may not conduct business with the public, but may contact other municipal dealers.

113. **D** The uptick rule was rescinded.

114. **B** This choice properly defines the gross domestic product.

115. **C** The markup is based on the current offering price of 37.75. The dealer's cost is not a relevant factor.

116. **D** The "additional bonds test" requires that earnings to provide proper coverage must be demonstrated before additional bonds of equal ranking can be issued.

117. **D** The reasoning here is no different than in stock options. To break even the client's long position must rise far enough for him to recapture his premium.

118. **A** The accepting of deposits is a function of a commercial banker not an investment banker.

119. **A** Writing a naked call is the same as shorting the stock. The loss potential is unlimited.

120. **C** See column 2 Alliance Technology C1.B has no sales charge; the others do.

121. **D** See column 5. This column shows the current value of a $10,000 investment made in 1998 Amer. Century Target 2020 Fund increased to $16,708. The others have risen less.

122. **B** See column 6. Alliance Americas Govt Inc., Trust C1.B shows a yield of 8.0%. The others show less.

123. **C** See column 2. All of these funds have a sales charge, but AIM Limited Maturity Treas Shs at 1.0% has the smallest.

124. **A** See column 2. AIM Intl. Equity C1.A has the highest maximum sales charge of 5.5%.

125. **D** See columns 3 and 4. Column 3 shows a capital gain distribution for 2003. Amer Century Growth Fund is the only one of these four that made no distribution in that year.

PART 2

NUMBER OF QUESTIONS: 125	TIME: 3 HOURS

Directions: Each of the questions or incomplete statements below is followed by four suggested answers or completions. Select the one that is best in each case and then blacken the corresponding space on the answer sheet.

1. Which of the following terms would only be used to describe an offering of corporate securities?

    (A) standby
    (B) firm commitment
    (C) all or none
    (D) best efforts

2. The purpose of a due diligence meeting in connection with a new issue is to:

    (A) prepare the registration statement
    (B) make the final price determination
    (C) review the SEC deficiency statement
    (D) establish that the underwriter and company officials have discussed the affairs of the company

3. Potential underwriters of a competitive municipal offering can obtain worksheets provided by:

    (A) the *Bond Buyer*
    (B) the MSRB
    (C) the *Wall Street Journal*
    (D) Standard & Poor's

4. Which of the following would appear on a confirmation of a "when issued" trade of municipal securities?

    (A) accrued interest
    (B) total money involved in the trade
    (C) capacity in which the dealer acted
    (D) settlement date

5. Which of the following best describes a double-barreled municipal security?

    (A) special tax bond
    (B) general obligation bond
    (C) limited liability bond
    (D) income bond

6. A bond rated "AA" by Moody's is considered to be:

    (A) highest investment grade
    (B) medium investment grade
    (C) speculative
    (D) low grade

7. A customer is long 200 shares of XON at $70 and 200 shares of GM at $80 in a margin account. The debit balance in the account is $18,000. The customer sells 50 of the XON shares for $3,500. The amount released to the SMA is:

    (A) -0-
    (B) $1,750
    (C) $3,500
    (D) $7,000

8. A customer sells short IBM stock at $125. The stock then declines to $110. To protect the profit the client could do all of the following EXCEPT:

    (A) buy an IBM call
    (B) place a buy-stop order
    (C) buy an IBM put
    (D) cover the short position

9. The MSRB rule dealing with quotations relating to municipal securities covers:

   (A) requests for offers
   (B) requests for bids
   (C) distribution of offers
   (D) all of the above

10. All of the following can affect the marketability of a municipal security EXCEPT:

    (A) call price
    (B) dated date
    (C) maturity
    (D) yield

11. Who is responsible for verifying that limited partners meet the net worth and income requirements?

    (A) the registered representative
    (B) the general partner
    (C) the SEC
    (D) the sponsor

12. The debt service on municipal revenue bonds may be paid from all of the following sources EXCEPT:

    (A) bridge tolls
    (B) airport revenues
    (C) hydroelectric plant revenue
    (D) ad valorem taxes

13. The intrinsic value of a call option is the:

    (A) out-of-the-money amount
    (B) time value
    (C) in-the-money amount
    (D) premium multiplied by 100

Questions 14–16 are based on the following information:

A client purchases one ABZ Jul 40 call at 7 and writes one ABZ July 50 call at 3. The market price of ABZ is 41.

14. The position created is known as a:

    (A) straddle
    (B) spread
    (C) strip
    (D) strap

15. The breakeven point for the client at expiration is:

    (A) 40
    (B) 44
    (C) 47
    (D) 50

16. How much of a deposit is required for the position?

    (A) $615
    (B) $1,015
    (C) $1,315
    (D) $400

17. A client opens a margin account and signs a customer loan consent and customer's agreement. Which of the following are true?

    I.   The stock will be kept in street name.
    II. The stock may be pledged for a loan at a bank.
    III. The stock may be loaned to other customers.
    IV. The customer pays interest on the debit balance.

    (A) I and III only
    (B) II and III only
    (C) II and IV only
    (D) I, II, III and IV

18. A customer buys securities and does not pay for the purchase within the five business days allowed under Reg T. Which of the following actions could the broker take?

    I. sell the securities
    II. request an extension for payment
    III. allow three additional days
    IV lend the customer the funds

    (A) I and II only
    (B) II and III only
    (C) I, II, and IV only
    (D) I, II, III, and IV

19. A technical analyst believes that XYZ stock currently trading at $52 has a resistance level at $55. Should the stock break out above $55 he feels that the shares will reach much higher prices. Which of the following orders would be the most appropriate?

    (A) market order to buy
    (B) limit order to buy at 55
    (C) stop order to buy at 53
    (D) stop order to buy at 55.25

20. The general partner of a DPP can be described as all of the following EXCEPT:

    (A) has limited liability
    (B) manages the business
    (C) is entitled to a portion of the profits
    (D) acts as fiduciary for the limited partner

21. Which of the following would *not* be included on a municipal "when issued" confirmation?

    I. settlement date
    II. accrued interest
    III. total dollar amount
    IV. extended principal

    (A) I and II only
    (B) III and IV only
    (C) I, II, and III only
    (D) I, II, III, and IV

22. A technical analyst states that the market is "consolidating." This means that the market trending is:

    (A) falling
    (B) rising
    (C) showing little movement
    (D) indeterminable

23. Which of the following is a lagging indicator of economic trends?

    (A) new housing permits
    (B) home appliances
    (C) natural gas
    (D) retailing

24. A technical analyst would be most interested in which indicator?

    (A) price-earnings ratio
    (B) current ratio
    (C) quick assets ratio
    (D) moving average

25. Which of the following actions by a registered representative would be a violation of the Conduct Rules?

    (A) trading of mutual fund shares
    (B) discussing the possibility of volume discounts on the purchase of mutual fund shares
    (C) sending a customer a prospectus after discussing a possible investment in a mutual fund
    (D) establishing a cash account for a customer without that customer's signature

26. A premium call on municipal securities is:

    (A) the amount paid to the issuer in excess of the par value of the security
    (B) a redemption provision that permits the issuer to call securities at a price in excess of par
    (C) a redemption provision that requires the issuer to call the securities if they trade at a premium in the secondary market
    (D) the amount by which the purchase price for the securities exceeds par value

27. An investor is short 100 shares of XYZ at 45 in a properly margined account. XYZ falls to 43, and the customer decides to sell 1 XYZ Oct 45 put at 3. What is the deposit required for the sale of the put?

    (A) $595
    (B) $495
    (C) $300
    (D) -0-

28. The effective federal funds rate is the:

    (A) highest rate at which trades occurred for the day
    (B) lowest rate at which trades occurred for the day
    (C) rate charged by the largest member bank
    (D) daily average rate throughout the country

29. A customer places an order to buy in a margin account 100 shares of ABC stock at $60 and 5 ABC Nov 65 calls at 2. The customer wishes to meet the Reg T requirement by depositing fully paid XYZ stock (NYSE listed) currently trading at $25. How many shares of XYZ must be deposited?

    (A) 250
    (B) 300
    (C) 320
    (D) 600

30. A registered representative erroneously enters an order to buy 900 shares of XYZ stock for a customer who has requested 700 shares. He discovers the error when he receives the report of execution. The registered representative should:

    (A) cancel the order
    (B) convince the customer to buy the extra shares
    (C) report the error to his manager
    (D) sell the extra 200 shares immediately

31. A customer shorts 1 XYZ Aug 20 put at 5 and 1 XYZ Aug 20 call at 3, when XYZ is at 18. At expiration, XYZ is trading at 15, and the position is closed at intrinsic value. What is the gain or loss?

   (A) $300 loss
   (B) $300 gain
   (C) $800 loss
   (D) $800 gain

32. Which of the following is the narrowest measure of the market?

   (A) NYSE Composite Index
   (B) Value Line Index
   (C) Dow Jones Industrial Average
   (D) Standard & Poor's 100 Index

33. Which of the following choices shows a zero plus tick?

   (A) 36.50   36.50   36.37   36.50
   (B) 36.50   36.37   36.75   36.37
   (C) 36.50   36.62   36.62   36.50
   (D) 36.50   36.37   36.75   36.37

34. Which of the following are possible federal tax consequences of call options that are purchased and subsequently sold?

   I.   capital gain
   II. capital loss
   III. regular income
   IV. no taxable income

   (A) I and II only
   (B) I and IV only
   (C) III and IV only
   (D) I, II, III, and IV

35. Which of the following positions would be considered in the same class of options?

   I.   long and short calls on the same underlying security
   II. long calls and short puts on the same underlying security
   III. long and short puts on the same underling security
   IV. short calls and long puts on the same underlying security

   (A) I and II only
   (B) I and III only
   (C) II and III only
   (D) II and IV only

36. The placement ratio of municipal securities is:

   (A) the total dollar volume of the new issue municipal securities placed by underwriting syndicates in the last 30 days
   (B) the amount of new issue municipal securities sold to underwriting syndicates as a percentage of the amount issued that month
   (C) the amount of new issue municipal securities sold to underwriting syndicates in the prior week
   (D) the total dollar volume of municipal securities expected to be issued over the next 30 days

37. A client of yours has recently retired and is looking for safety of principal and income. Which of the following mutual funds would be least suitable for your client?

   (A) special situation fund
   (B) balanced fund
   (C) bond fund
   (D) growth & income fund

38. A customer has the following position in his margin account: long market value of $21,000 and a debit balance of $10,000. What is the purchasing power in the customer's account?

    (A) $500
    (B) $1,000
    (C) $2,000
    (D) $6,500

39. The provisions of the Trust Indenture Act of 1939 apply to all of the following securities EXCEPT:

    (A) $30,000,000 U.S. treasury bonds due in 2005
    (B) $20,000,000 Shell Oil equipment trust certificates due in 2007
    (C) $40,000,000 Pacific Power mortgage bonds due in 2007
    (D) $35,000,000 Boeing debentures due in 2010

40. Which of the following has the greatest risk?

    (A) common stock
    (B) zero coupon bonds
    (C) debentures
    (D) preferred stock

41. All of the following are DPP programs EXCEPT:

    (A) oil and gas
    (B) real estate
    (C) equipment leasing
    (D) self-directed IRA

42. A customer's margin account has available SMA of $1,000. How much would the customer have to deposit to purchase listed options with a premium of $4,000?

    (A) $4,000
    (B) $3,000
    (C) $2,000
    (D) $1,000

43. If an investor sold stock for a loss and repurchased the same security within 30 days of the sale, which of the following statements would be true?

    (A) Under no circumstances can it be done.
    (B) The loss would not be allowed unless the stock was held long term on the date of sale.
    (C) The IRS will disallow the loss for tax purposes.
    (D) The loss would be allowed for all purposes.

44. Treasury bills:

    (A) are registered
    (B) are in book entry
    (C) have coupons attached
    (D) are callable

45. When a corporation buys a new computer for cash, each of the following effects is seen on the balance sheet EXCEPT:

    (A) working capital declines
    (B) net worth declines
    (C) cash declines
    (D) plant and equipment rise

46. Restricted stock is most often acquired through:

    (A) rights offering
    (B) merger
    (C) employee profit-sharing plan
    (D) private placement

Questions 47–49 are based on the following information: A customer buys 100 shares of XYZ common stock at $77 and on the same day buys one XYZ July 75 put at 1.50.

47. A customer will break even with this position when the market price of the stock is:

    (A) 73.50
    (B) 75.50
    (C) 77
    (D) 78.50

48. Prior to expiration of the option in July, what is the maximum potential of loss on this position?

    (A) $150
    (B) $350
    (C) $7,050
    (D) $7,350

49. What is the maximum possible gain to the customer upon expiration of the option?

    (A) $7,350
    (B) $7,550
    (C) $7,850
    (D) unlimited

50. In the analysis of a general obligation bond, an increase in all of the following events would be considered negative EXCEPT:

    (A) delinquent taxes
    (B) tax rates
    (C) assessed value of property
    (D) municipal operating expenses

51. A director of a public corporation wishes to sell some of his stock in the company. Under SEC Rule 144, which of the following may not be sold?

    (A) unregistered securities held for 12 months
    (B) unregistered securities held for 24 months
    (C) unregistered securities held for 36 months
    (D) registered securities held for 12 months

52. For a security not registered in state A to be sold to a customer in state A, which of the following must be true?

    I. the security is listed on a national stock exchange
    II. the stock is exempt from registration requirements
    III. the same security has been offered to the public for the past 12 months

    (A) II only
    (B) I and II only
    (C) II and III only
    (D) I, II, and III

53. Which of the following are progressive taxes?

    I.   estate taxes
    II. gasoline taxes
    III. income taxes
    IV. sales taxes

    (A) I and III only
    (B) I and IV only
    (C) II and IV only
    (D) I, III, and IV only

54. When considering bids submitted for a new municipal bond issue, which of the following is most important to the issuer?

    (A) par value
    (B) coupon rate
    (C) reoffering scale
    (D) net interest cost

55. The agreement among underwriters provides for all of the following EXCEPT:

    (A) establishment of the concession
    (B) appointment of the syndicate manager
    (C) appointment of bond counsel
    (D) establishment of the takedown

56. A corporation decides to write down the value of its current inventory because of technological obsolescence. Which of the following does not decline?

    (A) working capital
    (B) total assets
    (C) net plant and equipment
    (D) net worth

57. The document that stipulates the rights and obligations of the general and limited partners in a direct participation program is the:

    (A) agreement of limited partnership
    (B) certificate of incorporation
    (C) partnership papers
    (D) life tenancy agreement

58. Which of the following are true of negotiable certificates of deposit?

    I.   are guaranteed by the issuing bank
    II. are refundable
    III. have a minimum denomination of $5,000
    IV. can be traded in the market

    (A) I and IV only
    (B) II and IV only
    (C) I, II, and III only
    (D) I, II, III, and IV

59. Which of the following is not true regarding commercial paper?

    (A) it has a maximum maturity of 270 days
    (B) it generally trades at a discount
    (C) it is callable by the issuer
    (D) it can be sold directly to the public

60. Which of the following generally trades "plus accrued interest"?

    (A) zero coupon bonds
    (B) treasury bills
    (C) certificates of deposit
    (D) banker's acceptances

61. Which of the following are true regarding zero coupon bonds?

    I. interest is paid quarterly
    II. interest is not paid until maturity
    III. the discount must be accreted
    IV. the discount must be amortized

    (A) I and II only
    (B) I and III only
    (C) II and III only
    (D) II and IV only

62. A freelance writer earns $65,000 a year. Her husband works for her as an accountant making $40,000 a year. What is the total that they can contribute to individual retirement accounts? Both individuals are over 50 years of age.

    (A) -0-
    (B) $2,250
    (C) $10,000
    (D) $21,000

63. Which of the following statements regarding Eurodollar bonds is not correct?

    (A) The issuer of Eurobonds can be a corporation.
    (B) Payment of interest and principal may be made in U.S. dollars or designated foreign currencies.
    (C) Payment of interest and principal is made in U.S. dollars.
    (D) The bonds are issued in Europe.

64. After a registered representative sends a red herring preliminary prospectus to a customer for an issue whose registration is not yet effective, each of the following activities is permissible EXCEPT:

    (A) taking an indication of interest
    (B) guaranteeing the offering price to the customer
    (C) discussing the information in the preliminary prospectus
    (D) sending the final prospectus to the customer

65. A municipality has issued a double-barreled bond. The revenues generated by the facility have proven to be insufficient. Which of the following income sources may be used by the municipality to satisfy the obligation?

    (A) real estate taxes
    (B) franchise taxes
    (C) income taxes
    (D) any of the above

66. A customer writes one XYL June 60 call uncovered for a premium of 3 when the market price of XYL is 58. What is the required margin in the customer's account?

    (A) $1,170
    (B) $1,370
    (C) $1,260
    (D) $2,900

67. Free-riding and withholding are violations of the:

    (A) NASD Conduct Rules
    (B) the Securities Act of 1933
    (C) the Securities Exchange Act of 1934
    (D) NYSE constitution

<u>Questions 68–71 are based on the following information:</u> A customer writes 1 ABC June 50 put at 9, and buys 1 ABC June 40 put at 3. The customer has no position in the stock.

68. The customer will profit in all the following instances EXCEPT:

    (A) when both options are exercised
    (B) when both options expire
    (C) when the spread narrows
    (D) when the underlying security is at 47 at expiration

69. What is the maximum potential gain for the combined position?

    (A) $300
    (B) $600
    (C) $900
    (D) $1,000

70. What is the maximum potential loss for the combined position?

    (A) $200
    (B) $300
    (C) $400
    (D) unlimited

71. What is the breakeven point for the combined position?

    (A) 40
    (B) 42
    (C) 44
    (D) 47

72. The sale of a security long in a customer's restricted margin account would have which of the following results?

    (A) decreased market value and equity
    (B) decreased market value, increased SMA, and no effect on equity
    (C) decreased market value and decreased equity
    (D) increased equity

73. If the IRS determines that a tax shelter was abusive, what consequences may follow?

    I. the deductions are disallowed
    II. the taxpayer is charged interest on the back taxes
    III. the taxpayer may be charged penalties

    (A) I and II only
    (B) I and III only
    (C) II and III only
    (D) I, II, and III

74. If a limited partner in a DPP exercised control of the day-to-day business operation of the partnership, which of the following could occur?

    (A) Her limited partnership status could end.
    (B) She would be required to increase her contribution.
    (C) She would be entitled to a larger share of profits.
    (D) She would receive increased income offsets.

75. Which of the following would be considered to be an "accredited investor"?

I. a financial institution
II. an individual with net worth of $1,000,000 or more
III. an individual with income of $200,000 or more for the past two years
IV. a person who invests $150,000 or more in the program

(A) I only
(B) II and III only
(C) I and IV only
(D) I, II, III, and IV

76. The major objective of requiring dealers to report transactions in NASDQ National Market System issues within 90 seconds is to provide current information to:

(A) investors
(B) the SEC
(C) the NASD
(D) the SEC and the NASD

77. An OEX 200 call is purchased at 4, and is exercised on a day when the Standard & Poor's 100 Index closes at 207. The option writer's cash obligation to the owner of the call is:

(A) $400
(B) $700
(C) $1,000
(D) $2,070

78. Which of the following issuers of pass-through securities is restricted to purchasing only conventional residential mortgages from financial institutions insured by an agency of the U.S. government?

(A) Fannie Mae
(B) Ginnie Mae
(C) Sallie Mae
(D) Freddie Mac

79. A British pound option contract is quoted at 5.50. The size of the contract is 25,000 units. What would be the cost of one of the BP option contracts?

(A) $550
(B) $1,100
(C) $1,375
(D) $2,000

80. A customer purchased 1 June 220 Standard & Poor's 100 Index call for a premium of 5 when the Standard & Poor's 100 is trading at 219. The required deposit for this position is:

(A) $250
(B) $500
(C) $776
(D) $876

81. The strike price and premium of treasury bond options are stated as a percentage of the:

(A) current market value of the underlying bonds
(B) face amount of the underlying bonds
(C) aggregate call premium
(D) accrued interest

82. Which of the following would improve the U.S. balance of payments?

    (A) increased foreign investment in the U.S.
    (B) building of plant facilities abroad by U.S. companies
    (C) loans by U.S. banks to foreign corporations
    (D) Americans increasing their purchase of foreign securities

83. A customer has purchased $25,000 worth of ABC corporation over a period of time. Which of the following is true about his subsequent sale of $10,000 of ABC stock?

    (A) His capital gain is $10,000.
    (B) The IRS requires that LIFO be used to identify the shares sold.
    (C) The IRS requires that FIFO be used to identify the shares sold.
    (D) The investor is allowed to specify which shares are being sold to minimize his capital gain.

84. Which of the following statements about mutual funds and variable annuities are false?

    I.   they are regulated by the Investment Company Act of 1940
    II. property passes to the estate of the owner at death
    III. investment income and capital gains realized by the portfolio result in a current taxable income to the owner

    (A) I and III only
    (B) I and II only
    (C) I, II, and III
    (D) II and III only

85. Which of the following statements concerning a variable annuity during the annuity period is true?

    (A) The AIR varies, and the number of annuity units varies.
    (B) The value per annuity unit varies, and the number of annuity units is fixed.
    (C) The number of accumulation units is fixed, and the value per unit is fixed.
    (D) The value per annuity unit is fixed, and the number of annuity units varies.

86. Which of the following would establish a short position?

    (A) sale of borrowed stock
    (B) sale of stock "against the box"
    (C) a purchase and sale for arbitrage
    (D) all of the above

87. If an NASD member firm acts as an agent (broker) on a transaction the confirmation to the customer must provide for disclosure of which of the following?

    (A) the commission charged on the trade
    (B) the markup that was added
    (C) the markdown that was subtracted
    (D) any of the above that would apply

88. Which of the following would be a valid reason for calling an issue of municipal bonds?

    (A) the revenue-producing facility is destroyed by a hurricane
    (B) the authority issuing the securities develops excess funds
    (C) interest rates decline sharply
    (D) any of the above

89. In recommending an investment in a variable annuity contract to the client, what is the most important suitability factor to be considered by the registered representative?

(A) the fact that payments to the client may decrease
(B) the fact that the client's deposits may decrease
(C) the fact that there is a sales charge
(D) the fact that a management fee may be charged

90. The following transaction is reported on the tape.

ABC Pr
71 s 119

It would indicate that:

(A) 71 shares of ABC preferred traded at 119
(B) 710 shares of ABC preferred traded at 119
(C) 7,100 shares of ABC preferred traded at 119
(D) a short sale of 7,100 shares of ABC preferred had occurred

91. Mary Brown makes a gift of securities to her grandson, John Brown, Jr. Ms. Brown appoints her daughter, Caroline Brown, as custodian for John Brown, Jr., under the UGMA in the state of Ohio. Who is the owner of these securities?

(A) Mary Brown
(B) Caroline Brown
(C) John Brown, Jr.
(D) Caroline Brown and John Brown, Jr., as joint tenants

92. Using the facts in question 91, whose tax ID number would be needed to open the account?

(A) Caroline Brown
(B) John Brown, Jr.
(C) Mary Brown
(D) all of the above

93. When can a new equity issue first be quoted on the NASDAQ system?

(A) 10 days prior to the effective date (when-issued quotes only)
(B) the effective date
(C) 7 business days following the effective date
(D) 10 business days following the effective date

94. Which of the following statements regarding treasury stock is incorrect?

(A) Treasury stock does not receive dividends.
(B) Treasury stock is considered to be unauthorized stock.
(C) Treasury stock does not have voting rights.
(D) Treasury stock is not used in computing earnings per share.

95. Interest on a new issue of municipal securities is calculated beginning on the:

(A) trade date
(B) settlement date
(C) dated date
(D) offering date

96. The computerized system used on the floor of the NYSE that provides rapid execution of certain odd-lot and round-lot orders is known as the:

    (A) FOK system
    (B) DOT system
    (C) AON system
    (D) CQS system

97. An over-the-counter transaction takes place between two reporting dealers. The security is included in the National Market System. This trade must be reported within 90 seconds of occurrence by:

    (A) the seller
    (B) the buyer
    (C) both the buyer and the seller
    (D) the dealer that initiated the trade

98. A husband and wife have an account at a firm as joint tenants with right of survivorship. The wife calls the RR covering the account and asks him to sell 100 shares of XYZ stock. She tells the RR that as her husband is ill, the check for the proceeds of the sale should be made in her name only. What should the RR do in regard to this request?

    (A) comply with the wife's request
    (B) refuse to enter the order
    (C) accept the order but inform her that the check must be made out in both names
    (D) close the account

99. On Monday, May 5, a client purchases $18,000 worth of a listed stock in his margin account. On settlement date, Thursday, May 8, the value of these securities has risen to $24,000. What minimum deposit will be required for this purchase?

    (A) $3,000
    (B) $9,000
    (C) $12,000
    (D) $18,000

100. A client is long 500 shares of IBM. Which of the following orders could be used to protect his position?

    I.   buy IBM puts
    II. write IBM puts
    III. buy IBM calls
    IV. write IBM calls

    (A) I and II only
    (B) I and IV only
    (C) II and III only
    (D) I, II, III, and IV

101. A client holds a call on Swiss francs with an exercise price of 61. This permits the client to buy (call) the Swiss francs at:

    (A) $ .61
    (B) $ 6.10
    (C) $61.00
    (D) $ .061

102. An underwriter is offering a new issue of common stock at $31 per share. Which of the following would be an improper stabilizing quotation?

    (A) 30.50–30.75
    (B) 30.62–30.87
    (C) 30.75–31
    (D) 31–31.50

103. A bond is convertible into common stock at $50 a share. The bond is trading at 116. What is parity for the common stock?

   (A) $50
   (B) $66
   (C) $58
   (D) cannot be determined

104. In a period of declining interest rates, which of the following U.S. treasury securities would probably have the greatest increase in market value?

   (A) bills
   (B) notes
   (C) Series EE savings bonds
   (D) bonds

105. A client purchases 100 shares of DIS at $67 and writes 1 DIS Oct 70 call for a premium of 4. What is the maximum profit that may be made from this position?

   (A) $300
   (B) $400
   (C) $500
   (D) $700

106. At what point are accumulation units of a variable annuity converted to annuity units?

   (A) when the client's investment exceeds $100,000
   (B) when the client begins to receive payments
   (C) when the trust is dissolved
   (D) when the parent insurance company releases the funds

107. Under the offering terms of a new issue of municipal securities the stated concession is .375 and the takedown is .25. The total takedown would be:

   (A) .125
   (B) .25
   (C) .375
   (D) .625

108. A municipal dealer purchases $100,000 of State of Virginia 7½% GO bonds at par. The dealer immediately reoffers the bonds in the market. Which of the following would be deemed to be a bona fide offering?

   (A) 6.00 net
   (B) 7.25
   (C) 107½
   (D) 107½ less .50

109. A client writes 1 uncovered EK Jul 70 call for a premium of 3 and 1 uncovered EK July 70 put for a premium of 4. What is the maximum loss that can result from this position?

   (A) unlimited
   (B) $6,300
   (C) $7,700
   (D) $7,000

110. The bond attorney handling the legal details of an offering of municipal securities is employed by the:

   (A) underwriter
   (B) MSRB
   (C) issuer
   (D) transfer agent

111. Under the Tax Reform Act of 1986 income received from a limited partnership interest is called:

    (A) tax-exempt income
    (B) passive income
    (C) portfolio income
    (D) active income

112. Under the Tax Reform Act of 1986 a limited partner's portion of losses from a tax-sheltered investment can be used to offset income received from which of the following?

    (A) active income
    (B) portfolio income
    (C) passive income
    (D) any of the above

113. Which of the following orders cannot be executed in a customer's cash account?

    (A) a short sale
    (B) a purchase of municipal securities
    (C) the purchase of a listed put option
    (D) the sale of a listed call covered by the underlying security

114. XYZ stock is trading at $47 a share. Which of the following options would be considered to be "in the money"?

    (A) XYZ Oct 50 call
    (B) XYZ Oct 50 put
    (C) XYZ Oct 45 put
    (D) none of the above

115. A client owns an ABC June 60 call. Later the company declares a 14% stock dividend. On the ex date for this dividend the client's call will be:

    (A) unchanged
    (B) a contract for 114 shares with a strike price of 60
    (C) a contract for 100 shares with a strike price of 52.62
    (D) a contract for 114 shares with a strike price of 52.63

116. Under MSRB rules the advertising of a firm must be approved prior to use by:

    (A) the MSRB
    (B) a general securities principal
    (C) a municipal securities principal
    (D) all of the above

117. A client is considering an investment in a direct participation program. What factor would be most important for her to determine?

    (A) the economic viability of the project
    (B) the past record of the general partner
    (C) the value of anticipated tax advantages
    (D) the current level of tax rates

118. A client is making periodic purchases of units of a variable annuity. During the accumulation he would expect to receive which form of distribution?

    (A) dividends
    (B) interest
    (C) capital gains
    (D) none of the above

119. A real estate investment trust (REIT) must distribute what portion of its net income to its shareholders?

   (A) 50%
   (B) 90%
   (C) 95%
   (D) 100%

120. Which of the following securities pays interest on a monthly basis?

   (A) GNMA pass-throughs
   (B) income bonds
   (C) GO municipals
   (D) all of the above

Questions 121–123 are based on the following information: A client purchases 100 shares of LMN at $78 a share and writes 2 LMN Oct 80 calls for a premium of $3.

121. What is the client's breakeven point on the 100 shares of LMN stock?

   (A) $78
   (B) $72
   (C) $74
   (D) $75

122. What is the client's maximum profit on this position?

   (A) $200
   (B) $600
   (C) $800
   (D) unlimited

123. What is the customer's maximum loss on this position?

   (A) $7,200
   (B) $7,800
   (C) $8,000
   (D) unlimited

124. A customer purchases one municipal bond at a price of 111. The bond matures in exactly ten years. After holding the bond for four years the client sells it at a price of 108. What is the tax result of this sale?

   (A) nothing; municipals are exempt from taxes
   (B) $30 capital loss
   (C) $14 capital gain
   (D) $110 capital loss

125. A client purchases an XYZ July 70 call for a premium of 5. Shortly before expiration with XYZ stock trading at 72 he sells the call for its in-the-money value. What is the result of this sale?

   (A) $200 gain
   (B) $700 gain
   (C) $200 loss
   (D) $300 loss

PART 2 ANSWERS

1. **A** A standby offering refers to an offering made in connection with preemptive rights. This would only be done with corporate securities, not municipals or U.S. treasury securities.

2. **D** At the due diligence meeting, the underwriters and the issuing corporation discuss the offering.

3. **A** The *Bond Buyer* offers a service called the "New Worksheet and Record Service" that summarizes the contents of municipal notices of sales.

4. **C** The confirmation of a "when issued" trade could not include the accrued interest or total money as the settlement date needed to compute the interest is not known. The capacity in which the dealer acted, that is, as principal or agent, would be included on the confirmation.

5. **B** A double-barreled municipal security is first paid from a particular source of revenue, but should that fall short there is a general obligation behind it. For example, Massachusetts Dormitory Authority bonds are first paid from student fees, but further secured by a general obligation of the state.

6. **A** Moody's Ratings rates bonds as follows;

AAA and AA	highest investment grade
A	upper medium grade
BAA	medium grade
below BAA	speculative

7. **B** This account is restricted as the debit balance ($18,000) exceeds 50% of the market value ($30,000). A sale in a restricted

account releases 50% to the SMA. 50% of $3,500=$1,750.

8. **C** Buying a put would only allow the client to sell (put)s at an agreed price. As he is short, this option will be of no help to him.

9. **D** All of these choices are included in the MSRB rule dealing with a dealer's quotation.

10. **B** The dated date is only used to determine the amount of the first interest payment of a municipal security. It does not affect the marketability.

11. **A** In all cases the registered representative must determine the necessary facts regarding a client. In the case of limited partnerships this includes the income and net worth requirements.

12. **D** Ad valorem taxes are real property taxes. As they are generally paid to the town or county of residence they are not available for debt service of revenue bonds.

13. **C** The intrinsic value of an option is equal to the in-the-money amount. On a call it is the amount by which the market price exceeds the strike price. On a put it is the amount by which the market price is lower than the stock price.

14. **B** In a spread a client goes long one series in a class of options and short another series in the same class.

15. **B** The client has a debit of $4 (paid $7 and received $3). The stock is at 44. Upon expiration his long 40 call will have an intrinsic value of $4 and the short 50 call will be worthless.

16. **D** As the options have the same expiration and the long position has

the more favorable strike price the spread is covered. The client is required to deposit only the difference in the premiums.

17. **D** All of the choices are correct regarding a properly opened margin account.

18. **A** The broker can sell out the securities or request an extension if a valid reason exists. The other actions would not be permitted.

19. **D** The technician only wants to buy if the stock trades at $55. The buy stop at 55.25 would not be executed unless traded at or above 55.25.

20. **A** The general partner has unlimited liability not limited liability. All of the other choices correctly describe a general partner.

21. **D** In a when issued transaction the settlement date is not known. Therefore, the amount of interest, total amount of the trade, and extended principal could not be computed.

22. **C** The term "consolidating" indicates that the market on a particular stock is showing little price movement.

23. **B** Home appliance manufacture would be a lagging indicator of economic activity. The other choices are leading indicators.

24. **D** A technical analyst is not concerned with fundamental statistics found on the balance sheet or income statement. He is concerned with volume, trend, and price movement.

25. **A** Mutual funds are not proper vehicles for trading. A dealer cannot position these shares for later sale.

26. **B** A premium call is a provision in the bond whereby the issuer can buy back (call) bonds at a premium. Calls by issuers can never be at a price below par.

27. **D** Although the short is stock, a short put is not a covered position; thus, no margin is required under Federal Reserve rules.

28. **D** The federal funds rate is the interest rate charged by banks lending their excess reserve funds to other banks needing them. These loans are generally overnight loans. This is the most unstable rate in the money market. In fact, this rate can change from hour to hour during the day, and thus the average national daily rate is considered to be the effective federal funds rate.

29. **C** Options cannot be purchased on margin, with the exception of long-term LEAPS; therefore the 5 ABC calls must be paid for in full ($1,000). The market requirement on the 100 shares of ABC stock is $3,000 ($6,000×50%), so the customer could deposit $4,000 in cash or $8,000 in securities. The number of shares of XYZ stock currently priced at $25 per share that would cover this requirement is 320.

30. **C** Once an order has been executed, it cannot be canceled or changed. The appropriate action is to notify your manager, who will determine the proper course of action to take.

31. **B** When the customer shorted this straddle he received $800 in total premiums. When he closes it out, the call is out of the money and thus has no intrinsic value and he keeps the $300 premium he received. But the put is in the money by 5 points and he thus must buy it back for $500. The overall position results in a $300 profit.

32. **C** The Dow Jones Industrial Average contains 30 blue chip issues. The S&P 100 Index consists of 100

stocks that have options traded on the CBOE. The NYSE Composite Index consists of all common stock traded on the Big Board (about 1,600). Finally, the Value Line Index is the largest and most speculative index, consisting of some 1,700 stocks that trade on the NYSE, AMEX, or OTC market.

33. **C** A plus tick is a trade that occurs at a price higher than the previous trade. A zero-plus tick is a trade that is the same as the previous one, but that one was higher than the trade price prior to it.

34. **A** The purchase and sale of an option, as with any other capital asset, results in a capital gain or loss.

35. **B** A class of options refers to all types of options on the same underlying security. Puts are one type and calls are another type.

36. **C** By definition.

37. **A** The least appropriate fund offered is the special situation fund, which looks entirely to capital gains (growth) to attain its objectives.

38. **B** Purchasing power is two times excess equity. The regulation requirement is $10,500 (50% × $21,000), and he has $11,000 in equity. This gives him $500 in excess equity and thus $1,000 in buying power.

39. **A** The Trust Indenture Act does not apply to U.S. treasury securities.

40. **A** By definition.

41. **D** A self-directed IRA is simply a retirement plan wherein an investor makes her own investment decisions.

42. **B** Listed options must be paid for in full. The customer has available $1,000 in SMA to which he must add $3,000 in cash to meet the $4,000 requirement.

43. **C** The loss would not be allowed by the IRS since it is a wash sale. Losses are disallowed when an investor purchases the same security 30 days before or after the date of sale.

44. **A** Treasury bills are sold in book-entry form only, but the name of the purchaser is recorded.

45. **B** Net worth (or shareholder's equity) does not change. On the asset side of the balance sheet, cash is reduced, which reduces working capital by a like amount. Plant and equipment rise by the amount of the computer purchase. The net effect is that assets are shifted from more liquid to less liquid but are not otherwise altered.

46. **D** Private placements are exempt from registration with the SEC and thus are restricted. Choice (B) sometimes results in restricted stock; choices (A) and (C) have nothing to do with restricted stock.

47. **D** We simply add the cost of the put (1.50) to the cost of the stock (77).

48. **B** The maximum loss is the breakeven point minus the exercise price of the put (77–75 = 200+150 = $350).

49. **D** The maximum gain is unlimited. Once the stock goes above 78.50 all further appreciation represents profit to the customer.

50. **C** Increasing the assessed value of property will bring in tax revenue to the municipality in a way that does not increase tax rates. Since it reflects the increased value of real estate in the area, it would not be a problematic rise in tax rates. Choice (A) reduces receipts and Choice (D) increases expenses, both of which are negative.

51. **A** There is a two-year holding period for unregistered securities under Rule 144. There is no holding

period at all for the sale of registered securities.

52. **B** By regulation.

53. **A** Progressive taxes are those that increase with the wealth or income being taxed.

54. **D** The issuer's main concern is how much it will cost to borrow the money. This pretty much defines net interest cost.

55. **C** The agreement among underwriters has nothing to do with the issuer who is responsible for appointing bond counsel prior to offering the securities. The agreement spells out all the rights and responsibilities for the syndicate manager members.

56. **C** Inventories are part of current assets and a reduction in their value would likewise reduce working capital, total assets, and net worth. Plant and equipment remain unchanged as inventories are not included in that account.

57. **A** The agreement of limited partnership contains all rights, obligations and limitations of the partners to the agreement.

58. **A** Certificates of deposit are guaranteed by the issuing bank. As they are negotiable instruments they can be traded in market. The minimum denomination, however, is generally $100,000, and they cannot be refunded prior to maturity.

59. **C** Commercial paper cannot be called by the issuer prior to maturity. The other choices are correct.

60. **C** Most certificates of deposit trade plus accrued interest. The other choices are issued at and trade at a discount.

61. **C** By definition a zero coupon bond does not pay interest. At maturity the discount is considered to be

income on bonds bought in the open market. The discount must be accrued each year.

62. **C** As both the husband and wife are over 50, they can contribute up to $5,000 each for a total of $10,000.

63. **B** Although Eurobonds can be issued by either U.S. or foreign corporations, the payment of principal and interest is made only in U.S. dollars.

64. **B** Prior to the effective date of the registration statement, the registered representative cannot guarantee shares of an issue to a client. She can only take indications of interest.

65. **D** If the revenues on a double-barreled bond are insufficient it becomes a general obligation of the municipality. It may use any income source to accomplish payment.

66. **C** The margin required on an uncovered option is 20% of the Market Value, plus the premium and minus any out-of-the-money amount.

$1,660 (20% of $5,800)
+$ 300 (premium received)
$1,460
– $ 200 (out-of-the-money
$1,260   amount)

Note: The customer would only have to deposit $960 as the premium received is just left in the account.

67. **A** The prohibition against free-riding and withholding is found in the NASD Conduct Rules.

68. **A** The customer has a credit of $600 in this spread (paid $3 and received $9). If both options are exercised he will put at $50 and will exercise his put at $40 for a

loss of $1,000. Subtracting his premium credit, his net loss will be $400.

69. **B** If both options expire unexercised he will retain the original credit of $600. This is his maximum profit.

70. **C** As shown in question 68, his maximum loss is $400.

71. **C** If the stock is $44 and the customer is put at $50, he will lose $600. This would be offset by his original credit.

72. **B** The sale of a security held long in a restricted margin account reduces the market value and the debit balance. It also creates an increase in the SMA but has no effect on the customer's equity.

73. **D** If the IRS determines that a tax shelter is abusive, that is that it had no business purpose, they can disallow deductions and charge appropriate interest and penalties.

74. **A** If a limited partner exercises control over the partnership business, her status as a limited partner could be in jeopardy and she might lose her limited liability.

75. **D** All of those listed would be deemed to be accredited investors.

76. **A** Such information as volume and price of transactions is important to all investors and is the reason for the requirement.

77. **B** Index options settle on a cash basis. Quite simply, the loser pays the winner. In this situation the option has a strike price of 200 and the index is at 207 when exercised. The writer must pay the buyer the difference (its intrinsic value). Since the multiplier for OEX options is $100, the writer must pay $700 (7×$100).

78. **D** Ginnie Mae (Government National Mortgage Association) and Fannie Mae (Federal National Mortgage Association) issue pass-through mortgage securities, which are usually backed by government-guaranteed mortgages (FHA and VA). Sallie Mae (Student Loan Marketing Association) deals in student loans. Freddie Mac (Federal Home Loan Mortgage Corp.) issues pass-through securities backed by conventional (nongovernment-guaranteed) mortgages only.

79. **C** British pounds are quoted cents per BP, so a quote of 5.50 means $.0550 per BP. We simply multiply that quote value by the number of BPs in the contract, 25,000 ($.0550 × 25,000 = $1,375).

80. **B** Remember, you cannot buy options on margin, except long-term LEAPS. The premium (5 × $100 = 500) must be paid for in full.

81. **B** The option covers $100,000 par (face) amount of U.S. treasury bonds. Premiums and striking prices are quoted as a percentage of that amount.

82. **A** Foreign investment in the U.S. brings money to this country. All other choices are an outflow of U.S. funds.

83. **D** An investor may specify which shares are being sold at the time of the sale. If the investor chooses not to do so, the IRS requires that the FIFO (first in, first out) method be used.

84. **D** Statement I is true of both. Statement II is true only for mutual funds; annuities generally pass on to the beneficiary. Statement III is true of mutual funds but not annuities.

85. **B** Once you have finished paying into the annuity, it is annuitized.

The payout period known as the annuity period begins thereafter. Your payment each time is based on the fixed number of annuity units multiplied by the value of the unit. This value can vary from one payment to another.

86. **D** Any of these transactions would result in a short position.

87. **A** Note that the question states that the firm acted as an agent. Markups and markdowns would only apply if the firm acted as principal.

88. **D** All of the choices offered would be valid reasons for retiring an issue of municipal bonds. Note, choice (A) would lead to the implementation of any catastrophe call provision.

89. **A** As the term "variable annuity" indicates, the payments to the client upon withdrawal will rise or fall depending on the market value of the accumulation units. This is the most important consideration.

90. **C** In reporting trades of up to 10,000 shares in volume, the trade is abbreviated on the tape by eliminating the final two zeros. Thus 71s would indicate 7,100 shares. One cannot determine if stock was sold long or short by looking at the tape.

91. **C** In an account under the Uniform Gifts to Minors Act (UGMA), the securities are the property of the minor.

92. **B** As the securities are the property of John Brown, Jr., his tax ID number would be required.

93. **B** NASDAQ allows quotations for qualified issues to commence on the effective date.

94. **B** Treasury stock has been authorized and issued by the corporation, but it has later been reacquired.

95. **C** Interest will begin to accrue on the date on which the bonds are first dated until the settlement date of the trade.

96. **B** The DOT (designated order turn-around) system is employed on the floor to handle many odd-lot and round-lot market and limit orders through a computerized hookup with the specialists.

97. **A** In a trade of a National Market System security the seller must report the transaction within 90 seconds of occurrence.

98. **C** The registered representative may accept orders from either party of the joint account. However, any checks sent out must be in the name of both tenants.

99. **B** The client is required to deposit a minimum of 50% of the cost of the purchase, or $9,000.

100. **B** The purpose of IBM puts would allow the customer to sell (put) the stock at the exercise price if the market price declined. By writing calls the client would be paid a premium, which would provide partial protection should the market price decline.

101. **A** The exercise price is expressed in cents. A price of 61 would mean $.61 per franc.

102. **D** A stabilizing quotation must be at or below the public offering price. As the offering price is $31, a quotation of 31–31.50 would be improper.

103. **C** We determine the number of shares into which the bond is convertible by first dividing the face value of the bond ($1,000), by the conversion price of $50. The result is 20 shares. We then divide the market price of the bond (1160) by the number of shares (20) to determine the parity for the stock of $58 a share.

104. **D** As the treasury bonds have the longest maturity they would probably experience the greatest fluctuation in market value.

105. **D** If the client is called at 70 he will have a profit of $300 over his original cost of 67. In addition, he will retain the $400 premium for a total profit of $700.

106. **B** The accumulation units become annuity units when the payment period begins.

107. **D** The total takedown is the concession (.375) plus the additional takedown (.25).

108. **B** The dealer is entitled to a reasonable markup above his cost of par. An offering at 7.25 would be a markup of 25 basis points and would be reasonable. The other offerings are excessive.

109. **A** The customer is short an EK straddle. As one part of the straddle leaves her short an uncovered call, her potential loss is unlimited.

110. **C** The bond attorney is employed by the issuer of the securities.

111. **B** Income from limited partnerships are called passive income. Dividends and interest received is considered to be portfolio income while salary and bonuses are termed active income.

112. **C** Under the 1986 law, losses from passive investments can only be used to offset income from other passive investments. They cannot be used to offset income from other sources as was the case in the past.

113. **A** As the amount required to cover a short sale is unknown at the time of the trade, all short sales must be carried in margin accounts.

114. **B** An option is considered to be in the money if it has any intrinsic value. A put with a strike price of 50 allows the holder to sell (put) the stock at 50. As the stock is trading at 47 this put is 3 points in the money.

115. **D** When a stock dividend is paid that does not result in a multiple of 100 shares we simply increase the number of shares in the contract to reflect the stock dividend. This contract would now be for 114 shares. To determine the new strike price we divide the old strike (60) by the new number of shares (114) and round to the cent. Thus, 60 divided by 115 equals 52.631.

116. **C** Municipal advertising must be approved prior to use by a municipal securities principal.

117. **A** While all the choices contain important factors, the most important is the economic viability of the project.

118. **D** During the accumulation period no distributions are made to the holder of a variable annuity contract. When the payout period begins, distributions are then made.

119. **B** Under the Internal Revenue Code a REIT must distribute 90% of its net income to its shareholders.

120. **A** GNMA pass-throughs make interest and principal payments on a monthly basis. Other debt securities generally pay interest semi-annually and return principal at maturity.

121. **B** The client bought the LMN stock at $78. If it declines to $72 he will lose 6 points. This would be offset by the premiums ($3 for each contract written) received.

122. **C** If at expiration the stock is trading at $80 the client will not be called and will keep the $600 in premiums received. In addition, he will have a profit of $200 on the stock purchased at $78 for a total profit of $800.

123. **D** The customer has written two calls but as he only has 100 shares of stock one of the calls is uncovered. The maximum possible loss from writing an uncovered call is unlimited. (How high is up?)

124. **C** When bonds are purchased at a premium, the client can amortize that premium each year and reduce his cost on the bond. The bond was purchased at $1,110. We divide the premium by the number of years to maturity ($110 divided by 10 years equals $11 per year) and reduce the cost by an annual amortization. As the client held the bond for four years, his original cost of $1,110 is reduced by $44 and is now $1,066. A sale at 108 ($1,080) results in a gain of $14.

125. **D** As the call has a strike price of 70 the intrinsic, or in-the-money, value is $200 when the stock is trading at 72. However, as the call cost the customer $500 he would have a net loss of $300.

ANSWER SHEET FOR PRACTICE EXAMINATION 2

Part 1

1. Ⓐ Ⓑ Ⓒ Ⓓ	26. Ⓐ Ⓑ Ⓒ Ⓓ	51. Ⓐ Ⓑ Ⓒ Ⓓ	76. Ⓐ Ⓑ Ⓒ Ⓓ	101. Ⓐ Ⓑ Ⓒ Ⓓ
2. Ⓐ Ⓑ Ⓒ Ⓓ	27. Ⓐ Ⓑ Ⓒ Ⓓ	52. Ⓐ Ⓑ Ⓒ Ⓓ	77. Ⓐ Ⓑ Ⓒ Ⓓ	102. Ⓐ Ⓑ Ⓒ Ⓓ
3. Ⓐ Ⓑ Ⓒ Ⓓ	28. Ⓐ Ⓑ Ⓒ Ⓓ	53. Ⓐ Ⓑ Ⓒ Ⓓ	78. Ⓐ Ⓑ Ⓒ Ⓓ	103. Ⓐ Ⓑ Ⓒ Ⓓ
4. Ⓐ Ⓑ Ⓒ Ⓓ	29. Ⓐ Ⓑ Ⓒ Ⓓ	54. Ⓐ Ⓑ Ⓒ Ⓓ	79. Ⓐ Ⓑ Ⓒ Ⓓ	104. Ⓐ Ⓑ Ⓒ Ⓓ
5. Ⓐ Ⓑ Ⓒ Ⓓ	30. Ⓐ Ⓑ Ⓒ Ⓓ	55. Ⓐ Ⓑ Ⓒ Ⓓ	80. Ⓐ Ⓑ Ⓒ Ⓓ	105. Ⓐ Ⓑ Ⓒ Ⓓ
6. Ⓐ Ⓑ Ⓒ Ⓓ	31. Ⓐ Ⓑ Ⓒ Ⓓ	56. Ⓐ Ⓑ Ⓒ Ⓓ	81. Ⓐ Ⓑ Ⓒ Ⓓ	106. Ⓐ Ⓑ Ⓒ Ⓓ
7. Ⓐ Ⓑ Ⓒ Ⓓ	32. Ⓐ Ⓑ Ⓒ Ⓓ	57. Ⓐ Ⓑ Ⓒ Ⓓ	82. Ⓐ Ⓑ Ⓒ Ⓓ	107. Ⓐ Ⓑ Ⓒ Ⓓ
8. Ⓐ Ⓑ Ⓒ Ⓓ	33. Ⓐ Ⓑ Ⓒ Ⓓ	58. Ⓐ Ⓑ Ⓒ Ⓓ	83. Ⓐ Ⓑ Ⓒ Ⓓ	108. Ⓐ Ⓑ Ⓒ Ⓓ
9. Ⓐ Ⓑ Ⓒ Ⓓ	34. Ⓐ Ⓑ Ⓒ Ⓓ	59. Ⓐ Ⓑ Ⓒ Ⓓ	84. Ⓐ Ⓑ Ⓒ Ⓓ	109. Ⓐ Ⓑ Ⓒ Ⓓ
10. Ⓐ Ⓑ Ⓒ Ⓓ	35. Ⓐ Ⓑ Ⓒ Ⓓ	60. Ⓐ Ⓑ Ⓒ Ⓓ	85. Ⓐ Ⓑ Ⓒ Ⓓ	110. Ⓐ Ⓑ Ⓒ Ⓓ
11. Ⓐ Ⓑ Ⓒ Ⓓ	36. Ⓐ Ⓑ Ⓒ Ⓓ	61. Ⓐ Ⓑ Ⓒ Ⓓ	86. Ⓐ Ⓑ Ⓒ Ⓓ	111. Ⓐ Ⓑ Ⓒ Ⓓ
12. Ⓐ Ⓑ Ⓒ Ⓓ	37. Ⓐ Ⓑ Ⓒ Ⓓ	62. Ⓐ Ⓑ Ⓒ Ⓓ	87. Ⓐ Ⓑ Ⓒ Ⓓ	112. Ⓐ Ⓑ Ⓒ Ⓓ
13. Ⓐ Ⓑ Ⓒ Ⓓ	38. Ⓐ Ⓑ Ⓒ Ⓓ	63. Ⓐ Ⓑ Ⓒ Ⓓ	88. Ⓐ Ⓑ Ⓒ Ⓓ	113. Ⓐ Ⓑ Ⓒ Ⓓ
14. Ⓐ Ⓑ Ⓒ Ⓓ	39. Ⓐ Ⓑ Ⓒ Ⓓ	64. Ⓐ Ⓑ Ⓒ Ⓓ	89. Ⓐ Ⓑ Ⓒ Ⓓ	114. Ⓐ Ⓑ Ⓒ Ⓓ
15. Ⓐ Ⓑ Ⓒ Ⓓ	40. Ⓐ Ⓑ Ⓒ Ⓓ	65. Ⓐ Ⓑ Ⓒ Ⓓ	90. Ⓐ Ⓑ Ⓒ Ⓓ	115. Ⓐ Ⓑ Ⓒ Ⓓ
16. Ⓐ Ⓑ Ⓒ Ⓓ	41. Ⓐ Ⓑ Ⓒ Ⓓ	66. Ⓐ Ⓑ Ⓒ Ⓓ	91. Ⓐ Ⓑ Ⓒ Ⓓ	116. Ⓐ Ⓑ Ⓒ Ⓓ
17. Ⓐ Ⓑ Ⓒ Ⓓ	42. Ⓐ Ⓑ Ⓒ Ⓓ	67. Ⓐ Ⓑ Ⓒ Ⓓ	92. Ⓐ Ⓑ Ⓒ Ⓓ	117. Ⓐ Ⓑ Ⓒ Ⓓ
18. Ⓐ Ⓑ Ⓒ Ⓓ	43. Ⓐ Ⓑ Ⓒ Ⓓ	68. Ⓐ Ⓑ Ⓒ Ⓓ	93. Ⓐ Ⓑ Ⓒ Ⓓ	118. Ⓐ Ⓑ Ⓒ Ⓓ
19. Ⓐ Ⓑ Ⓒ Ⓓ	44. Ⓐ Ⓑ Ⓒ Ⓓ	69. Ⓐ Ⓑ Ⓒ Ⓓ	94. Ⓐ Ⓑ Ⓒ Ⓓ	119. Ⓐ Ⓑ Ⓒ Ⓓ
20. Ⓐ Ⓑ Ⓒ Ⓓ	45. Ⓐ Ⓑ Ⓒ Ⓓ	70. Ⓐ Ⓑ Ⓒ Ⓓ	95. Ⓐ Ⓑ Ⓒ Ⓓ	120. Ⓐ Ⓑ Ⓒ Ⓓ
21. Ⓐ Ⓑ Ⓒ Ⓓ	46. Ⓐ Ⓑ Ⓒ Ⓓ	71. Ⓐ Ⓑ Ⓒ Ⓓ	96. Ⓐ Ⓑ Ⓒ Ⓓ	121. Ⓐ Ⓑ Ⓒ Ⓓ
22. Ⓐ Ⓑ Ⓒ Ⓓ	47. Ⓐ Ⓑ Ⓒ Ⓓ	72. Ⓐ Ⓑ Ⓒ Ⓓ	97. Ⓐ Ⓑ Ⓒ Ⓓ	122. Ⓐ Ⓑ Ⓒ Ⓓ
23. Ⓐ Ⓑ Ⓒ Ⓓ	48. Ⓐ Ⓑ Ⓒ Ⓓ	73. Ⓐ Ⓑ Ⓒ Ⓓ	98. Ⓐ Ⓑ Ⓒ Ⓓ	123. Ⓐ Ⓑ Ⓒ Ⓓ
24. Ⓐ Ⓑ Ⓒ Ⓓ	49. Ⓐ Ⓑ Ⓒ Ⓓ	74. Ⓐ Ⓑ Ⓒ Ⓓ	99. Ⓐ Ⓑ Ⓒ Ⓓ	124. Ⓐ Ⓑ Ⓒ Ⓓ
25. Ⓐ Ⓑ Ⓒ Ⓓ	50. Ⓐ Ⓑ Ⓒ Ⓓ	75. Ⓐ Ⓑ Ⓒ Ⓓ	100. Ⓐ Ⓑ Ⓒ Ⓓ	125. Ⓐ Ⓑ Ⓒ Ⓓ

Part 2

1. Ⓐ Ⓑ Ⓒ Ⓓ	26. Ⓐ Ⓑ Ⓒ Ⓓ	51. Ⓐ Ⓑ Ⓒ Ⓓ	76. Ⓐ Ⓑ Ⓒ Ⓓ	101. Ⓐ Ⓑ Ⓒ Ⓓ
2. Ⓐ Ⓑ Ⓒ Ⓓ	27. Ⓐ Ⓑ Ⓒ Ⓓ	52. Ⓐ Ⓑ Ⓒ Ⓓ	77. Ⓐ Ⓑ Ⓒ Ⓓ	102. Ⓐ Ⓑ Ⓒ Ⓓ
3. Ⓐ Ⓑ Ⓒ Ⓓ	28. Ⓐ Ⓑ Ⓒ Ⓓ	53. Ⓐ Ⓑ Ⓒ Ⓓ	78. Ⓐ Ⓑ Ⓒ Ⓓ	103. Ⓐ Ⓑ Ⓒ Ⓓ
4. Ⓐ Ⓑ Ⓒ Ⓓ	29. Ⓐ Ⓑ Ⓒ Ⓓ	54. Ⓐ Ⓑ Ⓒ Ⓓ	79. Ⓐ Ⓑ Ⓒ Ⓓ	104. Ⓐ Ⓑ Ⓒ Ⓓ
5. Ⓐ Ⓑ Ⓒ Ⓓ	30. Ⓐ Ⓑ Ⓒ Ⓓ	55. Ⓐ Ⓑ Ⓒ Ⓓ	80. Ⓐ Ⓑ Ⓒ Ⓓ	105. Ⓐ Ⓑ Ⓒ Ⓓ
6. Ⓐ Ⓑ Ⓒ Ⓓ	31. Ⓐ Ⓑ Ⓒ Ⓓ	56. Ⓐ Ⓑ Ⓒ Ⓓ	81. Ⓐ Ⓑ Ⓒ Ⓓ	106. Ⓐ Ⓑ Ⓒ Ⓓ
7. Ⓐ Ⓑ Ⓒ Ⓓ	32. Ⓐ Ⓑ Ⓒ Ⓓ	57. Ⓐ Ⓑ Ⓒ Ⓓ	82. Ⓐ Ⓑ Ⓒ Ⓓ	107. Ⓐ Ⓑ Ⓒ Ⓓ
8. Ⓐ Ⓑ Ⓒ Ⓓ	33. Ⓐ Ⓑ Ⓒ Ⓓ	58. Ⓐ Ⓑ Ⓒ Ⓓ	83. Ⓐ Ⓑ Ⓒ Ⓓ	108. Ⓐ Ⓑ Ⓒ Ⓓ
9. Ⓐ Ⓑ Ⓒ Ⓓ	34. Ⓐ Ⓑ Ⓒ Ⓓ	59. Ⓐ Ⓑ Ⓒ Ⓓ	84. Ⓐ Ⓑ Ⓒ Ⓓ	109. Ⓐ Ⓑ Ⓒ Ⓓ
10. Ⓐ Ⓑ Ⓒ Ⓓ	35. Ⓐ Ⓑ Ⓒ Ⓓ	60. Ⓐ Ⓑ Ⓒ Ⓓ	85. Ⓐ Ⓑ Ⓒ Ⓓ	110. Ⓐ Ⓑ Ⓒ Ⓓ
11. Ⓐ Ⓑ Ⓒ Ⓓ	36. Ⓐ Ⓑ Ⓒ Ⓓ	61. Ⓐ Ⓑ Ⓒ Ⓓ	86. Ⓐ Ⓑ Ⓒ Ⓓ	111. Ⓐ Ⓑ Ⓒ Ⓓ
12. Ⓐ Ⓑ Ⓒ Ⓓ	37. Ⓐ Ⓑ Ⓒ Ⓓ	62. Ⓐ Ⓑ Ⓒ Ⓓ	87. Ⓐ Ⓑ Ⓒ Ⓓ	112. Ⓐ Ⓑ Ⓒ Ⓓ
13. Ⓐ Ⓑ Ⓒ Ⓓ	38. Ⓐ Ⓑ Ⓒ Ⓓ	63. Ⓐ Ⓑ Ⓒ Ⓓ	88. Ⓐ Ⓑ Ⓒ Ⓓ	113. Ⓐ Ⓑ Ⓒ Ⓓ
14. Ⓐ Ⓑ Ⓒ Ⓓ	39. Ⓐ Ⓑ Ⓒ Ⓓ	64. Ⓐ Ⓑ Ⓒ Ⓓ	89. Ⓐ Ⓑ Ⓒ Ⓓ	114. Ⓐ Ⓑ Ⓒ Ⓓ
15. Ⓐ Ⓑ Ⓒ Ⓓ	40. Ⓐ Ⓑ Ⓒ Ⓓ	65. Ⓐ Ⓑ Ⓒ Ⓓ	90. Ⓐ Ⓑ Ⓒ Ⓓ	115. Ⓐ Ⓑ Ⓒ Ⓓ
16. Ⓐ Ⓑ Ⓒ Ⓓ	41. Ⓐ Ⓑ Ⓒ Ⓓ	66. Ⓐ Ⓑ Ⓒ Ⓓ	91. Ⓐ Ⓑ Ⓒ Ⓓ	116. Ⓐ Ⓑ Ⓒ Ⓓ
17. Ⓐ Ⓑ Ⓒ Ⓓ	42. Ⓐ Ⓑ Ⓒ Ⓓ	67. Ⓐ Ⓑ Ⓒ Ⓓ	92. Ⓐ Ⓑ Ⓒ Ⓓ	117. Ⓐ Ⓑ Ⓒ Ⓓ
18. Ⓐ Ⓑ Ⓒ Ⓓ	43. Ⓐ Ⓑ Ⓒ Ⓓ	68. Ⓐ Ⓑ Ⓒ Ⓓ	93. Ⓐ Ⓑ Ⓒ Ⓓ	118. Ⓐ Ⓑ Ⓒ Ⓓ
19. Ⓐ Ⓑ Ⓒ Ⓓ	44. Ⓐ Ⓑ Ⓒ Ⓓ	69. Ⓐ Ⓑ Ⓒ Ⓓ	94. Ⓐ Ⓑ Ⓒ Ⓓ	119. Ⓐ Ⓑ Ⓒ Ⓓ
20. Ⓐ Ⓑ Ⓒ Ⓓ	45. Ⓐ Ⓑ Ⓒ Ⓓ	70. Ⓐ Ⓑ Ⓒ Ⓓ	95. Ⓐ Ⓑ Ⓒ Ⓓ	120. Ⓐ Ⓑ Ⓒ Ⓓ
21. Ⓐ Ⓑ Ⓒ Ⓓ	46. Ⓐ Ⓑ Ⓒ Ⓓ	71. Ⓐ Ⓑ Ⓒ Ⓓ	96. Ⓐ Ⓑ Ⓒ Ⓓ	121. Ⓐ Ⓑ Ⓒ Ⓓ
22. Ⓐ Ⓑ Ⓒ Ⓓ	47. Ⓐ Ⓑ Ⓒ Ⓓ	72. Ⓐ Ⓑ Ⓒ Ⓓ	97. Ⓐ Ⓑ Ⓒ Ⓓ	122. Ⓐ Ⓑ Ⓒ Ⓓ
23. Ⓐ Ⓑ Ⓒ Ⓓ	48. Ⓐ Ⓑ Ⓒ Ⓓ	73. Ⓐ Ⓑ Ⓒ Ⓓ	98. Ⓐ Ⓑ Ⓒ Ⓓ	123. Ⓐ Ⓑ Ⓒ Ⓓ
24. Ⓐ Ⓑ Ⓒ Ⓓ	49. Ⓐ Ⓑ Ⓒ Ⓓ	74. Ⓐ Ⓑ Ⓒ Ⓓ	99. Ⓐ Ⓑ Ⓒ Ⓓ	124. Ⓐ Ⓑ Ⓒ Ⓓ
25. Ⓐ Ⓑ Ⓒ Ⓓ	50. Ⓐ Ⓑ Ⓒ Ⓓ	75. Ⓐ Ⓑ Ⓒ Ⓓ	100. Ⓐ Ⓑ Ⓒ Ⓓ	125. Ⓐ Ⓑ Ⓒ Ⓓ

To remove answer sheet, cut along dotted line.

PRACTICE EXAMINATION 2 ━━━━━━━━━

PART 1

NUMBER OF QUESTIONS: 125   TIME: 3 HOURS

Directions: Each of the questions or incomplete statements below is followed by four suggested answers or completions. Select the one that is best in each case and then blacken the corresponding space on the answer sheet.

1. All of the following are used as sources of information about new offerings of municipal bonds EXCEPT:

   (A) *Bond Buyer*
   (B) Blue List
   (C) Munifacts
   (D) newspapers and periodicals

2. Which of the following investment company securities will genially have the largest expense ratio:

   (A) a unit invest trust
   (B) a closed-end fund
   (C) a front-end load fund
   (D) a 12B-1 mutual fund

3. ADRs are instruments that facilitate investments by:

   (A) foreign investors in U.S. securities
   (B) foreign investors in foreign securities
   (C) U.S. investors in U.S. securities
   (D) U.S. investors in foreign securities

4. Purchase of a zero-coupon treasury avoids which two of the following risks:

   I. credit risk
   II. interest rate risk
   III. reinvestment risk
   IV. purchasing power risk

   (A) I and II
   (B) I and III
   (C) I and IV
   (D) III and IV

5. A customer purchases 1 ABC Oct 30 put @ 2 and writes 1 ABC Oct 40 put @ 8. The customer will profit when:

   I. the spread widens to more than 6
   II. the spread narrows to less than 6
   III. both options expire
   IV. both options are exercised

   (A) I and III
   (B) I and IV
   (C) II and III
   (D) II and IV

6. Which of the following persons need their employer's authorization to open a margin account at an NYSE member firm?

   I. an employee of another NYSE member
   II. a clerical worker of an NASD broker/dealer
   III. a bank teller
   IV. an employee of the NYSE

   (A) I and II only
   (B) I, II, and III only
   (C) I, II, III, and IV
   (D) II and III only

7. A Swiss Franc 62 call option (62,500 francs) quoted at 1.5 would have a premium of:

   (A) $150.00
   (B) $500.00
   (C) $625.00
   (D) $937.50

8. The value of a variable annuity unit is determined from the value of which of the following:

   (A) Dow Jones Industrials
   (B) S & P 500
   (C) issuer's separate account
   (D) issuer's general account

9. A municipal bond purchased at a market discount will have a yield-to-maturity that is:

   (A) lower than the bond coupon rate
   (B) equal to the bond coupon rate
   (C) greater than the bond coupon rate
   (D) indeterminate if the bond is callable

10. Which of the following investment companies does *not* charge a management fee:

    (A) municipal unit investment trust
    (B) open-end growth fund
    (C) closed-end income fund
    (D) money market mutual fund

11. An institution requesting a quote on a block of 100 bonds from a government securities dealer receives a response of 98.02 bid, 98.06 ask. What is the dollar amount the institution will receive per bond if the bonds are sold to the government securities dealer?

    (A) $98,062.50
    (B) $98,187.50
    (C) $98.250.00
    (D) $98.750.00

Questions 12–14 are based on the following: With XYZ common stock trading at 72, an investor buys an XYZ 70 call for 4 and sells an XYZ 80 call for 1.

12. What is the breakeven point on the XYZ call position?

    (A) 73
    (B) 74
    (C) 77
    (D) 78

13. What is the potential maximum gain on the position, before commissions or other transaction costs, if held until expiration?

    (A) $300
    (B) $500
    (C) $700
    (D) $1,000

14. What will be the gain or loss on the position if XYZ is trading at 63 at expiration?

    (A) $300 gain
    (B) $300 loss
    (C) $700 gain
    (D) $700 loss

15. Which two of the following financial indicators are used to assess a company's liquidity?

      I. net working capital
     II. net tangible assets (book value)
    III. capitalization ratio
    IV. net quick assets

    (A) I and III
    (B) I and IV
    (C) II and III
    (D) II and IV

16. All the following actions by a corporation would lower working capital EXCEPT:

    (A) calling a bond 5 years prior to maturity
    (B) purchasing machinery without incurring debt
    (C) declaring a dividend
    (D) paying a dividend

17. MSRB rules permit municipal securities' dealers to use which of the following types of quotes?

      I. bona fide bids and offers
     II. nominal quotes (if clearly indicated as such)
    III. one-sided markets (bids only or offers only)
    IV. indications of interest (e.g., bids wanted)

    (A) I and II only
    (B) I and III only
    (C) II and IV only
    (D) I, II, III, and IV

18. NASD rules concerning OTC trades of NYSE listed securities:

    (A) require the selling broker/dealer to report the trade to the consolidated tape within 90 seconds of the transaction
    (B) require the buying broker/dealer to report the trade to the consolidated tape within 90 seconds of the transaction
    (C) require both the buying and selling broker/dealers to report the transaction to the consolidated tape
    (D) permit only broker/dealers that also belong to the NYSE to report such trades to the consolidated tape

19. A NYSE listed stock closed at 63.50 on a plus tick. The next day is the ex-date for a 65¢ per share dividend. What is the lowest price at which the stock may be sold short at the opening of trading on the ex-date?

    (A) 62.85
    (B) 62.75
    (C) 63.50
    (D) any price

20. A securities transaction executed directly between a pension fund and a trust company using the Instinet system would have been completed in the:

    (A) first market
    (B) second market
    (C) third market
    (D) fourth market

21. XYZ Corporation's 5% cumulative convertible preferred stock (100 par) is currently trading at 80. It is convertible into XYZ common stock at 60 per share. What is the current yield on the preferred stock?

    (A) 5.00%
    (B) 6.25%
    (C) 8.33%
    (D) 16.67%

22. An investor holds interests in two limited partnerships. One provides passive income of $10,000, and the other, passive losses of $12,000. Which of the following properly describes the tax treatment of these two entries?

    (A) The investor has a net loss of $2,000 for the year.
    (B) The investor may deduct $2,000 from current taxable income.
    (C) The investor may carry both amounts forward until he sells his partnership interest.
    (D) $10,000 of the losses offsets $10,000 of the gains, the remaining $2,000 of losses is carried forward to be offset against the future passive income.

23. Which of the following terms is unrelated to a municipal bond underwriting?

    (A) bond counsel
    (B) firm commitment
    (C) standby underwriter
    (D) undivided account

24. MSRB rules permit which of the following to approve advertising related to municipal securities?

    I. municipal securities principal
    II. municipal securities financial and operations principal
    III. general securities principal
    IV. bond counsel

    (A) I and IV
    (B) II and IV only
    (C) I and III only
    (D) II and III only

25. Which of the following must be completed before a customer can begin trading listed options?

    I. The customer must grant power-of-attorney to their registered representative.
    II. The customer must receive the OCC disclose document.
    III. The customer account must be approved by the firm's registered options principal.
    IV. The customer must return a signed option agreement to the broker/dealer.

    (A) I and II only
    (B) II and III only
    (C) III and IV
    (D) I and IV

26. A municipal securities dealer is quoting a two-sided market in a particular issue at 88.60 to 89.20 on blocks of 100 bonds. What is the spread per thousand dollars of par value?

    (A) $1.25
    (B) $2.50
    (C) $6.00
    (D) $7.50

27. A limited partnership is officially recognized as a legal entity with the filing of the:

    (A) registration statement
    (B) limited partnership agreement
    (C) subscription agreement
    (D) certificate of limited partnership

28. An investor writes an uncovered call option. The option expires unexercised. What are the tax consequences of the position?

    (A) The investor has a capital loss equal to the premium recognized as of the date of the opening sale.
    (B) The investor has a capital gain equal to the premium recognized as of the date of the opening sale.
    (C) The investor has a capital gain equal to the premium recognized at expiration.
    (D) The investor has ordinary income equal to the premium recognized at expiration.

29. An investor writes one uncovered ABC January 45 put for 3 when ABC common stock is trading at 47. In December, with ABC trading at 39, the put is exercised, and the investor buys the stock. What are the tax consequences of the events to the put writer?

    (A) $300 gain
    (B) $300 loss
    (C) $500 loss
    (D) cost basis of $42 per share in ABC stock

30. An investor has a margin account with long market value of $60,000 and a debit balance of $40,000. The investor directs his broker/dealer to sell 100 shares of ABC stock. The stock is sold at 12. How much money can the investor withdraw?

    (A) $0
    (B) $400
    (C) $600
    (D) $1,200

31. What is the buying power of a margin account in which the client has an SMA of 4,500?

    (A) $2,250
    (B) $4,500
    (C) $6,750
    (D) $9,000

32. Broker/dealers are required to obtain confirmation of a customer's financial condition prior to which of the following actions?

    I. opening a margin account
    II. approving an account for option trading
    III. handling an account on a discretionary basis
    IV. allowing the purchase of a DPP for a customer account

    (A) I only
    (B) II and III only
    (C) IV only
    (D) II and IV only

33. Which of the following would not be included on the confirmation of a municipal bond dealer acting as a principal to a retail customer?

    (A) the dealer's address and phone number
    (B) the accrued interest
    (C) the commission charged
    (D) the fact that the delivery is "ex-legal"

34. Federal Reserve Board margin rules prohibit broker/dealers from lending money for the purchase of which of the following securities?

    (A) short-term listed options
    (B) national market system securities
    (C) municipal bonds
    (D) treasury securities

Questions 35 and 36 are based on the following information: With ABC common stock trading at 64, an investor sells one ABC July 65 call at 2 and sells one ABC July 65 put at 3.50.

35. What are the two breakeven points on the position?

    I. 59.50
    II. 61.50
    III. 67
    IV. 70.50

    (A) I and III
    (B) I and IV
    (C) II and III
    (D) II and IV

36. What is the maximum possible gain?

    (A) $200
    (B) $350
    (C) $550
    (D) unlimited

37. Which of the following are NOT considered a type of investment company?

    (A) unit investment trusts
    (B) real estate investment trusts
    (C) open-end management companies
    (D) closed-end management companies

38. Authorization for the limited partners to shorten the term of a limited partnership and thus terminate the venture is an example of:

    (A) partnership democracy
    (B) common law rights
    (C) subscription privileges
    (D) proportionate sharing

39. An investor purchases 20 ABC Oct 75 calls for 6 when ABC common stock is trading at 77. ABC Corporation subsequently declares a 3-for-2 split. How would the investors option position be expressed after the split is effected?

    (A) 20 ABC Oct 50 calls
    (B) 20 ABC Oct 75 calls
    (C) 30 ABC Oct 50 calls
    (D) 30 ABC Oct 75 calls

40. Which best describes a Coverdell IRA?

    I. A savings account that is set up to pay the qualified education expenses of a designated beneficiary.
    II. It may be opened at any bank in the United States or other IRS-approved entity.
    III. Any beneficiary under 21 years of age.
    IV. The trustee must be an individual.

    (A) I and IV
    (B) II and III
    (C) I and II
    (D) III and IV

41. XRT Corporation issued debentures convertible into XRT common stock at $50 per share. What will be the conversion price of the bonds following a 10% stock dividend?

    (A) $45.00
    (B) $45.45
    (C) $54.55
    (D) $55.00

42. An investor purchased $10,000 face value of 6.75% municipal bonds with 7 years maturity at 96.50. The investor sells the bonds at 97 after holding them for two years. What is the gain or loss for tax purposes?

    (A) $50 gain
    (B) $50 loss
    (C) $100 gain
    (D) $100 loss

43. The standard margin agreement includes all of the following EXCEPT:

    (A) the pledge of portfolio securities
    (B) authorization for the broker/dealer to rehypothecate margined securities
    (C) a trading authorization for the RR
    (D) the right to sell out the account to protect the dealer's loan

44. Under Rule 144, a shareholder is allowed to sell what percentage of a corporation's outstanding shares?

    (A) 0.5%
    (B) 1%
    (C) 2%
    (D) 5%

45. A tombstone advertisement will normally show all of the following EXCEPT:

    (A) the issuer's identity
    (B) a description of the securities
    (C) the managing underwriter
    (D) the underwriter's compensation

46. What is the maximum number of non-accredited purchasers allowed in a private placement?

    (A) 15
    (B) 25
    (C) 35
    (D) 45

47. An investor owns XYZ common stock. What actions may the investor take to partially protect her position from an expected decline in XYZ stock?

    I. buy XYZ puts
    II. buy XYZ calls
    III. place sell stop orders on XYZ
    IV. sell XYZ common stock short against the box

    (A) II only
    (B) I and III only
    (C) II and IV only
    (D) II and III

48. When ABC stock is trading at 124, an investor buys an ABC 120 call for 5 and writes an ABC 130 call for 1. Which two of the following statements concerning the position are true?

    I. This is a bullish spread.
    II. This is a bearish spread.
    III. The investor will profit if the spread widens.
    IV. The investor will profit if the spread narrows.

    (A) I and III
    (B) I and IV
    (C) II and III
    (D) II and IV

49. What is the taxable equivalent yield on a 7.5% municipal bond for an investor in the 29% tax bracket?

    (A) 11.2%
    (B) 10.4%
    (C) 9.6%
    (D) 8.3%

Questions 50 and 51 are based on the following information: Each ABC Corporation convertible debenture ($1,000 par) is convertible into ABC common stock at $50 per share.

50. If the ABC convertible debenture is trading at 88 and is selling at parity, the price of the common stock is:

    (A) 42
    (B) 44
    (C) 48
    (D) 50

51. If the debenture is selling at 105, there would be an arbitrage situation if the common stock is selling at:

    (A) 50
    (B) 51
    (C) 52
    (D) 53

52. XYZ 6.25% preferred stock ($100 par), convertible at 25 and callable at 102, is currently trading at 90. What is the nominal yield?

    (A) 2.50%
    (B) 6.13%
    (C) 6.25%
    (D) 6.94%

53. The third market refers to:

    (A) exchange trading of listed securities
    (B) exchange trading of unlisted securities
    (C) OTC trading of listed securities
    (D) OTC trading of unlisted securities

54. List the following according to priority of claim in a liquidation of a corporation:

    I. preferred stockholders
    II. general creditors
    III. secured bondholders
    IV. subordinated debenture holders

    (A) I, II, III, IV
    (B) II, III, IV, I
    (C) III, IV, II, I
    (D) III, II, IV, I

55. Generally, the manager of a municipal syndicate will confirm orders in which priority (first to last)?

    I. group net order
    II. member takedown orders
    III. designated orders
    IV. pre-sale orders

    (A) II, IV, I, III
    (B) I, II, III, IV
    (C) IV, I, III, II
    (D) IV, III, I, II

56. A standby underwriter would be used in connection with a subscription to what type of securities?

    (A) options
    (B) municipals
    (C) governments
    (D) corporates

57. In a typical corporate underwriting, which of these activities occurs last?

    (A) the due diligence meeting
    (B) taking indications of interest
    (C) stabilization of the offering
    (D) the agreement among underwriters

58. All of the following statements are true EXCEPT:

    (A) All new accounts must be approved by a principal of the firm.
    (B) All discretionary orders prior to entry, must be approved by a principal, before they are entered.
    (C) All advertising must be approved by a principal of the firm prior to its first use.
    (D) All correspondence from registered representatives to customers must be approved prior to mailing.

59. Exercise of which one of the following will *not* change the number of shares outstanding?

    (A) options
    (B) rights
    (C) warrants
    (D) convertible debenture

60. All of the following are leading indicators EXCEPT:

    (A) GNP
    (B) stock market prices
    (C) money supply
    (D) changes in inventories

61. Stocks of companies in which of the following industries would be considered defensive issues?

    (A) autos
    (B) electric utilities
    (C) consumer durables
    (D) oil drilling

62. What percentage of preferred stock dividends received by a corporation must be included in taxable income?

    (A) 15%
    (B) 30%
    (C) 70%
    (D) 85%

63. The holder of a corporate security can sustain a loss only until:

    (A) the trade date of a sale
    (B) the day after the trade date
    (C) the day before the settlement date
    (D) the settlement date

64. A new issue of municipals has a takedown of 2 points and is to be reoffered at par. The manager's fee is $2; the additional takedown is $8; the selling concession is $10. If a member has a "group net" order confirmed, the member will take bonds out of the account at:

    (A) $980
    (B) $982
    (C) $990
    (D) $1,000

65. Which rating service bases its rating on liquidity of issues?

    (A) Fitch's
    (B) Moody's
    (C) Standard & Poor's
    (D) White's

66. The Federal Reserve sets initial margin requirements for all of the following EXCEPT:

    (A) preferred stocks
    (B) convertible bonds
    (C) government bonds
    (D) NASDAQ national market equities

Questions 67 through 69 are based on the following information: An investor purchased 100 shares of ABC common stock at 68 and simultaneously bought 1 ABC 70 put at 6.

67. What is the maximum possible loss on the position prior to the expiration of the option?

    (A) $400
    (B) $600
    (C) $1,480
    (D) unlimited

68. What is the breakeven point on the stock at expiration of the options?

    (A) 62
    (B) 64
    (C) 74
    (D) 76

69. What is the gain on the position if ABC stock is trading at 79 at expiration?

    (A) $300
    (B) $500
    (C) $600
    (D) $1,000

70. On Tuesday, August 11, an investor purchases an 8% municipal bond in a regular way transaction. The bond has interest payment dates of June 15 and December 15. For how many days of accrued interest must the buyer pay the seller?

    (A) 57
    (B) 59
    (C) 62
    (D) 63

71. The amount of municipal bonds sold in the previous week as a percentage of the municipal bonds offered during that week is called the:

    (A) placement ratio
    (B) percentage depletion
    (C) visible demand
    (D) inter-bank offered rate

72. Which of the following instruments are used to finance international trade?

    (A) BAs
    (B) ADRs
    (C) foreign currency options
    (D) euro–dollar bonds

73. Which of the following government securities have no collateral value?

    (A) Series EE savings bonds
    (B) T-notes
    (C) T-bills
    (D) T-bonds

74. In general, states use all of the following sources of revenue to retire bonds EXCEPT:

    (A) sales taxes
    (B) income taxes
    (C) real estate taxes
    (D) license fees

75. Which two of the following are not considered part of the "bonded debt" of a municipality?

    I. revenue bonds
    II. general obligation bonds
    III. tax anticipation notes
    IV. limited tax bonds

    (A) I and III
    (B) I and IV
    (C) II and III
    (D) II and IV

76. For how long is a Rule 144 filing effective?

    (A) 30 days
    (B) 60 days
    (C) 90 days
    (D) 120 days

77. With the S & P 100 index at 110, an investor sells 5 Sept OEX (S & P 100) 123 calls at 2. The index closes at 130 and the options are exercised. What is his gain or loss?

    (A) $2,000
    (B) $2,500
    (C) $3,000
    (D) $3,500

78. Which of the following will increase the SMA in a restricted margin account?

    I. sale of securities held long in the account
    II. cash dividend on securities held long in the account
    III. deposit of cash to meet a Reg-T requirement
    IV. deposit of securities to meet a Reg-T requirement

    (A) I and II only
    (B) II and III only
    (C) I and III
    (D) III and IV

79. The manager of a government bond portfolio fears a temporary rise in interest rates. To protect the securities from a drop in price and to earn income, she should consider:

    (A) buying calls
    (B) selling calls
    (C) buying puts
    (D) selling puts

80. A client's margin account has the following status:

    Long market value $53,000
    Debit balance $25,500

    Which of the following terms IS NOT applicable to this account?

    (A) special memorandum account credit
    (B) buying power
    (C) margin excess
    (D) maintenance deficiency

81. Mutual funds must offer their shareholders which of the following benefits if the fund wishes to charge the maximum sales load of 8.5%?

    I. forward pricing
    II. rights of accumulation
    III. discounts on volume purchases
    IV. dividend reinvestment at NAV

    (A) I and II only
    (B) II and IV only
    (C) II, III, and IV only
    (D) III and IV only

82. An investor has a margin account with securities held long valued at $26,000 and a $16,000 debit balance. How much money must the investor deposit to meet the margin requirements on a purchase of $7,000 of additional stock?

    (A) $0
    (B) $500
    (C) $3,500
    (D) $7,000

83. Moody's MIG rating would apply to which of the following types of securities?

    (A) BANs
    (B) T-bills
    (C) general obligation bonds
    (D) corporate debentures

Questions 84 and 85 are based on the following information: A real estate limited partnership has these revenues and expenses in its tax year:

Gross Revenue:	$600,000
Operating Expenses:	$425,000
Interest Expenses:	$125,000
Depreciation:	$75,000

84. What is the amount of income or loss that will be reported from partnership operations?

  (A) $25,000 passive loss
  (B) $50,000 passive income
  (C) $100,000 passive income
  (D) $175,000 passive income

85. What is the partnership's cash flow?

  (A) negative $25,000
  (B) positive $50,000
  (C) positive $100,000
  (D) positive $175,000

86. Depletion allowances would be associated with which of the following types of DPP?

  I. oil and gas drilling programs
  II. raw land programs
  III. real estate partnerships buying existing properties
  IV. oil and gas income programs

  (A) I and II only
  (B) I and IV only
  (C) II and IV only
  (D) III and IV

87. All of the following would be considered benefits to investors in DPPs EXCEPT:

  (A) depletion
  (B) depreciation
  (C) recapture
  (D) passive tax credits

88. During the first 90 days of apprenticeship, candidates for registration as a municipal securities representative may:

  (A) solicit buy/sell orders for government securities only
  (B) relay confirmations of trade to institutional clients
  (C) accept orders from public customers on a salaried basis
  (D) do anything RR may do provided it is under supervision

Questions 89 through 91 are based on the following information: With ABC common stock trading at 39, an investor writes one ABC April 45 put for 11 and purchases one ABC April 35 put for 4.

89. This spread could be described by all of the following terms EXCEPT:

  (A) credit
  (B) bull
  (C) money
  (D) diagonal

90. What is the position breakeven point at expiration?

  (A) 34
  (B) 38
  (C) 39
  (D) 42

91. The client will have the largest gain on this position if the underlying stock at expiration is at:

  (A) 45
  (B) 42
  (C) 38
  (D) 35

92. Which of the following situations results in overlapping debt?

    (A) The total debt of the localities within a state exceeds the state's legal debt limit.
    (B) Serial bonds from the same issuers have overlapping maturities.
    (C) Bonds are issued by an interstate authority for several states having common borders.
    (D) Coterminous taxing authorities have individually issued bonds that are based on ad valorem taxes on common real property.

93. Which two of the following terms describe the underwriter's commitment during a rights offering?

    I. firm
    II. best efforts
    III. standby
    IV. matched book

    (A) I and III
    (B) I and IV
    (C) II and III
    (D) II and IV

Questions 94 and 95 are based on the following information: A corporation in the 34% tax bracket that had $5,000,000 of operating income in the recently ended fiscal year reports the following capitalization on the fiscal year-end balance sheet:

Long-term Debit:

7% mortgage bonds	$10,000,000
10% convertible debentures	$10,000,000
(convertible at $40 per share)	

Equity:

6% preferred stock (100 par)	$2,000,000
common stock ($1 par)	$2,000,000
capital surplus	$12,000,000
earned surplus	$20,000,000
treasury stock	($5,000,000)
*(500,000 shares)	

94. What would be the corporation's earnings per share calculated on a non-diluted basis?

    (A) $0.77
    (B) $0.96
    (C) $1.03
    (D) $1.37

95. What would be the corporation's earnings per share calculated on a fully diluted basis?

    (A) $1.21
    (B) $1.36
    (C) $1.55
    (D) $1.81

96. A net lien revenue bond reported the following items:

Gross Revenue:	$15,000,000
Operating Expenses:	$5,000,000
Maturing Principal:	$2,000,000
Interest Expenses:	$3,000,000

What is the debt service coverage?

    (A) 2 to 1
    (B) 3 to 1
    (C) 3⅓ to 1
    (D) 5 to 1

97. Which of the following positions has the greatest dollar risk?

    (A) long stock – short call
    (B) long stock – long put
    (C) short stock – long call
    (D) short stock – short put

98. A corporation issued convertible debentures. Conversion of those securities would reduce all of the following for the issuing corporation EXCEPT:

    (A) leverage
    (B) capitalization
    (C) interest expense
    (D) long-term debt

99. The ABC Corporation has issued $8 convertible preferred stock ($100 par). Each share of preferred is convertible into 4 shares of common stock. The preferred is callable at 106. The preferred is currently trading at 112. The common stock is currently trading at 27. If ABC Corporation announced a call of its preferred, how would you advise a client that currently holds these securities?

   (A) sell the preferred immediately at 112
   (B) accept the call at 106
   (C) convert the preferred
   (D) hold the preferred because of its attractive dividend

100. Municipal securities dealers must disclose the existence of control relationships when executing which of the following types of transactions?

   I.   new issues sold on a principal basis
   II. new issues sold on an agency basis
   III. secondary trades executed on a principal basis
   IV. secondary trades executed on an agency basis

   (A) I and II only
   (B) I and III only
   (C) III and IV only
   (D) I, II, III, and IV

101. Retirement plans established by which of the following are subject to the requirements of the Employee Retirement Income Security Act?

   (A) public employers
   (B) private employers
   (C) both public and private employers
   (D) self-employed individuals

102. Which of the following investment instruments should provide the best protection against inflation?

   (A) T-bills
   (B) T-bonds
   (C) fixed annuities
   (D) variable annuities

103. An investor's margin account shows the following balances:

Long Market Value:	$60,000
Debit Balance:	$25,000
Short Market Value:	$18,000
Credit Balance:	$30,000

   What is the equity in the investor's margin account?

   (A) $35,000
   (B) $37,000
   (C) $47,000
   (D) $82,000

104. An oil and gas limited partnership is compensating its general partner with a percentage of all revenues. The general partner also shares in a different percentage of the partnership's expenses. How would this type of sharing arrangement be described?

   (A) carried working interest
   (B) functional allocation
   (C) overriding royalty interest
   (D) disproportionate sharing arrangement

402 • PRACTICE EXAMINATION 2

105. What is the most likely reason why a municipal securities dealer might use a broker's broker to effect a sale with another dealer?

(A) The dealer may wish to keep its activity confidential.
(B) The broker's broker can effect the trade more efficiently at a lower cost.
(C) This will allow the dealer to secretly manipulate the market price of the bond.
(D) The broker's broker would be willing to swap bonds from its inventory for those the dealer wishes to sell.

106. If a new municipal bond issue is to be sold through a competitive bid, the issuer will determine which of the following:

(A) maturities
(B) underwriter
(C) coupon rate
(D) re-offering yields

107. A new customer had her account approved to trade options and directed her registered representative to purchase a call option. Despite repeated phone calls, she failed to return a signed option agreement within the required 15 days. Which of the following statements is true concerning this situation?

(A) The broker/dealer must liquidate the option position immediately.
(B) The broker/dealer should exercise the option since a long position in the stock is permissible.
(C) The broker/dealer must notify the SEC.
(D) The broker/dealer may only accept closing transactions.

108. High P-E ratios and low dividend payout ratios would be typical of:

(A) defensive issues
(B) growth stocks
(C) blue chip corporations
(D) industries in decline

109. Your client's margin account shows the following balances:

Long Market Value:	$24,000
Debit Balance:	$16,000
SMA:	$10,000

How much money could the client withdraw without liquidating any of the existing security positions?

(A) $0
(B) $2,000
(C) $4,000
(D) $10,000

110. An investor's margin account has $24,000 of long market value and a $10,000 debit balance. If we presume no other source of SMA, how much money would the customer have to deposit to purchase $6,000 of common stock?

(A) $1,000
(B) $2,000
(C) $3,000
(D) $6,000

Questions 111 through 114 are based on the following information: With ABC stock trading at 23 an investor decides to buy 200 shares and sell 2 ABC 25 calls for 3.

111. What is the maximum possible loss on the investor's position?

(A) $4,000
(B) $4,600
(C) $5,200
(D) unlimited

112. What is the maximum possible gain on the investor's position?

    (A) $400
    (B) $600
    (C) $1,000
    (D) unlimited

113. What is the breakeven point for the investor's position?

    (A) $20
    (B) $22
    (C) $26
    (D) $28

114. By expiration, the stock has risen only one point. At that time, the investor sells the stock and closes out the option at its intrinsic value. What is the investor's gain or loss?

    (A) $400 loss
    (B) $200 gain
    (C) $400 gain
    (D) $800 gain

115. Which two of the following statements are true of inverted yield curves?

    I. They are positively sloped.
    II. They are negatively sloped.
    III. They reflect short-term yields lower than long-term yields.
    IV. They reflect short-term yields higher than long-term yields.

    (A) I and III
    (B) I and IV
    (C) II and III
    (D) II and IV

116. Which of the following securities is sold through a yield auction?

    (A) general obligation bonds
    (B) GNMAs
    (C) T-bills
    (D) ADRs

117. Which of the following is *least* likely to purchase municipal bonds?

    (A) a qualified pension fund
    (B) mutual fund
    (C) insurance company
    (D) bank

118. Which of the following organizations insure municipal bonds?

    (A) ABA
    (B) MSRB
    (C) AMBAC
    (D) FHLBB

119. Municipal double-barreled bonds would be rated and traded like:

    (A) revenue bonds
    (B) moral obligation bonds
    (C) general obligation bonds
    (D) treasury bonds

120. Which of the following would disclose the good faith deposit requirements and date, time, and place of sale for a competitive bid offering of general obligation bonds?

    (A) blue list
    (B) official statement
    (C) official notice of sale
    (D) agreement among underwriters

121. The purchase price of which of these assets cannot be depreciated?

    (A) land
    (B) used computers
    (C) 20-year-old building
    (D) new oil drilling equipment

122. Which of the following statistics would be of *least* interest to a technical analyst?

    (A) P-E ratio
    (B) short interest
    (C) puts and calls
    (D) advance–decline line

123. Which of the following has regulatory but not enforcement authority?

    (A) MSRB
    (B) ASE
    (C) CBOE
    (D) NASD

124. A T-bill with 180 days to maturity is sold with a discount yield of 8%. What is the price of a bill with a face value of $100,000?

    (A) $92,000
    (B) $94,000
    (C) $96,000
    (D) $98,000

125. A stock trades ex-dividend on Monday the 20th. What is the last day a customer can purchase the stock and be entitled to the dividend?

    (A) Monday the 13th
    (B) Thursday the 16th
    (C) Wednesday the 15th
    (D) Monday the 20th

PART 1 ANSWERS

1. **B** The Blue List, published each business day by Standard & Poor's, contains dealer offerings of municipal bonds—plus some convertibles and preferreds offered by the participating dealers.

2. **D** 12B-1 funds have no up-front sales charge. They do however, have both a distribution fee and a management fee. The distribution fee, which will average .50 to .75% per year causes them to have a substantially larger expense ratio.

3. **D** ADRs, which are registered receipts for foreign securities held by an American bank acting as a depository, greatly facilitate investment in foreign corporations.

4. **B** Zero-coupon treasuries have neither credit nor reinvestment risk. They are subject to both interest rate and purchasing power risk.

5. **C** The customer has a net of $600. Therefore, the spread is a credit spread. The customer wants the spread to narrow. If both options expire, the customer keeps the net premium of $600.

6. **C** All four of the restricted employees need their employer's permission (in writing) before a member firm may open a margin account for them.

7. **D** The premium is computed as follows:

Unit Number × Unit Price × Premium
62,500 × 0.1 × 1.5 = $937.50

8. **C** Since the owner accepts part of the capital risk of a variable annuity, the assets must be segregated from the general assets of the issuing insurance company. This segregated account is called the separate account.

9. **C** Current tax law permits the market discount on a municipal bond to be considered a capital gain (it is *not* such on governments and corporates; it is interest income on them). As such, it increases the total return from the investment; as a result, the YTM is greater than the coupon rate of interest.

10. **A** Unit investment trusts—unlike management companies—feature a *fixed* diversified portfolio. Thus, there is no day-to-day management of the portfolio and no fee.

11. **A** If the bonds are sold to the dealer, the institution will receive the bid price of 98.02 (98²⁄₃₂). On $100,000 this translates to $100,000 × .9806250 of the face value, or $98,062.50.

12. **A** The breakeven point on a debit call spread is

the lower strike price + the debit
$$70 \quad + \quad 3 \quad = 73$$

13. **C** On a debit call spread the maximum potential gain is always the difference between the strike prices and the net debit. Here:

10 points (80 − 70) − 3 (net debit) = 7
$7 × 10 shares = $700

14. **B** At a closing market price of 63 *both* options are out-of-the money; thus, the client will lose the total net debit of $300.

15. **B** Both the net working capital and the net quick assets of a corporation give an insight into its ability to meet current debts. Net tangible assets and capitalization ratio are used to assess value of the stock (II) or risk of bankruptcy (III).

16. **D** Paying a dividend—you'll be surprised to know—does not lower working capital. There is a dollar-for-dollar reduction of current assets and current liabilities as the dividend is paid. On the other hand, declaring a dividend introduces a new charge into current liabilities (the dividend), and working capital is reduced. In effect, corporate cash dividends are a two-step process: declaring (which lower working capital) and paying (which does not).

17. **D** All four are MSRB quote regulations.

18. **A** This is a factual requirement: NASDAQ trades of less than 5,000 shares must be reported to the consolidated tape (or to NASDAQ) within 90 seconds of the trade. The selling dealer normally makes this report.

19. **D** The any price uptick rule was rescinded.

20. **D** Instinet is the tradename of the subscription computer service whereby institutional clients can seek bids and offers for OTC trades of listed or unlisted securities. Instinet is registered with the SEC as a national exchange, and all such trades appear on the consolidated tape.

21. **B** The current yield is the annual dividend in dollars ($5) divided by the current price ($80), or 6.25%.

22. **D** The IRS permits passive losses to be used only to offset passive gains; the remainder is carried forward.

23. **C** The term "standby underwriter" is used only of rights offerings—it is not a municipal term.

24. **C** Advertising needs member firm approval. MSRB rules permit either a municipal or general principal to do this.

25. **B** To begin options trading, the customer must receive a copy of the risk disclosure document and the account must be approved by an ROP. A signed power-of-attorney is NOT required. The customer has 15 days within which to sign the option agreement.

26. **C** The spread between 88.60 (bid) and 89.20 (asked) is .6 of a point, or $6.

27. **D** Most partnerships are authorized in one of the 50 states. Their official authorization occurs when the certificate of limited partnership is filed with the date. Be careful of the working of the question: There is no partnership in practice until the general partner signs the subscription agreement.

28. **C** If an option expires, the writer has income and is taxed as such.

29. **D** The IRS has a simple rule: The writer of a put who is exercised has an adjusted cost of acquisition of:

Strike Price – Premium Received
$45 – $3 = $42

30. **C** In a restricted margin account (the case here because the debit balance of $40,000 exceeds the equity of $20,000), the client may always withdraw 50% of the proceeds of a long sale ($600).

31. **D** The buying power is twice the SMA if registered non-exempt marginable securities are purchased.

32. **D** The key word is "confirmation." All customer's financial conditions must be known as part of the "know your customer" rule. Confirmation, however, must be obtained for option trading and the sale of DPPs. In general, this will require a positive affirmation or signature from

the customer on the option information agreement or the subscription agreement.

33. **C** Municipal securities are subject to mark ups or mark downs when the dealer acts as the principal.

34. **A** Short-term listed options have no loan value; therefore, they are not marginable. The FED does approve for margin purchase all OTC securities on the NASDAQ national market. Muni and governments are exempt from FED restrictions and are regularly purchased on margin.

35. **B** The position is a short straddle; by agreement, the breakevens on a short straddle are the strike price plus (59.50) and minus (70.50) the premiums.

36. **C** The maximum possible gain on a short straddle is the sum of the combined premiums: $550.

37. **B** Although REITs are taxed like investment companies, they are not investment companies. The other three choices are.

38. **A** The partnership agreement specifies certain circumstances in which the limited partners have a vote; the decision to terminate the partnership is one of them.

39. **C** Multiply the number of calls by $3/2$. Multiply the strike price by $2/3$. Result: 30 calls at 50.

40. **C** I and II is correct by definition. III the beneficiary must be under 18 years old and IV the trustee or custodian must be a bank or entity approved by the IRS.

41. **B** Following a stock dividend multiply the number of shares by $11/10$ and multiply the conversion price by $10/11$.

$$50 \times \frac{10}{11} = \$45.45$$

42. **A** There is no evidence that this is an OID municipal bond; thus, presume that this is a market discount. On a market discount muni *do not* adjust the price upward. The gain on sale is the sale price minus the cost of acquisition: 9,700 – 9,650, or $50.

43. **C** The standard margin agreement does not include discretionary authorization for the RR; it does include the other three choices.

44. **B** The general rule on 144 sales is 1% of the outstanding shares. The exception: listed shares where the upside limit is the *greater* of 1% or the average of the last 4-week's volume.

45. **D** Tombstones do not show underwriters' compensation.

46. **C** On a private placement, the maximum number of non-accredited investors is 35. The number of accredited investors is unlimited.

47. **C** Of the choices given, only the long call will not hedge a long stock position; it adds to risk.

48. **A** This is a bullish spread. You can easily identify this: the client bought the lower priced option and sold the higher priced option. This is also true of put spreads. The spread was put on a debit ($5 out and $1 in on each share). Whenever a spread is put on at a debit, the client wants the spread to widen so that he can make a closing transaction at a greater price.

49. **B** To compute the equivalent taxable yield, use this formula:

$$\frac{\text{Non-taxable Yield}}{(28\% \text{ Tax Bracket}) - 100} = -\frac{7.5}{0.72} = 10.4\%$$

50. **B** You are told that the convertible, selling at 88, is at parity. Thus, take $440 and divide by the number of shares into which it is convertible. Answer is $880 divided by 20 = $44.

51. **D** An arbitrage situation occurs whenever the value of the underlying common stock *exceeds* the market value of the convertible bond. Here: $20 \times 53 = \$1,060$. This is greater than the bond's price of $1,050.

52. **C** Nominal yield and coupon yield are the same. Thus, the correct response is 6.25%.

53. **C** The over-the-counter trading of listed securities is said to take place in the third market.

54. **D** Creditors always take priority over owners; thus I is last. Of the creditors, the secured bondholders come first; the general creditors next; and the subordinated debenture holders just before the preferred stockholders.

55. **C** As a general rule, the order is: presale, group-net, designated (net), and member takedown. The syndicate manager must be prepared to explain if he departs from this priority.

56. **D** Standby underwriters are used in conjunction with rights subscriptions for corporate securities.

57. **C** Stabilization takes place only after the underwriting is effective. All of the other activities take place before the effective date.

58. **B** Discretionary orders must be reviewed promptly, but they need not be approved before they are entered.

59. **A** Options are a "derivative" product. They are independent of the issuer and its outstanding shares.

60. **A** The GNP is a coincident indicator. The other three are leading indicators. Of these, the money supply is the most important and the price of 500 stocks the most accurate.

61. **B** Industries mentioned in A, C, and D are quite cyclical. Only B is a defensive industry.

62. **B** Current tax law permits a domestic corporation to exclude 70% of the dividends received from any equity security of a domestic corporation. Thus, a maximum of 30% is taxable. Advice is needed because in some circumstances, larger amounts are excluded.

63. **A** A holder is at risk only until the trade date; after that, all risk goes to the new buyer. The holder is, however, the holder of record until the settlement date, and accrued interest is computed up to but not including the settlement date.

64. **D** "Group net" means that the entire takedown remains in the account to be divided up among the participants according to their participation. Answer: $1,000.

65. **D** White's rating services bases its ratings on the liquidity of issues.

66. **C** The Fed exempts governments from Reg-T. Any margin requirements are established by the SROs.

67. **B** As long as a put option is in effect, the maximum loss an investor can face is the premium paid for the option.

68. **C** At the expiration of the option, the client shall have paid out $68 for the stock and $6 for the put option; a total of $74. Thus, the client will breakeven if she can sell the stock at $74.

69. **B** If the stock is selling at 79 at expiration, the client's put will be out-of-the-money. However, the client will make $500: the market price of $70 minus the breakeven of $74.

70. **B** The accrued interest days are as follows:

    June   16 days   (15th through end of month)
    July   30 days   (entire month)
    August   13 days   (first up to 13th)
    Total   59 days

    You count up to but do not include the settlement date.

71. **A** The placement ratio gives an insight into the underwriting risk of an issue. If 85% are placed, 15% of the bonds are unsold and subject to interest rate risk for the underwriter. The *Daily Bond Buyer* publishes this ratio each week.

72. **A** Banker's acceptances, which are post-dated time drafts accepted by American banks, are used extensively in international trade.

73. **A** Series EE bonds are non-negotiable and have no collateral value because they may only be sold back to the government.

74. **C** States do not use real estate taxes—they use income and sales taxes—to generate income. On the other hand, cities and counties and school districts use limited tax bonds and retire them from real estate taxes.

75. **A** Revenue bonds are considered self-liquidating, and TANs will be paid off by taxes and no new security will be issued. They are not considered part of the bonded debt of a municipality.

76. **C** Rule 144 filings are valid for 90 days.

77. **B** The writer is liable for $700 in cash for each contract ($32,400 – $33,500). There are 5 contracts: therefore 5 × $700 = $3,500. However, the client received

$1,000 in premiums ($200 × 5). Net loss: $2,500.

78. **A** Both cash dividends (Resp. I) and long sales (Resp. II) will increase the SMA in a margin account. Deposits to meet Reg-T requirements will not increase the SMA.

79. **B** As the question is worded, the manager wants some downside protection to a portfolio of bonds. Thus, she is slightly bearish. Selling calls would be ideal: The premium gives some downside protection plus income. (This represents the best answer.)

80. **D** The account has excess over Reg-T. Therefore, it has an SMA credit and has buying power. It is neither restricted, nor does it have a maintenance deficiency.

81. **C** To legitimately charge the maximum NASD sales charge of 8.5%, the fund must give right of accumulation, breakpoint sales, and dividend reinvestment at NAV. Forward pricing is not an option; it is obligatory under SEC rules.

82. **C** The account is restricted, and there is no evidence of an SMA balance. Therefore, the investor will have a margin call for the Reg-T initial margin requirement of $3,500 (50% of $7,000).

83. **A** Moody's MIG (Moody's Investment Grade) ratings are issued only for municipal notes: BANS.

84. **A** The partnership will report a $25,000 passive loss to its partners. This loss will not have any taxable consequences until there is passive income to offset it, or at the time of the final sale of the partnership interests.

85. **B** There is, however, a positive cash flow of $50,000; the depreciation of $75,000 minus the loss.

86. **B** Depletion is a term associated with wasting mineral rights. Thus, it could only apply to the oil and gas programs. Note, however, that there is *no* depletion on the exploratory program (I) until such time as oil is found and sold. Depletion is only on income realized, not income potential.

87. **C** Recapture is a negative feature. Under current tax laws, recapture does not change the dollar amount of tax due—only the time when the tax is due. They are due sooner.

88. **B** RR candidates of MSRB firms may relay confirmations to institutional clients, and they may relay quotes if asked; they may do no other part of an RR's job until they are registered.

89. **D** This is a vertical credit bull spread. It is not a diagonal spread.

90. **B** On a credit put spread, the breakeven is the higher strike price (45) *minus* the net credit (7) for a breakeven of 38.

91. **A** This is a credit bull put spread. Thus, the client's maximum gain will occur if the stock closes at 45 or above.

92. **D** Overlapping debt results when two municipalities with coterminous taxing authorization are based on the same source of income—usually common real property. For example, a taxpayer has real property with an assessed valuation of $27,000. This is the basis of both county bonds and school district bonds.

93. **A** A *standby* underwriting in conjunction with a rights offering is a *firm* underwriting.

94. **C** We'll answers questions 94 and 95 together.

95. **A**

	Primary	Full-diluted
Operating income	5,000,000	5,000,000
Interest	−1,700,000	−700,000
Earnings before taxes	3,300,000	4,300,000
Taxes	−1,122,000	−2,838,000
Earnings after taxes	2,178,000	2,838,000
Pfd dividends	−120,000	−120,000
Available for:		
Common shares	2,058,000	2,718,000
Common shares	2,000,000	2,250,000
EPS	$1.03 primary	$1.21 fully diluted

Because of the large interest rate on the convertibles (10%), the fully diluted earnings are greater than the primary earnings per share. This does not usually happen.

96. **A** Gross revenues are $15,000,000. To get net revenues, subtract $5,000,000 to get $10,000,000 net revenues. Divide this by total bond debt service of $5,000,000. Coverage is 2 to 1.

97. **D** Short stock–short put has the greatest dollar risk of the choices given. The premium from the put protects the writer from the short sale price upward (the direction of the writer's risk). From that breakeven point upward, the writer has unlimited risk.

98. **B** Capitalization would remain the same following the conversion of the bonds. Leverage, interest expense, and long-term debt would all decrease.

99. **C** D cannot be correct; the bonds have been called. B loses money; it accepts the call at 106 and is the worst response. If it is possible, sell

the bonds at 112; this produces the greatest income for the holder. Otherwise, convert to get stock worth $1,080. In practice, once the preferred shares are called, the price will drop. C is the best answer.

100. **D** Any control relationship creates a conflict of interest and must be disclosed to customers.

101. **B** Private employer pension plans—in most circumstances—are subject to ERISA (Employee Retirement Income Security Act) rules. Such rules place fiduciary responsibility on plan managers.

102. **D** In general, T-bills and T-bonds give poor inflation protection. Fixed annuities are only slightly better because many give "bail-out" provisions if returns fall below a certain guaranteed percent. By far, the best response is variable annuities.

103. **C** Equity is easily computed.

+	LMV	60,000
–	SMV	18,000
–	DR	25,000
+	CR	30,000
+		47,000

104. **D** This is a definition of disproportionate sharing.

105. **A** As a general rule, broker's brokers are used to preserve confidentiality.

106. **A** It's a competitive bid. The issuer will determine the maturities and dollar amounts. The competition will determine the winning underwriter, the coupon rate, and the re-offering yields.

107. **D** If the customer is unwilling to sign the option agreement, only closing sales (purchases) may be made.

108. **B** The best response is growth stocks.

109. **B** The client's equity is $8,000, and the margin maintenance excess is only

$2,000. This is all of the SMA that may be used for withdrawing cash.

LMV	$24,000	
Debit	–16,000	
Equity	$8,000	
Maintenance	– 6,000	(25% of
M excess	$2,000	24,000)

Thus, $2,000 is all the SMA that is currently usable for a cash withdrawal. Of course, all the SMA could be used for purchases, but it would create a margin call.

110. **A** The customer's account is overmargined by $2,000.

LMV	$24,000	
DR	–10,000	
Equity	$14,000	
Reg-T	–12,000	
Margin excess	$2,000	Minimum
		SMA
		2,000)

A purchase of $6,000 will cause a Reg-T requirement of $3,000. With a minimum SMA of 2,000, the margin call will be $1,000.

111. **A** The maximum possible loss is the $4,600 spent to buy 200 shares of ABC minus the $600 received for 2 ABC 25 calls at 3. Answer: $4,000.

112. **C** The maximum possible gain is $5,000 (2 × $2,500) *plus* $600 received from the 2 calls *minus* the $4,600 spent for the 200 shares. Total out: $4,600; Total in: $5,600— maximum gain $1,000.

113. **A** The breakeven on a short call covered by long stock is the purchase price of the stock (23) minus the premium (3) received. Breakeven: $20.

114. **D** The stock has risen to $24; thus, the client has a $200 gain on 200 shares. He closes the option at its intrinsic

value which is zero (it is out of the money!!) Total gain: $200 + $600 on the options = $800.

115. **D** An inverted yield curve will have both II and IV correct.

116. **C** T-bills are sold through a yield auction. Competitive bids are awarded to the lowest yield (highest bid price), and non-competitive bids are awarded at the average yield of the winning competitive bids.

117. **A** A qualified pension fund is least likely to purchase municipals because it is already tax sheltered.

118. **C** AMBAC (American Municipal Bond Assurance Corporation) is an insurer of municipal bonds.

119. **C** The official guarantee from a taxing authority would cause double-barreled municipals to be rated like general obligation bonds.

120. **C** The official notice of sale would have the details of the good faith deposit and the competitive nature of the offering.

121. **A** Land, neither raw nor developed, can be depreciated—although if it is used for certain agricultural or mining endeavors, the value of the minerals may be depleted.

122. **A** Technical analysts are quite interested in short interest, put and call ratios, and the advance–decline line. They are not particularly interested in P-E ratios.

123. **A** The MSRB has regulatory authority, but it is not an enforcer; enforcement rests with the original reporting agency of MSRB members.

124. **C** To find the price:

Multiple $\$100,000 \times .08 \times \dfrac{180}{360} =$ $4,000 (the discount)

Subtract the discount from the face value:

$100,000,000 − $4,000 = $96,000

125. **C** You must purchase the stock prior to the ex-dividend date to be entitled to the dividend. Therefore, Wednesday the 15th would be the last day a customer could purchase and receive the dividend, since it is the business day prior to the ex-dividend date.

PART 2

NUMBER OF QUESTIONS: 125   TIME: 3 HOURS

Directions: Each of the questions or incomplete statements below is followed by four suggested answers or completions. Select the one that is best in each case and then blacken the corresponding space on the answer sheet.

1. Following an OTC trade for 400 shares, "good delivery" between brokers would *not* include:

   (A) 10 certificates for 40 shares
   (B) 8 certificates for 50 shares
   (C) 1 certificate for 400 shares
   (D) 4 certificates for 100 shares

2. Long-term corporate debt is called:

   (A) equity
   (B) funded debt
   (C) debt service
   (D) working capital

3. Accrued interest on *municipal bond* transactions is based on:

   (A) 30 day month/360 day year
   (B) 30 day month/365 day year
   (C) Actual days/360 day year
   (D) Actual days/365 day year

4. Which of the following are true of treasury stock:

   I. received dividends
   II. part of authorized stock
   III. carries voting rights
   IV. carried on the balance sheet at cost

   (A) I and II only
   (B) I and III only
   (C) II and IV only
   (D) III and IV only

5. The Blue List contains information on which of the following securities?

   I. rights and warrants
   II. common stock
   III. preferred stock
   IV. corporate bonds

   (A) I and III only
   (B) I and IV only
   (C) III and IV only
   (D) II and IV only

6. The Option Clearing Corporation (OCC) exercise limits state the maximum number of contracts that can be exercised:

   (A) on the same day
   (B) over two consecutive days
   (C) over five consecutive days
   (D) over seven consecutive days

7. Limited partnerships find it most difficult to avoid which two of the following corporate characteristics?

   I. centralized management
   II. pursuit of profit
   III. continuous life
   IV. limited liability for all owners

   (A) I and II only
   (B) I and III only
   (C) II and III
   (D) II and IV

8. List the following securities, according to their quoted yields, from lowest to highest yield:

   I. junk bonds
   II. mortgage bonds
   III. government bonds
   IV. municipal bonds

   (A) II, IV, III, I
   (B) I, II, III, IV
   (C) III, IV, II, I
   (D) IV, III, II, I

9. Which of the following statements concerning buy limit orders is true?

   (A) The order is activated as soon as the market trades at or above the limit price.
   (B) The order is guaranteed a fill at the limit price or better if the market trades above the limit price.
   (C) The order is guaranteed a fill at the limit price or better if the market trades at or below the limit price.
   (D) Once the order is activated, the order will be filled, but the price may be higher than the limit.

10. All of the following statements concerning REITs are true EXCEPT:

    (A) REITs must pay dividends equaling at least 80% of net investment income.
    (B) REITs may not pass through operating losses to shareholders.
    (C) REITs must invest at least 75% of assets in real estate or real estate related securities.
    (D) REITs may hold mortgages as investments.

11. A transaction executed on the floor of the NYSE is reported as XYZ $40 \frac{s}{s} 25$ on the consolidated tape. This shows that:

    (A) 400 shares were sold at 25
    (B) 400 shares were sold short at 25
    (C) 4,000 shares were sold at 25
    (D) 4,000 shares were sold short at 25

12. The penalty tax for premature withdrawals from an IRA or Keogh is:

    (A) 4%
    (B) 6%
    (C) 10%
    (D) 50%

13. The first transaction in a margin account is the purchase of 200 shares at 16. What is the customer's initial margin requirement?

    (A) $800
    (B) $1,600
    (C) $2,000
    (D) $3,200

14. A put option is in the money when the market price of the stock:

    (A) is higher than the strike price
    (B) is lower than the strike price
    (C) is higher than the strike price minus the premium
    (D) is lower than the strike price minus the premium

15. All the following may set margin requirements for corporate securities traded in the OTC market EXCEPT:

    (A) FED
    (B) the issuing corporation
    (C) NASD
    (D) individual broker/dealer firms

Questions 16 through 18 are based on the following information: In a margin account with no other positions or credits, an investor sells short 100 shares of ABC common stock at 122 and writes one ABC July 130 put at 12.

16. How much money is the investor required to deposit to meet the initial margin requirement:

   (A) $2,460
   (B) $3,640
   (C) $4,900
   (D) $6,100

17. What is the investor's breakeven point?

   (A) $110
   (B) $118
   (C) $134
   (D) $142

18. What is the investor's maximum possible loss?

   (A) $400
   (B) $1,200
   (C) $13,400
   (D) unlimited

19. Holders of GNMA pass through securities receive:

   I. interest on a monthly basis
   II. interest on a semi-annual basis
   III. principal on a monthly basis
   IV. principal only at maturity

   (A) I and III
   (B) I and IV
   (C) II and III
   (D) II and IV

20. An investor purchasing shares of a closed-end management company in a secondary trade would pay the:

   (A) market price plus a commission
   (B) market price plus a sales charge
   (C) net asset value plus a commission
   (D) net asset value plus a sales charge

21. Which of the following is a violation of the federal laws with regard to tender offers?

   (A) the tender of stock from a cash account
   (B) the tender of stock from a long margin account
   (C) the tender of a minor's stock from a custodian account
   (D) the tender of stock in a short margin account that has been borrowed by the customer

22. Which of the following, if done within 30 days of sale of XYZ common stock at a loss, would prohibit the deduction of the loss for tax purposes?

   I. purchase of XYZ common stock
   II. purchase of XYZ debentures
   III. purchase of an XYZ call option
   IV. purchase of an XYZ put

   (A) III only
   (B) I and II only
   (C) I and III only
   (D) I and IV only

23. A distribution of a new issue would likely be completed on a principal basis in all the following situations EXCEPT:

   (A) rights offering
   (B) negotiated revenue bond offering
   (C) competitive bid general obligation bond offering
   (D) DPP offering

24. The redemption price for most mutual fund shares is:

    (A) NAV minus any redemption fee
    (B) NAV plus any redemption fee
    (C) POP minus any redemption fee
    (D) POP plus any redemption fee

25. On October 3, an investor purchases $5,000 ABC 8% debentures at 91. The bonds have interest payable dates of January 15 and July 15. What amount of accrued interest must be added to the purchase price to settle the transaction?

    (A) $18.89
    (B) $89.91
    (C) $94.44
    (D) $95.55

26. Regular way settlement on government securities transactions occurs:

    (A) business day after trade date
    (B) 2 business days after trade date
    (C) 5 business days after trade date
    (D) 7 business days after trade date

27. An investor may verbally grant discretion over which of the following terms of an order:

    I. price
    II. quantity
    III. timing
    IV. security selection

    (A) I and II only
    (B) I and III only
    (C) II and III only
    (D) II and IV only

28. What is the tax consequence to an investor who purchases a municipal bond at a market discount and holds the bond to maturity?

    (A) capital loss equal to the discount
    (B) capital gain equal to the discount
    (C) ordinary income equal to the discount
    (D) no capital gain or loss

29. An investor purchased an 8% 20-year new issue municipal bond at 92. After 15 years the bond is sold for 98. What is the gain or loss per bond for tax purposes?

    (A) $20 loss
    (B) $20 gain
    (C) $60 gain
    (D) no gain or loss

30. Which two of the following statements characterizes investment in treasury bills?

    I. stable income
    II. fluctuating income
    III. stable principal
    IV. fluctuating principal

    (A) I and III
    (B) I and IV
    (C) II and III
    (D) II and IV

31. Assume that each of the following bonds is trading at a 7.25 basis. Which is most likely to be refunded?

    (A) 8.25% coupon callable in 2007 at 100
    (B) 7.75% coupon callable in 2010 at 104
    (C) 6.50% coupon callable in 2010 at 103
    (D) 5.75% coupon callable in 2007 at 102

32. In a period of stable interest rates, which of the following types of preferred stock is likely to exhibit the greatest price volatility?

    (A) guaranteed
    (B) callable
    (C) convertible
    (D) cumulative

33. A corporation calls a bond issue 6 years prior to its maturity. Which of the following would be reduced?

    I. current assets
    II. working capital
    III. total liabilities
    IV. capitalization ratio

    (A) I and II only
    (B) II and III only
    (C) I, III, and IV only
    (D) I, II, III, and IV

34. All the following will increase SMA in a margin account EXCEPT:

    (A) stock dividends
    (B) cash dividends
    (C) cash deposits to meet a maintenance call
    (D) cover a short position

35. SMA in a margin account can be used for which of the following:

    I. to buy stock long
    II. to sell stock short
    III. to meet a house call
    IV. to meet any maintenance call

    (A) I and II only
    (B) I and III only
    (C) II and III only
    (D) III and IV only

Questions 36 through 38 are based on the following information: With ABC common stock trading at 107, an investor buys 1 ABC April 100 call for 14 and sells 1 ABC April 120 call for 6.

36. How much money must be deposited by the investor to meet the margin requirement?

    (A) $800
    (B) $1,000
    (C) $1,200
    (D) $1,255

37. Assuming the spread is held until the option expiration, the investor will lose money if ABC common stock is trading below:

    (A) $106
    (B) $108
    (C) $112
    (D) $114

38. The maximum possible gain on the position is:

    (A) $800
    (B) $1,200
    (C) $2,000
    (D) Unlimited

39. What would be the most likely reason for a municipal securities dealer to avoid short selling municipal bonds?

    (A) Such practices are prohibited by the Securities Exchange Act.
    (B) MSRB rules state that such actions are against the buyer's best interest.
    (C) Commissions cannot be charged on short sales for the dealer's own account.
    (D) The same security might be difficult to obtain when the dealer wishes to close the short position.

40. Under the regulation A exemption from registration, an issuer can sell a maximum dollar amount of securities over 12 months of:

    (A) $500,000
    (B) $1,000,000
    (C) $1,500,000
    (D) $5,000,000

41. A limited partner may do which of the following without endangering limited liability?

    (A) play an active role in management
    (B) sue the general partner
    (C) allow his name to be used in the partnership
    (D) confess a judgment against the partnership

42. An investor short sells 1000 shares of ABC common stock at 1.50. What is the investor's margin requirement?

    (A) $750
    (B) $1,500
    (C) $2,000
    (D) $2,500

43. On corporate bonds, the accrued interest is calculated through the:

    (A) settlement date
    (B) settlement date minus one
    (C) trade date
    (D) trade date plus one

44. For regular way trades in common stock the ex-dividend date is:

    (A) the business day after the record date
    (B) the business day before the record date
    (C) two business days before the record date
    (D) four business days before the record date

45. The FED may be expected to be an active purchaser of securities through its open market operations under all the following circumstances EXCEPT:

    (A) rising wholesale prices
    (B) falling GNP
    (C) rising unemployment
    (D) falling interest rates

46. Detailed information of an investor's financial condition is required for the purchase of:

    (A) DPP private placements
    (B) index options
    (C) broker/dealer inventory securities
    (D) high yield municipal bonds

47. A corporation will increase which of the following through the issuance of convertible debentures?

   I. leverage
  II. capitalization
 III. working capital
 IV. potential for dilution

(A) I only
(B) II and III only
(C) II, III, and IV only
(D) I, II, III, and IV

48. Which two of the following are usually associated with the underwriting of municipal general obligation bonds?

   I. firm commitment
  II. best efforts
 III. negotiated
 IV. competitive bid

(A) I and III
(B) I and IV
(C) II and III
(D) II and IV

49. If bidders state the lowest discount yield they will accept, we have an example of:

(A) yield auction
(B) tender offer
(C) market offering
(D) competitive underwriting

50. An NASD member could justify the mark-up on a customer purchase of securities on all of the following EXCEPT:

(A) value of services rendered
(B) availability of the security
(C) current price
(D) dealer's cost

51. MSRB rules apply to which of the following?

   I. municipal issuers
  II. municipal employees
 III. municipal securities dealers
 IV. municipal securities registered representatives dealing solely with other municipal securities representatives

(A) I only
(B) II and III only
(C) III and IV only
(D) II and IV only

52. MSRB rules are enforced by which of the following:

   I. SEC
  II. NASD
 III. MSRB
 IV. NYSE

(A) I and II only
(B) I and III only
(C) I and IV only
(D) III and IV only

53. All of the following statements concerning zero coupon corporate bonds are true EXCEPT:

(A) Zero coupon bonds are traded flat.
(B) Zero coupon bond prices are more volatile than coupon bond prices.
(C) Zero coupon bonds pay no interest until maturity.
(D) Zero coupon bond holders incur no tax liability prior to sale or maturity.

54. An investor has possession of the certificates for a stock. If, following a long sale, the investor fails to deliver the certificates, the broker will buy in the account on:

    (A) settlement date
    (B) the business day following settlement
    (C) the day after the extension expires
    (D) the eleventh business day following settlement

55. The ex-dividend date for mutual funds is:

    (A) four business days prior to the record date
    (B) the first of each month
    (C) the business date after the record date
    (D) set by the mutual fund sponsor

56. Which of the following open orders would be reduced on the ex-date for a cash dividend:

    I. buy limit
    II. buy stop
    III. sell limit
    IV. sell stop

    (A) I and IV only
    (B) III and IV only
    (C) I and III only
    (D) III and IV only

57. An investor buys 1 BP Jan 135 contract for 7.50. What is the underlying value of the contract?
    (A) 10,000 British pounds
    (B) 12,500 British pounds
    (C) 10,000 U.S. dollars
    (D) 12,500 U.S. dollars

58. An investor purchased a $10,000 municipal bond in the secondary market at 106. The bond has 12 years remaining until maturity. After holding the bond for 6 years the bond is sold for 104. What is the capital gain or loss?

    (A) $100 gain
    (B) $200 gain
    (C) $200 loss
    (D) $400 loss

59. "Good delivery" is not effected if the certificate is:

    (A) assigned with power of substitution
    (B) accompanied by a stock power
    (C) accompanied by legal papers
    (D) "in street name"

60. All of the following are TRUE regarding accounts established under the Uniform Gift to Minor's Act EXCEPT:

    (A) Taxes are the responsibility of the minor.
    (B) Custodian makes all investment decisions in the account.
    (C) Custodian can use account positions to cover short sales in his own personal account.
    (D) Account must reflect the minor's social security number.

61. All the following statements are true concerning both stock splits and stock dividends EXCEPT:

    (A) Both increase the number of shares outstanding.
    (B) Both increase the par value of all the outstanding shares.
    (C) Both leave total equity unchanged.
    (D) Both may cause the market price to fall with the issuance of the additional shares.

62. At what age can individuals begin withdrawing funds from an IRA without incurring a penalty?

   (A) 59½
   (B) 62½
   (C) 65
   (D) 70½

Questions 63 through 66 are based on the following information: With ABC common stock trading at 62.75, an investor purchases 1 ABC June 60 call for 7 and purchases 1 ABC June 60 put for 4.

63. This strategy would be most consistent with what expectations about the price for ABC common prior to the June expiration?

   (A) rising prices
   (B) falling prices
   (C) volatile prices with uncertain direction
   (D) stables prices

64. What are the breakeven point(s) for this position?

   I. 49
   II. 56
   III. 67
   IV. 71

   (A) II only
   (B) IV only
   (C) I and IV only
   (D) II and III only

65. What is the maximum possible loss on the position?

   (A) $300
   (B) $1,100
   (C) $4,900
   (D) unlimited

66. What is the maximum possible gain on this position?

   (A) $300
   (B) $1,100
   (C) $4,900
   (D) unlimited

67. Purchasers of variable annuities have all the following rights EXCEPT:

   (A) the right to redeem the contract prior to annuitization
   (B) the right to vote on changes to the investment policy
   (C) the right to approve investment advisory contracts
   (D) the right to vote on changes in the security holdings of the separate account

68. The primary consideration in selecting a DPP investment should be its:

   (A) liquidity
   (B) debt ratings
   (C) economic viability
   (D) tax write-offs

69. Which of the following is the best definition of the crossover point?

   (A) A corporation's interest expense exceeds its operating income.
   (B) Income from a DPP investment exceeds its tax deductions.
   (C) The market value of stock one would receive from converting a bond exceeds the market value of the bond.
   (D) Coterminous jurisdictions of municipal taxing authorities lead to overlapping debt.

70. Which of the following is a means of protecting a municipal bond investment?

    (A) The investor could accept a lower yield on the bond in return for the right to put the bond back to the issuer at par value.
    (B) The dealer could offer a guarantee against any loss the investor may suffer.
    (C) The dealer could offer to repurchase the bond at a set price on a fixed date.
    (D) The dealer could offer to repurchase the bonds at a set price on any date selected by the investor.

71. An exporter is paid in Swiss francs for his merchandise. If the exporter wants to hedge his holdings in Swiss francs against a drop in the value of that currency, the exporter should:

    (A) buy calls
    (B) buy puts
    (C) sell calls
    (D) sell puts

72. All of the following are benefits of arbitration over litigation in the settling of securities related claims EXCEPT:

    (A) lower cost
    (B) quicker resolution
    (C) knowledgeable arbitrators
    (D) right to appeal

Questions 73 and 74 are based on the following information: ABC Corporation has outstanding an 8% convertible debenture issue. The bonds, which are convertible at 25 and are currently callable at 105, are trading at 114.50. ABC common stock is currently quoted at 28.

73. A client of yours owns some of the ABC convertible debentures. What should you advise your client to do if ABC Corporation calls the entire bond issue?

    (A) Sell the bonds immediately at the market price of 114.50.
    (B) Accept the call at 105.
    (C) Convert the bonds.
    (D) Continue to hold the bonds for the additional interest payments.

74. If ABC does not call the bonds, which of the following statements is true:

    (A) The stock and bond are trading at parity.
    (B) The stock is trading at 3 points over parity.
    (C) The bond is trading 2.50 points above parity.
    (D) Both B and C are true.

75. All of the following ratios can be calculated from information on a corporation's balance sheet EXCEPT:

    (A) bond debt service coverage
    (B) capitalization ratios
    (C) current ratio
    (D) book value

76. An analyst reviewing the investment merits of a revenue bond would be concerned with all of the following EXCEPT:

    (A) economic viability of the project
    (B) protective indenture provisions
    (C) ad valorem tax rates
    (D) existing and potential competitive facilities

77. Which of the following statements is not true of both mutual funds and variable annuities?

    (A) Issuers of both are subject to regulation under the Investment Company Act of 1940.
    (B) Maximum sales charges for both securities are 8.50%.
    (C) The value of both types of securities is based on the value of a portfolio of securities.
    (D) Both securities must make capital gains distributions annually.

78. The Employee Retirement Income Security Act (ERISA) sets rules for

    (A) the conduct of pension plan managers
    (B) the securities that may be purchased in an IRA account
    (C) the annual deductions in a Keogh account
    (D) 401(K) contributions

79. Which of the following orders must be filled in their entirety, either immediately or eventually?

    I. Fill or kill
    II. All or non
    III. At the opening

    (A) I only
    (B) II only
    (C) I and II only
    (D) I, II, and III

80. Treasury stock may be considered as:

    (A) issued and outstanding shares
    (B) unissued and authorized shares
    (C) authorized and issued shares
    (D) outstanding and unissued shares

81. Which of the following strategies will provide limited upside protection to a client?

    (A) writing uncovered calls
    (B) stop order to sell
    (C) buying puts
    (D) buy limit orders

82. Which means of credit control does the FRB use most frequently to affect the money supply?

    (A) open market operations
    (B) discount rate
    (C) reserve requirements
    (D) margin requirements

83. What type of fund would best suit an investor seeking maximum current income while minimizing tax liability?

    (A) Money market fund
    (B) Municipal bond mutual fund
    (C) Growth fund
    (D) Preferred stock and bond fund

84. Variable annuities are characterized by:

    I. fixed dollar investments acquiring a variable number of accumulation units
    II. variable dollar investments acquiring a fixed number of accumulation units
    III. a fixed number of annuity units giving a variable dollar payout
    IV. a variable number of annuity units giving a fixed dollar payout

    (A) I and III only
    (B) I and IV only
    (C) II and III only
    (D) II and IV only

85. Issuance of a bond by a corporation will cause all the following EXCEPT:

    (A) higher current ratio
    (B) lower book value
    (C) higher debt–equity ratio
    (D) lower common stock ratio

86. An investor purchased municipal bonds at 104. The bonds have 10 years to maturity. After 5 years the bonds are sold in the secondary market for 98. What is the loss for tax purposes?

    (A) no loss because the premium must be amortized
    (B) $20 per bond
    (C) $40 per bond
    (D) $60 per bond

87. Property with an assessed valuation of $100,000 and a rate of 38 mills would have to pay a tax of:

    (A) $38
    (B) $380
    (C) $3,800
    (D) $38,000

88. A limited partner contributed $50,000 to a partnership. Of this sum, $25,000 was his own funds, and $25,000 was derived from a non-recourse loan. At the end of the first year, he contributed another $20,000. At the end of the second year, he reinvested $10,000 of undistributed profits. At this point, what is the partner's "basis"?

    (A) $25,000
    (B) $50,000
    (C) $70,000
    (D) $80,000

89. All of the following terms are used in connection with a municipal bond underwriting EXCEPT:

    (A) managing underwriter
    (B) best efforts
    (C) selling concession
    (D) takedown

90. A "seller's option" settles in:

    (A) 5 business days
    (B) 2 business days to 60 calendar days
    (C) 7 calendar days
    (D) 6 calendar days to 60 business days

91. Which interest rate is considered the most volatile?

    (A) prime rate
    (B) discount rate
    (C) treasury bond rate
    (D) federal funds rate

Questions 92 through 94 are based on the following information: With the ABC common stock trading at 41, an investor writes 1 ABC September 35 put at 2 and buys 1 ABC September 45 put at 7.

92. What is the maximum possible gain on the position?

(A) $300
(B) $500
(C) $3,800
(D) unlimited

93. What is the breakeven on the position?

(A) 37
(B) 38
(C) 40
(D) 42

94. What is the gain or loss on the position if ABC stock is trading at 46 at the September expiration?

(A) $500 gain
(B) $500 loss
(C) $600 gain
(D) $600 loss

95. All of the following dates that occur in connection with a common stock dividend are set by the corporation EXCEPT:

(A) declaration date
(B) ex-date
(C) record date
(D) payment date

96. Dilution of a corporation's earnings may result from all of the following EXCEPT:

(A) warrants
(B) common stock
(C) convertible debentures
(D) call options

97. All of the following terms are used in connection with a corporate underwriting EXCEPT:

(A) managing underwriter
(B) selling group
(C) underwriter's discount
(D) tender offer

98. A 9% municipal bond maturing in 10 years is trading at 110. The bond is callable in 5 years at 104. What is the yield to call?

(A) 7.3%
(B) 7.4%
(C) 7.5%
(D) 7.6%

99. A municipal bond has coupon dates of April and October 15. A regular way trade made on Monday, January 10 will result in accrued interest of:

(A) 88 days
(B) 91 days
(C) 93 days
(D) 94 days

100. On an Industrial Development Revenue Bond (IDRB), the credit rating will be based on an analysis of the creditworthiness of the:

(A) underwriter
(B) lessee
(C) bond counsel
(D) issuer

101. SIPC is:

(A) government agency
(B) government-sponsored private corporation
(C) publicly traded private corporation
(D) policy-holder owner (mutual) insurance company

102. Compared to similarly rated municipal bonds trading at or above par, municipal bonds trading at a discount will normally have:

    (A) higher yields
    (B) lower yields
    (C) the same yields
    (D) all of the above

103. What is the most likely reason that a new AAA-rated bond is offered by the underwriters at a discount?

    (A) The discount reflects the market's opinion that the issuer is less creditworthy than the rating suggests.
    (B) The discount makes the bonds more attractive when tax considerations are taken into account.
    (C) The bond coupon is less than the market interest rate on bonds of similar rating and maturity.
    (D) It allows the underwriters bigger profits.

104. All of the following types of corporate bonds are secured by specific assets EXCEPT:

    (A) guaranteed bonds
    (B) mortgage bonds
    (C) collateral trust bonds
    (D) equipment trust certificates

105. Eurodollar bond is the popular name given to bonds:

    (A) issued in the U.S. but denominated in a foreign currency
    (B) issued in the U.S. and payable in U.S. dollars
    (C) issued in a foreign country but denominated in U.S. dollars
    (D) issued in a foreign country and payable in a foreign currency

106. Which of the following taxes would be considered progressive:

    I. income taxes
    II. sales taxes
    III. real estate taxes
    IV. estate taxes

    (A) I and III only
    (B) I and IV only
    (C) III and IV only
    (D) I and IV only

107. Mutual funds must provide financial reports to shareholders:

    (A) monthly
    (B) quarterly
    (C) semi-annually
    (D) annually

108. Which of the following bonds would be considered a double-barreled bond?

    (A) a local housing authority bond additionally backed by the federal government
    (B) a corporate bond guaranteed by the issuer's parent corporation
    (C) a corporate bond guaranteed by the federal government
    (D) a special tax bond additionally backed by the issuing municipality's full faith and credit

109. Which of the following debt securities trade flat?

   I. defaulted bonds
  II. income bonds
 III. T-bills
 IV. zero coupon bonds

(A) III only
(B) I and II only
(C) I, II, and IV only
(D) I, II, III, and IV

110. Who holds the legal title to the assets used to collateralize equipment trust certificates?

(A) issuing corporations
(B) bondholders
(C) trustee
(D) independent bond counsel

111. Which type of preferred stock must pay dividends in arrears before dividends may be paid to common stockholders?

(A) cumulative
(B) convertible
(C) guaranteed
(D) participating

112. All of the following terms have some connection with trades encountering settlement problems EXCEPT:

(A) recapitalization
(B) rejection
(C) reclamation
(D) don't know

113. The SEC requires broker/dealers holding customer assets to provide customers with financial statements:

(A) on demand
(B) quarterly
(C) semi-annually
(D) annually

114. Which of the following items will be included on the confirmation statement for a "when issued" transaction?

   I. price
  II. accrued interest
 III. total dollar amount
 IV. settlement date

(A) I only
(B) I and IV only
(C) II and III only
(D) I, II, III, and IV

115. A municipality has 8% bonds outstanding that are callable 5 years from now. If the municipality issues new 6% bonds and escrows the funds until the earliest call date, the original issue is said to be which two of the following:

   I. pre-refunded
  II. refunded
 III. defeased
 IV. defaulted

(A) I and III
(B) I and IV
(C) II and III
(D) II and IV

116. All of the following are certain to result from the conversion of a corporation's outstanding debentures into common stock EXCEPT:

    (A) increased equity
    (B) lower EPS
    (C) increased number of shares outstanding
    (D) lower interest expense

117. The most likely source of debt service on general obligation bonds issued by a local school district is:

    (A) sales taxes
    (B) income taxes
    (C) real estate taxes
    (D) excise taxes

118. To achieve level debt service for a bond issue, the issue must be structured so that over the life of the bonds:

    (A) interest payments increase as principal repayments decrease
    (B) principal repayments increase as interest rates decrease
    (C) combined interest and principal payments remain constant each year
    (D) the issuer issues new bonds in amounts equal to those maturing each year

119. A corporation is doing a rights offering through which it hopes to issue additional shares equal to 25% of the shares currently outstanding. The subscription price of the stock is $20 per share. The stock is trading at $24 cum rights. What is the theoretical value of the rights?

    (A) $0.80
    (B) $1.00
    (C) $1.25
    (D) $4.00

120. A bond was issued at par and was purchased by the holder. If the bond has a 7% coupon and is currently selling at 92.50, the current yield is approximately:

    (A) 7%
    (B) 7.5%
    (C) 8%
    (D) 8.5%

121. A client purchased 400 XYZ at 80 in a newly opened margin account and deposited the necessary margin. Some time later, XYZ goes to 90. What is the customer's SMA?

    (A) $2,000
    (B) $4,000
    (C) $6,000
    (D) $8,000

122. Which of the following statements are true of both warrants and call options?

    I. The holder has the right to buy at a fixed price.
    II. The holder can determine when to exercise the security.
    III. Exercise results in an increase in the number of shares outstanding.
    IV. Options and warrants may be perpetual.

    (A) I and IV
    (B) I and II only
    (C) II and IV only
    (D) I and III only

123. A DPP subscription agreement is considered accepted when it is:

    (A) signed by the investor
    (B) signed by the general partner
    (C) filed with the state
    (D) filed with the SEC

124. All of the following practices in connection with mutual fund sales are violations of the Conduct Rules of the NASD EXCEPT:

    (A) selling dividends
    (B) quantity discounts
    (C) short-term trading
    (D) 9.5% sales charge

125. The biggest portion of the spread on a corporate securities underwriting is typically the:

    (A) manager's fee
    (B) expense allowance
    (C) concession
    (D) reallowance

PART 2 ANSWERS

1. **A** NASD rules require that securities be delivered in units of 100 or multiples of 100. Thus, 10 certificates of 40 shares are not acceptable.

2. **B** Funded debt identifies corporate debt. Debt service is the annual total of interest and principal payable.

3. **A** Municipal bond interest is calculated on a 30/360 day calendar. Corporate bonds use the same 30/360 calendar. The U.S. government uses actual days to calculate the interest.

4. **C** Treasury stock is stock that has been repurchased by the corporation. It does not receive dividends, has no voting rights, and is carried on the balance sheet at cost.

5. **C** The Blue List is the major publication for the sale of municipal bonds in the secondary market; nevertheless, it also contains quotations on preferred stock and corporate bonds. The Yellow List is the primary source for the trading of corporate bonds in the secondary market.

6. **C** The maximum number of contracts that can be exercised over a period of five business days are 8,000 contracts on the same side of the market.

7. **D** Limited partnerships find it most difficult to avoid the pursuit of profit (II) and limited liability for all owners (IV). Avoiding continuous life (III) is easy: The partnership agreement sets the term of the partnership. Management of DDPs is not centralized; only the general partner has authority.

8. **D** Municipal bond yields the lowest due to the tax-free status, followed by government securities because of the safety. Mortgage bonds are third, and junk bonds yield the highest because of the risk factor involved.

9. **C** The simple definition of a buy limit order is when the investor wants a better price than the market price. When investors place a buy limit order, they want a better price than the market price; therefore, a price below the market price will be chosen—if that is possible.

10. **A** REIT must pay dividends equaling at least 90% of the net investment income.

11. **A** The symbol $\frac{s}{s}$ stands for units of 10 and not for sold short.

12. **C** If an individual withdraws money before 59½, the penalty on the investor is 10% of the amount withdrawn, plus he or she must pay taxes on the amount withdrawn.

13. **C** The LMV is $3,200. The initial margin 50% of $1,600 does not meet the NYSE/NASD minimum of $2,000.

14. **B** A put option becomes valuable when the market price drops below the strike price.

15. **B** The FRB was given the authority to establish margin requirements on listed securities and unlisted securities by the Securities Act of 1934.

16. **C** A margin of 50% of the short-market value, equal to $6,100, is required. No margin is required for the short put, since there is no risk involved. The investor can use the premium received, $1,200, to be $12,200 × 50% = $6,100 − $1,200 = $4,900.

17. **C** The price of the stock can rise to $134 per share before the customer will start to lose money. This is a breakeven question.

18. **D** The customer must close out the short account by purchasing the stock. The price of the underlying stock could rise to an unlimited amount, creating, therefore, an unlimited loss.

19. **A** GNMA investors receive interest and principal on a monthly basis. GNMA securities are U.S. government agency securities and are subject to federal, state, and local taxes.

20. **A** Closed-end management company shares trade in the secondary market like other securities. Commission is charged, and the asked price may be below the NAV.

21. **D** It is a violation of federal law for anyone to tender stock that a customer borrowed in a short margin account. The stock has been temporarily borrowed and does not belong to the customer; consequently, it cannot be tendered.

22. **C** The purchase of XYZ common stock or the purchase of convertible debentures would be covered under the 30-day wash sale rule. Investors cannot buy back securities sold at a loss within 30 days and take the loss for tax purposes. The purchase of a call option is also considered a wash sale. The purchase of a put is not.

23. **D** Many DPP offerings are executed through private placements and as such, will not use an underwriter's services. Rights offerings use standby underwriters, a form of principal underwriting.

24. **A** Mutual funds are redeemed at the NAV minus any redemption fees that may be charged by the fund.

25. **B** There are 81 days of accrued interest due. July 16 days, August 30 days, September 30 days, and October 3 days. Add 2 days for settlement. $400 interest per year based on 360 days in the year = $89.91.

26. **A** Regular way settlement for U.S. government securities is the next business day, T + 1.

27. **B** The client may give the RR discretion over price and time. The investor chooses the stock and the size. A Discretionary Account would give the trader the ability to choose the size, security, price, and time.

28. **B** The tax code treats municipal bonds trading in the secondary market at a discount in the same manner as any asset. The discount will be a capital gain, if the bond is held to maturity.

29. **D** Since the discount exceeds the norm (.25% per year) it qualifies as an OID (original issue discount). As such, the discount of $80 must be accreted. Each year's accretion is $4 and since the bond was held for 15 years, $60 is added to the cost of $920. The new basis is now $980 and the sale price is also $980. Thus, there is neither gain nor loss.

30. **C** Treasury bills are sold at a discount with the discount being the interest. The underlying face value remains stable.

31. **A** Since the 8.25s have the highest coupon and the lowest call price, they are the likely candidates for a call.

32. **C** Fixed income securities are interest rate sensitive. Convertible securities will have the most volatility when interest rates are stable because of the underlying common stock.

33. **D** When a bond is called, everything is affected. Current assets are reduced because cash is reduced; working capital is also reduced for the same reason. Long-term liability is reduced, and the capitalization ratio is changed.

34. **A** The distribution of stock dividends will not affect SMA in a margin account. The result will be an increase in the number of shares; current market value is not necessarily changed.

35. **A** Although excess equity is the source of SMA, they cannot be said to be "Excess Equity *or* SMA." *Technically*, when a broker *credits* SMA, he *debits* the account—this lowers equity. In other words, Reg-T considers the SMA *as used*. This *never* shows up on a customer's statement, but it can severely limit the practical use of SMA. SMA can be used to purchase stock or sell stock short. It can be removed and may be used to purchase options. Since short-term options are not marginable, the investor's purchasing power is a 1-to-1 ratio and not 2 times the amount.

36. **A** This is a debit spread, and to calculate the required margin, just net out the two premiums.

37. **B** This is a breakeven point question. To calculate the breakeven point on a debit spread, use the same formula for the buyer of a call and apply it to the buy side of the spread: Strike Price + Premium

($100 + 8 = 108$). The market price must be higher than $108 for the investor to make money.

38. **B** The most an investor in this position could make would be $1,200, and that would occur if the market value of the securities were trading at or above 120. The investor would exercise the 100-call option and buy the stock at $10,000. If the market goes above $120, the investor would be exercised by the holder of the 120 option and would have to sell the stock at 120. The $20 gain per share, adjusted for the $8 premium, leaves a $12 gain per share of $1,200.

39. **D** Municipal dealers avoid selling municipal bonds short because of the difficulty of buying the same bond to close out the position.

40. **D** Regulation A exempts from registration those issues that do not exceed $5,000,000.

41. **B** The partnership agreement allows limited partners to sue the general partner for failure to fulfill his responsibility to the partnership.

42. **D** The NYSE/NASD has a rule for selling stock short that has a market value of $5 or less. The investor must deposit the greater amount of either 100% or $2.50 per share.

43. **B** Interest accrues up to but not including settlement date.

44. **C** To identify ex-date, count two business days before record date.

45. **A** The FED purchases securities to pump money into the market. They want to stimulate the economy when the GNP drops, unemployment rises, or interest rates fall. Rising wholesale prices would indicate inflation. In this

case, the FED will sell securities in order to tighten credit.

46. **A** In general, DPPs require that the RR have verified information about the purchaser. This is particularly true of private placements of DPPs. Here most purchasers will be accredited investors.

47. **D** All the choices are correct. Debentures will increase leverage, will result in a larger capitalization base and, until the money is spent, more working capital. There is also the possibility of dilution if the bonds are converted into common stock.

48. **B** Most municipal general obligation bonds are issued under competitive bidding. Competitive bidding is always done as a firm commitment.

49. **A** This is a description of how U.S. treasury bills are sold.

50. **D** The NASD rules on fair pricing take into account the current market, difficulty of the trade, and the services rendered. The dealer cannot consider the cost of the securities as the basis of his mark-up.

51. **C** Municipal issues and employees are not regulated by any MSRB rules; the others are.

52. **A** The MSRB creates the rules and regulations but does not have an enforcement power and must rely on the SEC, NASD, Controller of the Currency, or the FDIC.

53. **D** In a zero coupon bond, the investor purchases the bond at a deep discount. The discount represents the final interest. However, the IRS requires an annual payment of taxes on the imputed interest.

54. **D** Although the broker is supposed to make sure that the client will deliver by settlement date, SEC does not require a buy-in until the morning of the eleventh business day following settlement.

55. **D** Ex-dividend date for a mutual fund is set by the sponsor.

56. **A** All orders entered below the market are reduced on ex-date. Open buy limit and open sell stop (limit) are reduced.

57. **B** British pound options have an underlying value of 12,500 British pounds.

58. **A** This is a municipal bond selling at a premium. The premium must be amortized over the remaining life of the bond. Thus, the $60 premium will be reduced to $30 in 6 years. If the client sells at $10,400, there will be a $100 gain.

59. **C** If a certificate is accompanied by legal papers—for example, tax waivers, or a certified copy of a will—it is the obligation of the selling broker to put the certificate "in street name" for good delivery. Responses A, B, and D are correct.

60. **C** The custodian cannot use securities in the custodian account to cover a short sale in his own personal account. All securities in the custodian account must be used for the benefit of the minor.

61. **B** In a stock split, the par value decreases. Stock dividends do not affect the par value.

62. **A** If an investor removes money before 59½, the amount removed is subject to a 10% penalty tax. In addition, the amount withdrawn is subject to tax as current income.

63. **C** This is an example of a long straddle. If the market price rises, the call will be exercised and the put will expire. If the market price drops, the put will be exercised

and the call will expire. An investor may purchase a straddle if he or she expects substantial market movement but does not know the direction.

64. **C** The total premium is 11:7 for the call, 4 for the put. The two breakeven points are calculated for a straddle: one for the call, 71; and one for the put, 49. Remember that the breakeven points for a straddle are the total premium on either side of the strike price.

65. **B** The maximum loss is the total premium of $1,100.

66. **D** The holder of a long straddle can theoretically have an unlimited profit. If the stock drops, the put will be profitable from breakeven down to zero. If the stock rises, the call will be profitable from breakeven upward. Only if the stock closes at the strike price will the straddle holder lose his entire premium paid.

67. **D** A variable annuity is managed in similar fashion to a mutual fund. The investor invests money into the fund and the investment advisor purchases the securities.

68. **C** The major consideration on a DPP is that is makes economic sense.

69. **B** The crossover point in a DPP is where income becomes a taxable event. This results from the fact that deductions are less than the operating profit.

70. **A** A put bond allows the investor to resell the bond to the issuer and receive par value. B, C, and D are not permitted by NASD rules.

71. **B** The exporter is long Swiss francs; to hedge his position, he should buy puts. The only other partially logical choice is to sell calls; this will moderate his risk, but it will not hedge against a sudden "spike downward" in Swiss francs.

72. **D** The Code of Arbitration is quicker and cheaper than litigation. An arbitrated decision is final.

73. **C** This question can be tricky. Your first thought is to sell the bond at 114.5 because this is above parity. But when a bond is called, the market price of the bond will drop to the call price of 105. The only practical action that the investor can take is to convert the bonds to the common stock. When bonds are called, future interest payments stop.

74. **C** In question 73, you had to calculate parity for the convertible bond. Remember the basic formula for finding parity is:

$$\frac{\text{Par Value}}{\text{Conversion}} = \frac{\text{Price of Convertible}}{\text{Price of Common Stock}}$$

$$\frac{\$1,000}{\$25} :: \frac{X}{\$28} = 25X = 28,000$$

$$X = \$1,120$$

Parity of the convertible security Since the market price is 114.5 for the bond and the parity of that bond to the common is 112; the market is 2.50 points above parity.

75. **A** To calculate the bond debt service coverage, the Income Statement must be used. The formula for finding the ratio is operating income divided by bond interest.

76. **C** Ad valorem taxes are used for general obligation bonds and not for revenue bonds. Revenue bondholders are paid from the revenue generated by the project.

77. **D** Choices A, B, and C are true about mutual funds and variable annu-

ities. Choice D is correct about mutual funds, and the investor is taxed on the distribution. Variable annuities do not distribute income.

78. **A** ERISA—although a complicated act—can be said to produce guidelines for the conduct of qualified pension plan accounts by their portfolio managers.

79. **D** All choices are correct. Each must be filled completely. No partial fillings are allowed. FOK and At the Opening are allowed only one try, whereas with an AON the trader can try again.

80. **C** Treasury stock is corporate stock that was issued but has been repurchased by the corporation. It does not have voting rights nor does it receive dividends.

81. **A** Of the choices given, only the uncovered call will provide limited upside protection (breakeven is the strike price PLUS any premium). All of the other strategies protect the client on the downside.

82. **A** Open market operations are conducted by the FOMC. This committee will either buy or sell U.S. government securities when they want to regulate the money supply.

83. **B** The key phrase in this question is "minimizing tax liability." Municipal bonds are exempt from federal taxation.

84. **A** Investors purchasing variable annuities buy accumulation units during the paying period. Usually they purchase a fixed dollar amount, either lump sum or on a periodic basis. During the payout period, the accumulation units are changed into a fixed number of annuity units. The number of

annuity units remains the same but the payout will vary.

85. **B** Bonds are debt instruments. Book value pertains to the value of common stock and is independent of bonded debt.

86. **C** An investor buying a municipal bond at a premium must authorize the loss over the life of the bond. After 5 years, the basis of the bond is 102. The bond is sold for 98; thus there is a $40 loss.

87. **C** 38 mills is, in effect, a rate of .038 per $1 of assessed valuation. Hence, the tax would be $100,000 × .038 or $3,800.

88. **D** All four contributions are part of his $80,000 basis.

89. **B** A best efforts commitment is associated with a corporate underwriting. In a best efforts underwriting, the underwriter acts as an agent and has no financial responsibility and liability. Municipal bonds are firm commitment underwritings.

90. **B** Settlement is done at the option of the seller. Settlement must take place between 2 business days and 60 calendar days. The seller is required to give the buyer a one-day written notice.

91. **D** The federal funds rate is the rate banks charge other banks for overnight loans and is the most volatile of all the rates. The effective federal funds rate quoted in the papers is the daily average rate throughout the country.

92. **B** This is a debit bear spread, and the investor will gain if the stock declines. The difference between the strike prices is $1,000. The net debt is $500. The maximum gain is $1,000 – $500 or $500.

93. **C** On a put debit spread, the

breakeven is the strike price of the long option (45) minus the net debit (5). Thus, the client will breakeven at 40.

94. **B** The client will lose the entire net debit of $500. The stock price is above the breakeven; hence, all options are out-of-the-money.

95. **B** Ex-date is set by the exchange or the NASD and not by the corporation. Ex-date is 2 business days before the record date.

96. **D** Warrants and convertible debentures have the potential of diluting the earnings. The issuance of common stock will immediately dilute the earnings. Listed options will trade on outstanding shares so no further dilutions will occur.

97. **D** Tender is basically a bid price. Underwritings are offerings.

98. **A** Calculation of YTC:

Step 1

−$1,100	Price Paid
+$1,040	Price Received
−60	Loss
$5	Years to Call = $12 loss per year

Step 2

$90	Annual Interest
−12	Loss
$78	Adjusted Income

Step 3

$1,100	Price Paid
+1,040	

$$\frac{2,140}{2} = \$1,070 \text{ average price}$$

Step 4

$$\frac{\$78}{\$1,070} = \frac{\text{Adjusted Income}}{\text{Average Price}} = 7.3\% \text{ YTC}$$

99. **A** The computation is as follows:

October	16 days
November	30 days
December	30 days
January	12 days
Total	88 days of accrued interest

100. **B** IDRBs are issued by municipalities, but the lessee signs a net lease agreement that guarantees payment of sufficient funds to pay the bond debt service. Therefore, the rating services look to the creditworthiness of the company that agrees to pay for the bond debt service.

101. **B** SIPC insures customer's accounts if a broker/dealer goes bankrupt. The maximum protection is $500,000 per separate account, with a maximum of $100,000 in cash.

102. **A** This question is similar to question 99. It tests the inverse relationship between the price of a fixed income security and its yields.

103. **C** The interest in the marketplace must have risen before the issue was sold. The managing underwriter will discount the price of the bond, thereby raising the yield to meet the market interest.

104. **A** Guaranteed bonds are not backed by a specific asset, but by a third party.

105. **C** With the large trade imbalance generated by the United States, there are large numbers of U.S. dollars in foreign hands. Bonds used to borrow these funds—thus they pay U.S. dollars—are called Eurobonds.

106. **B** A progressive tax is based upon an individual ability to pay. The greater income is, the higher the percentage. Sales tax and real estate

107. **C** Mutual funds must provide financial reports to shareholders semiannually. Corporations must submit quarterly reports to SEC.

108. **D** A double-barreled municipal bond is a revenue bond with the backing of a full faith and credit (general obligation) bond.

109. **D** All four choices are correct. A bond in default will not trade with interest, an income bond will only pay interest if there is a profit, T-bills are sold at a discount with the discount being the interest, and zero coupon bonds are also sold at a deep discount with interest received at maturity.

110. **C** The trustee holds the legal title for the equipment trust certificate. He or she will act on behalf of the bondholders.

111. **A** Cumulative preferred stock promises to pay all unpaid dividends in arrears before dividends may be paid to common stockholders. Except for variable rate preferred stock, almost all preferred shares are cumulative.

112. **A** This answer is derived by a process of elimination. Rejection is the refusal of a delivery of securities because of some problem; reclamation allows the buyer to recover costs if some problem arises in the delivery. A "don't know" is applied to a transaction where information is missing. Recapitalization is an alteration in a corporation's capital structure, such as exchanging bonds for stocks.

113. **B** The SEC requires statements to be sent out quarterly, though most will send them out monthly if there is activity.

114. **A** A "when issued" calls for settlement sometime in the future. Since settlement date is not known, accrued interest cannot be determined. Therefore, the total dollar amount cannot be calculated.

115. **A** The issuance of bonds to redeem a prior issue with the funds held in escrow until the earliest call date is called pre-refunding (I). As a result, the original issue—since the finds for repayment are in hand—is said to be defeased, or annulled.

116. **B** There is a possibility of a lower EPS, but this is not a certainty. The savings on bond interest might offset any possible dilution in the EPS.

117. **C** Ad valorem or property taxes are used to pay off school district bonds.

118. **C** The general rule of thumb is that payment of interest is higher in the early part of the repayment schedule. To maintain a level debt service, as interest decreases, the amount of principal repaid will increase. The combined total remains the same.

119. **A** The stock is selling cum rights before ex-date. The formula is market price minus subscription price divided by the number of rights plus 1 equal the value of the right. Since the additional share will equal 25% of outstanding shares, 4 rights are needed. 24 − 20 divided by 4 + 1 = $0.80.

120. **B** The current yield is the annual coupon yield in dollars divided by the current price in dollars. Here:

$$\frac{\$70}{\$925} \times 100 = 7.57\%$$

121. **A** The customer's account will appear:

LMV $36,000
Debit −16,000
Equity $20,000
Reg-T −18,000
+$2,000 Excess Margin

122. **B** Both I and III are true. Warrants and call options give the holder the right to purchase the stock. Warrants are long-term options, whereas listed options are short-term options. Warrants will result in an increase in outstanding shares, but listed options will purchase already outstanding shares. Only warrants can be perpetual.

123. **B** The subscription agreement in a DPP is considered accepted when the general partner signs the agreement. Now the general partner is responsible for all debts of the partnership.

124. **B** Quantity discount is another term for the breakpoint schedule. This must be part of the funds features if the fund wants to charge the maximum NASD 8.5% sales charge.

125. **C** This concession is the compensation earned by members of the selling group. This amount is the largest portion of the spread. Reallowance is the compensation received by a broker/dealer who is not a member of the selling group or the syndicate and sells a share to the public. It is a percentage of the concession.

INDEX

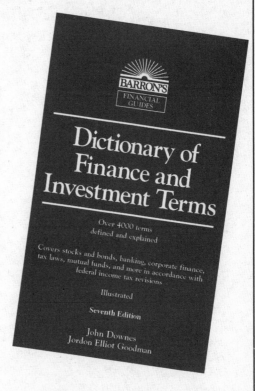